Managing the Testing Process

Practical Tools and Techniques for Managing Software and Hardware Testing

Third Edition

Rex Black

WILEY

Wiley Publishing, Inc.

Managing the Testing Process: Practical Tools and Techniques for Managing Software and Hardware Testing, Third Edition

Published by
Wiley Publishing, Inc.
10475 Crosspoint Boulevard
Indianapolis, IN 46256
www.wiley.com

ISBN: 978-0-470-40415-7

Manufactured in the United States of America

10 9 8 7 6 5 4 3

For general information on our other products and services please contact our Customer Care Department within the United States at (877) 762-2974, outside the United States at (317) 572-3993 or fax (317) 572-4002.

Wiley also publishes its books in a variety of electronic formats. Some content that appears in print may not be available in electronic books.

Library of Congress Control Number: 2009929457

About the Author

With a quarter-century of software and systems engineering experience, **Rex Black** is President of RBCS (www.rbcs-us.com), a leader in software, hardware, and systems testing. For more than a dozen years, RBCS has delivered services in consulting, outsourcing, and training for software and hardware testing. Employing the industry's most experienced and recognized consultants, RBCS conducts product testing, builds and improves testing groups, and hires testing staff for hundreds of clients worldwide. Ranging from Fortune 20 companies to start-ups, RBCS clients save time and money through improved product development, decreased tech support calls, improved corporate reputation, and more.

As the leader of RBCS, Rex is the most prolific author practicing in the field of software testing today. His popular first book, *Managing the Testing Process*, now in its third edition, has sold more than 30,000 copies around the world, including Japanese, Chinese, and Indian releases. His five other books on testing, *Critical Testing Processes, Foundations of Software Testing, Pragmatic Software Testing, Advanced Software Testing: Volume I, and Advanced Software Testing: Volume II,* have also sold tens of thousands of copies, including Hebrew, Indian, Chinese, Japanese, and Russian editions. He has contributed to 10 other books as well. He has written more than 25 articles, presented hundreds of papers, workshops, and seminars, and given about 30 keynote speeches at conferences and events around the world. Rex is a former president of both the International Software Testing Qualifications Board and the American Software Testing Qualifications Board.

When he is not working with clients around the world, developing or presenting a training seminar, or in his office, Rex spends time at home or around the world with his wife and business partner, Laurel Becker; his daughters Emma Grace and Charlotte Catherine; and his faithful canine friends Hank and Cosmo.

Acknowledgments

This book is a third edition, and that happens only when the first edition and second edition are successful. So, first off, I'd like to thank those of you who bought the first edition or second edition. I hope it's proven a useful reference for you. A special thanks goes to RBCS clients who used these books on their projects, attendees who provided evaluations of RBCS training courses, and readers who wrote reviews or sent me emails about the book. I have addressed your suggestions for improvement in this third edition.

A book gets into people's hands only through a lot of behind-the-scenes hard work by a publisher's team. A special thanks to the fine people at Wiley who helped bring this book to fruition, especially Kelly Talbot and Robert Elliott. RBCS associate Judy McKay provided valuable technical reviewing help. I'd also like to thank Ben Ryan, who shepherded *Managing the Testing Process* along through the first two editions, starting in 1998. I'd also like to thank my friends at Microsoft Press who helped me with the first edition: Erin O'Connor, John Pierce, Mary Renaud, Ben Ryan (again), and Wendy Zucker.

In the course of learning how to manage test projects, I have worked with many talented professionals as a tester, test manager, and consultant. The list of people who helped me is literally too long to include here, but my gratitude to all of my colleagues and clients is immense.

The material in this book appears in one-day, two-day, and three-day test management courses that RBCS associates and I have presented all around the world. I thank all the attendees of those seminars for their help making this material better in the third edition.

Of course, my appreciation goes out to all my past and current colleagues, subcontractors, employees, clients, and employers. I especially want to thank the clients who graciously agreed to the use of data and documentation from their projects to illustrate many of the tools and techniques I discuss.

Four people I want to name specifically in this regard are Judy McKay, Andrew Brooks, Jodi Mullins, and Steven Gaudreau. Judy is a director of quality assurance at large network equipment company. Andrew Brooks is vice president, CA Network and Voice Management Quality Assurance. Jodi Mullins is senior software engineer, CA Network and Voice Management Test Automation. Steven Gaudreau is software engineer, CA Network and Voice Management Test Automation. Each shared specific case studies, authored by them, about topics central to a chapter of each book. I really appreciate their valuable, practitioner insights.

Please attribute all errors, omissions, mistakes, opinions, and bad jokes in this book solely to me.

In the realm of "without whom," of course, I thank my parents, Rex, Sr. and Carolynn, for their love and support over the years. My greatest appreciation goes to my wife and business partner, Laurel Becker. *Managing the Testing Process* has taken me away from a lot of things in my life, three times now, but I especially appreciate my wife's support in terms of her own time given up for me.

I've changed a few of my ideas since I wrote the first and second editions, but the biggest changes in my life have involved the arrival of my daughters. Along with having a burst of wisdom that led me to marry Laurel, I have to say that Emma Grace and Charlotte Catherine are the greatest things to happen in my life. All parents have dreams for their children's success, and I hope that my two beautiful and inspirational daughters have the same luck and success in their careers that I have had. Whatever Emma and Charlotte choose to do, this book is dedicated to them, with the utmost of a father's love.

Contents at a Glance

Contents

Introduction

So, you are responsible for managing a computer hardware or software test project? Congratulations! Maybe you've just moved up from test engineering or moved over from another part of the development team, or maybe you've been doing test projects for a while. Whether you are a test manager, a development manager, a technical or project leader, or an individual contributor with some level of responsibility for your organization's test and quality assurance program, you're probably looking for some ideas on how to manage the unique beast that is a test project.

This book can help you. The first edition, published in 1999, and the second edition, published in 2002, have sold over 35,000 copies in the last decade. There are popular Indian, Chinese, and Japanese editions, too. Clients, colleagues, readers, training attendees, and others have read the book, writing reviews and sometimes sending helpful emails, giving me ideas on how to improve and expand it. So, thanks to all of you who read the first and second editions, and especially to those who have given me ideas on how to make this third edition even better.

This book contains what I wish I had known when I moved from programming and system administration to test management. It shows you how to develop some essential tools and apply them to your test project. It offers techniques that can help you get and use the resources you need to succeed. If you master the basic tools, apply the techniques to manage your resources, and give each area just the right amount of attention, you can survive managing a test project. You'll probably even do a good job, which might make you a test project manager for life, like me.

The Focus of This Book

I've written *Managing the Testing Process* for several reasons. First, many projects suffer from a gap between expectations and reality when it comes to delivery dates, budgets, and quality, especially between the individual contributors creating and testing the software, the senior project managers, and the users and the customers. Similarly, computer hardware development projects often miss key schedule and quality milestones. Effective testing and clear communication of results as an integrated part of a project risk management strategy can help.

Second, when I wrote the first edition, there was a gap in the literature on software and hardware testing. We had books targeting the low-level issues of how to design and implement test cases, as well as books telling sophisticated project managers how to move their products to an advanced level of quality using concepts and tools such as the Capability Maturity Model, software quality metrics, and so forth. However, I believe that test managers like us need a book that addresses the basic tools and techniques, the bricks and mortar, of test project management. While there are now a number of books addressing test management, I believe this book remains unique in terms of its accessibility and immediate applicability to the first-time test manager while also offering guidance in how to incrementally improve a foundational test management approach. It also offers a proven approach that works for projects that include substantial hardware development or integration components.

The tips and tools offered in this book will help you plan, build, and execute a structured test operation. As opposed to the all-too-common ad hoc or purely reactive test project, a structured test operation is planned, repeatable, and documented, but preserves creativity and flexibility in all the right places. What you learn here will allow you to develop models for understanding the meaning of the myriad data points generated by testing so that you can effectively manage what is often a confusing, chaotic, and change-ridden area of a software or hardware development project. This book also shows you how to build an effective and efficient test organization.

To that end, I've chosen to focus on topics unique to test management in the development and maintenance environments. Because they're well covered in other books, I do not address two related topics:

Basic project management tools such as work-breakdown structures, Gantt charts, status reporting, and people management skills. As you move into management, these tools will need to be part of your repertoire, so I encourage you to search out project management books — such as the ones listed in the bibliography in Appendix D — to help you learn them. A number of excellent training courses and certifications currently exist for project management as well.

Computer hardware production testing. If your purview includes this type of testing, I recommend books by W. Edwards Deming, Kaoru Ishikawa, and J. M. Juran as excellent resources on statistical quality control, as well as Patrick O'Connor's book on reliability engineering; see the bibliography in Appendix D for details on books referenced here.

Software production, in the sense of copying unchanging final versions to distribution media, requires no testing. However, both hardware and software production often include minor revisions and maintenance releases. You can use the techniques described in this book to manage the smaller test projects involved in such releases.

The differences between testing software and hardware are well documented, which might make it appear, at first glance, that this book is headed in two directions. I have found, however, that the differences between these two areas of testing are less important from the perspective of test project management than they are from the perspective of test techniques. This makes sense: hardware tests software, and software tests hardware. Thus, you can use similar techniques to manage test efforts for both hardware and software development projects.

Canon or Cookbook?

When I first started working as a test engineer and test project manager, I was a testing ignoramus. While ignorance is resolvable through education, some of that education is in the school of hard knocks. Ignorance can lead to unawareness that the light you see at the end of the tunnel is actually an oncoming train. "How hard could it be?" I thought. "Testing is just a matter of figuring out what could go wrong, and trying it."

As I soon discovered, however, the flaws in that line of reasoning lie in three key points:

- The tasks involved in "figuring out what could go wrong, and trying it" — that is, in designing good test cases — are quite hard indeed. Many authors have written good books on test case engineering, particularly in the last two decades. Unfortunately, my university professors didn't teach about testing, even though Boris Beizer, Bill Hetzel, and Glenford Myers had all published on the topic prior to or during my college career. As software engineering enters its sixth decade, that has begun to change. However, even at prestigious universities the level of exposure to testing that most software-engineers-in-the-making receive remains too low.

- Testing does not go on in a vacuum. Rather, it is part of an overall project — and thus testing must respond to real project needs, not to the whims of hackers playing around to see what they can break. In short, test projects require test project management.

- The prevalence of the "how hard can testing be" mindset only serves to amplify the difficulties that testing professionals face. Once we've learned through painful experience exactly how hard testing can be, it sometimes feels as if we are doomed — like a cross between Sisyphus and Dilbert — to explain, over and over, on project after project, why this testing stuff takes so long and costs so much money.

Implicit in these points are several complicating factors. One of the most important is that the capability of an organization's test processes can vary considerably: testing can be part of a repeatable, measured process, or an ad hoc afterthought to a chaotic project. In addition, the motivating factors — the reasons why management bothers to test — can differ in both focus and intensity. Managers motivated by fear of repeating a recent failed project see testing differently than managers who want to produce the best possible product, and both motivations differ from those of people who organize test efforts out of obligation but assign them little importance. Finally, testing is tightly connected to the rest of the project, so the test manager is often subject to a variety of outside influences. These influences are not always benign when scope and schedule changes ripple through the project.

These factors make it difficult to develop a *how to* guide for planning and executing a test project. As academics might say, test project management does not lend itself to the easy development of a canon. "Understand the following ideas and you can understand this field" is a difficult statement to apply to test management. And the development of a testing canon is certainly not an undertaking I'll tackle in this book.

Do you need a canon to manage test projects properly? I think not. Instead, consider this analogy: I am a competent and versatile cook, an amateur chef. I will never appear in the ranks of world-renowned chefs, but I regularly serve passable dinners to my family. I have successfully prepared a number of multicourse Thanksgiving dinners, some in motel kitchenettes. I mastered producing an edible meal for a reasonable cost as a necessity while working my way through college. In doing so, I learned how to read recipes out of a cookbook, apply them to my immediate needs, juggle a few ingredients here and there, handle the timing issues that separate dinner from a sequence of snacks, and play it by ear.

An edible meal at a reasonable cost is a good analogy for what your management wants from your testing organization. This book, then, can serve as a test project manager's cookbook, describing the basic tools you need and helping you assemble and blend the proper ingredients.

The Tools You Need

Several basic tools underlie my approach to test management:

A solid quality risk analysis. You can't test everything. Therefore, a key challenge to test management is deciding what to test. You need to find the important bugs early in the project. Therefore, a key challenge to test management is sequencing your tests. You sometimes need to drop tests due to schedule pressure. Therefore, a key challenge to test management is test triage in a way that still contains the important risks to system quality. You need to report test results in terms that are meaningful to non-testers. Therefore, a key challenge to test management is tracking and reporting residual levels of risk as test execution continues. Risk based testing, described in this book, will help you do that.

A thorough test plan. A detailed test plan is a crystal ball, allowing you to foresee and prevent potential crises. Such a plan addresses the issues of scope, quality risk management, test strategy, staffing, resources, hardware logistics, configuration management, scheduling, phases, major milestones and phase transitions, and budgeting.

A well-engineered system. Good test systems ferret out, with wicked effectiveness, the bugs that can hurt the product in the market or reduce its acceptance by in-house users. Good test systems mitigate risks to system quality. Good test systems build confidence when the tests finally pass and the bugs get resolved. Good test systems also produce credible, useful, timely information. Good test systems possess internal and external consistency, are easy to learn and use, and build on a set of well-behaved and compatible tools. I use the phrase *good test system architecture* to characterize such a system. The word *architecture* fosters a global, structured outlook on test development within the test team. It also conveys to management that creating a good test system involves developing an artifact of elegant construction, with a certain degree of permanence.

A state-based bug tracking database. In the course of testing, you and your intrepid test team will find lots of bugs, a.k.a. issues, defects, errors, problems, faults, and other less-printable descriptions. Trying to keep all these bugs in your head or in a single document courts immediate disaster because you won't be able to communicate effectively within the test team, with programmers, with other development team peers, or with the project management team — and thus won't be able to contribute to increased product quality. You need a way to track each bug through a series of states on its way to closure. I'll show you how to set up and use an effective and simple database that accomplishes this purpose. This database can also summarize the bugs in informative charts that tell management about projected test completion, product stability, system turnaround times, troublesome subsystems, and root causes.

A comprehensive test-tracking spreadsheet. In addition to keeping track of bugs, you need to follow the status of each test case. Does the operating system crash when you use a particular piece of hardware? Does saving a file in a certain format take too long? Which release of the software or hardware failed an important test? A simple set of worksheets in a single spreadsheet can track the results of every single test case, giving you the detail you need to answer these kinds of questions. The detailed worksheets also roll up into summary worksheets that show you the big picture. What percentage of the test cases passed? How many test cases are blocked? How long do the test suites really take to run?

A simple change management database. How many times have you wondered, "How did our schedule get so far out of whack?" Little discrepancies such as slips in hardware or software delivery dates, missing features that block test cases, unavailable test resources, and other seemingly minor changes can hurt. When testing runs late, the whole project slips. You can't prevent test-delaying incidents, but you can keep track of them, which will allow you to bring delays to the attention of your management early and explain the problems effectively. This book presents a simple, efficient database that keeps the crisis of the moment from becoming your next nightmare.

A solid business case for testing. What is the amount of money that testing saves your company? Too few test managers know the answers to this question. However, organizations make tough decisions about the amount of time and effort to invest in any activity based on a cost benefit analysis. I'll show you how to analyze the testing return on investment, based on solid, well established quality management techniques.

This book shows you how to develop and apply these basic tools to your test project, and how to get and use the resources you need to succeed. I've implemented them in the ubiquitous PC-based Microsoft Office suite: Excel, Word, Access, and Project. You can easily use other office-automation applications, as I haven't used any advanced features.

The Resources You Need

In keeping with our culinary analogy, you also need certain ingredients, or resources, to successfully produce a dish. In this testing cookbook, I show you how I assemble the resources I need to execute a testing project. These resources include some or all of the following:

A practical test lab. A good test lab provides people — and computers — with a comfortable and safe place to work. This lab, far from being Quasimodo's hideout, needs many ways to communicate with the development team, the management, and the rest of the world. You must ensure that it's stocked with sufficient software and hardware to keep testers working efficiently, and you'll have to keep that software and hardware updated to the right release levels. Remembering that it is a test lab, you'll need to make it easy for engineers to keep track of key information about system configurations.

Test engineers and technicians. You will need a team of hardworking, qualified people, arranged by projects, by skills, or by a little of both. Finding good test engineers can be harder than finding good development engineers. How do you distinguish the budding test genius from that one special person who will make your life as a manager a living nightmare of conflict, crises, and lost productivity? Sometimes the line between the two is finer than you might expect. And once you have built the team, your work really begins. How do you motivate the team to do a good job? How do you defuse the land mines that can destroy motivation?

Contractors and consultants. As a test manager, you will probably use outsiders, hired guns who work by the hour and then disappear when your project ends. I will help you classify the garden-variety high-tech temporary workers, understand what makes them tick, and resolve the emotional issues that surround them. When do you need a contractor? What do contractors care about? Should you try to keep the good ones? How do you recognize those times when you need a consultant?

External test labs, testing services providers, and vendors. In certain cases, it makes sense to do some of the testing outside the walls of your own test lab — for instance, when you are forced to handle spikes or surprises in test workloads. You might also save time and money by leveraging the skills, infrastructure, and equipment offered by external resources such as testing labs and testing services providers.

What can these labs and vendors really do for you? How can you use them to reduce the size of your test project without creating dangerous coverage gaps? How do you map their processes and results onto yours? How does outsourcing fit into your test effort?

Of course, before you can work with any of these resources, you have to assemble them. As you might have learned already, management is never exactly thrilled at the prospect of spending lots of money on equipment to test stuff that — in their view — "ought to work anyway." With that in mind, I've also included some advice about how to get the green light for the resources you really need.

On Context

I've used these tools and techniques to manage projects large and small. The concepts scale up and down easily, although on larger projects it might pay to implement some of the tools in a more automated fashion. In that case, the tools I've described here can be prototypes or serve as a source of requirements for the automated tools you buy or build.

The concepts also scale across distributed projects. I've used the tools to manage multiple projects simultaneously from a laptop computer in hotel rooms and airport lounges around the world. I've used these tools to test market-driven end-user systems and in-house information technology projects. While context does matter, I've found that adaptations of the concepts in this book apply across a broad range of settings.

Simple and effective, the tools incorporate the best ideas from industry standards such as the IEEE 829 Standard for Software and System Test Documentation and bring you in line with the best test management practices and tools at leading software and hardware vendors. I use these tools to organize my thinking about my projects, to develop effective test plans and test suites, to execute the plans in dynamic high-technology development environments, and to track, analyze, and present the results to project managers. Likewise, my suggestions on test resource management come from successes and failures at various employers and clients.

Because context matters, the final two chapters discuss the importance of fitting the testing process into the overall development or maintenance process. This involves addressing issues such as organizational context, the economic aspects of and justifications for testing, life cycles and methodologies for system development, and increasing test process capability, including test process assessment and maturity models.

Using This Book

Nothing in this book is based on Scientific Truth, double-blind studies, academic research, or even flashes of brilliance. It is merely about what has worked — and continues to work — for me on the dozens of test projects I have managed, what has worked for the clients that my company, RBCS, has the good fortune to serve, and what has worked for the thousands of people who have attended RBCS training courses. You might choose to apply these approaches as is, or you might choose to modify them. You might find all or only some of my approaches useful.

Along similar lines, this is not a book on the state of the art in test techniques, test theory, or the development process. This is a book on test management, both hardware and software, as I have practiced it. In terms of development processes — best practices or your company's practices — the only assumption I make is that you as the test manager became involved in the development project with sufficient lead time to do the necessary test development. Chapter 12 addresses different development processes I have seen and worked within. I cover how the choice of a development life cycle affects testing.

Of course, I can't talk about test management without talking about test techniques to some extent. Because hardware and software test techniques differ, you might find some of the terms I use unclear or contradictory to your usage of them. I have included a glossary to help you decipher the hardware examples if you're a software tester, and vice versa. Finally, the test manager is usually both a technical leader and a manager, so make sure you understand and use best practices, especially in the way of test techniques, for your particular type of testing. Appendix D includes a listing of books that can help you brush up on these topics if needed.

This book is drawn from my experiences, good and bad. The bad experiences — which I use sparingly — are meant to help you avoid some of my mistakes. I keep the discussion light and anecdotal. The theory behind what I've written, where any exists, is available in books listed in the bibliography in Appendix D.

I find that I learn best from examples, so I have included lots of them. Because the tools I describe work for both hardware and software testing, I base many examples on one of these two hypothetical projects:

- Most software examples involve the development of a browser-based word-processing package named SpeedyWriter, being written by Software Cafeteria, Inc. SpeedyWriter has all the usual capabilities of a full-featured word processor, plus network file locking, Web integration, and public-key encryption. SpeedyWriter includes various add-ins from other vendors.[1]

- Most hardware examples refer to the development of a server named DataRocket, under development by Winged Bytes, LLP. DataRocket is intended to serve a powerful, high-end database, application, and Web server. It runs multiple operating systems. Along with third-party software, Winged Bytes plans to integrate hardware from vendors around the world.

As for the tools discussed in this book, you can find examples of these at www.rbcs-us.com. These include templates and case studies from real projects. In those chapters that describe the use of these tools, I include information to guide you in the use and study of these templates and case studies should you want to do so. That way, you can use these resources to bootstrap your own implementation of the tools. These tools are partially shown in figures in the chapters in which I describe them. However, screen shots can only tell you so much. Therefore, as you read the various chapters, you might want to open and check out the corresponding case studies and templates from the Web site to gain a deeper understanding of how the tools work.

Please note that the tools supplied with the book are usable, but contain only small amounts of dummy data. This data should not be used to derive any rules of thumb about bug counts, defect density, predominant quality risks, or any other metric to be applied to other projects. I developed the tools primarily to illustrate ideas, so some of the sophisticated automation that you would expect in a commercial product won't be there. If you intend to use these tools in your project, allocate sufficient time and effort to adapt and enhance them for your context. For large, complex projects, or for situations where test management is an ongoing activity, you'll want to consider buying commercial tools.

For those wanting to practice with the tools before putting them into use on a real project, I have included exercises at the end of each chapter. For many of these exercises, you can find solutions at www.rbcs-us.com. These exercises make this book suitable as the test management textbook for a course on testing, software engineering, or software project management. Given that testing is increasingly seen by enlightened project managers as a key part of the project's risk management strategy, including material such as this as part of a college or certification curriculum makes good sense.

Finally — in case you haven't discovered this yet — testing is not a fiefdom in which one's cup overfloweth with resources and time. I have found that it's critical to focus on testing what project managers really value. Too often in the

---

[1]When I wrote the first edition and used this same example, a browser-based word processor might have struck readers as a bizarre concept. Well, to those at Google, I say, "You're welcome" for the idea!

past I've ended up wrong-footed by events, spending time handling trivialities or minutiae while important matters escaped my attention. Those experiences taught me to recognize and attend to the significant few and ignore the trivial many. The tools and techniques presented here can help you do the same, especially the risk-based testing elements. A sizeable number of test groups are disbanded in their first couple of years. This book will help keep you out of that unfortunate club.

Although it's clearly more than simply hanging onto a job, success in test management means different things to different people. In my day-to-day work, I measure the benefits of success by the peace of mind, the reduction in stress, and the enhanced professional image that come from actually managing the testing areas in my purview rather than reacting to the endless sequence of crises that ensue in ad hoc environments. I hope that these tools and ideas will contribute to your success as a testing professional.

What's New and Changed in the Third Edition?

For those of you who read the second edition and are wondering whether to buy this third edition, I've included the following synopsis of changes and additions:

- I've split the final chapter into two detailed chapters on the importance of fitting the testing process into the overall development or maintenance process. I address organizational context, the economic aspects of and justifications for testing, life cycles and methodologies for system development, test process assessment, and process maturity models.

- I have addressed the IEEE 829-2008 standard, which came out as I started work on this book. This new version of the IEEE 829 standard includes not only document templates, but also discussion on the testing process. While I'm not endorsing the complete adoption of this standard on your projects, I believe it does provide useful ideas and food for thought.

- I also added some new metrics. The templates include the tools to generate those metrics. Some of the templates originally published with the book, while usable, contained minor errors. Readers of the first and second editions — being test professionals — caught and pointed out these errors to me. I have corrected those mistakes.

- In addition to case studies, I have added some exercises. Some of these come from RBCS's live and e-learning course "Managing the Testing Process," some carried over from the second edition, and some are adapted from *Pragmatic Software Testing*. You can use these exercises for self-study, as part of a book club, or for classroom education. (Some professors have selected this book as a textbook for a software testing course.) Solutions to many of these exercises are now available at www.rbcs-us.com.

- Finally, little has changed in terms of the challenges facing those who manage test projects since I wrote the first and second editions. Every time my associates teach RBCS's "Managing the Testing Process" classes, which are drawn directly from this book, at least one attendee tells me, "It's amazing how every issue we've talked about here in class is something that has come up for me on my projects." However, I have learned some new tricks and broadened my mind. For example, Agile project methodologies are now quite popular, so I've incorporated material to discuss the challenges that Agile techniques pose for testing and how you can manage these challenges.

If you read the second edition, enjoyed it, and found it useful, I think these changes and additions will make this third edition even more useful to you.

Defining What's on Your Plate: The Foundation of a Test Project

Testing requires a tight focus. It's easy to try to do too much. You *could* run an infinite number of tests against any nontrivial piece of software or hardware. Even if you try to focus on what you think might be "good enough" quality, you can find that such testing is too expensive or that you have trouble figuring out what "good enough" means for your customers and users. Before I start to develop the test system — the testware, the test environment, and the test process — and before I hire the test team, I figure out what I *might* test, then what I *should* test, and finally what I *can* test. Determining the answers to these questions helps me plan and focus my test efforts.

What I might test are all those untested areas that fall within the purview of my test organization. On every project in which I've been involved, some amount of the test effort fell to organizations outside my area of responsibility. Testing an area that another group already covered adds little value, wastes time and money, and can create political problems for you.

What I should test are those untested areas that directly affect the customers' and users' experience of quality. People often use buggy software and computers and remain satisfied nevertheless. Either they never encounter the bugs or the bugs don't significantly hinder their work. Our test efforts should focus on finding the critical defects that will limit people's ability to get work done with our products.

What I can test are those untested, critical areas on which my limited resources are best spent. Can I test everything I should? Not likely, given the schedule and budget I usually have available.[1] On most projects, I must make

---

[1]You can find the first mention of this difficult test management problem in Glenford Myers's *The Art of Software Testing*.

tough choices, using limited information, on a tight schedule. I also need to sell the test project to my managers to get the resources and the time I need.

What You *Might* Test: The Extended Test Effort

On my favorite software and system projects, testing was pervasive. By this, I mean that a lot of testing went on outside the independent test team. In addition, testing started early. This arrangement not only made sense technically, but also kept my team's workload manageable. This section uses two lenses to examine how groups outside the formal test organization contribute to testing. The first lens is the level of focus — the *granularity* — of a test. The second is the type of testing performed within various test phases. Perhaps other organizations within your company could be (or are) helping you test.

From Microscope to Telescope: Test Granularity

Test *granularity* refers to the fineness or coarseness of a test's focus. A fine-grained test case allows the tester to check low-level details, often internal to the system. A coarse-grained test case provides the tester with information about general system behavior. You can think of test granularity as running along a spectrum ranging from structural (white-box) to behavioral (black-box and live) tests, as shown in Figure 1-1.

Ideal Testers:	Programmers DB/Net/System Admins Electrical/Mechanical Engineers	Test Engineers Test Technicians (Some) Programmers	Tech Support/Help Desk Sales/Marketing Business Analysts/Users
Test Granularity:	Structural (White-Box)	Behavioral (Black-Box)	Live (Alpha, Beta, or Acceptance)

Figure 1-1 The test granularity spectrum and owners

Structural (White-Box) Tests

Structural tests (also known as *white-box tests* and *glass-box tests*) find bugs in low-level structural elements such as lines of code, database schemas, chips, subassemblies, and interfaces. The tester bases structural tests on *how* a system operates. For example, a structural test might reveal that the database that stores user preferences has space to store an 80-character username, but that the field allows the user to enter only 40 characters.

Structural testing involves a detailed technical knowledge of the system. For software, testers create structural tests by looking at the code and the data structures themselves. For hardware, testers create structural tests to compare chip specifications to readings on oscilloscopes or voltage meters. Structural tests thus fit well in the development area. Testers in an independent test team — who often have little exposure to low-level details and might lack programming or engineering skills — find it difficult to perform structural testing.

Structural tests also involve knowledge of structural testing techniques. Not all programmers learn these techniques as part of their initial education and ongoing skills growth. In such cases, having a member of the test team work with the programmers as a subject-matter expert can promote good structural testing. This person can help train the programmers in the techniques needed to find bugs at a structural level.

Behavioral (Black-Box) Tests

Testers use behavioral tests (also known as *black-box* tests) to find bugs in high-level operations, such as major features, operational profiles, and customer scenarios. Testers can create black-box functional tests based on *what* a system should do. For example, if SpeedyWriter should include a feature that saves files in XML format, then you should test whether it does so. Testers can also create black-box non-functional tests based on *how* a system should do what it does. For example, if DataRocket can achieve an effective throughput of only 10 Mbps across two 1-gigabit Ethernet connections acting as a bridge, a black-box network-performance test can find this bug.

Behavioral testing involves a detailed understanding of the application domain, the business problem that the system solves, and the mission the system serves. When testers understand the design of the system, at least at a high level, they can augment their behavioral tests to effectively find bugs common to that type of design. For example, programs implemented in languages like C and C++ can — depending on the programmers' diligence — suffer from serious security bugs related to buffer overflows.

In addition to the application domain and some of the technological issues surrounding the system under test, behavioral testers must understand the special behavioral test techniques that are most effective at finding such bugs. While some behavioral tests look at typical user scenarios, many tests exercise extremes, interfaces, boundaries, and error conditions. Bugs thrive in such boundaries, and behavioral testing involves searching for defects, just as structural testing does. Good behavioral testers use scripts, requirements, documentation, and testing skills to guide them to these bugs. Simply playing around with the system or demonstrating that the system works under average conditions are not effective techniques for behavioral testing, although many test teams make the mistake of adopting these as the sole test techniques. Good behavioral tests, like good structural tests, are structured, methodical, and often repeatable sequences of tester-created conditions that probe suspected system weaknesses and strive to find bugs, but through the external interfaces of the system under test. Most independent test organizations perform primarily behavioral testing.

Live Tests

Live tests involve putting customers, content experts, early adopters, and other end users in front of the system. In some cases, we encourage the testers to try to break the system. Beta testing is a well-known form of bug-driven live testing. For example, if the SpeedyWriter product has certain configuration-specific bugs, live testing might be the best way to catch those bugs specific to unusual or obscure configurations. In other cases, the testers try to demonstrate conformance to requirements, as in acceptance testing, another common form of live testing.

Live tests can follow general scripts or checklists, but live tests are often ad hoc (worst case) or exploratory (best case). They don't focus on system weaknesses except for the "error guessing" that comes from experience. Live testing is a perfect fit for technical support, marketing, and sales organizations whose members don't know formal test techniques but do know the application domain and the product intimately. This understanding, along with recollections of the nasty bugs that have bitten them before, allows them to find bugs that developers and testers miss.

The Complementary and Continuous Nature of Test Granularity

The crew of a fishing boat uses a tight-mesh net to catch 18-inch salmon and a loose-mesh net to catch six-foot tuna. They might be able to catch a tuna in a salmon net or vice versa, but it would probably make them less efficient. Likewise, structural, behavioral, and live tests each are most effective at finding certain types of bugs. Many great test efforts include a mix of all three types.

While my test teams focus on behavioral testing typically, I don't feel bound to declare my test group "the black-box bunch." I've frequently used structural test tools and cases effectively as part of my system test efforts. I've also used live production data in system testing. Both required advanced planning, but paid off handsomely in terms of efficiency (saved time and effort) and effectiveness (bugs found that we might have missed). Test granularity is a spectrum, not an either/or categorization. Mixing these elements can be useful in creating test conditions or assessing results. I also mix planned test scenarios with exploratory live testing. I use whatever works.

A Stampede or a March? Test Phases

The period of test execution activity during development or maintenance is sometimes an undifferentiated blob. Testing begins, testers run some (vaguely defined) tests and identify some bugs, and then, at some point, project management declares testing complete. As development and maintenance processes mature, however, companies tend to adopt an approach of partitioning testing into a sequence of phases (sometimes called *levels*). Ownership of those various phases can differ; it's not always the test team. There are various commonly encountered test phases, although these often go by different names.

Unit Testing

Unit testing focuses on an individual piece of code. What constitutes an individual piece of code is somewhat ambiguous in practice. I usually explain to our clients that unit testing should focus on the smallest construct that one could meaningfully test in isolation. With procedural programming languages such as C, unit testing should involve a single function. For object-oriented languages such as Java, unit testing should involve a single class.

Unit testing is not usually a test phase in a project-wide sense of the term, but rather the last step of writing a piece of code. The programmer can use structural and behavioral test design techniques, depending on her preferences and skills, and, possibly, an organizational standard.

Regardless of which test design technique is used, unit tests are white-box in the sense that the programmer knows the internal structure of the unit under test and is concerned with how the testing affects the internal operations. Therefore, programmers usually do the unit testing. Sometimes they test their own code. Sometimes they test other programmers' code, often referred to as *buddy tests* or *code swaps*. Sometimes two programmers collaborate on both the writing and unit testing of code, such as the *pair programming* technique advocated by practitioners of the agile development approach called Extreme Programming.

Component or Subsystem Testing

During the component or subsystem testing, testers focus on the constituent pieces of the system. Component testing applies to some collection of units that provide some defined set of capabilities within the system.

Component test execution usually starts when the first component of the product becomes functional, along with whatever scaffolding, stubs, or drivers[2] are needed to operate this component without the rest of the system. In our SpeedyWriter product, for example, file manipulation is a component. For DataRocket, the component test phase would focus on elements such as the SCSI subsystem: the controller, the hard-disk drives, the CD/DVD drive, and the tape backup unit.

Component testing should use both structural and behavioral techniques. In addition, components often require hand-built, individualized test harnesses. Because of the structural test aspects and the custom harnesses required,

---

[2]For a discussion on stubs, drivers, and other such frameworks for component testing, you can refer to my book *Pragmatic Software Testing*.

component testing often requires programmers and hardware engineers. However, when components are standalone and have well-defined functionality, behavioral testing conducted by independent test teams can work. For example, I once worked on a Unix operating-system development project in which the test organization used shell scripts to drive each Unix command through its paces using the command-line interface — a typical black-box technique. We later reused these component test scripts in system testing. In this instance, component testing was a better fit for the test organization.

Integration or Product Testing

Integration or product testing focuses on the relationships and interfaces between pairs of components and groups of components in the system under test, often in a staged fashion. Integration testing must happen in coordination with the project-level activity of *integrating* the entire system — putting all the constituent components together, a few components at a time. The staging of integration and integration testing must follow the same plan — sometimes called the *build plan* — so that the right set of components comes together in the right way and at the right time for the earliest possible discovery of the most dangerous integration bugs. For SpeedyWriter, integration testing might start when the developers integrate the file-manipulation component with the graphical user interface (GUI) and continue as developers integrate more components one, two, or three at a time, until the product is feature-complete. For DataRocket, integration testing might begin when the engineers integrate the motherboard with the power supply, continuing until all components are in the case.[3]

Not every project needs a formal integration test phase. If your product is a set of standalone utilities that don't share data or invoke one another, you can probably skip this. However, if the product uses application programming interfaces (APIs) or a hardware bus to coordinate activities, share data, and pass control, you have a tightly integrated set of components that can work fine alone yet fail badly together.

The ownership of integration testing depends on a number of factors. One is skill. Usually, testers will use structural techniques to perform integration testing; some independent test teams do not have sufficient internal system expertise. Another is resources. Project plans sometimes neglect or

---

[3]Since this is a book on test management, not test design, I don't want to diverge into a long technical discussion of how to do this. Instead, I can recommend three books for your test engineers to read. If they can find a copy, Boris Beizer's *Software System Testing and Quality Assurance* remains one of the best. If they can't find that, my own book *Pragmatic Software Testing* contains a chapter on integration testing that summarizes Beizer's discussion as well as some other useful ideas. Finally, Rick Craig and Stefan Jaskiel's book, *Systematic Software Testing*, does a good job of explaining this topic as well.

undersize this important task, and neither the development manager nor the test manager will have the resources (human or machine) required for integration testing. Finally, unit and component testing tends to happen at the individual-programmer level when owned by the development team — each programmer tests her own component or swaps testing tasks with her programmer peer — but this model won't work for integration testing. In these circumstances, unfortunately, I have seen the development manager assign this critical responsibility to the most junior member of the programming team. In such cases, it would be far better for the test team to add the necessary resources — including appropriately skilled people — to handle the integration testing. When the product I'm testing needs integration testing, I plan to spend some time with my development counterparts working out who should do it.

String Testing

String testing focuses on problems in typical usage scripts and customer operational strings. This phase is a rare bird. I have seen it used only once, when it involved a strictly black-box variation on integration testing. In the case of SpeedyWriter, string testing might involve cases such as encrypting and decrypting a document, or creating, printing, and saving a document.

System Testing

System testing encompasses the entire system, fully integrated. Sometimes, as in installation and usability testing, these tests look at the system from a customer or end-user point of view. Other times, these tests stress particular aspects of the system that users might not notice, but are critical to proper system behavior. For SpeedyWriter, system testing would address such concerns as installation, performance, and printer compatibility. For DataRocket, system testing would cover issues such as performance and network compatibility.

System testing tends to be behavioral. When doing system testing, my test teams apply structural techniques to force certain stressful conditions that they can't create through the user interface — especially load and error conditions — but they usually evaluate the pass/fail criteria at an external interface. Where independent test organizations exist, they often run the system tests.

Acceptance or User-Acceptance Testing

From unit testing through to system testing, finding bugs is a typical test objective. Before you start acceptance testing, though, you generally want to have found all the bugs. The test objective is to demonstrate that the system meets requirements. This phase of testing is common in contractual situations, when successful completion of acceptance tests obligates a buyer to accept a system. For in-house IT development efforts, successful completion of the acceptance tests triggers deployment of the software in a production environment.

In commercial software and hardware development, acceptance tests are sometimes called *alpha tests* (executed by in-house users) and *beta tests* (executed by current and potential customers). Alpha and beta tests, when performed, might be about demonstrating a product's readiness for market, although many organizations also use these tests to find bugs that can't be (or weren't) detected in the system testing process.

Acceptance testing can involve live data, environments, and user scenarios. The focus is usually on typical product-usage scenarios, not extreme conditions. Therefore, marketing, sales, technical support, beta customers, and even company executives are perfect candidates to run acceptance tests. (Two of my clients — one a small software startup and the other a large PC manufacturer — use their CEOs in acceptance testing; the product ships only if the CEO likes it.) Test organizations often support the acceptance testing; provide test tools, suites, and data that they developed during system testing; and, with user "witnessing," sometimes execute the acceptance tests.

Pilot Testing

Hardware development often involves pilot testing, either following or in parallel with acceptance tests. Pilot testing checks the ability of the assembly line to mass-produce the finished system. I have also seen this phase included in in-house and custom software development, where it demonstrates that the system will perform all the necessary operations in a live environment with a limited set of real customers. Unless your test organization is involved in production or operations, you probably won't be responsible for pilot testing.

Why Do I Prefer a Phased Test Approach?

As you've seen, a phased test approach marches methodically across the test focus granularity spectrum, from structural tests to behavioral tests to live tests. Such an approach can provide the following benefits:

- Structural testing can build product stability. Some bugs are simple for developers to fix but difficult for the test organization to live with. You can't do performance testing if SpeedyWriter corrupts the hard disk and crashes the system after 10 minutes of use.

- Structural testing using scaffolding or stubs can start early. For example, you might receive an engineering version of DataRocket that is merely a motherboard, a SCSI subsystem, and a power supply on a foam pad. By plugging in a cheap video card, an old monitor, and a DVD drive, you can start testing basic I/O operations.

- You can detect bugs earlier and more efficiently, as mentioned previously.

- You can precisely and quantitatively manage the bug levels in your system as you move through the project.

- Phases provide real and psychological milestones against which the project team can gauge the quality of the system and thus the project's proximity to completion.

I'll explain the last two benefits in more detail in Chapters 4 and 9.

Test Phase Sequencing

Figure 1-2 shows a common sequence of the execution activities for various test phases. On your projects, the execution activities in these phases might be of different relative lengths. The degree of overlap between execution activities in different phases varies considerably depending on entry and exit criteria for each phase, which I'll discuss in Chapter 2, and on the project life cycle, which I'll discuss in Chapter 12. Quite a few organizations omit the test phases that I've shown with dotted lines in the figure. There's no need to divide your test effort exactly into the six test phases diagrammed in Figure 1-2. Start with the approach that best fits your needs and let your process mature organically.

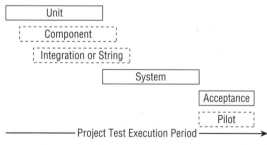

Figure 1-2 The test execution period for various test phases in a development project

When I plan test sequencing, I try to start each test phase as early as possible. Software industry studies have shown that the cost of fixing a bug found just one test phase earlier can be lower by an order of magnitude or more, and my experience leads me to believe that the same argument applies to hardware development.[4] In addition, finding more bugs earlier in testing increases the total number of bugs you'll find. On unique, leading-edge projects, I need to test basic design assumptions. The more realistic I make this testing, the more risk mitigation I achieve.

This rule of starting test phases as early as possible has some caveats. Since the nasty, hard-to-fix problems often first rear their ugly heads in behavioral testing, moving into integration or system testing early can buy the project more time to fix them. However, you need to make sure that the earlier phases of testing found and fixed enough bugs to adequately stabilize the product and make it ready for such testing. Otherwise, you'll enter a later phase of testing before the product is ready, and spend a lot of time working inefficiently, with many blocked tests and hard-to-isolate bugs.

This is complicated by another common project failing. One of the main challenges with unit testing and other phases of testing typically owned by the programmers relates to whether these tests actually get done. Rushed for time, and knowing an independent test team will get the code somewhere down the line, programmers sometimes are tempted to skip these tests. Even if such tests do get done, as I mentioned before, not all programmers know how to do them properly. So, it makes sense to have some amount of engagement between your test team with the development team to help ensure that these tests get done and get done properly.

The First Cut

At this point, you have some ideas about how other organizations attack the division of the test roles. Now you can look at the testing that already goes on in your organization and locate gaps. If you are establishing a new test organization, you might find that folks who tested certain areas on previous projects believe that they needn't continue testing now that *you're* here. (I touch on this topic more in Chapter 9 when I discuss how development groups can become "addicted" to the test team.) After identifying past test contributions, I make sure to close the loop and get commitments from individual contributors (and their managers) that they will continue to test in the future.

What You *Should* Test: Considering Quality

Once I've identified the areas of testing that might be appropriate for my test organization, my next step is to figure out what I should test. To do this, I must understand what quality means for the system, and the risks to system quality

---

[4]For example, see Stephen Kan's *Metrics and Models in Software Quality*, Jack Campanella's *Principles of Quality Costs*, and Capers Jones's *Estimating Software Costs*.

that exist. While quality is sometimes seen as a complex and contentious topic, I have found a pragmatic approach.

Three Blind Men and an Elephant: Can You Define Quality?

There's a management parable about three blind men who came across an elephant. One touched the tail and declared it a snake. Another touched a leg and insisted that it was a tree. The third touched the elephant's side and claimed that it was a wall.

Defining quality can be a similar process. Everyone knows what *they* mean by quality, but disagreements abound. Have you debated with developers over whether a particular test case failure was really a bug? If so, weren't these debates in fact about whether the observed behavior was a quality issue? What, really, is quality? What factors determine its presence or absence? Whose opinions matter most?

J. M. Juran, a respected figure in the field of quality management, defines quality as "features [that] are decisive as to product performance and as to 'product satisfaction'. ... The word 'quality' also refers to freedom from deficiencies ... [that] result in complaints, claims, returns, rework and other damage. Those collectively are forms of 'product *dis*satisfaction.'"[5] Testing should cover the decisive features, those that determine customer and user satisfaction, and try to find as many as possible of the bugs that would result in dissatisfaction.

As the project team develops or maintains a system, the project team is exposed to various risks related to not implementing all of the satisfying features and to implementing some of them improperly. These risks can collectively be called *quality risks*, since these risks relate to the possibility of a negative or undesirable outcome related to the quality of the system. As we execute our tests, we might discover failures related to these risks. At the most general level, the process of testing should allow the test organization to assess the quality risks and to understand the failures that exist in the system under test.

After a system is released, customers or users who encounter bugs might experience dissatisfaction and then make complaints, return merchandise, or call technical support. This makes the users and customers the arbiters of quality. Who are these people, and what do they intend to do with the system? For our purposes, let's assume that customers are people who have paid or will pay money to use your system and that they expect your system to do what a

---

[5]This is from Juran's book *Juran on Planning for Quality*. In his book *Quality Is Free*, Phillip Crosby argues that quality is conformance to requirements — nothing more and nothing less. But when was the last time you worked on a project with complete, unambiguous requirements?

similar system, in the same class and of the same type, should reasonably do. The users might also be customers, or they might be people who did not pay for the product or its development, but use it or its output to get work done.

Testing looks for situations in which a product fails to meet customers' or users' reasonable expectations in specific areas. For example, IBM evaluates customer satisfaction in terms of capability (functions), usability, performance, reliability, installability, maintainability, documentation/information, service, and overall fitness for use. Hewlett-Packard uses the categories of functionality, usability, reliability, performance, and serviceability.

The Perils of Divergent Experiences of Quality

As people use a product — a car, an espresso machine, a bar of soap — they form opinions about how well that product fulfills their expectations. These impressions, good or bad, become their *experience of quality* for that product. Test teams try to assess quality during test execution. In other words, you and your test team use the test system — the testware, the test environment, and the test process as discussed in Chapter 3 — to gauge, in advance, customers' experiences of quality. I refer to the extent to which the test system allows testers to do this as the *fidelity* of the test system.

Figures 1-3 and 1-4 provide visual representations of two test systems. In both figures, the circles represent the sets of quality risks for a product. In Figure 1-3, test system A allows the tester to cover a majority of the product's quality risks and also to cover those areas that affect user A's experience of quality.

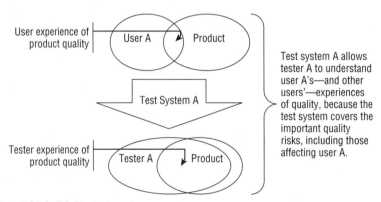

Figure 1-3 A high-fidelity test system

Test system B, shown in Figure 1-4, fails in both respects. It covers a smaller portion of the product's quality risks. Worse yet, the portion tested does not cover user B's experience of quality.

Figure 1-4 A low-fidelity test system

Two other scenarios are possible. First, suppose that you have a test system with the same degree of coverage as test system B, but that the coverage area aligns with user B's use of the product. In this case, your test team will do a fine job of catching critical defects — at least from user B's perspective. You'll also be able to explain how those defects will affect the users, which is important in terms of establishing priority. If most users, including your most important ones, use the product the same way user B does, then test system B, coverage limitations notwithstanding, is a good test system.

Second, suppose that you have a test system with the same degree of coverage as test system A, but that the coverage area does not align with user A's usage of the product. In this case, you fail to test the quality risks that user A cares about. In addition, you can't relate the results of the testing you do perform to real-world usage scenarios, which reduces the apparent priority of any defects you find. Since these features will probably reach the field buggy, user A will be dissatisfied. If user A is typical of your customer base — especially your important customers — you have a serious test coverage problem, even though the test system covers most of the product's quality risks.

Figure 1-5 represents these scenarios. Of course, you can't test all of the quality risks and none of the customer uses, or vice versa. In Figure 1-5, these unlikely or unreachable zones are shown in the dotted-line-enclosed areas in the upper left and lower right. The best test systems score on the right-hand side of the chart (covering customer usage), and the farther up the right-hand side you get (the more quality risks you cover), the better your test system. Those quality risks that relate most closely to actual customer usage are the critical quality risks.

Figure 1-5 Test system coverage and its ability to assess quality

So, how do you determine the customer-critical quality risks? You want to address as many of these quality risks as possible, developing and executing tests consistent with customer priorities in both order and emphasis. Various quality risk analysis techniques will allow you to do so, so let's look at them now.

What to Worry About: How to Analyze Quality Risks

The next few pages discuss risk-based testing. Let me start by clarifying some terms and concepts. First, *risk* generally means the possibility of a negative or undesirable outcome or event. Specific to our area of concern, testing, we can say that a risk is any possible problem that would decrease customer, user, participant, or stakeholder perceptions of product quality or project success.

When the primary effect of a potential problem is to impact project success, we can call it a *project risk*. For example, a possible test environment problem that could delay completion of a project is a project risk. When the primary effect of a potential problem is on the quality of the product itself, we can call it a *quality risk*. For example, a possible performance defect that could cause a system to respond slowly during normal operation is a quality risk. I'll cover how testing should deal with project risks in the next chapter. In this chapter, I focus on quality risks.

Risks differ in terms of importance, which I refer to as the *level of risk*. Later in this section, we'll look at some intricate ways to determine the level of risk, but we'll start with a simple approach that considers two factors:

- The likelihood of the problem occurring
- The impact of the problem should it occur

To determine likelihood, you generally focus on technical considerations, such as the programming language, network throughput, and so forth. To determine impact, you generally focus on business considerations, such as the potential financial impact of a problem, the frequency with which users or customers will encounter a problem, and so forth. While I refer to this as a simple approach to determine the level of risk, it is often sufficient for many organizations.

Analytical risk-based testing strategies start with quality risk analysis to identify risk items and determine the level of risk for each risk item. You then address the quality risks in four ways:

- **Allocation of effort.** During planning, preparation, and execution of testing, you allocate effort for each quality risk item based on the level of risk. Individual testers should match the rigor and extensiveness of the test techniques to the level of risk.

- **Test sequencing.** During planning, preparation, and execution of testing, test managers and testers attack the risks in risk priority order, starting with the most important quality risks first and working their way down to the less important ones.

- **Test triage.** If needed during test execution, should management reduce the time or resources available for testing, you can delete tests from the test plan in reverse-risk priority order, starting with the least important tests.

- **Reporting test results.** Test managers should report test results in terms of risk. You'll look at this more closely in Chapters 4 and 5.

With these preliminaries out of the way, let's get into the details. First I'll review some of the properties and benefits of analytical risk-based testing strategies. Next I'll show you a couple of checklists you can use as frameworks and mental aids for quality risk identification. I'll then discuss processes, techniques, and templates that you can use for quality risk analysis. Finally, I'll cover some tips and challenges associated with quality risk analysis.

Properties and Benefits of Analytical Risk-Based Testing

Analytical risk-based testing has six interesting and useful properties, two of which are fundamental, and four of which are incidental.

First and fundamentally, the testing effort is proportional to the level of risk. The higher the level of risk for any risk item, the more test effort you expend to develop and to execute test cases for that risk item.

Second and also fundamentally, test tasks are sequenced based on risk. The higher the level of risk for any risk item, the earlier you develop the test cases for that risk item. The test case inherits the level of risk belonging to the risk item from which you derive the test case. By using the level risk of risk associated with the test case to sequence the test cases, you can run the test cases in risk order.

The third property, an incidental one, has to do with the way test execution reduces the residual level of risk. This incidental property arises from the way the first two fundamental properties of risk-based testing influence the overall level of risk during the project. Because the test cases relate to risks items, and because you run them in risk order, the overall level of residual quality risk goes down as test execution continues, and the drop in the overall level of residual quality risk is most significant in the first quarter of the test execution period, when you're running the highest-risk test cases.

The fourth property, also incidental, enables risk-based test results reporting. Because the test cases relate to risk items, if you preserve traceability between test cases, bugs found by those test cases, and the risk items from which you derived those test cases, you can do risk-based test results reporting. This means that you report your test results not only in terms of bugs (found and fixed) and test cases (run, passed, and failed), but also in terms of the overall level of residual quality risk and in terms of specific risk items that have known failed test cases or known bugs. (You'll look at traceability in Chapter 3, and results reporting in Chapters 4 and 5.)

The fifth property, incidental as well, allows intelligent test triage. Since each test case inherits the level of quality risk from its parent risk item, if you find yourself forced to reduce the overall test execution effort due to schedule pressure, you can eliminate the cases in reverse risk order. You will run the most important tests (and will run them first) and will drop less important tests (which you would run later in any case) only if you find yourself squeezed at the end.

The sixth property, and the final incidental one, allows for self-correction of errors in the risk analysis. This property relates to a weakness inherent in all analytical test strategies. In any analytical test strategy, you perform an analysis early in a project and use that analysis to determine the test work you will do. However, any early analysis will often be based on incorrect assumptions and information, to some extent, and those invalid concepts become embedded in the testing. By blending reactive test strategies such as bug hunting, software attacks, and exploratory testing (discussed in Chapter 3), you introduce a self-correcting element into the test execution process, since these reactive strategies will tend to identify the holes and mistakes in your test set that arose due to problems with the analysis. In iterative life cycle models (which I'll discuss in Chapter 12), including agile models, you will do the analysis iteratively, which helps to address this problem as well.

Because of some of these properties, analytical risk-based testing strategies provide a number of benefits to you as a test manager and to the project team.

First, due to the ability to allocate effort, prioritize test cases, and, if necessary, to triage test cases, risk-based testing allows you to deal with the common situation of insufficient time, including the situation where you must make intelligent test case deletion decisions when management reduces the test execution period.

Second, due to the same priorities, risk-based testing helps you make smart coverage decisions. Remember that, at the outset of this chapter, I said that an infinite number of tests *could be* run against any system. So, test coverage, measured as a percentage of what *could be* tested, is always 0% because you must select a finite number of actual test cases from this infinite cloud of possible test cases. So, how do you choose a smart subset? Risk-based testing gives you a defensible method for doing this.

A third benefit arises from the process for risk analysis rather than from the properties of risk-based testing. Best practices for quality risk analysis involve a broad cross-section of business and technical stakeholders in the risk-analysis process. Due to this broad stakeholder involvement, even if you receive poor specifications documents, you can fill in the gaps in those documents based on what the stakeholders tell you.

A fourth benefit is one offered primarily to the project team, though you are the bearer of the benefit. Because you can report test results in terms of residual risk, rather than only bug and test counts, this allows you to give the project team a solid understanding of the risks associated with releasing the system at any point in time after test execution begins.

Kick-Starting Quality Risk Analysis with Checklists

In the next section, I describe processes you can use for quality risk analysis. These processes involve starting with a checklist and developing the list of quality risk items using that checklist as a framework. So, in this section, let's look at two checklists you can use.

The Usual Suspects

To develop the list of major quality risk categories, I start by breaking down the test process into the phases of component testing, integration testing, and system testing. Using the guidelines presented earlier in this chapter, you will have already determined which of these test phases you will run and which you can skip because other colleagues are covering them.

During unit and component testing, the following major quality risk categories apply:

- **States.** In some computer systems, especially telephony systems and embedded software of various types, the components or some set of components implement what is called a *state machine*. Incoming events cause a state machine to transition through clearly defined states, while the response (the associated output and the subsequent state) to an event depends on the current state, the event, and any conditions that might exist. State machines present a variety of quality risks related both to the state machine as a whole and to the individual states. Do the transitions from one state to another occur under the proper conditions? Does the system generate the correct outputs? Does the system accept and properly handle both legal and illegal event/condition combinations? Consider an alarm card in the DataRocket server that sends SNMP information over the network if problems arise. This component spends most of its time in a quiescent state, but if it senses that the CPU is overheating, it transitions to a CPU Overtemp Warn state, during which it sends out alerts at regular intervals. If the problem does not clear up, the component transitions to a CPU Overtemp Critical state, at which point it initiates a system shutdown. You will need to verify that the transitions occur at the right points and that the component can't get stuck in a given state. For example, if the CPU returns to a normal temperature but the alarm card remains in a CPU Overtemp Warn state, the alarm card will continue to send (now spurious) alerts over the network and might do something dangerous, such as transitioning incorrectly to the CPU Overtemp Critical state.

▪ **Transactions.** Components that have transactions with the user or with other components present various risks. For example, creating a new file is a transaction in SpeedyWriter. Can the user select the appropriate file template? How does the product respond to illegal file names?

▪ **Code coverage.** Untested code in a component presents unknown structural risks. These untested areas often handle unusual or hard-to-create conditions, which make it tempting to skip them. For example, simulating the CPU Overtemp Critical condition described earlier might result in damage to the test configuration. However, how else can you verify that the system shutdown will actually occur? If it is impractical — because of CPU placement, for example — to simulate the overheating using a hair dryer or a soldering iron, you might be forced to sacrifice one CPU to find out.

▪ **Data-flow coverage.** A data flow is the transfer of information — either through parameters, shared (global) data space, or a stored database — from one component of the system to another. The risks associated with data flows don't receive nearly the attention they deserve Programs allow you to import, export, and link data from other programs, creating complex data flows. Users sometimes report strange and counterintuitive failures while using these features. If SpeedyWriter, for example, includes a component that reads and writes Microsoft Word files, testers must evaluate this feature across multiple Word versions and with files that include more than just text. In the hardware world, signal quality testing is a form of component-level data-flow testing.

- **Functionality.** Each component exists to implement some set of functions, which are internal operations such as calculations and formatting. Functional quality risks are generally of two types: either the function behaves improperly, or the function behaves properly but has undesirable side effects.

- **User interface.** The quality risks in this area are similar to those encountered for functionality, but they also include questions of usability such as understandable prompts and messages, clear control flows, and appropriate color schemes and graphics. User interface testing during component testing often involves prototypes of the interface.[6]

- **Mechanical life.** Any object that can be flexed or moved has a limit to the number of motions it can endure: keys on a keyboard break, hinges fatigue, buttons snap off, latches crack, and contacts fail.

- **Signal quality.** Any circuit that processes data, whether digital or analog, is subject to the constraints imposed by signal quality. Lead times, lag times, rise times, fall times, noise, spikes, transients, and the like can be out of spec, causing a component to fail.

During integration testing, the following major quality risk categories apply:

- **Component or subsystem interfaces.** Every API, every method, every function, every bus, every connector represents an opportunity for misunderstandings between the two (or more) component development engineers. These misunderstandings manifest themselves when two otherwise-correct components fail to work together. Shared data files and especially dynamic data such as configuration files and multi-user databases are interfaces as well. Any place where one component transfers data or control to one or more components, whether immediately or in a delayed fashion, an interface exists that can cause trouble.

- **Functionality.** In integration tests, you again have risks related to the possibility of the wrong action, or the right action with the wrong side effect. Here you focus on functionality that requires the correct operation of two or more components or a flow of data between them.

- **Capacity and volume.** Think of software, a computer, or a network of computers as a system of pipes for bringing in information, operating on it, storing it, and sending it out. The capacities (static) and volumes (dynamic) of these pipes must match the requirements of the application and the expectations of the user. From a structural test perspective, every buffer, queue, storage resource, processor, bus, and I/O channel

---

[6]As Steve McConnell points out in the *Software Project Survival Guide*, these mock-ups are an excellent opportunity to get real users in front of the interface, and should actually be created during the requirements, design, or detailed design phase.

in the system has a theoretical limit and a (lower) practical limit. For a single-user program on a PC, this might be a simple, well-bounded set of risks. For SpeedyWriter, the effects of network traffic and the speed of the typist might be the only issues. For a network server such as DataRocket, however, a variety of risks can apply. Can the network card handle realistic traffic levels? Can the disk subsystem deal with realistic loads? Is the data-storage capability sufficient? In integration testing, you can begin to evaluate these risks.

▪ **Error/disaster handling and recovery.** Undesirable events happen. PCs lock up. Servers crash. Networks drop packets. Hard drives die. Building air conditioners and heaters go out. Electrical grids have power surges, brownouts, and failures. It might be depressing, but you should construct a list of such situations and how they can affect your system. Increasingly, people choose to use common PC-based office applications and operating systems in critical infrastructure. This implies a need for true disaster-recovery capability. Mostly, though, there are the mundane mini-catastrophes that will eventually afflict the system. You can start looking at these quality risks early in the integration test phase.

▪ **Data quality.** If your product stores, retrieves, and shares significant amounts of data — especially data that has delicate links, relationships, and integrity constraints — you should consider testing whether the product can handle that data reliably. For example, I once used an expense-reporting program that had a serious data quality bug in the way it handled the expense-report data file that it managed. Because I needed to analyze data across multiple reports, all reports had to reside in the same file. If the PC operating system crashed while the application had the expense-report file open, the application corrupted the file. The corruption was subtle; I could continue to use the file for quite a while afterward, but in the meantime, the corruption compounded itself. At some point, any attempt to add a new transaction caused the application to crash. The application did not include a file-repair utility. Because data storage and retrieval tend to be clustered in certain components or subsystems, you should start testing these areas as soon as these components are integrated.

▪ **Performance.** As with capacity and volume, performance concerns apply to most subsystems or components in a product. For real-time and mission-critical applications, performance can be the most important quality risk. Even for systems that are not real-time, important performance issues exist. Most product reviews address performance. Performance is not only "how many per second," but also "how long." Consider the battery life of a laptop. As the system is integrated, you can begin to measure performance.

- **User interface.** As more pieces of real functionality are integrated into the system, you can start to test these through the user interface. (If the user interface is a true throw-away prototype, then you might not have this option.)

During system and acceptance tests, the following major quality risk categories apply:

- **Functionality.** During system testing, you should consider functionality in terms of whole sequences of end-user operations (broad) or an entire area of functionality (deep). For example, with SpeedyWriter you might look at creating, editing, and printing a file, or at all the possible ways of creating a file, all the editing options, and all the printing options.

- **User interface.** If you or the programmers have a chance to work with a prototype in earlier test phases, the remaining usability quality risks during system testing are the irritating behaviors that crop up when everything is connected to the interface. Regrettably, though, the system test phase is often the first point of testing for the complete user interface with all the commands and actions available. (The prototyping I advocated earlier happens on the best projects, but not on all projects.) If you have the opportunity, you must address all usability quality risks at this stage.

- **States.** State machines can exist at the system level as well as at the component level. For example, a voice-mail system is a complex computer-telephony state machine.

- **Transactions.** Transaction handling can also occur at the system level. DataRocket, for example, handles transactions: printing a file, delivering a file (one chunk at a time), and so forth.

- **Data quality.** During the system test phase, I revisit the data quality risks initially covered in integration testing, since the complexity of the data often increases once the entire product is integrated. For example, if SpeedyWriter supports embedded pictures and other nontext objects, this feature might not be dropped in until the end of the integration test. Working with such complex data makes problems more likely.

- **Operations.** Complex systems often require administrators; databases, networks, and servers come to mind. These operators perform essential maintenance tasks that sometimes take the system offline. For DataRocket, consider the following quality risks: Can you back up and restore files? Can you migrate the system from a Windows server to a Linux server? Can you add an external RAID array? Can you add memory? Can you add a second LAN card?

- **Capacity and volume.** During a system test, you have the same kinds of quality risks related to capacity and volume risks covered in integration testing.

- **Reliability, availability, and stability.** Quality risks in this area include unacceptable failure rates (mean time between failures, or MTBF), unacceptable recovery times (mean time to repair, or MTTR), and the inability of the system to function under legitimate conditions without failure.

- **Error/disaster handling and recovery.** As in the case of capacity and volume, I revisit error/disaster handling and recovery from a behavioral perspective. I focus on the external failures.

- **Stress.** This risk category is often an amalgam of capacity, volume, reliability, stability, and error/disaster handling and recovery.

- **Performance.** First broached during integration testing, performance is another risk category that I revisit during the system test phase.

- **Date and time handling.** A decade ago, concerns about the year 2000 raised the level of awareness about these types of quality risks, but many programmers of today were not yet even in college at that point. You might also need to take account of the fact that some countries — for example, Taiwan — base their calendars on events other than the birth of Jesus. Additionally, your product might not work properly in different time zones, or even multiple time zones if it is a distributed system.

- **Localization.** Localization typically refers to problems associated with different languages. Even Romance languages, which use the Latin alphabet, often include special letters, such as the ñ in Spanish, that can generate quality risks if your product includes sorting or searching capabilities. Languages such as Chinese, Japanese, Russian, and Greek create bigger difficulties. Besides the software considerations, computers in these environments use different keyboards and different printer drivers. Moreover, language is not the only thing that changes at the border and can affect your system. Can your product handle 220 volts and 110 volts, 50 hertz and 60 hertz? How about the unique dial tones and ring signals found in Europe and Asia? Beyond the technical considerations, there are cultural issues and taboos. What is considered an acceptable way of indicating something in one culture might be a rude or obscene gesture in another.

- **Networked and distributed environments.** If your product works in a networked or distributed environment, you have some special quality risks to consider. For example, what if your system spans time zones? Can the constituent systems talk to each other without getting confused about Central Standard Time and Pacific Standard Time? If your systems must communicate internationally, will the telephone standards affect them?

▪ **Configuration options and compatibility.** Most PC software these days supports various configuration options. SpeedyWriter, for example, might need to remember a customer's name, address, and company to generate letter outlines. DataRocket might allow various CPU speeds and multiprocessor settings. In addition, many configuration options are dynamic. On-demand loading and unloading of drivers, libraries, and software; cold and hot swapping of devices; and power management can dynamically change the configuration of software and hardware. Moreover, when you look out past the internal variables, the PC world includes a bewildering variety of software, hardware, and network environments that can create problems for your system. Will the system talk to all the printers your customers own? Do network drivers cause your system to fail? Can your software coexist with leading applications?

▪ **Standards compliance.** In the hardware world, you might need to consider legal and market standards such as UL, FCC, CE, and others that might be required for your target market. In the software and hardware worlds, customers sometimes require compatibility logos such as Microsoft's "Designed for Windows." Innocuous bugs related to standards can have serious repercussions: your company might even find the product legally or effectively barred from the market.

▪ **Security.** Given your dog's name, your spouse's name, your children's names, and your birthday, I might be able to crack your computer accounts. On a larger scale, if your company has a web site, right now criminals might be trying to break into your network. If security is a feature of or concern for your product, you will need to think about the quality risks that exist.

▪ **Environment.** Because hardware products must live in the real world, they are subject to environmental risks. How do the shaking and bumping encountered during shipping affect a server? Can power sags and surges cause your system to crash and fail? What about the effects of temperature and humidity?

▪ **Power input, consumption, and output.** All computers take in electrical current, convert some of it to heat and some to electromagnetic radiation, and send the rest of it to attached devices. Systems with rechargeable batteries, such as laptops, might add some conversion and storage steps to this process, and some systems might use power in unusual modes such as 48 VDC, but ultimately the process is the same. This orchestration of electrical power can fail; insufficient battery life for laptops is a good example.

▪ **Shock, vibration, and drop.** All computers will at some point be moved. I have never worked with a system that was assembled on the floor on which it would operate. In the course of this movement, the computer will experience shocks, vibrations, and, occasionally, drops. Some computers are subject to motion while on, others only while packaged. The system test phase is the right time to find out whether the system misbehaves after typical encounters with the laws of Newtonian physics.

▪ **Installation, cut-over, setup, and initial configuration.** Every instance of a product has an initial use. Does the installation process work? Can you migrate data from an old system? Are there unusual load profiles during the first few weeks of use? These loads can include many user errors as people learn the system. In a multi-user situation, configuration will also include the creation of the initial accounts. Think about the entire process, end to end. Individual actions might work, but the process as a whole could be unworkable. In addition, consider the possibility that someone might want to uninstall the product. Finally, don't forget quality risks related to the licensing and registration processes.

▪ **Documentation and packaging.** If your product includes documentation, you have risks ranging from the possibly dangerous to the simply embarrassing. Consider instructions in DataRocket's manual, accompanied by an illustration, that led a user to set the input voltage selector for 110 volts in a 220-volt environment. On the less serious side, think of some of the humorous quotations from technical documentation that circulate on the Internet. Do you want your company singled out for such honors? Packaging, likewise, should be appropriately marked.

▪ **Maintainability.** Even if your system is too simple to require an operator, you might still have maintainability risks. Can you upgrade software to a current version? Can you add memory to your PC? If your software works in a networked environment, does it support remote (possibly automated) software distribution?

▪ **Alpha, beta, and other live tests.** For general-purpose software and hardware, no amount of artificial testing can cover all the uses and environments to which your customers will subject your product. To address these risks, I like to use a beta or early-release program of some sort.

As long as this list is, it is not complete. I could add other categories of quality risks. However, this list should serve as a good starting point for your quality risk analysis process.

Using the ISO 9126 Standard as a Checklist

If you work in an organization that tends to follow standards, you might want to consider the ISO 9126 standard's quality model as a checklist and framework for your quality risk analysis. The ISO 9126 quality model consists of six quality characteristics for systems, each of which has three or more subcharacteristics:

- **Functionality:** Attributes that bear on the existence of a set of functions and their specified properties. The functions are those that satisfy stated or implied needs. Its subcharacteristics are suitability, accuracy, interoperability, security, and compliance.

- **Reliability:** Attributes that bear on the capability of software to maintain its level of performance under stated conditions for a stated period of time. Its subcharacteristics are maturity, recoverability, fault tolerance, and compliance.

- **Usability:** Attributes that bear on the effort needed for use, and on the individual assessment of such use, by a stated or implied set of users. Its subcharacteristics are learnability, understandability, operability, and compliance.

- **Efficiency:** Attributes that bear on the relationship between the level of performance of the software and the amount of resources used, under stated conditions. Its subcharacteristics are time behavior, resource behavior, and compliance.

- **Maintainability:** Attributes that bear on the effort needed to make specified modifications. Its subcharacteristics are stability, analyzability, changeability, testability, and compliance.

- **Portability:** Attributes that bear on the ability of software to be transferred from one environment to another. Its subcharacteristics are installability, replaceability, adaptability, and compliance.

To use this as a checklist, you will identify one or more quality risks for each quality subcharacteristic. If you cannot identify one or more quality risks for a subcharacteristic, then you can delete it from your framework in the quality risks analysis document or, for auditability, make a notation that you could not identify any quality risks related to this subcharacteristic.

Identify and Assess: Process Options for quality risk Analysis

At a high level, the process for carrying out a quality risk analysis is straightforward:

1. Select a technique for identifying and assessing quality risks and the associated template to capture the information generated.

2. Assemble a cross-functional team to perform the quality risk analysis.

3. Perform the quality risk analysis, documenting the results in the template.

4. Verify the distribution of the risk-level ratings to ensure adequate dispersal, and adjust the ratings if necessary.

5. If specifications documents related to requirements, design, or use cases exist, establish traceability between the elements of these documents and the quality risk items.

6. If a set of test cases already exists, for example, in the case of an existing product for which a new version is being prepared, establish traceability between the existing test cases and the quality risk items.

7. Check the document into whatever repository you use for test system documents.

Let's take a closer look at each of these steps.

1. **Select a technique for identifying and assessing quality risks and the associated template to capture the information generated.** In the next section, I'll cover the various techniques you and your team can use to identify and assess quality risks. They vary in terms of the level of formality involved and in the amount of documentation they tend to produce, so you'll want to be careful here. Typically, I recommend that people start with an informal approach the first time. It's hard enough to institute quality risk analysis in its simplest form without adding additional difficulties related to large, complex documents and highly rigorous and formalized techniques. The selected technique will determine the template you need.

2. **Assemble a cross-functional team to perform the quality risk analysis.** A critical success factor for quality risk analysis is selecting the proper set of participants. You need a cross-functional team that includes technical stakeholders and business stakeholders. Technical stakeholders can include senior development team members, hardware engineers, network and database experts, help-desk or technical-support staff, and senior test staff, among others. Anyone who understands what is likely to go wrong with the system is a good candidate as a technical stakeholder.

   Business stakeholders can include sales people, marketing staff, business analysts, and product managers, among others. Anyone who understands the impact of potential problems in the system is a good candidate as a technical stakeholder. I must stress the importance of the cross-functional team. Having the right mix of participants will minimize the chances that your quality risk analysis will miss important quality risk items or assign improper risk levels to those items. In addition, keep in mind the human aspect of this process. Risk-based testing uses quality risk analysis to decide what to test, in what order, and how much. To put it another way, we are also deciding what not to test, what to test late in the project, and what to test very little if at all. If you successfully use the cross-functional team to build a cross-functional consensus around these decisions, you not only have the most accurate quality risk analysis possible, but also have support across the organization for these decisions.

The team should include the project manager and the development managers. By including them in the process, you'll build a level of comfort between these managers and you about what tests you plan to run. This mutual understanding prevents surprises and confrontations down the road, and assures the managers that you won't pull any "gotcha" maneuvers on them by running mysterious tests late in the game.

Finally, if your list of risk items somehow gets contaminated with any gross misunderstandings about what the product should do, the project manager and the development managers can help you clear up the misunderstandings at this early stage. This avoids the lost time and the potential embarrassment of developing new tests for — and even reporting bugs against — broken features that don't exist.

3. **Perform the quality risk analysis, documenting the results in the template.** With the team in place, you can now carry out the quality risk analysis. There are two general approaches to this. One approach is to hold a brainstorming session with the entire team. In this session, you use one or both of the checklists introduced earlier to facilitate the identification of quality risk items. Once the team has identified the quality risk items, you then assess each quality risk item to determine its level of risk, according to the rules of the technique you selected. This approach can work well, but the brainstorming session can consume the better part of day or even more than one day for a large product. You might not want — or be able — to hold such a session.

The other approach is to hold a sequence of one-on-one or small-group interviews with distinct stakeholder groups. In each interview, you identify quality risk items, again using one or both of the checklists to structure the interview. After the interviews, you organize a smaller focus group of stakeholders to review the list and, during that review, to assess the level of risk for each risk item. This approach can also work well, but you must remember to hold a final review with the whole team to achieve the consensus-building aspect of the process, since not all the participants will have seen the entire list of quality risk items or their assessed risk levels.

Whichever of these two approaches you use, you'll need to capture the results in the template associated with the selected technique. I usually save this information in a spreadsheet. I call the worksheet with the initial results something like "Initial Risk Analysis." As I update the analysis in the subsequent steps of the process or at later points in the project, I'll use a different worksheet with a different name, preserving the initial results for reference.

4. **Verify the distribution of the risk-level ratings to ensure adequate dispersal, and adjust the ratings if necessary.** One of the challenges of quality risk analysis, which I'll discuss in a subsequent section, is the tendency for the risk-analysis team to turn in initial risk-level assessments that do not do a good job of differentiating the levels of risk associated with risk items. In other words, the risk ratings are clumpy or skewed. Therefore, you should plan to check the distribution of the risk-level ratings. If you use Excel to capture the results, this is easy, because you can create a histogram that shows the distribution. You want to see an approximately normal or bell-curve type of distribution. If not, you should validate the ratings and adjust them.

5. **If specifications documents related to requirements, design, or use cases exist, establish traceability between the elements of these documents and the quality risk items.** At this point, you should evaluate specifications documents, if you have them. These documents could include requirements specifications, design specifications, or use cases. You should establish traceability between the elements of these documents and the quality risk items. This process might result in the discovery of additional risk items. With this traceability, should the specifications change during the project, rather than having to evaluate the effect of the changes on all of the quality risks, you can focus on those risk items related to the changed specification elements.

6. **If a set of test cases already exists, for example, in the case of an existing product for which a new version is being prepared, establish traceability between the existing test cases and the quality risk items.** You (or perhaps senior test engineers on your test team) should also evaluate any existing test cases. For example, with an existing product for which a new version is being created, you are likely to have a significant set of test cases inherited from the previous versions. You should establish traceability between the existing test cases and the quality risk items. This process also might result in the discovery of additional risk items. In addition, this process might result in the discovery of significant areas of under-testing and over-testing, relative to the level of risk associated with various quality risk items. You should plan to address those problems during development of the test system, which I'll discuss in Chapter 3.

7. **Check the document into whatever repository you use for test system documents.** At this point, you should finalize the document for the time

being. You'll need to adjust it later at major project milestones, but for the time being you have a solid foundation for your test estimate, your test plan, and your test system development. You should at least e-mail the final document around to the various project stakeholders, including the participants in the quality risk analysis. You should certainly make sure everyone on the test team has it, and understands how it will affect their work. You should check the document into whatever repository you use for test system documents.

quality risk analysis Techniques and Templates

You might select from any number of techniques for quality risk analysis. I've identified several major types of quality risk analysis techniques, each with significant variations, in use by project teams around the world.[7] These include the following:

- Informal
- ISO 9126
- Cost of exposure
- Hazard analysis
- Failure mode and effect analysis

I'm sure there are one or two more out there that I haven't encountered yet.

The two most commonly used techniques, though, are the informal technique and failure mode and effect analysis (FMEA). I have used these and seen them used more often than any other set of techniques. Because they are the most commonly used, I'm going to focus on these techniques in this chapter.

I'll start with the informal technique. I use this one most frequently. If you are new to risk-based testing, you should start with this one. As I mentioned previously, it's hard enough to institute quality risk analysis in its simplest form. If you add all the difficulties related to the large, complex documents and the highly rigorous and formalized technique associated with failure mode and effect analysis, you are making this process much harder. Why do something the hard way, unless you are required to do so by some regulatory agency or company standard?

I'll illustrate this technique and the template by example. Figure 1-6 shows an example of a portion of the quality risk analysis for SpeedyWriter. I'll explain each column.

---

[7]For a survey of these five techniques, see my article "Quality Risk Analysis," available in the Basic Library at www.rbcs-us.com. You can also find this article in *Fundamental Concepts for the Software Quality Engineer, Volume 2*, edited by Taz Daughtry.

	A	B	C	D	E	F	G
1							
2	#	Quality Risk	Likeli-hood	Im-pact	Risk Pri. #	Extent of Testing	Tracing
3	1.000	*Functionality*					
4	1.001	Can't open supported file	3	2	6	Broad	2.2.7
5	1.002	Can't save native file type	5	1	5	Extensive	2.1.1
6	1.003	Can't save supported file type	3	3	9	Broad	2.2.8
7	1.004	Font attributes don't work	4	2	8	Broad	2.3.1
8	1.005	Font sizes don't work	5	3	15	Cursory	2.3.1
9	1.006	Can't create a table	4	1	4	Extensive	2.4.1
10	1.007	Problems editing a table	3	2	6	Broad	2.4.2
11	1.008	Can't insert a picture	5	1	5	Extensive	2.5.1
12	1.009	Problems formatting pictures	4	2	8	Broad	2.5.2
13	1.010	Paragraph formating problems	2	2	4	Extensive	2.6.1
14	1.011	Doesn't load add-in features	4	5	20	Opportunity	2.7.1
15	1.012	Legacy styles not supported	5	5	25	Report bugs	2.8.1

Figure 1-6 Example of informal quality risk analysis for SpeedyWriter

The leftmost column is a unique identifier for each row. Each quality risk category appears at the top of a list of one or more quality risk items. Each quality risk category has a sequential number (1, 2, 3, and so forth). Each quality risk item listed for each quality risk category has a sequential number (1.001, 1.002, 1.003, and so forth). This number is useful in capturing traceability from test cases back to the risks.

The Quality Risk column shows the quality risk categories, and, within each category, the specific quality risk items. The quality risk categories thus serve as a framework for the quality risk items associated with them.

The Likelihood column captures the likelihood for each quality risk item. This is the quality risk analysis team's assessment of the likelihood of the risk item becoming an actual problem. In other words, how likely does the team feel it is that one or more bugs will exist for this item? The team should determine likelihood based primarily on technical considerations. In this example, the team rated the likelihood on a 1–5 scale as follows:

- **1: Very high.** Such bugs are almost certain to occur.

- **2: High.** Such bugs are more likely to occur than not to occur.

- **3: Medium.** Such bugs have about an even chance of occurring as not occurring.

- **4: Low.** Such bugs are less likely to occur than not to occur.

- **5: Very low.** Such bugs are almost certain not to occur.

Of course, you can use another scale if you'd like. I have found this five-point scale to work quite well, though.

The Impact column captures the impact for each quality risk item. This is the quality risk analysis team's assessment of the business impact that would result if the system had bugs related to this risk item that escaped. In other words, how bad would it be if we delivered one or more bugs for this item to the customers and users? (Remember, the focus here is on the quality risk analysis team's perception of business impact, not the test team's perception of impact.) The team should determine impact based primarily on business considerations. In this example, the team rated the likelihood on a 1–5 scale as follows:

- **1: Very high.** Such bugs would render the system unsalable.

- **2: High.** Such bugs would seriously impair users and significantly reduce sales.

- **3: Medium.** Such bugs would inconvenience some users and marginally reduce sales.

- **4: Low.** Such bugs would inconvenience a few users and might reduce sales.

- **5: Very low.** Such bugs would only rarely affect users and would not reduce sales.

As before, you can use another scale, but this five-point scale works quite well in practice.

The Risk Priority Number column shows the aggregate level of risk for each risk item. In this example, the spreadsheet calculates the number by multiplying likelihood and impact. You can adopt another formula for calculating the risk priority number if you like, including weighting likelihood or impact to emphasize technical or business considerations, respectively. When the test team develops test cases from the quality risk analysis, each test case inherits the risk priority number from its parent risk item. The test team can then run the test cases in risk-priority order, starting with the tests that have a risk priority number of one. If the testers must delete test cases due to schedule pressure, they can do so in reverse risk-priority-number order.

While the risk priority number allows you to sequence and, if necessary, triage test cases based on risk, you still need some way to determine the amount of effort to expend on testing a particular risk item. In other words, based on the risk priority number, what relative amount of test effort should we put into developing and executing tests against this risk item? The Extent of Testing column shows this determination. In this example, the team has used the following breakdown for the extent of testing, based on the range of the risk priority number:

- **1–5. Extensive.** Run a large number of tests that exercise many combinations and variations of interesting conditions.

- **6–10. Broad.** Run a medium number of tests that exercise many different interesting conditions for the risk item.

- **11–15. Cursory.** Run a small number of tests that sample the most interesting conditions for the risk item.

- ▪ **16–20. Opportunity.** Leverage other tests to explore the risk item with minimal effort and only if the opportunity presents itself.

- ▪ **21–25. Report bugs.** Only report bugs observed for this risk item if discovered during other tests.

As with the Likelihood and Impact columns, feel free to use some other breakdown if it makes more sense for you. Unlike with the Likelihood and Impact columns, I have quite frequently found it necessary to fine-tune this heuristic for allocation of effort. Of course, if you adjust the risk-priority-number calculation, you'll need to adjust this heuristic, too.

Finally, the Tracing column captures the relationship between the requirements specification elements and the quality risk item. The numbers given in the column in Figure 1-6 correspond to the section numbers in the requirements document. I have not shown tracing for test cases, because I'm assuming this is a new project. Tracing for existing tests, if they exist, would typically involve another column.

Having discussed the informal technique, let's move on to a formal technique for defining quality risks using an approach called *failure mode and effect analysis* (FMEA).

Fundamentally, FMEA is a technique for understanding and prioritizing possible failure modes (or quality risks) in system functions, features, attributes, behaviors, components, and interfaces. It also provides a means of preventive defect reduction and tracking process improvements. Preventive defect reduction arises because the technique is ideal applied not only to testing decisions, but to product design and implementation decisions. As these design and implementation decisions reduce the level of risk, iterative application of the technique shows the risk reduction, which allows us to re-focus our testing on the remaining higher risks.

Figure 1-7 shows the top page of a sample FMEA chart for DataRocket. Let's go through each of the columns in detail.

The System Function or Feature column is the starting point for the analysis. In most rows, you enter a concise description of a system function. If the entry represents a category, you must break it down into more specific functions or features in subsequent rows. Getting the level of detail right is a bit tricky. With too much detail, you can create an overly long, hard-to-read chart; with too little detail, you will have too many failure modes associated with each function.

In the Potential Failure Mode(s)-Quality Risk(s) column, for each specific function or feature (but not for the category itself), you identify the ways you might encounter a failure. These are quality risks associated with the loss of a specific system function. Each specific function or feature can have multiple failure modes.

	A	B	C	D	E	F	G	H	I	J	K	L	M	N	O	P	Q	R	S
1			Failure Mode and Effects Analysis (Quality Risks Analysis) Form																
3	System Name: DataRocket					Supplier Involvement: Seven Lucky					FMEA Date: 5/20/2002								
4	System Responsibility: Jim Johnson					Model/Product: DataRocket					FMEA Rev Date: 5/28/2002								
5	Person Responsibility: Bob Chen					Target Release Date:													
6	Involvement of Others:					Prepared By: Lin-Tsu Wei													
8															Action Results				
9	System Function or Feature	Potential Failure Mode(s)- Quality Risk(s)	Potential Effect(s) of Failure	Critical ?	Severity	Potential Cause(s) of Failure	Priority	Detection Method(s)	Likelihood	Risk Pri No	Recom-mended Action	Who/ When?	References	Action Taken	Severity	Priority	Detection	Risk Pri No	
11	Video Subsystem																		
12	Video Controller	Installation	Bad fit, blocked access to other cards, etc.	Y	1	PCI Slot Layout	1	Case/MB Design	1	1	Function Test	Test/ Product Test	Video Card Ref Guide, Pg 12 MB Ref Guide, Pg 15						
13		Palette Limit	Limited displays.	N	5	Memory size	5	Vendor HW Test	5	125	None		Video Card Ref Guide, Pg 10						
14		Performance	Slow screen displays.	N	4	Memory speed	5	Vendor HW Test	5	100	None		Video Card Ref Guide, Pg 10						
15		Reliability	Loss of functionality.	Y	1	Unreliable card, MB/card incompat	1	Vendor MTBF Test	3	3	MTBF Demo	Test/ System Test	Video Card Ref Guide, Pg 15						
16																			
17	Linux Video Drivers	Incompatiblity	Loss of functionality.	Y	1	Novell/Video chipset	2	Vendor driver Test	3	6	Compat Test	Test/ Product Test	Video Card Ref Guide, Pg 11						

Figure 1-7 A portion of the FMEA for DataRocket

In the Potential Effect(s) of Failure column, you list how each failure mode can affect the user, in one or more ways. I keep these entries general rather than trying to anticipate every possible unpleasant outcome.

In the Critical? column you indicate whether the potential effect has critical consequences for the user. Is the product feature or function completely unusable if this failure mode occurs?

In the Severity column, you capture the effect of the failure (immediate or delayed) on the system. This example uses a scale from 1 to 5 as follows:

1. Loss of data, hardware damage, or a safety issue

2. Loss of functionality with no workaround

3. Loss of functionality with a workaround

4. Partial loss of functionality

5. Cosmetic or trivial

Some books on FMEA show the use of a reverse scale, in which larger numbers denote greater severity. However, I prefer to use the scale shown here, which is more in line with the typical use of the term *severity* as I've encountered it.

In the Potential Cause(s) of Failure column, you list possible factors that might trigger the failure — for example, operating-system error, user error, or normal use. In my experience, this column is not as important as others when you are using an FMEA strictly as a test design tool.

In the Priority column, you rate the effect of failure on users, customers, or operators. This example uses a scale from 1 to 5, as follows:

1. Complete loss of system value

2. Unacceptable loss of system value

3. Possibly acceptable reduction in system value

4. Acceptable reduction in system value

5. Negligible reduction in system value

Because these are subjective ratings highly dependent on an understanding of the business, you should rely on input from sales, marketing, technical support, and business analysts.

In the Detection Method(s) column, you list a currently existing method or procedure, such as development activities or vendor testing, that can find the problem before it affects users, excluding any future actions (such as creating and executing test suites) you might perform to catch it. (If you do not exclude the tests you might create, the next column will be skewed.)

In the Likelihood column, you have a number that represents the vulnerability of the system, in terms of: a) existence in the product (e.g., based on technical risk factors such as complexity and defect history); b) escape from the current development process; and c) intrusion on user operations. This example uses the following 1-to-5 scale:

1. Certain to affect all users

2. Likely to impact some users

3. Possible impact on some users

4. Limited impact to few users

5. Unimaginable in actual usage

This number requires both technical judgment and an understanding of the user community, which makes participation by programmers and other engineers along with business analysts, technical support, marketing and sales important.

As with the informal technique, the RPN (Risk Priority Number) column tells you how important it is to test this particular failure mode. The risk priority number (RPN) is the product of the severity, the priority, and the likelihood. Because this example used values from 1 to 5 for all three of these parameters, the RPN ranges from 1 to 125.

The Recommended Action column contains one or more simple action items for each potential effect to reduce the related risk (which pushes the risk priority number toward 125). For the test team, most recommended actions involve creating a test case that influences the likelihood rating.

The Who/When? column indicates who is responsible for each recommended action and when they are responsible for it (for example, in which test phase).

The References column provides references for more information about the quality risk. Usually this involves product specifications, a requirements document, and the like.

The Action Results columns allow you to record the influence of the actions taken on the priority, severity, likelihood, and RPN values. You will use these columns after you have implemented your tests, not during the initial FMEA.

As with the informal technique, you can use a cross-functional brainstorming session to populate your FMEA chart. To do so, you gather senior representatives from each team — development, testing, marketing, sales, technical support, business analysts, and so forth — and fill in the chart row by row. This is certainly the best way, but it requires a commitment from each group to send a participant to a meeting that could consume a day or more. If you can't get people to attend a cross-functional brainstorming session like this, you can proceed with the interview approach discussed for the informal technique, too.

I have encountered a few pitfalls in using the FMEA method. In some cases, I have become distracted by quality risks that lie outside the scope of the test project. If I am working on SpeedyWriter, for example, I don't need to worry about operating-system bugs or underlying hardware failures. For DataRocket, I needn't analyze possible low-level failures in drives or chips. If I find a bug related to a given failure mode, will the development team — or some other group — address it? If not, it's out of scope.

The resulting FMEA document will be large. Be sure that you are ready to maintain this document after you create it. Otherwise, you won't be able to use it to focus test development and execution, which defeats the purpose.

Tips and Challenges of quality risk Analysis

I'll finish up this discussion on quality risk analysis by offering a few tips on how to best handle quality risk analysis. I'll also list some challenges you need to take into account.

The first tip relates to keeping the proper degree of detail. How precise should you be with your quality risk items? Sometimes you might feel a risk item covers too much ground. Should you separate it? The rule of thumb is to only separate one risk item into two or more risk items when necessary to distinguish between different levels of risk. Too much detail makes the documents hard to manage. Too little detail makes it impossible to prioritize test cases accurately.

The second tip relates to respecting your quality risk analysis team and their precious time. The quality risk analysis brainstorming sessions can require one or more entire days. Even the interviews can take up to two hours. Make sure people know what they are committing to when you ask them to participate.

My final tip relates to the type of quality risk analysis and thus quality risk management you are doing. It looks quantitative, since you have numbers. However, the numbers are just shorthand for classifications, used to allow you to calculate the risk priority number by using a mathematical equation rather than a table. You must understand that what you are doing is qualitative risk management. Based on the subjective opinions and collective wisdom of the participants, the process assigns relative priorities to risk items. Quantitative risk management is something that insurance companies and banks, armed with statistically valid data, can do. You don't have such data.

Let's look at some challenges. The first is building consensus on risk. Sometimes participants disagree about likelihood or priority ratings. You can try to use some of your political influence to broker a compromise. You can also see if the various participants can educate each other on how they should rate the risks. However, if you can't reach consensus, you need to escalate to some decision-maker who is ultimately responsible for the quality of the delivered system.

Another challenge is to avoid priority inflation. Sure, in the absence of constraints, everyone would want to test everything extensively. That's not connected to reality. If you see that priority inflation is happening, ask people what they would give up for additional test coverage. Is a week or a month of schedule delay acceptable? Is an extra $10,000 or $100,000 in test budget acceptable? Is dropping features that were not extensively tested acceptable? If the answers to these questions are no, no, and absolutely not, then perhaps you can apply a reality check to people's gold-plated test coverage aspiration.

The final challenge is getting the participants to make rational decisions about risk. Consider this example: Which is safer, air travel or driving? Most people know, rationally, that air travel is safer. In fact, on a distance-traveled basis, air travel is about 100 times safer. However, more people have a fear of flying than of driving. This same kind of irrationality can afflict the quality risk analysis process. If you think people are overstating or understating likelihood or impact during the process, you should try to question the reasons for a particular rating to see if you can get people to be more rational in their assessment.

What You *Can* Test: Schedule, Resources, and Budget

Whether you've used an informal approach or the more formal FMEA technique, you now have a prioritized outline of quality risks. This is analogous to the requirements for the overall project; the list of critical quality risks documents the essential requirements for my test effort. Now I need to figure out a test schedule and a budget that will allow me to test the scariest risks.

One of my first managers was fond of this saying: "Schedule, cost, and quality — pick two." This pithy remark means that while for a given feature set you can freely select any two of these variables, doing so determines the third variable. I call this rule, which is illustrated in Figure 1-8, the "Iron Box and Triangle" of system development. The clockwise arrow indicates refinement during the planning stage. These refinements balance features, schedule, cost, and quality. Once implementation begins, the feature set becomes more rigid, the schedule more painful to change, and budget increases less likely. Within the fixed box representing the feature set in Figure 1-8, the two lines that show the schedule and the cost determine the third line, quality, that completes the triangle.

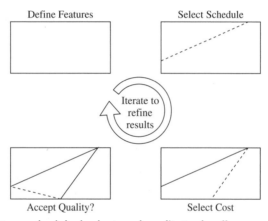

Define Features   Select Schedule

Iterate to refine results

Accept Quality?   Select Cost

Figure 1-8 The feature, schedule, budget, and quality trade-offs

This creates a planning conundrum in that you have only a rough idea of what your test project is about, but the window of opportunity that might allow a realistic schedule and an adequate budget is closing. And even this scenario assumes that you are on the project team during the planning phase. The situation is worse if you have joined the team later, during implementation, as you might have a fixed budget and schedule. There's no perfect solution, but some project management techniques exist to help.

Shoehorning: Fitting a Test Schedule into the Project

Often, software and hardware project schedules don't evolve according to any textbook approach. You might have to start with a ship date and a list of product features — the negotiability of both varies — and build the schedule from there. How can you construct a workable test schedule within these constraints?

I use a work-breakdown structure, which is a top-down approach.[8] I find it intuitive to start with big categories of work and iteratively decompose them into discrete tasks, especially at the early stages when I don't have a lot of details. I start by breaking the test effort into major phases such as these:

- Planning (the work discussed in this chapter and the next)
- Configuration (getting the necessary hardware and other resources and setting up the test lab)
- Staffing (if applicable)
- Test development (building or deploying the test tools, creating the test suites and the test case library, putting the reporting tools in place, and documenting how the test process is to put these testware items into action)
- Test execution (running the tests, recording test status, and reporting results)

Next, I divide each phase into activities. Within the planning category, for example, I set up activities such as defining quality risks, creating the schedule and the budget, writing test plans, and selecting test tools. Other activities might include getting bids from third parties for their help, or hiring test technicians, test engineers, and system administrators.

After that, I decompose each activity into tasks, and then subtasks if necessary. This decomposition continues until I have constituent tasks that are one or two days long and are the responsibility of one person. (I don't decompose the work-breakdown structure this way for test execution; instead I use the test case estimating and tracking method illustrated in Chapter 5.) These small task definitions allow me to ascertain whether I'm on track during the project. Big tasks can get dangerously out of control, and I won't discover such problems until a long period (a week or more) has slipped past me.

The activities in the configuration phase depend on the test environment I need. Even though I probably don't know all the details at this point, my list of quality risks usually has given me some ideas. Once I think through the quality risks, I have a high-level perspective on the test suites I must create, which gives me a good idea of my test environment needs.

For development, you must deploy your test tools and then develop the test suites themselves. I often list separate major tasks for each test phase and then enter the test suites as individual tasks within each phase. Test suite development should proceed in priority order. Developing test suites is a

---

[8]If you aren't familiar with work-breakdown structures, I recommend *Effective Project Management* by Robert Wysocki, et al., as a good introduction to the topic.

full-time job, so I'm careful not to set up work on various suites as parallel tasks unless I have multiple test engineers or can give a single engineer twice as long to finish. In addition, I take care to add a task for the test engineers to document how the test system works, both in terms of the design and functionality of the testware and the way the test process uses that testware to find bugs.

For test execution, there are two important questions to answer in coming up with a good estimate. First, how long will it take to run all the tests once (which I often refer to as a single *test pass*)? Second, how many times will I need to run the tests against successive test releases to find all the important bugs and subsequently confirm the fixing of those bugs (which I refer to as the *number of test cycles*)? Suppose I have six person-weeks of testing work defined for the system test phase and three testers allocated to run the tests. Then, each pass takes my test team two weeks. If I have found, on previous projects with the same project team, that we need to run six cycles to find and fix the important bugs, then I have six cycles, say one week each, with three passes in those cycles (see Figure 1-9).

Figure 1-9 System test passes, releases, and cycles

The time required to run the tests is something a test manager can control and measure. As long as I can come up with solid estimates of how long and how much effort each test case requires, I can add up those numbers across the entire test set and use simple math to predict test pass duration. However, the number of cycles is dependent on many factors outside my control as a test manager. If the quality of the software is poor, then more cycles will be required. If the programmers are slow to fix bugs, then more cycles will be required. If bug fixes tend to break other areas of the product (i.e., to introduce regression bugs), then more cycles will be required.

If I have no historical data with the project team, I have to take a guess on the number of cycles. I've successfully used six one-week cycles as a rule of thumb on a number of projects, although you'll need to consider your project's size and complexity carefully before adopting it. If the set of test cases is small enough, you can run a full pass in each cycle, which has benefits in terms of regression risk. (I'll talk more about test sets, suites, cycles, passes, phases, regression risks, and confirmation testing in Chapter 3.) More commonly, I estimate one week per test cycle, two or three cycles per pass, and three passes per phase. One of my clients, though, has a test set that requires about two person-decades of effort. The whole team runs each test case once as part of a year-long test pass.

However the passes and cycles work out, I break the rules a bit on the work-breakdown structure in the area of test execution, and assign the entire team to test tasks at the test cycle level of detail. I've found that trying to assign a single tester to a single test case in a work-breakdown structure doesn't work well. For one thing, I generally don't know all the tests I'm going to run during this early planning stage, so if I account only for the tests I know, I'll underestimate. Moreover, the project management tools I've worked with do a poor job of managing test cases as tasks. My usual rule of thumb is to estimate the test effort, increase it by 50 percent for the tests I don't know about yet, plan on between 20 and 30 hours of testing per tester per week, and just do the math.

In this first cut, I try to capture the basic dependencies. For example, I must develop a test suite before I can run it, and I can't start a test cycle until I receive something to test. Although some dependencies that loom far in the future won't jump out at me, my best effort will probably suffice. I try to build some slack and extra time into my schedule for the inevitable discoveries. Good project management process dictates that I track against and revise this schedule throughout my project, so I can add dependencies as they become apparent, but increases in schedule and budget numbers after the initial plan are often difficult to negotiate.

As I create the tasks, I also assign resources, even if I can't be complete at this point. I don't worry about staples such as desks, workstations, or telephones unless I have genuine concerns about getting an adequate budget for them. I focus on items such as these:

- Expensive resources such as networks, environmental test equipment, and test tools
- Resources that require long lead times, such as lab space that must be rented and set up, or ISDN and T1 lines
- Missing resources such as people I need to hire
- External resources such as third-party labs
- Scarce resources such as my test engineers and technicians

I'm careful not to over-utilize resources that have limited bandwidth or availability. People, for example, can do only one thing at a time, and you can easily overtax shared resources such as servers, printers, networking infrastructure, and the like if you're not careful. Certain types of tests, such as performance and reliability, require a dedicated set of resources for accurate results.

Accurate scheduling requires the participation of the actual contributors wherever possible. For example, it's better for the test engineer who'll design and implement an automated test suite to tell me how long it will take her than for me to guess myself, especially if she has experience doing test automation and I don't! The more experience the contributor has with the task in question and the tool to be used, the more accurate her estimate will be. There are also so-called Delphic oracle approaches where you poll multiple people on the team for best-case, worst-case, and expected-case task durations, then take the averages of those to come up with best-case, worst-case, and expected-case schedules. You might want to apply these types of approaches on long, complex projects where the consequences of error in the schedule are severe. No matter how careful you are, though, some studies have shown that initial estimates are off by 50 to 200 percent.[9]

One thing I do to improve the accuracy of my schedules is to refer to published rules of thumb to sanity-check my estimates.[10] Capers Jones, in *Estimating Software Costs*, includes an entire chapter of such rules. Various presentations and articles on test estimation, including rules of thumb, appear from time to time at conferences and in testing journals. You might want to accumulate a collection of estimation rules that you use to check your work-breakdown structure.

---

[9]See Rita Hadden's "Credible Estimation for Small Projects," published in *Software Quality Professional*.

[10]For example, see my article, "Software Test Estimation," originally in *Software Testing and Quality Engineering* magazine, now on the Basic Library page of our company web site, www.rbcs-us.com.

Test estimation is hard to do perfectly, but not terribly hard to do well. If you follow good project management practices in preparing your work-breakdown structure, don't forget key tasks, estimate conservatively, don't overload people and resources, involve your entire team in estimation, and focus on key dependencies and deliverables, you can construct a draft schedule for your test project that should prove relatively accurate. I also make sure that my milestone dates fit within the constraints of the project. As the project proceeds, I track progress against the schedule, adding details, adjusting durations, resolving resource conflicts, including more dependencies, and so on. Figures 1-10 and 1-11 show an example of this approach, applied to testing for SpeedyWriter.

Figure 1-10 The first page of a Gantt-chart view of the work-breakdown structure for SpeedyWriter

If you're new to management, you might feel a bit daunted by the prospect of doing a work-breakdown structure. I encourage you to jump in with both feet, picking up a good self-study book first and then cranking out your first test project schedule with one of the project management tools on the market. My ability to schedule projects continues to improve — partly as a result of acquiring skills with the tools, although mostly as a result of experience — but

I started with simple schedules and ran a number of test projects successfully. Scheduling and project management are not trivial skills, so keep it simple to start. Simple schedules are less precise but more accurate. If you try to create complicated 300-task schedules, you can get lost in the minutiae.

Figure 1-11 The second page of a Gantt-chart view of the work-breakdown-structure for SpeedyWriter

Estimating Resources and Creating a Budget

Given a work-breakdown structure with detailed resource allocations, I can hammer out a budget in a couple of hours. Again, I use a top-down approach. I first create a list of resources, starting with general categories such as these:

- **Staff.** This category includes permanent employees, contractors, and consultants.

- **Test tools.** If I'm testing software, I might need code-coverage analyzers, scripting utilities, GUI test automation systems, low-level diagnostic programs, and so forth. Hardware testing can involve oscilloscopes, shock and vibration tables, thermal chambers, and other equipment. Don't forget basic utilities for hardware and software testing.

- **Facilities and overhead.** Items in this category can include travel allowances, lab space, workstations, and infrastructure such as cabling, routers, hubs, bridges, ISDN terminals, and so forth.

- **Test environment.** This category includes the hardware, software, engineering samples, and experimental prototypes.

- **External labs.** I include this category if I intend to use external labs for environmental testing, localization, performance, or other purposes (see Chapter 10).

Within each category, I list the individual items I will need. I use placeholders to indicate where I might add items or quantities later.

To transform this resource list into a budget, I load it into a spreadsheet and line up columns to the right for each month of the project. For each item, I enter a cost figure — a monthly figure for variable costs or a one-time figure for fixed costs. Don't forget hidden or invisible costs such as burden rates for staff, agency markups for staff, application software, support contracts, and training.

If you find it difficult to estimate costs for tools, facilities, infrastructure, or the test environment, you can hit the Web or make some telephone calls. Estimating the cost of using an external lab might require an actual bid, although you can probably get a rough estimate by calling the lab. For unknown items — the placeholders on your resource list — you'll simply have to make an educated guess. Pick a comfortable figure with some wiggle room, but don't allow so much wiggle room that you'll be shot down when you approach management.

At this point, you can compare each line item against your schedule. When do you start using the resource? How long do you use it? Are ramp-up and ramp-down times associated with the resource? Answering these questions will tell you which months must absorb charges for each item, and what fraction of the charge applies in beginning and ending months. For fractions, I keep it simple; I find that halves and quarters are usually precise enough.

As I do for my schedules, I run a sanity check to ensure that all the numbers make sense. If allowed, I involve my staff in the process, making sure that they don't see each other's salary information. (Check with your management before circulating any proposed budget among your staff. Some companies don't allow individual contributors to see any budget information.) After coming up with the budget, I usually sleep on it and then review it the next day. I ask myself whether I've forgotten anything. If the budget contains a few gaping holes where I don't have enough information to even hazard a guess, I'll be honest and indicate that. Figure 1-12 provides an example of a budget for SpeedyWriter, assuming the schedule shown in Figures 1-10 and 1-11.

	A	B	C	D	E	F
1		SpeedyWriter Test Budget				
2		May	June	July	August	Total
3	**Staff**					
4	Jake--Test Manager	$12,500	$12,500	$12,500	$12,500	$50,000
5	Lin-Tsu--Sys Admin.	3,516	3,516	3,516	3,516	$14,063
6	Hitesh--Test Engineer	0	3,750	7,500	7,500	$18,750
7	Maria--Test Engineer	0	1,875	7,500	7,500	$16,875
8	New Hire--Test Engineer	0	12,100	12,100	12,100	$36,300
9	Technicians	0	0	0	10,500	$10,500
10	Staff Materiel Overhead	7,000	0	0	0	$7,000
12	**Total Staff**	$23,016	$33,741	$43,116	$53,616	$153,488
14	**Travel and Training**	$2,500	$2,500	$2,500	$2,500	$10,000
16	**Tools**					
17	GUI	$5,000	$0	$0	$0	$5,000
18	Code Coverage	7,500	0	0	0	$7,500
19	Training	5,000	0	0	0	$5,000
21	**Total Tools**	$17,500	$0	$0	$0	$17,500
23	**Test Environment**					
24	Solaris Client	$1,500	$0	$0	$0	$1,500
25	Windows XP Client	1,200	0	0	0	$1,200
26	Windows Vista Client	1,200	0	0	0	$1,200
27	Mac Client	1,200	0	0	0	$1,200
28	Solaris Server	2,500	0	0	0	$2,500
29	Windows Server	2,500	0	0	0	$2,500
30	Novell Server	2,500	0	0	0	$2,500
31	Solaris x86	1,000	0	0	0	$1,000
32	Novell	700	0	0	0	700
33	Windows Server OS	500	0	0	0	500
35	**Total Test Environment**	$14,800	$0	$0	$0	$14,800
37	**External Labs**					
38	Localization	$0	$0	$5,000	$20,000	$25,000
40						
41	**20% Contingency Padding**	$11,563	$7,248	$10,123	$15,223	$44,158
42						
43	**Grand Total**	$69,379	$43,489	$60,739	$91,339	$264,945

Figure 1-12 SpeedyWriter budget

Negotiating a Livable Test Project

With a quality risks list, schedule, and budget, I have a concise package that I can take to management. By speaking management's language, I can address four key questions that will arise:

- What type of risk management are we buying?
- How long will it take?
- What will it cost?
- What's the return on investment (see Chapter 11)?

Although each company has a different process for approving a test program, every project I've worked on has required some degree of discussion, explanation, and negotiation. Be flexible. If management insists on reduced costs or a faster schedule (or both), I eliminate tests in reverse priority order. If cost is the major concern but I can add a few weeks to the schedule, perhaps I can get by with one less employee. Outsourcing can also reduce costs when done wisely, as you'll see in Chapter 10. I make the case for what I believe needs to be done, but I'm prepared to do less. The only taboo is agreeing to do everything I initially proposed to do but in less time and/or for less money, unless management wants to cut out the contingency time (schedule slack) and money and run a high risk that later discoveries will break my budget or schedule. If I've created a realistic schedule and budget, then agreeing to some faster schedule and lower budget that fits management desire but not reality is hardly doing anyone any favors, and it certainly won't help my credibility. If handed a non-negotiable dictate — for example, "You will do this amount of testing in this period of time with this budget, end of discussion" — then I simply agree to do the best job possible within those parameters, and move on.

At the end of this negotiation, I have an approved budget and schedule and a mutual understanding of the scope and deliverables for my test project. Now it's time to move on to creating a detailed plan, building the testware, and putting the resources in place to carry out the project.

Case Study

On one project, we applied the failure mode and effect analysis (FMEA) technique to analyze possible ways that an application might fail. This application provided secure-file deletion functionality for PC users running some versions of the Windows operating system. We had a six-hour cross-functional meeting with the test team, the programmers, the project manager, a salesperson, and the marketing manager. In this meeting, we discussed ways in which the system might fail and possible approaches to mitigation. These included both testing and various programming-process improvements. Figure 1-13 shows the top portion of this 100-item document. The full document is available at www.rbcs-us.com.

Notice that while the DataRocket example shown earlier in the chapter broke down failure modes based on major subsystems of the server, in this case the analysis starts with major functionality and expected behaviors. You can also use categories of quality risk as the starting point.

	Potential Failure Mode(s)- Quality Risk(s)	Potential Effect(s) of Failure	Critical?	Severity	Potential Cause(s) of Failure	Priority	Detection Method(s)	Detection	Risk Pri No	Recommended Action	Who/ When?
Shreds Deleted Files	Fails to Shred	Security Breach	Y	1	Program Error	1	Test; Debug Trace; Code Review	2	2	Test; Debug Tracing; Code Review	
	Shreds Excessively	Data Loss	Y	1	Program Error	1	Test; Debug Trace; Code Review	2	2	Test; Debug Tracing; Code Review	
Temp File Recognition	Fails to Recognize	Security Breach	Y	1	Program Error	1	Test; Debug Trace; Code Review	2	2	Test; Debug Tracing; Code Review	
	Recognizes Incorrectly	Data Loss	Y	1	Program Error	1	Test; Debug Trace; Code Review	2	2	Test; Debug Tracing; Code Review	
Internet Files Recognition	Fails to Recognize	Security Breach	Y	2	Program Error	3	Test; Debug Trace; Code Review	4	24	Test	
	Recognizes Incorrectly	Data Loss	Y	1	Program Error	1	Test; Debug Trace; Code Review	2	2	Test; Rules Validation	

The above table is part of the "Failure Mode and Effects Analysis (Quality Risks Analysis) Form" shown in the figure.

Figure 1-13 A case study FMEA

Exercise

1. Based on your reading of the Omninet Marketing Requirements Document, the Omninet System Requirements Document, and your experience with testing and bugs, perform a risk analysis for Omninet.[11]

   a. What will determine how long it takes to finish test execution for the Omninet project? You have to consider the following:

   - The time required to run each test once
   - The time required to find, fix, and confirm the fix for each bug

   b. What other factors should you consider?

   c. What management/stakeholder-expectation issues might also affect the test schedule?

[11] This exercise and solution are adapted from Chapter 7 of my book *Pragmatic Software Testing*.

CHAPTER 2

Plotting and Presenting Your Course: The Test Plan

This chapter offers a practical approach to writing one or more test plans for your project. I'll walk through a sample template that I use to develop a solid test plan — and I'll look at the issue of getting the plan approved once I've drawn it up.

Why I Write Test Plans

In Chapter 1 I discussed how I set the scope, schedule, and budget parameters for my test projects. Given a budget, resource commitments, and a schedule, can you claim that you have a test plan? Some people do. In my experience, however, you need more detail to successfully manage a test project. Below the objectives and estimates featured in Chapter 1 lurks another layer of complexity, right above the specific details of test suites — and it pays to consider this complexity in advance.

Writing a test plan gives you a chance to collect your thoughts, your ideas, and your memories. Undoubtedly you've learned a great deal throughout the course of your career. Writing a thorough test plan gives you a chance to crystallize that knowledge into a concrete way of tackling the tasks ahead.

I see the test plan also as an opportunity to communicate with my test team, my development colleagues, and my managers. The most intense discussion of what testing is all about often occurs when I hold a test plan review. I appreciate the chance to have a forum focused solely on testing before a project enters the often-chaotic test execution periods, in which everyone can become so oriented toward minutiae that they lose sight of the big picture.

In some organizations, the test plan encompasses the entirety of the test effort, all the way down to defining all the individual test cases — often called the *test set* or the *test suites* — that the team will run. However, I recommend creating two distinct types of documents: first a test plan, and then an accompanying document, set of documents, or entries in a test-management tool that details the test cases. The difference between a test plan and a test suite is a matter of strategy versus tactics. The test plan describes how we intend to implement the test strategy on a particular project. The test cases in the test suite provide the specific steps the testers will carry out during test execution, which are the tactics necessary to implement the plan. This chapter focuses on the test plan itself. Chapter 3 discusses the process of creating test suites, test cases, and other testware.

How Many Test Plans?

Suppose that you are working on SpeedyWriter. Further suppose that, as the test manager, you have responsibility for the component, integration, and system test phases, with an aggressive beta-testing program during the system test phase. You thus have three distinct test subprojects to plan and manage. Do you write one plan or three? I favor using separate plans for test subprojects that are distinct in one or more of the following ways:

- **Different time periods.** If the test planning, test development, test-environment configuration, and test execution tasks for the subprojects start and end on different dates, I find that I have the information needed to plan some subprojects well before I get the necessary information for the other subprojects. (See Chapter 12 for more information on system life cycle models and test phase timing.) If I try to write only one test plan, I find myself forced to leave large sections of it marked "TBD" (to be determined), which can make the overall plan hard for people to understand and approve.

- **Different methodologies.** Detailed discussions of code coverage instrumentation and platform-independent automated GUI test tools don't really go together. Likewise, in the case of hardware, discussions of thermal chambers, accelerometers, and business application compatibility testing can create a rather eclectic mix of topics in a plan.

- **Different objectives.** If I'm trying to accomplish three different goals — in the current example, finding bugs in components, finding bugs in the relationships and interfaces between incrementally integrated components, and finding bugs in a fully integrated system — writing one plan each for the component test, integration test, and system test allows me to focus my thinking on each goal in turn.

- **Different audiences.** My test plan is not only my chance to inform my colleagues, my testers, and my managers of my vision; it is also a chance to discover their perspectives. This input is especially valuable to the extent that it gives me a better idea of how to focus my test efforts. If I write one lengthy test plan that addresses every issue, I might have trouble getting people to read it, not to mention getting them to participate in a three- or four-hour review. However, if I segment my planning, I'm better able to create documents that speak to the specific concerns of the individuals involved.

Multiple test plans can lead to overlapping content, though, which some people deal with by cutting and pasting shared sections such as test tracking, bug reporting and management, and revision control. Having the same information spread across multiple documents leaves you open to the possibility of inadvertent discrepancies or contradictory statements. When I have multiple test plans, I'll write a single *master test plan* that addresses these common topics and include references to them in the detailed test plans.

Using Drafts to Stimulate Discussion

I expect to release several versions of any test plan I write. Far from finding this frustrating, this sequence of drafts is a dialog that provides me an opportunity to pose questions to the readers. I use brackets in my plans (as opposed to colored fonts, which don't show up as well in hard copy) to indicate questions and open issues. My first drafts are always full of bracketed questions and statements such as these:

[TBD: Need to figure out what the hardware allocation plan is.]

[TBD: Need the Configuration Management team to define the revision numbering schema and the packaging.]

[TBD: Mary, please tell me how this should work.]

I find identifying and documenting these open issues and questions to be among the most useful aspects of the planning exercise. Writing the plan forces me to think through the entire test effort — tools, processes, people, and technology — and to confront issues that I might otherwise miss. I then use the first few drafts of the plan as a method of bringing these issues to the attention of my peers and my managers. If possible, rather than simply asking a question, I also include a suggested answer or a set of possible answers. These prompts or options tend to seed the brainstorming and problem-solving process needed to finalize the document.

Using a Test Plan Template

The template presented in Figure 2-1 is one that I often use for developing test plans. (I have also used the IEEE 829 test plan template, which I'll discuss a little later in this chapter.) It isn't a tool for cutting and pasting a test plan in little time with little thought; rather, it is a logical set of topics that I've found I need to consider carefully for my test efforts. Feel free to add or delete topics as your needs dictate. The following sections examine the parts of the test plan template one by one.

Overview
Bounds
    Scope
    Definitions
    Setting
Quality Risks
Proposed Schedule of Milestones
Transitions
    Entry Criteria
    Continuation Criteria
    Exit Criteria
Test Development
Test Configurations and Environments
Test Execution
    Resources
    Test Case and Bug Tracking
    Bug Isolation and Classification
    Test Release Management
    Test Cycles
    Test Hours
Risks and Contingencies
Change History
Referenced Documents
Frequently Asked Questions

Figure 2-1 A test plan template

Overview

The Overview section of a test plan allows me to introduce readers of the plan to my test project, including what we plan to test and the general test approach. I've found that oftentimes managers one or two levels above me don't have a good idea of what testing covers or how it works. In the overview, I present a concise explanation of my goals, methodologies, and objectives. I keep this section brief. I find it useful to include simple pictures or charts. You might want to illustrate concepts such as the architecture of the system under test, the decomposition or segmentation of the system for component or integration testing, or how this test effort fits into other test efforts that might precede, run concurrently, or follow.

Bounds

In this section, I set boundaries for the test plan by discussing what I will and will not test, by defining important terms and acronyms related to the testing I plan to perform, and by determining where and in what context the test efforts associated with this test subproject will take place.

Scope

Webster's Dictionary defines *scope*, in the context of a project or an operation, as the "extent of treatment, activity, or influence; [the] range of operation." When I describe the scope of my project, I tell the reader what I will and will not pay attention to during the course of the project. I often use an "Is/Is Not" table to define the scope of testing. The Is column lists the elements included within the scope of a particular test phase. The Is Not column does not specify all elements not covered by this test effort — just those elements some readers might think I'll cover. Table 2-1 is an example of such a table, used to describe the scope of the system testing for SpeedyWriter based on the risk analysis shown in Chapter 1.

This compact form allows me to present a precise statement of scope. I don't define each item at this point, as the details about each aspect of testing belong in the test cases themselves.

Definitions

Testing, like other disciplines in the computer world, has its own terms and phrases. Therefore, I include a table of definitions in my test plans. Such a table can help to clarify terminology for those who are not experienced in the field of testing, and can also help to ensure that everyone on the test team is operating from the same set of definitions.

I have included a glossary in this book that you can use as a reference for your own definitions if you like. You can also use the IEEE 610 glossary or the ISTQB glossary as a source. You should edit the definitions as necessary. Don't worry about using the "right" definition, as I have seen plenty of projects that use their own unique definitions without any harm. If you do use a standard glossary as a source, be sure to delete words and phrases that do not apply to your project. Putting a lot of extraneous verbiage in a test plan can lead to a severe case of MEGO ("my eyes glaze over") for readers and a lot of maintenance headaches for you. Speaking of making eyes glaze over, make sure you define all acronyms.

Table 2-1 Is/Is Not Format for Presenting Test Project Scope

IS	IS NOT
Functionality	File conversion
Localization (Spanish, French, and German)	Localization (other than Spanish, French, German)
Capacity and volume	Network compatibility
Basic file sharing	Network file sharing options
Configuration options	Security or privacy
Usability study Install, setup, initial configuration Update and uninstall	Other usability, including any time and motion study
Performance	Date handling
Windows XP, Windows Vista, and Unix (Solaris, Linux) compatibility and functionality	Older Windows versions, Unix (other than Solaris and Linux), or Mac compatibility and functionality
508 accessibility standard compliance	Structural testing
Error handling and recovery	
User interface (functional)	
Web browser compatibility	
Behavioral testing	
Beta testing by customers	

Setting

This section of the test plan describes where I intend to perform the testing and the way those organizations doing the testing relate to the rest of the organization. The description might be as simple as "our test lab." In some cases, though, you might have testing spread hither and yon. I once managed a test project in which work took place in Taipei and Lin Kuo, Taiwan; in Salt Lake City, Utah; and in San Jose and Los Angeles, California. In cases such as this, I would present a table or diagram (such as the one shown in Figure 2-2) that shows how the test team will allocate work among the various participants. (For more information on managing distributed test efforts, see Chapter 10.)

It's a good idea to place testing in an organization setting, too. I often consider what deliverables I need from other groups on the project and what deliverables I will give those groups. You can do this with a table, but I've found that doesn't work so well. An organizational setting diagram, like the one shown in Figure 2-3, will help clarify the situation pictorially.

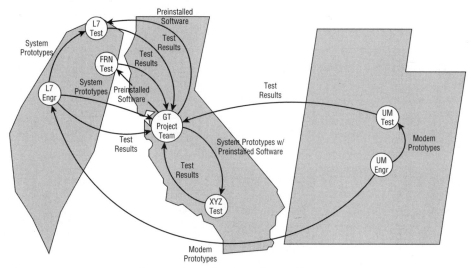

Figure 2-2 A test setting diagram for a distributed test effort

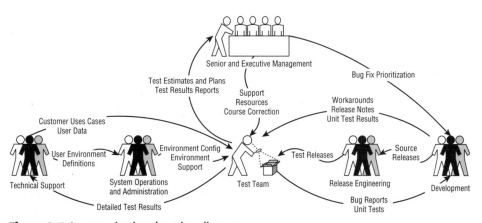

Figure 2-3 An organizational setting diagram

Quality Risks

If you followed the process discussed in Chapter 1, you already have the material you need for this section. You can summarize the quality risk documents you've prepared, or simply reference them in the test plan. If you suspect that many of your readers won't look at the referenced documents, it makes sense to summarize the quality risks here, given that your purpose is to communicate as well as to plan. However, if you know that people will read your quality risks analysis documents — or better yet, if all of the key audience members for the test effort participated in the quality risk analysis process — you can save yourself some work by referencing them.

I also like to cross-reference the test strategy and the test environments against the various risk categories. For example, suppose you have identified a particular configuration of a server for testing a particular quality risk category. You are using risk-based testing. You intend to run primarily behavioral, manual tests. For the most part, you intend to use scripted tests written in advance, blended with some reactive approaches such as software attacks and exploratory testing.[1] One row in your quality risks table might look as shown in Table 2-2.

Table 2-2 An Extract of a Quality Risks Table

QUALITY RISK CATEGORY	SERVER CONFIGURATION	TEST STRATEGY
Functionality	Solaris/Oracle/Apache	Risk-based Manual Behavioral Primarily scripted Some exploratory and software attacks

Proposed Schedule of Milestones

Most of my test plans contain a schedule for the test project's major milestones. You can extract these from the work-breakdown structure, which I discussed in Chapter 1. I focus on the high-level milestones and deliverables that are visible to management. Table 2-3 provides an example of such a schedule.

Transitions

For each test phase, the system under test must satisfy a minimal set of qualifications before the test organization can run tests effectively and efficiently. For example, it makes little sense to start extensive user-scenario testing of SpeedyWriter if the application cannot open or save a file or display text on the screen. Likewise, the DataRocket server can't undergo environmental testing — especially thermal testing — if you don't have even a

---

[1]You can find more information on exploratory testing in Cem Kaner, et al.'s book, *Lessons Learned in Software Testing*, while James Whittaker's books *How to Break Software* and *How to Break Software Security* discuss general methods for attacking software to reveal bugs. Of the two techniques, the software attack technique is more structured, more flexible with teams of variable levels of testing skill and experience, and easier to implement successfully.

prototype case. This section of the test plan should specify the criteria essential for beginning and completing various test phases (and for continuing an effective and efficient test process). I usually refer to these as *entry*, *continuation*, and *exit* criteria, respectively, but some test professionals use the terms *entry*, *suspension/resumption*, and *exit* criteria or *entry*, *stopping*, and *exit* criteria.

Table 2-3 An Example Schedule from a Test Plan

MILESTONE	DATE
Test Development and Configuration	
Test plan complete	8/9/2010
Test lab defined	8/12/2010
FMEA complete	8/16/2010
Test lab configured	8/26/2010
Test suite complete	9/5/2010
Test Execution	
System test entry	9/2/2010
Cycle 1 Complete	9/16/2010
Cycle 2 Complete	10/3/2010
Cycle 3 Complete	10/13/2010
System test exit	10/13/2010

As you write criteria for test phases and transitions, be aware of what you're actually saying: "If someone outside the test group fails to comply with these rules, I'm going to object to starting this phase of testing, ask to stop this phase of testing, or suggest that we not move this project forward." While these are technical criteria, invoking them can create a political firestorm. I include only criteria that I seriously believe will affect the test team's ability to provide useful services to the project. While test team efficiency is important to the project, making life convenient for the test team is not, so I'm careful to avoid criteria that could be construed as trying to shuffle work on to other departments. Finally, when test phase milestones — especially phase entry and exit meetings — occur, I explicitly measure the project against the criteria and report in those terms. I typically rate each criteria as *green* (totally satisfied), *yellow* (not entirely satisfied, but perhaps not a problem), or *red* (unsatisfied and creating a major problem). For the criteria identified as *yellow* or *red*, I bring the data I need to back up the criteria identified as yellow or red.

The data to substantiate each violated criterion's status is critical, and should connect to an important business reality. What I've seen with entry, continuation, and exit criteria is that any reasonable-sounding criterion will usually pass muster in the test plan review, but if that criterion isn't anchored in a solid business case for project delay, it will create all sorts of controversy when invoked.

Some people use hard-and-fast, bug-related exit criteria such as "zero open severity-1 bugs," "10 or fewer open severity-2 bugs," and so forth. I have found that these approaches can lead to counterproductive arguments about whether a bug is correctly classified in terms of severity, which ignores the bigger picture of quality and how quality fits into the other business issues such as schedule, budget, and features. However, in some contexts — for example, safety-critical systems, defense systems, outsource development, and so forth — using quantifiable exit criteria might be necessary.

Entry Criteria

Entry criteria spell out what must happen to allow a system to move into a particular test phase. These criteria should address questions such as the following:

- Are the necessary documentation, design, and requirements information available that will allow testers to operate the system and judge correct behavior?

- Is the system ready for delivery, in whatever form is appropriate for the test phase in question?[2]

- Are the supporting utilities, accessories, and prerequisites available in forms that testers can use?

- Is the system at the appropriate level of quality? Such a question usually implies that some or all of a previous test phase has been successfully completed, although it could refer to the extent to which code review issues have been handled. Passing a smoke test is another frequent measure of sufficient quality to enter a test phase.

- Is the test environment — lab, hardware, software, and system administration support — ready?

Figure 2-4 shows an example of entry criteria that might apply for Speedy-Writer.

[2]In the component test phase (assuming that the test organization is involved at that point), I usually accept whatever development is ready to provide as long as it includes sufficient scaffolding, or harnesses, to run my tests. Once I reach the system test phase, however, I ask for customer packaging, especially in the case of software, whose installation process has a significant impact on whether the system works at all.

System Test can begin when:

1. Bug tracking and test tracking systems are in place.

2. All components are under formal, automated configuration and release management control.

3. The Operations team has configured the System Test server environment, including all target hardware components and subsystems. The Test Team has been provided with appropriate access to these systems.

4. The Development Teams have completed all features and bug fixes scheduled for release.

5. The Development Teams have unit tested all features and bug fixes scheduled for release.

6. Less than fifty must-fix bugs (per Sales, Marketing, and Customer Service) are open against the first test release slated. (Fifty being the number of bug reports that can be effectively reviewed in a one-hour bug triage meeting.)

7. The Development Teams provide software to the Test Team three business days prior to starting System Test.

8. The Test Team completes a three-day "smoke test" and reports on the results to the System Test Phase Entry meeting.

9. The Project Management Team agrees in a System Test Phase Entry Meeting to proceed. The following topics will be resolved in the meeting:

    •   . Whether code is complete.

    •   . Whether unit testing is complete.

    •   Assign a target fix date for any known "must-fix" bugs (no later than one week after System Test Phase Entry).

Figure 2-4 Entry criteria for SpeedyWriter

Continuation Criteria

Continuation criteria define those conditions and situations that must prevail in the testing process to allow testing to continue effectively and efficiently. Typically, I find that the test environment must remain stable, the bug backlog manageable, and the tests for the most part unblocked (e.g., by large bugs); installable and stable test releases must be delivered regularly and properly; and the change to the system under test must be known and controlled. Figure 2-5 shows an example of continuation criteria that might apply to SpeedyWriter.

System Test can continue if:

1. All software released to the Test Team is accompanied by Release Notes.

2. No change is made to the system, whether in source code, configuration files, or other setup instructions or processes, without an accompanying bug report. Should a change be made without a bug report, the Test Manager will open an urgent bug report requesting information and escalate to his manager.

3. The open bug backlog ("quality gap") remains less than fifty. The average time to close a bug remains less than fourteen days.

4. Twice-weekly bug review meetings (under the Change Control Board) occur until System Test Phase Exit to manage the open bug backlog and bug closure times.

Figure 2-5 Continuation criteria for SpeedyWriter

Exit Criteria

Exit criteria address the issue of how to determine when the project has completed testing. For example, one exit criterion might be that all the planned test cases and the regression tests have been run. Another might be that project management deems your results "OK," by whatever definition they use to decide such questions. (I'll look at some metrics that can shed light on product quality in Chapters 4 and 5, and examine some political issues associated with results reporting in Chapter 9.) In the case of System Test exit criteria — provided System Test is the last test phase on your project — these exit criteria often become the criteria by which the customer-ship or deployment decision is made. An example of a business-driven set of System Test exit criteria for SpeedyWriter is shown in Figure 2-6.

System Test will end when:

1. No changes (design/code/features), except to address System Test defects, occurred in the prior three weeks.

2. No panic, crash, halt, wedge, unexpected process termination, or other stoppage of processing has occurred on any server software or hardware for the previous three weeks.

3. No client systems have become inoperable due to a failed update during System Test.

4. The Test Team has executed all the planned tests against the GA-candidate software.

5. The Development Teams have resolved all "must-fix" bugs per Sales, Marketing, and Customer Service.

6. The Test Team has checked that all issues in the bug tracking system are either closed or deferred, and, where appropriate, verified by regression and confirmation testing.

7. The test metrics indicate that we have achieved product stability and reliability, that we have completed all planned tests, and the planned tests adequately cover the critical quality risks.

8. The Project Management Team agrees that the product, as defined during the final cycle of System Test, will satisfy the customer's reasonable expectations of quality.

9. The Project Management Team holds a System Test Phase Exit Meeting and agrees that we have completed System Test.

Figure 2-6 SpeedyWriter System Test exit criteria

Test Development

In some cases, I find my test teams rerunning tests that we created in previous test efforts. In other cases, I've used a purely exploratory approach where I created the test data during testing and followed my muse in terms of procedures and specific test steps. Typically, though, my test projects include some amount of work to design and develop various test objects, such as test cases, test tools, test procedures, test suites, automated test scripts, and so forth. Collectively, I refer to these objects as *test systems*.

In this section I'll describe how my test team will create each of those objects. (I'll look at some particulars of test system development in Chapter 3.) If we're going to use manual testing, then I'll let the readers know if we intend to write detailed test cases or use test charters. If I need test data, then I'll explain how we're getting that data and why we picked those approaches. If we're doing test automation using existing (commercial or freeware) test tools, then I'll describe why we're using the particular tools we've chosen and how we intend to develop test scripts. If we're creating custom test tools or utilities, then I'll describe what those utilities are and how we intend to use them.

At some point, test system or testware development can become a software-development project in its own right. I've worked on custom tool projects for clients where we created completely free-standing test automation and management tools. Some of my test projects have included test development efforts that involved person-decades of work. In such cases, my preference would be to have a separate plan that describes that development effort. Various good templates are available for software development plans.[3]

Test Configurations and Environments

This section of the test plan is where I document which hardware, software, networks, and lab space I will use to perform the testing. For these various test systems, I'll describe whatever important configuration details bear mentioning, as well. For a PC application or utility, this task can be as simple as listing the half-dozen or so test PCs, the two or three test networks (assuming that networking is even an issue), and the printers, external drives, and other accessories you might require from time to time. For mass-market software or hardware, I find it useful to have competitors' systems available in my test lab as reference platforms. For example, when testing an Internet appliance (which provided Web and email features only), we had PCs configured with the various browsers and email clients so we could answer the question, "What happens when we run the same test using *X* (browser or email client)?" when confronted by potentially buggy behavior on the appliance.

Suppose, however, that you are testing a system with significant custom hardware elements (such as a new laptop or a server), one with many hardware elements (such as a network operating system or a network application), or one with expensive hardware elements (such as a mainframe, a high-availability server, or a server cluster). In these complex cases, using a simple table or a spreadsheet might not be sufficient. In Chapter 6 I'll introduce a database that

---

[3]For example, see www.construx.com for templates drawn on Steve McConnell's *Software Project Survival Guide.*

can help you stay on top of complicated situations such as these. In Chapter 7 I'll show how to extend this database to include managing lab space and equipment. This database also models human resources and network needs. You can include the reports produced by this database in this section of the test plan.

When custom hardware is involved, you can present a plan for hardware allocation in this portion of the test plan or in a separate document. Whatever the location, I've found it extremely important to prepare this hardware allocation plan. Failing to establish a detailed plan for allocating hardware is tantamount to assuming that the needed hardware will magically make itself available, properly configured and ready for testing, at the very moment I need it. If you lead a charmed life, such things probably happen to you all the time, but they never happen to me. I always worry about hardware allocation, and ensure I have a hardware allocation plan in place as part of the test plan.

What goes into a test hardware allocation plan? I usually list the test purpose or use, the systems needed (including the quantities and revision levels), the infrastructure, the time period, the location, and any other hardware necessary for a particular test. Table 2-4 shows a prototype allocation plan for DataRocket's integration test phase and system test phase.

Test Execution

This portion of the test plan addresses important factors affecting test execution. For example, in order to run tests, you often need to receive items from the outside world, primarily resources (or funding for those resources) and systems to test. In the course of running tests, you will gather data that you must track, analyze, and report to your team, your peers, and your managers. In addition, you will run through distinct test cycles in each test phase. I find that the level of detail required here varies from team to team and project to project. With my more senior test teams on well-run projects, I can leave some matters to the discretion of my crack team of testers. With junior testers, especially on chaotic projects, the more I can nail down the test execution realities during the planning phase, the more confusion I can anticipate and resolve ahead of time.

Resources

In this section I identify the key participants in the test effort and the role they'll play in testing, along with any other resources not identified elsewhere in the plan. I find it especially important to identify the external participants, the hand-off points, and each participant's contact information. This information complements the picture shown in Figure 2-3.

Table 2-4 A DataRocket Hardware Allocation Plan

TEST USAGE	SYSTEM [QTY]	NETWORK	WHEN	WHERE	OTHER[QTY]
Integration Test Phase					
Component interfaces	Engineering prototype [2]	Linux Samba, Sun Network File System, Windows 2003 Server	9/15–10/15	Engr lab	MS mouse, MS kbd, dual mon, USB mouse, USB mon, USB kbd, 3COM switch, Epson prn, Quantum HD, oscilloscope
Mechanical life	Engineering prototype [2]	None	8/1–10/1	Engr lab	None
Stress, capacity, volume	Engineering prototype [1]	Linux, NFS, Windows	9/15–10/15	Test lab	MS mouse, VGA mon
Performance	Engineering prototype [1]	Linux, NFS, Windows	9/15–10/15	Test lab	MS mouse, MS kbd, Dual mon, Quantum HD, solid state HD
System Test Phase					
MTBF demonstration	Validation prototype [4]	Linux	10/17–1/17	Engr lab	MS mouse, MS kbd, dual mon, MUX
Functionality	Validation prototype [2]	Linux, NFS, Windows	10/17–12/1	Test lab	MS mouse, MS kbd, dual mon
Stress, capacity, volume	Validation prototype [1]	Linux, NFS, Windows	10/17–12/1	Test lab	MS mouse, dual mon
Performance	Validation prototype [1]	Linux, NFS, Windows	10/17–12/1	Test lab	MS mouse, MS kbd, dual mon, Quantum HD, solid-state HD
Compatibility	Validation prototype [3]	N/A	10/24–12/1	System Cookers, Inc.	MS mouse [3], MS kbd [3], dual mon [3]
Environmental	Validation prototype [2]	N/A	10/24–12/1	System Cookers, Inc.	MS mouse [2], MS kbd [2], dual mon [2]

I often include an escalation process in this subsection. An *escalation process* defines what happens if some key participants do not or cannot fulfill their agreed-upon role. In the case of external participants, I work out the roles and hand-off points with the appropriate peer-level managers before putting that information in the test plan. Don't surprise fellow project team managers with new and urgent assignments for their staff.

Test Case and Bug Tracking

This section deals with the systems used to manage and track test cases and bugs. Test case tracking refers to the spreadsheet, database, or tool I use to manage all the test cases in the test suites and how I track progress through those tests. (If I don't track the tests I plan to run, how can I gauge my test progress and coverage later on?) Bug tracking has to do with the process my team uses to manage the bugs we find in the course of testing. Since these systems form your principal communication channels inward to your own team, outward to other teams such as development, and upward to your management, you should define them well here. Chapters 4 and 5 deal with these topics in more detail. Even if you choose not to use the approaches described there, you will find some ideas in those chapters that will help you complete this section of the plan.

Bug Isolation and Classification

This section of the test plan is where I explain the degree to which I intend to isolate bugs and to classify bug reports. *Isolating a bug* means to experiment with the system under test in an effort to find connected variables, causal or otherwise. I find it's important to be explicit about bug isolation. Otherwise, testers end up helping with debugging, a programmer task that can consume lots of my testers' time with very little to show for it in terms of test coverage (see Chapter 4).

Classifying a bug report assigns the underlying bug to a particular category that indicates how the bug should be communicated and handled. For example, I've used classifications such as the following:

- **Requirements failure.** The bug report concerns a failure of the system to meet its requirements. The appropriate party will resolve the problem.

- **Nonrequirements failure.** The reported bug is not covered by the system requirements, but it significantly affects the quality of the system in unacceptable ways. The appropriate party will resolve the problem.

- **Waiver requested.** The bug report does indeed describe a failure, but the programmers have requested a waiver because they believe that it will not significantly affect the customers' and users' experiences of quality.

- **External failure.** The bug report addresses a failure that arises from a factor or factors external to or beyond the control of the system under test.

- **Test failure.** The programmers believe that the test has returned a spurious or invalid error.

Rather than classifying bugs, some project teams use a single bug-management process. Many successful development projects I've worked on used a bug triage process (sometimes as part of the change-control board process) to assign bug priority and determine which bugs the project team must fix prior to release. In that case, you might want to describe that process here.

Test Release Management

One of the major interfaces between the overall project and testing occurs when new revisions, builds, and components are submitted to the test team for testing. In the absence of a predefined plan for this, I have seen this essential hand-off point degrade into absolute chaos. On one project, a software development manager was emailing a new version of the software out to the entire project team, including the test team, every time any member of his team of programmers fixed a bug. We received a dozen test releases a day! I find that kind of anarchy unacceptable on my test projects, so in this section of the test plan I define the key elements of the test release process that can affect my effort. In the ideal case, I try to create a test release process that looks as shown in Figure 2-7 (this figure also appeared in the previous chapter as Figure 1-7).

One element of that process is regular, predictable timing. How often will you accept a new test release into the testing process? My preference is once a week, which has worked well on most projects I've managed. Once-a-week test releases give me time to complete some scheduled tests and do some exploratory testing as part of each test cycle, rather than just doing confirmation testing of the bug fixes in that test release. Test releases that show up once a day — or more frequently — often leave my test teams little time for anything but confirmation testing the fixes. Test releases that come every other week or even less frequently can introduce major regressions and other changes in behavior that I'd like to know about sooner.

Every new release of a software or hardware component into the test lab should have a release (or revision) number or identifier attached. This identifier is essential so that testers can determine which version of the system contains a bug, which version fixes that bug, which pieces are compatible with other pieces, and which versions you have tested.

Figure 2-7 Test passes, test releases, and test cycles

You should also get release notes with the release. (The IEEE standards refer to these as *test item transmittal reports*.) These release notes should specify which bugs were fixed, what changes were made, how the changes will affect system behavior, and so forth. This is especially true for complex systems that interface with other systems. For example, if an application accesses a database, you might need to change the schema of the database to accommodate changes in the program. This creates challenges if multiple systems use this database, because you'll need to plan for the ripple effects.

In addition, I need to be able to count on receiving new releases in a certain format. I specify for each test phase — and therefore in each test plan — a specific process and format for delivering new releases. For example, for software delivered during component and integration test phases, we might allow programmers to deliver a .tar or .zip archive via email or posted to a project network drive. Once I enter system testing, however, I usually want the software releases to arrive in the same format and with the same installation process as the ultimate production or field delivery. I consider testing the installation process a key part of most system test efforts, so I cover that here.

I also find I need a defined uninstall process for many projects. The reason is two-fold. First, if an uninstall process exists for users or customers, then I need to test this capability. Second, if a test release comes along that, after installation, proves so unstable or unusable that further testing is pointless, then reverting to a release I know I can test is the only way to make forward progress. In the case of a simple application, an uninstall utility might be included, but complex systems — especially those that have shared databases — can have very complex installation and uninstallation processes.

In some cases, the proposed approach for accelerating a test process blocked or impeded by a bad test release is to install a new release. Therefore, you'll need to consider (for both software and hardware) whether you will accept new revisions in the middle of a test cycle. The key issues here are regression testing and the implications of the revision for the validity of your previous test cycle's results. Will you have to do a complete reset and start the test cycle over if a driver, a configuration file, or an application build shows up midway? These unexpected arrivals can cause real problems, especially toward the end of the system test phase, if you are receiving new releases every few days or even every few hours. Without a completely automated regression test system that can repeat every test flawlessly in a day or so, you will always have to worry about the possibility that the new release has introduced a major new bug. (For a discussion of coverage problems and regression testing, see Chapter 3.)

This problem occurs even in hardware development. It is true that motherboards, cases, and so forth have long lead times and that engineering prototypes cost a lot to produce. Nevertheless, you might still receive daily firmware or driver updates. My worst experiences with this kind of churn and burn have occurred on laptop development projects. Because of the manual nature of PC testing, you will probably have time for little more than confirmation testing on new releases if they come daily, leading to dismal test escapes. (I'll talk more about test escapes in Chapter 3.)

These chaotic releases have affected the logistics and operation of a number of my test projects. Some amount of effort is required for updating firmware, installing drivers or applications, or replacing a motherboard, especially when my lab contains half a dozen test platforms. If the process requires specialized skills, such as system administration, network administration, or database administration, I need to have the right person available to handle the job. Moreover, the system will be unavailable for test execution throughout the upgrade. Such abrupt, unexpected changes can also impose communication overhead and confuse testers. I have to inform everyone that a new release has dropped in, circulate the release notes (assuming that they exist), give my staff time to study them, and hope that everyone can keep straight just what the latest chunk of software is supposed to do.

As you can tell, I don't like midstream releases. However, it's also true that instituting significant, project-wide process changes from within the test team through the mechanism of the test plan can be difficult.[4] If your company's development "process" includes a system test phase composed of 18-hour days, with a warm DVD containing the allegedly final test release landing on your desk hourly, you can't transform that by fiat in the test plan.

Recently, my associates and I were doing an assessment for a client. We reviewed their test plans, which were excellent in their detail, their structure, and the processes they described. That didn't jibe with the stories I'd heard from people in the interviews, so I asked one of the managers how closely the test plans described what actually happened during a project. He replied, "Well, those test plans are mostly aspirational." This meant that he hoped that the project teams would follow the good ideas in the test plan, even though they never did.

Having "aspirational" test plans makes about as much sense as going on a road trip with the map of a country you'd like to visit rather than the country in which you really are driving. A test plan should describe what actually will happen. Does this mean that you accept whatever counterproductive nonsense goes on as a given? No, you can — and certainly should — attempt to persuade people there is a better way, if project realities are killing the test process. If you succeed, capture that in the test plan.

Test Cycles

In Chapter 1 I used the phrase *test cycle* rather cavalierly, but perhaps a more formal definition is in order. By a *test cycle*, I mean running one, some, or all of the test suites planned for a given test phase. I associate a test cycle with a single test release of the system under test, such as a build of software or a motherboard. Generally, new test releases occur during a test phase, triggering another test cycle. For example, if test suites 3.1 through 3.5 are planned for a three-cycle system test phase, the first cycle could entail executing 3.1 and 3.2; the second cycle, 3.3, 3.4, and 3.5; and the third cycle, 3.1, 3.2, 3.3, 3.4, and 3.5.

Any given test phase involves at least one cycle through the test suites planned for that phase. (As I mentioned in Chapter 1, during estimation you'll need to determine how many cycles you need in any given phase.) Each subsequent cycle generally involves a new release of one or more components in the system. This section of the test plan should spell out your specific assumptions and estimates about the number, timing, and arrangement of test cycles. A picture like Figure 2-7 can help.

---

[4] Aesop's fables include the apt story about belling the cat. The mice are tired of scurrying about in fear of the cat, and they convene a council to decide how to deal with the problem. One suggests that they put a bell on the cat's collar so that they can hear him coming. All agree this is a capital idea, until one young whippersnapper asks, "But who will bell the cat?" If you are trying to change the way other people work, remember that you are, in some sense, the mouse who is belling the cat.

Test Hours

In some cases, I find I need to define the specific hours of testing. In addition, on some projects I use multiple shifts to keep scarce resources humming 16 or 24 hours a day to accelerate the testing. In such cases, I'll include this section to define the specific hours and shifts that the team will use. I don't include this section unless I need it, though, and in many organizations it's unnecessary and maybe even counter-productive to have it; e.g., if your company has a flexible-hours policy you'll run afoul of that with your team by requiring work during certain hours.

Risks and Contingencies

In Chapter 1, in the discussion on quality risk analysis, I talked about how we can use testing to help manage risks to the quality of the system. However, like any other part of the project, testing is subject to risks. These risks are possible outcomes or events that could make the test plan difficult or impossible to carry out.

It's a good idea to try to identify the key project risks that could affect testing and to determine how you'll deal with those risks. For any risk, you have four options:

- **Mitigation.** Taking steps in advance that reduce the likelihood or impact of the event or outcome.

- **Contingency.** Being ready to act, should the risk become an actual event or outcome, to reduce its impact.

- **Transfer.** Getting another member of the project team or some other stakeholder to accept the impact of the risk should it become an actual event or outcome.

- **Accept or ignore:** Doing nothing.

Obviously, this last option works best when the likelihood and impact of the risk are low.

Let's look at some examples of project risks that can affect testing, along with various options for handling them.

- Logistics or product quality problems. Such problems can block tests. Mitigation steps include careful test and project planning as discussed in this chapter, along with robust test design (see Chapter 3). Contingency steps include good bug triage (see Chapter 4).

- Uninstallable test deliverables. Mitigation steps include ensuring that the programming or release engineering team practices continuous integra-tion and (at least) nightly builds. Ideally, these nightly builds include some kind of smoke test or sanity test, which can be built from automated unit tests if programmers use them. Contingency steps include a well-defined (and tested) uninstall process.[5]

■ Excessive change in the requirements, design, or implementation of the system. Unmanaged change can invalidate test results and possibly requires extensive test updates. Mitigation steps include robust test design and lightweight test documentation (see Chapter 3). Contingency steps include good change control processes (see Chapter 4) and defined escalation processes.

■ Insufficient test environments, resulting in test delays. Transfer steps include explaining the reasons for eventual project delay associated with test delays.

■ Unrealistic test environments, resulting in questionable test results. Since certain types of tests (such as compatibility, reliability, and performance tests) are particularly subject to these problems, mitigation steps include outsourcing these tests (see Chapter 10).

■ Unreliable test environment support. Contingency steps include having a good escalation process or having system administration skills in the test team (see Chapter 8).

■ Gaps in test coverage revealed during test execution (or, worse yet, *not* revealed during test execution). Mitigation steps include planning and executing a sufficient amount of reactive testing (bug hunts, software attacks, and exploratory testing), as discussed in Chapter 1, as well as providing for continuous test improvement during test execution.

■ Slips in test start dates or test releases reduce the total test execution time. Contingency steps include using risk priority to drop tests in reverse risk order, as discussed in Chapter 1. Transfer steps include escalation to management with a request for more test time or elimination of untested features.

■ Budget or staffing cuts reduce the total test effort. Mitigation steps include having a well-rounded test team or identifying inexpensive ways to outsource some areas of testing. Contingency steps include use of risk priority to drop tests.

■ Debugging in the test environment reduces the total available test-execution time. Mitigation steps include working with the programming to identify ways to avoid the use of the test environment for debugging. Contingency steps include escalation to management and the use of risk priority to drop or reschedule tests.

---

[5]See my article, co-written with Greg Kubaczkowski, called "Mission Made Possible," for a description of how this might work. You can find this article on the Library page of our company web site, www.rbcs-us.com.

Most advocates of good development processes encourage a global approach to risk management.[6] If you work on a project in which the entire team has a single risk management plan, you might be able to omit this section by including these concerns in that plan. However, my usual experience is that this section of the test plan is quite important.

Change History

This part of the document records the changes and revisions that have been made to the test plan itself to this point. Specifically, you can assign a revision number and record who made the changes, what those changes were, and when the revision was released.

Referenced Documents

As a rule, a test plan refers to other documents such as design specifications, requirements, the test suites, any quality risk analysis documents, and other pertinent information. Listing these documents in this section lets me avoid extensive repetition of their contents (which can create complications when these documents change).

Frequently Asked Questions

On projects where I use neophyte test engineers and test technicians, I find that a frequently asked questions section is useful. Many of these questions entail describing the importance of the escalation process or some other delicate matter.

That said, if you don't need this section, don't use it. As with the Test Hours section, using it inappropriately can waste your time and create problems. It can become a catch-all for any question anyone ever asked about testing, bloating your test plans into huge, unnavigable, and unmanageable documents.

The IEEE 829 Template: Compare and Contrast

The test plan template presented previously will capture the same information as a test plan that follows the IEEE 829 standard, shown in Figure 2-8. However, my template is organized a bit differently and tends to produce shorter documents. However, in some cases you might need to achieve IEEE 829 standard compliance, so here I'll describe each section in the IEEE 829 template briefly and how the information maps to my template.

---

[6]See, for example, McConnell's *Software Project Survival Guide*.

1. Introduction
   1.1. Document identifier
   1.2. Scope
   1.3. References
   1.4. System overview and key features
   1.5. Test overview
2. Details of the Master Test Plan
   2.1. Test processes
   2.2. Test documentation requirements
   2.3. Test administration requirements
   2.4. Test reporting requirements
3. General
   3.1. Glossary
   3.2. Document change procedures and history

Figure 2-8 IEEE 829 standard test plan template

The Introduction section covers a number of sections from my template. In most cases, the IEEE template provides for a more detailed discussion. The Introduction section includes subsections that address test organization, test schedule, and the overall level of quality risk associated with the project. Like in my template, an overview of the test resources, tasks, and techniques appear here.

The Document Identifier section includes information such as the date of release for the test plan, the organization that released the test plan, the author, the author's manager, the approvers, the reviewers, the document ID number or official name, and the version number. I tend to put most of this information in the Change History section rather than distract people in the opening pages of my test plan with minutiae like this. I do include the version number on the title page and in the footing of each page, though.

In the IEEE 829 template, the Scope section describes the purpose, goals, and scopes of the test effort in detail. In most of my test plans, the implicit scope is the entire system, and testing will focus on the high-risk areas of that system, which I cover in the Scope and Quality Risks sections. As discussed previously and as I'll show in the case study at the end of this chapter, my approach is to use a bullet item and tabular style of listing this information. The IEEE format is more narrative and more explicit.

The IEEE 829 test plan template recommends a description of the project and the project life cycle. This includes a discussion on whether a sequential or iterative life cycle applies and how the life cycle affects testing (see Chapter 12). Like my template, this template covers the features to test, the features not to test, and any assumptions and limitations. The features to test and the features not to test correspond to the "Is/Is Not" table you saw in my template, but, using the IEEE 829 template, you include more details.

This section also covers the order of testing, while I tend to address that in the Quality Risks section. If this test plan covers multiple test phases (which the IEEE standard refers to as *test levels*), it includes a discussion of the sequencing of those phases. If there are individual test plans for each level, then this test plan (which is a *master test plan* as discussed previously) should refer to those for the details.

The References section in this template is basically the same as the one in my template, though the IEEE recommends segmenting the documents into external and internal references. External references are those from outside the project, while internal references come from within the project.

The System Overview and Key Features section corresponds to the first half of what I typically put in an Overview section under my template. The Test Overview section corresponds to the second half of my Overview section. As I mentioned earlier, I want to keep this very short so that it can serve as an executive summary for senior managers reading the document.

However, the IEEE 829 standard provides for an extensive Test Overview section. It can include a description of the relationship of the test processes to other processes, such as programming, project management, the larger quality assurance processes, and configuration management or release engineering. It can cover the organizational issues I cover in the Setting and Resources sections, including escalation. It can also include a discussion of the schedule, including major test activities and milestones, information flows and dependencies between testing and the rest of the project, and how regression testing is triggered by project changes.

The Test Overview section also covers the IEEE 829 concept of an integrity level. This is roughly equivalent to the concept of risk-based testing covered in Chapter 1. Both the informal and FMEA approaches I described in Chapter 1 are more sophisticated and fine-grained than the integrity-level concept described in the IEEE 829 standard. However, you can use the quality risk-analysis technique with the IEEE 829 test plan template, in which case this section corresponds to the Quality Risks section in my template.

The Test Overview section also covers resources. This includes the people involved, along with tools, facilities, and hardware. It also includes any special procedural requirements like permissions levels for testers running particular tests. This is material that I tend to cover in the Test Configurations and Environments section in my template. The Test Overview section also includes a discussion of tools techniques, methods, and metrics.

To some extent, the IEEE description of this section seems to overlap the Resources subsection in the Test Execution section of Figure 2-1. It includes a discussion on how the test team will acquire, develop, and re-use the test cases and test tools, similar to the section Test Development in my own template. It also includes a discussion on metrics and results reporting, which I'll cover in Chapter 4.

With the overview (which is quite large for what I'd call an overview) in place, the template moves on to the Details of the Master Test Plan section. This section consists of four major subsections: Test Process, Test Documentation Requirements, Test Administration Requirements, and Test Reporting Requirements. Let's look at each one.

First, the Test Process section discusses test activities and tasks for each level. The assumption here is that this master test plan describes all test levels, and might be complemented by level or detail test plans. This document starts by describing the levels.

For each level, it groups the activities discussed together in a set of steps similar to the ones I described in Chapter 1. Each step is discussed in its own subsection in the IEEE 829 template. First is Management, roughly equivalent to what I call planning. Next is Acquisition, which includes buying and deploying test tools, test environments, and test data. So, it includes elements from my own Test Development and Test Configurations and Environments sections. Next is a section on Test Development, which is similar to my template's Test Development section. That is followed by a section on running the tests, which corresponds to my template's Test Execution section. Finally, there is a section on capturing the tests for use in maintenance testing, which I do not explicitly cover in my template.

For each set of activities, there is a discussion of risks and assumptions. The risks discussion corresponds to the Risks and Contingencies section of my template. Additionally there are discussions of resources, roles, and responsibilities, which I also cover in my template.

The section on test documentation specifies the purpose, format, and content of the test documentation produced. In my template, I might address this to some extent in my Test Development section, but I do not tend to spend a lot of time on it in the test plan. Typically, I provide the test team with templates for these documents and guide them in the use of those templates (see Chapter 3).

The section on test administration deals with a number of important issues that I typically address in my Test Execution section. One of those issues is the reporting and management of bugs, which I cover in two subsections of my template. Another issue is the approach for regression testing and confirmation testing, which I cover in the Test Cycles subsection. The IEEE 829 template addresses managing deviation from the test plan, which I usually handle as a matter of course in various test-tracking spreadsheets (see Chapter 5) and a change management database (see Chapter 6). The IEEE 829 template includes a discussion on control procedures, corresponding roughly to my Release Management section. Finally, there's a discussion on standards and practices, which I address in various sections of my plan wherever they apply.

The Details of the Master Test Plan section concludes with a major sub-section on test reporting. This section discusses the purpose, content, format, recipients, and timing of all test reports. This includes all test logs, bug reports (which they call *anomaly reports*), and interim and final test status reports. I'll discuss test logs in Chapters 5 and 6, bug reports in Chapter 4, and test status reports in Chapter 4 and especially Chapter 5.

Finally, we have the General section. It includes a glossary, which I cover in my Definitions section. It also includes a discussion on change procedures and history. I keep the change history at the end of my own test plans. As for the procedure, I typically don't document that unless there is some critical need to do so.

Selling the Plan

Regardless of the template I use, after finishing a test plan, I want to obtain approval from project management and development peers. I have used the approach of attaching a formal sign-off sheet to the plan. The approach I usually prefer, though, is that of holding a review meeting with all the involved managers.

If your company tends to become mired in politics, you might need a sign-off to protect yourself. If such formalism is rare in your company, there are other ways to document approval, such as a circulation list that you keep. In any case, I recommend a tactful approach if you pursue a formal sign-off. Goose-stepping around the office with a document, requiring management signatures before you proceed with the test project, is not likely to endear you to your colleagues.

You might be tempted to send the test plan via email, demanding that the recipients speak now or forever hold their peace. After failing to receive any criticisms or concerns, you might assume that everyone has read your plan and agrees with it. This assumption is typically false. Lack of response usually means that no one has read it.

Review meetings are my favorite way to get people to read plans. One benefit of writing and circulating the plan is to provide a forum for discussing the test part of the project. What better way to achieve that than to assemble the appropriate parties to hash out the plan?

Before I hold a review, I email the test plan with a note mentioning that we'll hold a meeting to review it in the next week. (Since email attachments are notoriously flaky, I offer to print a hard copy for anyone who can't open the file.) I invite every manager who is directly affected by the plan — usually the development manager, the project manager, the product manager, the build/release manager, the technical support manager, the sales and marketing managers, the business analysts or other in-house domain experts, and my own manager — as well as the lead test engineer on the project. I send courtesy invitations to others who might have an interest, but I try to limit the total list to 10 or fewer. I then schedule the review.

At the meeting, I provide extra hard copies of the plan for forgetful participants. As the test manager, I lead the group through the plan section by section or page by page. If anyone has concerns, we discuss — and try to resolve — them on the spot. My goal is to leave the meeting with a marked-up copy of the test plan that will enable me to produce a final version. Shortly after the review, I make the requested changes to the document and re-circulate it, this time marked as "Released for Execution" or "Release 1.0" to flag the fact that we intend to proceed according to this plan.

Clarity, Pertinence, and Action

Some of my clients refer to long, dry test documents as *shelfware*. Many of us have seen too many test managers and senior test engineers spend too much of their time filling enormous binders that then sit on shelves, untouched during test execution. This is a cautionary tale: veer off into a morass of documentation for its own sake — just to follow a standard or to fill in the blanks of a template — and you can lose focus, relevance, and credibility.

The style of writing matters, too. Avoid passive verbs. Don't say that something "is to be done;" instead, say exactly who is to do what and when. Defining roles and responsibilities keeps you out of the trap I saw one client's test manager fall into when she wrote a test plan that was just a collection of statements of principle and pieties ("Testing is good," "Bugs are bad," etc.). Keep jargon, buzzwords, and so forth limited to those appropriate for the audience, and use a Definitions section to promote further clarity.

I keep my test documents practical, focused, and short, and they work well for me. This approach to planning, customized to fit your particular needs, will help you write effective test plans that you can really use.

Case Study

On one project, my test team and I tested a browser-based program that provided home-equity-loan-processing capabilities to call-center banking agents. The project was somewhat quirky, since we executed tests developed by another team and didn't have a chance to do a formal risk analysis. However, this plan gives an example of how I applied the template shown earlier to a large in-house IT project. The document, "Case Study Loan Processing Test Plan.doc," is available on the Basic Library page of www.rbcs-us.com.

I thank my client on this project, a major midwestern financial institution, and the executive in charge of development for allowing me to share this example with readers of this book. I have purged all identifying and otherwise private information from this document. My client contact has asked that the organization remain anonymous.

Exercises

1. Use either of the templates presented (or your own template) to create a rough first draft of a test plan. Use the Omninet Marketing Requirements Document and your risk analysis from the previous chapter as the basis for the plan. Write down two to five bullet items or high-level statements in each section. Be sure to note any open issues that you would want to discuss with the project team.

2. Expand the rough draft of the test plan you created in the first exercise into a complete test plan.

3. You are responsible for the System Test phase for a calculator program, as discussed in Chapter 1.

   ▪ Assume that you are working in the same location (e.g., same cubicle or adjacent tables) as the sole programmer working on the calculator. How would you document the entry criteria, bug reporting, and test release process?

   ▪ Assume that the development team is in another city. What are the entry criteria and the bug-reporting and test release implications?

4. Translate the test plan you wrote in exercise 2 into the IEEE 829 format. Was there any particular information in one that was not accounted for in another? Which one do you prefer? Justify your answers.

CHAPTER 3

Test System Architecture, Cases, and Coverage

Chapters 1 and 2 provided a practical look at the process of defining a test organization's purview, understanding the risks to system quality that fall within that purview, and drawing up an overall plan for testing the most important of those risks. Now that you have a grasp of what's involved in these initial tasks, let's turn our attention to the specifics of building the test system itself.

First, we'll take a step back for a conceptual view of a test system and the relationships among the test system component parts. This section provides some definitions and describes the basic operation of a model test system. I use the phrase *test system architecture* to emphasize the fact that solid design and implementation are just as important for test systems as they are for the software and hardware we're testing.

After laying this foundation, I'll look at a method of defining test cases. This discussion presents a few test case templates that I find useful. In addition to some informal templates I've used, I'll cover the IEEE 829 templates. Whatever template you use, you'll need to decide how precisely to document your tests, so I'll also examine the level of detail required when writing test cases, including options that minimize the documentation, such as software attacks, bug hunting, and exploratory testing. Finally I'll analyze the issue of test coverage, discussing different approaches to measuring coverage, as well as appropriate steps you can take to fill the inevitable gaps.

Test System Architecture and Engineering

By *test system*, I mean the organizational capability for testing created by the testing processes, the testware, and the test environment. The testing processes include both written and unwritten procedures, checklists, and other agreements about the way the test team does its testing. The testware includes all those tools, documents, scripts, data, cases, tracking mechanisms, and so forth that the test team uses to do its testing. The test environment includes the hardware, software, networking and other infrastructure, paper and other supplies, facilities, lab, and so forth that the test team procures, installs, and configures the system under test in order to test it. See Figure 3-1 for a pictorial representation.

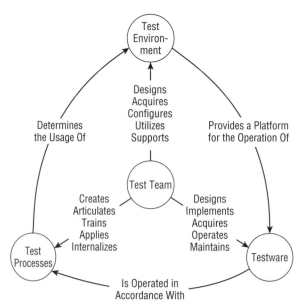

Figure 3-1 The composition of the test system

A competent test team with a good test system can consistently provide effective and efficient test services to a (supportive) project. A good test system helps the tester focus her testing efforts on the key quality risks, and find, reproduce, isolate, describe, and manage the most important bugs in the software or hardware being tested, as well as capturing and analyzing key metrics.

Chapters 4 and 5 focus on the reporting and data management aspects of this system. Chapters 6 and 7 focus on the test environment, including the test hardware, software, and network and the test lab. In Chapter 12 I discuss project context for testing, supportive and otherwise. I look at the principles and practices that underlie effective and efficient, integrated and maintainable test systems, especially the testware. Figure 3-2 is a visual representation of the testware, a model that I find useful in thinking about and communicating the structure and mechanics of test systems.

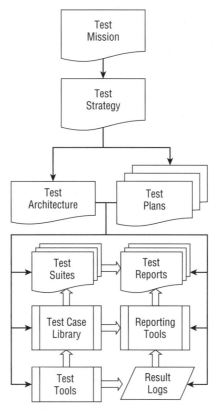

Figure 3-2 A logical decomposition of typical testware components

Let me explain the model shown in Figure 3-2 from the bottom up. Testware often involves one or more test tools — for example, operating systems, scripting languages, GUI test automation systems, API test harnesses, oscilloscopes, or thermal chambers. Using these tools produces result logs, which are either created automatically from the tool or logged manually by the tester.

Because the test team uses the tools to execute test cases, these tools support the test case library. The relationship between the two elements is many-to-many — that is, each tool can appear in multiple test cases, and any one test case can involve the use of multiple tools. Both the test case library and the result logs feed into reporting tools, with a greater or lesser degree of automation. Test engineers assemble test suites from the test case library; the relationship between cases and suites is also many-to-many. From the test suites and the reporting tools come test reports.

Above these, the test architecture is a document that defines the design principles, the structure, and the tools that apply for the testware and test environment, as well as the interrelationships between the constituent pieces; it is project-independent, but it reflects the system under test. The test plan harnesses the test system to the project.

At the very top are the test mission and the test strategy. The test mission or test policy is a document that defines the goals of testing. For example, do the goals of testing include finding defects? Building confidence? Reducing risk? In addition to these goals, the key process indicators or metrics are defined for determining whether the test team is meeting the goals. The test strategy document tells how — in a project-independent way — to go about fulfilling the goals.

The test plan implements the test strategy in a way that fits the project and that achieves the mission as appropriate to the project. The test architecture implements the test strategy in a way that defines how the testware supports the guiding principles of testing in the test strategy.

The Action Components: Definitions

Figure 3-2 zeroes in on three elements of the testware: the test tools, the test case library, and the test suites. These are the action components, the testware parts that do something. Figure 3-3 presents a hypothetical — and simplified — example of how these three components fit together. In reality, you might have a dozen or so test tools, a few hundred or maybe thousands of test cases, and a score or more test suites. Moreover, the lines between the test tools and the test conditions they create and measure are blurrier than those shown in Figure 3-3.

On the left side of Figure 3-3 are four test tools. In the software world, these might be a GUI test tool, a batch scripting language, a load generator, and an external performance monitor. In the hardware world, imagine an oscilloscope, a thermal chamber, a vibration table, and a keyboard tapper. A test tool can be any general-purpose hardware, software, or hardware/software system used during test case execution to set up or tear down the test environment, to create test conditions, or to measure test results. A test tool is also separate from the test case itself.

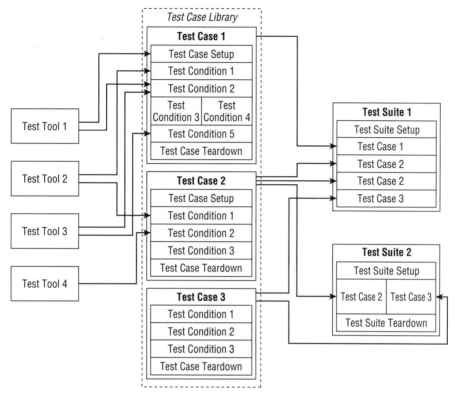

Figure 3-3 The action components of testware, and how they relate

In the center of Figure 3-3 is the test case library, which is a collection of independent, reusable test cases. Each test case consists of a sequence of three stages:

- The *test case setup* describes the steps needed to configure the test environment to run the test case. Connecting a loopback device, making sure that a certain amount of disk space is available, and installing an application are examples of test case setup.

- The point of running a test case is to create a set of *test conditions*. The creation of these conditions allows the tester to assess the quality of the system in relation to particular risks to system quality and customer usage scenarios. Some of the conditions exist in parallel, and others exist in series. In the software world, running a test tool to consume all the buffers while submitting transactions is a specific condition that I might create as part of a performance test. In the hardware world, each cycle of the power switch is a test condition that might occur as part of a mechanical-life test. (I discuss the issue of the actions, data, and expected results associated with test conditions a little later in this chapter.)

- The *test case teardown* specifies the steps required to restore the test environment to a clean condition after execution of the test case (or test suite). Disconnecting a loopback device, deleting temporary files, and removing an application are examples of test case teardown.

Figure 3-3 also illustrates the role of test suites. Because test cases are reusable, I can incorporate a test case into one or more suites. In testware, a test suite provides a framework for the execution of test cases, a way of grouping cases. The test suite allows you to combine test cases to create unique test conditions. Test suite 2, for example, calls for the tester to run test cases 2 and 3 in parallel, which can lead to situations that neither test case could produce alone. As you can see in the figure, test suites, like test cases, can have setup and teardown activities associated with them.

It's Not Saint Paul's, But . . . Principles for Test System Architecture

One of the most stately, impressive buildings in Europe is Saint Paul's Cathedral in London. With understated elegance and restrained majesty inside and out, it has reliably provided a place of worship for generations of Londoners since its completion in 1710, shortly after the Great Fire of London. It withstood the Nazi bombing of South Britain in the early part of World War II and the V-1 and V-2 rocket attacks as the war drew to its close.

Those of us who design test systems for a living could learn a lot from Sir Christopher Wren, the prolific architect who designed and built Saint Paul's Cathedral (as well as much of the rest of old London after the Fire). He built a cathedral that survived the Nazi Blitz even though the structure was more than 200 years old at the time. How many of our test systems can withstand the tight deadlines and project pressure that occurs as the planned project end date approaches (often referred to as *crunch mode*) on even three or four projects? The design and layout of London still work after all these years, although the city had a little trouble adjusting to the technological advance of the automobile. Do our test systems respond well to changes? Wren's works also have an elegance and simplicity that make them simultaneously powerful and obvious. Can we sit down with a typical test system and easily understand how to use it?

All too often, testware is a mess. When creating new test systems, I consider both function and form. Careful engineering creates the functions, and pervasive design decisions produce the form. Good test system architecture means well-designed testware and a well-designed test environment.

What constitutes good test system architecture? I can't offer specific statements that apply to all situations. If you use oscilloscopes, vibration tables, thermal chambers, and a hardware/software library to test PCs, you face a different set of test engineering challenges than if you need to automate the testing of a GUI application that runs on multiple operating systems. Nevertheless, some general principles apply.

Not an *Objet d'Art*: Test System Quality

What would it mean for a test system to have quality? You can use the same quality risk analysis techniques discussed in Chapter 1 to try to answer this question for your specific test system, since test systems should reflect the software and hardware being tested. To state some general principles, I'll look to the ISO 9126 characteristics for software quality: functionality, reliability, usability, efficiency, maintainability, and portability. I discuss usability specifically in the next subsection, but first let's look at the other five characteristics.

Most important, a well-designed test system provides the functionality you need for your testing projects. This might go without saying except that in reality, too many test systems don't meet this criterion. I find that developing testware with all the needed functions requires that I — like my engineering colleagues who must develop the right features in their software and hardware systems — focus on the tasks that the testers need to perform with the testware. This focus must inform the initial design of the test system and persist throughout its development and subsequent maintenance. Unfortunately, it's easy to get distracted by crises, minutiae, and the temptation to add bells and whistles. In fact, Dorothy Graham and Mark Fewster identify not providing a suitable tool for the most pressing test development and execution tasks as a leading cause of failure for automated testing efforts.[1]

What are these essential test tasks? Well, let's go back to the quality risk analysis I discussed in Chapter 1. In that analysis, I said that I try to identify the risks to system quality, prioritize those risks, and put an estimate in place for how much time and money I'll need to cover the critical quality risks. Therefore, quality test systems allow testers to cover all the critical quality risks effectively and efficiently. (I'll return to the mechanics of measuring this coverage later in this chapter.)

[1]For this and other important observations, see Fewster and Graham's book, *Software Test Automation*.

Another key element of test system functionality is a consideration I brought up in Chapter 1, test system fidelity. The test system should accurately model end-user hardware, software, and interface environments, and simulate end-user conditions. Low-fidelity systems introduce probe effects (where the test or test tool distorts the results), misleading system behaviors, or misleading results reported by the testware. For example, suppose that a SpeedyWriter test fails with the result *Can't open file*. That's a bug, right? Not if your tests caused the system under test to hit its open file limit immediately before trying to open the file in question.

Alternatively, test systems can cause the tester to fail to report real problems. Suppose that the tester in charge of environmental testing for a laptop computer reports that the computer passed the drop test. However, the test case specifies only a level drop on the bottom of the laptop. When the computer is dropped in the field on its edge, corner, or top, the case cracks or the LCD breaks.

Especially challenging types of fidelity and probe effect issues arise in performance, stress, capacity, error handling and recovery, and accelerated-life testing. In these types of tests, you will by necessity fake it: simulating failures by pulling power and network cables; trying to make a lifetime of use transpire by shaking, baking, sweating, pounding, and shocking a system; using scripts to generate loads; and using programs and instruments to measure cycle times. Numerous books on test case design devote attention to these topics. It's a good idea to consult the ones pertinent to your field before you spend a lot of time developing such tests.[2]

Moving beyond functionality, consider reliability. One attribute implied by a reliable test system is that you can produce the same result repeatedly, over an extended period of time. Repeatable, dependable test results are part of a reliable test system.

A low degree of coupling between test cases and activities is another attribute of reliability. The failure, blockage, or skipping of one test case shouldn't prevent you from running others. (However, a test case failure can indicate a problem in the *system under test* that is blocking other tests from running — a predicament quite different from one in which the *test system* is blocking test cases.) Imagine two unrelated features, A and B, in a system under test. Test cases TC_A and TC_B cover these features, respectively, and in that order in the test system. Feature B works, but A is broken. The test system should run TC_A and report the problem in feature A. It should then proceed to run TC_B and report its results for feature B. However, if TC_A's success in finding a bug renders the test system incapable of executing TC_B, the test system is not reliable.

---

[2]Two of the best discussions are found in Boris Beizer's *Software System Testing and Quality Assurance* (for software) and Patrick O'Connor's *Practical Reliability Engineering* (for hardware).

PROBE EFFECT FROM HELL

Although it's obvious that probe effects are bad and test system fidelity is good, desirability does not always translate into implementation. This is especially true when the probe effect arises from what appears to be a small, harmless, simplifying assumption during test design but hopelessly compromises your test results during test execution.

My test team and I once designed a stress and performance transaction generator for a telephony system (an interactive voice response or IVR server). It simulated lots of incoming phone calls. The telephony driver and utility software included a special program — a Unix daemon — to manage communication to the telephony hardware. We chose to invoke one instance of the daemon per simulated call to make the programming easy, although the daemon was designed to support approximately 24 callers. "So what?" we thought. "As long as the operation is legal, it shouldn't matter."

It *did* matter. When we started testing, we learned immediately that the daemon was a hungry little devil, devouring about 1 megabyte of memory per invocation. Consequently, we could simulate only 300 or so calls before the daemon filled the memory. We needed to simulate approximately 800 calls, but when we tried to do this, the resulting resource contention (swapping) created a ferocious probe effect that rendered our test results meaningless. We had to reengineer the test tool to multiplex 24 simulated caller programs into one daemon.

Because test resources and schedules are tight, efficiency matters. Continuing the preceding example, an efficient test system will allow the testers to run TC_B before TC_A if that's what makes sense, or even run TC_A without running TC_B. When creating any test system, but especially one that involves scalability, you should also consider test system performance. The system's performance is mostly a product of the speed of your tools, but it can also be determined by how efficiently you can schedule tests. Tests that you must run in a particular sequence (for whatever reason) are less efficient than tests that you can run in parallel. Automated tests that can run (reliably) without human intervention for hours or even days are more efficient than those that require constant care, minor repair, and mid-course adjustment. If your test system takes weeks to run through all your defined tests, you will face a lot of hard choices about what to skip.

The test system should be portable to the same extent that the system under test is portable. External conditions that don't affect the operation of the system under test should not perturb or impede the operation of the test system or the results it reports. A classic example of this problem arises when you develop a test system that requires network access in order to run, even though the product, which is able to access network resources, is not inherently networked. If the network goes down, you can't test. Your painful alternative is to transfer a local copy to the marooned system and modify the tests to run in a standalone fashion.

Good test system architecture also implies maintainability. One aspect of this is flexibility over time. A minor change in the operating environment or an insignificant change in the behavior of the system under test should not topple the test system. For example, a networked test system that can't handle outside load on the network or file server bandwidth is inflexible. Similarly, some capture-playback test tools for command-line and GUI programs suffer from an inability to handle changes in screen resolution, a one-pixel shift in a window, or even changes in the date.

As a special case of flexibility, consider scalability, the extent to which the test system's parameters of operation can expand without necessitating major changes or fundamental redesign. If the system under test can support up to 60 transactions per second for the first release, your test system must be able to hit the upper boundary and simulate 60 transactions per second. However, you should design it to expand easily to accommodate 600 or maybe even 6,000 transactions per second for subsequent releases. Achieving such versatility might sound difficult, but you can often create it by devoting adequate care to design and initial implementation.

Maintainable test systems are consistent, which is significant in many ways. All the tools in your test system should work in as similar a fashion as possible. If you buy various tools that must work together, be sure that they do. Remember that off-the-shelf tools, like the tools you develop, have paradigms; they are based on assumptions about what you should and shouldn't do. These assumptions will, of course, enable or impede certain operations.

Reliability, efficiency, and maintainability are enabled by simplicity. The more bells and whistles you introduce into a test system, the wider its footprint. To stretch the metaphor a tiny bit, as objects become wider they lose the ability to fit into narrow spaces. In addition, a proliferation of test system features tends to result in tight coupling of the test system to particular operating environments, and can, if you're not careful, cause interdependence between test cases as well. Generality is usually desirable, but it's a smart move to make simplifying assumptions that don't impair the functionality of the test system.

That said, you'll often find a trade-off between simplicity on one hand and portability and functionality on the other. By making a test tool a bit more general (and thereby more complex), you might be able to get it to do double duty, saving the effort of developing another tool. In addition, two similar tools can be hard to maintain, especially if consistency of operation across the two is important.

No Test System Is an Island: Testers and the Test System

Considerations of consistency and simplicity bring us to the human side of the equation. No matter how automated your test system, it does not create, use, or maintain itself; people do. I put the test team in the center of Figure 3-1 to emphasize this fact. Testers must set up the test environment, start the tests, interpret the results, reproduce anomalies manually, isolate bugs by experimentation, and restore the test environment to a known state at the end of the testing.

In addition, the testers will usually need to maintain the test system, especially the test cases and suites. This is especially true any time development adds new features to the product being tested, changes the definition of correct behavior for the product, or supports new configurations or environments. Maintenance is also necessary when you decide to enhance the test system to get better test coverage. My test teams have found a well-designed test system easier to maintain than one that is a mess.

In the area of consistency, it's helpful to limit your tool set. I once developed a test system that was implemented in four languages — Tcl, iTcl, C, and Silk — running on Solaris and Microsoft Windows NT. The complexity made the development difficult. Technical challenges arose from getting the disparate interfaces to cooperate, while human difficulties ensued from the need to have such varied skill sets in a small team. Nevertheless, we were forced to use all four languages because of the architecture of the system under test. To preserve what little consistency we had left, we rejected a tool from an outside party that they had written in Perl. Although the tool would undoubtedly have been useful, the Tower of Babel was too high to add another level.

In contrast, my test team and I on another occasion supported a test system implemented almost entirely via Korn shell scripts, with only a few localized tests and utilities written using a specialized batch utility and a GUI test automation tool. Nonetheless, the system ran on three or four variants of Unix, iSeries, and Windows, and it supported about 10 databases. The commonality of the test system components made maintenance technically straightforward and kept the team's skill set requirements simple.

Simplicity of the test system is also essential to usability. The best test systems are easy to learn and easy to use. I also try to make the test system difficult to misuse, although I find I need to balance this objective against the costs of complexity. It shouldn't require a cabal of wizards knowledgeable in mystic scripting secrets and magical keyboard incantations to operate and maintain a test system. When outside people join your team, take advantage of the opportunity to quiz them about how easy — or how difficult — it is to learn the test system.

Miscellaneous Best Practices and Principles for Quality Test Systems

Often, test systems need documentation. This is especially true with automated test systems. The more complex the system is, the more documentation is needed. The document should cover three main topics. First, you should tell the testers how to use the test system. Second, you should tell the testers how the test system works. Third, you should tell the testers why you built the test system the way you did.

The test system should also document itself. Largely, this happens through internal consistency. Testers should find filenames, result logs, and the like easy to read, giving some clue about their purpose. Use intuitive and consistent variable names in programs and scripts, even if people won't read these files and logs during normal operation. When the test system doesn't work, a test engineer will have to figure out the problem, and obscure error messages such as *SYS40: Wrong at 252.351.37.92* and files with names like TST001.TXT will make the job difficult.

On the subject of files, try to ensure that your test system software doesn't become full of junk such as non-test-related documents, unidentifiable log files, output files associated with old bug isolation operations, and so forth. I once worked on a test system that tended to accumulate temporary files with charming names like `zit.txt` and other less printable garbage. To encourage cleanliness, I wrote a script that ran once a week, examining the test system and identifying every unexpected file, who created it, and when it was created. The script then mailed the list of junk files to the entire team, and I followed up with the owners of these extraneous files. If the files in fact represented new tests, I simply changed the script. Often, however, the testers had failed to clean up a test directory after running tests.

A well-designed test system promotes accountability. It should identify, usually through the logs and the result files, who ran specific tests. Using a generic *tester* login can cause frustration when you need to ask questions or investigate a problem. Testers should identify themselves when they log in so that the logs and the result files will bear date/time and owner information.

Finally, if your test organization develops special tools, you'll want to avoid two common software development mistakes. First, don't forget the importance of configuration management and release engineering. You should have your testers check in, check out, and manage the software and documentation portions of the test system just like any other software. Second, remember to test the tests. A standard test plan and suite should exist for the test system. A tester should revise and execute the plan any time changes are made to the test system. You should employ quality assurance best practices such as reviews.

To close the topic of test system architecture, let me point out that the quality of the test system, like the quality of software and hardware systems, follows from a good underlying test system design. Test system quality is a key factor in the number of result interpretation errors your testers will make. While test team competence and diligence are also factors, quality guru W. E. Deming's famous red-bead/black-bead experiment demonstrates that system capability results in some amount of unavoidable variation in results. As test managers, we are responsible for putting the most appropriate and capable systems in place for our test projects.[3]

The Bricks and Mortar of the System: Test Cases

In a sense, everything in the test system — the test processes, the test tools, the reporting formats, the test environment, and so forth — exists to support the execution of test cases. The test case — at least in my model of the test system — is where the test takes actions on the system under test, the tester supplies data to the system under test, and the system under test ends up in some state or states, with resulting outputs and behaviors that testers can compare to expected results. These three things — action, data, and expected results — are the heart of test execution, since they create the test conditions.

Creating Test Conditions

How exactly can testers use test cases to create test conditions? At the highest level, I think of test cases as consisting of a sequence of actions, each action having potentially some associated test data and some associated expected result. Figure 3-4 is a graphical illustration of the process, which I'll walk through in detail in the next few paragraphs.

Assume that we start at step one of a test case, the first action to take. The system is in whatever initial condition is reached from the test suite and test case setup steps. Following our test procedures, system documentation, or inspiration, we deliver some data to the system under test. Some of that data comes from persistent databases, some from various input devices, including from our creative fingers on keyboards, mice, and so forth. We have created the test condition. The system under test responds. It processes this data, going through whatever computation steps occur. The system generates output and enters some subsequent state. The output, the subsequent state, and the way

[3]In this experiment, two teams are given ping-pong paddles with holes drilled into them and told to use those paddles as filters to separate large buckets containing beads of different colors. The beads of one color are slightly larger than the beads of the other color and are slightly larger than most (but not all) of the holes. The person representing the manager in the experiment specifies the exact procedure for separating the beads. Of course, any difference between the two teams in terms of effectiveness and efficiency results from random variations in the size of the holes and from the luck of one team. This exercise is described in Mary Walton's book, *The Deming Management Method.*

in which the system behaves during its response comprise the results. At this point, we evaluate the results, using automated tools, documented expected results, system documentation, and our own reasonable expectations about how our system should respond. After we make our determination, we can proceed to the next test step or substep.

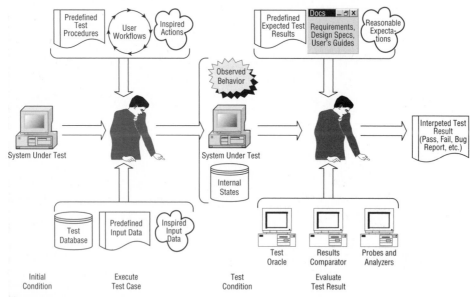

Figure 3-4 Creating test conditions through test case execution

Let's move from the general to the specific — that is, from the architecture of the overall test system and generic test cases to the construction of specific test cases. Since I find examples most compelling in illustrating specific points, I'm going to present a couple of templates in this section that I use to document test cases. I'll examine each part of each template and then look at an example of its use.

A Basic Testing Template

Figure 3-5 shows a basic test case template that can be used for either manual or automated testing. Each test step includes the action to be taken, the associated data, and the expected results. Let's look at each piece a little more closely.

I refer to the first 10 rows of the template, which identify and describe the test case, as the *header* section. It's a good idea to name the test case with both mnemonic and numeric identifiers. The mnemonic name is a short description that conveys the essence of the test — for example, Stress, 1m Drop, or Network Performance. For the numeric identifier, I use a Dewey decimal–style notation: for example, a test case that is used in the fifth test suite and that is the second test case is assigned identifier 05.002. Alternatively, you can use a pure sequential numbering.

	A	B	C	D	E
1	Test Case Name:	Mnemonic identifier			
2	Test ID:	Five-digit ID, XX.YYY: XX suite number, YYY test number.			
3	Test Suite(s):	The name of the test suite(s) that use this test case.			
4	Priority:	From quality risk coverage analysis			
5	Hardware Required:	List hardware in rows			
6	Software Required:	List software in rows			
7	Duration:	Elapsed clock time			
8	Effort:	Person-hours			
9	Setup:	List steps needed to set up the test			
10	Teardown:	List steps needed to return SUT to pretest state			
11					
12	ID	Test Step/Substep	Result	Bug ID	Bug RPN
13	1.000	Major step			
14	1.001	Minor step (substep)			
15	1.002	Minor step (substep)			
16	2.000	Major step			
17					
18					
19	Execution Summary	Status			
20		System Config ID			
21		Tester			
22		Date Completed			
23		Effort			
24		Duration			

Figure 3-5 A basic test case template

The next entry in the header lists the name of the test suite (or suites) in which the test case will be used. Because you might use a given test case in multiple suites, this entry could potentially be large. However, in practice most test cases are used in only one test suite, so including the name of the suite provides some useful information with only infrequent confusion.

Assuming you follow the risk-based testing strategy discussed in Chapter 1, each test case will derive from a specific quality risk. So, to achieve the test sequencing benefits of risk-based testing, each test case should inherit the risk priority number of its parent risk item. In some cases, you might decide to modify these priorities, and, if so, I recommend documenting that decision.

The next entries in the header address resource requirements. For two of these entries, I list, row by row, the hardware and software needed to run the test. You might want to restrict these lists to the non-obvious. For example, if you are testing a Windows-based application and the standard test environment includes the most recent version of Microsoft Windows, Microsoft Office, Trend Micro AntiVirus, and GoToMyPC, you needn't duplicate that listing for every test case.

The entries for Duration and Effort specify how long it will take to run the test, in clock time and in person-hours, respectively. In creating these estimates, you have two alternatives. You can assume that the test will pass. In this case, you will need to include additional time for expected bug finding and reporting in your estimation process. Alternatively, you can build expected bug finding and reporting time estimates into each test case, which allows you to estimate test passes based on the total test case estimation, plus additional time for confirmation testing and reactive testing. You might refer back to Chapter 1's section on estimation, "What You *Can* Test," for a moment to refresh your memory on how this works.

Based on the relationship between duration and effort, you can infer the human resources needed to run the test. For example, do you need two people to run the test, one in front of each terminal? You would if you were testing the multiplayer features in video game. Do you need one person for just an hour, even though the test runs for 12 hours? You might if you were describing an automated test that runs unattended overnight.

In the final two entries of the header, I specify the setup procedures and the teardown procedures. Sometimes there are none, but typically you'll need two or three steps at the beginning and end of a test, such as installing or uninstalling an application. For example, when the tester concludes a test, she might need to delete sample files created during the test in order to return the system under test to its original state.

With the preliminaries out of the way, let's move on to the test case proper. A test case is fundamentally a sequence of actions, performed serially, in parallel, or in some combination, that creates the desired test conditions. The template breaks down these actions into steps and substeps. Each step or substep might involve the use of special test data, either entered as part of running the test step or prior to starting the test case during the setup steps. During test design, the test engineer determines the expected results of each step or substep, which might be in an output, a system state, a timing or sequencing result, or some other observable behavior. Alternatively, the test engineer might determine how the test system should determine the expected result; e.g., the test system might use a legacy system or other program to generate the expected result during test execution.

Each step or substep has a numeric identifier. Again using a Dewey decimal–style notation, I number steps sequentially starting from 1 and then number their subordinate substeps decimally (1.001, 1.002, and so forth). This numbering allows me to refer to specific test steps by combining the test case's numeric identifier (from the header) with the test step identifier — for example, the second substep of step 5 in test case 9.010 can be unambiguously identified as 9.010.5.002. This method is useful in bug reports and in discussions with testers. (The bug-tracking database discussed in Chapter 4 includes a field that captures this value.)

To the right of the list of steps are three columns that allow testers to record the results of their testing. Following the execution of a test case, one of three statements will typically hold true for each step or substep:

- The tester ran the test step or substep and observed the expected result, the whole expected result, and nothing but the expected result. The test step or substep did not locate any bugs. The tester should record *Pass* in the Result column.

- The tester ran the test step or substep, and the outcome was, to a greater or lesser extent, unexpected. The test case successfully identified some untoward behavior that the tester can now report in the bug-tracking database. How to classify the test case? If the unanticipated result was something along the lines of a CPU catching fire, a program crashing, or a system lockup, the tester should enter *Fail* in the Result column. However, what if the unexpected result doesn't affect the correct operation of the functionality under test? Development might see your team as unfair and alarmist if the tester classifies this test as *Fail*. It is important, however, to keep track of the test case that did find a new bug, so I don't want my testers to record it as a *Pass*. For these situations, I like to use the word *Warn* as the documented result. A *Warn* entry can also cover some of the gray areas between complete failure and tangential failure — for example, if system under test performs the functionality under test correctly but also displays an incorrectly spelled help message.

- The tester did not run the test step or substep. If the tester could not run the step or substep — for example, because a known bug prevented the specified action or because the test environment lacks necessary resources — the tester should record *Block* in the Result column. If the tester chose not to run the test step or substep, the test should mark the step or substep as *Skip*. In either case, the tester should explain this omission.

If a test step is marked *Fail* or *Warn*, the tester should also indicate, in the Bug ID column, the identifier for the bug report filed as a result of the observed failure. In the Bug RPN column, the test should record the risk priority number for the bug. Chapter 4 covers the topic of bug reporting in depth, including bug RPNs (risk priority numbers). For now, suffice it to say that you need a facility for recording bugs, that each reported bug report needs a unique identifier, and that bugs should include some metric of risk that they pose.

At the bottom of the template is a summary section in which the tester indicates an overall assessment of the test case. The tester should mark the

Status entry *Pass*, *Warn*, or *Fail*, depending on the results of the test case. The tester might also record *Block* or *Skip* if applicable. Since test cases consist of multiple steps, I find that I need a hierarchical rule for assigning test case status based on test step status, such as the following:

1. If any test step or substep is in progress, then record the entire test case as *IP*.

2. Else, if any step or substep is blocked, then record the entire test case as *Block*.

3. Else, if any step or substep failed, then record the entire case as *Fail*.

4. Else, if any step or substep warned, then record the entire case as *Warn*.

5. Otherwise, all the steps must have passed, so record the entire case as *Pass*.

I don't have a rule for *Skip* because generally the tester (or perhaps test manager) would make this decision at the test case level. The tester should next note the specific system configuration used for the test. (Chapter 5 introduces the idea of assigning an identifier to different system configurations.)

In the final part of the summary section, the tester should record his or her name or initials (depending on your custom), the date on which the test case was completed, the actual effort expended in terms of person-hours, and the duration. The latter three pieces of information allow you to track progress and understand variances from the plan that result from fast — or slow — test progress. Be careful, though, not to use these duration and effort numbers as a cudgel. Testers are not motivated by an angry boss who yells at them for not achieving (possibly unrealistic) targets. Instead, they quickly learn to manipulate these numbers, which prevents you from seeing a realistic picture of your test operation in this area.

A Stress Test Case for DataRocket

Let's look at a brief example of how you might use the test case template. Figure 3-6 shows a test case designed to evaluate DataRocket's response to CPU and memory loads while running under Sun Solaris, Microsoft Windows Server 2008, and Red Hat Linux. A tester (initials LTW) has run the test case and recorded the results.

Suppose that, when LTW installed the LCV test tool on the Windows server from the CD, the DVD drive failed to read the CD on the first two tries. The third try succeeded, but this ratio of two failures out of every three tries held up on subsequent retests. Because the failure doesn't materially affect the CPU or the memory subsystem, LTW classified it as a *Warn*.

Worse, however, Solaris, a key network operating system in the target market, did not install or run reliably. About half the time, the system panicked during the installation. The rest of the time, it panicked later, sometimes under load, sometimes while idle. This result is a *Fail*, as it obviously does materially affect the CPU and memory response to stress.

In the summary section, the overall test case result is marked *Fail* because of the failure of the Solaris installation. System configurations B, A, and C are not identified in Figure 3-6. I typically use a separate worksheet in the spreadsheet to describe the exact composition of particular test configurations and to assign a convenient ID to each one. Also note that the two bugs seem to have consumed a lot of LTW's time; the Effort and Duration entries are well over the allocated times.

	A	B	C	D	E
1	Test Case Name:	CPU and Memory			
2	Test ID:	2.001			
3	Test Suite:	Load, Capacity and Volume			
4	Priority:	High			
5	Hardware Required:	One Datarocket Service			
6	Software Required:	Load, Capacity and Volume Test Suite			
7		Windows Server 2008			
8		Solaris			
9		RedHat Linux			
10	Duration:	4			
11	Effort:	4			
12	Setup:	Install Windows Server 2008			
13		Install Linux			
14		Install Solaris			
15	Teardown:	Burn drive images of each OS installation.			
16	**ID**	**Test Step/Substep**	**Result**	**Bug ID**	**Bug RPN**
17	1.000	Test CPU load on Windows Server 2008.			
18	1.001	Install Windows Servcer 2008	Pass		
19	1.002	Install LCV Test Suite.	Warn	760	6
20	1.003	Run LCV Test Suite, CPU Module, for one hour. Check log file for failures on exit.	Pass		
21	2.000	Repeat steps 1.001-1.003 for Solaris.	Pass		
22	3.000	Repeat steps 1.001-1.003 for Linux.	Fail	762	1
23	**Overall**	**Status**	Fail		
24		**System Config**	B,A,C		
25		**Tester**	LTW		
26		**Date Completed**	7/12		
27		**Effort**	5.5		
28		**Duration**	5.5		

Figure 3-6 The basic test case template used for a DataRocket stress test

CONFESSIONS OF AN OVERZEALOUS TEST MANAGER

I once worked at an organization where the testers, who were mostly contractors, had their billable hours capped by the planned effort of the test cases they ran. If they tried to bill more hours than the total effort allocated to their assigned test cases, the project leads rejected their time cards. The leads

(continued)

CONFESSIONS OF AN OVERZEALOUS TEST MANAGER *(continued)*

had an incentive to enforce these limits because they received bonuses based on completing the project on or under budget. Since this organization worked primarily with fixed bids, this method effectively aligned the test technicians with a key corporate objective: meeting or exceeding the profit margins for each project. What you measure is what you get.

Conversely, what you *don't* measure is what you *don't* get. In the absence of corresponding quality assurance pressures such as audits of test results, some testers adopted a "see no evil" attitude. Tests that fail take longer to analyze and complete than tests that pass. Remarkably, most testers remained conscientious and spirited trackers of bugs.

In addition to the quality problems caused by linking pay to planned test effort, it was unfair to penalize the testers so heavily. Test case delays and time overruns often have more to do with the management hierarchy, the support organizations, and the developers than with lackadaisical or featherbedding attitudes on the part of test technicians. Furthermore, there was nothing but downside for the test technicians, while the project leads were motivated to hoard hours in an attempt to make their bonuses as big as possible. I admit to being an exacting enforcer of hour limits in those days, but I wouldn't make the same mistake today.

Another Useful Test Case Template

Some test cases involve entering data into fields on a well-defined sequence of screens. This is especially the case with transactional components or systems. Registration screens, application wizards, and many e-commerce sites follow very specific sequences of screens that implement the workflow with few if any opportunities for variation, except where the values entered on one screen determine which of two or more subsequent screens will be followed. (In other words, where the system has a tree-type workflow.) A typical word processor is an example of a test that's very much *not* that way, as there is an almost infinite number of workflows, each very different, that could result in an identical document.

In the case of screen- and field-oriented systems, I have used test templates such as the one shown in Figure 3-7. In this template, you can put many test cases on a single worksheet, because the screen and field names remain the same. I once managed a test project for a bank where we tested a browser-based home-equity-loan application-processing system. The software had six or seven screens, each with well-defined, invariable fields that had to be filled in before the user could proceed to the next screen. Our test case definitions consisted of a sequence of columns in the worksheets that identified the inputs for those fields, and, below each input, the expected result, if appropriate.

	A	B
1	Test Case Name:	Mnemonic identifier
2	Test ID:	Five-digit ID, XX.YYY: XX suite number, YYY test number.
3	Test Suite(s):	The name of the test suite(s) that use this test case.
4	Priority:	From quality risk coverage analysis
5	Hardware Required:	List hardware in rows
6	Software Required:	List software in rows
7	Duration:	Elapsed clock time
8	Effort:	Person-hours
9	Setup:	List steps needed to set up the test
10	Teardown:	List steps needed to return SUT to pretest state
11		
12	**Screen/Field**	**Test Step/Substep**
13	Screen1	Screen name
14	Field1	Input value for field1.
15	Field2	Input value for field2.
16	Screen2	Screen name.
17	Expected Results	The result at the final (test condition) input.
18		
19	**Execution Summary**	
20	**Status**	
21	**Bug ID**	
22	**System Config ID**	
23	**Tester**	
24	**Date Completed**	
25	**Effort**	
26	**Duration**	

Figure 3-7 A screen- and field-oriented test case template

Suppose that one of the tests we need to run against DataRocket involves configuring the server with each of three bundled operating systems. A quick-start CD is included with the server that gathers the user's information into memory, and then drives the OS-installation process. At the end, upon rebooting, the system should contact a server at Winged Bytes offices to register the product and the bundled OS. The test case for these three sets of related test conditions is shown in Figure 3-8.

IEEE 829 Test System Templates

The IEEE 829-2008 standard provides three levels of templates for documenting test suites, test cases, and what the IEEE calls test procedures. I find adherence to this documentation standard rare in practice. In addition, as with the IEEE 829 test plan template, I find that these templates produce heavier-weight documentation than my own templates. However, they can provide interesting and useful ideas.

	A	B	C	D
1	Test Case Name:	Congifure/Register Windows	Configure/Register Solaris	Configure/Register Linux
2	Test ID:	3.001	3.002	3.003
3	Test Suite(s):	Basic Functionality	Basic Functionality	Basic Functionality
4	Priority:	High	High	High
5	Hardware Required:	One DR Server	One DR Server	One DR Server
6	Software Required:	Windows Server 2008	Solaris	Linux
7	Duration:	4	4	4
8	Effort:	2	2	2
9	Setup:	Install blank HD.	Install blank HD.	Install blank HD.
10	Teardown:	Save "Clean" WS2008 drive.	Save "clean" Solaris drive.	Save "clean" Linux drive.
11				
12	**Screen/Field**	**Test Step/Substep**	**Test Step/Substep**	**Test Step/Substep**
13	Welcome Screen			
14	Welcome Message	Check against docs.	Check against docs.	Check against docs.
15	Operator Name	Enter first, MI, last.	Enter first, MI, last.	Enter first, MI, last.
16	Company Name	Enter Name (min/max).	Enter name (min/max).	Enter name (min/max).
17	Company Address	Enter various options.	Enter various options.	Enter various options.
18	Next Button	Mouse or tab/enter.	Mouse or tab/enter.	Mouse or tab/enter.
19	Install Screen			
20	Select OS	Windows Server 2008	Solaris	Linux
21	Enter Disk Registration	Try invalid, then valid.	Try invalid, then valid.	Try invalid, then valid.
22	Confirm CD-ROM Insert	Try no, see CD request, then try yes w/o CD, see error message, then try yes w/CD.	Try no, see CD request, then try yes w/o CD, see error message, then try yes w/CD.	Try no, see CD request, then try yes w/o CD, see error message, then try yes w/CD.
23	Confirm Install Start	Confirm no start if "YES" not entered exactly as spelled.	Confirm no start if "YES" not entered exactly as spelled.	Confirm no start if "YES" not entered exactly as spelled.
24	Complete Screen			
25	Success Message	Check against docs.	Check against docs.	Check against docs.
26		Reboot; verify WS2008 load. Verify automatic call to reg server.	Reboot; verify Solaris load. Verify automatic call to reg server.	Reboot; verify Linux load. Verify automatic call to reg server.
27	*Repeat above using a bad disk.*	Verify failed install, "Fail" message, no registration.	Verify failed install, "Fail" message, no registration.	Verify failed install, "Fail" message, no registration.
28				
29	**Execution Summary**			
30	**Status**	Warn	Fail	Pass
31	**Bug ID(s)**	772	774	
32	**System Config ID**	B	A	C
33	**Tester**	LTW	HS	LTW
34	**Date Completed**	7/19	7/20	7/21
35	**Effort**	3	5	2
36	**Duration**	6	7	4

Figure 3-8 A screen-oriented registration test case

Let's start with the test design template, shown in Figure 3-9. This template describes a logical collection of test cases, which I refer to as a test suite. In Chapter 5, you'll see how I document test suites (and their results).

The first section, Introduction, identifies the test team that created the test suite and gives its status. The document identifier is some unique document name or ID number, consistent with the organization's standards. The Scope subsection summarizes the product, items, or features addressed by this collection of test cases. If you are following the IEEE 829 standard, you should ensure that everything listed in the scope of the Master Test Plan (see Chapter 2) appears in one or more test design documents. The References section, logically enough, lists the applicable reference documents, often divided into external references (those outside the project) and internal references (those inside the project).

	A	B	C	D	E
1	**1.0**	**Introduction**			
2	1.1	Document identifier			
3	1.2	Scope			
4	1.3	References			
5					
6	**2.0**	**Details of the Level Test Design**			
7	2.1	Features to be tested			
8	2.2	Approach refinements			
9	2.3	Test identification			
10	2.4	Feature pass/fail criteria			
11	2.5	Test deliverables			
12					
13	**3.0**	**General**			
14	3.1	Glossary			
15	3.2	Document change procedures and history			

Figure 3-9 The IEEE 829 test design template

The Details of the Level Test Design section, as you'd imagine, provides the real core of the document. It addresses the features to be tested, including potential combinations of features if we're talking about a test of a use case, an end-to-end test case, or a configuration test. As I mentioned a moment ago, if you are following the IEEE 829 standard, you should ensure that everything listed as a feature tested in the master test plan (see Chapter 2) appears in one or more test design documents. Similarly, the Approach Refinements subsection of the test design document should expand upon the approach described in the master test plan, at least as it relates to these features. You should mention any common attributes of the test cases covered by this test design document. The Test Identification subsection lists the test cases this test design document covers. The Feature Pass/Fail Criteria subsection elaborates on how you intend to check the results of these test cases. The Test Deliverables subsection explains the results logging, bug reporting, and results reporting associated with this test suite.

Finally, the General section includes a glossary of terms specific to this test design, as well as the change history for the document.

Let's move on to the test case template, shown in Figure 3-10. The test case should provide the information the testers need to run the test case. (The level of detail can vary, as I'll discuss later in this chapter.) The way the IEEE 829 test case templates work now, a single document contains multiple test cases, ideally all the test cases associated with a single test design document. If this is the situation, the first and third sections exist once in the document, with the second section repeated for each test case. However, since a test case may do duty in multiple test suites, the test engineer should produce the document in such a way as to support that.

	A	B	C	D	E	F
1	**1.0**	**Introduction (once per document)**				
2	1.1	Document identifier				
3	1.2	Scope				
4	1.3	References				
5	1.4	Context				
6	1.5	Notation for description				
7						
8	**2.0**	**Details (once per test case)**				
9	2.1	Test case identifier				
10	2.2	Objective				
11	2.3	Inputs				
12	2.4	Outcome(s)				
13	2.5	Environmental needs				
14	2.6	Special procedural requirements				
15	2.7	Intercase dependencies				
16						
17	**3.0**	**Global (once per document)**				
18	3.1	Glossary				
19	3.2	Document change procedures and history				

Figure 3-10 IEEE 829 test case template

The first section, Introduction, contains the same type of information as discussed for the test design introduction. The Context subsection supplies information not covered elsewhere about the context of the test case, such as a third party that might be involved in the testing. The Notation for Description subsection explains how the test cases and test suites are numbered.

The second section, the Details section (which is repeated for each test case in the test suite), provides a number of pieces of information. Each test case has a unique identifier, as I described earlier. It also has an Objective subsection, which includes information like risk, priority, and the intent of the test. This is a bit more extensive than the information I tend to include in the headers of test cases shown earlier, but if the readers of the test case included people outside the test team, such detail would certainly help.

Next, for each test case, the template includes the inputs. These can be specific values (which might include tolerances), tables, files, databases, or any other values or events provided to the system under test during execution of the test case. Similarly, the test case should include outputs and expected behaviors. This can also involve tolerances and a wide range of types of behaviors, beyond merely values displayed on screens.

After the inputs and outcomes, the test case template includes information about the specific test environment needs associated with the test case. If all tests run in the same environment and the test plan already described that environment, then you can omit this section. Otherwise, the test case should include a description of the hardware, software, operating systems, networks, facilities, and other such information. If the same environments cover all the test cases in this test suite, then you can have a single instance of this section for the entire test suite.

For each test case, there are two additional subsections. The first has to do with any special procedural requirements. This can include pre-conditions and post-conditions, but should not repeat anything covered in the test procedure documents, which I'll discuss in a minute. The second subsection covers intercase dependencies, which are those tests that must run before or after this test case. As a general rule, intercase dependencies can create more inefficiencies than efficiencies. While the idea of having a sequence of test cases set up the pre-conditions for the subsequent tests seems quicker, the problem is that, should the preceding tests fail, then the dependent tests could suffer false positives when they appear to fail due to improper initial conditions.

The third section, the Global section, contains the same kind of information discussed for the General section of the test design document. Of course, it should focus on information not previously provided in the test design document.

Let's move on to the test procedure template, shown in Figure 3-11. According to the IEEE 829 standard, the test procedure documents should specify the steps to execute a set of test cases. I find this usage unusual in practice. Generally, for manual tests, people combine the inputs, expected outcomes, and the actions required to submit those inputs and evaluate those outcomes in a single document. The IEEE 829 approach of separating these documents makes sense for automated tests where data, scripts, and expected results reside in different files.

	A	B	C	D	E	F	G	H	I
1	1.0	Introduction							
2	1.1	Document identifier							
3	1.2	Scope							
4	1.3	References							
5	1.4	Relationship to other procedures							
6									
7	2.0	Details							
8	2.1	Inputs, outputs, and special requirements							
9	2.2	Ordered description of the steps to be taken to execute the test cases							
10									
11	3.0	General							
12	3.1	Glossary							
13	3.2	Document change procedures and history							

Figure 3-11 IEEE 829 test procedure template

Most of the Introduction section is much the same as discussed previously for other IEEE templates. The References subsection should cover all the test cases covered by the test procedure. The Relationship to Other Procedures subsection, like the Intercase Dependencies subsection for the test case template, should describe test procedures that must run before this one. It should also describe test procedures that run concurrent with and subsequent to this one.

The Details section, as you'd expect, provides the central information for the test procedure. It should list all the test cases, output files, databases, external systems, prerequisite steps, skills, and environmental needs, beyond any covered in the associated test cases. It should provide, in order and in sufficient detail, the steps required to run the test cases. This includes information for the test to capture and log. It describes how to set up and start the tests. It describes how to run each step of the test and how to measure the results. It also describes shutdown information if needed to suspend the test (and information about how to restart suspended tests), wrap-up actions to complete the tests, and contingency information on how to deal with any anomalies expected during testing.

The third section, the General section, contains the same kind of information discussed for the test design and test case documents. Of course, it should focus on information not previously provided in those documents.

On Test Design and the Smart Use of Templates

In the last few pages, I've talked about ways to document test cases. That might have left you scratching your head at points, saying, "Where did this test come from?" Since this book is for test managers, not test engineers, the immediate answer to that is, "The test engineers wrote them."

If you are persistent, you might ask, of course, "Fine, wise guy, but how did the test engineers do that?" In general, there are five main categories of test design techniques:

- **Behavioral tests of functionality:** Those tests that focus on what the system does, the real-world problems it solves. Such tests check the accuracy, suitability, interoperability, security, and compliance with applicable standards of the functional elements of the system.

- **Behavioral tests of non-functional elements:** Those tests that focus on how the system does what it does, the behaviors it displays while it solves problems. Such tests check usability, reliability, resource utilization, performance, maintainability, and portability of the system.

- **Structural tests:** Those tests based on internal design and implementation of the system. Such tests look at control flows, data flows, architecture, and the like.

- **Experience-based tests:** Those tests based on the experience and skills that testers have gained from testing similar systems. *Similar* in this case can mean similar domain, similar technology, or similar types of tests.

- **Defect-based tests:** Those tests based on defects typically found in similar systems. *Similar* in this case again can mean similar domain, similar technology, or similar types of tests.

As a test manager, you should ensure that your test engineers know how to design tests using each of these five techniques (see Chapter 8). You should also ensure that your test suites use the appropriate mix of techniques. Each of these techniques has strengths and weaknesses, and only a good blend of all five techniques can produce truly excellent results.

I once had a discussion with a test engineer about test design techniques. He became frustrated with the details and said, "Look, I don't need to know any of that. I just need a template for fill in." Sorry, wrong answer. Test engineers do need to know good test design techniques. Templates themselves are merely tools, not magic. Templates provide a convenient format to capture the information needed for certain kinds of tests, but they do not substitute for test design skills.

There are many, many different ways to document test cases. Myriad templates have been developed and used by various test teams. What's not important are the particular templates you choose, if any. What is important is that if you do choose templates for your test cases, they are suitable for the kind of system you're testing. It's also important that you and your team use the templates consistently.[4]

How Detailed? The Effects of Precision

An important decision when thinking about documenting test cases is how much detail the test engineers should include. How precisely should the test engineers document the actions, data, and expected results? The decision involves a set of trade-offs.

On the one hand, extensive, detailed, precise test documentation assumes less knowledge on the part of the testers, which often allows me to use testers with lower levels of skill than I might otherwise require. It also supports reproducibility: if nothing is left to the judgment of an individual tester, I usually see less variability in two evaluations of the same test by two different people, or even by the same person at different times. In addition, if development is involved in the review process for test cases as my team constructs them, spelling out the details serves to communicate, clearly and unambiguously, what types of failures we're looking for and what behaviors we'll consider buggy.

On the other hand, writing precise, detailed, unambiguous test documentation can involve considerably more work than writing a laconic one. The difference in effort involved in creating a concrete set of test specifications (those that leave little to the discretion of the tester) or a logical set of test

---

[4]For more on test design techniques, see my books *Pragmatic Software Testing* and *Advanced Software Testing: Volume I*. Paul Jorgensen's book *Software Testing: A Craftman's Approach* is another excellent reference for test engineers. Most of the other books on test design are domain-specific, technology-specific, or strategy-specific, and of various degrees of usefulness.

specifications (those that require tester skill, experience, and judgment) is about ten times the effort. Obviously, you have to write more, but you also must unlearn information that seems obvious to you and your test engineers but could mystify or confuse the test technicians and any others who might become involved in testing. If you've ever tried to explain what testing is all about to someone with no experience in the field, you already know that this can be quite difficult. Understanding the level of detail required for the test team you have assembled (or intend to assemble) is, I find, the key to writing effect test cases.

Beyond the effort required to write unambiguous test cases, consider the effort needed to maintain them. In one example test case, step 1.001 tells the test technician, *Install Windows Server. Confirm proper install*. The instruction *Install Windows Server 2008. Confirm proper install* might have been better, but it would require me to update the OS version before using this test case in the future. Or, suppose that I had launched into an exposition, dozens of steps long, about how to install Windows Server 2008 and then how to confirm the proper install. As soon as the next version of Windows Server comes out and totally changes the installation procedure (say), the test case will require an extensive rewrite.

There is a test strategy called *reactive testing* or *dynamic testing*, which I alluded to briefly in Chapter 1. With reactive test strategies, such as bug hunting, software attacks, and exploratory testing, testers design, develop, and execute tests during test execution.

Most reactive strategies include written test documentation, but generally it is of the *logical* type. Reactive test documentation doesn't tend to include specific values for input data and expected results. Instead, it gives a high-level statement of the area to test, some heuristics for testing that area (often by reference), and some general guidelines for checking the results. For example, James Whittaker's concept of *software attacks* provides generalized test cases, including logical descriptions of data, actions, and bugs to watch for, in his approach to reactive testing.[5]

Such strategies certainly have a lot to recommend them. As I mentioned in Chapter 1, reactive approaches introduce a self-correcting element into the test execution process, since these reactive strategies will tend to identify the holes and mistakes in your test set that can arise due to gaps and holes in analytical test strategies.

---

[5]For example, see James Whittaker's books *How to Break Software*, *How to Break Software Security*, and *How to Break Web Software*. These books are the most practical texts on how to apply reactive techniques to your projects, but they do seem mostly applicable to PC-based applications.

Reactive tests tend to do a good job of finding bugs, particularly compared with following detailed manual test cases. Reactive tests do not require a lot of effort to create or maintain, so they are efficient. This is always good, since test budgets are always constrained.

Lastly, but certainly not last in importance, testers find such reactive tests fun and creative. I certainly do. I like to kick off a session of testing, guess where the bugs are, apply my testing skills and experience, follow the signs, and — as I always do — find bugs.

That said, nothing is perfect, including reactive test strategies. I have seen a number of problems arise with such strategies, and you should be aware of these problems.

First, notice that the more the test manager relies on tester discretion, judgment, and experience in testing, the more she risks the possibility that a tester might forget something. Under pressure, it's all too easy to forget something. The guidance of some amount of documentation prepared prior to test execution can help avoid that.

If you think back to Chapter 1, you probably can see that the techniques discussed there for test estimation won't work so well without some analysis going on in parallel. As a test manager, having no idea how long test execution will last is not a career-boosting situation, particularly since test execution lies on the critical path for project completion. By doing some amount of analysis in parallel with test planning, you can better anticipate the test effort.

Another problem with purely reactive approaches is the loss of opportunities to prevent bugs during testing. As I've observed again and again with clients, the cost of finding and fixing a bug goes up the later in the project you find that bug. Since most reactive strategies focus on finding bugs in the system ultimately presented rather than analyze the system during development, you can't expect to find and remove bugs early in the project. By creating some amount of test documentation prior to test execution, you can often find and remove bugs before test execution starts.

Yet another issue is the problem of scalability. If the test cases are too lightweight in terms of documentation, you'll have to spend a lot of time as a test manager talking with your testers. What did they test? What did they find? What should they do next? While such conversations might be interesting, the problem is that, as a test manager, you'll have a lot going on during test execution. Time you spend managing inwards is time you don't spend managing upwards and outwards, as I'll discuss in Chapter 9. By providing more detailed test cases, you can let your testers operate on their own most of the time and have a single debrief session with the entire team once a day or so.

Finally, since reactive tests rely on experience and skills, remember that you can use only experienced, skilled testers to do such tests. Good reactive testing requires a significant understanding of the business problem the system solves, the technology by which it solves it, and the testing of dozens of similar systems. Many test managers do not have the luxury of staffing their team exclusively with people with such experience. By providing more detailed test cases, you can substitute for some of the skill that purely reactive strategies require.

I want to reiterate — with a bit of refinement — a metaphor I used in the first edition of this book. Ten years ago I wrote, "Testing without written test cases and documented expected results has a lot in common with the Hispanic party tradition of letting blindfolded children pummel a hanging piñata with a stick to get at the candy inside. Would you bet your job and the quality of your company's product on this methodology?" Those were then, and they are now, strong words. However, I would bet that most of the reactive testing that occurs in practice is risky, because it does not adequately manage the risks I just mentioned. Be careful.

So, does that mean you shouldn't use reactive techniques at all? No, you should use them. Reactive testing is a best practice for most test projects. I suggest reserving about 10 to 20 percent of test execution effort for such testing.

To some extent, you can integrate reactive testing right into the written test cases. I often tell testers that a test case is a road map that takes them to interesting places in the system under test, and when they get somewhere interesting, they should stop and look around.

As H.L. Mencken said, for every complicated question there is an answer that is simple, obvious, and wrong. So there is no simple right answer to the question of how much precision you should include in your test cases. Of course, there is no single right answer. Every test operation has different constraints in terms of the resources and time available to develop test cases, the technical and product expertise possessed by the engineers and technicians, the concern with strict reproducibility, traceability, and auditability, and the effort that you can have your team spend maintaining test cases. In addition, you needn't pick a single answer. I usually allow my skilled test engineers to run reactive tests while I make sure that test technicians have ample guidance in well-documented test cases. Decisions about level of detail, like much of management, must move on a continuum (see Figure 3-12).

No documentation; often associated with immature test processes and teams
Pros: Cheap and quick
Cons: No coverage measurements

Used for highly regulated industries; follows specific templates
Pros: Traceable and auditable
Cons: High initial and ongoing costs, not always followed

"Pure Reactive" | Logical test documentation

Many test teams balance precision and detail, with adequate reproducibility and traceability in realistic budgets.

Concrete test documentation | "Pure Scripted"

Lightweight documentation; a sophisticated technique
Pros: Inexpensive but measurable
Cons: Requires skilled testers and managers

Detailed documentation; a widely described technique
Pros: Reproducible and traceable
Cons: Significant resources to develop and maintain

Figure 3-12 The logical/concrete test case continuum

Avoiding the Dreaded Test Escape: Coverage and Regression-Test Gaps

A common metric of test team effectiveness measures whether the test team manages to find a sizeable majority of the bugs prior to release. The production or customer bugs are sometimes called *test escapes*. The implication is that your test team missed these problems but could reasonably have detected them during test execution. You can quantify this metric as follows:

$$\text{Defect Detection Effectiveness} = \frac{\text{bugs (test)}}{\text{bugs (test)} + \text{bugs (production)}}$$

We'll look at this metric again in a little more detail in Chapter 4 when we have a database in place for gathering the underlying data.

Note the word *reasonably*. You are probably not going to score 100% on this metric consistently. If your testers could have found the bug only through unusual and complicated hardware configurations or obscure operations, that bug should not count as a test escape. Moreover, the count of the bugs found in the field should not include bugs previously detected by testing; in other words, if the testers found the bug during testing, but project management deferred fixing the bug, that bug should count as a bug found by test. Finally, note that in many environments one can assume that most field bugs are found in the first three months to a year after deployment, so you can estimate the defect detection effectiveness after that period.

Test escapes usually arise through one or a combination of the following types of problems:

A **low-fidelity test system.** While a low-fidelity test system might cover a significant chunk of the product's features and operations, it doesn't cover the ones most important to your customers, usually as a result of poor engineering.

A **regression-test gap.** The test suite does contain test cases covering the operation in which the bug surfaced, but the team ran the test cases before the bug was introduced in the system under test. Regression-test gaps arise from schedule or resource limitations or from planning errors (see the paragraph following this list).

A **test-result interpretation error.** A tester fails to detect or report incorrect system behavior, assigns an excessively low priority or severity to the bug, or otherwise understates the significance of the problem.

Chapter 6 discusses result interpretation errors in more depth. For now, let's look at how low-fidelity test systems and regression-test gaps create test escapes. Imagine for a moment that defects are fish (not bugs), that tests are fishnets, and that testers are the crew on a fishing boat. When you have a low-fidelity test system, the fish escape by swimming through holes in the fishnets. When regression-test gaps occur, the fish swim under a fishnet that is only half deployed. Prosperous fishing crews have an efficient fishing system. Flourishing test teams have powerful test systems and use them effectively. The following sections discuss some ways to maximize your catch. First, though, a cautionary tale to illustrate the stakes.

Bad Coverage Decisions with the Best Intentions

Coverage mistakes are easy to make, even if you spend time thinking about the issue. Some years ago, I took over as a test manager in a company that had developed a neat way of automating testing, using a portable scripting language and the command-line functionality of the system under test. For two years my team and I worked with that test system, polishing it to a bright luster. We wrote an intelligent output comparison program. We had clean, maintainable test tools, under strict revision control. The system was robust, reliable, and fast. Furthermore, we analyzed test coverage in terms of the crucial databases and operating systems supported by the system under test, and we had most of them nailed. Nevertheless, we had significant test escapes, and the customers were unhappy. Accordingly, my managers were unhappy, and they made my team and me very unhappy by liquidating the test organization.

What happened? I let the test tool determine my decisions about test coverage. As the saying goes, "Give a child a hammer and the whole world becomes a nail." We had only two test suites that evaluated the user interface. We barely tested the utilities included with the package. We spent insufficient time understanding the unique uses and the special boundary conditions that plagued our customers.

I took a couple of lessons away from this experience. The most important was to be sure that I decided on test coverage based on the quality risks that matter to my customers, my end users, and my colleagues in such areas as marketing, technical support, sales, business analysis, the help desks, and any others who are close to the users. If you follow the risk-based testing approach from Chapter 1, it should help you avoid this problem. I also learned that coverage is not a one-time consideration, so I constantly revisit my coverage goals.

Are You Testing What Development Is Building?

If you are lucky enough to get written requirements and design specifications for your product, you probably already use them as a basis for test planning and test system development. You should also close the loop and ascertain the coverage. You can use a numeric approach, such as the one outlined for quality risk coverage in the following section, or you can use a cross-reference approach. To create a cross-reference document, carefully go through the requirements or specifications, and note (in a soft copy) the specific test cases that verify each requirement or specification. For those requirements not paired with a test case, decide whether there's a good reason to skip testing in that area. If there isn't, you have found a coverage problem you need to address. Apply this approach iteratively until you are happy with your test system's coverage. You can also circulate this marked-up cross-reference to your peers, especially key testing stakeholders, to be sure they're comfortable with what you plan to test.

You can apply this approach even if you don't have requirements or design specifications documents. By listing the functional areas of the product at a general level and then subdividing them into more specific areas, you have a black-box decomposition of what the system is supposed to do. (This is analogous to building the requirements and design specifications documents from the product itself, which is reverse-order but not unusual.) Then proceed as just described, using either a numeric or a cross-reference approach. Iterate until you're satisfied, and circulate the document for review.

Remember two caveats about using such a functional coverage approach, however. First, it measures testing of what the system *does*. Don't forget about what it *doesn't* do, *shouldn't* do, and *should* do — these factors are equally important to your customers. You'll want to add coverage analysis based on the risks you identified to check these areas, as described in the following section.

Second, if you are focused narrowly on functions, you can easily overlook factors such as stability, performance, data quality, error handling and recovery, and other such system problems. My mistake in the cautionary tale related earlier was, at least in part, that of depending solely on a narrow functional coverage analysis to validate my testing approach. As your coverage analyses move further away from customer requirements and more into the minutiae of system functionality, you need to augment your approach by looking at what the customers care about.

Relating Quality Risks to Test Cases

Chapter 1 introduced (or maybe reintroduced) you to a list of generic risks that apply to the quality (i.e., quality risks) of many computer systems, and I used that list to develop a prioritized set of quality risks for our SpeedyWriter case study. That chapter also explained the use of various other risk analysis techniques, including the *failure mode and effect analysis* (FMEA) approach for defining quality risks. Whichever approach I use for test case development, I need to ensure quality risk coverage. After I have generated my list of quality risks, I benchmark my test system against it.

One way to do this is to list test case identifiers as column heads to the right of the FMEA chart itself. In each cell where a quality risk row intersects a test case column, I enter one of the three values shown in Table 3-1. (In Chapter 5, I'll show you a variation on this technique that also ties coverage to test case status, providing data for a very interesting chart we can create to measure test coverage during test execution.)

Table 3-1 Relative Test-Coverage Analysis

VALUE	COVERAGE MEANING
0 (or blank)	The test case does nothing to address the quality risk.
1	The test case provides some level of indirect coverage for the quality risk.
2	The test case provides direct and significant coverage for the quality risk.

In addition to rating individual test case and quality risk intersections, I aggregate this information. When I total the numbers by quality risk category and by test suite, I am measuring, respectively, whether I'm covering particular risks and whether tests are providing an adequate return on investment. Remember, though, to relate these numbers to the risk priority numbers. High coverage numbers should correspond to high risk, low coverage numbers to low risk.

If you were careful to capture the pertinent data in the References column of the FMEA (as explained in Chapter 1), you could also generate the coverage analyses for requirements and design specifications discussed in the previous section. You could then use this cross-reference to prepare a set of documents that, because they are less information-dense than an FMEA, will allow your peers to review your coverage. It is sometimes difficult to get people outside test to review FMEA charts, but requirements, specifications, and functional decompositions are easier to digest.

These quality risk coverage numbers are relative and subjective. No hard-and-fast rule separates a 0 rating from a 1, or a 1 from a 2. However, as long as you and your engineers use the ratings consistently, and you use peer reviews to ensure agreement, the numbers have meaning. Be careful, though, to avoid bias in one direction or the other. If your team is consistently too optimistic, assigning 1s and 2s gratuitously, you can overestimate your coverage. Conversely, you can also underestimate it.[6]

Configuration Coverage

Let's suppose that you are testing SpeedyWriter, and your manager tells you to run only the installation and file-open tests. You not only will be allowed to retain your current level of staff and resources, but also will be given even more resources — an unlimited hardware budget. In return, all you have to do is test SpeedyWriter against every possible combination of client computer, platform (Web browser, operating system, and network), and I/O peripheral. Would you do it?

For purposes of illustration, let's assume 20 possible variations of each variable: 20 different client computers; 20 operating system, browser, and network combinations; and, 20 combinations of printers, mice, keyboards, scanners, and video controllers. Figure 3-13 shows the test space created by this scenario.

As you can see from Figure 3-13, you would have to test 8,000 different configurations, give or take a few hundred impossible configurations, such as the use of a particular peripheral with an operating system that doesn't support it. If the two tests (installation and file-open) take about an hour, including

---

[6]A number of test management tools include the ability to measure coverage. This is better than trying to do this with a spreadsheet, if you can afford the tools. Most of them refer to this as requirements coverage, but by recasting the risk items — or anything else you want to be sure to cover — as a requirement, you can use the tools to accomplish the same thing.

setup and teardown time, you have about 2.75 person-years of work ahead of you. In addition to the time, imagine the expense. This simple example could easily cost $100,000 in hardware, operating systems, and server software alone. (Chapter 10 discusses how to reduce the expense of covering multiple configurations by leveraging the capital expenditures of external test labs.)

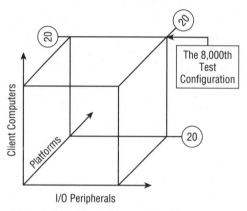

Figure 3-13 An intractable configuration coverage problem

Even this discouraging example simplifies the matter. In reality, the platform and I/O-peripheral dimensions are themselves multiple dimensions. In general, any time you confront the issue of configuration coverage, you are faced with a truly ugly *N*-dimensional matrix of configuration combinations that you have no hope whatsoever of covering completely. What to do?

First, forget about covering combinations of configurations. This is a chump's game. With just a few memorable exceptions, most of the configuration-related bugs I've seen in my 20-plus years of testing experience related either to specific, important configurations or to a single configuration option that didn't work with the system under test at all. Every now and then I've seen a bug that related to a pair of configuration options together, and just once was a bug specific to three configuration options together.

You can effectively manage this problem by using one or more of the following five techniques. The first is to be sure that you pick the key configurations. For each configuration variable, identify a handful of hardware, software, or infrastructure items that you really care about. Factors to consider in this decision include customer usage, the risk to the product if that particular item does not work, and your gut feeling for where the bugs are. You should also consider the long-term usefulness of the item in your lab and, naturally, its price. Expect to spend some time negotiating your list with management, and be ready to justify each purchase. In addition, keep in mind that configuration testing is but one of the many types of testing you must do. By trying to cover too many configurations, you might end up with too little time and money and too few staff resources to test other important quality risks.

Even if you had only five variations of each configuration variable in the SpeedyWriter example, completely covering the matrix would take three person-weeks. That's probably a significant chunk of time in your project unless configuration testing is your main quality risk. Rather than trying to cover every single cell in the matrix, you might choose a second technique, known as *shotgunning*. In shotgunning, you will make sure that every important configuration option is represented at least once in some test case. You can choose the test case associated with a particular configuration option specifically to check for a particular problem, or, if you have no idea how a particular option might cause problems, you simply distribute your tests randomly across the options.

The third technique offers an opportunity to increase test configuration coverage through careful use of test cycles. By reshuffling the configuration used with each test in each cycle, you can get even closer to complete coverage. Continuing our SpeedyWriter example, suppose that you had 250 test cases to run and three test cycles. This gives you 750 case/cycle combinations. You could test each configuration combination against six cases. This isn't exhaustive, but at least you've sampled each one.

A fourth technique, called *all-pairs* or *orthogonal arrays*, allows you to test not all possible combinations across all options, but all possible combinations across all possible pairs of configuration variables. For example, if each configuration variable has five options, and you have three configuration variables, instead of testing 125 combinations, you test 25 combinations. In some cases, there might be plenty of test cycles and test cases available to distribute these pairs across. Going back to the SpeedyWriter example, notice that you would have 20 times 20 (or 400 pairs) across the three variables there, which you could easily cover in the 750 case/cycle combinations we just discussed.

Finally, a last technique you can apply is the use of widespread beta testing. By picking potential customers who can, collectively, help you cover many of the key configurations, you should locate many of the remaining configuration-specific bugs that matter to your customers and users. This also provides the benefit of testing in the customer environment and with customer data, although this added level of complexity can make isolating bugs challenging. Finally, you'll need to find beta testers who will stay engaged enough in the process to provide good feedback, which also implies that beta testing must happen only when the product is stable enough not to frustrate and drive away your beta testers.[7]

---

[7]I'm grossly simplifying this technique to keep this discussion down to a paragraph, and, before any purist should spontaneously combust, let me say that, yes, I know that orthogonal arrays and all-pairs tables are not the same. For a more extensive and precise description of this technique, see my book *Pragmatic Software Testing*.

Bug Coverage

So far, we've discussed several ways to analyze coverage: by requirements specifications, by design specifications, by functional areas, by quality risks, and by configurations. All these methods address the question, "Have we tested *X*?" From a confidence-building perspective, coverage of the key test areas is important.

However, when you consider another objective of testing — to find bugs — the real question is, "Have we found enough bugs?" The approaches we've covered provide indirect information about this question, since bugs usually relate back to one or more of these areas. Nevertheless, important bugs could remain because we haven't tested *enough*.

Unfortunately, we can't know what we don't know. If it were possible to know all the bugs in advance, the entire test effort would be unnecessary. Suppose, though, that you could estimate the total number of bugs in the system under test. Or, perhaps you could measure the bug-finding effectiveness of your test system. There are three techniques for solving these problems.

The most commonly cited and, in my experience, commonly used technique for estimating bug numbers relies on historical data. Based on the size of the current project, the sizes of past projects, and the number of bugs found in past projects, the test manager can estimate the number of bugs in the current project. Suppose the current project is estimated at 5,000 lines of code. Further, suppose that historical data indicates one bug found in system test or, failing that, in the first six months following release for every 100 lines of code. In this case, we can estimate that either we find 50 bugs during system test or resign ourselves to the remainder surfacing after release. Line-of-code estimates being notoriously unreliable early in the project, though, this estimate is subject to considerable error.

Alternatively, we can measure project size in function points. Function points are a software-sizing technique that assigns a given number of points to certain activities that the developers must build into a program, based on a detailed requirements specification. Users of this technique claim it is more reliable as an estimating tool. Suppose we expect — based on the requirements — that we'll implement 100 function points. Suppose further that we expect 1.5 bugs per function point, so 150 bugs would escape into the system test phase. We can either find about 150 bugs during system test, or deliver those bugs to the customers and users. The problem is that you'll need to have function point counts. Most projects and clients I've worked with don't have these.

A more practical technique involves estimating the number of bugs based on development effort. Suppose you know, from historical data, that for a given person-month of development effort, the programmers will introduce 30 bugs that will either surface during system test or after release. In that case, if the development manager estimates the total development effort at 10 person-months, then you'd expect 300 bugs.

To ascertain bug coverage during test execution, you then could use a chart showing the number of bugs found and the number of bugs resolved to see how close you'd come to covering most of the bugs. We'll look at charts like this in Chapters 4 and 5.

However, you — and more importantly, your project management colleagues — might be just as curious about how long it will take to find and resolve the bugs during the initial project planning and preparation phases of the project. To do so, you'd need to use historical data to predict the rate of bug finding and the lifetime of the typical bug. In both cases, you can use metrics like those in Chapters 4 and 5 to derive such predictions. If you can make such predictions, you should do so when creating your test estimate, as discussed in Chapter 1, and make sure that the estimate reflects this bug find/resolve time.

These techniques — which have many variants — are called *defect removal models*. Simple ones like the one shown in Figure 3-14 deal only with the final phase of testing. However, you can extend these to deal with all phases of testing.

Figure 3-14 Predicting bugs and bug find/resolve time

Such models assume that, during each phase of the project, some number of defects are *injected* into the system by developer error, some number of defects are *removed* through testing and quality assurance, and the difference *escapes* to the next phase of the project. Suppose we follow a sequential software development life cycle model for our project (see Chapter 12 for a discussion of life cycle models) with five phases: requirements, design, implementation, unit test, and system test. If we have historical data not just for the defect detection effectiveness of system testing, but also for all the previous phases, we can estimate the bugs delivered to our users as the number of bugs that escape at the end of the system test phase.

Whether simple or sophisticated, defect removal models can be accurate. One of our clients, who uses a lines-of-code model to predict bugs, can predict the number of bugs and the duration of test execution to within 10 percent. To achieve this, you'll need good defect and project management metrics. Furthermore, changes in the process, the technology, and the team can invalidate these models for future projects.[8]

Regression-Test Gaps

The concept of regression is straightforward but sometimes misunderstood. Formally, you can say that if, as a result of a change in the system under test, a new revision of the system, S_{n+1} contains a bug not present in the previous revision, S_n, the quality of the system has regressed. Plainly speaking, regression occurs when some previously correct operation misbehaves. If a new revision contains a new piece of functionality that fails without affecting the rest of the system, that's not regression.

Usually, you'll detect regression when test cases that passed previously now fail. Some regression, though, is so obvious that no test is required to find it — flaws in a system's case or a glitch in software installation, for example. Or, you can have Zen regression: if a bug crawls into the system but no one detects it, you will find this regression, like the sound of the unattended falling tree, hard to prove!

There are two instructive ways to think about regression. The first has to do with the feature-space separation between the change introducing the regression bug and the regression failure associated with it. The most painless is the local regression, where a fix or change creates a regression failure in the same feature area where the programmer made the change. I call this painless because a confirmation test of the fix might well reveal the new failure. Similarly, when a change or fix exposes an existing bug, for example by making a particular area of the system accessible for the first time, that's not too hard to detect, either. The tougher situation is when you're dealing with a remote regression, where a fix in one area breaks something in another area. The classic example here is where a change affects the data stored by one feature, and this new format or type of data causes failure of another area of the system that uses the data.

---

[8]If you're curious about how to build a model like this, I can recommend Stephen Kan's *Metrics and Models in Software Quality Engineering*.

Another way to think about regression has to do with the separation in time between the introduction of a feature and the introduction of a regression bug that breaks that feature. The two main variants are the regression of a new feature and the regression of a release feature. I'll illustrate with an example.

Suppose you are working on the first release of a product, release 1.0. This release has five features. You receive a feature-complete test release and start testing. You test features 1 and 2 without any problems. You find a bug in feature 3, which the programmers duly fix. You confirmation test the fix, which is fine, but you don't re-test the features tested so far. Oops, big mistake, because the fix to feature 3 broke feature 1, as shown in Figure 3-15. (This example assumes you are following a sequential life cycle, but the problem is even worse in iterative life cycles, as discussed in Chapter 12.) At least no one was using feature 1 to do real work before you broke it.

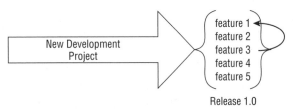

Figure 3-15 Regression of a new feature

Well, suppose you successfully delivered release 1.0 and got feature 1 fixed via a patch before too many customers started howling. You now are working on a major update, release 1.1. This involves three new features. You test each of these features, without finding any bugs. However, because you did not completely re-test the features from the first release, you miss the fact that one new feature broke two previously released features, as shown in Figure 3-16.

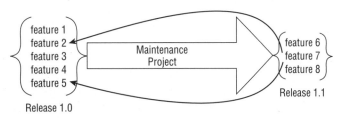

Figure 3-16 Regression of existing features

Existing feature regression really is unforgivable from the point of view of existing customers. It's one thing to not deliver a new feature that you promised or to deliver it broken. It's an entirely different and more serious issue when you take away a feature that used to work. I had this happen to me a couple of years ago when my iPod, a recent gift from my wife, downloaded a software update for itself and became an unreliable piece of musical trash that would not shut down properly after charging. It took over a year before another update apparently fixed that problem, and in the meantime I suffered through a number of situations where the battery died prematurely because I had to wait for it to time out after charging it, rather than being able to shut it down.

Okay, so we can probably agree that regression sucks. So, how do we deal with regression?

In an ideal setting, the test team would have the time needed to execute all the test cases during each cycle of each test phase. This would ensure that within days (or even hours) you would catch any regression in a new release. However, running all the test suites in such a way that every configuration is covered could take forever, stretching test cycles into weeks, months, or even years rather than days. Few organizations (except those developing safety-critical systems) have such luxurious time frames. Pesky realities such as budgets and deadlines tend to compress test phases.

In addition to the "do it all by tomorrow" urgency that prevails on many development projects, you can become a victim of your own success. When you first start developing tests, you'll only have enough tests to cover the most critical items. As your test system and your team grow and mature, however, you'll find that you have more tests to run than time in which to run them.

One or both of these factors usually forces me to select a subset of the test suites for each test cycle. Yet each test case omitted might create a regression-test gap. (If you can drop a test case without affecting test coverage, you should consider deleting the test case from your test suite. It is probably redundant, assuming that your measurement of coverage is valid.) Unless you execute every test case in every test suite against every revision and configuration, you are exposed to regression-test risks — to follow an earlier analogy, some fish will swim around a partially deployed fishnet. What can you do?

Is Automation a Complete Solution?

Some people suggest test automation as a solution to this problem, and it can be — at least partially. An automated test system runs more tests in a given period than a manual system does (at least if it works effectively and efficiently). Consequently, the regression test gap is reduced. Nevertheless, automation is not a panacea. As a test manager, you will receive lots of brochures touting (expensive) test automation tools, so bear the following in mind when you read them.

For a stable system, you can develop automated tests and run them repeatedly, with some minor modifications to one or two test cases each time.

However, when interfaces, major functions, or supported environments evolve and change rapidly, automated tests can require significant maintenance.

It's great if you can anticipate how these changes will affect your automated regression tests. Sometimes you can. In my experience, though, most automated regression-test failures aren't failures at all, at least not in the sense of a failure as symptom of a bug. Rather, many of these mismatches between expected and actual results arise from unexpected, but correct, consequences of other changes. Try as I might, I usually cannot change the all of the expected results for the automated tests prior to starting test execution.

So, you're often forced to wait until test execution to see the exact effects of the changes on the tests and their results. During the thick of test execution, though, you won't always have the time and resources to fix the tests. This might tempt you to wait until the product is released to maintain and/or develop automated tests for the functionality just developed, but systems in major development run the highest risk of regression, since the level of code change is high. This is just a cruel irony of life in a test organization, I'm afraid.

That said, the most practical approach is, in my experience, to focus most functional automation efforts on functionality introduced in the previous release, as these features will — we hope — tend to remain stable from one release to the next after initial release. This means that, often, we can apply automated testing only to features already in the production or released system. The new features will require manual regression testing prior to release, as the system changes.

Furthermore, test automation automates only the creation of test conditions, not the setup and teardown of test cases and suites, nor the analysis of the results. Testers can spend a significant amount of time getting the test environment, test data, and test tools configured. Moreover, glitches encountered in setting up the tests usually come from the test system itself, not from the system under test. Any time spent setting up the tests or chasing down probe effects disguised as bugs is time not spent testing. Large numbers of failed test cases can result from a single bug, leading to extensive analysis efforts beyond what would be required in the case of manual testing, where test failures are noted, isolated, reproduced, and reported in real time.

In the hardware world, automation can help only in certain areas. For stress, capacity, and performance testing, for example, automation is essential. However, when you test multiple applications — imagine compatibility testing Windows-based applications against a new desktop computer — the time needed to install the application and verify the installation can make up the bulk of the test. You can't effectively automate these operations. Even in the software world, installation of the program and its ancillary utilities, followed by configuration and verification of the install, are by necessity manual activities for most systems. (I have worked on a few projects in which automated distribution of the software and the test system itself made these costs of automation low. Most test projects, however, involve a manual installation, configuration, and verification process as the first — and often nontrivial — step of a new test cycle.) You can automate the testing of the application itself, but this might save you only a few dozen hours per project. Test automation won't help if installation and configuration eat up half the time in your test cycle.

I don't mean to disparage test automation. It is useful, and it will often help to reduce regression-test gaps. Testing for certain quality risks, such as performance, stress, capacity, and volume, almost always requires the assistance of automated test tools. Despite some claims to the contrary by some test automation tool vendors, though, it is not a silver bullet for functional regression testing.

Four Ways to Spread Tests Across Cycles

Test automation or no, the time will probably come when you will be forced to select only a subset of the test system for certain test cycles — or even test projects. When this happens, you can use these four alternative tactics to minimize regression-test gaps:

- Assigning an aggregate risk priority number to each test suite in advance, based on the risk priority number for each test case, and then running the test suites in a way that favors the higher-priority tests. I call this the *static priority* approach.

- Assigning the risk priority numbers to each test suite in advance, but adjusting them dynamically as each test cycle begins, and then running the test suites in priority order. I call this the *dynamic priority* approach.

- Randomly distributing the test suites across the test cycles. I call this the *shotgunning* approach.

- Running the entire set of test suites straight through as many times as possible (definitely more than once). I call this the *railroading* approach.

The next few pages use a DataRocket example to illustrate each of these approaches, demonstrating practical ways of slicing and dicing the test suites in a test phase under tight — but not quite unreasonable — schedules. Of course, if you are receiving releases of software every few hours, the regression risk will overwhelm all of these approaches. (The most chaos-resistant technique is railroading, as you'll see.) Remember, too, that although these scheduling methods might appear clever and efficient, they are nevertheless only fancy ways of making compromises: I'm trading added regression risk for saved time and resources. Any time I plan a test cycle that includes anything less than a full pass through every test suite in the current test phase, I create a regression-test gap relative to the quality risk analysis established earlier in the project (as shown in Chapter 1).

For our example, let's assume that you have one month to run system testing for DataRocket. During that period, you are scheduled to receive two motherboard revisions and 10 BIOS releases. You plan to run 10 cycles, the first and the tenth lasting one week and the intervening cycles lasting two days. The entire system test takes about four days to run, depending on the number of bugs you find. Table 3-2 shows the test schedule with milestones.

Table 3-2 A Frenetic DataRocket System Test Schedule

CYCLE	START	END	MB REV	BIOS REL	% TESTS
1	7/1	7/7	A	X1	100
2	7/8	7/9	A	X2	50
3	7/10	7/11	A	X3	50
4	7/12	7/13	A	X4	50
5	7/14	7/15	B	X5	50
6	7/16	7/17	B	X6	50
7	7/18	7/19	B	X7	50
8	7/20	7/21	B	X8	50
9	7/22	7/23	B	X9	50
10	7/24	7/30	B	X10	100

Static Priority

Let's start by using the static priority approach. Suppose we use an averaging technique across the test cases to determine the average risk priority for the test suite. Based on a three-level division of priority, let's suppose that the high-priority subset of the test system consists of test suites STS1, STS2, STS5, and STS7, and takes two days to run. The medium-priority subset containing STS3 and STS6 takes one day. The low-priority portion containing STS4 and STS8 also takes one day. Figure 3-17 shows a road map for running these tests in priority order. (The higher-priority tests are shown with darker shading.)

Notice that the road map in Figure 3-17 starts and ends with a complete pass through the test system. The complete first pass provides a baseline for the rest of the testing and alerts development to every bug I can find in the system right from the start. The three-day hiatus from organized test suite execution allows testers to isolate all the bugs revealed by the first run of the test suites and gives the developers access to the test lab for debugging purposes. (See Chapter 7 for some tips on how to do this without invalidating subsequent tests.)

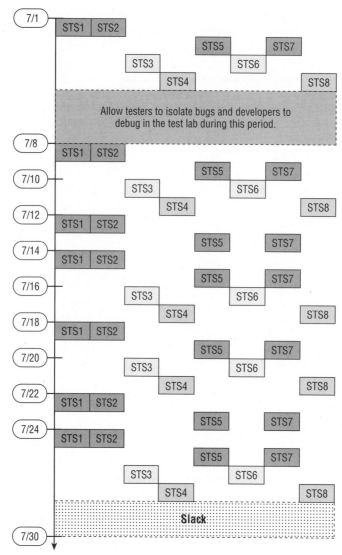

Figure 3-17 A road map for test selection based on static prioritization

The complete last pass gives you a chance to yell "Stop!" before your organization embarrasses itself with a buggy release. Of the two complete passes, the last pass is the most important in terms of preventing test escapes. It is also the one most likely to receive short shrift as a result of resource redirection and project fatigue. I try to run a complete last pass even if management declares the final cycle formally complete. Because of the ramp-up time, I usually still have a chance to stop a bad release before it hits the customers.

In the middle of the road map, you can spread your test suites across the other test cycles. The high-priority test suites are run seven times in total, while the medium- and low-priority test suites are run five times. This arrangement comes fairly close to totally rerunning all of the test suites in every cycle, yet it is 14 days shorter.

Of course, this road map suffers from two obvious defects. The first is that it is simplified to make a point. In the real world, you won't have eight test suites that divide into three neat groups of four, two, and two, with each suite taking exactly a day to run. Life seldom works out as neatly as this example. The second problem is the absence of slack except at the end. On real projects, deliverables slip frequently. (At the risk of sounding inordinately cynical, I can't remember a single project in which every single major deliverable into test hit its target date.) This road map won't handle those slips well. Instead, I would hide a day of slack in each cycle, or at least insist on keeping the weekends. (Think of weekends as "hidden slack" that you can draw on every now and then if you have a motivated team.)

Dynamic Priority

The priority-order approach might have raised a question for you: how do you know in advance which test suites should have a high priority? Of course, the quality risk analysis is an educated guess, and you sure hope you got that right. However, the odds are pretty good that you will be proven partially wrong. Suppose that you assign a high priority to DataRocket's thermal test (STS1) because an early engineering evaluation unit caught fire at one point. Also suppose that you assign a low priority to the USB, FireWire, serial, and parallel port test (STS4) because development has found no problems in this area.

By the end of July 4, though, you discover that you have the priorities backward: the thermal test passes with headroom to spare, but the USB test is a target-rich environment. It turns out that the developers forgot to test the interaction of power management with USB hot plugging and hot unplugging, and the system crashes when you try this. Now, suddenly, STS4 is a high-priority suite, and STS1 is a low-priority suite.

You can handle this situation by conceding in advance that the priorities you come up with ahead of time might change. With this concession, you simply plan to run four test suites, selected based on the priorities of the moment, during the second through ninth test cycles (with complete passes at the beginning and the end, as before). See Figure 3-18 for a road map of testing under this plan.

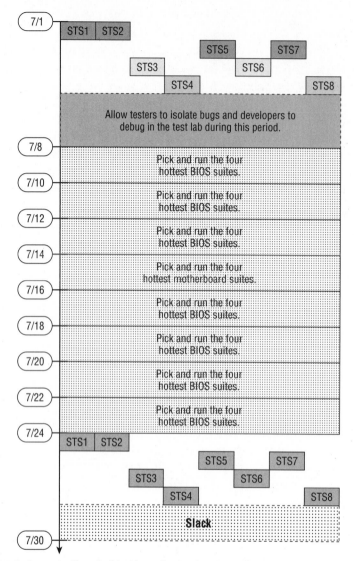

Figure 3-18 A dynamically prioritized road map for test selection

Certainly, you should adjust your quality risk analysis as you go along. That's smart and should result in changing the effort allocation and prioritization of test cases for the rest of the test effort. However, there is a risk that this approach will devolve into an ad hoc, figure-it-out-as-you-go test methodology.

The difference between the static priority and dynamic priority approaches is one of data versus gut. Chapters 4 and 5 discuss the use of bug metrics and test metrics, respectively, to adjust test priority. You can use such metrics to select tests that yield the most important bugs. That's data-driven. When the selection of test suites gets into subjective assessments, then you have a more visceral approach to test case importance.

As a manager, I've learned to listen to my gut, but not to obey my gut, if you know what I mean. I don't like managing solely by gut. Your gut will lie to you. Sometimes what seems reasonable is wrong.

Maybe you can't foresee everything or assign the priorities perfectly, but refusing to plan leaves you totally crisis-driven. Caught up in the emergency du jour, you could easily reach the end of the test phase and find that you have spent all your time running fewer than half of your test suites. If you then run all the test suites in the last cycle (which you should) and find a slew of nasty bugs, you deliver a Hobbesian choice to the project team: fix the bugs and slip the schedule, or ship the bugs and keep the schedule.

Personally, in most situations, I find the dynamic priority approach to be the ideal one, when driven by data. I avoid any attempt to do this by gut. In certain circumstances, without enough data to re-evaluate risks properly during test execution, I might fall back on the following two approaches.

Shotgunning

Suppose that you want to have a plan in place to help impose some discipline, but you do not have sufficient data to finalize the sequencing of tests in advance. At the time of test planning, you are forced to consider all test suites equally important. So, you can distribute the suites randomly in test cycles 2 through 9. (Cycles 1 and 10 remain total coverage cycles as before.) Figure 3-19 shows the road map for this scattering of test cases.

This shotgun approach is more robust than the previous two approaches in the face of rapid, unpredictable change. Since you are decoupling your test suite selection from the specific test deliverables, a change in those deliverables doesn't affect your plan. What if the BIOS release doesn't show up on July 10? With the previous schedules, you might have wondered what to do next. With a shotgun road map, however, four test suites have not yet been run against the X2 BIOS release, so you can simply continue with your plan to run those tests.

Railroading

The shotgun approach looks clever on paper, but the premise might strike you as flawed. After all, if the test suites are equally important, why go to the trouble of randomizing their run order? You could just as easily use the test suite numbering — STS1 through STS8 — as the sequence. In this case, the testing rolls on regardless of what's going on in the project. Figure 3-20 shows a road map for this railroad approach.

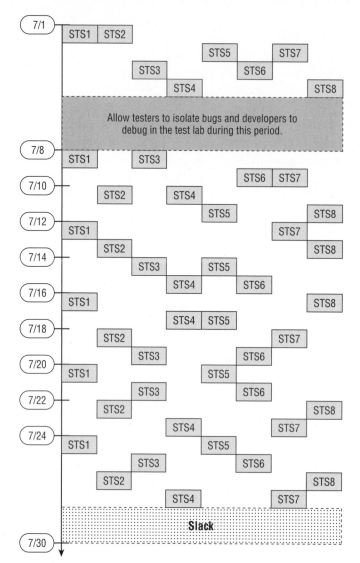

Figure 3-19 A road map for test selection based on shotgunning

Like the shotgun method, the railroad approach to test selection is resistant to rapid change and slips in delivery dates, and can include other forms of project chaos. For example, if the X3 BIOS release arrives on July 11 instead of July 10, you needn't be concerned; you can just install the new BIOS on the test systems and run STS7 and STS8. If a deliverable slips by a long enough period, you can start to use reactive techniques, as discussed earlier.

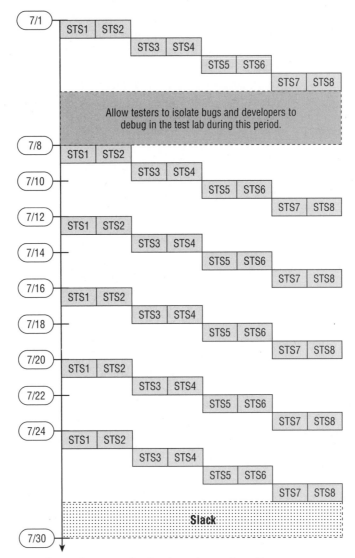

Figure 3-20 A road map for test selection based on railroading

Avoiding Mistakes

What I most want to avoid is a situation in which I never get to run an entire set of tests — or in which I run them only once early on and never return to them — because they keep getting preempted by new releases. This can happen if I run in test suite order, as in the railroad approach, but start over with the first test suite every time a new release shows up. Figure 3-21 shows the result of this approach. Obviously, large regression-test gaps are created in the middle of the system test phase, while the test team repeats STS1 through STS4. The bill for this mistake comes due around July 27, when STS5 and STS6 are run for the first time in about 20 days. These tests, as well as STS7 and STS8, are likely to reveal significant problems that, because of the looming ship date, give management the unpleasant choice of delaying the product or shipping known bugs. People will blame the test manager for this situation, and rightly so.

Figure 3-21 A road map for bonehead test selection

Two additional points are key to good test selection. First, for every new release of software or hardware, I have my testers perform thorough *confirmation testing* against each bug that has allegedly been fixed in the release — and I have them do this first. Confirmation tests check for bugs related to the failure of a bug fix to address the reported issue fully, and they usually involve rerunning the test procedure and isolation steps, per the bug report.

The fixes are where the new and changed stuff lives. In software, for example, bugs abound in new and changed code. The parts not changed, although perhaps not directly tested, at least have been subjected to incidental tests along the way. The new stuff is truly untested and unseen.

Second, I take into account the inevitable ups and downs of the process. When my plan encounters reality, I want it to bend, not break. I try to create robust plans that handle changes well, which is why I prefer the dynamic approach to the other approaches. Be flexible, though, when your plan is forced to change, and remember that you can mix and match the test suite selection methods — for example, you can use the railroad approach and still preempt some of the test suites for others you feel are more important. Plans are good, but keep the goal in mind and be ready to adapt to changes as they happen. (Chapter 6 provides a tool to help you track and manage those changes effectively.)

What if I Can't Repeat All the Tests? Alternative Regression Risk Mitigation Strategies

The standard technique — you might say the brute force technique — to mitigate regression risk is to repeat the tests you have, over and over, against each release to the test team organization and against each release to the customers or users. This is the technique illustrated in the last few sections. Extensive automation or simple products with simple feature sets make this possible, but in some cases such test repetition is impractical.

One of my clients tests geological modeling software, an extremely complex application with an almost unlimited potential number of data sets and workflows. The entire set of tests used for system test takes about two person-decades to run. With a 20-person test team, they have no time to repeat tests, with the exception of some very basic functionality tests that don't even come close to exercising a thousandth of the possible workflows and data sets. What to do?

One simple approach is, in each test cycle, to rerun every test case that failed the last time it was run, whether in the last cycle, the cycle before that, or even in the first test cycle. A slightly more risk-averse approach would be to rerun every test that has ever failed during the entire test phase during every test cycle or every other test cycle. The rationales here are that the tests that have failed before are likely to fail again, that bugs tend to cluster together, and that changes tend to be localized and break features that are nearby.

But is it really true that failures are localized? Imagine a client/server family of applications with a shared database. The development team might change a table in the database to accommodate a new report. Testing might find a bug or two in the new report, but, if we don't regression-test broadly enough, fail to find a huge set of bugs in another application that also uses that same table. To handle this problem, some test teams resort to change analysis.

In change analysis, we sift through what we know about the system as it exists now and what we know about the proposed changes. We look at our risk assessments, our coverage information, and our past bug logs. Based on this data, we conclude that the changes increase the level of risk attendant to some set of quality risks in the system. We re-run the tests that cover those risks.

But what a luxurious amount of data and time I need for this process! While I've done this informally, based on gut, I've never — nor have any of my employers, clients, or seminar attendees — been able to do the kind of detailed analysis that would be required to draw solid, logical, quantifiable inferences about what to test and what to ignore. Usually, change analysis involves asking the developers what to regression-test. The problem with that approach, of course, is that if the developers could figure out what they might have broken, wouldn't they simply have not broken it?

This leaves me with the approach my geological modeling software client uses. Start by assuming that the system is a minefield, and each mine a bug. Testing detects some of the mines — by hitting them — but each subsequent change can (and many changes definitely will) introduce new mines. If we create test cases that are limited and isolated in their test conditions, then each test case is like walking gently through the minefield. But what if our tests are broad in coverage — for example, based on various workflows, usage scenarios, and data sets — then wouldn't each test case be more like dragging a wide iron bar across the minefield? This is exactly my client's experience. They use structural coverage — in other words, "How much of the code have we tested?" — as their key metric for assessing regression risk. By measuring structural coverage, they find they cover 60 to 70 percent of the modules in a given four-week period.

Over the course of the year-long test period, code coverage is close to 100 percent. Are there regression risks? Certainly, but this method of test design and their metric for checking up on regression risks assures them that the level of risk is acceptable, given that the alternative is to multiply the test team size by 25 or so to achieve a complete test pass against every other (weekly) test release.

"There's a Lesson to Be Learned Here ... ": Test Case Incremental Improvement

No matter how good a job I do on my first crack at developing test cases and suites, my test systems always have holes. Budget and time pressures, along with human mistakes, result in incomplete testing. Some test cases won't cover conditions they should, or some test suites won't include important test cases, or the overall test system won't have all the test suites it needs.

In the case of most consumer software and hardware products, a few omissions won't prove fatal to the product, provided you are careful to test the critical features. (The issue of test escapes takes on a different meaning when you are dealing with safety-critical systems such as traffic-light, medical, or power-plant control computers or with situations that involve people's privacy and security. A higher standard of quality is required in safety- or mission-critical systems.) Nonetheless, I attempt to improve my test system for each subsequent release. A few techniques for doing this involve responding to the failures in the shipping product, incorporating the practices of others into your test system, and using exploratory testing.

Responding to Failures

One obvious way of enhancing a test system is to plug gaps that come to light when some poor customer or user is whacked in the forehead by a test escape. Of course, this doesn't mean that you or anyone else in your company will celebrate test escapes. You'd rather your customers were dazzled by your product's quality. However, a bug found in the field is the perfect candidate for inclusion in the test system. You know that it's important to your customers, or to at least one of them, because they wouldn't bother to report it if it weren't. Assuming that development is fixing the problem, it's also important to your management. As an added bonus, the test case should be relatively easy to write. Given a field report, you should have the steps to reproduce the bug and any ancillary test data at hand.

In addition to learning from your own test escapes, how about learning from someone else's? As the saying goes, Any fool can learn from his (or her) own errors, but a wise person learns from the mistakes of others. Reading trade journals, keeping up on pertinent Internet newsgroups and web sites, and networking with your peers in the test profession and your niche of the computer business will allow you to learn from their blunders.

Adopting Best Practices

Beyond merely learning from others' mistakes, you also want to learn from their successes. I'm not suggesting industrial espionage, but rather research.

For example, simply by reading this book you are learning new test techniques, even though the book is primarily about *managing* testing. Likewise, trade journals might print articles that evaluate your competitors' products, often including sidebars on "how we tested" that you can use to benchmark your own testing.

Training sessions, conferences, and seminars provide great opportunities to expand your test system as well as your skills. If you purchase test tools, you almost certainly have training options. Even if you believe that your team understands the use of a purchased tool, it might make sense for one person to attend the training session and bring back good ideas. Likewise, seminars are opportunities for cross-pollinating your test system with your peers. Every presenter at a reputable conference or training session is an expert chosen by the organizers of the event to offer unique knowledge and skills.[9]

Some practicing test professionals write off the academic world. It's true that research literature is not always practical. However, today's research is tomorrow's state-of-the-art product or process. I try to read at least one or two advanced books every year. It's worth remembering that James Whittaker's very practical techniques for reactive testing, documented in *How to Break Software*, grew out of research he did while he was a professor.

Using Reactive Testing

Speaking of reactive testing, remember that some people have a knack for rooting out errors, like a bird dog on a quail or a pig after truffles. Glenford Myers, in *The Art of Software Testing*, refers to this process as *error guessing*. This might sound like a precise technique, but Myers admits that no technique exists — it's simply intuition. Part of what I want to do as a test manager is to find bugs, so reactive testing is great for that — provided I have the right people — but I'd also like reproducibility for subsequent test cycles.

My challenge as a test manager is to convince my intrepid reactive testers to write down their brilliant ideas. Many of these testers tend to have a problem understanding the value of documentation. I, however, know when they've come up with a particularly good test: they find a bug. Since I capture defect data in my bug-tracking database, I can ensure that any problems found during exploratory testing turn into a documented test case.

You Can't Do It All: Deciding What Not to Do

As a final note on test cases, let me revisit a point made in earlier chapters. As much as it pains test professionals to do so, we have to make choices

---

[9]From my own consulting practice, I can recommend *Pragmatic Software Testing* and the corresponding live and e-learning training course as a good way to learn how to create better test systems. There are a number of other training courses on test design out there from other companies, of varying degrees of quality, so choose wisely.

about what we will and won't test. With luck, you can get others to help you make those choices (as described in the material on risk analysis in Chapter 1), thereby making your life easier and providing you with some political cover at the same time. External support for your test goals, and the management backing it brings, is something you can't have too much of.

Nonetheless, at times you have to make tough decisions. On most projects, eventually someone asks you whether, in your professional judgment, a feature needs to be tested. What they are asking you is a question about bug coverage: "Do you think we will find critical bugs in this if we test it?"

There is no magical heuristic that will prevent me from making the wrong decisions. Hard choices are hard because no solution is obvious and the stakes are high. When faced with these types of choices, I approach them with an open mind. I question my assumptions about what *has* to be tested. Why do I feel that way? I trust my gut, but I confirm my intuition. Then I talk it over. I ask my test team what they feel is essential, and why. I consult test stakeholders, peers, and colleagues. I quiz my development associates on the project. I review any pertinent references in books and articles.

After going through this analysis process with an open mind, I make my decision. I document what I intend to keep and what I intend to drop. I'm prepared to answer why. When I feel confident in my decision, I communicate it. And then I'm prepared to start all over again if need be.

Case Study

In this section, I illustrate two styles of test case documentation. The first follows the screen-oriented template introduced earlier, which my team and I used for testing the browser-based program for home equity loan processing described in the case study for Chapter 2. Note that the test procedure (actions taken) is implied by the flow of the screens, but that the input data and the expected results are defined very precisely. The document, "Case Study Loan Processing Test Cases.xls," is available on the basic Library page at www.rbcs-us.com.

I thank my client on this project, a major midwestern bank, and the executive in charge of development, for allowing me to share this example with readers of this book. I have purged all identifying and otherwise private information from this document. My client contact has asked that the organization remain anonymous.

The second set of tests show a data-driven approach used for a custom automated test harness. This test harness sent the data to the subsystem under test — in this case, small programs running across a network providing security and access control — and then checked the return values. Note the use of HTML-style "tags" to define stanzas that control the harness. The documents "Case Study Functionality.suite" and "Case Study AddValidUser.case" are also available on the basic Library page at www.rbcs-us.com.

Bonus Case Study

A number of RBCS clients find that obtaining good test data poses many challenges. For any large-scale system, testers usually cannot create sufficient and sufficiently diverse test data by hand; i.e., one record at a time. While data generation tools exist and can create almost unlimited amounts of data, the data so generated often do not exhibit the same diversity and distribution of values as production data. For these reasons, many of our clients consider production data ideal for testing, particularly for systems where large sets of records have accumulated over years of use with various revisions of the systems currently in use, and systems previously in use.

However, to use production data, we must preserve privacy. Production data often contains personal data about individuals which must be handled securely. However, requiring secure data handling during testing activities imposes undesirable inefficiencies and constraints. Therefore, many organizations want to anonymize (scramble) the production data prior to using it for testing.

This anonymization process leads to the next set of challenges, though. The anonymization process must occur securely, in the sense that it is not reversible should the data fall into the wrong hands. For example, simply substituting the next digit or the next letter in sequence would be obvious to anyone — it doesn't take long to deduce that "Kpio Cspxo" is actually "John Brown" — which makes the de-anonymization process trivial.

In addition, Kpio Cspxo and other similar nonsense scrambles make poor test data, because they are not realistic. The anonymization process must preserve the usefulness of the data for localization and functional testing, which often involves preserving its meaning and meaningfulness. For example, if the anonymization process changes "John Brown" to "Lester Camden," we still have a male name, entirely usable for functional testing. If it changes "John Brown" to "Charlotte Dostoyevsky," though, it has imposed a gender change on John, and if his logical record includes a gender field, we have now damaged the data.

Preserving the meaning of the data has another important implication. It must be possible to construct queries, views, and joins of these anonymized data that correspond directly to queries, views, and joins of the production data. For example, if a query for all records with the first name "John" and the last name "Brown" returned 20 records against production data, a query for all records with the first name "Lester" and the last name "Camden" must return 20 records against anonymized data. Failure to honor this corollary of the meaning and meaningfulness requirement can result in major problems when using the data for some types of functional tests, as well as any kind of performance, reliability, or load test.

Even more challenging is the matter of usefulness of the data for interoperability testing. Consider three applications, each of which have data gathered over years and describing the same population. The data reside in three different databases. The three applications interoperate, sharing data, and data warehousing and analytical applications can access the related data across databases. These applications can create a logical record for a single person through a de facto join via de facto foreign keys, such as full name, Social Security number, and so forth.

If the anonymization process scrambles the data in such a way that these integrity constraints break, then the usefulness of the anonymized data for interoperability testing breaks. Meaningful end-to-end testing of functionality, performance, throughput, reliability, localization, and security becomes impossible in this situation. For many of our clients, preserving the usefulness of the data for interoperability testing poses the hardest challenge.

In addition, the anonymization process must not change the overall data quality of the scrambled data. This is subtle, because most production data contains a large number of errors. Some have estimated the error rate as high as one in four records. So, to preserve the fidelity of the test data with respect to production data, the same records that have errors must continue to contain errors. These errors must be similar to the original errors, but must not allow reverse engineering of the original errors.

A good test data set has the property of maintainability, and so the anonymized data must also. Maintainability of test data means the ability to edit, add, and delete the data. This includes at the level of individual data fields and records, and, if applicable, across the logical records that might span multiple databases. To have the property of maintainability, the anonymization of the production data should not make maintenance of the data impossible, of course, but furthermore it should not make maintenance of the data any more difficult or time-consuming than maintenance of the production data.

Two other practical challenges arise with the process of anonymization itself. The first is the time and effort required to carry out the anonymization process. One client told an RBCS consultant that they only refreshed their test data from production every 12 to 18 months, because the test data refresh process, including the anonymization, required 4 to 6 person-months of effort and typically took an entire month to complete. In an organization where staff must charge the time spent on tasks to a particular project, few project managers felt compelled to absorb such a cost into their budgets.

The next practical challenge of anonymization relates to the need to operate on quiescent data. In other words, the data cannot change during extraction of the to-be-anonymized data. This is nothing more complex than the usual challenge of backing up databases, but the people involved in producing the anonymized test data must be aware of it.

Options for production data anonymization include both commercial and custom-developed tools. The selection of a data anonymization tool is like the selection of any other test tool. One must assemble a team, determine the tool options, identify risks and constraints for the project, evaluate and select the tool, and then roll out the tool. In this case, these activities would typically happen in the context of a larger project focused on creating test data entirely or in part through the anonymization of production data. Our experience with RBCS clients has shown that such a project requires careful planning, including identification of all requirements for the anonymized data and the anonymization process. An organization planning such a project should anticipate investing a substantial amount of time and perhaps even money (should commercial tools prove desirable). Trying to do a production data anonymization project on the cheap is likely to result in failure to overcome many of the challenges discussed here. However, with careful planning and execution, it is possible for an organization to use anonymized production data for testing purposes.

Bonus Case Study

Ross Collard, principal consultant of Collard and Company and fellow testing expert, provided me with the following interesting case study that examines degrees of test case documentation details and precision. In this case study, Ross enumerates five points on the precision spectrum I showed as Figure 3-12, with an additional level for automation. Note that Ross uses the phrase *test specification* where I would probably use *test case*. I thank Ross for his permission to use this case study.

- **Level 0:** No documentation is prepared before trying the test case; just do it.

- **Level 1:** A brief description of the overall purpose and nature of the test. Typical length of the documentation: one or two lines.

- **Level 2:** A list of the conditions and items to be tested, with the description of each condition limited to one line. Typical length: a quarter page to a full page.

- **Level 3:** An outline of how to test each condition on the list in level 2. The outline includes the input data, initial conditions, and expected results for each condition. Typical length: a quarter to a half page for each condition, for a total of one to three pages.

- **Level 4:** A step-by-step description of how to perform the test manually, including every action, click, and keystroke. Typical length: a half page to two pages for each condition, for a total of 3 to 20 pages.

- **Level 5:** An automated test program. The typical length varies based on the conciseness or density of the test scripting language: if the language is concise, there typically can be 10 to 100 lines of code (instructions) in the test script language, but if it is wordy, there can 5 to 50 pages of source code in this language.

An example of these various levels of detail follows.

Example of Test Specification Levels of Detail

Level 1

Verify that the search function works correctly in the *ABC* system.

Level 2

Verify that the search function works correctly in the *ABC* system, by testing these conditions:

1.1 Click the search button without entering any search parameters.

1.2 Attempt to enter invalid search keys.

1.3 Enter a valid search key for which no matching records are found.

1.4 Enter a valid search key for a record which the user is not authorized to access.

1.5 Enter a full or partial search key which is unique, and ensure that the matching record is displayed for this search key.

    1.5.1 Full last name, all other parameters blank.

    1.5.2 Full last name, first initial.

    1.5.3 Full last name, first initial, date of birth.

    1.5.4 Full last name, first initial, age range (from *x* to *y*).

    1.5.5 Partial last name, all other parameters blank.

    1.5.6 Partial last name, first initial.

    1.5.7 Partial last name, first initial, date of birth.

    1.5.8 Partial last name, first initial, age range.

    1.5.9 Soundex (sound-alike name) retrieval; e.g., "Smythe" is considered a match for "Smith."

    1.5.10 Full customer ID#.

    1.5.11 Partial customer ID# (an asterisk can be used as a "wild card" for one or more digits in the customer ID#).

1.6 Enter a full or partial search key that is not unique, and ensure that a list of all matching records is displayed for the search key.

   1.6.1 Full last name, all other parameters blank.

   1.6.2 Full last name, first initial.

   1.6.3 Full last name, first initial, date of birth.

   1.6.4 Full last name, first initial, age range (from x to y).

   1.6.5 Partial last name, all other parameters blank.

   1.6.6 Partial last name, first initial.

   1.6.7 Partial last name, first initial, date of birth.

   1.6.8 Partial last name, first initial, age range.

   1.6.9 Soundex (sound-alike name) retrieval; e.g., "Smythe" is considered a match for "Smith."

   1.6.10 Full customer ID#.

   1.6.11 Partial customer ID#.

1.7 Enter a partial search key that matches more than the maximum number of records that are allowed to be retrieved (for example, more than 1,000 matching records), and ensure that the response is the message "Too many matches to display."

1.8 Refresh the search window after a search has been completed (by pressing the Alt-F4 key combination), change the value of one search parameter, and initiate a new follow-up search.

1.9 Terminate a search after it has been initiated but before it has been completed and before the responding matches have been displayed.

Level 3

For brevity, this next level of detail is limited to one condition (1.5.1) from the prior list.

   1.5.1 Enter a full last name as the search key that is unique, leave all other search parameters blank, and ensure that the matching record is displayed for this search key.

   ▪ **Description:** Search based on complete last name, with no first name and no suffixes, with one matching record in the search database.

   ▪ **Initial conditions:** *ABC* system running under the latest version of Windows, with the search window open.

- **Input:** Full last name, followed by the Enter key.
- **Expected results:** Search results window opens and displays the customer that matched the search key on the last name.

Level 4

For brevity, this next level of detail is limited to one condition (1.5.1) from the prior list.

1.5.1 Enter a full last name as the search key that is unique, leave all other search parameters blank, and ensure that the matching record is displayed for this search key.

Initial conditions:

- Platform: Latest version of Windows.
- ABC system running, version: 5.06.04.
- No other applications running.
- Blank screen.
- Search window open.
- No other windows open.
- Initial location of cursor is in the first position of the last name.
- All parameters in the search window are set to blank or null values.
- Test database: SSIMENU.
- Test case table: Y2KAPL3, with the table pointer set to the correct next test case.
- Customer SMITH, JOHN exists and is the only SMITH entry in the test database.
- Caps Lock is not set and is assumed to have no effect (i.e., upper- or lowercase data entry does not matter).

Input search key:

- Last name: SMITH.
- Enter key.
- Process (to run the test case).
- Retrieve the next set of inputs (last name: SMITH) from the table of test cases.

- Edit the test case to ensure the inputs are valid.
- Enter the data from the table (last name: SMITH) in the appropriate data entry fields of the search window.
- Click on the Search key or press the Enter key (either should work).
- Verify the correct list of customers is displayed in the search results window.
- Press Escape, Cancel, or Ctrl-C to terminate the search.
- Return to the search window ready for the next search.

Expected behavior:

- Search results window appears.
- List of the matching customers with the specified search parameters appears in the window.
- For this test case, the list should contain only one member: SMITH, JOHN.
- After pressing the Escape or Cancel key, the search results window disappears and the search window reappears with the cursor in the Last Name field.

Level 5

In level 5, you would translate the step-by-step instructions given in level 4 into the instructions that the automated tool would use. That would typically entail creating three distinct types of objects. The first is a set of scripts, using the automated tool's capabilities and language, that would know how to run and log tests and navigate the user interface. The second is a repository of test data, some pre-loaded into the application database and some used by the scripts as they navigate the application. The third is a set of expected results, which the scripts can cross-check against the actual results.

Exercises

1. You are responsible for the system test phase for a calculator program, as discussed in Chapter 2. Write a test case for the multiplication feature (assume standard rather than scientific mode) in three formats:

   a. The sequential step template.

   b. The screen-oriented template.

   c. The IEEE 829 template.

   How do the three test cases compare?

2. The other dyadic operators (those that take two operands, like addition, division, and subtraction) can be tested using the same format. How would you change your approach for the unary operators (those that take one operand, like square root, inverse, and change sign)?

3. The expected result for a calculator must be known very precisely to ascertain pass or fail status for tests of mathematical correctness. What if we were testing the user interface (appearance, functionality, etc.) of the calculator? Can we describe precisely all the attributes that make a user interface good? Comment on whether we can describe precise pass and fail criteria for user interface tests, and whether pass or fail status is an absolute for user interface tests.

An Exciting Career in Entomology Awaits You: A Bug-Tracking Database

You now have a thorough test program put together. Time to relax, exchange the quadruple espressos for a few nice cold Warsteiners, and coast, right? After all, the only work that remains is executing the test plan, and surely your test technicians, with a little guidance from the test engineers, can handle that.

Definitely not. Your job as test manager remains as important as ever when you move into the stage of implementing the test plan and gathering data related to that plan.

Once test execution begins, even the most organized approach will not save you from the excitement of the project going on around you. A quality risk analysis, test estimate, test plan, test cases, test tools, test architecture, measures of test coverage, and all the other program components you've developed are proactive objects. If your analysis was correct, they should only require minor, incremental adjustments during test execution.

With test execution underway, though, you enter the world of the reactive and the dynamic. Following a test plan diligently and using a test system properly but flexibly require continual adjustments in your priorities, meticulous attention to details both clear and subtle, and adaptation to the endless changes in the project.

You will soon find yourself awash in the data generated by your shiny new test system. This is good, because this is the objective. Testing should generate useful information about the quality of the system. Testing is about risk management, and you can't manage risk without data.

Raw test data, however, tend toward the amorphous, the confusing, and the hard to categorize. Moreover, the quality of the system under test is a moving target during test execution. Therefore, there's a real challenge ahead for you in terms of extracting information from all that data.

Worse yet, remember all those commitments people made in terms of entry criteria, system delivery dates, acceptable turnaround times for test results, and so forth? Be prepared for otherwise honest and upstanding citizens to go back on their word shamelessly. This is not because they are out to get you. Eagles and sharks live at the top of the food chain, and every toxin that trickles into the ecosystem ends up sickening or killing the hapless predators disproportionately. Likewise, test is at the end of the development schedule, and every failure, delay, and slip-up can manifest itself in test, concentrated along the way into a noxious slime of confusion and missed dates that can make you very ill indeed.

Clearly, you need a way to track, analyze, and present what's going on in your once-peaceful test domain. The following three chapters provide some tools and techniques that will keep you on top of the test results and help you minimize the damage from the inevitable bombshells.

As a start, this chapter introduces a tool that supports a critical and visible role played by test organizations: the finding, documenting, and tracking of bugs. The role is critical because, if it is done right, the project team will fix many of the bugs you find, making test a direct contributor to increased product quality. Because bug reports provide tangible evidence of quality problems, they are visible not only to developers, but also often all the way up to the executive level. I have used a variety of bug-tracking systems and have seen the task done well and not so well by clients, vendors, and test labs. The approach outlined here handles the necessary tasks, is easy to implement, and provides information appropriate to all levels of an organization.

Why Bother? The Case for a Formal Bug-Tracking System

To start, let me explain some of the terms I'll use to be sure you can understand what I'm talking about. By *defect* or *bug*, I mean some problem present in the system under test that would cause it to fail to meet a customer's or user's reasonable expectations of quality. To tie back to Juran's definition of quality in Chapter 1, a bug is a potential source of product dissatisfaction.

A *bug report* is a technical document that describes the various symptoms or failure modes associated with a single bug. A good bug report provides the project management team the information they need to decide when and whether to fix a problem. A good bug report also captures the information a programmer will need to fix and debug the problem. Because a bug report is so specific and discrete, it is the most tangible product of testing and represents a well-defined opportunity for the project team to make a decision to increase the quality of the system.

Because we want to focus on problems in the system under test, not in the development or maintenance process, testers should not file bug reports against process breakdowns such as late delivery of test releases. We'll look at a database you can use for that purpose in Chapter 6.

There is also the possibility that not everything that at first appears to be a bug symptom is determined, ultimately, to arise from an actual problem in the system under test. When the expected results and the actual results of a test differ, some people refer to that situation as an *anomaly*. These same people refer to the observation of an anomaly as an *incident*. They distinguish an incident from an actual bug-related failure, and prefer to talk about incident reports rather than bug reports. In my experience, the phrase *bug report* is common and harmless, but you should keep in mind that false positives can and do happen. We'll talk about that further in Chapter 6, because this issue has implications beyond merely complicating the process of tracking bugs.

A *bug-tracking system* is some program or application that allows the project team to report, manage, and analyze bug reports and bug trends. Functionally, most bug-tracking systems provide a form that allows us to report and manage specific bugs, a set of stored reports and graphs that allow us to analyze, manipulate, and output this bug data in various ways, and a customizable workflow or life cycle that provides for orderly bug management. (I'll talk more about each of these items later in this chapter.)

Architecturally, bug-tracking systems run the complexity gamut. Sophisticated systems allow clients to connect to the corporate network, intranet, or Internet, and communicate with databases on a server or set of servers, depending on the exact implementation. Simple systems run on a single, standalone PC or workstation. I'm going to use the simple architecture to illustrate the ideas in this chapter, but those ideas scale to the most complex of networked, distributed systems.

Perhaps you don't see the value in having a bug-tracking system. You might be thinking, "Spending all that time and effort documenting bugs is too much hassle, especially with the developers right across the hall." It's true that creating, evolving, and using a bug-tracking database take significant effort and discipline. However, don't skip this chapter yet. I think you'll find that a systematic approach to bug tracking provides some important benefits:

- A bug-tracking database facilitates clear communication about defects. Well-written, standardized reports tell the story much better than free-form emails or shouts across a hallway or to the next cubicle.

- Using a database allows automatic, sequential bug numbering (a useful way to keep track of and refer to bugs), and it provides a number of analysis and reporting options that are not available with a flat file. If you have never looked into the various types of product and process metrics that can be derived from defect information, be ready to be surprised.

- A bug-tracking database allows the development team to fix problems based on importance to the project team, project management, the customers, and the users. With a more informal approach, the tester who has the best rapport with the most developers is often the one whose bugs get fixed, which is hardly a good strategy for focusing scarce project resources on the most important bugs.

- You can manage bugs throughout their life cycle, from the initial report to the final resolution. This ensures that bugs don't fall through the cracks, and it keeps attention focused on the important bugs that need to be fixed as quickly as possible.

- As bugs progress through their life cycle, developers, testers, and managers learn new information. A well-designed bug-tracking database allows you to capture this history and then refer to it later when you are looking at the status of the bugs.

- Every bug report that is closed in your database is a defect that might otherwise have gone into production, causing support calls, bad reviews, and lost sales. Every bug report that is not closed when the product ships provides technical support with useful advance warning and proves that your testers found the bug in the event that it crops up in the field. (In Chapter 11 we'll look at how this data can help us measure the return on the testing investment.)

In this chapter, I'll present a simple bug-tracking system that realizes these benefits. You can use this database, which is included with the templates for this book, or use the ideas in this chapter to develop a requirements list for a bug-tracking system you build or buy yourself.

As with some previous chapters, you can look to the IEEE standard for some additional ideas on bug tracking, ideas you might consider including in your bug-tracking system. IEEE 829 includes suggestions on information to capture in a bug report.

So, What Seems to Be the Problem? The Failure Description

Bug-tracking systems allow you to capture a lot of information about each bug. Some of this information is classifying data, generally selected from some set of values. For example, severity and priority ratings for bugs often run from 1 (most serious) to 5 (least serious). Other information is more narrative, describing what happens when the bug symptoms appear, how the bug was fixed, and so forth.

I'll discuss all of these possible pieces of information in detail, but let's start with the narrative data that captures the account of the problem as told by the report's author. This is the heart of any bug-tracking and reporting system, the *failure description*. The failure description is the message of the bug report. The failure description is the tester's first and best opportunity to communicate clearly with the programmers and the project team about a problem. Done properly, the failure description captures in simple prose the essentials of the bug. Done poorly, the failure description obfuscates the bug and misleads the reader.

What does a good failure description look like? Figure 4-1 shows the failure description for a nasty bug in the SpeedyWriter product. The failure description contains three basic sections: summary, steps to reproduce, and isolation.

```
Summary
Arial, Wingdings, and Symbol fonts corrupt new files.
Steps to Reproduce
1. Started SpeedyWriter editor, then created new file.
2. Typed four lines of text, repeating "The quick fox jumps over the lazy
brown dog" each time.
3. Highlighted all four lines of text, then pulled down the font menu,
and selected Arial.
4. All text converted to control characters, numbers, and other
apparently random binary data.
5. Reproduced three out of three tries.
Isolation
New to build 1.1.018; same test case passed against builds 1.1.007
(System Test entry) through 1.1.017.
Reproduced with same steps using Wingdings and Symbol fonts.
On vague suspicion this was a formatting problem, saved file, closed
SpeedyWriter and reopened file, but data corruption remained.
Saving file before changing font prevents bug.
Bug does not occur with existing files.
Only happens under Windows XP, not Solaris, Mac, or other Windows
flavors.
```

Figure 4-1 A good SpeedyWriter bug report

The *summary* is a one- or two-sentence description of the bug, emphasizing its impact on the customer or the system user. The summary tells managers, developers, and other readers why they should care about the problem. The sentence, "I had trouble with screen resolutions" is a lousy summary; the sentence, "Setting screen resolution to 800 by 1024 renders the screen unreadable" is much better. A succinct, hard-hitting summary hooks the reader and puts a label on the report. Consider it your one chance to make a first impression.

The *steps to reproduce* provide a precise description of how to repeat the failure. For most bugs, you can write down a sequence of steps that re-create the problem. Be concise yet complete, unambiguous, and accurate. This information is critical for developers, who use your report as a guide to duplicate the problem as a first step to debugging it. As a test manager and as a consultant, I have heard many teams of programmers complain bitterly about the poor job the test team was doing in terms of bug reporting. In most cases, their complaints centered around the poor quality of the steps to reproduce.

Reproducibility varies considerably. In many cases, failures are reproducible 100 percent of the time only for simple functional bugs. When repeating a test case three times reproduces the identical (incorrect) behavior three times, the bug is reproducible. Nevertheless, the possibility remains that the next run of the test case will produce a different symptom or perhaps no failure whatsoever. Moving to a different environment — from the test lab to the development lab, for example — often affects reproducibility, as can seemingly unrelated version changes. (In Chapter 7 I'll discuss the use of a test lab to provide a controlled test environment.) Therefore, it's important for the author of the bug report to verify reproducibility. Good bug reports include statements such as, "I tried the above steps four times and observed the error three times."

Isolation refers to the results and information the tester gathered to confirm that the bug is a real problem and to identify those factors that affect the bug's manifestation. What variations or permutations did the tester try in order to influence the behavior? For example, if the problem involves reading the CD-ROM drive on DataRocket, what happens when the CD-ROM is on a different SCSI ID? Did the tester check the SCSI termination? If SpeedyWriter can't print to a laser printer, can it print to an inkjet? Good isolation draws a bounding box around a bug. Documenting the isolation steps performed will assure the programmers and the project team that the tester isn't simply tossing an anomaly over the wall, but is instead reporting a well-characterized problem.

More Like Hemingway than Faulkner

Two of the great writers of the early 20th century, Ernest Hemingway and William Faulkner, reportedly hated each other. Like their personalities, their prose differs dramatically. Hemingway created a muscular style of prose that used short sentences, focused on actions, and spelled out events clearly and sequentially. Faulkner, conversely, wrote long sentences, made the prose the point as much as the story, used metaphors, and changed points of view. A remarkable capacity and appetite for alcoholic beverages is one of the few known common interests between them.

Had he tried his hand at computer testing, I suspect that Hemingway would have written great bug reports (provided he was sober). I doubt that Faulkner would have. It's not simply a matter of style, though. Even if you write like Hemingway, it takes concentration, practice, and discipline to describe bugs well. Over the years, I have read literally hundreds of bug reports that had significant problems.

How can you write better descriptions? Most important, remember that good bug reporting starts with good testing. Testers who have a disorganized approach to testing tend to write rambling, confusing bug reports. Testers who follow a sequence of test steps carefully (or apply thoughtful reactive testing techniques), take detailed notes, and isolate bugs using a methodical process tend to write concise, clear bug reports.

On a similar note, testers should write bug reports concurrent with or immediately following testing. A tester who runs many tests, takes notes on various bugs that arise, and then waits to write a report until a dozen or so problems have piled up not only endangers the overall schedule — delaying the day the bugs are reported delays the day the bugs are fixed — but also tends to write poor bug reports. The tester is likely to forget pertinent details and might lose access to the test configuration needed to repeat the test. If the tester must then re-run the test to gather more information on the bug, this results in either inefficiency or a poor bug report.

When it comes to writing the report, make sure that it's accurate, complete, and concise. A report that gets major details wrong is embarrassing at best. A report that omits important information is misleading. A report that takes 400 words to describe a bug won't be read. After the report is written, invest a little extra time and effort in a review. As the test manager, you can either review all the reports yourself or use a peer review process. I prefer a peer review process as part of a daily test team debrief meeting. That way, people learn how to write better bug reports by studying each other's bug reports, and they also learn what works and what doesn't.

Finally, good bug reports tell the reader what the tester found, not what the tester did. Some organizations use a test report approach, documenting every step taken, every behavior observed. There's a place for this level of detail, but it's the test case description itself, not the bug report. When I write reports, I document the minimal number of reproduction steps, and I include only isolation information that yielded an interesting data point. If I run one test and see two independent bugs, I write two reports.

Figure 4-2 and Figure 4-3 show two failure descriptions that might describe the same bug reported in Figure 4-1. The report in Figure 4-2 is vague and incomplete, with a misleading summary, missing steps, and no isolation. The report in Figure 4-3 babbles on and on, with a rambling summary, extraneous steps, and information on isolation that doesn't help the reader understand the bug.

```
Summary
SpeedyWriter has trouble with Arial.
Steps to Reproduce
1. Open SpeedyWriter.
2. Type in some text.
3. Select Arial.
4. Text gets screwed up.
Isolation
N/A
```

Figure 4-2 A vague, incomplete bug report

```
Summary
I ran SpeedyWriter for Solaris, Windows XP and Mac, and with certain
fonts it seems to screw up some data.
Steps to Reproduce
1. I opened SpeedyWriter on Windows XP, then edited a couple existing
files. These files contained a mix of fonts.
2. Printing of the files worked fine.
3. I created and printed a graphic, which worked okay. Some of the lines
aren't real sharp, though.
4. After this, I created a new file.
5. Then, I typed in a whole bunch of random text.
6. After I typed the text, I then highlighted a few lines of it. Next, I
pulled down the font menu and picked Arial out of the list.
7. The text I changed got screwed up.
S. I was able to reproduce this problem three times, which was every time
I tried it.
9. I reran steps one through six on Solaris and didn't see any problems.
10. I reran steps one through six on Mac and didn't see any problems.
Isolation
I tried selecting a few of the different fonts, but only Arial has this
bug.
However, it might still occur in the other fonts I didn't test.
```

Figure 4-3 A verbose and confusing bug report

Ten Steps to Better Bug Reports

I once heard someone at a conference say that in his organization, programmers kicked back almost half of the bug reports filed to the test team as irreproducible, no fault found, works as designed, or otherwise not actionable. If I saw such a rate of bug report rejection on one of my projects, I would take that as indicating a process breakdown requiring immediate resolution: all that time wasted writing those bug reports; the frustration and damage to team cohesion between programmers and testers; and, worst of all, no opportunity to improve product quality.

Some number of bug reports will always be irreproducible or contested. Some bugs exhibit symptoms only intermittently, under obscure or extreme conditions. In some cases, such as system crashes and database corruption, the symptoms of the bug often destroy the information needed to track down the bug. Inconsistencies between test environments and the programmers' systems sometimes lead programmers to respond, "works fine on my system." On some projects without clear requirements, there can be reasonable differences of opinion over what is correct behavior under certain test conditions. Sometimes testers misinterpret test results and report bugs when the real problem is bad test procedures, bad test data, or incorrect test cases. We'll look at all of these non–bug-related causes of non-actionable bug reports in the next few chapters, but in the meantime I'll just say that, as a rule of thumb, less than 20 percent of bug reports should fall into such categories. If I saw that 50 percent of my team's bug reports were ending up in the garbage can, I'd suspect a bad bug-reporting process.

To prevent such problems, I have developed a 10-step process that I use as a guideline and checklist for experienced testers, and as a training tool for people new to testing.

1. **Structure:** Test thoughtfully and carefully, whether you're using reactive techniques, following scripted manual tests, or running automated tests.

2. **Reproduce:** My usual rule of thumb is to try to reproduce the failure three times. If the problem is intermittent, report the rate of occurrence; for example, one in three tries, two in three tries, and so forth.

3. **Isolate:** See if you can identify variables — for example, configuration changes, workflow, data sets — that might change the symptoms of the bug.

4. **Generalize:** Look for places that the bug's symptoms might occur in other parts of the system, using different data, and so forth, especially where more severe symptoms might exist.

5. **Compare:** Review the results of running similar tests, especially if you're repeating a test run previously.

6. **Summarize:** Write a short sentence that relates the symptom observed to the customers' or users' experiences of quality, keeping in mind that in many bug review or triage meetings, the summary is the only part of the bug report that is read.

7. **Condense:** Trim any unnecessary information, especially extraneous test steps.

8. **Be clear:** Use clear words, avoiding especially words that have multiple distinct or contradictory meanings; for example, "The ship had a bow on its bow," and "Proper oversight prevents oversights," respectively.

9. **Neutralize:** Express yourself impartially, making statements of fact about the bug and its symptoms and avoiding hyperbole, humor, or sarcasm. Remember, you never know who'll end up reading your bug report.

10. **Review:** Have at least one peer, ideally an experienced test engineer or the test manager, read the bug report before you submit it.

The point of this process is to ensure that every bug report that comes out of my team is accurate, concise, well-conceived, and of the highest quality. By working through this process with my test teams, I instill a focus on writing good bug reports. By applying this process on my projects, my testers consistently produce bug reports that are clear to project management, actionable by the developers, and quickly repaired.

Because of the quality of our bug reports, my test teams enjoy improved communication to senior and peer management, which enhances credibility, standing, and our access to needed resources. My testers have excellent relationships with their programmer peers, because we provide the programmers with useful information as well as avoiding pointless arguments over bug reports. Faster, more efficient bug life cycles mean quicker fixes, fewer reopens, less time spent retesting, and quicker conclusion to each test phase. Altogether, focusing on writing good bug reports is one of the most important things the test manager can do to support increased product quality.[1]

Flexible Reporting: Beginning to Construct a Database

You could implement every piece of advice in the previous section in a bug-reporting system that relies on email or a flat file. I have seen projects that use spreadsheets or word processors to track bugs, but the reporting options were sparse, limited to little more than a printout of the worksheet or document. (Spreadsheets can summarize and graph data, as discussed later in this chapter, but they have poor text-reporting capabilities. Word processors have good text formatting, but poor analysis and graphical abilities.) To store, manipulate, search, analyze, and report large volumes of data flexibly, you need a database.

There are certainly many options for commercial and freeware bug-tracking databases. However, many companies do build their own. In this section, I'll explain how to build a bug-tracking database. Later sections of this chapter build on this foundation to enhance the database's capabilities. I used Microsoft Access for the database shown here, but you can use StarOffice, FileMaker, Oracle, or any other relational-database application. In the course of these discussions, you'll see how to build a bug-tracking database if you want to do so, or what you should look for in a commercial or freeware bug-tracking system if you decide to acquire one.

Minimally, a bug-tracking database stores narrative information about the failure (e.g., the summary, steps to reproduce, and isolation) together with

---

[1] I benefited from an online discussion with Bret Pettichord when I was thinking through these 10 steps, and I thank him for his input.

classifying information such as a sequential ID number, the project name, the author of the report, and the date the report was filed. Figure 4-4 shows the design view of an Access table (tblBugs) that stores this basic information. I've used the memo data type in Access for the Steps to Reproduce and Isolation fields because entries in these fields can be rather long. If you want to restrict these entries to a particular size to prevent excessive verbiage, you can use a text field rather than a memo field. The Bug ID identifier is a sequential number assigned by the AutoNumber feature in Access. The Date Opened field uses the standard Access date/time data type, formatted as a short date because you don't need to capture the specific time when the bug report was filed.

Field Name	Data Type	Description
Bug ID	Auto Number	The bug identifier.
Project Name	Text	The Project against which the bug appeared.
Tester	Text	The tester's name.
Date Opened	Date/Time	The date the report was opened.
Summary	Text	The bug report summary.
Steps to Reproduce	Memo	How the tester was able to reproduce the bug.
Isolation	Memo	what the tester did to determine the bug was real, and to find influencing factors.

Field Properties

General | Lookup |

Field Size	Long Integer
New Values	Increment
Format	
Caption	
Indexed	Yes (No Duplicates)
Smart Tags	
Text Align	General

A field name can be up to 64 characters long, including spaces. Press F1 for help on field names.

Figure 4-4 The design for a basic bug-tracking database

Because entering text directly into an Access table is cumbersome, you can set up a form for entering bug reports. I used the Form Wizard to create the bug entry form shown in Figure 4-5, and then entered the SpeedyWriter bug report you saw earlier, in Figure 4-1.

Once you've put a bug report into your database, you'll probably want to get it out at some point. I used the Report Wizard (with a few design adjustments) to create two reports in about five minutes. The simplest is the bug detail report, which prints all the information about the bug; Figure 4-6 provides an example. I usually produce a more compact report for management that has just the summary, the tester, and the date opened, too.

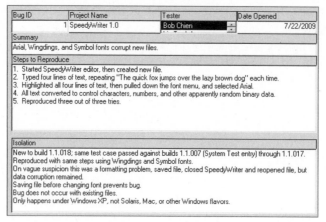

Figure 4-5 A bug report in the SpeedyWriter bug database, using a bug entry form

SpeedyWriter Bug Detail

Bug ID	Project Name	Tester	Date Opened
1	SpeedyWriter I.0	Bob Chien	7/22/2009

Summary
Arial, Wingdings, and Symbol fonts corrupt new files.

Steps to Reproduce
1. Started SpeedyWriter editor, then created new file. 2. Typed four lines of text, repeating "The quick fox jumps over the lazy brown dog" each time. 3. Highlighted all four lines of text, then pulled down the font menu, and selected Arial. 4. All text converted to control characters, numbers, and other apparently random binary data. 5. Reproduced three cut of three tries.

Isolation
New to build 1.1.018; same text case passed against builds 1.1.007 (System Test entry) through 1.1.017. Reproduced with same steps using Wingdings and Symbol fonts. On vague suspicion this was a formatting problem, saved file, closed SpeedyWriter and reopened file, but data corruption remained. Saving file before changing font prevents bug. Bug does not occur with existing files. Only happens under Windows XP. not Solaris. Mac. or other Windows flavors.

Figure 4-6 A bug detail report

The Vital Few and the Trivial Many: Ranking Importance

This database can capture details about bugs found by test, but it doesn't yet contain a mechanism that allows you to assign levels of importance to bugs. To solve this problem, you can add two metrics of importance — severity and priority — and then aggregate them to create a third, compound metric.

The first metric is *severity*. By severity, I mean the impact, immediate or delayed, of a bug on the system under test, regardless of the likelihood of occurrence under end-user conditions or the effect such a bug would have on users. I often use the same scale I used for failure mode and effect analysis (FMEA; see Chapter 1):

1. Loss of data, hardware damage, or a safety issue
2. Loss of functionality with no workaround
3. Loss of functionality with a workaround
4. Partial loss of functionality
5. Cosmetic or trivial

The second metric is *priority*. I use priority to capture the elements of importance not considered in severity, such as the likelihood of occurrence in actual customer use and the subsequent impact on the target customer. When determining priority, you can also consider whether this kind of bug is prohibited by regulation or agreement, what kinds of customers are affected, and the cost to the company if the affected customers take their business elsewhere because of the bug. Again, I find a scale like the priority scale used in the FMEA useful:

1. Complete loss of system value
2. Unacceptable loss of system value
3. Possibly acceptable reduction in system value
4. Acceptable reduction in system value
5. Negligible reduction in system value

Priority and severity are not completely independent, but it is possible to have low-priority, high-severity bugs, and vice versa. If DataRocket, for example, doesn't pass the Microsoft Windows standards certification test, the product's advertising, promotional materials, and sales pitches can't use the "Designed for Microsoft Windows" logo. This can be the kiss of death for a computer system, since logos are often checklist items for corporate purchasers. Even if the bug that crops up in the Windows certification test is entirely cosmetic — a severity 5 — it is a priority-1 bug if it blocks certi-fication.

Conversely, suppose that to re-create SpeedyWriter's hypothetical bug mentioned earlier in this chapter, the tester had to type one line of Arial text, followed by one line in a symbol font and then another line of Arial. The problem is a severity-1 bug because data is lost. However, what are the odds of a user typing exactly three lines of text, formatting the first as Arial, the second as symbols, and the third as Arial without saving at any point in the process? Despite its severity rating, I would assign this bug a priority of 4 or 5.

What you need is a single number that captures the overall importance of a bug. We created a similar number in Chapter 1 as part of ranking quality risks: in both informal methods and in FMEA, you multiply risk ratings to create a risk priority number. So, for the bug-tracking database, you can multiply severity by priority to calculate a risk priority number (RPN) for the bug. Using this approach, the RPN can range from 1 (an extremely dangerous bug) to 25 (a completely trivial bug).

The database modifications associated with adding these metrics of importance are straightforward. In the bug table, you can add three fields: Severity, Priority, and Risk Priority Number.

Next, you should make the corresponding changes in the bug entry form, adding the three fields and then automating the calculation of the risk priority number. To include the measures of importance in the detail and summary reports, simply insert the appropriate fields. Of course, if you include these fields in your table from the beginning, the Report Wizard can pick them up automatically.

Putting the Tracking in Bug Tracking: Adding Dynamic Information

So far, you have a database that is fine for *reporting* bugs but not for *tracking* them. It still lacks a way to include dynamic information, a mechanism to trace the steps through which a bug must move on its way to resolution. Having this information available would allow you to answer questions such as these: Who is currently responsible for pushing the bug toward closure? Is the resolution process stuck or moving forward smoothly? When will the bug be fixed?

Using States to Manage Bug Life Cycles

The aim of reporting problems is to bring them to the attention of the appropriate people, who will then cause the most important bugs to be fixed — or will at least attempt to have them fixed. The test organization then must either confirm or rebut the proposed fixes. Other possible outcomes for a particular bug report include its cancellation as a non-problem, its closure as a duplicate, or its indefinite deferral because of a lack of interest. In other words, a bug report should go through an identifiable life cycle, with clear ownership at each phase or state in its life cycle.

While the appropriate life cycle for your organization might vary, here's one life cycle I've used:

Review. When a tester enters a new bug report in the bug-tracking database, the bug-tracking database holds it for review before it becomes visible outside the test team. If non-testers can report bugs directly into the system, then the managers of those non-testers should determine the review process for those non-tester bug reports.

Rejected. If the reviewer decides that a report needs significant rework — either more research and information or improved wording — the reviewer rejects the report. This effectively sends the report back to the tester, who can then submit a revised report for another review. The appropriate project team members can also reject a bug report after approval by the reviewer.

Open. If the tester has fully characterized and isolated the problem, the reviewer opens the report, making it visible to the world as a known bug.

Assigned. The appropriate project team members assign it to the appropriate development manager, who in turn assigns the bug to a particular developer for repair.

Test. Once development provides a fix for the problem, it enters a test state. The bug fix comes to the test organization for confirmation testing (which ensures that the proposed fix completely resolves the bug as reported) and regression testing (which addresses the question of whether the fix has introduced new problems as a side effect).

Reopened. If the fix fails confirmation testing, the tester reopens the bug report. If the fix passes confirmation testing but fails regression testing, the tester opens a new bug report.

Closed. If the fix passes confirmation testing, the tester closes the bug report.

Deferred. If appropriate project team members decide that the problem is real but choose either to assign a low priority to the bug or to schedule the fix for a subsequent release, the bug report is deferred. Note that the project team can defer a bug at any point in its life cycle.

Cancelled. If appropriate project team members decide that the problem is not real, but rather is a false positive, the bug report is cancelled. Note that the project team can cancel a bug at any point in its life cycle.

Figure 4-7 shows these states and the flows between them. Terminal states — in other words, states in which a bug report's life cycle might terminate and the bug report become legitimately inactive with no further action required or expected — are shown with heavy lines.

I've shown the typical flows with solid lines and atypical flows with dotted lines. Any time a bug report traverses an atypical flow, some degree of inefficiency has occurred, which you as a test manager can and should measure.

The project team determines the way in which a bug report traverses the flows through a process that is sometimes called *bug triage*. I'll discuss that process later in this chapter.

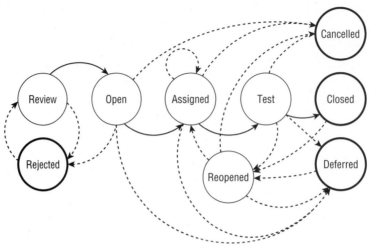

Figure 4-7 A bug report life cycle or workflow

Emphasizing Ownership and Accountability

While the state of a bug gives hints about what needs to happen next, tracking the assigned owner of a bug as well as the intended fix date provides a rudder to keep the process sailing toward a conclusion. Emphasizing personal ownership of a problem and setting an estimated fix date serve to cement commitments and support accountability. In addition, a bug sometimes blocks forward progress in the testing effort, and having some idea of its fix date allows you to plan the resumption of the blocked tests.

As the state diagram in Figure 4-7 shows, bugs can be reassigned, and such changes often shift the estimated fix date. If this is a problem in your organization, you can use an assignment history, similar to (or part of) the status log discussed in "Putting the Dynamic Fields in Place," below. I refer to this as the *bouncing-ball bug report* problem, and it can be a source of significant inefficiency on large, multi-organization projects.

The bug-tracking system should track not only developer ownership, but also tester ownership. When a bug returns to the test organization, the bug-tracking system should assign a tester to perform the confirmation and regression tests. In other words, as soon as the fix arrives in the next build or test release, the tester verifies the fix and then closes or reopens the bug. The tester should open a new bug report — not reopen the existing one — if regression testing indicates that the programmer has broken something new in the course of attempting the fix. This use of ownership in the test organization helps the test manager track expeditious resolution of bugs, and identify and resolve any blockages that arise in the bug life cycle.

Good bug-tracking systems often allow owners and stakeholders to log notes and history for a bug report as it progresses along its life cycle. That is, the appropriate testers, programmers, and managers can add a log entry to the bug report, especially when a bug reports goes through a state change. After a bug is assigned, for example, the development manager might note to whom it was assigned, when, and under what circumstances. When the fix comes back to the test organization, the test manager might enter a comment that development believes the problem is resolved. However, don't feel compelled to make a log of everything. The status entry "7/16: Muhammad assigned the bug to John" is useful; the entry "7/17: Had a five-minute discussion in the lunchroom with John about how the bug manifests itself" is not. The status log should capture significant events in the life cycle of the bug, not serve as a detailed diary.

Ultimately, the states in a bug report life cycle or workflow represent the key players in the bug find and repair cycles that arise naturally on most development and maintenance efforts. The transitions between states represent handoffs between those key players. A good bug-tracking system should allow you to implement whatever workflow will work best on your particular projects. The more automation the tool can provide — for example, sending email to the stakeholders when a bug changes state — the better the tool can support the workflow. However, process automation is only half the battle. Each project team member, the project managers (including the test manager), and the appropriate people in charge of the bug triage process must all play their parts with diligence and alacrity to ensure that each bug report moves expeditiously through the life cycle to a terminal state.

One Key Handoff: Isolation to Debugging

One key bug-reporting handoff exists between the tester and the programmer when the underlying bug report goes from being isolated to being debugged. The responsibilities of the test organization and the developers meet at this boundary. Because of the frequency with which this handoff occurs during most test projects, and because of the opportunity for miscommunication over the boundary between isolation and debugging, the sharpness of the distinction you draw between the two has a lot to do with the control you have over your scarce test resources.

Any time a tester observes a difference between actual and expected results or behavior, that observation should set in motion the appropriate bug life cycle. Along this life cycle, the participants must answer a series of questions:

1. What is the exact and minimal sequence of steps required to reproduce the symptoms of the bug? How often do these steps successfully reproduce it?

2. Does the failure indicate a test bug or a system bug? In other words, does the anomalous result originate from a test artifact or a tester error, or from system misbehavior that could affect customers?

3. What external factors influence the symptoms? In the SpeedyWriter example, one way the tester looked for influential factors was by trying different fonts.

4. What is the root cause of the problem, in the code, the electronics, the network, or the environment? Root causes are internal factors.

5. How can the problem be repaired without introducing new problems?

6. Are the changes properly debugged?

7. Is the problem fixed? Does it now pass the same test it failed before, and does the rest of the system still behave properly?

Step 1 checks for intermittence and refines the experiment. Steps 2 and 3 isolate the bug. Steps 4, 5, and 6 are debugging tasks. Step 7 involves confirmation and regression testing. Figure 4-8 shows these questions in the context of players and handoffs.

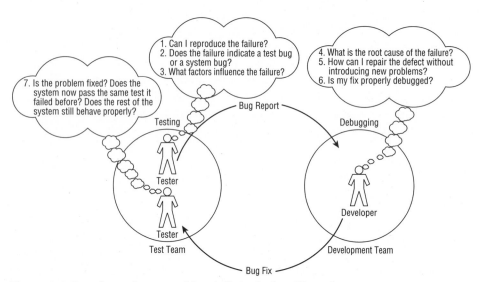

Figure 4-8 Questions, players, and handoffs in the bug life cycle

In moving through the life cycle, the bug moves through and out of the test team (steps 1, 2, and 3), into the development team (steps 4, 5, and 6), and then back into the test team (step 7). While this flow of responsibility might seem straightforward and obvious, defining and consistently observing it, especially the boundary between steps 3 and 4, can involve a significant amount of rigor, discipline, and will power.

In the excitement and pressure of test execution, the first four steps can get mixed up. Testers sometimes fail to characterize and isolate bugs completely, which results in uncertainty about the reproducibility, veracity, and nature of the bugs. The programmers and engineers then involve the testers in ongoing question-and-answer sessions as part of their debugging work or return the bug report to the testers for clarification. The testers, who have plenty of other work on their plates, are sucked into debugging, which is a development responsibility. The developers are forced to ask the testers a lot of central questions that the testers should have answered when they wrote their reports. The result is squandered time and effort, those most precious resources during test execution. I refer to this problem as *bug report ping-pong*. Through failure of clear handoffs, the productivity-enhancing tactics of division of labor and specialization of roles are defeated. To me, that's unacceptable.

When you review bug reports, or when you have your staff review one another's reports, check for clear answers to the questions in steps 1, 2, and 3 of the bug life cycle. This way, you can draw the line between isolation and debugging distinctly and keep your testers focused on testing.

Every rule has exceptions, of course. Testers must sometimes assist developers in debugging activities, especially when the test team has unique hardware items tied up in the test network, when the test system — data, tools, scripts, and environment — requires special expertise to operate and is essential to reproducing the bug, or when a bug, for whatever reason, proves irreproducible in the development lab. Most of the time, though, when I have observed testers becoming involved in debugging, it was for dysfunctional reasons. In some cases, it was my fault as the test manager for not adequately communicating the difference between isolation and debugging to the project team. In other cases, the tester wrote a poor bug report (this set of circumstances became less of a problem for me when I implemented the bug-reporting process and techniques outlined in this chapter). Sometimes programmers or engineers don't accept bugs reports as complete and accurate even though they are. These three cases are typically process problems that I can resolve as a test manager. The fourth case is a motivational or personnel management issue that arises when testers find it more interesting to work with the programmer or engineer on debugging than to move on to other testing. For all these cases, you must either limit the extent to which this happens or accept the significant drain it will impose on your resources.

Guiding the Bug Life Cycle: The Bug Triage Process

In Figure 4-7, you might have noticed multiple arrows coming out of a single state. These represent decision points happening within the state. A variety of such important decisions must occur during the life cycle. Should we fix a bug or defer it? Is this actually a problem or correct behavior? How do these decisions get made?

In some cases, this is a small, obvious decision. If a bug's symptom is obviously a high priority (e.g., very visible and/or dangerous to many users), if the bug is obvious in its fix (e.g., a misspelled message or a simple logic error), and the impact to the tester and programmer of fixing the bug is minimal (e.g.,

15 minutes to repair the code and five minutes to confirm the fix in the next test release), then such bugs can be resolved at the discretion of the testers and programmers involved. At some point, a large number of these types of bugs becomes a management issue, but often I've seen this be a process that can proceed in the background with minimal management attention.

However, some bugs have unclear priority, might well require an unknown and possibly extensive effort to fix, might require significant effort (including build and test effort) to integrate and confirm, or some combination of these three factors. In such a case, the project management team must intervene in some fashion to make the fix/defer decision. There are two common approaches that I've seen, and both can work. One is the bug triage or bug review committee, and the other is a change-control board (CCB).

A bug triage or bug review committee is a subset of the overall project team. Typical attendees include the test manager, the project manager, the development manager, the release engineering or build manager, and some senior technical experts. There are often attendees to represent the users and customers. On a mass-market system, these might include the sales, marketing, and technical support managers. For an in-house IT project, the project sponsor and senior users of the system might attend. In custom development efforts, I have seen the client send attendees.[2]

The committee meets regularly — as often as once a day — to review the bugs opened or reopened since the last meeting, and to decide, for each bug, whether and when to fix it. The primary driver of this decision is the bug's priority, which the committee might adjust upward or downward. However, the committee should also consider schedule and budget implications. For example, the triage committee should schedule the repair of a bug that blocks significant chunks of testing ahead of other bugs, because finishing text execution is on the critical path for finishing the project.

A CCB serves a similar function, but has a broader scope. Not only will a CCB decide on whether to fix certain bugs, but they generally also decide on changes proposed for the requirements, design, user interface, supported configurations, and other significant adjustments to the project plan. CCBs sometimes have broad powers to decide on changes in budget and schedule, too, although in some organizations these decisions are reserved for senior managers. CCBs are often composed of the same sort of people as a bug triage committee, although more powerful CCBs tend to include more senior managers, too.[3]

There are plenty of possible variations to the bug triage process. I am not a partisan for any particular approach, because each organization needs to adopt a bug triage process that works in its context. The important aspect to me is

---

[2]Even though it's a book ostensibly for children, Robert Sabourin's *I am a Bug!* includes an insightful discussion of the bug life cycle, including the triage process.
[3]A good discussion of change-control boards can be found in Steve McConnell's *Software Project Survival Guide.*

that the bug triage process includes the input of the major stakeholders. (The participants in the quality risk analysis discussed in Chapter 1 might be a good place to start.) Part of keeping all these busy professionals involved is having a CCB or bug triage meeting duration and frequency that work for the entire team. Keeping the meeting focused on bugs and moving quickly through a tight list of bugs is essential. To help with that, I have three suggestions:

- All participants should come to the meeting either prepared to make a recommendation on any particular bug, or prepared to abstain from discussion about that bug. These meetings will last too long if extensive Q&A sessions are required to explain each bug to the participants.

- Limit the discussion on each bug to five minutes or less, and discuss only bugs and the direct ramifications of bugs. Schedule the meetings frequently enough that the meeting takes an hour or less. Even allowing for five minutes per bug, this should be possible for any project where the bug find rate does not exceed 60 per week.

- Make the decision to fix or defer each bug exactly once and in the first meeting in which that bug is addressed. Avoid analysis paralysis or a Hamlet-like debate ("to fix or not to fix, that is the question") that allows a single bug report to eat up an hour of the team's time over the course of a dozen meetings.

Like all rules of thumb, exceptions will arise, but in my experience, few bugs really need an exception to one or more of these rules. If you find that more than, say, 10 percent of the bugs require extensive discussion, Q&A sessions, or revisiting during the project, ask yourself if there's not a change you could make to some other process to reduce that number. Bug triage committees and CCBs are powerful techniques for balancing quality, schedule, budget, and features on a project, but they can easily become bureaucratic, time-wasting tar pits. Once that happens, people will find (rightfully so) convenient excuses not to attend.

Putting the Dynamic Fields in Place

You can easily add all this dynamic information to your bug-tracking database. You'll need to add four fields to the table and the form: State, Owner, Estimated Fix Date, and Log. *State* and *Owner* are text fields, with the entry selected from a list box. *Estimated Fix Date* uses a standard Access date/time data type, formatted as a short date. It's probably most useful to define *Log* as a memo field, although you can, for reasons of space, use a text field. You could also use an external table linked through a foreign key with a separate row for each entry. Implementing such a database, however, involves database programming, which is beyond the scope of this book.

Figure 4-9 shows the bug entry form with the four new fields; Figure 4-10 shows the updated version of the bug detail report. I include all four of these fields in all my reports, including the bug summary report. Doing so crowds the detail report a bit, but it's worth it because I use that report as a management tool, and the addition of these fields makes the report even more valuable.

Figure 4-9 A bug entry form with dynamic information

SpeedyWriter Bug Detail

Bug ID	Project Name	Tester		State	Date Opened
1	SpeedyWriter I.0	Bob Chien		Assigned	7/22/2009
Severity	**Priority**	**Risk Priority Number**	**Owner**		**Estimated Fix**
1	2	2	Muhammad Zamanzadeh		8/12/2009
Summary					
SpeedyWriter for Windows XP scribbles on the file under edit if Arial font is selected.					
Steps to Reproduce					
1. Open SpeedyWriter and create a new file. 2. Type in two or mere lines of random text. (It doesn't matter what) 3. Highlight the text, pull down the font menu, and select Arial. 4. Text is transformed into meaningless garbage. 5. I was a able reproduce this problem three out of three tries.					
Isolation					
On the vague suspicion that this was just a formatting problem. I saved the file, closed SpeedyWriter and reopened the file. The garbage remained. If you save the file before Arializing the contents, the bug does net occur. The bug does not occur with existing files. This only happens under WindowsXP This bug doesn't recur with other fonts.					
Status					
7/23: Reviewed and opened this issue. 7/29: Assigned to Muhammad. who thinks he can fix it in a couple weeks.					

Figure 4-10 A bug detail report with dynamic information

Finishing Touches: Capturing Bug Data for Analysis

You now have a fully adequate bug-tracking database that you can use to manage bugs through their entire life cycle, to produce summary reports for management and detail reports for developers, and to keep track of who is responsible for moving bugs forward. You might want to design additional reports or make some cosmetic changes, but the database is essentially complete. To gather some additional data that can bring bugs into sharper focus, however, I recommend that you add a few more fields.

What the Bug Relates To: Subsystem, Configuration, and Quality Risks

Some of the data you might want to gather would help you understand what the bug is related to. In other words, what is the context for the bug? There are a number of data elements you could gather here, but I prefer to focus on three.

Adding a Subsystem field allows you to captures which component of the system bears the brunt of each bug's symptoms. In our DataRocket case study, for example, subsystems might break down as follows:

Mainboard. The CPU, the motherboard, the memory, the on-board fans, and common built-in controllers for the USB, IEEE 1394, and serial ports.

Video. The video card and, if bundled, the video cable and monitor.

SCSI. The SCSI adapter, the internal cables, the external cables, the RAID hardware, the tape drive, and the DVD drive.

Network. The controller configuration, which can involve one or more cards.

Telecommunications. The optional bundled modem, the wireless wide area network (WWAN), or the computer-telephony-integration hardware.

Other hardware. The case, the power supply, the mouse, and the keyboard.

BIOS. The features controlled by the BIOS, especially power management and boot-up passwords.

Other software. Any custom drivers, such as bundled custom network drivers, as well as any preinstalled network operating systems that might ship on the system.

For SpeedyWriter, you might choose to decompose the subsystems this way:

User interface. The behavior of the graphical user interface (GUI), including video, mouse, and keyboard aspects, such as screen painting, print previews, windowing, and all command selection sequences.

Tools. The ability to check spelling, use a thesaurus, track revisions, create tables, display graphs, insert files and other objects, draw pictures, and so forth.

File. Create, open, save/save as, and export and import features.

Edit engine. The formatting, editing, font selection, footnote/endnote features, and so on.

Install/config. The installation, configuration, reconfiguration, and upgrade processes.

Docs/packaging. The documentation, help files, or packaging.

In addition to system-dependent components, you might include three catchall subsystems to deal with exceptional situations:

Other. The bug affects a particular subsystem, but not one that is listed.

Unknown. The bug doesn't appear to have anything to do with any subsystem.

N/A. No subsystem applies.

Usually a small fraction — less than five percent on most of my projects — of the total bugs will fit into each of these three categories. If the number is larger, the Other category is probably picking up too many bugs that should have their own subsystem category.

As you've probably noticed, the division of a system into subsystems is arbitrary. In some cases, especially projects in which different teams work on each subsystem, the task is easier. Regardless, you need to establish a subsystem breakdown that is meaningful for each project, because you can't categorize if everyone decides for themselves what subsystems exist in the system under test.

Moving on to the next data element, consider adding a Configuration field or fields to track the test release and test environment in which the bug was observed. Projects usually involve multiple revisions of software and hardware, many of which must operate in multiple software, hardware, LAN, WAN, and database environments. Capturing configuration information in the bug-tracking database can help you understand the setting in which failures occur.

I often employ multiple configuration fields. These parallel the subsystem values, but it's seldom a complete overlap. For example, with DataRocket you might track the BIOS revision, the mainboard revision, the case version, and the bundled software version.

Alternatively, you can use a lookup table approach. For SpeedyWriter, you might use a combination of letters and numbers to indicate software revisions and the test environment. Suppose that the SpeedyWriter internal revisions are identified in *X.YY.ZZ* format, such as 0.01.19. The systems in the test lab are labeled A, B, C, and D; the three networks (Linux, Sun Solaris, and Microsoft Windows) are assigned the identifiers X, Y, and Z, respectively. A test configuration of a Windows workstation connected to a Solaris server with the second major and thirty-third minor revision might thus be designated A.Y.0.2.33. Of course, you must record details about how to decode or read these designations. Such a sequence of letters and numbers doesn't exactly explain itself.

The third data element traces the bug back to the test basis that it relates to. (The test basis is the foundation for the testing we intend to do.) I generally use quality risks as the basis of my testing, as discussed in Chapter 1. Therefore, I have added a field for this in the bugs table. Assuming you use a hierarchical approach with risk categories and then risk items within categories, you should keep this decomposition of risk breakdowns so you can aggregate at the higher level or focus on the lower levels at will.

Some people use requirements, designs, implementation details, and other data as the test basis. In some test approaches, the test basis is derived from these items by creating an inventory of test objectives. In such a situation, you could trace back to the test objective inventory instead of quality risks.

Either way, if you have prioritized the risks, the test objectives, or whatever your chosen test basis, you can set up the database to suggest the associated priority of the basis as the default priority for the bug report. This can help your testers decide what the bug priority should be.

Where the Bug Came From: Resolution and Root Cause

The simplest way to keep track of where bugs come from is to ask the programmers and other engineers who fix the bugs to take a note. By adding a Resolution field, this note can be entered to describe how the problem was solved. (Alternatively, you could use the Status field for this purpose, but a separate field is more useful for reports.) Through database programming, you can force completion of this field. Any time a bug is closed, some notation should be made.

The problem with free-form resolution fields is that it's hard to do analysis on them. In addition, if people forget to write anything down — or write something so cryptic that no one but the engineer who wrote it can figure it out — then you might be missing data for many bugs. The solution to this problem is for the project team — specifically, the development or project manager — to institute a root cause analysis process and a bug taxonomy.

If you are the first test manager your company has ever had, with no exposure to root cause analysis, and your development process consists of hacking and flailing away until the product appears to work, root cause analysis is probably beyond the level of process maturity at your company.

(See Chapter 12 for more on development processes and process maturity.) You might want to read this section as information only. Doing root cause analysis is not a trivial undertaking. Furthermore, it requires the assistance of the developers and the support of management.

Simply put, a root cause is the underlying reason for a bug. When you are doing behavioral (black-box) testing, a bug makes its presence known through an observed behavior, a symptom, an anomalous output, data transformation, slow response time, a system crash, an inexplicable delay, or some other visible program transgression. (During structural (white-box) testing, you can observe bugs that don't involve program output or behaviors because you have access to internal program states and other information that tells you whether something has gone awry.) Therefore, when a tester doing behavioral testing observes a bug, he sees only the symptom. Taking cough medicine to stop hacking or aspirin to lower a fever doesn't cure a cold because it doesn't address the root cause, the virus that is making you sick.

You can think of the connection between root causes and bugs with the sequence of events shown in Figure 4-11. An anomaly occurs when a tester observes an unexpected behavior. If the test environment and the tester's actions were correct, this anomaly indicates either a system failure or a test failure. The failure arises from a bug in either the system or the test. The bug comes from an error committed by a software or hardware engineer (while creating the system under test) or a test engineer (while creating the test system). That error is the root cause.

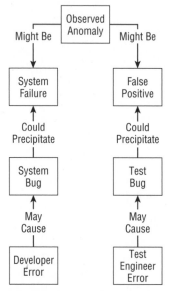

Figure 4-11 Bugs and their root causes

This model illustrates the connection between bugs and their root causes in an elegant way, but it suffers from some flaws. First, errors, bugs, and failures don't have one-to-one relationships. The trickiest bugs — stability problems, for example — often arise from complex interactions of components, any one of which is not necessarily an error. Next, the conditional language points out that while many events might possibly transpire, sometimes nothing happens at all. Errors don't always cause bugs, bugs occasionally remain hidden in programs, and failures aren't always observed. Therefore, the model has limitations, but it does create a useful mental picture. That intellectual image can help you think about root causes.

Usually, the aim of performing a root cause analysis isn't to determine the exact error and how it happened. Other than flogging some hapless engineer, you can't do much with such information. Instead, root cause analysis categorizes bugs into a taxonomy. For DataRocket, you might, in a root cause analysis, assign hardware bugs to one of three categories: design, production, or material. A design bug results from the misuse of a component, a failure to understand the limitations of a chip, inappropriate airflow, or other such errors. A production bug ensues from an error on the production line — for example, a CPU is improperly inserted and falls out during shock and vibration testing. A material bug occurs when a component misbehaves or fails. (These categories are relative to whether your company buys or sells the failed item. A producer's design failure can cause the consumer to experience a material failure. For example, the Pentium floating-point bug was Intel's design failure, but computer makers experienced a component failure.) In addition to these hardware failures, you need to include at least one category for software failures arising from BIOS bugs.

For software, you might consider the following bug taxonomy, which is based on one originally published by Boris Beizer.[4] While retaining the essentials of the original, I have added two features to the list: explanations and examples associated with the various root causes, and a few bookkeeping categories that will help you deal with unusual cases (Duplicate, NAP, Bad Unit, RCN, and Unknown).

Functional

Specification. The specification is wrong.

Function. The specification is right, but implementation is wrong.

Test. The system works correctly, but the test reports a spurious error.

---

[4]This taxonomy is based on the appendix, "Bug Taxonomy and Statistics," in *Software Testing Techniques, Second Edition*, by Boris Beizer. Copyright © 1990 by Boris Beizer. Reprinted by permission of the author.

System

Internal Interface. The internal system communication failed.

Hardware Devices. The hardware failed.

Operating System. The operating system failed.

Software Architecture. A fundamental design assumption proved invalid.

Resource Management. The design assumptions are OK, but some implementation of the assumption is wrong.

Process

Arithmetic. The program incorrectly adds, divides, multiplies, factors, integrates numerically, or otherwise fails to perform an arithmetic operation properly.

Initialization. An operation fails on its first use.

Control or Sequence. An action occurs at the wrong time or for the wrong reason.

Static Logic. Boundaries are misdefined, logic is invalid, "can't happen" events do happen, "won't matter" events do matter, and so forth.

Other. A control-flow or processing error occurs that doesn't fit in the preceding buckets.

Data

Type. An integer should be a floating point, an unsigned integer stores or retrieves a negative value, an object is improperly defined, and so forth.

Structure. A complex data structure is invalid or inappropriate.

Initial Value. A data element's initialized value is incorrect. (This might not result in a process initialization error.)

Other. A data-related error occurs that doesn't fit in the preceding buckets.

Code

A typo, misspelling, stylistic error, or other coding error occurs that results in a failure.

Documentation

The documentation says the system does X on condition Y, but the system does Z — a valid and correct action — instead.

Standards

The system fails to meet industry or vendor standards, follow code standards, adhere to naming conventions, and so forth.

Other

The root cause is known, but fits none of the preceding categories.

Duplicate

Two bug reports describe the same bug. (This can happen when two testers report the same symptom, or when two testers report different symptoms that share the same underlying code problem.)

NAP

The behavior described in the bug report is not a problem. The report arises from a misunderstanding on the part of the tester about correct behavior. This situation is distinct from a test failure (whose root cause is categorized as *functional/test*) in that this is *tester* failure.

Bad Unit

The bug is a real problem, but it arises from a random hardware failure that is unlikely to occur in the field. (If the bug indicates a lack of reliability in some hardware component, this is not the root cause.)

RCN

A root cause is needed; the bug is confirmed as closed by test, but no one in development has supplied a root cause.

Unknown

No one knows what is broken. This root cause usually fits best when an intermittent failure doesn't appear for quite a while, leading people to conclude that some other change fixed the bug as a side effect.

Why go to the trouble of capturing this information? First, gathering root cause data allows you to apply the Pareto principle — focus on the vital few, not the trivial many — when the time comes to try to improve your development process. For example, if most DataRocket failures result from bad components, you should revisit your choice of suppliers. Next, if you use industry-standard bug taxonomies, you can compare root cause statistics for your projects against the averages. You can also accumulate historical data over the course of your projects that you can use for in-house comparisons.

Finally, if you know where bugs are apt to originate, you can tailor your test effort to hit those areas particularly hard. By combining root cause data with subsystem breakdowns, you can get a good idea of what breaks in which parts of the system.

How Long Was the Bug Around? Close Date and the Injection, Detection, and Removal Phases

In addition to tracking where the bug came from, it's useful to know how long it was in the system. We can capture a couple of different sets of data to answer this question. The easiest is to keep track of the length of time the bug is known active — in other words, the time from initial discovery to confirmation of closure, deferral, or cancellation — which we can do by capturing not only the open date but also the date on which the bug report entered a closed or deferred state. Entering this date in the Close Date field is more than simply tidying up your records. You'll see how this piece of information comes into its own later in this chapter, when we discuss extracting metrics from your database.

The more sophisticated set of data we can track has to do with when the bug was originally created, when we found it, and when we confirmed it fixed. While we could do this by date, the more typical way to handle this is by project phase. The specific phases that you have in your projects will vary depending on your system life cycle (see Chapter 12), but for the moment let's assume that your projects consist of eight phases:

Requirements. The activities in which the project team figures out what the system is to do.

Design. The activities in which the project team figures out how the system will do what it does.

Implementation. The activities in which the project team implements the requirements according to the design.

Component test. The activities in which the project team looks for and repairs bugs in the constituent pieces of the system.

Integration test. The activities in which the project team looks for and repairs bugs in the interaction of components.

System test. The activities in which the project team looks for and repairs bugs in the entire system, fully integrated.

Acceptance test. The activities in which the project team demonstrates that the system meets requirements.

Post-release. The activities in which the project team supports the system in the field.

A *defect removal model* analyzes, for all eight phases, the bugs *injected* (or created), the bugs *detected* (found through testing or quality assurance), and the bugs *removed* (through repair, confirmation testing, and regression testing) in each phase of testing. The concept of defect removal models is a sophisticated one, well beyond the scope of this book.[5] However, in order to support the data collection needed, the bug management process will need the engineering team to identify the *phase injected*, and the test team to identify the *phase detected* and *phase removed*. The bug-tracking system will need to capture these three values for each bug.

The reason for capturing these two sets of data is to look for opportunities to improve our processes. Bugs found and fixed in the same phase in which they're created are much less dangerous to the project in terms of schedule and budget. Therefore, defect removal models allow us to analyze the number of bugs that *escape* from one phase to the next. Keeping this metric small reduces the likelihood of schedule slips and budget overruns. Similarly, within a phase, the shorter the period of time the bug is open, the less risk there is of delay in meeting the exit criteria for that phase. I'll show you ways to present a bug lifetime metric in the last section of this chapter, but first let's finish up our bug-tracking database.

The Finalized Bug-Tracking Database

The data-capturing fields that we'll add now all allow us to categorize a bug report. In a database, we can do this in a couple of ways. One is to pick from a fixed list of possible items. This works for values that won't change over time. In this case, the Phase Injected, Phase Detected, Phase Removed, Severity, Priority, and Root Cause fields won't change, so we can implement them as Microsoft Access combo boxes that present a list of valid values to the user.

For values that will change over time, having the database look up the valid values and present that list to the user is the way to go. This involves providing a separate table and using a query to retrieve the information from that table. For our database, there are five fields that fall into this category: Tester, Owner, Configuration, Subsystem, and Quality Risk. Let's look at Subsystem for an example of how this works, as all five work in substantially the same fashion.

Figure 4-12 shows the subsystem lookup table. It's just two text fields, one with the subsystem mnemonic, the other with a more complete description of the subsystem. Figure 4-13 shows the definition for the subsystem combo box on the bug entry form. Finally, you can see the added fields in Figure 4-14, which shows the completed bug entry form. (Try it on your own system to see how the table lookup shows up in the pull-down combo box.) I include all of these fields in the bug detail report, but might leave them out of the bug summary report for brevity.

---

[5]Stephen Kan's *Metrics and Models in Software Quality Engineering* addresses this topic in details, including the schedule and budget implications of these metrics.

Subsystem ▾	Description
⊞ Docs/Package	The documentation or packaging.
⊞ Edit Engine	The formatting, editing, font selection, footnote and end note features, and such.
⊞ File	Create, open, save/save as, export and import features.
⊞ Install/Config	The installation, configuration, reconfiguration and upgrade processes.
⊞ N/A	No subsystem applies to this bug.
⊞ Other	A subsystem not listed applies.
⊞ Tools	The ability to spell-check, use a thesaurus, track revisions, create tables, display graphs, insert files and other objects, draw pictures, and so forth.
⊞ Unknown	The bug does not appear to depend on the subsystem.
⊞ User Interface	The GUI video, mouse and keyboard behavior, including screen painting, print previews, windowing, and all command-selection sequences.
✳	

Figure 4-12 The subsystem lookup table

Property Sheet ✕
Selection type: Combo Box

Combo34 ▾

Format	Data	Event	Other	All

Control Source	Subsystem
Row Source	SELECT DISTINCTROW [tblSubsystem].[Subsystem], [tblSubsystem].[Description] FROM [tblSubsystem];
Row Source Type	Table/Query
Bound Column	1
Limit To List	No
Allow Value List Edits	No
List Items Edit Form	
Inherit Value List	No
Show Only Row Source Valu	No
Input Mask	
Default Value	
Validation Rule	
Validation Text	
Enabled	Yes
Locked	No
Auto Expand	Yes
Smart Tags	

Figure 4-13 Subsystem combo box definition on bug entry form

Field Name	Data Type	Description
⌄► Bug ID	AutoNumber	The bug identifier.
Project Name	Text	The project against which the bug appeared.
Tester	Text	The tester's name.
State	Text	The current state of the issue.
Date Opened	Date/Time	The date the report was opened.
Severity	Number	The severity of the bug, 1-5.
Priority	Number	The priority of the bug, 1-5.
Risk Priority Number	Number	The product of the severity and the priority, 1-25.
Owner	Text	The person currently responsible for moving the bug to the next state.
Estimated Fix Date	Date/Time	When the bug will be fixed, by the "owner's" estimate.
Summary	Text	The bug report summary.
Steps to Reproduce	Memo	How the tester was able to reproduce the bug.
Isolation	Memo	What the tester did to determine the bug was real, and to find influencing factors.
Status	Memo	What has happened to date to fix the bug.
Subsystem	Text	The subsystem affected, from the look-up table.
Configuration	Text	The configuration tested, from the look-up table.
Close Date	Date/Time	The date on which the bug was closed.
Resolution	Memo	The resolution of the bug.
Root Cause	Text	The root cause, from the pick-list.

Figure 4-14 A complete bug entry form

The IEEE 829 Standard

The IEEE publishes a standard with some potentially useful and interesting suggestions for information to include in your bug reports. This standard is IEEE 829, and Chapters 2 and 3 provided some ideas on using it with test plans and test systems.

The IEEE 829 standard contains a template for bug reports, shown in Figure 4-15. Now, IEEE doesn't actually call it a template for bug reports, but rather a template for anomaly reports. As they state in the standard, "The purpose of the [anomaly report] is to document any event that occurs during the testing process that requires investigation. This may be called a problem, test incident, defect, trouble, issue, anomaly, or error report." I find it strange that they chose to leave out the phrase *bug report* as a synonym. Carping about terminology notwithstanding, what ideas can we glean from this document?[6]

1. Introduction
    1.1. Document identifier
    1.2. Scope
    1.3. References
2. Details
    2.1. Summary
    2.2. Date anomaly discovered
    2.3. Context
    2.4. Description of anomaly
    2.5. Impact
    2.6. Originator's assessment of urgency
    2.7. Description of the corrective action
    2.8. Status of the anomaly
    2.9. Conclusions and recommendations
3. General
    3.1. Document change procedures and history

Figure 4-15 The IEEE 829 standard's anomaly report template

Section 1, the introduction, includes a report ID number, which is pretty obvious. It includes a section listing references, which is useful when a bug report is pointing out a clear discrepancy between some documents that describe the expected behavior and whatever the actual behavior is. The Scope section is less obvious, and the standard doesn't help much when it says that this section should "briefly describe any contextual information not covered elsewhere in the AR [anomaly report] that is needed to make this AR understandable," which might lead you to ask, "Well, what wouldn't fit into section 2.3 that would require it to go here?"

Getting into the second section, you'll see some fields that look familiar. The Summary and Date Anomaly Discovered fields are exactly as I discussed earlier in this chapter.

The Context field here makes sense. This includes the information about the particular item or system being tested, and the version of it, when we saw

[6]Stranger still, nowhere in the IEEE 829 standard does the word *bug* occur, even though it must be one of the most common terms in testing. Perhaps the standards committee was trying to make some kind of terminological statement — or perhaps a termitological statement. Even though these sages do not say that you "may call" an anomaly report a bug report, I certainly say that you may — in fact, you may call it an apple tart as far as I'm concerned, provided the details are correct.

the bug. It also includes information about the software or system life cycle process underway at that time (more on this in Chapter 12). It also includes references to other test documents, especially the test procedure or test case the tester was running when we saw the bug, and any test results logs that document the test case result (see Chapter 5). It should also identify the phase or level of testing underway.

The Description of Anomaly field is basically the same as the failure description I described earlier in this chapter. It should indicate reproducibility, and provide detailed steps to reproduce. It should provide or reference the inputs given, the expected results, the actual results, what was unexpected about the outcome, the specific step in the test cases or procedure that failed, the test environment used, how many times the failure was reproduced, who ran the test, and who observed the results.

Note that, while the IEEE 829 standard allows you to reference these items elsewhere — e.g., in a test case — I consider it a high point in rudeness to make the reader of a bug report poke around distant documents to figure out what I'm complaining about. As bad as it is to do a copy-paste of a test case into the failure description of bug report, it's worse to say something as cryptic and unhelpful as "see test 10.145."

The 829 standard and I agree that this section should describe related activities and observations that can help the programmer isolate and correct the bug. We also agree that you should reference previous executions of the same test case or similar test cases if that helps indicate whether the bug is a regression.

The 829 standard encourages you to include a section on impact, which is not quite the same as the priority classification information I mentioned earlier. Here, they are looking for the way the problem affects various business and technical considerations, in narrative form. They are also looking for workarounds, if they exist. Once the development organization estimates the time required for a fix, that should go here as well.

The section on the originator's assessment of urgency is actually closer to what I meant by *priority*. They also include the idea of risk related to the bug, possibly involving a reference back to the quality risk item associated with the bug, as I mentioned earlier. The IEEE 829 standard encourages the use of a consistent set of classifications for urgency, like the ones I used for priority.

The Description of the Corrective Action section corresponds to what I called *resolution*. The Status of the Anomaly field is as I discussed in the section on life cycles. The Conclusions and Recommendations field includes recommendations for improving the development or testing processes to prevent this kind of bug in the future. As with my discussion about defect removal models earlier, they recommend identifying the source or injection point for the bug.

Finally, section 3, the General section, is similar to that described in Chapter 2 regarding the same section in a test plan.

Extracting Metrics from the Bug-Tracking Database

The bug reports just described are useful in and of themselves, but the bug tracking database can be a source of even more information. Bug data forms the basis of various quality control charts in a number of industries, and software and hardware are no exception. Using this bug-tracking database, you can generate bug analysis charts that allow you to see patterns in your bug data. These charts are also excellent for communicating with management because they highlight and illustrate test results that are difficult to explain with raw data.

The following sections introduce some powerful and easy-to-generate charts. These charts will allow you to communicate testing status related to bugs in terms of trends. By communicating in terms of trends, you can summarize key facts. This allows you to get your points across quickly and visually. It also promotes management of the project by key indicators, rather than whatever crisis happens to be going on at the time. These defect charts make up a key part of what I refer to as the *test dashboard*, which I'll discuss again in Chapters 5 and 9.

I create these charts typically by exporting data from a bug-tracking database into a spreadsheet. I set up the example spreadsheets for these charts using the Access bug-tracking database we built in this chapter. I've populated the sample spreadsheets with various dummy data sets to create these charts. The data is manipulated to illustrate points, so don't assume that these charts necessarily represent a typical project. If you already have a bug-tracking database, or have bug data in some other format that you can easily get into a spreadsheet, I'd encourage you to load your own data into the Bugs worksheet of the spreadsheet and see what these charts look like for your projects. These spreadsheets are available in the RBCS Library at www.rbcs-us.com.[7]

How Defect Removal Proceeds: The Opened/Closed Chart

The most basic defect analysis chart plots the total number of bugs opened against the total number resolved on a daily basis. It's a common chart, and widely referred to as either the *convergence, opened/closed, found/fixed,* or simply *bug* chart. Figure 4-16 presents a sample chart, which offers a general view of the development project's status, taken during the middle of the system test phase.

This information-rich chart provides answers to a number of questions. How close are we to being ready to ship the product? In this chart, you see that I used the predicted number of bugs — created during the estimation work that I discussed in Chapter 1 — to show where I expect the total number of

---

[7]For more charts that might be useful, see Kan's *Metrics and Models in Software Quality Engineering* or my own book *Advanced Software Testing: Volume II.*

opened bugs to converge. Test projects eventually hit a point at which further testing produces diminishing returns. When the Total Opened curve — the top curve on the chart in Figure 4-16 — levels off to an expected number of bugs, testing is winding down, at least for the phase currently underway.

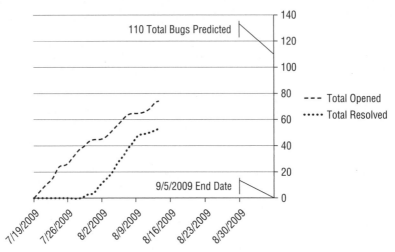

Figure 4-16 An opened/closed chart for SpeedyWriter

The leveling off indicates the fading of the test system's ability to find bugs in the current phase. Given a good test system, such as the kind produced by the test strategies discussed in this book, the bugs found represent the bugs most likely to torment the customer, and the fading of the test system is consistent with customer indifference. Conversely, a Total Opened curve that refuses to flatten indicates that you have plenty of problems left to find.

The chart in Figure 4-16 shows that we are not through finding bugs yet. However, since we are at the middle of the project, that's not a problem. We'll examine how this chart looks in dysfunctional projects in a moment.

Next, have you finished fixing bugs? Once development completes, developers usually start to catch up with the problems. Shortly afterwards, the opened curve should start to flatten. Consequently, the Total Resolved curve — the lower curve on the chart in Figure 4-16 — begins to converge with the Total Opened curve. (Referring back to Figure 4-7, *deferred, rejected, cancelled*, and *closed* bugs are counted as *resolved* for purposes of this chart.)

Figure 4-17 shows a project where, barring any other worrisome metrics or findings, we are ready to ship. Of course, there are plenty of other worrisome metrics or findings that could arise, beyond just problems related to bugs. For example, suppose we flattened the Total Opened curve by stopping testing? We'll discuss balancing this chart with other charts in Chapter 5. However, this chart is quite useful, and every test manager should have it as part of their analytical arsenal.

Figure 4-17 A good-looking opened/closed chart

THE FIX DATE PRECEDES THE CLOSE DATE

If you were to draw a *Total Fixed curve* based on the dates when developers actually repaired bugs, you would see that the Total Resolved curve lags behind it by a week or so. This lag results from delays incurred in getting the fix into the next test release, delivering that release to the test team, and doing confirmation testing. These various delays cause the convergence at the last day of testing shown in the sample chart in Figure 4-17.

At a more general level, is the bug management process working? It is working well in both Figure 4-16 and Figure 4-17: the Total Resolved curve follows right behind the Total Opened curve, indicating that the project team is moving the bugs quickly toward resolution.

Finally, how do milestones in the project relate to inflection points, changes in the slope of the opened or closed curves? The overlapping of the phases in these examples obscures this relationship somewhat, but often when you move from one test phase to the next, you will see a spike in the Total Opened curve. Such rises are gentle in our idealized example, but these transitions can be dramatic and even downright scary on some projects. As developers move from writing new code or engineering new hardware to fixing bugs, you should see an upward turn in the Total Resolved curve. Sometimes, when the bug triage process falls behind, a *bug scrub* meeting, where the technical and management leaders of a project gather to decide the fate of all known bug reports, can result in a discontinuous jump in the Total Resolved curve

To explore the use of opened/closed charts, let's look at three nightmare scenarios that represent those unpleasant projects in which most test managers eventually participate. Assume that, in each case, we're working on a project where the scheduled ship or deployment date is September 5. For the first nightmare, imagine that during the system test phase, the bug find rate remains high and refuses to level off. The opened/closed chart that results appears in Figure 4-18. Notice the deceptive leveling in the second cycle (8/23 through 8/29), where the Total Opened curve appears to flatten, only to leap up sharply in the third cycle (8/30 through 9/5). If the project team ships the product as scheduled, they can expect many failures in the field.

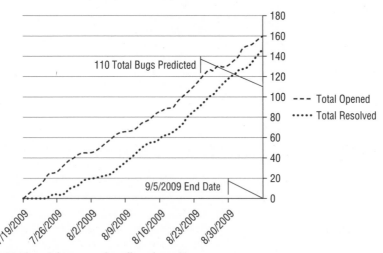

Figure 4-18 The nightmare of endless bug discovery

For the second nightmare, let's assume that development is ignoring some of the bugs. The developers have convinced themselves that about 25 of the bugs that test has reported are not really problems and can be disregarded. Figure 4-19 shows the opened/closed chart for this scenario. Until about August 20, the chart in Figure 4-17 (the idealized example) and the chart in Figure 4-19 are not radically different: on that date, the opened/closed gap is about 20 in the former chart, whereas it is about 30 in the latter. Ten bugs out of 100 one way or the other three weeks before the first customer ship is not a catastrophe. However, as the final two cycles of system testing unfold (8/23 through 8/29, and 8/30 through 9/5, respectively), it becomes clear that the gap is not narrowing. Unless you bring the pernicious bugs to project management's attention around August 23, the development team will deliver a *fait accompli*. Overturning their decision to ignore these bugs even a week later will require a slip in the delivery date.

As a final nightmare — well, okay, just a disquieting dream, actually — let's suppose that the developers and the testers are both doing the right things at a technical level, but the bug management process isn't working. The development manager doesn't notify you when bugs are fixed and ready for re-testing, and you don't follow up with your testers to make sure they close bugs that they have re-tested. In addition, testers don't bother to report bugs when they find them, but instead wait until Thursday or Friday each week. Then they enter their findings, some dimly remembered, into the bug-tracking database. Figure 4-20 shows how the opened/closed chart looks in this example. The trouble here is that you can't tell whether a jump in a curve represents a significant event or simply indicates that some people are getting around to doing what they should have done earlier. If you use this chart as part of your project dashboard or scorecard, your vision is blurred.

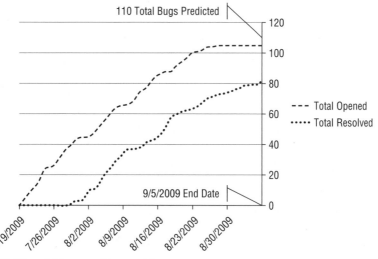

Figure 4-19 The nightmare of ignored bugs

Figure 4-20 The nightmare of mismanaged bugs

Why Bugs Happen: The Root Cause Chart

Root cause data is most interesting in the aggregate. Listing the closure of one bug with a specific root cause might not mean much, but seeing the breakdown for 100 — or 1,000 — bugs can tell an engaging story. Figure 4-21 presents a root cause breakdown for the SpeedyWriter example, showing the contribution of each type of error to the total number of bugs found and fixed so far. (During test execution, many bugs will not have root causes assigned to them because they are still under investigation.) As discussed earlier, analyzing a breakdown of root causes can serve to focus not only test efforts, but also development attention on those areas that are causing the most serious and frequent problems. As you might imagine, a chart such as the one in Figure 4-21 grabs management's attention more effectively than a table would.

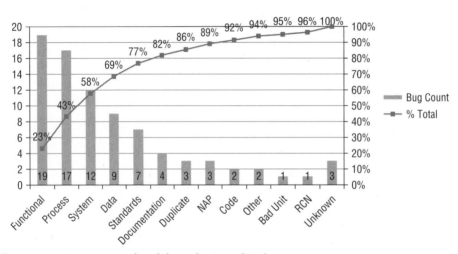

Figure 4-21 A root ;cause breakdown for SpeedyWriter

How Development Responds: The Closure Period Chart

Closure period (a.k.a. *closure gap*) is complicated to calculate, but it has a simple intuitive meaning: the closure period gauges the programming and engineering teams' responsiveness to the test team's bug reports. *Daily closure period* refers to the average number of days between the opening of a bug and its resolution for all bugs closed on the same day. *Rolling closure period* is the average for all closed bugs, including the current day and all previous days. Figure 4-22 shows the closure period chart for the SpeedyWriter project. As you can see, the daily plot tends to pull the rolling plot toward it, although the ever-increasing inertia of the rolling average makes it harder to influence as the project proceeds.

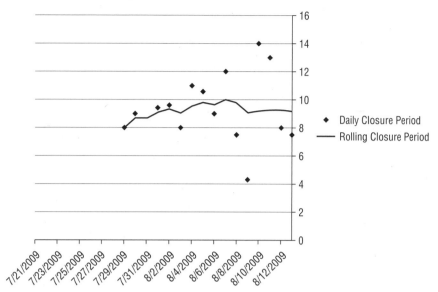

Figure 4-22 A closure period chart for SpeedyWriter

It's useful to look at closure period in terms of stability and acceptability. A stable closure period chart shows a relatively low variance from one day to another, with the slope of the rolling closure curve remaining almost constant and close to zero. In addition, to the extent that the daily closure period changes, it fluctuates randomly around the rolling closure curve, staying within a few days in either direction.

On an acceptable closure period chart, both the daily and rolling closure curves fall within the upper and lower limits set in the project or test plan for bug turnaround time. Although the pressures of the typical project make it hard to believe, there is indeed a lower limit for an acceptable closure period. Bugs deferred the day they are opened pull the daily closure curve toward zero, but the bug remains in the product. I audited a project once where the team took test releases two or three times a day for bugs identified just hours before. Although the closure period was very quick (a little over a day), that project had a significant number of bug reports that had been reopened multiple times, one of them 10 times. Haste makes waste, as the cliché goes. Finally, an acceptable daily closure curve does not exhibit a significant trend toward either boundary.

A closure period chart that is both stable and acceptable indicates a well-understood, smoothly functioning bug management process. The ideal is a low number with a downward or level trend, since an efficient bug management process drives bugs through their state transitions to closure with all deliberate speed. The closure period in Figure 4-22 is stable and, if management is realistic in its expectations, acceptable. Bugs tend to get fixed and confirmed closed in about a week and a half, which is a good pace if you assume one-week cycles and don't admit experimental bug fixes into the lab during cycles. Note that if the developers could fix bugs instantly, the lower bound on the process would be four days, given weekly releases into the test environment and about a day of confirmation testing per test release.

What Was Broken: The Subsystem Chart

Like the root cause breakdown, the subsystem breakdown is a simple chart with an important message: it tells you which subsystems experience the most bugs. Like the root cause chart, it's useful to format this as a Pareto chart, as shown in Figure 4-23, because usually two or three subsystems suffer the most problems.

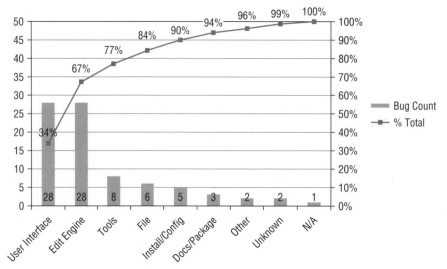

Figure 4-23 A subsystem breakdown for SpeedyWriter

You can use a subsystem chart in the same way you use a root cause chart, to focus process and product improvement efforts. The fact that the user interface and the edit engine account for two out of every three bugs found in SpeedyWriter, for example, indicates that an effort to make fewer mistakes in these areas would pay off handsomely. Moreover, if you are dividing your test effort evenly among the six subsystems, you should consider spending most of your testers' time on these two problem areas.

This conclusion might seem counterintuitive — after all, if you didn't find many bugs in the other four subsystems, maybe you should have spent more time looking in those four categories. And you certainly should do this if post-release field problems indicate a disproportionate number of test escapes in these four areas. However, as Glenford Myers points out in *The Art of Software Testing*, where you find many bugs, you will find more bugs. Therefore, you can predict from the SpeedyWriter data that most of the field bugs will also come from the user interface or the edit engine. For subsequent SpeedyWriter releases, you should spend even more time and resources looking for bugs in these subsystems.

However, this advice comes with a caveat. Let's suppose that we know, through a magic crystal ball, that a given release of SpeedyWriter contains 400 bugs. Further, suppose we have two test teams, Test Team A and Test Team B, each running SpeedyWriter system test. After the first test cycle, Test Team A looks at Figure 4-23. They decide to focus the rest of the testing effort on the user interface and the edit engine, and they succeed in finding all the bugs in those subsystems. Conversely, Test Team B decides that the current test approach is fine, and they end up finding the same percentage of bugs in each subsystem in the rest of the bugs they find. Both teams find 238 bugs (see Table 4-1). Which team did a better job?

Table 4-1 A Tale of Two Test Teams

SUBSYSTEM	ACTUAL BUGS	TEST TEAM A	TEST TEAM B
User Interface	100	100	74
Edit Engine	100	100	66
Tools	50	10	20
File	50	8	28
Install/Configuration	50	7	28
Documentation/Packaging	25	7	12
Other	10	2	4
Unknown	10	2	4
N/A	5	2	2
Total	400	238	238

The answer depends on risk. If the user interface and the edit engine are the highest-risk subsystems, and bugs in other subsystems will cause little if any trouble to users, operators, and other system stakeholders, then Test Team A is doing the right thing. However, in the case of a typical mass-market application like a word processor, users do care about file operations, installation and configuration, tools, documentation, and even packaging. In this case, what we know about the risks for mass-market applications tells us that Test Team

B is on the right track. Therefore, while Figure 4-23 can tell you about technical risk — where the most bugs live — it doesn't tell you about business risk, which is an important consideration in my approach to using testing to help manage the risks to the quality of the system.

An After-the-Fact Metric: Defect Detection Percentage

So far, we've been looking at metrics and charts that we generate during the project, but there is one very important defect metric that you might want to examine shortly after the project concludes. This metric is called the *defect detection percentage* or *defect detection effectiveness*, and was briefly mentioned in Chapter 3. Remember that I said that mathematically, the defect detection percentage is defined as follows:

$$DDE = \frac{\text{Test bugs}}{\text{Test bugs + Production bugs}}$$

In this equation, test bugs are the unique, true bugs found by the test team. This number excludes duplicates, non-problems, test and tester errors, and other spurious bug reports, but includes any bugs found but not fixed due to deferral or other management prioritization decisions. Production bugs are the unique, true bugs found by users or customers after release that were reported to technical support and for which a fix was released; in other words, bugs that represented real quality problems. Again, this number excludes duplicates, non-problems, customer, user, and configuration errors, and other spurious field problem reports, and excludes any bugs found but not fixed due to deferral or other management prioritization decisions. In this case, excluding duplicates means that production bugs do not include bugs found by users or customers that were previously detected by testers, developers, or other prerelease activities but were deferred or otherwise deprioritized, because that would be double-counting the bug. In other words, there is only one bug, no matter how many times it is found and reported.

To calculate this metric, we need to have the bug-tracking system discussed in this chapter, but we also need a way to track bugs found in production. Most help-desk or technical support organizations have such data, so it's usually just a matter of figuring out how to sort and collate the information from the two (often) distinct databases. We also have to decide on a time window. That depends on how long it takes for your customers to find 80 percent or so of the bugs they will find over the entire post-release life cycle of the system. For laptop computers, for example, the rate of customer encounters with new bugs (unrelated to new releases, patches, and so forth) in a release tends to fall off very close to zero after the first three to six months. Therefore, if you perform the calculation at three months, adjust upward by some historical factor — say 10 to 20 percent — you should have a fairly accurate estimate of production bugs, and furthermore one for which you can, based on your historical metrics, predict the statistical accuracy if need be.

Note that this is a measure of test effectiveness as a bug-finding filter. Finding bugs and giving the project team an opportunity to fix them before release is typically one of the major goals for a test team. Ideally, this metric would be 100 percent, because we'd like to find all the bugs before release. Realistically, though, we have to distinguish between what we *should* test and what we *can* test, as discussed in Chapter 1. To adjust for that, we can eliminate customer-identified bugs that are outside the scope of testing as defined in Chapters 1 and 2. In other words, we only count bugs found by the customer if they could have reasonably been found by the test team during the test project agreed to with the project management team.

A Note on Metrics and Charts

As you accumulate historical defect data — on both good and bad projects — you can compare charts from your current projects with charts from previous projects. Such comparisons can be enlightening. Even within a single class of projects such as laptop-computer development, I have seen variances of 600 percent in the total number of bugs found. Beyond the simple totals, the shapes of the curves can also differ. If you use these charts consistently across a few projects, you will soon recognize virtuous and evil shapes.

Avoid blind faith in your charts, though. One key assumption of the opened/closed chart is *ceteris paribus* (all things held equal). You can arbitrarily flatten any cumulative opened curve by stopping the test effort. You can cause the opened and closed curves to converge by deferring bugs rather than fixing them. You can spoof opened and closed dates in the database to make the opened/closed chart fit any profile you choose (as I did to create the sample charts in this section). You can easily rig the closure period chart, too. Breakdowns in the bug triage process, recording phony opened and closed dates, opening new bug reports rather than reopening existing ones when fixes fail in confirmation testing, and other manipulation of the opened and closed dates will defeat your purpose. Finally, carelessness when assigning subsystems and root causes to bugs renders these charts worse than pointless. Nothing good can come of making resource allocation decisions — or any decision, for that matter — based on phony data.

Similar cautions apply to any other analysis of defect or test data. For your analyses to have meaning, the underlying data must be accurate, complete, and free from gerrymandering. Only honest data yields worthwhile information.

The reports, charts, tables, and forms presented in this chapter are just starters. With a little imagination, you can extract all types of useful data and reports from a bug-tracking database. Start with simple tasks, learn the tool, and then expand it to meet your needs. In Chapters 5 and 9, we'll revisit this topic, augmenting bug data with test result data to build what I call a balanced scorecard or dashboard for the test operation.[8]

Managing Bug Tracking

When projects are in a test execution phase, I probably spend 10 to 20 percent of my time working with bugs, either those already reported or those about to be reported. Because testing should mitigate quality risks, and because a bug report documents the transition of a quality risk into a known bug, I consider bug reports one of the most important products of the test effort. Time devoted to understanding and managing bug data is time well spent.

The preceding section on metrics might have given you the impression that managing bugs consists mostly of analyzing data and gleaning meaning. I wish it were! You'll soon discover two other areas of concern. The first is staying aware of the politics and potential misuse of the bug data. The second is dealing with certain types of problematic bug reports that can consume a disproportionate share of your time.

Politics and Misuse of Bug Data

Chapter 9 deals with management considerations and the politics of the test manager's position in detail. Here, however, we should briefly examine political issues that are specifically related to bug data. From the most adversarial point of view, for example, you can see every bug report as an attack on a developer. You probably don't — and certainly shouldn't — intend to offend, but it helps to remember that bug data is potentially embarrassing and subject to misuse. Candor and honesty are critical in gathering clean bug data, but developers might distort the facts if they think you might use the data to slam them with the bug reports. Think of the detailed bug information your database captures as a loaded gun: an effective tool in the right hands and used with caution, but a dangerous implement of mayhem if it's treated carelessly.

Don't Fail to Build Trust

Most experienced developers support bug-tracking efforts. Nevertheless, some individuals — especially those who have experienced highly adversarial test/development relationships — won't disclose any more information to you than required, and they might do so with an uncooperative attitude. I once worked with a development manager who wanted to argue over every bug report. Bug triage meetings with this guy were a misery of semantic

---

[8]For more on these kinds of analyses, see my other book, *Critical Testing Processes*.

arguments punctuated with repeated assertions that any bug he had succeeded in ignoring for the past three or four weeks had probably been fixed in some recent release and should be retested by my team. In his mind, our relationship was by nature purely adversarial. There was no trust.

Some situations are irretrievable. Developers who are convinced that a written bug report is one step removed from a written warning in their personnel files probably will never trust you. Most developers, though, approach testing with an open mind. They understand that testing can provide a useful service to them in helping them fix bugs and deliver a better product. How do you keep the trust and support of these developers?

- Don't take bugs personally, and don't become emotional about them. The times I have anointed myself the defender of quality and acted holier-than-thou with my colleagues are moments in my professional life that I look back on with embarrassment and regret. Even if you're right on the issue, you're doing the wrong thing because you end up alienating people with whom you need to maintain a professional and trusting relationship.

- Submit only quality bug reports: a succinct summary, clear steps to reproduce, evidence of significant isolation work, accuracy in classification information, and a conservative estimate in terms of priority and severity. Also try to avoid cheap shot bug reports that can seem like carping.

- Be willing to discuss bug reports with an open mind. No matter how convinced you are that a program or a computer is malfunctioning, you should listen to developers when they explain that the bug is actually correct behavior. If you make the extra effort to discuss their opinions, it goes a long way toward keeping the flow of information moving.

- If developers want you to change something in your bug-reporting process, be open to their suggestions. They are, after all, some of the key customers for your bug report product. If they want reports delivered in a different fashion, advance warning before summaries go to management, or additional information in the reports, try to accommodate them whenever it's practical to do so.

Most of these suggestions are simple common courtesy and professionalism. You don't have to compromise your role in order to keep reasonable developers satisfied that you aren't grinding an ax.

Don't Be a Backseat Driver

The test manager needs to ensure that testers identify, reproduce, and isolate bugs. It's also part of the job to track the bugs to conclusion and to deliver crisp bug status summaries to senior and executive management. These roles differ, though, from managing bug *fixes*. In most of the organizations I've worked in, managing the bug fix process was the development manager's job; ensuring that this process moves at a satisfactory pace was the program manager's job. Even if some managers encourage you, don't get sucked into doing either.

If you, as an outsider, make it your job to nag developers about when a specific bug will be fixed or to pester the development manager about how slow the bug fix process is, you are setting yourself up for a highly antagonistic situation. Reporting, tracking, re-testing, and summarizing bugs are your worries. Whether any particular bug gets fixed, how it gets fixed, and when it gets fixed are someone else's concerns.

Don't Make Individuals Look Bad

It is a bad idea to create and distribute reports that make individuals look bad. There's probably no faster way to guarantee that you will have trouble getting estimated fix dates out of people than to produce a report that points out every failure to meet such estimated dates. Creating reports that show how many bug fixes resulted in reopened rather than closed bugs, grouped and totaled by developer, is another express lane to bad relationships. Again, managing the developers is the development manager's job, not yours. No matter how useful a particular report seems, make sure that it doesn't bash individuals.

Sticky Wickets

Challenging bugs crop up on nearly every project. The most vexing are those that involve questions about correct behavior, prairie dog bugs that pop up only when they feel like it, and bugs that cause a tug-of-war over priority.

Bug or Feature?

Although a perfect development project provides you with clear and unambiguous information about correct system behavior in the form of requirements and specifications, you will seldom have such good fortune. Many projects have only informal specifications, and the requirements can be scattered around in emails, product road maps, and sales materials. In such cases, disagreements can arise between development and test over whether a particular bug is in fact correct system behavior.

How should you settle these differences? Begin by discussing the situation with the developers, their manager, and your testers. Most of these disagreements arise from miscommunication. Before making a major issue out of it, confirm that all the parties are clear on what the alleged bug is and why your team is concerned.

Suppose that everyone understands the problem the test team is reporting, but the development team insists that the system is behaving properly, while you remain unconvinced. At this point, you might want to get other groups involved. Technical support, help desk staff, marketing, business analysts, sales, and the project manager might have strong opinions. Even if consulting with other people doesn't resolve the dispute, it at least escalates the problem to the proper level of attention.

If, after all the jawboning is over, you are the lone skeptic, now what? Insisting that the bug remain assigned to the recalcitrant developer won't help. If the bug remains active, you'll be forced to rehash this discussion every time you circulate your bug list. My preference is to cancel the bug — in other words, in the bug database I introduced in this chapter, put it in a *Closed* state with a root cause of *NAP* — but make a notation on the record that I disagree.

Irreproducible Bug

The challenge with irreproducible bugs comes in two flavors. First, some bugs simply refuse to reproduce their symptoms consistently. This is especially the case in system testing, in which complex combinations of conditions are required to re-create problems. Sometimes these types of failures occur in clusters. If you see a bug three times in one day and then don't see it for a week, has it disappeared, or is it just hiding? Tempting as it is to dismiss this problem, be sure to write up these bugs. Random, intermittent failures — especially ones that result in system crashes or any other data loss — can have a significant effect on customers.

The second category of irreproducible bugs involves problems that seem to disappear with new revisions of the system, although no specific fix was made for them. I refer to these as "bugs fixed by accident." You will find that more bugs are fixed by accident than you expect, but that fewer are fixed by accident than some project Pollyannas suggest. If the bug is an elusive one, you might want to keep the bug report active until you're convinced it's actually gone.

Deferring Trivia or Creating Test Escapes?

While bug severity is easy to quantify, priority is not. Developing consensus on priority is often difficult. What do you do when bugs are assigned a low priority? Bugs that will not be fixed should be deferred. If you don't keep the active bug list short, people will start to ignore it. However, there's a real risk that some deferred bugs will come back to haunt you. For this reason, a bug triage committee or CCB should make the final call on priority and deferral. In many cases, though, I didn't have the benefit of a bug triage committee, and so had to build consensus around bugs via email and face-to-face discussions. In these cases, when a bug was assigned a low priority and then ignored, I pressed for a clear decision about whether the bug would be fixed or deferred rather than discussing it repeatedly. What if a deferred bug pops up in the field as a critical issue? Is that a test escape? Not if my team found it and then deferred it on the advice or insistence of the project manager.

After you institute a bug-tracking system, including the database and metrics discussed here, you will find yourself the keeper of key indicators of project status. As I've emphasized, *fairness* and *accuracy* should be your watchwords in this role. Your peers and your managers will use your database and charts to make both tactical (day-to-day) and strategic (project-wide) decisions. If you take these activities seriously and apply the tools introduced in this chapter conscientiously, you and your test organization will provide invaluable assistance to the project team in creating the best possible product.

Case Study

Prior to my team getting involved in the loan processing application project discussed in the case study for Chapter 2, another team ran a test project against a previous release of the application. The test project ran from August 20 to November 12. The case study bug metrics document, "Case Study Loan Processing Bug Metrics.xls," is available at www.rbcs-us.com. Please note that, due to a lack of root cause data, only three of the four charts mentioned in this chapter are shown.

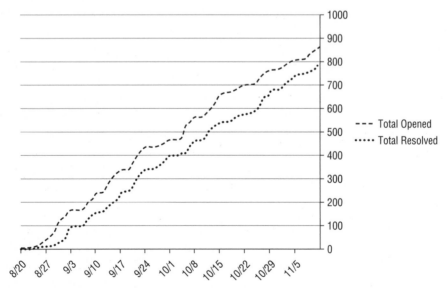

Figure 4-24 Case study opened/closed chart

The opened/closed chart in Figure 4-24 resembles Figure 4-18, and this was indeed the situation: the bug reports just never stopped coming. A number of factors contributed to the inability of the project team to stabilize the system's quality. One was frequent change in the requirements. Another was excessive regression; for example, one bug report was re-opened 10 times. Another was too-frequent (daily and sometimes hourly) test releases, which prevented the test team from getting through the planned tests. Ultimately, the release was cancelled in lieu of the subsequent project, which was the one my team worked on.

I thank my client on this project, a major Midwestern financial institution, and the executive in charge of development for allowing me to share this example with readers of this book. I have purged all identifying and otherwise private information from this document. My client contact has asked that the organization remain anonymous.

Exercises

1. Refer to Figure 4-25, which shows a poorly written bug report for the Omninet project. Referring to the discussion earlier in this chapter on good bug reporting, what improvements are needed? What additional testing might you do to gather information?

> Summary: Session lasts too long.
> Steps to Reproduce:
> 1. Swipe credit card in payment subsystem.
> 2. Buy some blocks of time.
> 3. Start a stopwatch when surfing starts.
> 4. Session will last between one and five minutes too long.

Figure 4-25 A bug report with problems

2. Using either exploratory testing or the test cases you created in Chapter 3, find a functionality bug in an application or utility running on your PC or workstation. (Sadly, this will not be hard.)

   ▪ Write a bug report following the 10-step process outlined in this chapter.

   ▪ Have a colleague or fellow student review your bug report. How many changes did you make based on the review?

   ▪ Repeat steps the preceding two steps for a user-interface or usability bug.

3. In the case study, I mentioned three factors outside the test process that contributed to the failure of the case study system to achieve stable quality Frequent requirements change, excessive regression, frequent test releases interfering with timely planned test completion). Refer to Figure 4-26 and note that almost 20 percent of the bug reports are opened more than once. What change to the test process could we make to help the development team spend less time in rework?

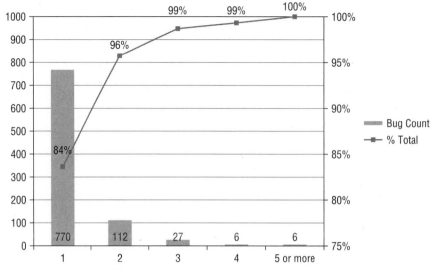

Figure 4-26 Bug opened count for the case study

4. One important — and difficult — part of estimating for a test project is predicting how long it will take to find and fix all the important bugs. Notice that, if we can predict when the cumulative opened curve will flatten and when the cumulative closed curve will intercept the cumulative opened curve, then we can predict this key indicator of quality. Given enough historical bug-tracking data, along with information about the size of the project, you can develop models using a spreadsheet to make these predictions in your organization, provided the teams and processes remain stable over time. These models are simple but effective forms of defect removal models, which I referred to earlier in this chapter. While such a model is not 100-percent accurate, such a model is at least based on data, not on wishful thinking, and can be improved over the course of multiple projects.

   ■ To know when we'll be done finding bugs, we have to know how many bugs we are going to find. Suppose we know that during system test we find two defects per person-month of estimated team effort on average for our projects. If we have 150 person-months of effort estimated for this project, how many bugs do you expect to find? (Note: While thousands of source lines of code [KSLOC] and function points [FP] are often considered to be more accurate units for sizing projects, estimated person-months of effort is perhaps the most easily gathered metric of project size.)

   ■ Suppose we find on average 1.25 bugs per tester day, and you have eight testers assigned. How many working days will it take to find all the bugs you'll find in system test? Assuming weekly test cycles, how many test cycles is this?

▪ Suppose half of the bugs in each test release are found during each test cycle that covers that test release. Suppose that the remaining predicted bugs are found in the last test cycle. In other words, the first test cycle finds half of the bugs that will be found in system test, and each subsequent cycle finds half the remaining bugs, until the last cycle finds all the remaining bugs. Calculate and graph the expected cumulative opened curve.

▪ Based on a histogram of closure periods from previous projects such as the one shown in Figure 4-27, suppose that roughly three-quarters of the bugs found in the previous test release are fixed in the next test release. Further suppose that three-quarters of any bugs remaining from any previous test release are likewise fixed in each release. Assume that the last test cycle results in the closure of all remaining bugs. Calculate and graph the expected cumulative closed curve.

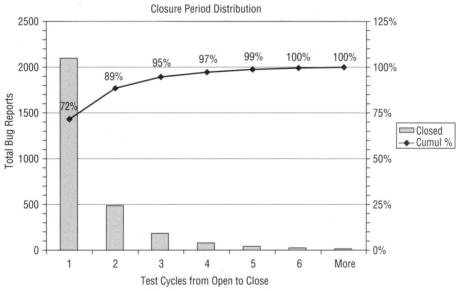

Figure 4-27 Closure period distribution for exercise 4

▪ Based on this model, how long will it be before you are ready to exit system test, assuming the exit criteria include finding and closing all bugs?

CHAPTER 5

Managing Test Cases: The Test Tracking Spreadsheet

Quick! For your last three test projects, answer the following questions:

- How many test cases did you plan to run?
- How many test cases did you actually run?
- How many tests failed? Of those, how many later passed when the bug was fixed?
- Did the tests take less or more time, on average, than you expected?
- Did you skip any tests? If so, why?
- Did your tests cover all the important risks to system quality?
- Did your management ever ask for a cumulative summary of test results, both passed and failed? If so, did you provide an accurate summary, or did you take a SWAG (scientific wild-ass guess)?

On any given project, I can answer these questions by checking my test tracking spreadsheet, a tool I use to manage test execution. This chapter shows you how to create and utilize this tool.

In its most basic form, the test tracking spreadsheet is a to-do list, with the added capability of status tracking. Using DataRocket as a case study, this chapter demonstrates how to build an abbreviated test tracking spreadsheet for system testing. We'll begin our example with a minimalist, or stripped-down, model of the spreadsheet. As you learn to add enhancements and to adapt this tool to fit your own needs, you should eventually be able to implement a complete set of test tracking and reporting capabilities using the spreadsheet as the foundation. As you'll see, you can also integrate individual test cases constructed with the approach outlined in Chapter 3. Finally, we'll pull in the bug metrics discussed in Chapter 4, combine them with some important test metrics, and build a simple but powerful and balanced test dashboard.

WHAT IF YOU USE A TEST MANAGEMENT TOOL?

This chapter and the previous chapter describe the construction of simple tools, using common desktop applications, to create a simple test management system. However, you might already use a tool like HP's Quality Center. Or you might prefer to buy such a tool.

In that case, you should look at Chapter 4 and Chapter 5 as defining the requirements for such a tool. A good test management tool should provide the capabilities I'm discussing in these two chapters. You might choose to use two tools, one to track bugs and another to track tests. In some cases, you might need to extend one or both of these tools to add the capabilities I describe here.

Building a Minimalist Test Tracking Spreadsheet

Let's start by building a very simple test tracking spreadsheet, and then see how we can adapt it to our case study.

The Basic Spreadsheet

To keep our sample worksheets relatively small, let's suppose that you have defined a simple four-suite system test phase. You intend to run these four test suites:

- Environmental
- Load, Capacity, and Volume
- Basic Functionality
- Standards

You want to track the status of each test case, the configuration against which the test was run, and who ran the test. You also want to summarize the test status numerically.

Figure 5-1 shows an example of a test case summary worksheet as it might appear halfway into the first cycle of system testing. The first column of the Excel worksheet (Test Suite/Case) contains the names of the test suites and, within each suite, the test cases. The names are short mnemonics that convey an idea of the test's purpose. In the second column (State), you can record the state of each test case. A blank entry in this column means that the test case is still queued for execution. A *Pass* entry signifies that the test case did not identify any bugs; *Fail* indicates that one or more bugs were found.

	A	B	C	D	E	F	G	H	I
1		DataRocket System Test Tracking							
2			System	Bug				Roll Up	
3	Test Suite/Case	Status	Config	ID	By	Comment	T	F	P
4	*Environmental*								
5	Operating Thermal Profile	Pass	D		HS		1	0	1
6	Operating Temp/Humid Cycle	Pass	D		HS		1	0	1
7	Nonoperating Temp/Humid Cycle	Fail	D	017	HS		1	1	0
8	Nonoperating Drop	Pass	D		HS		1	0	1
9	Nonoperating Shock	Pass	D		HS		1	0	1
10	Nonoperating Thermal Shock	Pass	D		HS		1	0	1
11	Packaging Drop					Package not ready yet	1	0	0
12	Packagin Shock					Package not ready yet	1	0	0
13	**Suite Summary**						8	1	5
14									
15	*Load, Capacity, and Volume*								
16	CPU and Memory	Pass	A,B,C		JR		1	0	1
17	FDD/USB/DVD Drive	Fail	A,B,C	020	JR		1	1	0
18	RAID	Pass	A,B,C		JR		1	0	1
19	Tape	Fail	A,B,C	020	JR		1	1	0
20	Network	Pass	A,B,C		JR		1	0	1
21	Modem Bank	Pass	A,B,C		JR		1	0	1
22	USB/Parallel/Firewire	Pass	A,B,C		JR		1	0	1
23	**Suite Summary**						7	2	5
24									
25	*Basic Functionality*								
26	Configure/Register Windows						1	0	0
27	Configure/Register Solaris						1	0	0
28	Configure/Register Linux						1	0	0
29	FDD/USB/DVD Drive						1	0	0
30	RAID						1	0	0
31	Tape						1	0	0
32	Network-Windows						1	0	0
33	Network-Linux						1	0	0
34	Network-PC-NFS						1	0	0
35	Modem Bank						1	0	0
36	USB/Parallel/Firewire						1	0	0
37	UI (Video/Kbd/Mouse)						1	0	0
38	**Suite Summary**						12	0	0
39									
40	*Standards*								
41	Solaris Certification						1	0	0
42	Window Certification						1	0	0
43	Linux Certification						1	0	0
44	**Suite Summary**						3	0	0

Figure 5-1 A test case summary worksheet, halfway through the first cycle of system testing

The System Config column lists an identifier for the system configuration used in each test case. A separate worksheet that serves as a lookup table, shown in Figure 5-2, allows you to record important details about each configuration, such as the motherboard revision, the BIOS level, the operating system, the specific network setup, and any additional software or hardware involved in the test.

	A	B	C	D	E	F	G
1							
2	System Config ID	MB Rev	BIOS	OS	Network	Other SW	Other HW
3	A	ST-01	X.015	Solaris	100MB		
4	B	ST-01	X.015	Windows Server	100MB		
5	C	ST-02	X.016	Linux	1GB		
6	D	ST-01	X.015	Windows Server	1GB		

Figure 5-2 A configuration lookup table in the System Config worksheet

Returning to the test case summary worksheet in Figure 5-1, notice the Bug ID column. For any test case that finds a failure, this column should contain the bug identifier from the bug tracking database. If a test finds more than one failure — in other words, more than one bug is reported based on the test's outcome — then I use one extra row per additional bug report directly below the test case row to track the bug IDs. I find this approach more elegant than letting the Bug ID column get wider and wider to accommodate a few test cases that have five or 10 bugs reported against them.

The By column on the worksheet contains the initials of the tester(s) who ran the test, and the Comment column allows you to enter text to provide more information on the test case status.

The last three columns of the worksheet in Figure 5-1, which I refer to as the Roll Up columns, help you summarize the status information. Each test case can be assigned three numeric values based on its state:

- The T column contains the value 1 if the row lists a test case. For example, in Figure 5-1, there is a 1 in cell G5 because cell A5 contains the name of a test case, Operating Thermal Profile, and the rest of the information in row 5 concerns that test case. Conversely, cell G4 is blank because cell A4 contains the name of a test suite, Environmental, not a test case.

- The F column contains a formula that computes the value 1 if the test case in that row has a Fail state (and computes the value 0 otherwise). For example, in Figure 5-1, there is a 1 in cell H7 because the corresponding test case, Nonoperating Temp/Humid Cycle, has the word *Fail* in cell B7 (column B is the State column). Conversely, Cell H6 contains a 0 because the corresponding test case, Operating Temp/Humid cycle, has the word *Pass* in cell B6.

- The P column contains a formula that computes the value 1 if the test case in that row has a Pass state (and computes the value 0 otherwise). To turn the preceding example around, in Figure 5-1 there is a 1 in cell I6 because the corresponding test case, Operating Temp/Humid Cycle, has the word *Pass* in cell B6. Conversely, Cell I7 contains a 0 because the corresponding test case, Nonoperating Temp/Humid Cycle, has the word *Fail* in cell B7.

In the Suite Summary rows — rows 13, 23, 38, and 44 in Figure 5-1 — you can add these three columns to see how many test cases are in the test suite and how many test cases are in each state. For easiest reference, you should also set up a third worksheet that will display the test case counts for each test suite. Figure 5-3 offers an example of such a test suite summary worksheet.

	A	B	C	D	E
1					
2					
3					
4		Total			In
5	Suite	Cases	Fail	Pass	Queue
6	Enviromental				
7	Load, Capacity, and Volume	8	1	5	2
8	Basic Functionality	7	2	5	0
9	Standards	12	0	0	12
10		3	0	0	3
11	Total				
12	By Pct	30	3	10	17
13			10%	33%	57%

Figure 5-3 A test suite summary worksheet

At this point, you have a simple but informative test tracking spreadsheet that provides test case details, with a reference to the bug tracking database for more data on failures. (Adventuresome types might want to use advanced features to allow you to "click through" the bug ID on the test case summary worksheet to the database. In the bug tracking database, you could even add the ability to track the test cases associated with a particular bug, and "click through" from the bug tracking database to the test case summary worksheet.) This spreadsheet offers, in the test suite summary, a management-level perspective of the test execution results. The spreadsheet also contains information about the test environment that will be useful in attempting to reproduce failures, in debugging, and in analyzing root causes. In addition, the spreadsheet identifies the tester(s) in case you need to follow up with questions about the testing performed.

Using the Test Tracking Spreadsheet on Test Projects

You might recall that in Chapter 1 (see the "Shoehorning: Fitting a Test Schedule into the Project" section) and Chapter 2 (see the "Release Management" section) I discussed the concepts of test passes, test releases, and test cycles. I refer to one complete execution of all the planned test cases as a *test pass*, while a *test cycle* is the subset of the test pass run against a single test release. I've reproduced that illustration from Chapter 1 as Figure 5-4 for convenient reference. In this figure, you can see that the test team intends to run each test three times during the test phase shown there, with half the tests run in each of the six cycles against the six test releases. How does this plan affect the test tracking spreadsheet?

Figure 5-4 Test passes, test releases, and test cycles

There are a few ways you can handle it. The most obvious way is to have one test case summary worksheet and one test suite summary worksheet for the entire test phase. The problem with this approach is that test case status will change at least with each pass, and you will lose information about how tests behaved in the first two passes as you update the worksheets. Therefore, another approach is to have one pair of worksheets (test case summary and test suite summary) for each test cycle. However, now you'll see that only half of your tests are planned to be run in each worksheet, which can create some problems with gathering metrics and summarizing results. (I'll talk about test case metrics and charts toward the end of this chapter.)

My preference is to have one pair of worksheets for each pass. That way, each test case summary shows all the test cases ready to run for that pass. Based on the date on which the test was run — which I'll discuss in the next section — I can tell which test release I ran each test against, although you could also add a column to track release IDs if you'd prefer. The downside to this approach is that test case status is not really a snapshot of an assessment of quality, since I've accepted a new test release in the middle of the pass if I'm following the approach just described. (If you think of testing software as analogous to testing a new drug, accepting a test release before you've run all the tests is similar to changing one or two ingredients in the drug during your drug trial before you've finished assessing the drug's safety and efficacy.) However, I've found that I can deal with that situation provided the new release doesn't result in excessive regression of previously passed tests; I just take a calculated risk that I can wait to catch any regressions in the next cycle. If, by having a compact test set, lots of testers, or good automation, I can make my pass and cycle lengths the same, this problem goes away.

In terms of how I use this tool, my approach is to have a once-a-day test team debriefing, usually at the end of the day, where I sit down with each tester one-on-one. In this debriefing, I ask about the tests run over the course of the day, the findings of those tests, and what tests remain to be run. I review each bug report filed. As I go through the debriefing, I update the test case summary worksheet. That way, that worksheet serves as a structured agenda for my debriefing session. If I have too many people reporting to me on a project to make this practical, I assign two or more lead test engineers to do the debriefing. I ask them to report significant findings that affect the outcome of the test project to me after their debriefing sessions. I generally find that if the end-of-day debriefing includes five or fewer people, it can be done in an hour or less.

Making Enhancements

Although the basic test tracking spreadsheet you've just seen is useful, you can certainly improve it to record and analyze even more information. Figure 5-5 and Figure 5-6 show an extended version of this tracking spreadsheet, with lots of useful enhancements that I've added over the years. The following sections describe how these data items help me manage my test projects. You might want to incorporate some of them (or come up with others on your own).

Assigning Identifiers and Testers to Test Suites and Cases

In addition to using short names for test suites and test cases, you can assign a Dewey decimal–style ID number to each. In a Test ID column, inserted to the left of the Test Suite/Case column, you can number each test suite, starting with 1.000, then 2.000, and so on. Each test case carries the suite number to the left of the decimal and its own sequential ID to the right of the decimal. For example, in the test case summary shown in Figure 5-1, the Load, Capacity, and Volume test suite would have the test ID 2.000, and the test ID for the CPU and Memory test case would be 2.001; likewise, the test ID for the Tape test case in the Basic Functionality test suite would be 3.006.

	A	B	C	D	E	F	G	H	I	J	K	L	M	N	O	P	Q	R	S	T	U	V	W
1			DataRocket System Test Case Summary																				
2					Pass One																		
3		Test			System	Bug	Bug		Plan	Act	Plan	Act	Plan	Act					Roll Up Columns				
4	Owner	ID	Test Suite/Case	Status	Config	ID	RPN	By	Date	Date	Effort	Effort	Dur	Dur	Comment	T	S	P	F	FW	Q	I	B
5	System Cookers. Inc.																						
6		1.000	*Environmental Test*																				
7		1.001	Operating Thermal Profile	Pass	D			SC	7/13	7/14	4	4	72	72		1	0	1	0	0	0	0	0
8		1.002	Operating Temp/Humid Cycle	Pass	D			SC	7/13	7/14	4	4	72	72		1	0	1	0	0	0	0	0
9		1.003	Non-operating Temp/Humid Cycle	Pass	D			SC	7/13	7/14	4	4	72	72		1	0	1	0	0	0	0	0
10		1.004	Non-operating Drop	Pass	D			SC	7/13	7/14	2	2	2	2		1	0	1	0	0	0	0	0
11		1.005	Non-operating Shock	Pass	D			SC	7/13	7/14	2	2	2	2		1	0	1	0	0	0	0	0
12		1.006	Non-operating Thermal Shock	Pass	D			SC	7/13	7/14	2	2	72	72		1	0	1	0	0	0	0	0
13		1.007	Packaging Drop	Pass	D			SC	7/13	7/14	2	2	2	2		1	0	1	0	0	0	0	0
14		1.008	Packagin Shock	Pass	D			SC	7/13	7/14	2	2	2	2		1	0	1	0	0	0	0	0
15			Suite Summary						7/13	7/14	22	22	296	296		8	0	8	0	0	0	0	0
16	Winged Bytes																						
17	LTW	2.000	*Load, Capacity, and Volume*																				
18		2.001	CPU and Memory	Fail	A,B,C	009	2	LTW	7/10	7/6	4	6	6	7		1	0	0	1	1/2	0	0	0
19						010	6													1/6			
20		2.002	FDD/USB/DVD Drive	Pass	A,B,C			LTW	7/10	7/6	4	4	4	4		1	0	1	0	0	0	0	0
21		2.003	RAID	Pass	A,B,C			LTW	7/10	7/6	4	4	4	4		1	0	1	0	0	0	0	0
22		2.004	Tape	Pass	A,B,C			LTW	7/10	7/7	4	4	4	4		1	0	1	0	0	0	0	0
23		2.005	Network	Pass	A,B,C			LTW	7/10	7/7	4	4	4	4		1	0	1	0	0	0	0	0
24		2.006	Modem Bank	Pass	A,B,C			LTW	7/10	7/8	4	4	4	4		1	0	1	0	0	0	0	0
25		2.007	USB/Parallel/Firewire	Pass	A,B,C			LTW	7/10	7/8	4	4	4	4		1	0	1	0	0	0	0	0
26		2.008	All Subsystems	Pass	A,B,C			LTW	7/10	7/10	4	4	4	4		1	0	1	0	0	0	0	0
27			Suite Summary						7/10	7/10	32	34	34	35		8	0	7	1	0.6667	0	0	0
28																							
29	JC	3.000	*Basic Functionality*																				
30		3.001	Configure/Register Windows	Pass	A,B,C			JC	7/9	7/7	2	2	2	2		1	0	1	0	0	0	0	0
31		3.002	Configure/Register Solaris	Pass	A,B,C			JC	7/9	7/7	2	2	2	2		1	0	1	0	0	0	0	0
32		3.003	Configure/Register Linux	Pass	A,B,C			JC	7/9	7/7	2	2	2	2		1	0	1	0	0	0	0	0
33		3.004	FDD/USB/DVD Drive	Pass	A,B,C			JC	7/9	7/7	2	2	2	2		1	0	1	0	0	0	0	0
34		3.005	RAID	Pass	A,B,C			JC	7/9	7/7	2	2	2	2		1	0	1	0	0	0	0	0
35		3.006	Tape	Pass	A,B,C			JC	7/9	7/7	2	2	2	2		1	0	1	0	0	0	0	0
36		3.007	Network-Windows	Pass	A,B,C			JC	7/9	7/7	2	2	2	2		1	0	1	0	0	0	0	0
37		3.008	Network-Linux	Pass	A,B,C			JC	7/9	7/9	2	1.5	2	1.5		1	0	1	0	0	0	0	0
38		3.009	Network-PC-NFS	Pass	A,B,C			JC	7/9	7/9	2	1.5	2	1.5		1	0	1	0	0	0	0	0
39		3.010	Modem Bank	Pass	A,B,C			JC	7/9	7/9	2	2.5	2	2.5		1	0	1	0	0	0	0	0
40		3.011	USB/Parallel/Firewire	Pass	A,B,C			JC	7/9	7/9	2	2.5	2	2.5		1	0	1	0	0	0	0	0
41		3.012	UI (Video/Kbd/Mouse)	Pass	A,B,C			JC	7/9	7/10	2	1	2	1		1	0	1	0	0	0	0	0
42			Suite Summary						7/9	7/10	18	17	18	17		12	0	12	0	0	0	0	0
43																							
44	HL	4.000	*Standards*																				
45		4.001	Solaris Certification	Pass	A			HL	7/8	7/7	8	8	16	16		1	0	1	0	0	0	0	0
46		4.002	Window Certification	Pass	B			HL	7/8	7/5	8	8	16	16		1	0	1	0	0	0	0	0
47		4.003	Linux Certification	Warn	C	005	25	HL	7/8	7/10	8	8	16	16		1	0	1	0	1/25	0	0	0
48			Suite Summary						7/8	7/10	24	24	48	48		3	0	3	0	0.04	0	0	0

Figure 5-5 An extended test case summary worksheet

	A	B	C	D	E	F	G	H	I	J	K	L	M	N	O
1				DataRocket System Test Suite Summary											
2					Pass One										
3															
4		Total	Planned Tests Fulfilled				Weighted	Planned Tests Unfulfilled				Earned Value			
5	Suite	Cases	Count	Skip	Pass	Fail	Failure	Count	Queued	IP	Block	Plan Eff	Act Eff	% Effort	% Exec
6															
7	Environmental Test	8	8	0	8	0	0.00	0	0	0	0	22.00	22.00	100%	100%
8	Load, Capacity and Volume	8	8	0	7	1	0.67	0	0	0	0	32.00	34.00	106%	100%
9	Basic Functionality	12	12	0	12	0	0.00	0	0	0	0	18.00	17.00	94%	100%
10	Standards	3	3	0	3	0	0.04	0	0	0	0	24.00	24.00	100%	100%
11															
12	Total	31	31	0	30	1	0.71	0	0	0	0	96.00	97.00	101%	100%
13	By Percentage		100%	0%	97%	3%		0%	0%	0%	0%				

Figure 5-6 An extended test suite summary worksheet

When more than one person will run tests, I find it useful to add an Owner column to the test case tracking worksheet. The owner might be the organization responsible for running the test, the engineer writing the test, or the test technician running the test. A test can have multiple owners over time. For example, a different tester might run each test in each test pass to get multiple perspectives.

Adding Date and Hours Information: Plan versus Actual

Your overall schedule is based in part on projected test completion dates, and one important component of your budget is projected effort (person-hours) per test case. Adding information about completion dates and effort to your test tracking spreadsheet can help you perform a reality check if your test project starts to deviate from the schedule or budget.

You can add two date columns, *Plan Date* and *Actual Date*, to the test case summary. The plan date comes from the schedule, based on when you expect to complete the test case. Remember that, if you're doing risk-based testing, the planned date should follow from the priority of the risk item that generated the test case. (If you don't use a planned date, then you should include a column with the risk priority number for the test case to help your testers sequence the tests.) Actual Date, the second date column, indicates when the tester actually completed the test.

You can also track actual and planned effort. I do this in person-hours. If you estimated that a test case would require 5 person-hours, but instead it took 10, that bears explaining. Conversely, you might find that another test case takes less effort than predicted. By accumulating these numbers and analyzing them, you can refine your plans for test cycles, improve your test cases, and figure out which test cases are consuming the most effort.

Now, two questions often come up in this context. One is whether you should count time spent on writing bug reports as part of the test execution effort. Another is whether to count time spent on re-running a test if you do run a test more than once in a given test pass. (You might choose to re-run a test in the second cycle of a test pass to carry out both confirmation testing and regression testing if the new test release contains a fix for a bug found in the first cycle.) Typically, I would count both, so I include a little extra time in the planned test effort to allow for these categories. The correct amount of time will depend on how many bugs you think you'll find — especially in your first test pass — and the percentage of tests you'll need to re-run. I spread the time evenly over all the tests. Those tests that pass should come in under time, and those that fail should tend to go a little over.

A neat trick you can do when you add tracking of actual and planned person-hours is to look at *earned value*. To illustrate the concept of earned value, suppose that you offered to wash 10 cars for $100. You plan on spending half an hour per car, so you'll make $20 per hour. However, at the end of four hours, you've only washed five cars. While you've expended 80 percent of the planned effort, you've only achieved 50 percent of the milestones. The idea of earned value allows you to see that you will not finish all 10 cars in the remaining hour, because it's taking you 48 minutes per car. At this rate, you will actually earn $12.50 per hour rather than $20.

To return to the testing world, consider test cases instead of cars to be units of work, and that you planned to get 75 test cases done by five testers in two weeks, assuming 30 hours of testing time per tester per week. (In my experience, I have found a 75 percent on-task productivity rate during test execution to provide a pretty good rule of thumb on my test teams, although some test managers have told me they have productivity rates more like 20 hours per tester per week.) If your team has completed 30 test cases, but all told they've expended only 100 person-hours of effort, your earned value situation is good. You are 40 percent through the planned test execution, but have used only 33 percent of your planned effort. I'll show you more ways to track whether you're on schedule with earned value in the section "Putting the Test Tracking System in Motion."

Using test cases as a unit of work assumes that the effort and duration of each test case are relatively uniform. It doesn't matter if some test cases are a little longer and some a little shorter, but if some test cases are an hour long and others are 10 hours long, that can make the results misleading. If you finish all the hour-long tests first, it might look like you're making great progress in terms of milestones, but you might not have time left over for the 10-hour tests.

Understanding How Long Tests Run

In some cases, the amount of effort required to run a test is less than the time the test takes to run. For example, if you use automated tools for functional regression or performance testing of your software, you might start the tests, leave them, and then return later to analyze the results. In the case of hardware, life tests, reliability demonstrations, and burn-in tests are the same way. To know how long tests take to run, it's a good idea to gather duration information as well. Adding Planned Duration and Actual Duration columns that capture the duration in the test tracking spreadsheet is a relatively straightforward way to do this.

In addition to the planning benefits of knowing how long tests take to run, test duration is commonly used when testing hardware to generate "mean time between failures" (MTBF) figures. It is also used similarly in various reliability models for software.[1]

Increasing the Precision of a Test Case State

The basic test suite summary introduced earlier records three possible states of a test case: Pass, Fail, or In Queue. (The In Queue state is indicated by a

---

[1]For some ideas on software reliability, see Stephen Kan's *Metrics and Models in Software Quality Engineering*. For hardware reliability, see Patrick O'Connor's *Practical Reliability Engineering*.

blank entry in the State column of the test case summary.) However, I prefer to use more precise states in the life cycle of a typical test case. While the appropriate life cycle for the way you test might vary, here's a test case life cycle I've used:

Queue. The test case is ready to run, assigned to a tester for execution in this test pass.

In Progress. The test is currently running and will probably continue to do so for a while. If a test takes less than a day, I don't bother to mark a test *In Progress* since I track test case status daily.

Block. Some condition — such as a missing piece of functionality or a lack of a necessary component in the test environment — has prevented the tester from executing the test to completion. I usually document the blocking condition in the Comments column of the test case summary worksheet. One way to think of the Block state is "I wanted to run the test, but I couldn't."

Skip. You've decided to skip the test for this pass, typically because it's a relatively low priority. Again, the Comments column of the test case summary worksheet should reflect why the test is not run. One way to think of the Skip state is "I could have run the test, but I didn't want to."

Pass. The test case ran to completion and the tester observed only expected results, states, and behaviors.

Fail. In one or more ways, the tester observed unexpected results, states, or behaviors that call into question the quality of the system with respect to the objective of the test. The tester reported one or more bugs.

Warn. In one or more ways, the testers observed unexpected results, states, or behaviors, but the underlying quality of the system with respect to the objective of the test is not seriously compromised. I usually count Warn in the Pass category in the test suite summary rather than adding another column to that worksheet. Another way to think about this is that Warn means that the tester only saw trivial bugs or bugs that did not affect the feature under test. The tester reported one or more such bugs. A handy rule of thumb I use is that a test associated only with deferred and non-must-fix bugs (per the bug triage committee) should be marked as Warn, not Fail.

Closed. After being marked as Fail or Warn in the first cycle of a test pass, the next test release included a fix to the bug(s) that afflicted this test case. Upon re-running the entire test case, the tester did not observe any bugs (see the sidebar "What Is Confirmation Testing?"). Marking such tests as Closed rather than Pass allows you to track the fact that the test did fail against one of the releases tested in the test pass. As with Warn, I count Closed test cases in the Pass category in the test suite summary.

Figure 5-7 shows this life cycle. Dotted lines indicate uncommon flows, while heavy circles indicate states that are typically final for the test case in that pass. From a point of view of the mechanics of the test case tracking worksheet, you'll need to add a few more columns for the extra roll-up fields, which you can see in Figure 5-5.

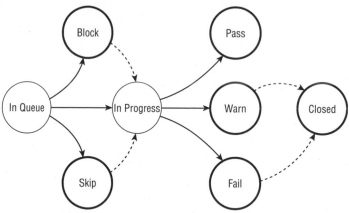

Figure 5-7 One possible test case life cycle

WHAT IS CONFIRMATION TESTING?

In Chapter 3, I discussed regression and regression test strategies. Any change to the system under test — including changes to fix bugs — can potentially create a regression. So, when you receive a test release with a bug fix in it, what are your options?

In terms of regression, as I mentioned in Chapter 3, you can either re-run all of your tests or some portion of them. The approach discussed in Chapter 1 and reviewed in this chapter (see Figure 5-4) involves re-running all tests, but not against every single test release. This approach might not work as the size and complexity of the product grows, though, unless you have complete test automation.

In addition to making sure that bug fixes and other changes didn't break anything, you also need to check that whatever the change was to accomplish, it did. This is confirmation testing. The name is intuitive: you run confirmation tests to confirm a change, typically a bug fix.

How do you run a confirmation test? There are two common variants that I've used and seen used in practice. The more efficient approach is to re-run the steps to reproduce the failure from the bug report. As described in Chapter 4, a bug report can also include isolation and generalization steps that expand the

(continued)

WHAT IS CONFIRMATION TESTING? *(continued)*

scope of the report. Typically, I'd want to see those generalization and isolation steps re-run as well, if appropriate.

The more conservative approach, albeit somewhat more expensive (effort-wise), is to repeat not only the bug report's steps, but also all the steps from the test case or test cases that initially identified the bug. Of course, this requires the time to re-run not only the steps in the bug report, but also the entire test case. Depending on the size of your test cases, this could constitute a serious investment of time. This is especially true if you allow some amount of reactive testing as part of your test cases, as I discussed in Chapter 3.

Now, if you think about it, this conservative approach to confirmation testing is not purely confirmation testing. The extra areas of test coverage are actually focused on the types of regression that I discussed in Chapter 3, *local regression*, *exposed regression*, and *new feature regression*. In fact, some people use this approach for both confirmation and regression testing, and do nothing more. That is not conservative, but rather risky, because this approach will not work against the types of regression I called *remote regression*, or, in most cases, *existing feature regression*.

Note that this life cycle is tightly coupled with the entire test pass, test release, and test cycle approach shown in Figure 5-4. For example, suppose that you use a less regression-averse approach than shown in Figure 5-4. You decide not to re-run tests after they have passed. In other words, you'll re-run failed or warned tests against subsequent releases, but only until they pass. Once all the tests are marked *Pass*, *Closed*, or *Warn*, you declare victory. In that situation, you would have a test case life cycle that applied to the entire test phase, rather than pass-by-pass, and it would include arcs from Fail and Warn to In Progress. In the approach shown in Figure 5-4, whatever state the test case is in at the end of the pass, it remains in that state. In subsequent passes, it starts anew with an *In Queue* state. I bring up this example to encourage you to consider how your testing strategies and test project realities will affect your use of this tool.

One possible complication is that, as I discussed in Chapter 3, a test case is an amalgamation of test steps and substeps. Test cases generally cover multiple test conditions. If one test condition fails and the rest pass, what to do? At one point, I tried having compound states such as Block/Fail and so forth, but found that made the test suite summary and other metrics very hard to gather. Do I count the test as Block, as Fail, or as both? It was too confusing for me, and impossible to explain to the rest of the project team. Therefore, I use the simple hierarchical rule introduced in Chapter 3:

1. If any test step or substep is in progress, then record the entire test case as *IP*.

2. Else, if any step or substep is blocked, then record the entire test case as *Block*.

3. Else, if any step or substep failed, then record the entire case as *Fail*.

4. Else, if any step or substep warned, then record the entire case as *Warn*.

5. If the test was marked *Fail* or *Warn* in the first cycle, was re-run in the second cycle, and the tester must have observed only expected results, states, and behaviors, mark the test *Closed*.

6. Otherwise, it must be the first time the tester ran the test in this pass, and further, the tester must have observed only expected results, states, and behaviors, so I mark the test *Pass*.

Since I usually make the decision to skip tests at the test case level of granularity, I don't need a rule for handling skips. My testers and I discuss test findings and assign these test states during the daily debriefing.

Prioritizing Test Suites and Cases

The discussion of regression gaps in Chapter 3 raised the issue of how to select or prioritize test suites to be re-run in multiple pass situations — that is, how to select the test suites that find the most important bugs. I suggested that a dynamic prioritization approach would make sense, where you re-evaluate the level of risk associated with your tests at the beginning of each pass.

You can find a numerical technique for this re-evaluation in the concept of *test suite yield*. This method considers not only the number of bugs found by the suite, but also the severity and priority rankings of the bugs (the risk priority numbers from the bug tracking system discussed in Chapter 4). By calculating a weighted failure number for each suite, you obtain a numeric yield that you can use to select test suites.

It's easy to add such a feature to a test tracking spreadsheet. In Figure 5-5. you see a column in the test case summary worksheet to store the risk priority number (RPN) for the corresponding bug ID. Then, in the Roll Up area, there's a column named FW (for Failure Weight) that holds a formula calculating the reciprocal of the RPN in each row. Finally, in Figure 5-6, there's a column in the test suite summary worksheet that references the sum of the failure weights for each suite. Now you have a test suite summary column that starts at 0 and increases as the yield — RPN-weighted — of the test suite increases. You can now figure out at a glance which test suites in your test system are most effective. You can also add something similar for test cases or simply do it by inspection.

If you want to look at test suite bug finding efficiency as well as overall effectiveness, then you might want to use a normalized value. By *normalized*, I mean adjusting for the size of each test suite. For example, when speaking of automobile efficiency, we don't talk about how many miles or kilometers are traveled per tank of gas — which varies from one model to the next — but rather in terms of miles per gallon or liters per hundred kilometers. You can use the number of test cases in the suite, if test case effort and duration are relatively uniform as I mentioned earlier in relation to earned value. If they are not, then you can normalize by effort or duration, depending on which is more meaningful in your situation. For heavily automated test regimens, for example, duration is likely to be more meaningful.

You might question my choice to add the failure weights rather than, say, multiplying them, squaring the sums, or using another more exotic function. If you believe that such an approach is more appropriate, try it. I would argue that multiplying overstates the importance of RPN-1 bugs while downplaying the importance of other bugs. Is a test suite that yields one RPN-1 bug eight times better than a suite that yields three RPN-2 bugs? I would deem the latter test suite better, a conclusion that supports the additive approach. Squaring the sums also emphasizes the bugs with smaller RPNs, although in a more appropriate way. However, it makes the number more difficult to explain, without adding much information. As always, however, follow your muse; if you have a better idea, go ahead and implement it.

As with the subsystem-breakdown chart in Chapter 4, failure weight is a measure of technical risk; in other words, where the bugs are most likely to occur. Again, any method of prioritizing that relies strictly on technical risk ignores the very important aspect of business risk. Business risk derives from what the users will do with the system, what value the customers are paying to receive from the system, and so forth. Business risk is closely connected with what it would mean for the system to have quality as discussed in Chapter 1. Therefore, if you want to use a formula to completely re-prioritize your tests from one pass to the next, then I suggest you pull in the original impact score that the test case inherits from its associated risk item. You might need to go back to the risk items using traceability, unless you carry this information forward for each test case.

Scrutinizing the Roll Up Columns

Let's look closely at the roll up columns on the rightmost side of Figure 5-5, so that you can better understand how the test suite summary worksheet works. I suggest you download the spreadsheet from the RBCS web site and follow along with me for a moment.

The T roll up column is just a constant value. It is 1 if the cell to the left in column C — the Test Suite/Case column — is a test case, not a test suite, a blank line, or a suite summary. The S, P, F, Q, I, and B columns, however, all contain formulas that check whether the Test State column contains the text *Skip*, *Pass*, *Fail*, blank (for *In Queue*), IP (for *In Progress*), or *Block*, respectively. If the formula finds matching in that column, then the formula returns a 1; if not, then it returns a 0. (I count Warn as a Pass. If you don't like this, you might want to add another roll up column to count the warns separately, or change the formula to count Warn as Fail.) These columns are summed in the Suite Summary rows and then referenced in the suite summary worksheet.

If you prefer to use other names for the same states, abbreviations for the states, or a different set of states entirely, you'll need to change these roll up columns, both the headings and the formulas. I encourage you to spend some time studying how the current formulas work before you start hacking on them, because they're fragile and not exactly self-documenting. You'll also need to change the test suite summary worksheet to reflect any states you add or rename.

The FW column contains the failure weight, which, as discussed earlier, is the inverse of the RPN for any bugs found by that test case. This is also added up in the Suite Summary rows and referenced in the suite summary worksheet.

One important part of using this tracking spreadsheet is keeping the formula references correct, especially in the Roll Up columns and in the suite summaries. It's not too hard after a little practice, but the first few times you get bitten by a broken cell reference it does eat up some time. As the carpenter's adage goes, "Measure twice and cut once." Check the references often when you first start using this tool, and you'll learn how to avoid stubbing your toe on spreadsheet quirks.

Other Ways to Summarize and Group Data

Beyond just summarizing by test state and failure weight, you can analyze more of the data you're gathering. For example, I usually include an Earned Value section of the test suite summary worksheet that looks at planned versus actual test effort and associated test case completion. You can also look at planned versus actual dates or durations, assigned owner versus tester, and so forth. The test tracking spreadsheet is a flexible tool, and it lends itself to extensions. Just remember that the more bells and whistles you attach, the bigger the file gets, the slower the updates become, and the more impenetrable the data seems to many managers and developers.

You also might want to think twice about certain types of metrics — in particular, those that address questions such as "Who found the most bugs overall?", "Who spent the most time testing?", and "Who found the most bugs per hour spent?" I find these numbers dangerous, and I don't generate them. As soon as you begin analyzing employee performance data, you take risks. If people know you are measuring them this way, they will soon figure out how to manipulate the numbers.

The test case summary worksheet shown earlier grouped data primarily by test suite. Alternatively, you could use test phases, owner, or organization as major groups. (Multiple organizations are sometimes involved in test efforts, especially those that include outsourcing. I'll discuss applying the test tracking spreadsheet to such virtual test teams in Chapter 10.) You can make the grouping as flat or as hierarchical as you want. If you use too many levels, you'll make the chart difficult to read. If you use too few — for example, 1,000 detail rows but no grouping — the chart will be monotonous and hard to scan. If in doubt, try out a few different arrangements and see what looks most readable and accessible.

Extending the Spreadsheet by Including Test Case Details

Chapter 3 provided a template for writing test cases, constructed with a spreadsheet. It has probably already occurred to you that you can integrate the test cases with the test tracking spreadsheet. By doing so, you gain automatic summaries of the test cases as you update them with test results. You can use links or references between worksheets to automatically transfer information such as the test ID, the test case name, and so forth from the test case template to the test case summary, or vice versa.

By creating a separate worksheet for each test case, you can include all the tests, along with the summaries, from a given test phase in a single spreadsheet. By establishing links up to the test case summary and down into each test case worksheet, you can create a complete, self-summarizing test tracking system. The feasibility of building such a system depends on how many test cases you intend to run. If you have too many to fit into a single spreadsheet, you can link them across multiple files. For very large projects, however, in which you would need to tie together a great many spreadsheets, this effort might prove too complex, and the system might be too difficult to maintain.

If you decide to use this approach, you'll need to establish a process for updating the worksheets. An approach I've used is to print the test cases and test case summary worksheet, have test engineers and technicians make notes on the hard copies, and input the results myself as part of the daily debriefing. This ensures that the data is more consistent, and it prevents mistakes in using the formulas. Personally, I find that staying intimately acquainted with test execution at a test case level makes a lot of sense. However, if your management style is better suited to focusing at a higher level, let your testers update the test case worksheets, and then you can audit the test case summary and test suite summary after the updates.

Tracking Coverage

I discussed coverage in Chapter 3. You can expand the spreadsheet we've discussed here so that, in addition to using the test case summary to track test case information, you can also use that worksheet to tie test cases back to the test basis. This is similar to including the Quality Risk field in the bug tracking database as discussed in Chapter 4. In the test case summary worksheet, I can include a set of columns to the right of the roll up columns that I can use to assess quality risk coverage.

Figure 5-8 shows the test coverage analysis for our DataRocket case study. I've identified seven broad categories of risks to system quality, plus a catchall category called Other. In each category, I look at planned and actual coverage. The planned coverage, as in Chapter 3, is a 2 if the test case directly addresses the risk, a 1 if the test case indirectly addresses it, and blank (counted as 0) if there is no coverage. The actual coverage uses the same weighting, but counts only if the test has been run and resulted in a Pass, Warn, or Fail. Blocked, skipped, and queued tests don't count toward actual coverage.

						DataRocket System Test Case			Quality Risk Coverage Columns										
						Install	Functionality		Reliability		Performance		Compatibility		Environmental		Standards		Other
Owner	ID	Test Suite/Case	State	Pln	Act	Pln	Act	Pln	Act	Pln	Act	Pln	Act	Pln	Act	Pln	Act	Pln	Act
System Cookers, Inc.																			
	1.000	Environmental Test																	
	1.001	Operating Thermal Profile	Skip					1	0					2	0				
	1.002	Operating Temp/Humid Cycle	Skip					1	0					2	0				
	1.003	Non-Opertng Temp/Humid Cycle	Skip											2	0				
	1.004	Non-Oprtng Drop	Skip											2	0				
	1.005	Non-Oprtng Shock	Skip											2	0				
	1.006	Non-Oprtng Thermal Shock	Skip											2	0				
	1.007	Packaging Drop	Skip											2	0				
	1.008	Packaging Shock	Skip											2	0				
		Suit Summary		0	0	0	0	2	0	0	0	0	0	16	0	0	0	0	0
Winged Bytes																			
	2.000	Load, Capacity and Volume																	
LTW	2.001	CPU and Memory	Fail			1	1	2	2	2	2	1	1						
						0	0	0	0	0	0	0	0						
						0	0	0	0	0	0	0	0						
						0	0	0	0	0	0	0	0						
						0	0	0	0	0	0	0	0						
LTW	2.002	FDD/CD-ROM/DVD	Closed			1	1	2	2	2	2	1	1						
LTW	2.003	RAID	Warn			1	1	2	2	2	2	1	1						
LTW	2.004	Tape	Pass			1	1	2	2	2	2	1	1						
LTW	2.005	Network	Warn			1	1	2	2	2	2	1	1						
LTW	2.006	Modem Bank	Pass			1	1	2	2	2	2	1	1						
LTW	2.007	USB/Parallel/Firewire				1	0	2	0	2	0	1	0						
LTW	2.008	All Subsystems				1	0	2	0	2	0	1	0						
		Suite Summary		0	0	8	6	16	12	16	12	8	6	0	0	0	0	0	0

Figure 5-8 Tracking test coverage

If you remember the DataRocket failure mode and effect analysis (FMEA) chart from Chapter 1, you can see that I'm tracking test coverage using broad categories of quality risks, not the type of low-level details shown in the FMEA chart. This makes sense here, because I intend to use this data to look at coverage at a high level for results reporting purposes. If I wanted to analyze the test execution in detail to look for gaps in coverage and the related risks to system quality, then I'd need to use the FMEA chart level of detail. In my experience, if you need tracking to that level of detail, you're better off doing the test and quality risks tracking in a database (see one of the case studies in this chapter).

Putting the Test Tracking System in Motion

To illustrate how the test tracking spreadsheet can work for you, this section presents three short case studies, using the DataRocket information shown earlier. In all scenarios, assume that you are about halfway through the scheduled system test phase. The first two scenarios represent test projects in some amount of trouble, one with a minor problem, and the other in serious difficulty. The third scenario describes a successful project.

Little Trouble

It's July 16. Life is pretty good on the test project. All the systems showed up on time — a small miracle — and you have yet to run into any major bugs. You sent the systems out to an external test lab named System Cookers, and most of the environmental tests finished almost a week early; this was a major stroke of luck since these tests were considered the most risky. Nevertheless, you do have a few problems, as your current test case and test suite summary worksheets (shown in Figure 5-9 and Figure 5-10) indicate.

Owner	Test ID	Test Suite/Case	State	System Config	Bug ID	Bug RPN	By	Plan Date	Act Date	Plan Effort	Act Effort	Comment	T	S	P	F	FW	Q	I	B
		DataRocket System Test Case Summary																		
																	Pass Two			
System Cookers, Inc.																				
	1.000	*Environmental Test*																		
	1.001	Operating Thermal Profile	Pass	D			SC	7/16	7/10	4	5		1	0	1	0	0	0	0	0
	1.002	Operating Temp/Humid Cycle	Pass	D			SC	7/16	7/10	4	6		1	0	1	0	0	0	0	0
	1.003	Non-Operating Temp/Humid Cycle	Pass	D			SC	7/16	7/10	4	4		1	0	1	0	0	0	0	0
	1.004	Non-Operating Drop	Pass	D			SC	7/16	7/10	4	6		1	0	1	0	0	0	0	0
	1.005	Non-Operating Shock	Pass	D			SC	7/16	7/10	4	6		1	0	1	0	0	0	0	0
	1.006	Non-Operating Thermal Shock	Pass	D			SC	7/16	7/10	4	3		1	0	1	0	0	0	0	0
	1.007	Packaging Drop	Block					7/16		4		Package redesign IP.	1	0	0	0	0	0	0	1
	1.008	Packaging Shock	Block					7/16		4		Package redesign IP.	1	0	0	0	0	0	0	1
		Suite Summary						7/16	7/10	32	30		8	0	6	0	0.00	0	0	2
Winged Bytes																				
	2.000	*Load, Capacity, and Volume*																		
LTW	2.001	CPU and Memory	Pass	A,B,C			LTW	7/10	7/10	4	5		1	0	1	0	0	0	0	0
LTW	2.002	FDD/CD-ROM/DVD	Pass	A,B,C			LTW	7/10	7/10	4	5		1	0	1	0	0	0	0	0
LTW	2.003	RAID	Pass	A,B,C			LTW	7/10	7/11	4	5		1	0	1	0	0	0	0	0
LTW	2.004	Tape	Pass	A,B,C			LTW	7/10	7/11	4	5		1	0	1	0	0	0	0	0
LTW	2.005	Network	Pass	A,B,C			LTW	7/10	7/12	4	5		1	0	1	0	0	0	0	0
LTW	2.006	Modem Bank	Pass	A,B,C			LTW	7/10	7/13	4	5		1	0	1	0	0	0	0	0
LTW	2.007	USB/Parallel/Firewire	Pass	A,B,C			LTW	7/10	7/14	4	5		1	0	1	0	0	0	0	0
LTW	2.008	All Subsystems	Pass	A,B,C			LTW	7/10	7/14	4	5		1	0	1	0	0	0	0	0
		Suite Summary						7/10	7/14	32	40		8	0	8	0	0.00	0	0	0
	3.000	*Basic Functionality*																		
JC	3.001	Configure/Register Windows	Pass	A,B,C			JC	7/5	7/5	4	8		1	0	1	0	0	0	0	0
JC	3.002	Configure/Register Solaris	Pass	A,B,C			JC	7/5	7/6	4	8		1	0	1	0	0	0	0	0
JC	3.003	Configure/Register Linux	Pass	A,B,C			JC	7/5	7/7	4	8		1	0	1	0	0	0	0	0
JC	3.004	FDD/CD-ROM/DVD	Pass	A,B,C	005	6	JC	7/9	7/16	2	4		1	0	1	0	1/6	0	0	0
JC	3.005	RAID	Pass	A,B,C			JC	7/9	7/16	2	4		1	0	1	0	0	0	0	0
JC	3.006	Tape	Pass	A,B,C			JC	7/9	7/16	2	4		1	0	1	0	0	0	0	0
JC	3.007	Network-Windows	Pass	A,B,C			JC	7/9	7/16	2	4		1	0	1	0	0	0	0	0
JC	3.008	Network-Linux	Pass	A,B,C			JC	7/9	7/16	2	4		1	0	1	0	0	0	0	0
JC	3.009	Network-PC-NFS	Pass	A,B,C			JC	7/9	7/17	2	4		1	0	1	0	0	0	0	0
JC	3.010	Modem Bank	Pass	A,B,C			JC	7/9	7/17	2	4		1	0	1	0	0	0	0	0
JC	3.011	USB/Parallel/Firewire	Pass	A,B,C			JC	7/9	7/17	2	4		1	0	1	0	0	0	0	0
JC	3.012	UI (Video/Kbd/Mouse)	Pass	A,B,C			JC	7/9	7/17	2	4		1	0	1	0	0	0	0	0
		Suite Summary						7/5	7/17	30	60		#	0	12	0	0.17	0	0	0
	4.000	*Standards*																		
HL	4.001	Solaris Certification	IP	A				7/8		8			1	0	0	0	0	0	1	0
HL	4.002	Window Certification	IP	B				7/8		8			1	0	0	0	0	0	1	0
HL	4.003	Linux Certification	IP	C				7/8		8			1	0	0	0	0	0	1	0
		Suite Summary						7/8	1/0	24	0		3	0	0	0	0.00	0	3	0

Figure 5-9 A worrisome test case summary

	A	B	C	D	E	F	G	H	I	J	K	L	M	N	O
1				DataRocket System Test Suite Summary											
2				Pass Two											
3															
4		Total	Planned Tests Fulfilled				Weighted	Planned Tests Unfulfilled				Earned Value			
5	Suite	Cases	Count	Skip	Pass	Fail	Failure	Count	Queued	IP	Block	Pln Hrs	Act Hrs	% Effort	% Exec
6															
7	Environmental Test	8	8	0	6	0	0.00	2	0	0	2	32.00	30.00	94%	75%
8	Load, Capacity and Volume	8	8	0	8	0	0.00	0	0	0	0	32.00	40.00	125%	100%
9	Basic Functionality	12	12	0	12	0	0.17	0	0	0	0	30.00	60.00	200%	100%
10	Standards	3	0	0	0	0	0.00	3	0	3	0	24.00	0.00	0%	0%
11															
12	Total	31	26	0	26	0	0.71	5	0	3	2	118.00	130.00	110%	84%
13	By Pct		84%	0%	84%	0%		16%	0%	10%	6%				

Figure 5-10 A worrisome test suite summary

First, and worst, the standards testing is taking longer than planned. Hitesh, the test engineer in charge, is deluged with other systems in the lab and probably won't wrap up that work for a few more days. This isn't a big deal — assuming that all the tests pass. Given the difficulty of predicting *that*, however, you're a little nervous.

Second, you seem to have underestimated the size of the effort. All of these tests are taking longer, in person-hours, than you expected. You are incurring some overtime costs associated with your contractor, Jim, and an irritated employee, Lin-Tsu, who has had to work overtime for two weeks. You can see this most clearly in the earned value section of the suite summary.

Third, the packaging was given a last minute facelift, delaying that portion of the environmental testing. Fourth, the floppy drive doesn't read 1.2MB (Japanese) formatted disks. You mark this as a Warn because this problem might delay shipment in Japan, although nowhere else.

The latter two problems, of course, are system-related issues, which you can't really affect. However, you do have two lessons to learn. The first is that you should cross-train your staff on standards testing so that you don't get held up there again. Next, you should be careful to adjust your planned effort for the next test project.

Big Trouble

It's July 26. You have big problems. Engineering samples showed up for testing a week late, but the project release date remains unchanged. You lost a week from your first test cycle. You don't have all the drivers you need for the supported operating systems, which blocks three very important test cases. On top of that, Solaris, an important network operating system for your customers, won't install or run reliably with DataRocket. The system panics during installation in nearly half the tests; at other times, it panics under load. This bug, which is referenced in the test case shown in Figure 5-11, blocks completion of most tests.

	A	B	C	D	F
1	Test Case Name:	CPU and Memory			
2	Test ID:	2.001			
3	Test	Load, Capacity and Volume			
4	Priority:	High			
5	Hardware	One DataRocket Server			
6	Software Reqired:	Load, Capacity and volume Test Tool			
7		Windows Server			
8		Solaris			
9		Linux			
10	Duration:	3			
11	Effort:	4			
12	Setup:	Install Windows Server			
13		Install Linux			
14		Install Solaris			
15	Teardow	None necessary.			
16	**ID**	**Test Area/Condition**	**Result**	**Bug ID**	**Bug RPN**
17	1.000	Test CPU load on Windows Server.			
18	1.001	Install Windows Server. Confirm proper install.	Pass		
19	1.002	Install LCV Test Tool from LCV CD-ROM. Confirm proper install.	Warn	9	3
20	1.003	Run LCV Test Tool, CPU Module, for one hour. Check log file for failures on exit.	Pass		
21	2.000	Repeat step 1.001-1.003 for Solaris.	Fail	10	1
22	3.000	Repeat step 1.001-1.003 for Linux.	Pass		
23	**Overall**	**Status**	Fail		
24		**System Config**	B,A,C		
25		**Tester**	LTW		
26		**Date Completed**	7/14		
27		**Effort**	16		
28		**Duration**	16		

Figure 5-11 A test case showing a serious problem

You also have problems with the Environmental test suite. The CPU exceeded its temperature specification in the thermal profile test. The CPU vendor tells you that the chip will suffer a serious degradation in its MTBF at this temperature, making the system prone to failure in a few months. In addition, the motherboard cracked during the temperature/humidity cycle test. Although the system still ran after the test, the damage indicates that the board is improperly mounted. To add insult to injury, the cardboard box, the padding, and the system case suffered cosmetic damage during the packaging drop test, indicating a need to redesign the package. All of these difficulties are reflected in the test case summary worksheet shown in Figure 5-12.

These problems are very serious. Does it even make sense to move on to the third pass of system testing? Probably not. You are effectively blocked until you have a fix for the Solaris bug, and you can't finish all the tests until the rest of the missing drivers show up. The environmental test — an expensive operation — will need to be re-run, but only after the mounting and temperature problems are resolved. You almost certainly won't exit the system test phase until weeks after the scheduled date, delaying first customer shipment. The severity of the problems is evident in the test suite summary worksheet shown in Figure 5-13. In my experience, this is the type of situation

Owner	Test ID	Test Suite/Case	State	Config	Bug ID	Bug RPN	By	Plan Date	Act Date	Plan Hrs	Act Hrs	Comment	T	S	P	F	FW	Q	I	B
		DataRocket System Test Case Tracking Spreadsheet																		
			Pass Two																	
	Test			System	Bug	Bug		Plan	Act	Plan	Act						Roll Up Columns			
Owner	ID	Test Suite/Case	State	Config	ID	RPN	By	Date	Date	Hrs	Hrs	Comment	T	S	P	F	FW	Q	I	B
System Cookers. Inc.																				
	1.000	*Environmental Test*																		
	1.001	Operating Thermal Profile	Fail	D	005	1	SC	7/16	7/19	4	5		1	0	0	1	1	0	0	0
	1.002	Operating Temp/Humid Cycle	Fail	D	006	1	SC	7/16	7/19	4	6		1	0	0	1	1	0	0	0
	1.003	Non-Operating Temp/Humid Cycle	Pass	D			SC	7/16	7/19	4	4		1	0	1	0	0	0	0	0
	1.004	Non-Operating Drop	Pass	D			SC	7/16	7/19	4	6		1	0	1	0	0	0	0	0
	1.005	Non-Operating Shock	Pass	D			SC	7/16	7/19	4	6		1	0	1	0	0	0	0	0
	1.006	Non-Operating Thermal Shock	Pass	D			SC	7/16	7/19	4	3		1	0	1	0	0	0	0	0
	1.007	Packaging Drop	Fail	D	012	5	SC	7/16	7.19	4	2		1	0	0	1	1/5	0	0	0
	1.008	Packaging Shock	Pass	D			SC	7/16	7/19	4	2		1	0	1	0	0	0	0	0
		Suite Summary						7/16	7/19	32	34		8				2.20			0
Winged Bytes																				
	2.000	*Load, Capacity, and Volume*																		
LTW	2.001	CPU and Memory	Fail	B,C	010	1	LTW	7/10	7/21	4	16	Solaris panics.	1	0	0	1	1	0	0	0
					009	3											1/3			
LTW	2.002	FDD/CD-ROM/DVD	Block	B,C			LTW	7/10		4		Solaris panics.	1	0	0	0	0	0	0	1
LTW	2.003	RAID	Block	B,C			LTW	7/10		4		Solaris panics.	1	0	0	0	0	0	0	1
LTW	2.004	Tape	Block	B,C			LTW	7/10		4		Solaris panics.	1	0	0	0	0	0	0	1
LTW	2.005	Network	Block	B,C			LTW	7/10		4		Solaris panics.	1	0	0	0	0	0	0	1
LTW	2.006	Modem Bank	Block	B,C			LTW	7/10		4		Solaris panics.	1	0	0	0	0	0	0	1
LTW	2.007	USB/Parallel/Firewire	Block	B,C			LTW	7/10		4		Solaris panics.	1	0	0	0	0	0	0	1
LTW	2.008	All Subsystems	Block	B,C			LTW	7/10		4		Solaris panics.	1	0	0	0	0	0	0	1
		Suite Summary						7/10	7/21	32	16		8			1	1.33			7
	3.000	*Basic Functionality*																		
JC	3.001	Configure/Register Windows	Block					7/12		4		Not all Win drv avail.	1	0	0	0	0	0	0	1
JC	3.002	Configure/Register Solaris	Block					7/11		4		Not all Sol drv avail.	1	0	0	0	0	0	0	1
JC	3.003	Configure/Register Linux	Block					7/10		4		Not all Lnx drv avail.	1	0	0	0	0	0	0	1
JC	3.004	FDD/CD-ROM/DVD	Block	B,C			JC	7/9		2		Solaris panics.	1	0	0	0	0	0	0	1
JC	3.005	RAID	Block	B,C			JC	7/9		2		Solaris panics.	1	0	0	0	0	0	0	1
JC	3.006	Tape	Block	B,C			JC	7/9		2		Solaris panics.	1	0	0	0	0	0	0	1
JC	3.007	Network-Windows	Pass	B			JC	7/9	7/16	2	1.5		1	0	1	0	0	0	0	0
JC	3.008	Network-Linux	Pass	C			JC	7/9	7/16	2	1.5		1	0	1	0	0	0	0	0
JC	3.009	Network-PC-NFS	Block	A	010	1	JC	7/9		2		Solaris panics.	1	0	0	0	1	0	0	1
JC	3.010	Modem Bank	Block	B,C			JC	7/9		2		Solaris panics.	1	0	0	0	0	0	0	1
JC	3.011	USB/Parallel/Firewire	Block	B,C			JC	7/9		2		Solaris panics.	1	0	0	0	0	0	0	1
JC	3.012	UI (Video/Kbd/Mouse)	Block	B,C			JC	7/9		2		Solaris panics.	1	0	0	0	0	0	0	1
		Suite Summary						7/12	7/16	30	3		#				1.00			#
	4.000	*Standards*																		
HL	4.001	Solaris Certification	Block	A	010	1	HL	7/13		8		Solaris panics.	1	1		0	1	0	0	0
HL	4.002	Window Certification	IP					7/13		8			1	0		0	0	0	1	0
HL	4.003	Linux Certification	IP					7/13		8			1	0		0	0	0	1	0
		Suite Summary						7/13	1/0	24	0		3	1			1.00			0

Figure 5-12 A test case summary indicating major problems

Suite	Total Cases	Planned Tests Fulfilled				Weighted Failure	Planned Tests Unfulfilled				Earned Value			
		Count	Skip	Pass	Fail		Count	Queued	IP	Block	Pln Hrs	Act Hrs	% Effort	% Exec
Environmental Test	8	8	0	5	3	2.20	0	0	0	0	32.00	34.00	106%	100%
Load, Capacity, and Volume	8	1	0	0	1	1.33	7	0	0	7	32.00	16.00	50%	13%
Basic Functionality	12	2	0	2	0	1.00	10	0	0	10	30.00	3.00	10%	17%
Standards	3	1	1	0	0	1.00	2	0	2	0	24.00	0.00	0%	0%
Total	31	12	1	7	4	5.53	19	0	2	17	118.00	53.00	45%	37%
By Pct		39%	3%	23%	13%		61%	0%	6%	55%				

Table title: DataRocket System Test Suite Summary — Pass Two

Figure 5-13 A test suite summary reporting major problems

that arises when too little component and integration testing was done prior to starting system test. A few large functionality and test-blocking bugs come up right away, preventing further progress. Once these bugs are resolved, a whole host of serious bugs affecting finer-grained areas of functionality and behavior will become visible.

No Problem!

It's July 15, and the living is easy. You received a telephone call this morning from the lab manager at System Cookers informing you that DataRocket passed all the environmental tests as of yesterday. This is only a day late, which is good, since the systems got to the lab three days late. The first pass of system test is now finished. The only problem found was a minor glitch during Linux certification testing, for which you just received a waiver. Your test suite summary worksheet shows that you have run 100 percent of the tests, with 100 percent passing. Better yet, you were within 1 percent of your estimated effort. The test suite summary worksheet (see Figure 5-14) also reflects this smooth sailing.

A	B	C	D	E	F	G	H	I	J	K	L	M	N	O
1				DataRocket System Test Suite Summary										
2					Pass One									
3														
4		Total	Planned Tests Fulfilled			Weighted	Planned Tests Unfulfilled				Earned Value			
5	Suite	Cases	Count	Skip	Pass	Fail	Failure	Count	Queued	IP	Block	Pln Hrs	Act Hrs	% Effort	% Exec
6														
7	Environmental Test	8	8	0	8	0	0.00	0	0	0	0	32.00	32.00	100%	100%
8	Load, Capacity and Volume	8	8	0	8	0	0.00	0	0	0	0	32.00	32.00	100%	100%
9	Basic Functionality	12	12	0	12	0	0.00	0	0	0	0	30.00	31.00	103%	100%
10	Standards	3	3	0	3	0	0.04	0	0	0	0	24.00	24.00	100%	100%
11														
12	Total	31	31	0	31	0	0.04	0	0	0	0	118.00	119.00	101%	100%
13	By Pct		100%	0%	100%	0%		0%	0%	0%	0%				

Figure 5-14 A test suite summary for a product that will ship soon

Based on these fantastic results, you have the enviable job of walking down to the project manager's office today and waiving the remaining scheduled system testing, as DataRocket now satisfies the system test exit criteria. The product will ship about a month early, provided all goes well during pilot testing.

The IEEE 829 Test Log

So far, I've referred to this chapter's topic as *test tracking*. The IEEE 829-2008 standard calls this *test logging*, and provides a template for documenting test results. As with the other IEEE 829 templates, I find strict adherence to this documentation standard rare in practice, and, as with the other templates, it can produce heavyweight documentation. However, it does give you some food for thought.

The IEEE test log template is shown in Figure 5-15. The IEEE intends that testers use this log to record relevant details about the execution of tests in a chronological format. The standard allows for the use of an automated tool to capture all or part of this information. While test management tools can capture test-by-test information of the sort discussed previously, there are some event-by-event details which I have not seen a tool successfully capture. (I'll talk about manual methods for capturing event-by-event information in Chapter 6.)

	A	B	C	D
1	**1.0**	**Introduction**		
2	1.1	Document identifier		
3	1.2	Scope		
4	1.3	References		
5	**2.0**	**Details**		
6	2.1	Description		
7	2.2	Activity and Event entries		
8	**3.0**	**General**		
9	3.1	Glossary		

Figure 5-15 An IEEE 829 Test Log template

The first section, the Introduction, is very similar to the same sections in the IEEE 829 template discussed in earlier chapters. The document ID is much the same, though IEEE notes that the log ID should have some clear mapping to the test procedure ID so that the relationship between the test resulting in the log entry is clear. (Remember that in the IEEE 829 parlance the *test case* consists of inputs and expected results, while the *test procedure* consists of the sequences of steps to take to execute the test case; most of us tend to combine all three — inputs, expected results, and steps to carry out — into a single document referred to as a *test case* or a *test procedure*.) In the test case summary worksheet shown earlier in this chapter, that mapping is quite clear. The IEEE says the Scope section should describe the scope of the log, both in terms of its focus and its relationship to other test documents. The header rows on the test case summary worksheets and test suite summary worksheets show this information.

Unsurprisingly, the Details section is the core of the test log and provides the essential information. It starts with a Description section, which provides general information for all entries in the log. IEEE suggests the following topics:

- The test items, including version numbers. In the case of the worksheets shown earlier, this is provided indirectly by the date of the test, which should suffice if the test releases are weekly. If that's not precise enough, you can add a column for this information to the test case summary worksheet.

- Information about the test environment, which is explicitly documented in the test case summary worksheet.

- The date and time of starting and stopping the test, which is a bit more fine-grained than I tend to get.

- The name of the tester who ran the test, for which I use initials.

- Any blocking issues that stop the test from completing, which I would show in the comments field.

At this point, matters get a bit mixed in the description of the template. It talks about recording activities and events, but then goes back to talking about information that is pertinent to test-by-test logging. As I mentioned, I'll discuss event-by-event logging at the end of Chapter 6, since I think it is quite important to log events that interrupt testing or interfere with your ability to carry out the plan. I don't think that mixing that information in with the test tracking information is the best way to go.

For each test, IEEE encourages you to identify the test procedure being executed. (As I mentioned a bit earlier in this section and in the discussion on IEEE 829 templates in Chapter 3, the IEEE 829 standard uses the term *test procedure* where I would typically use the term *test case*.) The log should record all of the people involved in running the test, though I usually consider logging the tester alone to be sufficient. Next, they call for logging the results of the test, including the status of the overall test (e.g., pass, fail etc.). I showed examples of this at the test case level and at the individual test step level in Chapter 3 and earlier in Figure 5-11.

They also call for the capture of information about anomalous events. They allow that you can capture this information in a bug report (which they call an *anomaly report*, you'll recall from Chapter 4). If you do capture the information in a bug report, they ask that the log reference the bug number, which you saw in my test case summary worksheets earlier in this chapter. For anomalies that results from problems other than those in the system under test, they call for logging of that. I agree with this wholeheartedly, and suggest the approach I discuss at the end of Chapter 6.

Finally, the template includes a General section, which has a glossary in it. The IEEE describes these sections as having the same information as similar sections in previously discussed templates.

Extracting Metrics from the Test Tracking Spreadsheet

Like bug reports, test cases are important details for test managers to stay on top of. However, the test case summary worksheet is probably not something you'll want to present to managers — there's just too much data there. Unless you're fortunate enough to work for a former test manager, the odds are that your manager will find the detail either confusing, or, in some cases, an irresistible temptation to micromanage your work.

Therefore, as with bug reports, extracting a set of metrics is a good idea. The test suite summary is one possible way to present this data. It is clearly management oriented, summarizing the key details of test execution.

However, the test suite summary suffers from similar problems as a management reporting tool. For one thing, it's just a snapshot; it doesn't tell us much about how things have gone or where things are headed. The Earned Value columns do show some trend information, but not every manager I've worked with has been able to interpret that easily, and as with the test case summary, misinterpretation of that set of columns can lead to micromanagement. In addition, while it seems to tell us something about quality, it is a great myth of testing that the percentage of passed and failed test cases is a reliable surrogate metric for product quality. Therefore, I generally don't include the test suite summary as part of my testing dashboard. Instead, I graph three sets of data that are easy to extract daily using the test management tools we've already developed.

Can We Get Any Work Done? Charting Test Progress

The first of these charts is the test progress chart, which looks at how many test hours have been achieved daily. By *test hours*, I mean the actual effort measured against all the tests. Based on my "30 hours per tester" rule of thumb that I quoted earlier, I can multiply six times the number of testers assigned to my test project and come up with a planned number of test hours per day. I might see some variation around that number one way or the other — tests sometimes take more time than planned because of bugs, and less time than planned when things go smoothly — but I should see a regular pattern of achievement of planned test hours every day. If not, then I can only assume that serious stability problems with the system under test, some logistical problems with the test environment, or other issues are interfering with my ability to get testing done. If I can't get through my testing, why should management think that the users would be able to use the system to get real work done?

Figure 5-16 shows an example of this chart for a two-tester effort. This team is clearly having trouble getting through the tests. Because I count test hours only when testers complete the associated test cases, this chart seems to indicate a lot of tests going over schedule. In addition, we have a couple of weekdays in the test schedule where no testing gets done at all. Most likely, the test environment is out of action or a bad test release has brought the testing down. Finally, you can see testing happening over the weekend, which is always a sign to me as a manager that a project is out of control. Whenever projects start to eat into people's personal time, you can be sure that burn-out and staff turnover are not far behind, leading to even greater losses in efficiency.

Figure 5-16 A chart of system test progress (test hours achieved)

Are We Getting as Much Work Done as Planned? Charting Planned Test Fulfillment

The second chart is the test fulfillment chart, which looks at whether we're getting through all the tests we planned. Given some stable number of test cases and a fixed period to complete a test pass, we can plan how many tests should get done, on average, every day. For example, if we have 50 test cases planned for the test phase, the phase is eight weeks long, and we intend to run four test passes for this phase, we have to complete five test cases per day to stay on track. Even if I'm achieving the test hours, if I can't get through all my tests, then that tells me that tests are taking longer than planned. That could be because I underestimated, but it could also be because the tests are finding more bugs than anticipated. If so, is it likely the system will be ready for customers on the planned ship date?

Figure 5-17 shows an example of this chart. This test team has 31 tests planned per pass, spread across 10 days as four tests on the first day and three tests every day after. The first pass didn't go too well; we didn't make it through all the planned tests. Pass two looks better, except that you can see we've planned on skipping eight of the tests, which hopefully does not include any of the tests we didn't get to in pass one. In pass one, also, more tests failed than passed, which is a bad sign if our tests are well aligned with customer usage. If Figure 5-16 and Figure 5-17 are the same project, then as a test manager I would probably go to the project manager and explain to her why the project is in trouble.

As a matter of fact, Figure 5-16 and Figure 5-17 *are* from the same hypothetical test project. Now, to illustrate the point I was making earlier about the test suite summary, see Figure 5-18. This doesn't look too bad, does it? We're behind schedule in the Earned Value area, but hey, just make your testers work over

Figure 5-17 A chart of system test fulfillment (completion of planned tests)

the weekend. We've gotten through 64 percent of the planned effort. Only around 10 percent are failing, so surely we can fix that. This is the problem with snapshots. Figure 5-18 creates the illusion that there's only a temporary problem that a little extra effort can resolve, while Figure 5-16 and Figure 5-17 show that we have a long-term trend that has played out over three weeks that indicates the project is in trouble.

	A	B	C	D	E	F	G	H	I	J	K	L	M	N	O
1					DataRocket System Test Suite Summary										
2						Pass Two									
3															
4		Total	Planned Tests Fulfilled				Weighted	Planned Tests Unfulfilled				Earned Value			
5	Suite	Cases	Count	Skip	Pass	Fail	Failure	Count	Queued	IP	Block	Pln Hrs	Act Hrs	% Effort	% Exec
6															
7	Environmental Test	8	8	8	0	0	0.00	0	0	0	0	0.00	0.00	0%	0%
8	Load, Capacity and Volume	8	6	0	5	1	2.45	2	2	0	0	32.00	30.00	94%	75%
9	Basic Functionality	12	2	0	1	1	1.30	10	8	1	1	30.00	6.00	20%	17%
10	Standards	3	2	0	1	1	1.25	1	0	1	0	24.00	19.00	79%	67%
11															
12	Total	31	18	8	7	3	5.00	13	10	2	1	86.00	55.00	64%	43%
13	By Pct		58%	26%	23%	10%		42%	32%	6%	3%				

Figure 5-18 A snapshot of the system test effort in tabular form

Are We Testing What We Promised? Charting Test and Bug Coverage

So far, in Chapter 4 and this chapter, we've looked at metrics that measure findings and results. Test cases, test effort, and bug metrics are all interesting sets of data, but they really only tell us something to the extent that our testing is an accurate assessment of quality. In other words, to understand what these metrics and the bug metrics in Chapter 4 really mean, we have to look at how they tie back to the risks to system quality risks we said we would address in Chapter 1. By using the quality risks coverage information I set up earlier in this chapter, and extracting the Quality Risk field from the bug tracking data discussed in Chapter 4, I can create the chart shown in Figure 5-19.

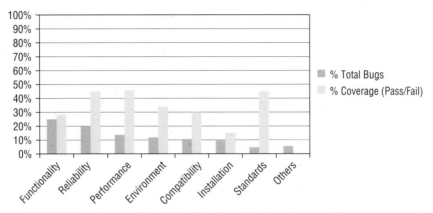

Figure 5-19 Relating bugs and tests back to the risks to system quality

This chart includes a set of light-gray bars that plot the percentage of planned coverage we've achieved against each of the quality risk categories. This data set is based on the weighted coverage figures shown in Figure 5-8. Since we plan on three passes, the total planned coverage is three times the numbers shown in the Pln columns along the bottom of Figure 5-8. Dividing the totals from the Act columns for the passes run so far by that total planned coverage yields the percentage for each category shown in the graph. If we have to add subsequent passes because of schedule slips, then the percentage we achieve either can exceed 100 percent or you can refigure the planned coverage. The problem with the latter approach is that people will be confused when they see coverage go down — perhaps dramatically — after you've added more test passes. I prefer to let the coverage exceed 100 percent, because I measure my percentage against the baseline or original planned test coverage.

Next to each coverage bar you see a dark-gray bar. These bars are calculated looking at the percentage of bugs found in each quality risk category. As the testing proceeds, a project on a path to success will show the taller dark-gray bars next to the taller ligh-gray bars; this means that testing is effective at finding bugs where it looks. Taller dark-gray bars near shorter light-gray bars are a trouble sign, because that might well indicate that many more bugs lurk in an area not fully tested yet. At the beginning of a test phase, note that test coverage will be low, but the total percentage of all bugs found will always add up to 100 percent, so the dark-gray bars might look kind of scary towering over the stubby little light-gray ones. If that chart unduly alarms management, you can plot bugs and test coverage on two different scales, and perhaps use a count rather than a percentage for bugs.

From the chart in Figure 5-19, we can draw a number of conclusions. We can see that functionality is only partially tested but very buggy. Adding some new test cases, doing some exploratory testing, and accelerating the planned testing in that area if possible would be good ideas. Since standards testing is mostly complete but not finding many bugs, perhaps we can shift some of the resources planned for further standards testing in the immediate future to functionality? Notice that once again, though, as with focusing on affected subsystems based on the chart discussed in Chapter 4, we have to consider business risk. If nonconformance to standards is the highest risk and functionality is the lowest, then perhaps you don't want to reallocate resources based on this chart.

Test Status in a Nutshell: Building a Balanced Scorecard or Dashboard

The three charts I just introduced, together with the opened/closed chart discussed in Chapter 4, often make up my dashboard — what some refer to as a *balanced scorecard* — for a test project. These are referred to as "balanced" because any misleading trend or data in one chart will be balanced out or further explained by another chart.

In Chapter 4 I said that, in an opened/closed chart like Figure 5-20, we want to see the opened curve flatten out and the closed curve turn up to intercept the opened curve from below. Suppose we saw such a trend? That could be because we're almost done testing, but it could also be because all the testers are spending all their time on confirmation testing bugs being fixed and released to the test team hourly.

Figure 5-20 An opened/closed chart for DataRocket, completing our dashboard or balanced scorecard for system test

However, if that were the case, Figure 5-16 would catch that, because we wouldn't be achieving any hours of test progress. (I count only hours spent against planned test cases, not against overheads such as installing new builds, confirming bug fixes, going to meetings, and so forth.) Still, it could be that I was getting plenty of planned testing hours done, but not finding many bugs due to a bunch of pernicious existing bugs that made every test take twice as long as I had planned.

However, in that case, Figure 5-17 points out the problem, because that chart will show that I'm not fulfilling my planned test cases. If we have a bunch of bugs making us unable to test areas of the system, then those blocked test cases will show up as a gap between planned and fulfilled tests. Remember, though, that I count skipped tests as fulfilled, because I planned to skip them. If I skipped a bunch of tests and declared victory, wouldn't that fake out the charts?

Nope. If I do that, then Figure 5-19 gives me away, because my achieved coverage measured against the quality risks will be low. If it is low in particular areas while a disproportionate number of bugs have been found there, I know that the charts together — far from telling us that we're about to ship as the opened/closed chart might have misleadingly done — tell me that some specific area or areas of quality are severely hindered by bugs.

As you've seen in these two chapters, this balanced scorecard doesn't require buying any complex or expensive test management tools — you can build it with a spreadsheet and a database. If you want to get fancy, you can post these charts on the company intranet via some automated refresh schedule. If so, you'll need to have a way to get the bug and test data into the appropriate repositories at regular intervals and in sync with each other so the charts match up. Because the dashboard is balanced, discrepancies between source datasets can show up as conflicting figures on two charts. Such mismatched charts will at best lead to questions, and at worst can damage the test team's credibility.

You can buy test management tools that can capture bug, test, and coverage information. Some of those can generate reports like these for you. However, I've found that few of the test management tools can provide really good analytical dashboard reports like these. You might still need to add some post-processing via Excel and some scripting or programming data manipulation. Scripts or programs can then generate the charts, post them to the intranet, and keep the data sets in sync, all automatically.

Questioning Dashboards: Dissent and Disputes

As you've probably guessed by this point in the book, I'm a numerical, analytical type of manager. A "what gets measured gets done" sort of guy. I like metrics, charts, and data. Chapters 4 and 5 of this book were fun for me to write, because I got to crawl around in a bunch of test data, hypothetical and real, and tease meaningful information out of it. Many of the managers I've worked for have also been inclined toward these types of charts and graphs, so these charts have served me well.

However, there are dissenters out there. Not everyone is as excited by these charts. Let me spend a few minutes discussing their concerns with you, along with telling you why I'm still a believer.

Charts, graphs, and numbers tend to give people — especially managers — a feeling of mastery, control, and insight. If the dashboards are well constructed, I would argue that those are not just feelings; those are realities. We are in control. However, how do we know that the dashboards are well constructed? Perhaps we're fooling ourselves, our peers, and our managers, driving multimillion-dollar projects with faulty gauges? Perhaps gathering all these numbers is a distraction from real testing work?

Let me deal with the distraction argument first. Yes, creating these charts can involve some effort, at least at first. Once you get the analytical templates set up, I've found that these usually do not involve more than routine updates. All the data gathered is data I'd need to manage anyway. Most importantly, I think that those who say that analyzing and reporting test metrics is a distraction forget that delivering useful, credible, timely information is a key role for a test team.

How about this argument that the gauges are faulty? It is true, the metrics I've proposed do not directly measure quality, test plan fulfillment, test progress, or residual risk. These measure things which are measurable and which are related to quality, test plan fulfillment, test progress, or residual risk. The scientific name for that is the use of a *surrogate metric*. That is, we measure something we can measure — or can more easily measure — to shed light on something we could not measure (at least not easily) and which is the actual area of interest.

Let me illustrate this with an example. Let's suppose that I gave you a measuring tape and sent you into the parking lot of a nearby grocery story with the instructions, "Please weigh the vehicles in that parking lot." Yes, I said *weigh*. Could you do it?

No, of course; not directly. But notice that you can use a surrogate metric. You can measure the height, width, and length of the vehicles to calculate the volume. You can then make a simplifying assumption that the density of the vehicles — the number of kilograms per cubic meter or pounds per cubic inch — is about the same. Voila! You can use volume as a surrogate metric.

Now, some would say, "No, that's not okay. What about the sports car? What about the bus?" True, a sports car is a small vehicle with a relatively high density due to the large engine. A bus is a big aluminum tube full of air, and thus has a relatively low density. But, provided that we can recognize where the use of a surrogate metric breaks down, we can exercise due caution in its use.

While most of my experiences with dashboards are good, I have had some problems with them that I should mention as cautionary tales. I have worked with a few managers that used test metrics as a means to achieve political ends, often against the test team. In one case, a development manager explained away an enormous bug backlog by saying, "Those bugs aren't customer-facing. The test team is just wasting everyone's time filing all these trivial bug reports." After release, it turned out he was wrong, but by that time the damage was done — to the project and to the test team! One project manager took up valuable project status time — the time I was supposed to spend explaining to everyone what the test status was — talking about how confusing he found the test charts. What a coincidence that those charts, interpreted correctly, showed the project to be in serious trouble and nowhere near on track to hit the current schedule!

Sometimes people find these charts confusing, especially if they don't know much about testing. One project manager was very perplexed by why the test case count changed from one test pass to the next. I explained that we were adding new test cases as we found areas needing further testing. This wasn't okay from her point of view, as she was thinking of the test project in terms of, "Okay, we have 247 test cases; as soon as all of those pass, we can ship." It's more complicated than that, of course, and her confusion indicated that I needed to do a better job of explaining testing and the charts to her.

At this point, it's time for me to admit that I've entered this entire discussion about metrics and charts from the backdoor, as it were. What should really drive the choice of metrics and charts is one of the goals of the test project: to provide the project team with information that helps the team manage the risks to the quality of the system. This includes especially an accurate, meaningful, and timely assessment of system quality, along with data about the project. I create this information by developing tests that address the important quality risks, deploying the system under test in the test environment, running the tests I developed, and reporting my findings in a way that communicates effectively with the project team.

So, what questions would I need to be able to answer for management to serve that goal? Often times, the questions are as follows:

- How is the quality of the system? Are we fixing the quality problems we know about?

- How is the progress of the test effort?

- Are we running all the planned tests?

- Did we address the important quality risks, and what did we find related to those risk?

What trends are developing in these four areas, and what do those trends tell us about when we'll get to an acceptable level of quality?

If these are the questions management has, then the four charts I've just outlined — or variations on them — should suffice. However, your manager might have different questions. Or, you might find that these charts, for whatever reason, don't help you communicate effectively with your colleagues. Charts, metrics, and reports are a means of providing information. Since providing information is the service that testers are rendering, it is incumbent on us to find ways to deliver information that is not only accurate and timely, but also in a format and presentation that our colleagues can understand.

The process of developing usable metrics is an iterative one. I find that there's a continual process of

1. Reassessing the questions that need to be answered, and putting together charts that answer those questions.

2. Making sure that people understand what the metrics mean — and what they don't mean.

3. Getting buy-in to use the metrics as useful information, even when that information does not match desired outcomes or results.

4. Managing the perceptions people have about the usefulness, accuracy, credibility, and timeliness of the information.

Only part of the first step involves the technical tasks we've looked at in Chapter 4 and in this chapter. We'll return to the bigger, interpersonal and managerial issues associated with this process in Chapter 9.

First, though, I'll close this chapter with another discussion of an IEEE 829 template. Then, in the next chapter, we'll move on to a few more tools and techniques. We'll examine what you need to know to manage the dynamic period of test execution, and some tools that can help you plan and track some of the moving parts.

IEEE 829 Test Reporting: Interim, Level, and Master

The IEEE 829 standard includes three templates for test results reporting. You can integrate the test dashboard metrics I covered in this chapter with these reports. As with the other IEEE 829 templates, rigid adherence to the standard can result in documentation-heavy deliverables. I recommend you see these templates as a source of ideas rather than as a document you must use in its entirety, unless you are required to comply with the standard.

The Level Interim Status Report

The first template is called the Level Interim Test Status Report. This is a report designed to summarize the results of testing so far on a given phase or level of testing. Depending on the phase of testing, the IEEE recommends you call this report the System Interim Test Report, Acceptance Interim Test Report, and so forth. They also recommend that the details of each report vary depending on level. This makes sense. I'd expect the Unit Interim Test Report to be less formal and detailed than the System Interim Test Report. The template for such Interim Test Reports is shown in Figure 5-21.

1. Introduction
    1.1. Document identifier
    1.2. Scope
    1.3. References
2. Details
    2.1. Test status summary
    2.2. Changes from plans
    2.3. Test status metrics
3. General
    3.1. Document change procedures and history

Figure 5-21 An IEEE 829 Level Interim Test Status Report template

The first section, Introduction, is much like the same section in other IEEE 829 test templates. The IEEE recommends that the Scope section reference reports and metrics from automated test management tools rather than putting that information into the report. If you can accomplish that with simple links to URLs on the company intranet or to the tool itself, that's fine. However, if the readers of the report cannot easily access these metrics and charts, thus making key elements of the report hard to locate, that's not fine at all. Further, if the quality of the reports and metrics from the tools are poor, making key findings hard to understand, then that's really not fine. In these cases, I recommend that you put the pertinent charts and metrics directly in the report, using the data from the test management tools as a source of the data but spreadsheets like the one shown in this chapter to prepare the charts and metrics.

The Details section includes the main body of the report. The Test Status Summary section gives the current test status in relation to the overall plan. You can combine this information with the test status metrics information. For example, you can see in Figures 5-16 and 5-17 that the current test status is compared against the planned status, and in Figures 5-19 and 5-20 the current status is compared against the ultimate targets. If the deviation from the plan is serious enough to require adjustments, this would result in information for the changes from plans section.

The final section, General, is basically the same as similar sections in other IEEE 829 test templates.

The Level Test Report

At the conclusion of a particular level or phase of testing, the IEEE recommends that you issue a Level Test Report. Depending on the phase of testing, the

IEEE recommends you call this report the System Test Report, Acceptance Test Report, and so forth. As with the Interim report, they also recommend that the details of each report vary depending on level. They also say that, on smaller projects, you can merge reports for multiple levels into a single report. The template for such Level Test Reports is shown in Figure 5-22.

1. Introduction
    1.1. Document identifier
    1.2. Scope
    1.3. References
2. Details
    2.1. Overview of test results
    2.2. Detailed test results
    2.3. Rationale for decisions
    2.4. Conclusions and recommendations
3. General
    3.1. Glossary
    3.2. Document change procedures and history

Figure 5-22 An IEEE 829 Level Test Report template

The first section, Introduction, is much the same as the Introduction section of the Interim Test Report. The References section should refer to the test plans, test design specifications, test case and procedure specifications, test logs, and anomaly reports for the test level in question.

The Details section is the main body of the report. The Overview of Test Results section summarizes the test results for the various test items. It includes information on the specific test items delivered for testing, the versions received, and the test environments used for testing.

The Detailed Test Results section summarizes the results of testing for this level. The IEEE recommends that this section identify all resolved and unresolved bugs, including those which were deferred. Now, this seems to me likely to result in a very long report. I've managed plenty of projects where we found hundreds or even thousands of bugs. So, I would tend to summarize this information here, with a reference to the bug tracking database for those who want the details.

This section should also include a summary of all major testing activities and any events that occurred. For example, you should summarize the results of major test suites like performance tests, reliability tests, and functionality tests. As with the interim report, you should summarize the metrics and the variances from plan (along with the reasons for variance). You should address the issue of completeness of coverage, based on the scope of the test level.

The Details section of the Level Test Report should include more analysis than the Interim Level Report. For example, the IEEE recommends some of the bug analysis I discussed in Chapter 4, such as bug cluster analysis and root cause analysis. That makes sense, to the extent that I want to make recommendations for future projects as well as for this project. However, I often reserve such analysis and the accompanying process improvement recommendations for a project retrospective report.

This Details section should conclude with the rationale for any decisions, along with conclusions and recommendations. For each test item, are the results good or bad, and what limitations exist? The IEEE recommends referring to the pass/fail criteria in the other test documents for this level. You should also discuss the residual level of quality risk, which is easy if you follow the approach discussed in this book.

The IEEE template calls for a go/no-go recommendation from you in this section, but I tend to resist that. If I recommend delay, then I might take the blame for the consequences of late release. If I recommend moving forward, then I might take the blame for the consequence of later failures. I prefer to provide solid information, and let that speak for itself.

The final section, General, is basically the same as similar sections in other IEEE 829 test templates.

The Master Test Report

At the conclusion of all the testing for a project, the IEEE recommends that you issue a Master Test Report. The template for such reports is shown in Figure 5-23. This report should summarize the results of all levels or phases of testing that occurred. In fact, if you wrote a Master Test Plan that describes multiple levels of testing and their relationships (as described in Chapter 2) the IEEE says that you "need … a corresponding Master Test Report that describes the results" of executing the Master Test Plan. I suppose that makes sense, but in many organizations I've worked and consulted with, it would be hard to organize such a report across the various groups responsible for the various levels of testing.

1. Introduction
    1.1. Document identifier
    1.2. Scope
    1.3. References
2. Details of the Master Test Report
    2.1. Overview of all aggregate test results
    2.2. Rationale for decisions
    2.3. Conclusions and recommendations
3. General
    3.1. Glossary
    3.2. Document change procedures and history

Figure 5-23 An IEEE 829 Master Test Report template

The first section, Introduction, is much the same as the Introduction section of the Interim and Level Test Reports. However, the References section in this case refers to the Level Test Reports across all levels of testing for this project.

As you'd expect, the Details section is the core of the report. The Overview of All Aggregate Test Results section gives an evaluation of all the test levels. The IEEE recommends the following information:

- An executive summary of all test activities and tasks, paralleling the test activities and tasks described in the Master Test Plan.

- A summary of all bugs found during testing, including their resolution (or lack of resolution).

- An assessment of the quality as of the end of the testing, along with a justification for that assessment. I would exercise caution while writing this part of the report, because one ill-advised or unfounded statement here could stir up a real hornet's nest. This seems to me tied to the Rationale for Decisions section, in that this rationale section gives the reasons for the assessment made.

- A summary of the overall metrics collected. Presumably this would focus on metrics related to the test project itself, but might also include test process metrics.

Like the Level Test Report, the Master Test Report template includes a section for conclusions and recommendations. This is similar information, albeit spanning all test levels. However, it also includes information about lessons learned and process improvements made during the testing. The IEEE especially recommends a discussion of bug clusters and root causes and how that affected the overall development effort, along with a discussion for the process by which the team made bug triage decisions.

The final section, General, is basically the same as similar sections in other IEEE 829 test templates.

Case Study One

On the loan processing application project discussed in the case studies in Chapters 2 and 4, it was very important to ensure that various specific conditions were evaluated. Banks have lots of business rules about who can and can't get a loan, as well as being heavily regulated by individual states and the United States federal government. Failure to test all these conditions could have resulted in situations such as making loans to bankrupt or unemployed applicants, getting sued for not being able to prove a legitimate business reason for denying a loan to an applicant, and so forth. Therefore, the test team built an Access database to keep track of all these conditions, and to trace the conditions back to specific test cases that covered them. The case study's test coverage tracking database, "Case Study Loan Processing Test Coverage Tracking," is available at www.rbcs-us.com.

This database contains two tables, TestCases and TestConditions, with a one-to-many relationship between the two based on the Sequence field, which was one unique test case identifier (see Figure 5-24). The tests were built to cover all the conditions. Various queries exist in the database to check that all conditions were covered, to verify that most test cases mapped to a condition, to identify the test cases that covered particularly high-risk conditions, and so forth. You could extend this database with result and bug tracking information, which would then allow an integrated view of the test status, including coverage, in a single database.

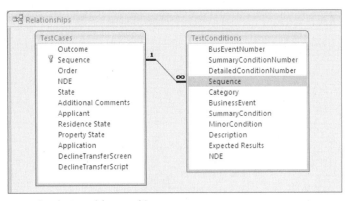

Figure 5-24 Two database tables tracking test case coverage

However, such integrated test management databases are a major under-taking to construct. (RBCS built a test management system for one client that also included an automated API-testing harness, and the entire application required more than two person-years of effort.) Therefore, on this project I used my usual test tracking spreadsheet. The case study test tracking document, "Case Study Loan Processing Test Tracking," is available at www.rbcs-us.com. Please note that I do not have an integrated dashboard in this spreadsheet, as I used the separate bug metrics spreadsheet that was the topic of Chapter 4's case study. Also note that I did not import data from the coverage-tracking database to analyze coverage into this spreadsheet. Finally, note that the lay-out and format is less polished than the examples in this chapter. Sometimes, polish is sacrificed for utility and speed on real projects, so you shouldn't feel bad if your spreadsheets, reports, templates, and tools don't look as fancy as many of the ones in this book!

A few noteworthy details bear discussion. Notice in Figure 5-25 that the planned and actual effort hours (columns L and M) are very small numbers.

Most test cases involved submitting a single loan application into the system, which took between 15 and 30 minutes. This is really about the finest-grained level of detail you can effectively track using this technique. If you start tracking one- and two-minute tasks, you'll spend as much time updating the worksheets as getting any work done. My usual rule of thumb is to build test cases between one and four hours long, though, as in this case, that rule has to bend sometimes. For this system, the test case duration was driven by the workflows being tested.

	A	B	C	D	E	F	G	H	I	J	K	L	M	N
1			Some Loan App Release 1.0 System Test Case Tracking Spreadsheet											
2					Pass 3									
3														
4		Test		Test	System	Bug	Bug	Bug		Plan	Act	Plan	Act	
5	Owner	ID	Test Suite/Case	State	Config	ID	RPN	State	By	Date	Date	Hrs	Hrs	Comment
48		2.000	*UAT Scripts*											
49	HD	2.001	1.1.0 More than 4 Stips Approved	Warn	018994/Train	1009	2	Assigned	HD	5/18	5/14	0.50	0.50	
50	HD	2.002	1.1.1 Basic App / Co App	Warn	018994/Train	1009	2	Assigned	HD	5/18	5/14	0.50	0.50	
51	HD	2.003	1.1.2 Direct mail, No ID	Warn	018994/Train	1009	2	Assigned	HD	5/18	5/14	0.50	0.25	
52	HD	2.004	1.1.2.2 Collateral for sale	Pass	018994/Train				HD	5/18	5/14	0.50	0.25	
53	HD	2.005	1.1.3. Collateral Type is 2-4 Dup/Tri/Quad	Warn	018994/Train	1009	2	Assigned	HD	5/18	5/14	0.50	0.25	
54	HD	2.006	1.1.4 Property is located in	Warn	018994/Train	1009	2	Assigned	HD	5/18	5/14	0.50	0.25	
55	HD	2.007	1.1.5 Dischared BK < 36 months	Pass	018994/Train				HD	5/18	5/14	0.50	0.25	
56	HD	2.008	1.1.5.2 Non-dischared bankruptcy	Pass	018994/Train				HD	5/18	5/14	0.50	0.25	
57	HD	2.009	1.1.6 Joint	Warn	018994/Train	1009	2	Assigned	HD	5/18	5/14	0.50	0.50	
58	HD	2.010	1.1.7 Warm Transfer	Pass	018994/Train				HD	5/18	5/14	0.50	0.25	
59	HD	2.011	1.1.7.4 Co-App is under 18 years old	Pass	018994/Train				HD	5/18	5/14	0.50	0.25	
60	HD	2.012	1.1.8 CA cond. Approve < 1 acre	Warn	018994/Train	1009	2	Assigned	HD	5/18	5/14	0.50	0.50	
61	HD	2.013	1.1.8.2 CA cond. Approve 5-25 acres	Warn	018994/Train	1009	2	Assigned	HD	5/18	5/14	0.50	0.50	
62	HD	2.014	1.1.8.3 SLA calculates DTI factoring in payoff of prior lies	Fail	018994/Train	1067	2	Review	HD	5/18	5/15	0.50	0.50	
63	HD	2.015	1.1.9.4 Application has rental income	Warn	018994/Train	1009	2	Assigned	HD	5/18	5/15	0.50	0.25	
64	HD	2.016	1.1.10 App has Non-Discharged BK	Pass	018994/Train				HD	5/18	5/15	0.50	0.25	
65	HD	2.017	1.1.11 Co-App Self Empd < 12 months	Pass	018994/Train				HD	5/18	5/15	0.50	0.25	
66	HD	2.018	1.1.13 DTI to High	Warn	018994/Train	1067	2	Review	HD	5/18	5/15	0.50	0.50	

Figure 5-25 Case study test case summary for pass three

In Figure 5-26, you can see that most of the passes were defined as one week. This corresponded to the test release cycle, which was weekly. However, the first pass took three weeks, and it seems that we planned it that way. In actuality, we had to react as well as we could to the fact that we violated the entry criteria in terms of having a stable system. As a result, we could not get any testing work done until the middle of the second week, and even then it was slow. This inefficiency also shows up in the Test Progress chart, which you can find as a worksheet in the spreadsheet if you care to look at it.

Notice also that the test case counts changed from 274 in passes one and two to 299 in passes three through five. This happened primarily because we added some new test cases for debt consolidation in pass three. This was related to a change in the system's functionality.

I thank my client on this project, a major midwestern financial institution, and the executive in charge of development for allowing me to share this example with readers of this book. I have purged all identifying and otherwise private information from this document. My client contact has asked that the organization remain anonymous.

Figure 5-26 Case study test fulfillment chart

Case Study Two

This case study comes from a major RBCS client, CA. It describes how one of their teams moved from an Office-based test tracking approach to a more automated one. The authors are Andrew Brooks, vice president, CA Network and Voice Management Quality Assurance; Jodi Mullins, senior software engineer, CA Network and Voice Management Test Automation; Steven Gaudreau, software engineer, CA Network and Voice Management Test Automation; and, Rex Black.

Introduction

There are many questions that are asked during the life cycle of a project as it begins the development cycle, enters testing, and ultimately is released to the customer. The project team must consider, estimate, and track the status of new features, existing features, and milestones. To support the project team in this work, the test organization must understand what needs to be tested, allocate resources, assess risk, and track progress.

Not only must the test organization carry out its work effectively and efficiently, but it must also gather test tracking information to answer the usual questions, such as, "What are you testing (and not testing)?" "What are you testing first (and last)?" and, "When will the testing complete?" So, the test plan must address how the testers will assess pass/fail status for the tests and how it will report all aspects of the project under test. The test tracking process must support continuous quality improvement *and* the timely delivery of a product.

Software test execution consists of many small tasks — the individual test cases — that testers must execute during the course of a development project. Due to the fine-grained nature of the work, we have found that the test manager cannot easily capture and track these test execution tasks in project planning tools such as Microsoft Project. This commonly observed problem has led test managers to implement a wide range of test tracking and summarization approaches, ranging from simple spreadsheets (such as those described earlier in this chapter) to custom-built applications to commercial test management tools. This case study describes how our team at CA evolved from a spreadsheet-based approach to a more sophisticated custom-built application.

The Evolution of a Tool

We started our journey with rather modest goals. We needed a quick, concise way to track test progress during a release, to know exactly what we had tested, what the test results were, and what remained to test. We initially employed a simple spreadsheet per functional area. Each functional area was a logical collection of test cases, which were referred to as a *test suite* throughout this chapter.

This worked, to a point. The test engineer responsible for each functional area could keep track of their work. The test managers knew exactly what the engineers had tested. This didn't work perfectly, though. With as many as 40 separate spreadsheets, project managers had quite a task when they wanted to correlate these disparate spreadsheets to evaluate test team progress against a plan of record.

The next phase of refinement had various spreadsheets feeding into a master spreadsheet. The master spreadsheet served as a dashboard (like the test suite summary worksheet shown in this chapter), and better facilitated project level tracking of a given release.

This worked quite well for a few years, but also was imperfect. The integrated multitude of spreadsheets, feeding into a master spreadsheet, involved a lot of cross-referencing links. These links updated sluggishly and were fragile. With multiple test engineers updating the same spreadsheet or related spreadsheets, this made file sharing tricky. To avoid damaging the fragile links, engineers had to adhere to a tight set of rules. Violating these rules could not only break the links — causing the status not to roll up properly into the master spreadsheet — but could also invalidate the data representation, so that the roll-up suffered from the classic *garbage in garbage out* problem.

Finally, the spreadsheet did not include automatic correlation of data from previous releases, a potentially useful feature for simplifying planning of future releases. However, trying to add yet another feature to this sprawling, fragile collection of spreadsheets could be the proverbial straw on the camel's back. It was clear to us that the spreadsheet platform for test tracking had reached — and perhaps exceeded — the limits of its scalability. It was time for the next step in the evolution of test tracking in our test organization.

Requirements for Moving Forward

To point that next step in the right direction, we decided to gather requirements for the new test tracking approach we wanted to build. We came up with the following:

- Full capabilities of the previous, spreadsheet-based tool, including test case level tracking of planned versus actual execution and functional area roll-up into a dashboard.

- High scalability, allowing hundreds of thousands of concurrent test cases to be active in the database across multiple concurrent releases.

- High performance, without any multi-minute wait times traversing screens.

- Real-time, automated status updating.

- Multi-user access with fine-grained access control.

- Inter-release correlation.

- Multiple views depending on role, including test planner/administrator, auditor, and test engineer.

- Ease of use for the test engineer, including test cases auto-populated from test plans. (Note: In this group at CA, the test plan includes a complete set of test cases, which contrasts with the contents of a test plan as was described it in Chapter 2.)

- Integration with test planning, bug tracking and automation tools.

- Common reporting for manual testing and automated testing, including a tie-in to Test Case Builder, our test automation tool.

- A dashboard for multiple active release visibility.

- Built-in support for risk-based testing.

With these requirements defined, we were ready to move forward.

Design and Implementation

We decided on a web-based architecture with a back-end database (see Figure 5-27). This supports the requirements of maintaining all of the capabilities of our spreadsheet-based approach while improving performance and scalability. This architecture also provides real-time reporting and greatly improves multi-user access via a standard role-based web-server design. The integral database also facilitates tracking and comparison between releases. As discussed in Chapter 4 (in the context of comparison of previous results for the same or similar test cases during bug reporting) and this chapter (in the context of evaluating the yield of a test case), the ability to compare across releases allows us to measure the effectiveness of regression test cases. We can then adjust or remove ineffective tests to maximize our bug finding efficiency while still providing the necessary regression risk mitigation.

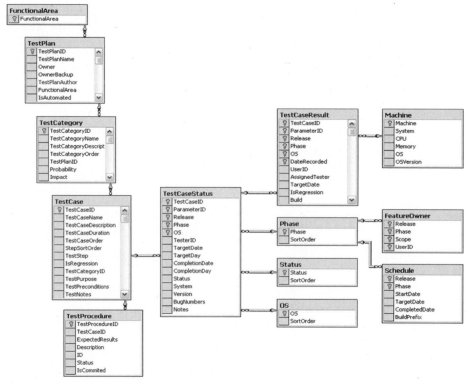

Figure 5-27 Database architecture diagram

The database architecture allows us to create and maintain a test case library. We organized this library on the feature hierarchy and the product release in which the feature was added. The test engineer classifies each test case in the database as a new feature test case or regression test case. This allows for dynamic planning of a test cycle. Before each test cycle, the test manager can determine whether a feature requires full testing using all available test cases (such as for a new feature or where significant changes occurs in a functional area) or whether only running the regression test cases will suffice (such as when no changes occurs to the feature).

In the role of test planner, the test manager can then fine-tune the proposed testing based on risk, time to test, and available testers. The nature of the database architecture allows managers to relate and represent cross-functional testing aspects. The test planner can make educated decisions about which test cases to schedule for the project, considering the current project to be tested and past testing results for previous projects.

At the start of the test cycle, the test planner enters these scheduled test cases into a status table, associated with the feature under test. This table provides the historical reference point that tool users can access to see real-time updates. They can also utilize this reference to review the overall success of a released project. During test execution, the tester (test engineer) will enter data into this table.

We created the design and layout of the web-based architecture based on standard web technologies. It allows for portability, ease of use, and broad simultaneous access. We carried over the hierarchical design at the database level into the structure of the web interface. The web interface provides the input mechanism for all test data in the database.

The hierarchical approach within the web-based architecture provides for several layers of drill-down navigation from the top-level view down to the individual test case results. If you would like more details on a data point, you can navigate through the links to see exactly what failed and any associated bug numbers created. The tool can provide statistical information at each level of the hierarchy. This gives the users at-a-glance reporting and visual status as to the current state of a test case. In addition, the tool provides a graphical summary at multiple levels on the project as well.

Let's take a look at some of the reporting facilities it provides, from the top-level view to the bottom:

Release View: At the top level, the tool provides a high-level summary of the status of all releases undergoing testing at a given time for our organization. This view provides a tabular summary of testing as well as a graphical dashboard of testing status.

Functional Area: This view breaks down the test status by its primary component areas. This allows an auditor to understand the test status of a release not only against overall test coverage but against a breadth of coverage (see Figure 5-28).

Test Plan: The Test Plan level highlights test plans associated with the functional area to which it belongs. This is important for future capabilities, since we'll want the tracking tool to create a new test plan from an existing test plan by adding new test cases. Such incremental addition of test cases can occur, for example, in response to triaging a customer bug or as we grow our automated test set.

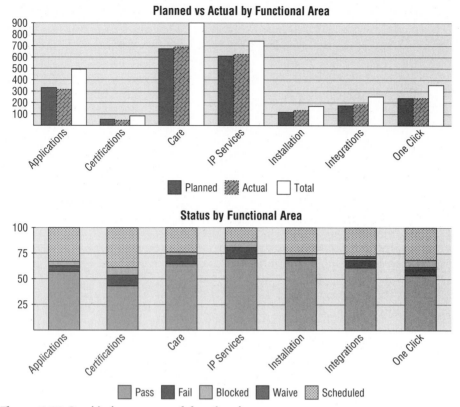

Figure 5-28 Graphical summary of functional areas

Test Category: This is the logical grouping of test cases within a test plan. This layer is primarily used to associate the level of risk with our tests. Similar to what is described in Chapter 1, our test organization defines the level of risk as the product of the likelihood of a failure and impact if there is a failure. We wanted this risk level association with tests to occur at a level fine-grained enough to be meaningful but not so fine-grained that we would have to do risk analysis individually on each of the thousands of existing test cases associated with a test project.

Test Case: This is the atomic layer where test cases are given a planned date, the date tested is tracked, and the time to execute is logged. Similar to what was discussed in this chapter, test engineers track the test status as *pass*, *fail*, *blocked*, or *waived*.

Thus, we can support the information needs of a number of different stakeholders, which is a big improvement over the primarily tactical reporting available in our previous spreadsheet-based approach.

Managing Risk

As discussed in Chapter 1, having risk levels associated with tests (in this case, test categories) allows us to choose what test cases we run first. It also allows us to understand the test effort required of the project. When entering a test cycle, we assess risk based on code changes in the test category, the criticality of the functional area under test, historical trends, and so forth. As previously stated, the tool displays risk metrics at the category level and automatically associates that risk with the underlying test cases.

We associate a numeric value to likelihood and impact (each having a scale of 1 to 5) for each test category. (Notice that this group in CA uses an ascending scale, for risk values, with 5 being the most serious, rather than a descending scale as described in Chapter 1.) We apply a risk weight to the category. We can then roll up the risk weight across the category's associated test cases to see the total risk coverage achieved as a function of total tests executed (see Figure 5-29). To achieve the same kind of proper dispersion of risk levels as discussed in Chapter 1, we force these risk levels for the categories into a normal curve. We can now prioritize test case execution based on risk, and we can track and report test status based on risk (see Figure 5-30).

Figure 5-29 Risk assessment vs. tests complete

Showing the Big Picture *and* the Details

As the test cycle involves several different aspects of planning, testing, and reporting, the need for multiple views based on a user's role is a fundamental design consideration. By creating different views for the test planners and test engineers, we streamlined the workflow of each role. Planners see the larger picture of the test cycle and the test cases for that cycle. Testers see a simplified view that displays only the tests that they need to execute. Likewise, there is an auditor view for managers and other members of the cross-functional

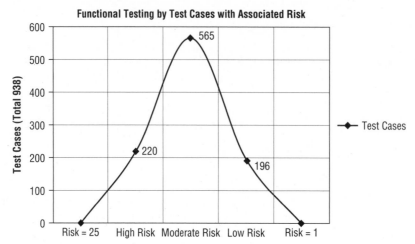

Figure 5-30 Risk-based standard deviation

project team who generally want read-only access to drill down into a project to understand how the team is tracking to plan and identify collections of test tasks that might delay the end of the test execution.

A test planner has the ability to see across functional areas to the test cases. This allows for assiduous planning with a broad perspective. A tester can use the tool to help in focusing on assigned test cases (see Figure 5-31). An interested party or auditor can use the tool for at-a-glance updates on the test cycle and current test status (see Figure 5-32).

Of course, this was not an entirely new development project, but rather it builds on existing test assets. Moving from the spreadsheet-based approach to a fully functional database posed another challenge. We needed to import the test cases from the spreadsheets into the database while adhering to the test plans for each functional area and maintain the relationships between features, test plans, and test cases. Further, as we implement new features in the product, the defined test cases can expand, decrease, or become obsolete. To address the migration of the tracking mechanism and to support setting up new test plans or expanding test plans, we implemented the capability of importing test cases from these existing test plans based on a standard test plan template. This simplifies setup for the test planner to a test case selection activity that can be expedited even further by importing a previous test plan and applying changes.

By defining a standard test plan template we can set expectations on the formatted data to make logical decisions on what the data represents and what database it belongs in, and maintain the hierarchy defined in the test plan. We first take an existing test plan and then convert it to an HTML document. HTML provides the advantage of applying tags to elements of the plan to identify the textual content. We utilize these tags to identify the sections of

Figure 5-31 Planner and tester view

the document we are interested in. During the importation process, the tool assigns the values to variables based on our definitions and incorporates the values into the appropriate database structure.

In order to have a full picture of all executed test cases, not just manual ones, we integrated automated test case status information. By creating a connector to tie the tracking tool to our automated test tools, we can continuously update this information without any additional effort. By assigning the value of *Automated* to the *tester* variable for a test case, the tracking tool can extract status information from the automated test tool for that test case. This not only assists with tracking and reporting, but also with planning, as the test planner can see the entire test set, both automated and manual.

The database architecture and the resulting web-based views provide many levels of detail, depending on the information needed by the product delivery team. We designed the layout and data results in a way that provides the desired information without inundating people with unnecessary detail. This ability to provide information to test stakeholders and participants at the

Figure 5-32 Auditor view

appropriate level of detail and abstraction is consistent with the discussion of test dashboards throughout this chapter.

Summary

Test tracking and reporting are key responsibilities for test organizations. A test organization can start with a simple approach, as we did, and evolve that approach to provide ever-increasing value to the test organization, as illustrated in this case study. The key is to make a commitment and stick with it. Once test engineers (who were initially skeptical) realized that the tool could actually save them time and facilitate continuous improvement, they came to support it.

As you've seen in this case study, we implemented a web-based planning and tracking tool as the next generation of test tracking. Through careful requirements specification and design, we integrated the tool with test plan templates, manual and automated testing, risk-based analysis, and a tracking dashboard. This tool has a built in database that allows a great degree of flexibility for reporting and correlation analysis.

The tracking tool provides a mechanism to correlate historical regression testing and test case execution time to allow for better estimation and planning. It also answers the common question as to how a bug escaped from the test process to beta or released product. If a customer bug presents itself, we can go back to the tool to see who, if anyone, tested this area. We can use that insight either to fix the test case or to better educate the test engineer as to how our customers use our product.

Given the real-time nature of the tool, test managers can easily forecast deviations from the plan and re-allocate resources accordingly to ensure that tall poles are knocked down and releases stay on schedule. This can include automatic notification of missing tests. It also includes, through a mechanism like the earning value technique discussed in this chapter, the ability to evaluate the evolving risks of missing target dates based on the amount of testing completed versus the amount of test execution time elapsed. Other benefits include a clear mechanism to proactively share test planning with a cross-functional project team. Finally, by having a strong tie-in to test plans, the tool facilitates audits by following a requirement all the way through test planning and test results.

Exercises

1. Consider ways of structuring test tracking for Omninet. Would you track tests for each subsystem (kiosk, call center, and data center) separately? How would you track end-to-end tests? Draw a picture of the various tracking documents and their relationships.

2. When you are a test manager, it's easy to walk into a project status meeting and deliver good news, but what happens when you have to tell people what they don't want to hear? For this exercise, you are given three scenarios that each describes a bad situation with the SpeedyWriter project. The following information is common to all three scenarios:

   ▪ The project is SpeedyWriter, the browser-hosted word-processing application that is used as an example in this book.

   ▪ The Development ran (or was to have run) the component and integration test phase, with component test from December 11 through 29 and integration test from December 18 through January 12. The project is now in the system test phase. The first cycle ran from January 8 through 14. Today is January 15. The system test phase exit meeting is planned for January 29 (after two more one-week test cycles).

   For each of these, propose ways to manage the presentation of the test status to the project team. Keep in mind that while you are presenting bad news, you want to portray the test team as part of the solution. Here are the three scenarios:

   a. The first scenario is that there are too many bugs and not enough time. In this scenario, the system test team is working productively and finding a few more bugs than expected. Furthermore, a large backlog (about 30 bugs) exists. Given the current bug find rate — which is not decreasing — and the backlog, the plan to finish testing in two weeks is in jeopardy. The high bug find rate forced you to skip a large number of tests in cycle one. The test dashboard charts for this scenario are shown in Figure 5-33, Figure 5-34, Figure 5-35, and Figure 5-36.

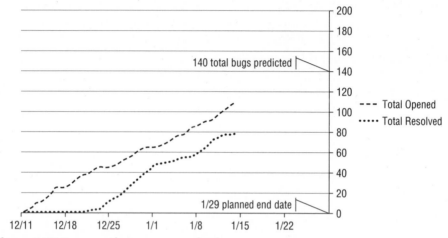

Figure 5-33 Too many bugs: open-resolved

Figure 5-34 Too many bugs: hours progress

b. The second scenario is that there is no stable test environment. The system test team is totally blocked. The operations and development teams were unable to install a working build during the entire week.

Figure 5-35 Too many bugs: test fulfillment

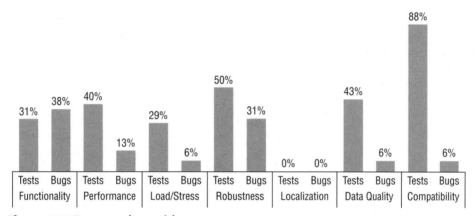

Figure 5-36 Too many bugs: risk coverage

On Monday it turned out that the wrong software version was on the web server. On Tuesday the operations team had to reinstall the operating system on the web server to install the proper software. On Wednesday the development team delivered five un-installable builds. On Thursday testing finally started, but none of the clients could see the servers on the network. On Friday running the Speedy-Writer application caused the server to crash repeatedly. On Saturday and Sunday, in an attempt to catch up, your team came in to run tests but the browser kept aborting during testing. Pages and mobile-phone calls to operations and development staff were not returned. Testing would start but then stop as the onion-peeling exercises occurred each day. The test dashboard charts for this scenario are shown in Figure 5-37, Figure 5-38, Figure 5-39, and Figure 5-40.

Figure 5-37 Onion-peeling: open-resolved

Figure 5-38 Onion-peeling: hours progress

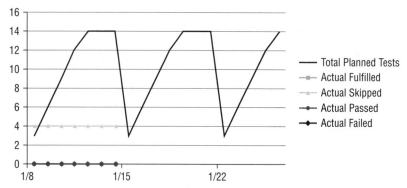

Figure 5-39 Onion-peeling: test fulfillment

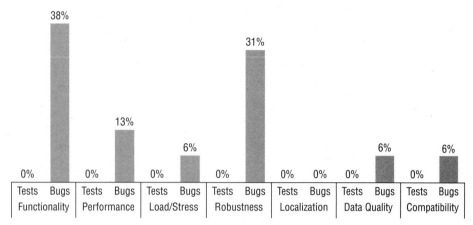

Figure 5-40 Onion-peeling: risk coverage

c. The third scenario is that there is inadequate testing of components and integration. The system test team found many bugs in cycle one. You added extra testers to meet the plan, but the problems are myriad and even exist in basic areas that simple testing should have caught. For example, you can't save a document longer than one page. The number and nature of the problems blocks many more-sophisticated tests. The development team has been warning the system test team informally that no time was in the schedule for sufficient component and integration testing. The test dashboard charts for this scenario are shown in Figure 5-41, Figure 5-42, Figure 5-43, and Figure 5-44.

Figure 5-41 Inadequate: open-resolved

Figure 5-42 Inadequate: hours progress

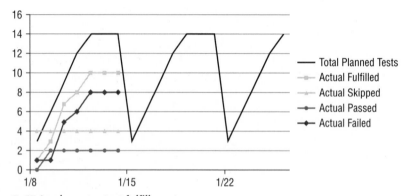

Figure 5-43 Inadequate: test fulfillment

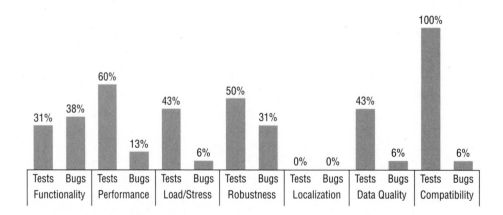

Figure 5-44 Inadequate: risk coverage

3. Assume that you are working on a large development project, leading a test team, and reporting to a project manager. Because of the large number of bugs found in the latest test cycle, your colleague, the development manager, thinks that the testing effort was not started in earnest until recently. You believe that the increase in the number of bugs is because the quality of fixes put in this release of the software is not good, specifically that there are many regressions. Can you use the test tracking spreadsheet to demonstrate this? If so, sketch a test tracking spreadsheet that might illustrate this point.[2]

4. Suppose that your project's regression testing strategy is to re-run only test cases that have failed against previous releases, rather than re-running every test case in the test set for the test phase as shown in this chapter. In other words, in each cycle you have an ever-increasing (hopefully) number of tests that you skip because they have already passed. If you use the tracking spreadsheet shown in this chapter, this growing number of skipped tests will eventually distort the test summary and the planned test fulfillment chart, because skipped tests are counted as fulfilled. (A further complication is that skipped tests are not counted in earned value calculation, because they do not involve any planned or expended effort.) How could you modify this technique to accommodate tracking such a project?

5. Export the coverage tracking data from the TestConditions table in the case study coverage tracking database into a worksheet in the case study test tracking spreadsheet. Match the sequence numbers in the table against the sequence numbers embedded in the test case names in most of the test suites. (You can ignore test cases that don't map to specific test conditions for this exercise.) Produce a chart that shows coverage of these conditions, similar to the chart shown in Figure 5-19 but without the bug data. In any of the three passes for which the test tracking spreadsheet contains test results, do any conditions remain uncovered? Is there any explanation of this in the test tracking spreadsheet?

6. In the templates and case studies provided with this book, there are three files that have test tracking data from multiple test passes: "Case Study Info Appliance Client Test Tracking.xls," "Case Study Info Appliance Server Test Tracking.xls," and "Case Study Loan Processing Test Tracking.xls." For the passes for which you have data on each project, produce a single graph that shows how the total weighted failure counts from the test suite summary worksheets behaved during the project. Compare this chart with the find-fix charts found in "Case Study Info Appliance

---

[2]This exercise was contributed by Dr. Deepti Suri of Milwaukee School of Engineering.

Bug Metrics.xls" and "Case Study Loan Processing Test Tracking.xls." Do you think that charting the total weighted failure from one pass to the next might serve as an equally good or better measure of quality and project progress? Explain.[3]

---

[3]I thank Ken Sommerville of XLR8 Technology for asking the perceptive question that led me to create this exercise.

Tips and Tools for Crunch Mode: Managing the Dynamic

Ah, crunch mode. That period of the project, usually starting during test execution, where people begin to suspect that the project team might not meet the schedule, the project might exceed budget, the system under test might not meet the desired level of quality, or not all the features might make it in. If you are unlucky, crunch mode might entail two, three, or all four of these problems.

If you've been through a test project once or twice, you know that a project in crunch mode is both hectic and confusing: facts prove elusive, plans change, and previously unknown dependencies emerge to delay and impede tasks. To some extent, the planning, preparation, and structured information gathering I've recommended in previous chapters can help you alleviate these problems. However, test execution is always a challenge, and you can't document your way out of whatever amount of chaos exists elsewhere in the project, because it will naturally leak into the test project.

This chapter offers two new tools specifically geared toward managing the goat rodeos that can consume your life during test execution. One is a logistics database that tracks the locations, configurations, and test requirements for hardware, software, infrastructure, and staff. The other is a simple change management database that helps you respond to the inevitable course corrections, both smooth and jerky, that occur on any test project. First, though, let me offer some observations on crunch mode that might aid you in maintaining your professionalism and sanity during this high-pressure period.

Do Sweat the Details: Staying on Top of Everything

The common thread running through all the tips in this section is the importance of remaining in control of the details swirling around you. During test execution, you will have many items to attend to, all of them urgent, but you should be sure to set aside some time to look at where your testing is taking you. Are you on track? What risks and roadblocks loom? In that spirit, here are some suggestions that should help you survive crunch time.

Moving Forward While Getting All the Facts: The Desire for Certainty, the Imperative of Progress

Imagine that you and I have two conversations. In the first, we're standing near a brick house, and you point to the wall and say, "Look at that chameleon! It changed color to match the brick." I look, I see the lizard, I notice its red hue, and I agree. In the second, you say, "Did you know that my golden retriever Gertrude can talk?" In the absence of hearing the dog talk myself, I'm not likely to believe you.

Often, the most interesting bug reports start out along these lines: *I did X, and everything seemed to be going fine. Then, all of a sudden Y happened, and the system crashed.* Sadly, you then discover that repeating action X doesn't repeat consequence Y. The failure is intermittent. You try a dozen times, but you can duplicate the failure only once or twice. You change some variables that might be related, and you can't reproduce the failure. But maybe it's not gone. It's hard to tell these types of stories to developers without triggering incredulity.

A solid bug report is satisfying and goes a long way toward building credibility with developers. Certainty — "this is the truth, and I can demonstrate it" — is a good feeling. A clean, reproducible bug report is indisputable. In many cases, though, the price of certainty is too high. If you've ever had to perform a reliability test of software or hardware, you know how time-consuming such demonstrations of statistical confidence can be. If you tried to investigate every bug to the level of certainty, you'd never find half of them. It's important to keep in mind the need to progress. Testing computers, like all engineering, is not a search for truth — that's science. Engineering is about producing things, about making useful objects. Often as not, close enough must be good enough.

This is not to say that sloppy work or a lack of attention to details in developing test systems, running test cases, or writing bug reports is acceptable. As I pointed out in the case study in the last chapter, though, there are certain levels of polish that can be skipped in the interests of time. If you're writing a bug report about a low-priority problem, you should certainly write a good report, as described in Chapter 4. However, you needn't try every single possible isolation step or reproduce the bug a dozen times.

Dependencies, Schedules, and Reminders: The Importance of Follow-Up

One of the more daunting challenges of managing a test project is that so many dependencies converge at test execution. You can often kludge your way through test development, but you can't execute tests unless all the myriad details and external components come together at the right time. One missing configuration file or hardware device can render all your test results meaningless. You can end up with an entire platoon of testers sitting around for days.

This type of incident is hardly the test manager's fault. You probably have your hands full managing your own team, and you can't be expected to manage others. This is cold comfort, however, when you are spending a weekend in the lab with your testers. All too often, missing components show up or prerequisite tasks are completed at 5:00 on a Friday afternoon, followed by a pep talk from a manager who stresses that it's the responsibility of the team players in the test organization to help compensate for the schedule hit. It's true that you can't manage other groups, but you should try to keep an eye on project-wide events and trends that can negatively impact your test schedule, and make sure you clearly communicate the potential or pending difficulties to your management.

Beyond simply staying in the loop concerning other parts of the project, it's essential that you learn to manage time and to set reminders and milestones for yourself. I've used scheduling programs such as Outlook to do so. The particular tool you choose doesn't matter much, as long as you set reminders about when external events that affect testing are scheduled to occur, and then follow up with the appropriate person:

Phone switch should be configured today. Check with John.

Three systems due to ship from Lucky Bit today. Check with Lin-Tsu and then verify customs broker with Jack.

Muhammad's team to deliver first cut of the XYZ software today. Follow up.

Keeping apprised of schedule slips, feature changes, and other modifications to the plan allows you to react in advance, which gives you more options. Wouldn't you rather know at 4:00 on Wednesday afternoon that you have to line up staff for weekend coverage, instead of finding out at 4:00 on Friday afternoon? By being proactive, you will earn some recovery or contingency time.

It Won't Deliver Itself: Revisions and Release Processes

Between the completion of a hardware or software subsystem and its delivery for testing lie various degrees and types of heavy lifting. Someone must assemble the software into a package of some sort, either physical or electronic. Someone must configure, pack, and send the hardware. If applicable, someone must deal with the shipping and customs clearance issues. People don't tend to volunteer to carry out these activities, which are not heroic, rewarding, or easy to keep straight.

Because you are on the receiving end, it behooves you to drive the definition of the process. For each subsystem or system, you should ensure that someone is responsible for delivering usable, testable items to your test group. I'm not suggesting that you take ownership of such tasks — far from it; you have enough to do. Often a well-worded email, sent to your manager and some of the people you suspect *might* be appropriate owners, will suffice.

In extreme cases, you might need to develop and promulgate a plan yourself. Such a plan would assign ownership of various stages of the delivery process to specific people, based on your understanding of their roles. This is dangerous ground politically, however. Be sure that you have sufficient clout before you attempt it.

As discussed in earlier chapters, you'll also face the issues of frequency and configuration management as new builds are released. Within a few weeks of initial delivery, you should seek renewed commitments from your development counterparts that they intend to adhere to the release plan agreed upon previously.

It Won't Install Itself, Either: Configuring the Test Environment

In some cases, testing covers the process of installing software or hardware components. When you test operating systems or applications, for example, the first step of testing a new build is to test the installation or upgrade procedures, which should result in a configured test environment. Unfortunately, however, it often leaves you with a broken mess, especially at the beginning, so you must have contingency plans in place whenever possible. One way to do this is to keep hard drive images of known good systems either on the network, on DVDs, on tape, or on spare drives. There are also commercial configuration management tools available for complex networks.

You can't always put such plans in place, of course. Obviously, access to a stable, completely installed version of the system under test is essential for effective testing. If you can't install the software or you can't get an operating system running on the computer you're testing, you are blocked. Since you'll find such announcements unpopular with management, always double-check to make sure you have your facts straight.

Sometimes the task of installing and configuring the test environment is too complex for a typical tester to handle. In such instances, you have two alternatives: either have the necessary level of system administration support available within your team, or have the expertise available on call from the project team, information systems, technical support, or another appropriate group.

My preference is the former. The best way to ensure that someone's priorities are aligned with yours is to have that person on your team. If you do use external system administration support, do your best to get a guarantee of response times and a clear process for escalating problem situations up the management chain to prevent them from festering. I have worked with some excellent support staff, but I have also had some negative experiences with relying on outside help. These problems were usually not the other team's fault. When a limited set of people must support half a dozen groups, eventually your request will languish in a queue. That will not happen if the support resource works on your team.

"The Hobgoblin of Small Minds" Is Your Friend: Auditing and Updating Test Results

The plethora of information, sometimes conflicting, can make test execution confusing. Except for the simplest of functional bugs, it's seldom clear exactly what has gone wrong when an anomaly first comes to light. Significant time might elapse between the first muttered, "What the heck?" and the completion of a bug report. Of course, since a bug report is a description of symptoms, further research is usually needed. A certain lack of clarity comes with the territory. Indeed, since tests are experiments, you could say that testing is about *creating* a lack of clarity, about raising questions in people's minds, about challenging beliefs and opinions that people think are facts.

When you challenge preconceived notions, you must back up your assertions with data. This requires spending a lot of time keeping your internal data — especially bug tracking and test tracking — as consistent and current as possible. When you're asked about status, you'll want to provide management with clear answers.

Chapters 4 and 5 introduced two linked tracking mechanisms, for bugs and for test cases. The linkages exist in both directions: the bug reports reference test case identifiers, and test cases — at both a detail level and a summary level — reference bug reports and their risk levels. The test project dashboard summarizes information from both, creating another set of linkages.

Figure 6-1 provides a visual representation of these linkages. I have not shown the linkages between quality risk items and test cases, bug reports, and the test dashboard, although such linkages should exist, as discussed in Chapters 3, 4, and 5. The quality risk items tend to evolve more slowly during test execution than the test status and bug reports.

By going through the bug reports, the test-tracking worksheets, and the dashboards at the same time to ensure consistency, you can keep your data consistent. Because bug reports and the status of test cases change over time, the two will get out of sync if you don't review the linkages regularly. This can happen quickly. When test execution is at full bore, you should audit the spreadsheets and the reports once or twice a week. I find that the daily debriefing process I described in Chapter 5 allows me to integrate this work into my daily routine.

Figure 6-1 The linkages between test-tracking and -reporting documents

Admittedly, auditing all these documents, charts, graphs, and data can be a painstaking exercise. If you are truly motivated, you might decide to implement a complete integrated test management system as I discussed in Chapter 5 or rely on a commercial test management tool. Either approach would automate the linkages. However, reconciling the bugs, the tests, and the charts manually actually provides an interesting side benefit: by forcing yourself to crawl through the details of every active bug, every planned test, and every chart and metric, you become intimately aware of what's going on. The ritual can reward you by identifying a number of important issues that you need to address.

You might start by going through the spreadsheet. If testers make notes on hard-copy test cases, you should enter this data in the worksheets. If testers update the worksheets themselves, you should review the results in the test case summaries and the test suite summaries. If you have questions, drill down to the test case level or across to the bug-tracking database. For each test case that has identified a bug, check the status of the bug report: Is it still open? Is the risk priority number correct? Does the configuration and tester information in the bug report match the test case summary?

After checking the spreadsheet, move on to the bug reports. Although you would have already audited many of the reports as part of auditing the spreadsheet, it's a good idea to walk through the bug reports at the detail level. Seeing a bug report might remind you to follow up on an item with a colleague or to schedule a confirmation test that you somehow missed.

Defining a Test Execution Process

You've probably seen an assembly line on TV, in a newspaper or magazine article, or perhaps even in person. On early automotive assembly lines, cars were built in one spot, with workers moving around to assemble them. Henry Ford revolutionized not just car assembly, but the entire manufacturing process when he introduced the idea of bringing the car to the worker on a moving line. All the tools were ready at hand in the right places, the parts came to the worker as needed, and the workers built the car piece by piece as it moved along the line.

Now, test execution is more creative than working on an assembly line, true. However, you'll need some process for assigning tasks, gathering results, recognizing and intervening in process breakdowns, and collecting metrics on how effective and efficient your process is. This means that you and your team need to come up with a process, and as a test manager you'll need to manage it.

Even the reactive test techniques discussed in Chapter 3 involve some type of process. For example, exploratory testing often involves the use of *test charters*, which are short, one-to-three-sentence logical test cases. Using this technique, the test manager assigns a test charter to a tester; for example, "test the printing capabilities." Each charter is allocated a certain amount of time, say 90 minutes. At the end of the period, the test manager debriefs the tester, gathering details about what was tested and what was found. At that time, the test manager either tells the tester to continue exploring that area for another set period of time or assigns a new test charter to the tester.

Test Result Misinterpretation: Minimizing False Positives and False Negatives

Despite your best efforts, it sometimes happens that the test system itself produces errors. On the one hand, testers sometimes report correct system behavior as a bug, assign an excessively high severity or priority to a bug, or otherwise overstate the significance of a problem. These are false positives. Although they don't jeopardize product quality, such errors can damage the credibility of the test organization. Developers and project managers tend to adopt a *boy who cried wolf* attitude toward the test team when the test team reports too many false positives. I have seen this happen on my own test teams, and on a number of test teams I have assessed as a consultant. You can measure this problem by measuring the percentage of rejected bug reports, which should not exceed five percent as a rule of thumb.

On the other hand, testers sometimes fail to detect or report incorrect system behavior, assign an excessively low priority or severity to a bug, or otherwise understate the significance of a problem. These are false negatives. This type of error often leads to a test escape, which is a direct risk to system quality. If you have too many false negatives, your defect detection percentage and thus your test team's value both go down, as discussed in Chapter 4.

One cause of both types of errors is MEGO, the affliction in which "my . . . eyes . . . glazed . . . over." Overly detailed written test cases are notorious for creating this problem. A tester running a test will always notice if the system catches fire or the program crashes, but an inattentive tester can miss subtle signs of system failure. Likewise, a lack of attention to specifications or other system documentation during bug isolation can cause the tester to mistake correct behavior for a bug.

Test automation provides a partial solution to this problem. Automated tests, unlike testers, never get too bored to notice that an error message is misspelled or a transaction takes 50 milliseconds too long.[1] It is, however, quite possible — indeed, all too common — for a test developer to embed result interpretation errors in automated tests.

Even if your testers don't suffer from shrinking attention spans after 12 grueling hours of running tests, they can misinterpret test results by guessing wrong about what was supposed to happen. As I mentioned in Chapter 3, you don't want your test case library to turn into a groaning bookshelf of totally unambiguous — and totally unmaintainable — pages stuffed into binder upon binder. Nevertheless, if you leave questions of correct behavior to the judgment of testers, they will make some mistakes. There is no perfect solution to this quandary, but appropriate automation, continual test case enhancement in response to test escapes, avoiding working people beyond their limits of concentration, and careful assignment of team members for test execution all help.[2]

On the topic of assigning testers, one of your jobs as a manager is to know the strengths and weaknesses of your team members. One of the most important variables in preventing errors is skill level. If, for example, you assign the Microsoft Windows logo certification test to a tester who has no experience with Windows, the poor fellow will probably not succeed in running it. If you ask a software test engineer to run a shock and vibration test on DataRocket, don't be surprised when she botches the job. I'm not arguing for career stultification; assigning new tasks keeps testers challenged and ensures a well-rounded test team. When you do cross-training, though, it's important not to set up the tester — and the project — for failure. Provide

---

[1] Bill Perry and Randy Rice, in their fine book *Surviving the Top Ten Challenges of Software Testing*, make a similar point when discussing test automation.

[2] As a manager, you should not expect perfect work from your team, either. If you set unachievable targets in terms of false positives and false negatives, you'll simply demotivate your team. You can read my article, "No More Bad MBOs," on the RBCS web site, www.rbcs-us.com, for a dramatic case study of this problem.

adequate instruction first, and then supply support from an experienced engineer during cross-training.

In addition to skill levels, you need to consider less tangible attributes when assigning testers. If the test is complicated and somewhat tedious, can the tester focus? If the test is a group effort, do the assigned testers work well together? If you suspect that the tester will need to contact a developer at some point, will the tester be able to make that contact?

Of course, in the real world, you'll have to make many test assignments based on who's free. Like any team, yours will contain some stars and some solid but unspectacular performers. As much as you want star quality work on all the jobs in your bailiwick, there's only so much star power to go around. Moreover, demand for a tester's particular skills can vary depending on the types of tests you need to run. When these realities force you to select a less-than-perfect tester, be sure to put in place safety nets such as peer reviews and the support of experienced engineers.

Here I must also inject a note of business reality. In some fields, any failure to detect a bug is totally unacceptable. If you are in charge of testing a system such as the Therac nuclear medicine device (see the sidebar *When Test Escapes Turn Deadly*), every test engineer and technician on your team must be top-notch, experienced, and deeply knowledgeable about the system under test. In contrast, if you test a typical consumer software or hardware product, you will probably have to accept a few result interpretation errors on both sides of the coin as part of the business. Of course, at some point, the business model for computer hardware and software could change if customers, legislatures, or regulatory agencies decide that buggy products are unacceptable. However, the reality today is that you won't have the time, the budget, the staff, or the management focus to achieve perfect testing or perfect products.

WHEN TEST ESCAPES TURN DEADLY

If you are not familiar with the Therac story, brace yourself. The Therac-25 nuclear medicine device was designed to administer precise dosages of radiation to hospital patients. Because of a software glitch that made it to the field, the device overdosed a number of patients, some of whom died as a result. Incidents such as this have fueled efforts by some in the computer industry to institute mandatory licensing or certification programs for computer professionals.

For a complete discussion of this and other dangerous test escapes, check out Peter Neumann's book *Computer-Related Risks*. You might also want to subscribe to the online forum *Risks Digest*, available through the *comp.risks* Usenet newsgroup and via email at `risks-request@csl.sri.com`.

"I Wish You a Merry Dragon Boat Festival ... ": When Crunch Time, Holidays, and Cultures Collide

Remember to consider holidays when you schedule crunch periods. Needless to say, you'll encounter major impediments to getting work done during holidays. Your testers will be both reluctant and less able to work long hours. Even if everyone on the team does come in to the office on a holiday, they won't be working the 60- to 80-hour weeks that are common during crunch mode. Holidays mean time spent with family, which implies a break from 14-hour days. Even more important, the people who carry the most water for your team — the men and women who consistently pull the all-nighters when the going is tough — have a debt to repay to themselves and their families during holidays. Not coming home on an ordinary Wednesday night during a big push is making a sacrifice, but not coming home for Passover or Christmas Eve can create serious issues in a tester's family life.

Testers are not the only ones who face these problems. In Chapter 11 I discuss what I call *gas pedals* and *brake pedals* for test operations. One major class of brake pedals is lack of proper system administration, infrastructure, and development support. Convincing system administrators and developers to respond to mobile phone calls at any hour is difficult enough under any circumstances. During holidays, people might well refuse the request. Even if you do have contact information, it might not do you any good. A system administrator who is visiting relatives in Buffalo, New York, without a laptop computer isn't much help when your test server goes down at 8:00 p.m. on December 31 in San Jose, California, even if you do find that individual answering their mobile phone and sober.

If you do business internationally, you also need to consider cultural issues related to crunch periods. The most obvious is that different countries observe different holidays. Asking a Taiwanese testing lab to squeeze in a rush test job from December 22 through December 31 might not create a problem. However, you might get an education about the Chinese (Lunar) New Year if you schedule a month of crunch time at the same lab in January or February. Calendar software such as Microsoft Outlook often includes support for foreign holidays.

In addition, you will find that the workaholic traditions that seem to accompany high-tech jobs in some countries do not apply the world over. Asking people to work until midnight or come in over a weekend can be a cross-cultural *faux pas*. Indeed, in France, the standard work-week is 35 hours. I have often been struck by the extreme demands of US and Canadian work habits in comparison with the attitudes prevalent in some of the foreign countries where I have worked. Also bear in mind that in some countries, formal work hours end strictly on time so that informal work — building relationships with colleagues over dinner or drinks and solving the problems of the day in a frank and relaxed environment — can occur regularly.

Before you begin to conduct business internationally, I encourage you to study the cultures and work styles of your new foreign colleagues. (One of my clients organized an off-site culture course for employees and consultants working in Taiwan — a valuable experience.) Such study can help you build more productive working relationships, and you will also enjoy a unique chance to immerse yourself in the culture of another country without the artificiality that comes with seeing that country as a tourist.

A Spider's Web of Connections: Managing Test Hardware and Software Configuration Logistics

If your system under test is used in a limited setting with a tightly defined list of possible hardware peripherals and software applications, the management of test hardware and software configuration is simple. I once consulted with a client who was working on a Microsoft Windows CE computer for an automobile. The system was installed in the dashboard, connected to only three or four peripherals, had a very simple BIOS, ran only one operating system, and supported a small set of applications. From the point of view of hardware logistics and software configuration management, the test organization merely needed to track BIOS levels, Windows CE releases, the hardware revision levels of the handful of peripherals, and the motherboard and chassis releases. A few very simple tables, implemented in Microsoft Word, were sufficient.

Not all projects are this straightforward, however. Whether you work on software or hardware development projects, you might find yourself managing a complicated and changing array of hardware devices, especially during test execution. In addition, the software installed on these devices can vary. You must allocate this hardware, make sure that the right software is deployed on it, track its movements, understand who needs it and for what, and ensure that all the appropriate connections are available.

Perhaps your system supports many different configurations or is deployed in a large setting, but you test with only a basic setup. For example, if you have an e-commerce application, maybe you only test with one or two clients browsing the site at once. Alternatively, if you have a client server system that supports 100 clients in a call center, perhaps you test only with one client talking to the servers.

While this might suffice for functional testing, some bugs show up exclusively in more complex configurations. Performance, data quality, reliability, load, and error handling are some of the risks to system quality that really can only be effectively explored in configurations that are as close to real world as possible.

The topic of test hardware is connected to software configuration management — which is a major issue during crunch time. Chapter 7 expands this discussion by focusing on test lab management, but for now we'll take a look, using SpeedyWriter as a case study, at a database that will help you manage hardware logistics and software configuration for your project. This database tracks the following:

- Hardware installation, locations, and moves
- Current, historical, and planned software configurations
- Hardware interconnections and networking
- Test locations
- Test infrastructure
- Test engineer assignments and locations
- Human resource deployment

The Pieces and How They Connect: An Entity-Relationship Diagram

Because this database is complex, it's useful to begin with a conceptual overview of the elements and how they relate. Figure 6-2 shows an entity-relationship (E-R) diagram for the database. Those of you who have some familiarity with database design or administration probably recognize this format. However, if it's new to you, don't worry; you don't have to understand database design to use this tool.

The rectangles in Figure 6-2 represent entities, which are objects of some kind. Each entity has a set of properties, represented by labeled lines. One (or more) of these properties, called the *key*, uniquely identifies an individual entity. In Figure 6-2, lines with solid endpoints indicate key properties, whereas lines with open endpoints indicate nonkey properties. For example, *HW Name* is a key property of the *Hardware* entity, while *Quantity* is a nonkey property of this entity.

The diamonds represent relationships between pairs of entities. Relationships can also have properties. (Not all relationships have properties, though; relationships are identified by the entities they associate.) There are three types of relationships: one-to-one, one-to-many, and many-to-many. In a one-to-one relationship between entities X and Y, any one Y can have a relationship with one and only one X at any given time, and vice versa. A one-to-many relationship between X and Y would allow any one X to have relationships with multiple Ys, but each Y could have a relationship with only one X. For example, you can have a number of coins in your pocket, but a given coin can be in only one pocket at one time. In a many-to-many relationship, both X and Y are unrestricted in terms of the number of associations that can exist between them. A corporation can have many shareholders, and a person can own stock in many companies at once. In the case of this database, all the relationships are many-to-many, as I'll explain in detail later on.[3]

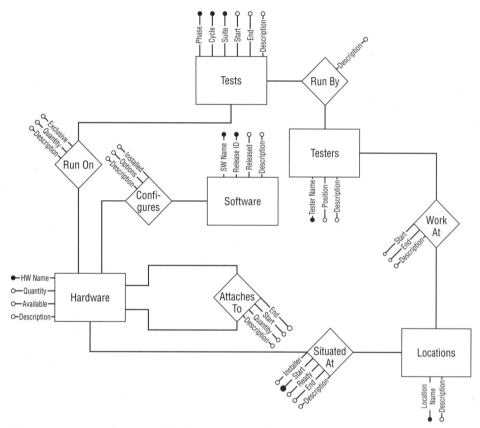

Figure 6-2 An entity-relationship diagram for test logistics

Let's look more closely at each entity and relationship in Figure 6-2. The *Tests* entity, with six properties, appears at the center top of the chart. The value of the *Phase* property can be Component, Integration, or System. *Cycle* is the sequence number of the test cycle in that phase. I use cycles rather than passes because we're going to track software revisions with this tool, which are the basis of test cycles in my approach. The *Suite* property is the name of the suite. (Alternatively, you could use an ID number for the Suite property, although a number is less descriptive.) These first three properties taken together uniquely identify an individual test, as in Integration Test, 2, GUI/Edit Engine.

---

[3]For a complete explanation of entity-relationship modeling of databases, targeted at beginning database users, data modelers, and business analysts, see *Conceptual Database Design*, by Carlo Batini, Stefano Ceri, and Shamkant Navathe.

In this implementation of the database, I've chosen to use a coarse-grained approach, planning and managing test suite by test suite. A finer-grained approach would involve planning and managing test case by test case, separately accounting for each test case in the test suite. I suspect that is excessively detailed in most situations. However, if you tend to interleave the test cases from test suites quite a bit, in an attempt to run the test cases precisely in risk priority number order, you might find a need to add the key property *Case* to this table and then plan and manage on a test-case-by-test-case basis.

The *Start* and *End* properties indicate the scheduled run dates for that suite in that cycle. *Description* includes any other pertinent information. There is a description field included for free-form notes with each entity and relationship.

Proceeding clockwise around the diagram, you can see that the entities *Tests* and *Testers* are linked by the relationship *Run By* — in other words, tests are run by testers. Testers are uniquely identified by their names. Testers have a position, generally either a test engineer or test technician. Because each test is run by one or more testers, and each tester runs one or more tests, the relationship is many-to-many.

Testers work at locations — that is, the *Testers* and *Locations* entities are linked by the *Work At* relationship. In some cases, locations are temporary, within the time frame of the project, so the relationship includes start and end dates. Testers might work at more than one location during a given period of time. Furthermore, a single location might have 0, 1, or more testers working at it at any given time. Therefore, the relationship is many-to-many.

Let's return to the top of the diagram and work our way counterclockwise and down. Tests run on one or more items of hardware, each of which in turn runs one or more tests. A test requires a given quantity of each hardware item, usually one but sometimes more, and the test's relationship with the hardware can be either exclusive or nonexclusive, depending on whether the test requires dedicated use of that piece of hardware during its execution. For a hardware item, the properties of interest are *HW Name*, *Quantity*, *Available* (the date of availability), and *Description*.

Software configures most hardware items — that is, the particular combination of one or more software items installed on a piece of hardware, and the way in which they are installed, determines the hardware's functionality. The same piece of software might be installed on multiple hardware items, too; for example, you might run Linux on multiple servers in your server farm. The *Software* entity has four properties of interest: *SW Name*, *Release ID* (the release number), *Released* (the release date), and *Description*. The software configures the hardware on the date on which it is installed with particular options.

In a networked environment, a given piece of hardware attaches to one or more other pieces of hardware. Routers, hubs, and switches attach to many devices at once. Wireless WAN modems, keyboards, and mice attach to one computer at a time. Such attachments have start and end dates, and the quantity required is also relevant.

Finally, hardware items are situated at a particular location during certain periods of time. In the *Situated At* relationship, an installer sets up the hardware, starting on a particular date. The hardware will be ready for test on a date shortly thereafter, and the hardware will end its sojourn at that location at a later date. More than one piece of hardware might well be situated at a particular location, and a piece of hardware might move around during the course of the test effort.

From Diagram to Schemas: Implementing the Logistics Database

To implement the logistics database, I have used Microsoft Access, but you can use any relational database. Begin by creating a table for each entity. Each table should contain a field for each entity property.

Because each relationship is many-to-many, the relationships in the diagram also translate directly into tables. A table for a many-to-many relationship includes the keys from the two related tables, with the combined keys and possibly some relationship properties used as the key for the relationship table. The relationship table also contains fields for each property in the relationship.

I have not provided the design details for each table, but they are not complex. Most of the fields are basic text, integer, or date fields, except for the Exclusive field in the Run On table, which is a yes/no field. Figure 6-3 shows the tables and their relationships.[4]

Budgeting and Planning: Using the Logistics Database Ahead of Time

One of most important uses of the logistics database is as a planning tool. The following sections walk through an example of how to use the database, based on a case study of SpeedyWriter test logistics. The example illustrates how you can enter data in the database's tables and then display it in simple but powerful reports. This database does not support form-based data entry, although you might want to add this and other enhancements if you choose to make the logistics database part of your standard toolkit. To keep the data minimal in this example, I have omitted test development, but you might need to allocate hardware and people for test development on most of your projects.

---

[4]Database purists and data modeling professionals might not like this translation. Access, with its cascading update feature, allows me to avoid the use of surrogate keys for the joins while retaining the ability to change values in key fields without having to do extensive database updates. If you use a database without cascading update capabilities, however, you might be stuck with surrogate keys.

Although this case study is a simplification, I have used this database to plan hardware, software, network, and human logistics for test projects much more complex than this.

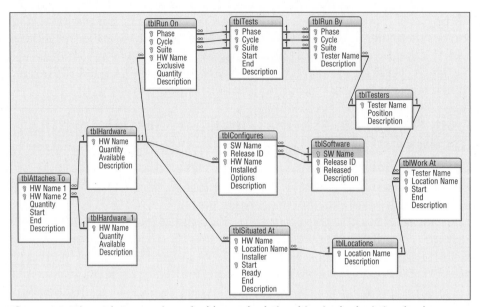

Figure 6-3 Microsoft Access view of tables and relationships in the logistics database

The Work, Who Does It, and Where It Happens: The People Side

To begin planning the SpeedyWriter test project, you can start with individual tests and who will run them. Figure 6-4 shows the table created for the Tests entity, detailing the test suites to be run during the various phases, along with their constituent cycles. A table of testers appears in Figure 6-5, and the table in Figure 6-6 represents the Run By relationship, which matches testers to tests. Note that some tests require more than one tester, and that some testers run more than one test. Also note that two of the "testers" aren't people. STC is a fictional but not atypical external test lab that specializes in software/hardware compatibility testing. Sales/Marketing refers to the internal sales and marketing staff and those special users they choose to involve in testing.

Alone, the three tables don't do a good job of telling you who's doing what and when. Why manually cross-reference the three tables when you can create reports based on a query that joins all three? In Figure 6-7, for example, you'll find a report titled Tester Assignments that documents which tester performs which tests, and when. This report is organized by phase, cycle, and start date, and also shows the overall length of time the tester is scheduled to work on the project.

	Phase	Cycle	Suite	Start	End	Description
⊞	Component	1	Edit Engine	7/19	7/21	
⊞	Component	1	User Interface	7/22	7/23	
⊞	Component	2	Edit Engine	7/26	7/28	
⊞	Component	2	File	7/26	7/27	
⊞	Component	2	Tools	7/28	7/28	
⊞	Component	2	User Interface	7/29	7/30	
⊞	Component	3	File	8/2	8/3	
⊞	Component	3	Tools	8/4	8/4	
⊞	Integration	1	Edit Engine-UI	8/2	8/4	
⊞	Integration	2	Edit Engine-File	8/9	8/10	
⊞	Integration	2	File-UI	8/11	8/12	
⊞	Integration	3	Edit Engine-UI	8/16	8/18	
⊞	System	1	Documentation/Packaging	8/16	8/20	
⊞	System	1	Install/Configure	8/16	8/20	
⊞	System	1	Performance	8/16	8/18	
⊞	System	2	Beta	8/23	9/5	
⊞	System	2	Compatibility	8/23	8/29	
⊞	System	2	Error Handling/Recovery	8/23	8/24	
⊞	System	2	File Sharing	8/25	8/27	
⊞	System	3	Compatibility	8/30	9/5	
⊞	System	3	Documentation/Packaging	8/30	9/3	
⊞	System	3	Error Handling/Recovery	8/30	8/31	
⊞	System	3	File Sharing	9/1	9/3	
⊞	System	3	Install/Configure	8/30	9/3	
⊞	System	3	Performance	8/30	9/1	

Figure 6-4 The SpeedyWriter tests

	Tester Name	Position	Description
⊞	John Goldstein	Technician	
⊞	Lin-Tsu Woo	Engineer	
⊞	Liz Campbell	Technician	
⊞	Muhammad Zamanzadeh	Manager	
⊞	Sales/Marketing	Sales, Marketing, and Users	
⊞	STC	Test Lab	

Figure 6-5 The SpeedyWriter testers

Phase	Cycle	Suite	Tester Name	Description
Component	1	Edit Engine	Lin-Tsu Woo	
Component	1	User Interface	Lin-Tsu Woo	
Component	2	Edit Engine	Lin-Tsu Woo	
Component	2	File	Liz Campbell	
Component	2	Tools	Liz Campbell	
Component	2	User Interface	Lin-Tsu Woo	
Component	3	File	Liz Campbell	
Component	3	Tools	Liz Campbell	
Integration	1	Edit Engine-UI	Lin-Tsu Woo	
Integration	2	Edit Engine-File	Lin-Tsu Woo	
Integration	2	File-UI	Lin-Tsu Woo	
Integration	3	Edit Engine-UI	Lin-Tsu Woo	
System	1	Documentation/Packaging	John Goldstein	
System	1	Install/Configure	Lin-Tsu Woo	
System	1	Install/Configure	Liz Campbell	
System	1	Performance	Lin-Tsu Woo	
System	2	Beta	Sales/Marketing	
System	2	Compatibility	STC	
System	2	Error Handling/Recovery	Lin-Tsu Woo	
System	2	File Sharing	Lin-Tsu Woo	
System	3	Compatibility	STC	
System	3	Documentation/Packaging	John Goldstein	
System	3	Error Handling/Recovery	Lin-Tsu Woo	
System	3	File Sharing	Lin-Tsu Woo	
System	3	Install/Configure	Lin-Tsu Woo	
System	3	Install/Configure	Liz Campbell	
System	3	Performance	Lin-Tsu Woo	

Figure 6-6 The SpeedyWriter test assignments

Tester Assignments					
Tester Name	Position	Phase Cycle Suite		Start	End
John Goldstein	**Technician**				
		System Test			
		1	Documentation/Packaging	8/16	8/20
		3	Documentation/Packaging	8/30	9/3
		John Goldstein works on this project from		**8/16** to	**9/3**
Lin-Tsu Woo	**Engineer**				
		Component Test			
		1	Edit Engine	7/19	7/21
		1	User Interface	7/22	7/23
		2	Edit Engine	7/26	7/28
		2	User Interface	7/29	7/30
		Integration Test			
		1	Edit Engine-UI	8/2	8/4
		2	Edit Engine-File	8/9	8/10
		2	File-UI	8/11	8/12
		3	Edit Engine-UI	8/16	8/18
		System Test			
		1	Performance	8/16	8/18
		1	Install/Configure	8/16	8/20
		2	Error Handling/Recovery	8/23	8/24
		2	File Sharing	8/25	8/27
		3	Error Handling/Recovery	8/30	8/31
		3	Performance	8/30	9/1
		3	Install/Configure	8/30	9/3
		3	File Sharing	9/1	9/3
		Lin-Tsu Woo works on this project from		**7/19** to	**9/3**

Figure 6-7 The Tester Assignments report

An alternative view of the same information, shown in Figure 6-8, documents when and who runs each test. You might notice that in this Test Schedule report, the tests run finish-to-start with no downtime in between. This is fine if you have built slack into the duration of each test suite; for example, three days are scheduled for the Edit Engine test suite during the component test phase, even though it is likely to take only two days. However, if you use a best-case estimate for each suite and pack the tests as shown here, you will find yourself either slipping the schedule or requiring lots of weekend work from your testers when expectations aren't met.

Next you need to address the question of where the test work happens. The Locations table in Figure 6-9 is populated with four places where testing will occur or where test hardware will be located. "JG Home" is John Goldstein's home, where he works between bouts on the road. "SC Engr" is the Software Cafeteria engineering offices. "SC SM" is the Software Cafeteria sales and marketing offices. Finally, "STC Lab" is the independent test lab.

The table in Figure 6-9 represents the Work At relationship, which matches testers with locations. (While the years don't show in the figure, I've used *1/1/1900* to indicate, "as far in the past as is relevant to this project" and *12/31/9999* to indicate, "for the duration of this project." Rest assured that Lin-Tsu, Liz, and Muhammad will not spend 8,100 years at Software Cafeteria, although on some late nights it might feel that way.) The real globetrotter of the team, you can see, is John Goldstein, the resident technical writing evaluator. He spends the first week testing at the Engineering office, stays for a week of meetings related to another project, returns to his home office for what he hopes will be a final review of the documentation, and then jets off to the Sales and Marketing office to help with the product launch.

Test Schedule					
Phase	*Cycle*	*Suite*	*Tester Name*	*Start*	*End*
Component Test					
	1				
		Edit Engine		7/19	7/21
			Lin-Tsu Woo		
		User Interface		7/22	7/23
			Lin-Tsu Woo		
		Component Test, Cycle 1 runs from		**7/19** to	**7/23**
	2				
		Edit Engine		7/26	7/28
			Lin-Tsu Woo		
		File		7/26	7/27
			Liz Campbell		
		Tools		7/28	7/28
			Liz Campbell		
		User Interface		7/29	7/30
			Lin-Tsu Woo		
		Component Test, Cycle 2 runs from		**7/26** to	**7/30**
	3				
		File		8/2	8/3
			Liz Campbell		
		Tools		8/4	8/4
			Liz Campbell		
		Component Test, Cycle 3 runs from		**8/2** to	**8/4**
		Component Test runs from		**7/19** to	**8/4**

Figure 6-8 The Test Schedule report

Tester Name	Location Name	Start	End	Description
John Goldstein	JG Home	1/1	8/8	
John Goldstein	JG Home	8/21	9/3	
John Goldstein	JG Home	9/6	12/31	
John Goldstein	SC Engr	8/9	8/20	
John Goldstein	SC SM	9/4	9/5	
Lin-Tsu Woo	SC Engr	1/1	12/31	
Liz Campbell	SC Engr	1/1	12/31	
Muhammad Zamanzadeh	SC Engr	1/1	12/31	
Sales/Marketing	SC SM	1/1	12/31	
STC	STC Lab	1/1	12/31	

Figure 6-9 The testers at their locations

Rather than putting together a report that merely correlates testers and locations — the table is simple enough, after all — you can generate two reports that tie together tests, testers, and locations, as shown in Figures 6-10 and 6-11. The first is location-oriented, organized by place; the second is test-oriented, providing the location last. As you can see, these reports can replace the previous reports, unless you find the location information distracting.

Tests by Location and Tester						
Location	Tester Name	Start	End	Phase		Cycle Suite
JG Home						
	John Goldstein	8/21	9/3			
		8/30	9/3	System Test	3	Documentation/Packaging
SC Engr						
	John Goldstein	8/9	8/20			
		8/16	8/20	System Test	1	Documentation/Packaging
	Lin-Tsu Woo	1/1	12/31			
		7/19	7/21	Component Test	1	Edit Engine
		7/22	7/23	Component Test	1	User Interface
		7/26	7/28	Component Test	2	Edit Engine
		7/29	7/30	Component Test	2	User Interface
		8/2	8/4	Integration Test	1	Edit Engine-UI
		8/9	8/10	Integration Test	2	Edit Engine-File
		8/11	8/12	Integration Test	2	File-UI
		8/16	8/18	Integration Test	3	Edit Engine-UI
		8/16	8/18	System Test	1	Performance
		8/16	8/20	System Test	1	Install/Configure
		8/23	8/24	System Test	2	Error Handling/Recovery
		8/25	8/27	System Test	2	File Sharing
		8/30	8/31	System Test	3	Error Handling/Recovery
		8/30	9/1	System Test	3	Performance
		8/30	9/3	System Test	3	Install/Configure
		9/1	9/3	System Test	3	File Sharing
	Liz Campbell	1/1	12/31			
		7/26	7/27	Component Test	2	File
		7/28	7/28	Component Test	2	Tools
		8/2	8/3	Component Test	3	File
		8/4	8/4	Component Test	3	Tools
		8/16	8/20	System Test	1	Install/Configure
		8/30	9/3	System Test	3	Install/Configure

Figure 6-10 The Tests by Location and Tester report

A certain amount of magic is required in the query for the reports shown in Figures 6-10 and 6-11. That query is shown in Figure 6-12. The database join by itself does not restrict the testing by location, since it is the date on which the tester performs the test, together with the tester's location at that time, which determines where the testing happens. Therefore the two date-matching criteria shown in the join are essential to making the query — and the reports that use it — work.

The Assets, How You Use Them, and Where They Live: The Hardware and Infrastructure Side

Let's move on to the issue of managing hardware and infrastructure, starting with hardware. Chapter 2 introduced the idea of a hardware allocation plan.

(See ''Test Configurations and Environments'' in that chapter.) Now you can expand this concept by using the logistics database to plan for the hardware, software, and infrastructure items you need, to organize how these items will be assigned and shared, and to track various configurations.

Locations by Test and Tester

Phase	Cycle	Suite	Tester Name	Start		End	Location
Component Test							
	1						
		Edit Engine					
			Lin-Tsu Woo	1/1		12/31	
				7/19		7/21	SC Engr
		User Interface					
			Lin-Tsu Woo	1/1		12/31	
				7/22		7/23	SC Engr
		Component Test, Cycle 1 runs from		**7/19**	to	**7/23**	
	2						
		Edit Engine					
			Lin-Tsu Woo	1/1		12/31	
				7/26		7/28	SC Engr
		File					
			Liz Campbell	1/1		12/31	
				7/26		7/27	SC Engr
		Tools					
			Liz Campbell	1/1		12/31	
				7/28		7/28	SC Engr
		User Interface					
			Lin-Tsu Woo	1/1		12/31	
				7/29		7/30	SC Engr
		Component Test, Cycle 2 runs from		**7/26**	to	**7/30**	
	3						
		File					
			Liz Campbell	1/1		12/31	
				8/2		8/3	SC Engr
		Tools					
			Liz Campbell	1/1		12/31	
				8/4		8/4	SC Engr
		Component Test, Cycle 3 runs from		**8/2**	to	**8/4**	
		Component Test runs from		**7/19**	to	**8/4**	

Figure 6-11 The Locations by Test and Tester report

Figure 6-12 A query to show locations, tests, and testers

For the SpeedyWriter case study, hardware and infrastructure come in three flavors: clients, servers, and networking devices. Let's assume that you want to cover five operating systems on the client side: Mac OS, Windows XP, Windows Vista, Linux, and Solaris. As noted earlier, SpeedyWriter testing starts in mid-July and runs through early September. Suppose that three client systems are available in the test lab during this time: a Sony laptop, a Macintosh laptop, and a Dell desktop. By purchasing two other clients — say, a Hewlett-Packard and a Panasonic — you can cover all five target client platforms.

Two questions might occur to you at this point. First, why not simply plan to use the testers' workstations as test platforms? Sometimes you should do this. In our example, John Goldstein uses his Macintosh PowerBook to do the documentation and packaging testing. Testers will undoubtedly install SpeedyWriter on their workstations and use these for isolation. Usually, however, you want your test clients to be clean configurations. Using an individual's workstation can create questions about bugs. For example, did the software under test corrupt the Registry, or does the problem stem from the open source application the user installed six months ago that never would completely uninstall?

Second, could you save money by allocating only two or three systems and using partitioning and virtual machines to install and select multiple operating systems on each? Again, this is sometimes a good idea. When testing software, you indeed might want to be able to boot different operating systems on a single platform to determine whether bugs are hardware-related. However, don't plan on saving money by getting too clever with your test hardware allocation. Do you want one bug on a single platform/operating system combination to bring other scheduled testing to a halt because you have a platform shortage? How many wasted hours of a tester's time will pay for a $500 computer? Of course, when you're talking about $50,000 servers, the story is different, but those servers can frequently support multiple users simultaneously. A client computer running tests is generally exclusively allocated for those tests for the duration of the tests.

Let's assume that you will use four different network types: 10 Mbps Ethernet TCP/IP, 100 Mbps Ethernet TCP/IP, 1 Gbps Ethernet TCP/IP, and 802.11 wireless. Figure 6-13 shows the test lab configuration with these clients, servers, and network types.

Although you have now defined a test network without much regard to the specific tests you will run on it, this is not a case of putting the cart before the horse. Your test network definition grew out of your coverage goals for the clients, servers, and network types. Having met these goals, you can now distribute test suites across the various client configurations, either randomly or based on which ones you think are most likely to find bugs against a particular configuration. Notice that by spreading the testing over the clients, you can also cover the servers and networks easily, provided you make sure that tests actually do exercise all the network connections available to the clients.

Figure 6-13 The test hardware and network environment for SpeedyWriter testing

Your next task is to set up some reports. You can begin by creating tables based on the Hardware entity and the Run On and Attaches To relationships from Figure 6-2. In much the same way you created reports for the tests and the testers, you can create two reports for tests and hardware, including the attached hardware in this case. Figure 6-14 shows the Hardware Assignment report, organized by hardware. Figure 6-15 shows the Test Hardware report, organized by tests. The former is useful for system administrators and for preparing budgets, while the latter helps testers and test managers understand what hardware they will use to run tests (and also helps you spot missing hardware).

You will also need to situate the hardware. In the Situated At table in this case study, I've shown all the hardware located at the Software Cafeteria Engineering headquarters in Austin, Texas (see Figure 6-16). Typically, I use a finer granularity for locations than this example allows, which enables me to track places such as Second Floor Lab, Thermal Chamber, and so forth. If you want to use this database to manage tight or limited spaces, you should consider this level of detail. In addition, you might want to include footprint areas and overall dimensions for servers and other lab equipment so that you can compare the space taken up by the hardware in a lab to the space available in the lab (see Chapter 7 for more on this idea.)

Hardware Assignment

Client	Network	Server	Phase	Cycle Suite	Exclusive	Start	End
Dell WXP Client						7/15	
	100 Mbps TCP/IP					7/19	
		Sun Solaris Server				1/1	
			Component Test				
				1 Edit Engine	Yes	7/19	7/21
				2 User Interface	Yes	7/29	7/30
			Integration Test				
				1 Edit Engine-UI	Yes	8/2	8/4
				2 Edit Engine-File	Yes	8/9	8/10
				2 File-UI	Yes	8/11	8/12
				3 Edit Engine-UI	Yes	8/16	8/18
			SystemTest				
				1 Install/Configure	Yes	8/16	8/20
				1 Performance	Yes	8/16	8/18
				2 Error Handling/Recovery	Yes	8/23	8/24
				2 File Sharing	Yes	8/25	8/27
				3 Error Handling/Recovery	No	8/30	8/31
				3 File Sharing	No	9/1	9/3
				3 Install/Configure	No	8/30	9/3
				3 Performance	No	8/30	9/1
HP Solaris Client						7/14	
	10 Mbps TCP/IP					7/19	
		Sun Solaris Server				1/1	
			Component Test				
				1 User Interface	Yes	7/22	7/23

Wesdnesday, December 24, 2008   Page 1 of 4

Figure 6-14 The Hardware Assignment report

Test Hardware

Phase	CycleSuite	Client	Network	Server	Exclusive	Start	End
Component Test							
	1						
		Edit Engine				7/19	7/21
		Dell WXP Client			Yes	7/15	
			100 Mbps TCP/IP			7/19	
				Sun Solaris Server		1/1	
		User Interface				7/22	7/23
		HP Solaris Client			Yes	7/14	
			10 Mbps TCP/IP			7/19	
				Sun Solaris Server		1/1	
			100 Mbps TCP/IP			7/19	
				Sun Solaris Server		1/1	
	2						
		Edit Engine				7/26	7/28
		Mac Client			Yes	7/12	
			10 Mbps TCP/IP			7/19	
				Sun Solaris Server		1/1	
		Tools				7/28	7/28
		Panasonic Linux Client			Yes	7/6	
			10 Mbps TCP/IP			7/19	
				Sun Solaris Server		1/1	
			100 Mbps TCP/IP			7/19	
				Sun Solaris Server		1/1	
		User Interface				7/29	7/30
		Dell WXP Client			Yes	7/15	
			100 Mbps TCP/IP			7/19	
				Sun Solaris Server		1/1	

Figure 6-15 The Test Hardware report

HW Name	Location Name	Installer	Start	Ready	End	Description
1 GB TCP/IP	SC Engr	James Sakayeda	7/17	7/19	12/31	
10 Mbps TCP/IP	SC Engr	James Sakayeda	7/17	7/19	12/31	
100 Mbps TCP/IP	SC Engr	James Sakayeda	7/17	7/19	12/31	
Acer Win Server	SC Engr	Sharif al-Hassan	8/12	8/13	12/31	
Dell WXP Client	SC Engr	Rajesh Gupta	7/15	7/15	12/31	
DSL Line	SC Engr	Rajesh Gupta	7/24	8/2	12/31	
HP Linux Server	SC Engr	N/A	1/1	1/1	12/31	
HP Solaris Client	SC Engr	Rajesh Gupta	7/14	7/14	12/31	
IBM Win Server	SC Engr	N/A	1/1	1/1	12/31	
IBM Wireless	SC Engr	James Sakayeda	8/8	8/10	12/31	
John's Powerbook	SC Engr	N/A	8/16	8/16	12/31	
Linksys Router	SC Engr	James Sakayeda	7/24	8/1	12/31	
Mac Client	SC Engr	Rajesh Gupta	7/12	7/12	12/31	
Panasonic Linux Client	SC Engr	Sharif al-Hassan	7/6	7/6	12/31	
Sony Vista Client	SC Engr	Rajesh Gupta	7/19	7/19	12/31	
Sun Solaris Server	SC Engr	N/A	1/1	1/1	12/31	
Wireless LAN	SC Engr	James Sakayeda	7/31	8/2	12/31	

Figure 6-16 Where the hardware is situated

As a final note, let me point out another simplification contained in this section. This example does not account for the hardware that the sales and marketing beta sites will provide, nor does it include the STC lab's hardware. To use this database to ascertain hardware coverage, you would certainly need that level of detail. However, I usually capture that type of data in the test-tracking spreadsheet.

What's Running Where? Tracking Software Configurations

In general, you can use the logistics database to track all types of software configurations on test hardware. You can trace the BIOS, operating-system versions, applications, virtual machines and interpreters, compilers, utilities, test tools, test scripts, and other software revisions. To keep our case study simple, though, this section shows only SpeedyWriter software revisions.

Unlike the hardware and human logistics planning discussed in the preceding sections, this section focuses on a dynamic aspect of the database. (After all, this chapter is about crunch mode!) In this example, software is arriving according to a release schedule but rather unpredictably within a one- or two-day window. Table 6-1 shows the planned release schedule for each flavor of SpeedyWriter (that is, for each of the five host, or target, client systems: Mac OS, Windows XP, Windows Vista, Linux, and Solaris), with the associated test phase and cycle. In addition, releases of SpeedyWriter for each host system are planned for the same day.

The plan shown in Table 6-1 looks good, but it probably won't survive its first encounter with reality. Good tests will find bugs, which often delay releases. Some bugs hold up the releases to the point that entire revision levels will be skipped for certain cycles. Logistical problems — lack of proper build platforms, compiler glitches, and so forth — will also detain releases. Every now and then, releases will come in early; and some releases might be skipped because the previous test cycle did not find any bugs in them.

Table 6-1 Planned Releases for Target Platforms

REVISION IDENTIFIERS	RELEASE DATE	PHASE	CYCLE
C.1.Mac C.1.WXP C.1.Vista C.1.Linux C.1.Sol	7/19	Component	1
C.2.Mac C.2.WXP C.2.Vista C.2.Linux C.2.Sol	7/26	Component	2
I.1.Mac I.1.WXP I.1.Vistal. 1.Linux I.1.Sol	8/2	Component Integration	3 1
I.2.Mac I.2.WXP I.2.Vista I.2.Linux I.2.Sol	8/9	Integration	2
S.1.Mac S.1.WXP S.1.Vista S.1.Linux S.1.Sol	8/16	Integration System	3 1
S.2.Mac S.2.WXP S.2.Vista S.2.Linux S.2.Sol	8/23	System	2
S.3.Mac S.3.WXP S.3.Vista S.3.Linux S.3.Sol	8/30	System	3

Let's take a hindsight view of what actually happens. Figure 6-17 shows a snapshot of a table based on the Software entity. If you are using the railroad method of spreading test suites across configurations (see Chapter 3), you can assume that delayed and even skipped releases do not affect the planned execution of tests. Figure 6-18 shows the Tested Configurations report, which cross-references tests against hardware and the software running on those platforms. (Of course, you could also produce a report that was organized by software and showed the tests run against the software configurations.) Since SpeedyWriter runs on the client side, this report does not show the networks or servers.

SW Name	Release ID	Released	Description
⊞ SpeedyWriter	C.1.Mac	7/19	
⊞ SpeedyWriter	C.1.Sol	7/20	
⊞ SpeedyWriter	C.1.WXP	7/19	
⊞ SpeedyWriter	C.1.Vista	7/19	
⊞ SpeedyWriter	C.1.Linux	7/19	
⊞ SpeedyWriter	C.2.Mac	7/26	
⊞ SpeedyWriter	C.2.Sol	7/30	
⊞ SpeedyWriter	C.2.Linux	7/28	
⊞ SpeedyWriter	I.1.Mac	8/2	
⊞ SpeedyWriter	I.1.WXP	8/1	
⊞ SpeedyWriter	I.1.Vista	8/3	
⊞ SpeedyWriter	I.1.Linux	8/1	
⊞ SpeedyWriter	I.2.Sol	8/9	
⊞ SpeedyWriter	I.2.WXP	8/11	
⊞ SpeedyWriter	I.2.Vista	8/10	
⊞ SpeedyWriter	I.2.Linux	8/8	
⊞ SpeedyWriter	S.1.Mac	8/16	
⊞ SpeedyWriter	S.1.Sol	8/17	
⊞ SpeedyWriter	S.1.Vista	8/17	
⊞ SpeedyWriter	S.1.Linux	8/17	
⊞ SpeedyWriter	S.2.Mac	8/23	
⊞ SpeedyWriter	S.2.Sol	8/23	
⊞ SpeedyWriter	S.2.WXP	8/26	
⊞ SpeedyWriter	S.2.Vista	8/25	
⊞ SpeedyWriter	S.3.Mac	8/30	
⊞ SpeedyWriter	S.3.WXP	9/1	
⊞ SpeedyWriter	S.3.Vista	8/31	
⊞ SpeedyWriter	S.3.Linux	8/30	

Figure 6-17 Release of software for SpeedyWriter

You can also expand this database to track hardware changes as they occur. To do that most effectively, you would need to bifurcate every date field into Planned Date and Actual Date fields. You can even use *deleted* and *added* flags to indicate those records that were dropped or inserted after the initial plan was formulated. Such an approach might constitute the beginnings of a very precise change management database for testing. I prefer, however, to use the more flexible approach introduced in the following section.

Tested Configurations

Phase	CycleSuite	Client	Software	Release ID	Released	Installed
Component Test						
1						
Edit Engine: Starts on 7/19 and ends on 7/21						
Dell WXP Client (Available 7/15)						
			SpeedyWriter	C.1 WXP	7/19	7/19
User Interface: Starts on 7/22 and ends on 7/23						
HP Solaris Client (Available 7/14)						
			SpeedyWriter	C.15ol	7/20	7/21
2						
Edit Engine: Starts on 7/26 and ends on 7/28						
Mac Client (Available 7/12)						
			SpeedyWriter	C.2 Mac	7/26	7/26
File: Starts on 7/26 and ends on 7/27						
Sony Vista Client (Available 7/19)						
			SpeedyWriter	C.1 Vista	7/26	7/19
Tools: Starts on 7/28 and ends on 7/28						
Panasonic Linux Client (Available 7/6)						
			SpeedyWriter	C.1 Linux	7/19	7/19
User Interface: Starts on 7/29 and ends on 7/30						
Dell WXP Client (Available 7/15)						
			SpeedyWriter	C.1 WXP	7/19	7/19
3						
File: Starts on 8/2 and ends on 8/3						
HP Solaris Client (Available 7/14)						
			SpeedyWriter	C.25ol	7/30	7/30
Tools: Starts on 8/4 and ends on 8/4						
Mac Client (Available 7/12)						
			SpeedyWriter	1.1 Mac	8/2	8/2

Figure 6-18 The Tested Configurations report, which relates tests, hardware, and the software running on the hardware

Expect the Unexpected: A Change Management Database

No matter how well you plan, no matter how carefully you follow up, no matter how effectively you work with your testers, colleagues, and managers, you will have to respond to the unexpected. Change is unavoidable, and not all changes can be foreseen. Last-minute course corrections, external errors, and internal omissions occur on every development project.

Change is often a manifestation of the learning process. As the development team — including the test team — proceeds through design, implementation, and testing toward the released product, individuals, groups, and the entire team learn more about how the product should function and behave. Changes related to such acquired wisdom are opportunities to be welcomed, since these changes result in a better product.

Sometimes changes are the result of someone's mistake. A failure to plan or follow up in one group can cause problems in other groups. Because the test process is on the receiving end of many project deliverables — and also because the test process needs extensive infrastructure, hardware, and software resources and support — your team is probably more susceptible to the vagaries of the unexpected than other development teams. Thus, you might find yourself in need of a way to track and manage incoming changes that threaten to rock — if not tip over — your boat.

Change management is seen by most system professionals as a project-wide function, not the role of the test organization. For example, Steve McConnell recommends that the project manager or the project management team establish a change control board (CCB). This board manages — monitors, assesses, and accepts or rejects — alterations in any portion of the project plan that is under change control, which includes the test plans and the schedule.[5]

If you are fortunate enough to work on a project that has a formal CCB, you can use that mechanism to track both deliberate and accidental alterations in the test plan and the schedule. However, if you work in environments such as those I'm most used to, where change management is an informal or even nonexistent process, the following sections might help you find a way to track the changes that affect your team, the consequences and the impact of those changes, and the recovery plans you put in place.

So What? Using (and Misusing) Change Management Data

By gathering data on changes, impact, and recovery plans, you can fulfill several important communication and planning responsibilities. Gathering this data provides a structured way to communicate to project management the consequences that certain decisions and events have for the test organization. Using a database also allows you to assemble persistent data that is especially helpful in post-project analysis meetings (variously called *project retrospectives*, *project post-mortems*, and *project post-partums*). In addition, committing recovery plans to writing helps to ensure that you aren't simply reacting on the spur of the moment — and it can also save you from having to formally update the test plan, the schedule, and other documents in the midst of crisis conditions. (Significant unexpected changes often happen in time-crunched situations, which rules out spending an hour checking out documents from the repository, modifying them, and then recirculating them for comments, sign-off, or approval.)

Bear in mind, however, that a change management database is not a place to record a laundry list of complaints. You will probably want to track only those changes that gain or cost a few hours or more, not five or ten minutes. Note that you should include gains. Some changes are for the better: deliverables show up a day early, software is so good that test cycles are dropped, external support

---

[5]See Chapter 6 of McConnell's *Software Project Survival Guide* for an excellent discussion of how such a CCB should work and what it should do.

is beyond expectations. The database described here supports capturing the good as well as the bad and the ugly.

Simple Is Good: The Change Management Database

This change management database is actually quite simple because the needs it serves are straightforward. Figure 6-19 shows the underlying table definition in Access, including a brief description of each field. You can insert data directly into the table using the Access datasheet view, but if you find lengthy text (memo) fields difficult to work with in this view, you can use a form such as the one shown in Figure 6-20, which presents a sample entry for DataRocket.

Field Name	Data Type	Description
ID	AutoNumber	Unique identifier for the change.
Project Name	Text	Name of project on which the change occurred.
Date Noted	Date/Time	Date on which the change was first noted.
Impact Date	Date/Time	Date on which the change will first affect testing.
Change Description	Memo	Short summary of what changed.
Change Type	Text	Type of change that is affecting testing.
Cross-References	Memo	List of the specific test documents that are affected by the change, with page and paragraph numbers.
Impact Description	Memo	Short description of what this change will mean for testing.
Schedule Impact	Number	Number of calendar-days delay or advance as a result of this change.
Resource Impact	Number	Number of person-days lost or saved as a result of this change.
Other Costs/Savings	Currency	Other costs/savings associated with this change.
Test Impact	Memo	Short list of the test case IDs affected by this change.
Recovery Plan	Memo	Short description of how we intend to accommodate this change, including any contingency plans identified
Status Log	Memo	Log of progress toward recovering from this problem.

Figure 6-19 A simple table for capturing test changes

Figure 6-20 A form for entering change data, with a DataRocket sample

The Change Type field shown in Figure 6-20 captures information that categorizes the changes. Your list of possible values might include categories such as these:

Early Deliverable. Some piece of hardware or software — a part of the system under test — showed up early.

Late Deliverable. The converse of the preceding category: the piece of hardware or software showed up late.

Feature Addition. A new feature that will, presumably, require testing, was added to the product.

Feature Change/Deletion. An existing feature was dropped or significantly changed. Any test tools, cases, or suites written primarily or partially for this feature must either change (requiring more time) or be dropped (meaning that the time already spent was wasted).

Test Addition. An existing feature, not previously planned for testing, must now be tested. Such a reversal is often a result of a change in test priorities: what was once considered unimportant suddenly became an important feature in the product.

Test Change/Deletion. An existing test is dropped, not because the feature was omitted, but because someone decided that time or resources should be spent otherwise.

Schedule Slipped. You have been granted more time to complete testing. Note that project schedule slips that do not move the planned ship date actually result in an opposite type of change from the test team's point of view, since testing starts later but must conclude at the previously agreed time.

Schedule Shortened. You have less time to complete testing. This often results when you are unable to start testing on time, but planned test exit dates remain unchanged.

Dependency. Some dependency (a factor other than the system under test) was not available or did not perform as expected.

Budget Increased. You received additional funds for testing, which, for example, allow you to purchase additional tools or hire more staff.

Budget Reduced. You lost funds previously committed.

Quality Exceptional. The system under test arrives with such a high level of quality that exit criteria are met ahead of schedule, allowing a planned cycle or pass of testing to be skipped.

Quality Problem. The system under test arrived on time, but with such abysmal quality levels that the continuation criteria in the test plan are violated, large numbers of tests are blocked, tests identify many bugs and take longer than planned, and so forth.

Because this tool is primarily text-based, it is certainly possible to use a word-processing program to maintain it. However, I find that I value the reporting, categorizing, and analyzing options available in a database. I can produce a report that summarizes positive and negative impacts and totals hours gained and lost. I can also export this data to a spreadsheet for analysis by date, category of change, and so forth.

Often, keeping track of changes is the best you can do during crunch time. This chapter's tips and tools notwithstanding, you will probably find yourself responding to events for the most part. Project crunch times can be managed by the entire project team when the project managers are careful to consider the effects of changes, overtime, pressure, and deadlines on the project team. You can play a more effective role within any project team, chaotic and reactive or orderly and mature, by developing and exercising the softer management skills involved in working with your team, your peers, and your managers. During crunch time especially, personal attributes such as grace under pressure, respect for your colleagues, and an even temper will serve you well, too. I'll discuss these skills in Chapters 8 and 9. First, though, let's look at stocking and managing a test lab, which will build on the discussion of test logistics in this chapter.

Case Study

On one project, my test team and I tested an interactive-voice-response (IVR) network connected to a central call center. The IVR network allowed people to access and exchange information and interact in various local communities. The call center gave these people access to technical and personal help with their use of the IVR network. The project involved building a large test IVR/call center network.

For this project, I used a variation of the test logistics database introduced in this chapter. The database, "Case Study IVR Network Test Logistics.mdb," is available at www.rbcs-us.com. You'll need to download that database to follow along with these examples.

In the Installed At table, notice that we have a specific system administrator assigned to install each piece of equipment (see Figure 6-21). This might be necessary when multiple people are involved in supporting the test environment.

When I discovered hardware availability issues or problems with this database, I would work with the project management team to resolve them somehow, and then update the database. This is why you don't see a lot of issues with hardware not being ready in time for a given test, testers being unavailable or double-booked for assignments, or any of the other issues mentioned in this chapter. If you wanted to track such problems, you'd need to add tables that track historical status as well as current status.

Hardware Name	Location Name	Administrator	Start	Ready	End
10 MBPS E'net 1860 B1	1860 B1	James McIntyre	7/1/1998	7/1/1998	12/31/9999
10 MBPS E'net 1860 H3	1860 Heat Lab	James McIntyre	7/1/1998	7/1/1998	12/31/9999
1860 Network	1860 B1	James McIntyre	7/1/1998	7/1/1998	12/31/9999
Beta	1860 B1	James McIntyre	7/15/1998	7/15/1998	12/31/9999
Cisco 3810/1010	IRU	Todd Harrington	10/9/1998	10/19/1998	10/19/1998
Cisco 3810/1010	IRU	Todd Harrington	12/1/1998	12/15/1998	12/15/1998
Cisco 3810/1010	STC	NTS	10/26/1998	10/26/1998	11/30/1998
Dev Agent	1860 Test	Barbara Jefferson	9/23/1998	9/23/1998	12/31/9999
Dev IVR #1	1860 B1	James McIntyre	8/23/1998	8/23/1998	12/31/9999
Dev SVR	1860 B1	Natasha Illyanov	6/22/1998	6/22/1998	12/31/9999
ES 3500 CSA	1777 Windy City	James McIntyre	12/28/1998	1/1/1999	12/31/9999
ES 3500 CSA	1860 B1	James McIntyre	9/28/1998	9/28/1998	12/27/1998
ES 4500 CDR	1860 B1	James McIntyre	9/28/1998	9/28/1998	12/31/9999
Full MAN	1777 Windy City	James McIntyre	11/1/1998	11/1/1998	12/31/9999
Full MAN	1860 B1	James McIntyre	11/1/1998	11/1/1998	12/31/9999
Full WAN	1325 Capone	James McIntyre	11/20/1998	11/20/1998	12/31/9999
Full WAN	1777 Windy City	James McIntyre	11/20/1998	11/20/1998	12/31/9999
G3 "R" PBX	1777 Windy City	James McIntyre	11/20/1998	11/20/1998	12/31/9999
Half WAN	1860 B1	James McIntyre	11/16/1998	11/16/1998	12/31/9999
Live PRI ISDN 1325-V	1325 Capone	James McIntyre	12/31/9999	12/31/9999	12/31/9999
Live PRI ISDN 1860 B1	1860 B1	James McIntyre	12/31/9999	12/31/9999	12/31/9999
Live T1 1325-V	1325 Capone	James McIntyre	12/31/9999	12/31/9999	12/31/9999
Live T1 1860 B1	1860 B1	James McIntyre	12/31/9999	12/31/9999	12/31/9999
Lucent Open IVR	1777 Windy City	James McIntyre	12/31/9999	12/31/9999	12/31/9999
Null WAN	1860 B1	James McIntyre	10/7/1998	10/7/1998	12/31/9999
PCS PBX	1860 B1	James McIntyre	9/23/1998	9/23/1998	12/31/9999
PL 3000 (WF)	1777 Windy City	James McIntyre	12/28/1998	1/4/1999	12/31/9999
PL 6500 CM/CSA	1777 Windy City	James McIntyre	12/28/1998	1/1/1999	12/31/9999
PL 6500 CM/CSA	1860 B1	James McIntyre	10/15/1998	10/15/1998	12/27/1998
Prod 1	1860 B1	James McIntyre	8/3/1998	8/3/1998	12/31/9999
Prod 10	1325 Capone	James McIntyre	12/7/1998	12/14/1998	12/31/9999

Record: I◄ ◄ 48 of 48 ► ►I   No Filter   Search

Figure 6-21 Installed Hardware table with explicit supporting system administrator assignments

If you look at the "Test Hardware Usage by Hardware" report, you'll see on pages 8 through 11 and 13 that we had an ongoing problem with getting sufficient PRI ISDN and T1 lines for testing. The database isn't completely up-to-date, as we did finally resolve those problems partially — enough to complete testing. On page 26, you'll notice that we did not have the live agent workstations to perform the CSA System Test (CSA stood for *Customer Service Application*). We ended up running those tests in a simulated agent workstation environment, and then running the integration tests that involve the agent workstations in a real environment. Because those tests revealed bugs in the agent workstations' interaction with the CSA database, it would have been preferable to find those bugs a few weeks earlier. This illustrates the danger of running high-level test phases in simulated environments.

Some of the tables in this database are not populated; for example, those related to specific projects and hardware attachment. I have left these in the database in case you want to experiment with them.

For this project, I also used the change management database introduced in this chapter. The database, "Case Study IVR Network Test Change Management.mdb," is available at www.rbcs-us.com.

As you page through the Changes report or the Changes form, you'll see that this project was significantly affected by a variety of changes. You might at first surmise that this reflects poorly on the project teams involved, but the truth is much more subtle than that. It's true that some players did drop the ball on certain tasks, and those problems rippled through to the test team. However, the project was based entirely on cutting-edge technology, which, as we'll discuss in Chapter 9, is always risky. In addition, the project had three major subsystems and a number of smaller and constituent subsystems that had to come together, meaning lots of interconnections and dependencies that affected the project — and testing. Finally, there were significant conversion issues that arose from the legacy data. All in all, this was one of the most complicated systems development undertaking I've ever worked on, lasting over 2 years, executed by teams in about 10 different companies involving hundreds of person-months of effort, and charged with achieving a huge leap in technology using brand-new components. This database reflects the type of change and fast thinking that is involved when smart people work on complex systems development projects. If I had one thing to do over again on this project, I'd have built more resilience and robustness into my test plan so that changes rippling through the project didn't have a more significant impact on testing than they should have.

I thank my client on this project, a regional entertainment services firm, and the project managers in charge of development for allowing me to share these examples with readers of this book. I have purged all identifying and otherwise-private information from this document, including changing the names of the participants in a random fashion. No client confidential information or information covered by nondisclosure agreement is contained in these documents. My client contact has asked that the organization remain anonymous.

Exercises

1. Identify the days on which you are unavailable for cultural, religious, or personal reasons. (There are no wrong answers here.) Compare your list with a peer's list, ideally someone with a different cultural or religious background. Describe at least one way that diversity in a project team can accelerate the schedule.

2. In exercise 1 in Chapter 3 and exercise 2 in Chapter 4, how much time did you decide to spend on each exercise? Discuss the time management

decision you made in terms of certitude versus progress. Note that there is no "right" answer in terms of time spent on either exercise, and that the right answer for this question depends not on justifying how much time you did spend, but rather on whether you might or might not make those decisions differently on a real project where certitude/progress trade-offs are more acute.

3. Using the change management data in the case study, find the most important types of changes using a Pareto chart as shown in Chapters 4 and 5. To identify the most important types of changes, analyze the data as follows:

- Based on the number of changes
- Based on the schedule impact
- Based on the resource impact
- Based on the other costs

Stocking and Managing a Test Lab

In many organizations, the test manager is responsible for stocking and managing the test lab. If you are taking over an existing operation, this might not present much of a challenge. Once you've seen a test lab in action, it's fairly obvious how to run one. However, for a first-time test manager in a new organization, getting a test lab up and running can be something of a mystery.

Simply put, a test laboratory is a place where testing is conducted. I use the word *laboratory* deliberately to emphasize that testers must perform controlled experiments, dealing with measurements and known quantities. They must be equipped with solid tools and a skeptical outlook in their attempt to establish facts. The test lab is an engineering laboratory, of course, not a scientific research laboratory, so the testers are seeking practical knowledge. Nevertheless, like a research laboratory, the test lab should be a place where structured, methodical, calm approaches prevail, not the center of a maelstrom where chaos reigns.

A test lab is also a physical location — or locations. When you have more than one test lab, it's useful to assign a name to each lab: a designation indicating its location ("B1"), a meaningful description ("the heat lab"), or just a whimsical name ("Gretchen"). When you conduct distributed testing (more on this in Chapter 10), you might even have multiple labs spread out over several continents.

This chapter describes the process of planning, establishing, and running a test lab. We'll look at questions such as these: Do you need a test lab? How do you select and plan the physical space? How do you outfit the lab? What about security? How do you manage the configuration of the test lab? What about the human factors? Before we begin, however, let me point out several considerations to keep in mind.

First, remember that testing can be conducted in settings other than test labs. You might recall John Goldstein, the documentation tester from the SpeedyWriter example in Chapter 6, who performed tests at his home, at the engineering office, at the sales and marketing office, even on an airplane in transit. Beta testing often takes place at customers' sites. Testing is still testing when it occurs outside the lab — although a less calm and collected atmosphere often prevails in a setting other than the lab.

Second, this chapter focuses on garden-variety test labs: labs that test hardware for environmental factors, reliability, electromagnetic radiation, sound, and software compatibility; and labs that test software for compatibility, performance, system behavior, and the like. This discussion does not deal with setting up clean room environments, testing battlefield conditions, dealing with toxic chemicals, doing radiation hardness testing, or working in other such exotic or dangerous settings. If your job requires you to test in these situations, you'll need to consult other references.

Finally, note that throughout the chapter I use the phrase *test platform* to refer to any piece of hardware on which testers run tests. In the case of hardware testing, this is often the system under test, but this is not always so. For example, a network switch can be a test platform when you are testing server connections to a network. In the case of software testing, the test platform is the host for the system under test (the software).

Do You Need a Test Lab?

Not every test organization needs a test lab. Some organizations need a lab only at certain times. Others can't test without a test lab. Because setting up and especially maintaining a decent test lab is an expensive proposition, you should carefully evaluate whether or not you actually need a lab.

Let's look at our two hypothetical companies. If you are the test manager for Winged Bytes, working on DataRocket and other servers, you will want a test lab. Environmental testing often requires thermal chambers and tables for shock and vibration tests. Electronic testing involves oscilloscopes, spectrum analyzers, and voltage meters. Reliability testing requires keyboard tappers and accelerated life test chambers. Compatibility testing calls for a library of hardware and software. These types of test tools — especially bulky tools such as chambers and space-consuming collections of software — require a home of their own, away from general circulation.

If you are the test manager for Software Cafeteria, working on SpeedyWriter, however, you might not need a test lab. Your setup involves only a few workstations and some operating-system software in open areas. The network infrastructure and servers are probably hidden away in a server room (or at least in a wiring closet) and thus don't require a separate lab.

The following questions can help you decide whether to establish or to forego a test lab:

- Do you need large test tools such as heat chambers? Are some of your test tools non-portable ones — a shock and vibration table, for example — that need a special permanent location?

- Is a special environment required? If your test platforms have strict environmental requirements (as servers do) or unusual voltage needs (as telephone switches do), you will need at least a server room, if not a separate test lab.

- Is security an issue? For example, when testing new software or hardware, confidentiality is a big concern. Secrets stay secret only when as few people as possible know about them. Moreover, if you perform compatibility testing with a variety of software packages, the CDs and DVDs with the software are valuable, as are the CPUs, laptop computers, tape drives, hard drives, and the like. Keeping them in a restricted access test lab — especially in a locked cabinet — can save thousands of dollars in shrinkage (from loss, damage, or theft) over the years.

- Do you need to prevent non-testers from fiddling with your test environment? You might find that some individuals from other teams can't help themselves; they insist on loading quick patches or trying to hook up some device to the test platform "just to see if it works." They then forget to undo whatever they did. If you work with people like this, the formalism of a test lab might deter such well-intentioned but counterproductive hacking on your test platforms.

- Do you need access to the test facility for an extended period of time? Can multiple projects — concurrent, sequential, or both — leverage the cost of the lab to lower the total cost to the organization? Better yet, can you make the test lab a profit center by selling tools and services from the lab to outside, noncompeting companies? (This is less unlikely than you might expect. For example, if you have a printer compatibility test lab for SpeedyWriter, you might sell printer compatibility test services to other companies.)

If you really need a test lab, you will be able to make a business case for it based on these (and possibly other) factors. Try preparing a budget specifically for the test lab; you'll be surprised at how much it can cost. Remember, too, that money and effort are required not only to set up a lab, but also to maintain it. If the costs seem prohibitive, you almost always have alternatives. By carefully using external resources such as third-party test labs and your vendors, as described in Chapter 10, you can leverage their investments in labs and lab materiel to minimize or eliminate the need for your own. Even expensive testing budgets might prove wise investments, though, as we'll see in Chapter 11.

Selecting and Planning a Lab Area

Once you've decided that a test lab is necessary, you'll need to select a location for the lab and plan its configuration. As you consider the factors outlined here, try to sketch a scaled floor plan of the lab, along the lines of the example shown in Figure 7-1. Make this floor plan as large as possible if you sketch it on paper, or use graphing or drawing software such as Visio. Either way, you should count on developing the floor plan iteratively; you might even need to start all over if you discover that the space you initially selected is unsuitable.

Figure 7-1 An example of a floor plan sketch for a test lab

Size. Is the potential lab space large enough? When the shape of the room is anything other than square or rectangular and wide, you must consider size in conjunction with layout — that is, you must look at the actual working space. Also consider the height of the ceiling. How high will you want your racks of equipment? Also consider the wiring ladders or wiring racks that you might need. Pay attention to the doors — everything in the lab must come in and, eventually, go out through them. Begin your sketch of the lab by drawing the lab area, including the location of the doors and the direction in which they open.

Lighting. Windows can provide both aesthetic benefits and a welcome break for testers. Some of the most pleasant test labs I ever worked in had high-rise views, one of downtown Taipei and the other of Santa Monica. Unfortunately, these same labs were also quite unpleasant when the afternoon sun came streaming into them in the summer. Beyond the heat it generates, direct sunlight can make screens difficult to read and, in some cases, damage valuable equipment. You'll want to have tinted windows in your lab with effective shades installed. Also note the level of the windows: if they are at ground level or close to it, they can create a security problem.

As for artificial lighting, fluorescent lights are the most common type and are probably the best. Incandescent lights tend to throw light in limited areas. Spot lights, track lights, and the like look cool, but they are a better choice for conference rooms than for labs, again because of the type of light they give off. Even and consistent lighting is important when testers are reading documents and screens or evaluating the quality of a display. On your floor plan, indicate the locations of both lighting fixtures and windows (if any).

Layout. When you select a lab space, keep in mind the types of tables and equipment racks you need to install. If you rack-mount most of your equipment, or if it is freestanding, a square room might work very well. If you use tables or desks, a rectangular room might be a better choice, as long as it is wide enough. Remember to leave enough open space to allow people to come and go freely. Populate your floor plan sketch with a scale layout of the chairs, desks, cabinets, shelves, tables, racks, and equipment you intend to install. To keep your floor plan less cluttered, you can use a legend to describe some of these objects.

Climate control. The test lab must have sufficient air conditioning and heating to preserve a stable, normal operating temperature and humidity for your equipment and your testers. Although the testers might go home, the equipment does not — which means continuous (24-hour, year-round) climate control. Your lab might also need automated shutdown capabilities if the temperature or humidity exceeds operational limits. If you have multiple labs or workspaces on the same system, ensure that each lab has its own thermostat. Locate the thermostat on your floor plan.

Fire safety and prevention. Every workplace should have a smoke or fire detector, either battery-powered or backed up by a battery. You should test this detector regularly. To control a fire, a test lab must have, ready at hand, portable fire extinguishers that are electrically safe and rapidly effective. If the lab contains large equipment such as mainframes or telephony switches, you will also need sophisticated, automatic fire suppression equipment that can put out a large electrical fire on its own while staff members attend to their personal safety. Include the fire detection and extinguishing equipment in your sketch, and make sure that your layout doesn't impede access to these devices or impede their use or flow. If objects in the lab get in the way, you should revisit your layout.

Power. You'll need appropriate electrical power in one form or another (120 VAC, 240 VAC, 480 VAC, 48 VDC, and so on) in any test lab, and you'll need the power outlets or connections in the right places. In addition, the incoming power must be conditioned and uninterruptible, immune from the spikes, surges, sags, brownouts, and blackouts that can plague the power grid. If it isn't, you will need to provide such conditioning and backup power in the lab, or be prepared to suffer the consequences. Indicate all the various power outlets on your floor plan.

Static. If you decide to carpet your lab, you will need to take extra precautions to inhibit static. Tile, linoleum, cement, and raised floors tend not to suffer from this problem to the same degree, but even clothing can generate static. The lab should contain static mats and other grounded metal objects to help testers dissipate static when they accumulate it.

Facilities. Facilities for your staff, such as restrooms, stairways, elevators, and so forth (including handicap accessibility) are important not only because you might be legally obligated to provide them, but also because they affect the productivity of the team. In addition, remember that you will need to connect the lab to the outside world using telephone lines (PSTN, BRI ISDN, PRI ISDN, T1, OC3, and so on); network infrastructure such as category-5 Ethernet, category-6 Ethernet, optical, WWAN, or ATM; and possibly other connections. If the proposed lab site does not already have the appropriate wiring installed, you will need to build it in, possibly at considerable expense. (A raised floor configuration can make wiring within the lab painless, but the wiring must still be brought into the lab space, either through a wall or through a crawl space above the ceiling or below the floor.) You should also identify connections for running water if your planned tests require water for cooling. Indicate all facilities and connections on your drawing.

To track many of the factors listed here, you can enhance the logistics database introduced in Chapter 6. Figure 7-2 shows a Locations table that can capture descriptive data about an individual lab site. As shown in Figure 7-3, a Hardware table can track the requirements and specifications of the lab's hardware.

Field Name	Data Type	Description
Location Name	Text	The name of the location.
Description	Text	The description of the location.
Length	Number	Length of the the lab in feet.
Width	Number	Width of the lab in feet.
Height	Number	Height of the lab in feet.
Entrance Width	Number	Width of the entrance.
Entrance Height	Number	Height of the entrance.
Lights	Text	The type and wattage of the lighting.
Floor Plan	OLE Object	An image file picture of the floor plan.
Climate Control	Text	The air conditioning and heating facilities.
Fire Control	Text	The fire detection and suppression facilities.
Power	Text	The power available in the lab (120 VAC, 240 VAC, 480 VAC, 48 VDC, etc.) including number of each.
Connection	Text	Phone (PSTN, BRI ISDN, PRI ISDN, T1 OC3, etc.), network (Ethernet, WWAN, ATM, etc.), others.

Figure 7-2 Extending the logistics database to include test lab locations

Field Name	Data Type	Description
HW Name	Text	Short name of the hardware item.
Quantity	Number	Number of these items available in this lot.
Available	Date/Time	The date on which this lot of these items becomes available for configuration.
Length	Number	Length in inches.
Width	Number	Width in inches.
Height	Number	Height in inches.
Min Temp	Number	Minimum (operating) temperature.
Max Temp	Number	Maximum (operating) temperature.
Min Humidity	Number	Minimum (operating) humidity.
Max Humidity	Number	Maximum (operating) humidity.
Power Requirements	Text	Input power (120 VAC, 240 VAC, 480 VAC, 48 VDC, etc.).
ESD Safe?	Yes/No	Can withstand ordinary electrostatic discharges?
Connections	Text	Phon (PSTN, BRI ISDN, PRI ISDN, T1, OC3, etc.), network (Ethernet, WWAN, ATM, etc.), others.
Description	Text	Any other information for this hardware item.

Figure 7-3 Extending the logistics database to include test lab hardware

The Test Lab Inventory

What items will you need to operate your test lab? Every test lab has different needs, depending on the systems under test. In addition, the importance of any specific item depends on the importance of the particular tests it supports.

Suppose that you are setting up a test lab for Winged Bytes in order to perform testing not only for DataRocket, but also for the entire line of servers, desktops, and laptops produced by the company. You will use System Cookers, a third-party test lab, to do the environmental testing, so you don't need to buy thermal chambers, shock and vibration equipment, or HALT chambers.[1] Assume that your team will focus primarily on behavioral (black-box) tests. Based on this information, let's try to put together a list of the things we'll need for the lab.

A Sample Inventory Template

The following sections might represent a first pass at developing a shopping list for equipping the Winged Bytes test lab. You would need to buy one or more items in each category listed below. For software and hardware items, the choice of which specific ones to buy could be driven by the sales and marketing staff's projections about the target customers, technical support's input on what the current customers use, and the test team's ideas on what is most likely to find bugs, design and requirements statements about support configurations, and so forth.

Software

Operating systems. You will need a wide representation of significant operating systems, which your team will use primarily for compatibility testing.

Applications. Your team will need a variety of software applications for compatibility testing and for use on tester workstations.

Test tools and utilities. Your team will use test tools and utilities to diagnose problems, create simple automated tests, send faxes and files, make system images (i.e., snapshots of system hard drives), back up critical data, measure system performance, and generate background loads on systems.

Hardware

PC Cards. PC Cards and ExpressCards tend to expose a lot of bugs in laptop systems, especially those that arise in conjunction with power management.

Monitors/video cards. The video subsystem is a frequent source of headaches. Consider using a variety of monitors and video cards.

---

[1]HALT is an acronym for *highly accelerated life testing*, which, through a combination of software operation and extreme environmental stress, simulates an entire lifetime for a computer. Some computer vendors use HALT testing to predict the failures that will occur in the system under test as well as the life expectancy of the system. See *HALT, HASS & HASA Explained: Accelerated Reliability Techniques* by Harry McLean.

Printers/scanners. Printers and scanners are not typically a source of hardware trouble, but you will find these items useful for verifying the functionality of USB, parallel, serial, and infrared ports, and for testing wireless connectivity to such devices.

Connectivity cards. You will need a fairly wide variety of Wireless Wide Area Network (WWAN) cards, Local Area Network (LAN) cards, and (802.11) wireless cards to test servers. Each card should be different to get as much test coverage as possible.

Data storage. In addition to items such as external hard disks, external removable storage, external CD/DVD drives, and external tape drives, you will need a fairly complete contingent of hard drives and other options.

Surge protectors/UPS units. In a good test lab, the wall current should be conditioned and backed up, but sometimes you have to make do with whatever power you can get. Surge protectors and uninterruptible power supply units can help.

Reference platforms. When you are conducting tests, the priority assigned to a bug often depends on whether the same failure occurs on multiple industry standard platforms. In many cases, a reference platform is not just hardware, but also a particular PC with a particular OS and set of applications installed.

Cables. Because cables are relatively expensive for such small items, it's tempting to skip them. However, the first time an engineer wastes an hour trying to copy a group of files from one system to another because you don't have the right cable to use for a network or to connect a USB or FireWire device, cables will start to look like a bargain.

Networking. In order to avoid testing on the corporate network, I recommend setting temporary or permanent dedicated test networks in your test lab. Network infrastructure and equipment are fairly inexpensive, but make sure you pay the extra money to get a reliable brand. I had a cheap Ethernet hub once that would crash when new systems were added to the network — either by plugging them in or just powering them on — and tremendous amounts of my time went up in smoke trying to figure out the problem.

Consumables

Be sure to have a plentiful supply of all consumables on hand. This saves time and prevents the loss of focus that occurs when your staff members become embroiled in wild goose chases searching for supplies. Remember that a missing $50 tape or $100 toner cartridge can cost you double that amount in an engineer's wasted time.

Computer media. This category includes such basics as blank CDs and DVDs, removable storage device media, and backup tapes.

Desk necessities. These items are the old standbys: notebooks, paper, pens, pencils, transparent tape, sticky notes, staplers, and paper clips.

Printer supplies. For all the printers involved in either testing or reporting results, you will need the appropriate types of toner, printer paper, printer cartridges, and ribbons.

Furnishings

Copiers and printers. Every test lab needs its own printer; you shouldn't count on using your test printers. Having a small copier isn't a bad idea, either.

Shredder. A shredder is a good idea if you work with confidential papers.

Benches, desks, stools, and chairs. It goes without saying that you will need places for your team to sit and work, but you'd be surprised how many labs have uncomfortable or inappropriate furniture.

Mouse pads. These often allow more precise, smooth motion than moving a mouse across a Formica lab counter. Even optical mice can have problems with certain colors or textures of surfaces.

Static pads. You should provide a few of these in every lab to minimize the occurrence of static discharge damage to hardware.

Tools

Specialized hardware. For basic electrical testing in the hardware test lab, you will need certain specialized hardware, such as an oscilloscope or a voltage meter.

Test management software. If you decide not to create your own systems for bug tracking, test tracking, estimating, and similar management tasks, you should plan to buy commercial software packages that implement such systems.

Computer toolkit. A fully stocked computer toolkit — including screwdrivers, wrenches, chip-pullers, and so on — is a necessity in every test lab.

Reference Materials

The classics. For every type of testing, a small set of books defines the current best practices. Be sure to have copies of these books on hand.

Standards. If industry or government standards apply to any of the systems under test, you will need to have up-to-date editions of these standards available.

Using Risk Analysis to Pick the Right Inventory

In some cases, the potential inventory for your test lab can be enormous. If you're testing a PC application such as a video game or accounting software, there are literally millions of potential supported configurations. (I covered this issue in Chapter 3 in the section "Configuration Coverage.") For a browser-based application, you have a number of different browsers if you consider the versions of each browser, plus you have various security settings and software on the client PC, along with many different possible back-end configurations. Problems related to configuration can arise in just about any quality risk category. I've seen variations in configuration lead to the discovery of bugs related not just to functionality, but also to performance, reliability, data quality, the user interface, and operations, among others. I once saw variations in the firmware on an embedded modem lead to a significant difference in connection stability on otherwise-identical versions of an information appliance.

In Chapter 3 I said that picking the key configurations was a function of the impact to the system if a particular configuration doesn't work, customer usage of that particular configuration, and the likelihood of problems in that particular configuration. (The same idea applies to any inventory item you would need to set up one of these configurations.) If you think back to my discussion of risk analysis in Chapter 1, you'll recognize that these factors map to likelihood and impact ratings in quality risk analysis. Therefore, if you have used this risk analysis technique, you can add a section analyzing the various inventory items you might purchase.

Given a risk priority number (RPN), you now have an assessment of the importance of including a particular item in your inventory. However, you also need to consider cost. An item might pose a relatively high risk, but if it's so expensive that it consumes the entire lab budget, then you'd be foregoing all other configuration coverage to address just this one item. That's not likely to be an intelligent risk management decision. You might want to add a cost column to your risk analysis chart, and then sort by RPN first and cost second, both on an ascending scale. The high-, medium-, and even some low-risk items that are low-cost you might as well buy, the high- and medium-risk items that are of medium cost you probably should buy, and the high-risk items that are highly expensive you should try to buy if possible.

Your cost factors should take into account depreciation across multiple or subsequent projects, too. In other words, the potential for re-use of an item should be an important consideration in whether you decide to purchase it. If you buy an item that you can use across 10 different projects, only one-tenth of the purchase price should accrue as a cost to your project. (This is one reason why buying lots of cables makes sense. Not only are they cheap in general, but they can be leveraged across hundreds or even thousands of projects, making their cost per project well under a penny.) Of course, depreciation is all well and good, but you are dealing with a fixed amount of money to outfit your lab. Just because you can depreciate a $100,000 server across 100 projects doesn't relieve your budgetary problems if you have only $100,000 to outfit your lab.

Since the number of potential items could be enormous, you might want to group equivalent items together in a class. For example, you could consider all models of laser printers from a single vendor equivalent. To pick a specific item out of this class, you can look at the risk, cost, and potential for re-use for that specific item compared with other items in the same class. Your sales and marketing staff, business analysts, users, technical support, and help desk staff might have strong opinions about which specific items represent certain classes, too. It is a good idea to take their ideas into account if practical.

Again, remember that configuration testing is but one of the many classes of testing you must do. Even if you have an almost unlimited budget for lab inventory, you probably don't have an unlimited number of people you can fit into that lab. By trying to cover too many configurations, you might end up with too few people to test other important quality risks.

Finally, keep in mind that beta testing and the use of third-party test labs (discussed in Chapter 10) can help keep your inventory costs down. A third-party test lab can re-use even expensive items with short life spans — servers, for example — across multiple projects in a fairly short period of time, due to their volume of testing business. If you can get enough beta copies into the hands of a representative subset of customers, you might be able to cover an enormous variety of items.

Further Thoughts on Stocking Your Lab

No matter what you are testing, some general observations about your lab's inventory apply. Most importantly, maintain some extra money in your test lab budget. You can't foresee everything, and you are sure to be caught off guard by a sudden need at some stage of the project. When that arises, you might find the need urgent and unavoidable. It's easier to include $5,000 in a contingency fund during budgeting than to go begging to management for another $2,500 in the middle of crunch mode — when everyone has innumerable other crises to attend to.

Along these lines, don't forget to budget for maintenance. Some companies will give you free upgrades to software and firmware for life, but most will not. If your hardware is three, four, or more firmware revisions out-of-date, and your software one or two major releases in the past, how well are you modeling the real world in your test lab? Even one revision can make a big difference in software or hardware behavior. As a tester, you know this implicitly for your own products, but it's easy to forget that we're all in the same boat.

Finally, as you estimate quantities for certain test equipment such as mice, keyboards, printers, and monitors, remember that these items are often shared. You must have a sufficient number of these items on hand so that people don't waste time waiting to use them. When working with software, make sure to have enough licenses for every concurrent user.

Security and Tracking Concerns

Over time, you can spend millions of dollars outfitting a test lab. With accumulated assets worth that much, you need to protect your investment from damage, theft, and other losses. In hardware testing, for example, your assets might include some big ticket items such as thermal chambers and oscilloscopes. A thermal chamber isn't terribly easy to steal, but one person with a car can easily make off with an oscilloscope. In software testing, you often use test platforms such as laptops that anyone with a decent-sized briefcase could sneak out of the building.

No matter how honest your team and your other colleagues are, you have a responsibility as a manager to take steps to prevent theft and the loss of valuable assets. That said, you also don't want your security system to impede your team's productivity. I have seen this dilemma resolved though the use of a library system, in which one or more people fill the role of asset librarian. The asset librarian assumes responsibility for ensuring the secure storage of every valuable asset when not in use, possibly in a locked cabinet or safe (for small hardware and software items) or a locked room (for larger items). When a tester needs to use an item for testing, for example, the tester checks it out from the librarian and then checks it back in when the test is completed. As you'll see in the next section, a simple database can track assets as they are checked in and out.

The beauty of this system is that one person is always accountable for each article at any given time. (You might need several asset librarians if you have multiple test shifts.) In the absence of accountability, a situation sometimes called the *tragedy of the commons* evolves as everyone mistreats a shared set of resources because no one has ownership. In a library system, signing out a piece of equipment indicates ownership, and the individual who has signed it out must take special care that the item doesn't become lost or damaged.

You should also consider the issue of insurance as the value of your lab assets increases. Even if your company has corporate insurance, you might need to declare these lab assets specifically in order to protect them. Understand the terms of coverage. For example, if your lab is in a location that is subject to floods, are you insured against such events?

In addition to considering theft, loss, or damage to physical property, you must also worry about intellectual property. I once worked at a third-party testing company where most clients had their own separate labs, each accessible only with a card key. Each tester had an individual card key, and a printer in a locked room logged the use of that card to enter a lab. Only staff members who were actively working on a client's project had card key access to that client's lab. Some clients insisted on labs without windows. Locked filing cabinets held specifications and other confidential documents. Even people not directly involved in testing, such as the sales staff and the bid writers, had to clean off their desktops and lock up the contents of their desks before leaving each day.

Managing Equipment and Configurations

The sample test lab inventory for Winged Bytes, presented earlier in this chapter, contains categories of items that you can classify as either consumable or durable. Most of the consumable items don't need any serious management — it's silly to try to keep track of pencils, for example. For such items, the only management concern is ensuring an adequate supply. However, for durable items such as desks, switches, computers, software, and the like, you'll need to manage them individually.

A common approach is to use asset tags. You affix a sticker or plaque emblazoned with a unique identifier to each valuable item. Your company might already use this method for managing desks, chairs, and other durable office furnishings. Such durable items can be either portable or nonportable. A desk, for example, is fairly nonportable; once you place it, it is likely to stay put. In contrast, a laptop computer or a switch that your team uses for testing might move around. In this case, the ownership concept discussed in the preceding section becomes important. You probably don't care, for example, which asset tag is on a tester's chair, but you do care which of the three copies of Microsoft Office she has at her workstation.

Note, however, that it makes sense to consider value when using this approach. Cables are a perfect example. Putting asset tags on USB cables and then trying to track who has them is absurd. It'll cost you more in time than it would cost to replace the cable. In this case, I recommend that you accept some shrinkage of your cable inventory, whether from loss, damage, or even theft, rather than descend into incidents reminiscent of Captain Queeg's farcical inquisition into "who ate the strawberries" in *The Caine Mutiny*.

In addition to asset management issues, the question of asset configuration is important for some items. In the case of an oscilloscope, for example, you probably don't need to worry about revisions of the component boards.

However, for each DataRocket in your lab, you must know not only the revisions for all the boards, but also the BIOS releases, the software installed, the disk drives present, and so forth. This is also true if you test software: because you test it on test platforms, you'll need to know exactly how each platform is configured.

You can adapt the logistics database introduced in Chapter 6 to meet your configuration and asset management needs as well as for test lab logistics. Figure 7-4 shows the entity-relationship diagram for an adapted database. The Hardware entity you saw in Figure 6-2 now becomes the *Asset* entity, with the asset tag number (*Asset ID*) as its key property. In practice, serial numbers make decent asset identifiers, or you can use your own system. This entity also has a *Name* property, for the manufacturer name and specific model name, and *Board Revs* property for the board revisions in the hardware. Adding a *Project* property to the *Tests* entity enables you to manage multiple projects in this one database. With the addition of the *Checked Out To* relationship, you can also track responsibility for assets as your testers check hardware and software assets in and out of the library.

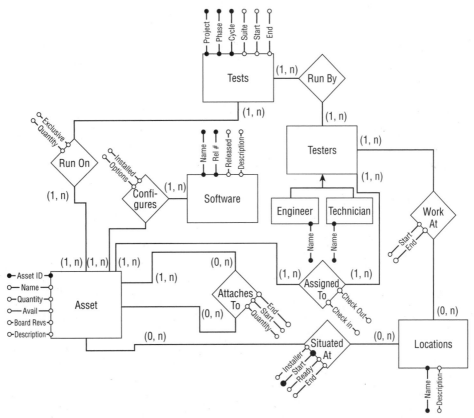

Figure 7-4 An entity-relationship diagram for managing logistics and lab assets

Beyond software and hardware configurations, another important dimension exists for test platform configuration, that of data (see Figure 7-5). The data dimension includes items such as databases and configuration files (the Windows Registry, for example, or Unix cron tables) as well as test input, output, and log files. Data can affect the behavior of the system as much as the software and the hardware can. Moreover, data presents a unique challenge in that the data configuration of the test platform is often changed, both deliberately and inadvertently, over the course of test execution.

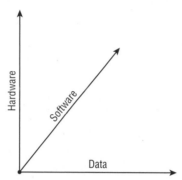

Figure 7-5 The dimensions of test-system configuration

Figure 7-6 shows the various data configuration states through which a test platform might move. These different states can be extremely complex. For each data state D_i, every byte of storage in system memory, video memory, the hard drive, networked storage, and any other secondary storage available to the test platform can be significant. In addition, the actions that cause data transformation are discrete keystrokes, mouse movements, network transactions, and so forth. Literally millions of such actions take place as part of a fairly straightforward test. Given this complexity, scaling up to, say, a 72-hour reliability test run on a network of two dozen servers and clients means that you have reached the point where capturing all data configurations in any meaningful sense is impossible.

Figure 7-6 Data configuration changes resulting from setup and test actions

Fortunately, being able to re-create any arbitrary data configuration D_i doesn't add much value. The two data states you care most about are D_0 and D_n. D_n is particularly important if you are testing data quality. D_0 is important because, if you want to re-run a set of test suites against a particular configuration, you must restore all three dimensions of that configuration, data included. For this reason, it is often helpful to use DVDs or CDs, tape, stored networked images, or removable storage media to take a snapshot of the test platform's data configuration before you begin to test. This step might add a few minutes to test suite setup time, but it is very helpful if you need to reproduce a particular result.

Keeping the Test Environment Clean

As I've stressed before, it is important to know precisely what is on each test system at any given time during test execution. Otherwise, failures prove irreproducible and bug reports become inaccurate. Although this might sound obvious, many people underestimate the importance of strict configuration management in test environments.

In my experience, the fastest way to let your test environment deteriorate into a mysterious state is to allow someone with a hacker mentality to work on your test systems. Just one letter altered in one configuration file, one cable disconnected, one software package installed can change the whole demeanor of a bug. Unless everyone working on your test system logs all changes to every test platform, your test environment will quickly become uncertain. The frustration engendered by bugs that change shape daily has made me a firm believer in scrupulous configuration management.

Most developers want to be able to make changes and try quick experiments when they're debugging; having to document every single step they try slows them down. Unfortunately, this often puts the goal of preserving test platform configuration in conflict with the goal of rapidly debugging a problem. From the test perspective, the best possible solution to this problem lies in preventing any debugging activities from taking place on the test platforms. In a perfect world, the development team has its own development labs — or at least development systems and networks — which reduce or eliminate the need to work in the test lab.

As a practical matter, however, some bugs will occur only in the test environment. Remember that the test environment is as user-environment-like as possible, while the development environment tends to be less controlled, with a narrower range of systems available. If a SpeedyWriter bug occurs only on a PowerBook computer, and the test team has the only PowerBook in the company, the developers must use test's hardware to debug the problem. Likewise, a performance problem on a wireless network will likely have to be verified in the test lab if all the development networks are wired Ethernet.

I'm afraid there is no simple solution here. On the one hand, dogmatically clinging to the notion that all debugging must happen outside the test lab can have a dangerous impact on a product's ship schedule. On the other hand, letting any developer who needs to track down a bug start hacking away on the test environment is an invitation to chaos. Loaning test equipment to developers isn't much of a solution, either. On occasion, I have loaned hardware to development tiger teams for debugging, only to find it borrowed on a nearly permanent basis. Don't assume that there is such a thing as the test team's hardware; project management can reassign it at a moment's notice. So, before you decide to let another group use your hardware — particularly on a promise that is it "only for a while," consider the possibility that "a while" might be the remainder of the project.

If you do have a situation where you share the test lab with the development team, and you can make this work in terms of shifting the use of the hardware, the DVD, CD, tape or network drive image strategy discussed previously for capturing useful data configurations can help you and the development manager. You can accumulate a library of useful configuration and data snapshots. You might want D_0, while the developers want D_i and D_j. This is certainly no panacea, and conflicts will arise, but you can at least prevent chaos in terms of the data state of the lab hardware.

Human Factors

Although the focus of this chapter has been on material objects and information related to them, you need to remember that *people* test in the test lab. The safety of the people who work in your lab must be of special concern to you as a manager. In addition, you need to consider the issues of how testers interact with your lab equipment (including possible damage to the equipment), and how to run the lab so that the testers are as productive as possible.

A Safe Lab Is a Productive Lab

As noted earlier, I assume that you are working in a typical test lab, where no extraordinary chemical, electrical, radiological, or mechanical hazards exist. If your staff must handle, use, or store dangerous chemicals; radioisotopes; radiation-emitting devices; sharp or heavy test probes or tools; high-voltage or high-current components; mechanical presses, punches, or drills; extremely hot or cold articles; or any other compound or object that can injure, electrocute, burn, blind, deafen, sterilize, poison, genetically damage, cut, or kill, you will need to take precautions beyond those discussed in this book.

Most of the test labs I've worked in were less dangerous than the typical garage, bathroom, or kitchen. Nevertheless, everyone working in the lab must understand basic safety considerations and practice common sense.

Thoughtless or careless behavior can result in harm to personal property, injury to oneself or others, or damage to the tools, systems, and facilities in the lab.

For example, if your testers work on the interior portions of computers, with computer peripherals, or with add-on devices, you might want to have them wear lab coats. If lab coats are considered excessive, at least make sure that people do not wear billowy or very loose clothing, and insist that they tuck in or bind any loose items such as ties, bandannas, and scarves. I once ran into a colleague who was wearing a silk tie that looked as if a puppy had used it for a chew toy for about a week. When I asked about it, he explained that he had been leaning over an open computer and had failed to notice that his tie had become entangled in protruding pins on the back of a card in the PC. When he straightened up, the little wires shredded the end of the tie.

Hair and jewelry can cause similar problems. Beards, long hair, and handle-bar mustaches can, under certain circumstances, get caught in a computer or in moving parts. Moist or sweaty hair can also create a short circuit on a live board. Loose necklaces can get snagged; rings (especially if they are large or numerous) can catch on notched and hooked items. In addition, dangling earrings and other uncovered jewelry stuck through sensitive body parts can get snared, leading to painful or dangerous injuries.

Speaking of painful and dangerous injuries, keep in mind that the inside of a computer often has sharp edges and is not sterile. I have taken more skin off my knuckles and the back of my hands while working inside a computer than I care to recall. Gloves might help, but it is cumbersome to work on small chips, jumpers, and screws while wearing any glove thick enough to make a difference. Testers must be careful and should wash cuts thoroughly and immediately.

Many test labs include eye wash stations. Drilling, machining, or filing any metal or plastic component can create shards that can lodge in the eye. Broken glass is always a possibility when working with computer monitors. A reversed capacitor, an overworked resistor, or a chip pushed beyond its specifications can smoke, snap, or even explode. Eye protection is an especially good idea when working with prototype hardware.

Earlier in this chapter, I discussed the need for smoke detectors and fire extinguishers in the lab. At the risk of belaboring the point, make sure to test those smoke detectors as specified in the owner's manuals. In addition, a fire extinguisher does no good if no one knows where they are or how to use them. Finally, people should know the evacuation route if a serious fire breaks out.

As a last note on safety, keyboards and mice must be positioned to minimize the risk of repetitive stress injuries. Likewise, work surfaces, chairs, and stools need to be set up so that people can work at comfortable angles, with proper wrist support and proper posture.

Damage to Lab Equipment

Working on computers can cause injury to a person, but a person can also inflict damage on software and hardware. In a lab where I worked, someone spilled an entire cup of coffee on a keyboard. The keyboard survived, but it required a complete disassembly and cleaning. On another occasion, I saw someone destroy a laptop computer by allowing a few drops of condensation to drip from the outside of a water bottle directly onto the mainboard through the keyboard. Greasy fingers can render a laptop's touchpad unreliable. If you decide to allow food in your lab, be sure that people understand the need to keep it away from the equipment, and institute rules against working on the equipment while eating or drinking.

Other objects that require caution in the lab include magnets, which can wipe out removable magnetic media. Carelessly dropped paper clips, pins, and other small objects can become lodged in a computer, which will eventually cause a short and damage the unit. Should this occur, the tester must power off the unit immediately and retrieve the lost item before powering it on again.

Shock, vibrations, and drops are also concerns. Don't precariously perch equipment in positions from which it can fall. Badly placed wires can trip and injure a tester, but they can also bring an attached component crashing to the ground or tear out a part of the system. I once seriously damaged an integrated modem in a laptop by inadvertently yanking the RJ-11 cable attached to it. On a similar note, I once saw someone attempt to seat a recalcitrant computer board using a two-by-four and a ball-peen hammer. This type of activity, along with slapping, pounding, or kicking any delicate electronic object, is always a bad idea. And, while you can hurl a pen or pencil at a glass-screened computer monitor in a fit of pique, doing the same to an LCD panel is likely to damage or destroy it.

When working on a computer, a tester or engineer must have the proper tools available. Trying to use a flathead screwdriver to tighten a Phillips-head screw might strip the head of the screw, leaving the component improperly seated and impossible to remove. Pliers or the wrong wrench can round the edges of a nut. Removing a chip without the proper chip-puller invites damage to a very valuable piece of equipment. If partial or complete disassembly is a possibility, you should provide trays to hold and categorize screws, jumpers, and other small components that can easily get mixed up or roll off the table.

In addition to providing proper tools, you should also train your staff to apply the carpenter's adage *measure twice, cut once* — that is, paying proper attention to each task and double-checking before taking action. When I first started working with computers, before the days of reprogrammable static memories, I installed a one-of-a-kind ROM backward in its socket. When I powered up the computer, I fried the chip and had to wait two days for a replacement. The client was not amused. Proper grounding when working on any electronic equipment is also a must. Be sure to provide grounding straps and static pads liberally throughout the lab.

Finally, you need to take care when cleaning computers, test tools, and the like. Spraying ammonia-based window cleaners on display screens might not be a good idea, depending on what the screen is made of and where the overspray ends up. Cleaning a laptop keyboard requires special attention because excess moisture can easily work its way into the system enclosure.

Productivity in the Lab

The setup of your test lab plays an important role in the productivity of the people working in it. Set up the tools and workstations to minimize the need for people to move around the lab. Having all the necessary components for completing a task close at hand helps avoid breaking the tester's concentration (or the concentration of colleagues). During an intricate test, any interruption can cause the tester to lose a critical train of thought, thereby omitting an important step or missing an indication of an error.

The idea of breaking one's concentration raises the issue of radios, TVs, and personal music players like the iPod. If all the denizens of the lab agree on a definition of *good music*, allowing some low-volume background music can make for a pleasant environment. However, the more people who are involved, the more likely it is that a conflict will ensue about what is tolerable. In addition, although listening to music can be enjoyable and improve morale, it doesn't necessarily improve productivity. Having people use headphones to listen to music is a good choice.

Similarly, mobile phones seem to pose an irresistible temptation to people. A rule that says, "No personal calls in the lab, and all incoming mobile phone calls to be answered outside of the lab" should help to reduce this problem. In addition, if someone needs to be on a conference call, especially on a speaker phone, that should happen outside the test lab if possible.

Radios, of course, play more than just music. Listening to talk radio might create a stimulating debate among those in the lab, but it is almost certainly a distraction. Even worse, a television, especially when tuned in to those daytime spectacle shows, is nothing but an electronic attention magnet. People simply aren't focused on testing if they're watching TV. In general, it's probably best that people use headphones and that the listening be confined to music.

Finally, your lab setup can contribute to productivity by ensuring that at least two network workstations are available to those working in the lab. This workstation should provide testers with access to the bug-tracking database, the test-tracking spreadsheet, the system configuration-tracking database, and any other reporting and information resources the testers need to execute the tests and report results efficiently.

Case Study

In the course of various projects, I've had the opportunity to see a number of medium- to large-sized hardware and software test labs. In the next few paragraphs and figures, I'll describe and sketch some common layouts for test labs, including some key features, pros, and cons of each layout. To keep the figures simple, I've omitted the furniture, facilities, and other details shown in Figure 7-1. The dimensions are fairly arbitrary, so please don't use these as floor plans for your test lab without making sure the layouts make sense for you.

Figure 7-7 shows a software test lab layout that would be fairly typical for an independent test lab that was organized based on technology areas. The main lab areas are classified by the type of testing that goes on in each location: Windows, Unix, and Networking. The test engineers and technicians work in one of these labs, depending on the skills and assignments. (Chapter 8 will discuss tester skills and ways of organizing test teams.) I also have shown a dedicated lab for one client. Clients often request dedicated labs when they will have ongoing testing happening and need a secure, separate space, away from the potentially prying eyes of competitors visiting the company (see Chapter 10). The overall space also includes some work areas for visiting clients and for the salespeople, who might need private spaces to meet with clients or have conference calls. The reception area will include a receptionist's workstation and a waiting area, and often letters of appreciation from clients. The common area might include shared printers, a copier, a workstation or two, and, in some companies, a Ping-Pong table or some other games. Finally, there is a software/hardware library, probably under control of one or more librarians, a kitchen and lunch area, and the managers' cubicles.

Figure 7-8 shows the same overall lab space for a company that has chosen a project-centric way of organization. The left and right sides at the top of the figure are now common lab areas where one or more projects will occur at one time. There's no privacy or separation for the clients, but this is economical in terms of space usage. The large lab space on the center right is split into two dedicated project labs. These labs aren't dedicated to any one client permanently, but they are dedicated to a single project for the duration of that project. This gives the client some of the benefits of the dedicated client lab space, but that does not include the ability to store prototypes, software, and documents long-term at the lab facility.

Figure 7-7 A technology-centered lab layout

For labs that do a lot of hardware testing — by this I mean primarily various types of hardware reliability testing — the layouts tend to be test-type-centric, as shown in Figure 7-9. The building is split into two main areas, the office area and the testing area. For safety and noise reasons, these areas will be separated by sound-proof, fire-proof, smoke-proof, and possibly projectile-proof walls and doors. (Hardware testing always has the possibility of resulting in physical failure of the system under test, which, if catastrophic, can result in fire, toxic vapors, and flying chunks of the system.) Walls also separate the main testing area into smaller areas dedicated to particular types of tests. Sliding garage-type doors — typically quite tall, say 10 or 12 feet — allow large pieces of equipment such as mainframes and telephone switches to be offloaded directly into the appropriate lab space from a truck.

Figure 7-8 A project-centered lab layout

Figure 7-9 A test-centric lab layout

Exercises

1. Draw a lab space sufficient for the test environment shown in Chapter 6 as Figure 6-13 (reproduced here as Figure 7-10 for convenience). Draw your figure to the same level of detail as Figure 7-1. Make sure to show power and networking connections along with space for testers to sit.

Figure 7-10 SpeedyWriter test environment

2. All the other relationships in the entity-relationship diagrams in Chapters 6 and 7 have been many-to-many. However, what type of relationship must the "Checked Out To" relationship be to implement the asset-tracking database discussed in this chapter?

3. Not all asset-tracking systems are high-tech. Implement an asset-tracking system with index cards. What information goes on each index card?

CHAPTER 8

Staffing and Managing
a Test Team

Hiring, motivating, and retaining an excellent staff are among the most important tasks any manager performs. The extent to which a manager does a good or poor job at these tasks largely determines the extent to which he or she is a good or poor manager. Although these are survival issues for all managers, from those at the neighborhood steak house to corporate CEOs to successful politicians, staffing and managing a test team has its own unique quirks. This chapter offers some pointers on a few of the issues that are particularly deviling:

- What personal attitudes, behaviors, and work styles make for good testers?

- How do you avoid hiring the wrong people for your test team?

- How many people do you need, what skills should they have, and what positions do they fill?

- Do you want to organize your staff by projects or by areas of test specialization?

- How do you find, interview, and hire good test team members?

- What motivates test staff, and what demotivates them?

- How can you use interim staff such as temporaries, contractors, and consultants?

If you reached your current position as a test manager by rising from a technical position, you are particularly likely to find this chapter useful.

The Right Person for the Job: What Kind of People Make Good Test Engineers

Let's start with personal traits for testers, because there's no point in worrying about someone's skills, position, or career goals if that person just isn't cut out to be a tester. The following are some traits I look for — and look out for — when I interview potential testers. After hiring someone, I encourage and cultivate these qualities in my team during test projects.[1]

Professional Pessimism

A Pollyanna attitude is the wrong attitude on a test team. In fact, testers are professional pessimists. Management pays them to explore the dark side of the project. One development engineer told me that he "felt very depressed" after reading the risk analysis documents my test staff had prepared. I find it more depressing, however, to ignore the possibility of failure during development, only to live with the reality of preventable failure after release. Testing involves anticipating the worst possibilities in order to achieve the best possible outcome, given realistic project constraints.

Everyone wants to release products of high quality. I have heard project managers comment that testing budgets are a waste of money because those development scoundrels should be building software or hardware that works in the first place. Those managers do care about quality, but they don't understand the process of software development.[2] Development engineers, especially the good ones, want to create products of elegance and quality.

Nevertheless, a test team must foresee and evaluate the ways in which a product might fail. I believe that this pessimistic, depressing function should live in an independent test group — mostly because it *is* depressing and pessimistic, at least to developers. Having constructed a beautiful piece of software or hardware, developers can hardly be expected to turn around and beat it, torture it, subject it to cruel boundary conditions, stress it, and force it to handle errors they consider unlikely.

---

[1]Bill Hetzel, in Chapter 11 of *The Complete Guide to Software Testing*, identifies the "five Cs" as important characteristics of a good testing specialist: controlled (organized and systematic), competent (aware of proper test techniques), critical (focused on finding problems), comprehensive (attentive to details), and considerate (able to communicate well with development peers). Judy McKay, in her book *Managing the Test People*, also has some excellent suggestions on selecting, hiring, and growing test teams.

[2]Scott Adams's series of Dilbert cartoons about testing put the following words into a development manager's mouth: "If a tree falls in the forest, and we've already sold it, does it have quality?" Actually, I've never heard anything quite that cynical. I believe that most failures to understand and appreciate the value proper testing brings to a project arise from ignorance, not apathy.

The test organization plays this difficult and, in many ways, noble role. One computer consultant referred to testing as the point in the project at which people's "depraved mind[s] ... can be usefully employed."[3] A good test engineer does not mind thinking about ways the product can fail. You might hope that nothing will go wrong, but relying on this hope denies the entire history of computing. Thus, the tester creates failures in a safe environment, allowing the project team to fix them. Testing requires a pessimistic mind-set in the pursuit of a lofty goal: company success through better products.

That said, professional pessimism differs from obnoxious behavior. A tester should focus on catching bugs in the product, not on catching the project team member who might have introduced the bug. Furthermore, the tester must be sensitive to the possibility that a developer will see negative test results as a personal attack. Pointing out specific flaws in a balanced, fair way is helpful. Attacking the product categorically and in general terms is not.

Everyone on the test team must maintain open, frank, and courteous relationships with the entire project team. If, through repeated conflicts, you reach the point where influential players on the project team refuse to listen to you, disbelieve what you say, or bear a grudge against you, your effectiveness will suffer. Being a tester is not a license to be offensive. It is a challenge to be positive, pleasant, and the bearer of bad news, all at the same time.

Balanced Curiosity

During test development, a tester must spend time learning to understand the system under test in order to write high-yield test cases. During test execution, a tester must isolate bugs — as discussed in Chapter 5 — to create good reports. However, it's important to differentiate between a tester who takes the time needed to develop a thorough test or write a good bug report, and one who goes off on a snipe hunt.

A good test engineer develops test cases the way an expert spelunker goes into a cave. Dead ends abound, but the test engineer understands the situation and writes test cases that lead to important bugs, deal with important risks, and build confidence in important features. This requires curiosity. The test engineer must read the specifications, discuss "what-if" scenarios with the developers, and mentally twist and turn the system under test, examining all the angles. Without curiosity, a fascination with the goal, the engineer will write superficial test cases.

A good test engineer also knows how to chase down a problem, trying the smart variations first, with an innate sense of what levers affect the anomalous

---

[3]I regret that I cannot properly attribute this quote. I no longer remember who said it, I only remember the comment. However, since it has become widely attributed to me on the Internet, I should acknowledge here that I am not the source.

behavior. Such an engineer willingly spends an hour or two rerunning a test case with minor variations to get at the essence of a bug, if that's appropriate.[4] This same type of curiosity leads scientists to spend time in a lab looking through a microscope or in an observatory staring at stars. A person who possesses this trait and uses it wisely is an irreplaceable asset.

However, if a tester becomes engrossed in unlikely failures and spends hours writing test cases to expose them, you end up with low-yield test cases. A tester who spends long hours investigating trivial bugs is squandering a precious resource: the test team's time. Curiosity motivates a tester to perform otherwise-tedious isolation steps against bugs, to research obscure and possibly undocumented aspects of the system under test, and to sift through ambiguity for understanding. A tester who rushes to write up a serious and complex bug report after reproducing the symptom once, without additional research, probably isn't curious enough. In contrast, a tester who spends hours on each bug, trying dozens of variations to find the root cause, is going too far.

What divides "curious enough" from "not curious enough" and "too curious?" Good judgment. Some testers can balance the need to finish developing a test suite in time for test execution with the thrill of writing a clever, effective test case. They can balance the pressure to move forward with the desire to know why a bug occurs.

Focus: No Space Cadets

One Saturday morning I went into the test lab and found absolutely no progress being made. A test engineer had brought everything to a standstill for more than an hour by pulling the two other engineers in the lab into isolating a problem. He had found a serious bug, but it didn't require the attention of three test engineers, and it really didn't need to hold up restarting the stress test, whose completion gated the product release. No one could question this engineer's dedication — he frequently spent the night in the lab, curled up in a sleeping bag — but his lack of focus put schedules in danger. He had also managed to defocus two other test engineers.

This situation exemplifies two types of focus problems. First, the engrossed engineer pursued the bug before him so narrow-mindedly that he lost sight of the more important priority. He should have realized after a few minutes that he needed to take a break, restart the stress test suite, and then continue analyzing the failure. Imagine a cook who produces perfect, lump-free gravy while the roast in the oven becomes the culinary equivalent of shoe leather. He was too focused. Second, the distracted engineers broke away from their tasks

[4]Glenford Myers, in *The Art of Software Testing*, refers to the ability to write high-yield test cases and to isolate bugs as "error guessing."

to gaze upon this wondrous bug, just for a moment. The moment passed, but they forgot what they were supposed to be doing until I arrived. They weren't focused enough.

Testers should re-evaluate the appropriateness of their choice of tasks every so often. Testers need quiet, focused periods to solve difficult problems, so you don't want to encourage scatterbrained behavior. However, especially during test execution, every tester should frequently examine whether the task on the table is the most important way to spend time at the moment.

Most testers will go off on a tangent from time to time. As the test manager, you must stay on top of your staff's activities to ensure that the tester who strays is herded back quickly. Recognize that the dynamic nature of the project can lead to frequent shifts in priority, making the task that was right yesterday the wrong task today. If your entire team has problems focusing on the right tasks, ask yourself whether you are communicating priorities clearly and effectively.

Some testers need more redirection — either from the task at hand to more pressing issues, or from the chimera back to their assignments — than others do. At the least, these people shouldn't hold leadership roles in your organization because they misdirect others as well as themselves. For the most hardened offenders, you might need to consider whether they should remain in the test group. Someone who consistently makes the wrong decision about which task to focus on might not be someone you can change.

Avoid the Aspiring Hero

Part of the problem with getting good test engineers lies in the fact that, compared to other software engineering disciplines, relatively fewer people choose testing as a specialty. Test work is perceived — wrongly, I believe, but widely nonetheless — as unglamorous drudgery in many companies, which creates two problems for you. First, you might end up hiring people who view the test organization as an extended period of hazing they must endure in order to join the fraternity of developers. These folks can work out, providing that the would-be programmer or motherboard designer is qualified for a development position, is on a career path toward that goal, and has skills you need. However, this type of situation gets ugly when it becomes obvious to everyone except the employee that a future as a developer isn't in the cards. Second, you might find that some of your test staff deal with formal or informal caste systems by adopting an inappropriate attitude toward the development staff, who sometimes treat testers with disdain in companies that foster an exaggerated pecking order. This situation can turn into a feeding frenzy of recrimination and backstabbing that will make your life difficult and damage your team's productivity. Be sure that candidates for test positions understand their prospects and can deal with their place on the company totem pole.

Shun the Sloth

I worked with a test engineer who was intelligent and capable of good work, but who had no drive. He would sit in the lab and browse the Internet for hours, neglecting important test tasks. In response, some of his colleagues wrote a program that checked whether he was running Internet-related processes on the test network. If he was, the program would kill the offending process and send a message to his screen that read, "Get back to work." In addition to his Internet vice, he had an aversion to hard work. He would work an eight-hour day, no more and often less when he could get away with it. I liked the guy personally, but he did not add a lot of value to the test organization. Eventually, he quit and moved on to a different job.

Don't misunderstand — a test operation shouldn't be run like the Bataan death march, nor does blowing off steam by playing a video game or surfing the Web cause an immediate schedule slip. Moreover, people who put in eight solid hours of work at a high level of productivity and then leave the lab are not shirking. They are engaged in what is sometimes called having a life. Some high-tech companies have a reputation for demanding ridiculous hours and slavish devotion, to the exclusion of a normal existence. In my experience, tired people do poor-quality work, and unrealistic schedules are seldom met.

Nevertheless, testing does involve hard work. Tight schedules, last-minute slip-ups, late hours, and weekend test runs call for people who will go the extra mile. If you find that a tester consistently misses deadlines or sets individual deadlines that allow far more time than required, or evades every bit of overtime or weekend work on flimsy pretenses, you have a sloth on your hands and should set about reforming this employee if possible. Of course, if you see any indication during the hiring process that a person won't work hard, you're better off not hiring that individual in the first place. Slothful test engineers force their colleagues to carry their weight.

Reject Casper Milquetoast

The flip side of the obnoxious, confrontational jerk discussed earlier is the tester who is just too mild-mannered. Rather than becoming ineffective by being in everyone's face, this engineer is too retiring, too confrontation-averse. Such a person will have real difficulties in testing. In order to promote quality, a tester must advocate, argue, assert, and defend, without hesitating to bring problems to the attention of management. A tester who files a bug report and then backs down at the slightest hint of controversy can't contribute to the quality of the product.

Although it's important to avoid undue obstinacy, testers must have the courage to make waves when the situation calls for it. As a colleague once said, "If you're not making people upset, you're not doing your job." This is different from saying, "Your job is to upset people." Rather, it means that testers necessarily cause controversy and distress when they uncover problems that have negative implications for project schedules, resource requirements, and so forth — or when they point out the possibility of those problems. A person afraid of upsetting others makes a poor test engineer. Test engineers should never go out of their way to upset people, but should be willing to deliver and defend bad news in spite of the reaction it might cause.

Defining the Test Team: How Many Whos Do What?

Now that we've looked at testers as individuals, let's expand our perspective and look at how testers fit into a test team. If you were assembling a sports team, the game you intended to play would define the team: you would know how many players were required, what skills they needed to possess, and what positions they would play. When assembling a development team, you can base your decisions on certain models that indicate how many coders, engineers, architects, and so forth you will need. These various models don't all agree on every point, but you can pick an approach secure in the knowledge that someone — if only the author of the book or paper that explains the model — has successfully applied it to one or more projects. The following sections outline some workable methods of defining a test team.

Size

If you are running a one-off test project — in other words, you intend to assemble a team that lasts only for the duration of the current project you're running — then sizing is pretty simple. Use the estimation techniques discussed in Chapter 1, and then go out and hire however many contractors you will need for the duration of the project, taking into account any outsourcing you can do, as discussed in Chapter 10. (Hire contractors, not employees, because you don't intend to keep anyone long-term, right?) However, because most companies and IT organizations intend to produce and maintain systems over time, most of us have to think longer-term.

There is a range of possibilities for sizing the test team long-term. At one extreme is a very deliberate, structured approach. In this technique, you look at the long-range (18 months, 2 years, 3 years, etc.) plan for the company's system projects (in many high-tech companies, this is called the *product road map*). Based on this road map, you can do rough estimation following the discussion in Chapter 1, including plenty of caveats for unforeseen overlap, scope creep, and missing projects. You hire however many testers for your test team as are needed to handle the heaviest project load that will exist at any one time. This is sometimes called *staffing for the peaks*.

A variation on this approach is to staff for the valleys in workload rather than the peaks, and then bring on contractors to handle the peaks. You have a lot more flexibility this way, because unforeseen changes in scope, slips in schedules that cause overlap, and so forth aren't the cause of huge logistical dilemmas and painful quality-versus-schedule tradeoffs. Instead, we trade off money for quality by hiring short-term contractors. However, this does tend to reduce test team effectiveness and efficiency during projects, because these contractors will need to go up the learning curve for each project.

Another variation is using a rule of thumb such as the tester-to-developer ratio discussed in Chapter 1. Based on the size of the development team, the test team is established. The theory here would seem to be that, since testers will only have to test what the developers build, we can piggy-back off the development manager's estimates. Any variation in workload due to the natural error inherent in ratios will come out in the wash over enough projects. This is a common approach, but it tends to break down when outsourcing or integration of commercial off-the-shelf components is involved. However, if the test manager has latitude to augment the test team with contractors, this should work as well as the previous approach.

At the other extreme, the approach that is most painful and generally demonstrates the lowest level of management commitment to the test team as an organization — and often to quality products — is the approach summed up in the words of many RBCS seminar attendees. "We don't estimate how many people we need. Management tells us how many people and who exactly we can have, and then tells us what to do with those people." These same people are often the ones who tell our instructors about how their managers keep loading them down with extra work because they have lots of free time in their groups. We'll discuss these interrelated phenomena further in Chapter 11.

Now, just about any staffing level can work, provided you clarify expectations through the *might test, should test, can test* process outlined in Chapter 1. You'll need to have at least enough people to make some tangible contribution — I would guess that absolutely no less than one tester per 10 developers is a good rule of thumb for this threshold in most contexts I've worked in — but from that point up, you can do some meaningful testing, find some dangerous bugs, and help get them fixed. Be careful about that expectation thing, though: I have seen test managers get themselves into serious, deep, irreparable trouble when management anticipated dramatic, immediate improvements in product quality because of their team's efforts in spite of minimal staffing levels. It's also true that, while an organization can reduce test team size through orderly processes, solid support, and quality deliverables, assuming that these and other facilitative traits will exist in the project without any effort is wishful thinking (see Chapter 12).

If you don't receive all the staff you need the first time around, don't give up hope immediately. Your logic might not have won this time, but it might well have sensitized management to your real staffing needs. As I mentioned, you should look at ways to accomplish some of your test tasks without relying on permanent staff. The last section of this chapter, "Bringing on the Experts," offers some ideas on retaining temporary staff to get through busy periods, and Chapter 10 discusses external resources. Use of temporary or external resources can resolve your real problem — getting the work done — while addressing management's concern that a test organization, once grown, will become a big, unproductive black hole.

Skills

You can think of tester skills in four categories. The first, general professionalism, I see as most important in the areas of basic skills such as reading, writing, and mathematics.

Testers must know how to *really* read — not superficially but with intense focus, meticulous attention to detail, and nearly masochistic capacity. Engineering prose is often dense, sometimes takes liberties with the mother tongue, and occasionally does a poor job of pointing out salient topics. Test case development involves a thorough reading of the specifications, the requirements, the product documentation, and myriad other detailed references. Test engineers and technicians often read hundreds of pages over the course of a project. Furthermore, these product documents often contradict one another. Whether trying to develop tests or looking for documentation bugs, testers must find and report these discrepancies, which is a painstaking process.

Since email is a primary communication channel in the high-tech world, people on a hot project — testers, developers, and managers alike — can receive dozens of project-related emails each day. Especially during the period of test execution, they must read these messages with care and comprehension in order to act on them with due speed. Test execution also requires the ability to understand possibly ambiguous instructions, grasp the goals, and take the right actions. A tester can't run tests without being able to read a test case, test tool documentation, and output logs.

Test personnel must also know how to write. I'm not talking about perfect grammar and spelling, although poor use of language can certainly distract and confuse readers. The most important issue is the ability to communicate effectively in writing. When testers find a problem, they must communicate the symptoms they observe. Finding bugs is useless if you can't write a good bug report. The bug report is the most tangible product of testing and the foundation of most quality metrics. Just as you wouldn't hire a chef who can't cook, you shouldn't hire test staff who can't write bug reports. The task of communicating blockages and breakdowns in the test process itself, often via email, also requires writing ability. Poor written communications can cause you, as a test manager, some real heartburn.

Interestingly, I have found the ability to communicate clearly in writing to be nearly independent of whether the tester is using his or her native language. I've worked with some Taiwanese test engineers who were tough to communicate with in spoken English, but who nevertheless wrote excellent bug reports in perfectly clear, if not always grammatically correct, English. I've also known some American test engineers whose bug reports, in English, required extensive editing. The difference lies more in the degree of care taken in expressing one's thoughts than in knowledge of the language.

The application of metrics in testing, such as a reliability growth model for software or MTBF calculations for hardware, can entail a sophisticated understanding of statistics and mathematics. If your test organization uses such metrics, you will need at least one person — in addition to yourself — who understands how these metrics work. For the rest of the team, a simple understanding of some basic mathematical and statistical concepts will suffice. It's not possible to give hard-and-fast rules for which specific concepts testers need to know in all cases, but you'll usually want the engineers on your staff to be familiar with statistical concepts such as distribution functions, means and standard deviations, and the like.

Beyond basic professionalism, there are three other specific categories of skill to consider:

Technology. Since bugs often are technology-dependent — or at least influenced by the technology the system was built with — testers should understand how systems are built, including having a grasp of the underlying programming languages, system architectures, operating system features, networking, presentation layers, database functionality and implementation, and so forth.

Application domain. Other bugs arise less from how the system was built than from what the system is supposed to do. Especially when it's most difficult to predict what a correct result would look like, testers need to understand the business, technical, or scientific problem that the system solves.

Testing. In addition to knowing where bugs live and what they look like, testers need to know how to find them, effectively and efficiently. In some cases, this is just a matter of sitting down in front of the system with adequate technological or application domain insight, but often it is not. I once saw a multimillion-dollar project fail in no small part due to the lack of knowledge of some otherwise-talented technical people who tried to perform load and performance tests that were well beyond their knowledge of that art. When test engineering and execution requires special skills, the test team must have an ample number of people with such skills.

The first two categories are well recognized, but I find the third category of skill, testing, to be often underappreciated as a unique, distinct skill that must be well represented within a strong test team.

This disconnect strikes me as somewhat strange, because I'm hardly the first person to note the importance of test-specific skills in a test team. Glenford Myers made a case for having a test staff composed of system test experts — that is, people whose careers are focused on testing as a specialty. However, I think the devaluation of test expertise might arise from a gap in testing as practiced in some organizations.[5]

I've reproduced a portion of Figure 1-1 here as Figure 8-1. In some organizations, very little true behavioral testing occurs. In these organizations, whatever independent testing occurs — in other words, testing outside of the unit testing done by developers — is called *system test* or *integration test*, but consists primarily of live testing techniques and is a variant of acceptance testing. In these cases, those people doing testing are either technologically savvy programmers and developers unit testing their own code, or application domain experts testing the system under end user conditions. The application domain experts are often temporarily assigned from the marketing, sales, help desk, business analyst, or technical support ranks.

Ideal Testers:	Programmers DB/Net/System Admins Electrical/Mechanical Engineers	Test Engineers Test Technicians (Some) Programmers	Tech Support/Help Desk Sales/Marketing Business Analysts/Users
Test Granularity:	Structural ("White-Box")	Behavioral ("Black-Box")	Live ("Alpha/Beta")

Figure 8-1 The test granularity spectrum, from a skills perspective

Don't misunderstand me. I definitely do see understanding the technology and the application domain as important for testers. However, you should recognize that testing does have its own set of special skills, especially when it comes to nonfunctional tests such as error handling, capacity, performance, and so forth. Just because you have a test organization now that includes only technology and application domain experts doesn't mean that's necessarily a good idea. Revisit the list of critical risks to system quality that you put together back in Chapter 1. Are there any high-priority risks you're not testing because you don't have the right skills in your test team? If so, you need to revisit the importance of testing skills in a balanced, effective, and efficient team.

[5]Myers discusses this in his pioneering book, *The Art of Software Testing*.

What are the critical skills for your projects and your test team? That's a question only you can answer. I like to look at the tasks that I identify on the work breakdown structure for my projects and ongoing maintenance efforts. Based on these tasks, what skills do I need in my test team to perform those tasks competently? Given a list of these critical skills, I can then assess the current team's capabilities against those skills — or better yet, have people self-assess.

Figures 8-2 through 8-5 show a skills assessment for the SpeedyWriter test team, based on the project schedule shown in Chapter 1. As you can see, the rightmost column defines the critical skills, grouped into the four categories discussed in this section. The next-rightmost three columns define desirable and required levels of experience for positions within the test team (more on positions in the next section). The middle five columns define where the various test team members stand on those skills, from no knowledge (0) to expert knowledge (3). The leftmost two columns show the team minimums and averages in each skill and in each skill category, allowing me to see relative strengths and weaknesses.

A	B	C	D	E	F	G	H	I	J	K
1					Software Cafeteria Test Team					
2					Skills Assessment and Management Worksheet					
3										
4	Legend	0 = No Knowledge		1 = Some Knowledge		2 = Knowledgeable		3 = Expert Knowledge		
5		Fi = Required		D = Desirable						
6		TT = Test Technician		TM = Test Manager		MTE = Manual Test Engineer		ATE = Automated Test Engr		
7 Skills and Qualifications	TT Minimum Ratings	ATE Minimum Ratings	MTE Minimum Ratings	TM Jake	MTE Lin-Tsu	ATE Bob	MTE Hitesh	ATE Maria	Team Minimum	Team Average
8 **General Qualifications**										
9										
10 Education										
11 Bachelor Science Degree (0r+)	D	D	D	BS (CSE)	Ph.D. (CS)	BS (Math)	MA (Psych.)	BS (Bus)		
12 Test Training or Certification	D	D	D	CSQE	ISEB					
13 Other							LFC	CPA		
14										
15 work Experience (Years)										
16 Test Roles	D	5R	5R	7	5	6	11	12		
17 Non-Test, Computer	D	D	D	3	2			4		
18 Non-Computer, Domain	D	D	D							
19 Non-Computer, Non-Domain							10	6		
20 Total / Any / Other	ID	5R	5R	10	7	6	21	22		
21										
22 Professionalism										
23 Oral Communication	IR	2R	2R	3	1	2	3	2	1	2.2
24 Written Informal Communication	IR	3R	3R	3	3	2	3	3	2	2.8
25 Written Formal Communication	D	D	D	3	0	1	3	1	0	1.6
26 Continuing Education	D	R	R	Yes	Yes	Yes	Yes	Yes	Yes	Yes
27 Test Team Building / Cross-training	D	2R	2R	3	2	1	3	2	1	2.2
28 Cross-functional Relationship Building	D	2R	2R	3	2	1	3	2	1	2.2
29 Reading (Retention, Reasoning, and Analysis)	IR	2R	2R	3	2	2	3	2	2	2.4
30 Business / Technical Trends (Journal Reading)	D	1R	1R	3	1	3	1	1	1	1.8

Figure 8-2 The first page of a skills assessment worksheet

I find that doing this skills analysis on a spreadsheet is nice. I like the measurement of skills at the individual and team level, although it is admittedly subjective and of limited precision. This makes an excellent hiring tool, as you'll see in a minute. I can also set goals for team skills growth as part of a quarterly team skills assessment, and then use education, training, and task assignment options to help the team and each person on it grow their skills over time.

Skills and Qualifications	TT Minimum Ratings	ATE Minimum Ratings	MTE Minimum Ratings	TM Jake	MTE Lin-Tsu	ATE Bob	MTE Hitesh	ATE Maria	Team Minimum	Team Average
Software Cafeteria Test Team										
Skills Assessment and Management Worksheet										
Legend	0 = No Knowledge			1= Some Knowledge		2 = Knowledgeable		3 = Expert Knowledge		
	Fi = Required			D = Desirable						
	TT = Test Technician			TM = Test Manager		MTE = Manual Test Engineer		ATE = Automated Test Engr		
Testing Skills										
General										
Testing Standards	D	2R	2R	3	3	3	3	3	3	3.0
Software Development Life Cycles	D	2R	2R	3	3	3	3	2	2	2.8
Testing / Development Process / Maturity	D	1R	1R	2	2	3	1	1	1	1.8
Change Management	D	1R	1R	2	2	3	1	1	1	1.8
Relating Testing to Business/SDLC	D	1R	1R	3	3	3	2	1	1	2.4
Planning										
Estimation		D	D	3	1	1	2	1	1	1.6
Documentation		D	D	3	1	3	2	1	1	2.0
Cost of Quality		D	D	3	2	2	1	1	1	1.8
Quality Risk/Failure Mode and Effects Analysis		D	D	3	2	1	1	1	1	1.6
Quality Risk Analysis and Management		D	D	3	2	1	1	1	1	1.6
Design and Development										
Behavioral (Black-box)	D	2R	2R	2	3	3	3	2	2	2.6
Strutural (White-box)	D	D	1R	1	3	2	1	2	1	1.8
Static (Requirements, Specifications, Documentation)	D	D	2R	2	3	1	3	2	1	2.2
Reliability (Statistics)		2R	D	1	1	3	1	2	1	1.6
Performance (Modeling/Simulation/Testing)		2R	D	1	2	3	1	3	1	2.0
Code/Dataflow Coverage		2R	2R	2	3	1	3	3	1	2.4
Quality Risk/Requirement Coverage (Traceability)		1R	2R	3	2	3	1	1	1	2.0
Automation Development										
COTS Execution (Silk, Validor, etc.)		3R	D	1	1	3	1	3	1	1.8
COTS Test Management		D	D	3	1	2	1	1	1	1.6
Custom Toolsmithing		3R	D	3	1	3	1	3	1	2.2
Configuration										
Test Data Generators		1R	D	1	1	2	1	2	1	1.4
Version Control		1R	1R	2	2	2	1	3	1	2.0
Configuration Management		D	1R	1	2	2	1	1	1	1.4
Ingration Testing		D	1R	3	2	2	1	1	1	1.8
Execution										
Manual Scripted	D	D	3R	3	3	1	3	1 1	1 1	2.2
Manual Exploratory	D	D	3R	3	3	1	3	1 1	1 1	2.2
Automated		3R	D	1	1	3	1	3 3	1 1	1.8
Bug Isolation	D	3R	3R	3	3	3	3	3 3	3 3	3.0
Bug Reporting	D	3R	3R	3	3	3	3	3 3	3 3	3.0
Test Status Reporting	D	2R	2R	3	2	3	3	2 2	2 2	2.6
Test Metrics (Dashboard)	D	1R	1R	3	2	3	1	3 3	1 1	2.4
Average Testing Skills				2.4	2.1	2.3	1.7	1.9	1.3	2.1

Figure 8-3 The second page of a skills assessment worksheet

Education, Training, and Certification

The topic of education and training for testers is something of a briar patch, and I'm sure to brush up against some thorns in the next few paragraphs. In general, we in the testing world are plagued by a number of problems in this area, which hark back to some comments I made in the introduction. One is that there is no generally accepted, standard body of knowledge for testing. Another is that, with a few notable and satisfying exceptions, testing is not widely taught in colleges and universities. Furthermore, some people don't believe that we know enough about testing at this point to adopt the types of licensure and certification options that doctors, lawyers, and other professionals have. Therefore, the best I can do here is comment briefly on the state of education, training, and certification for testers, and hope that the offerings in this area ultimately catch up with the need.

	A	B	C	D	E	F	G	H	I	J	K
1					Software Cafeteria Test Team						
2					Skills Assessment and Management Worksheet						
3											
4			Legend	0 = No Knowledge		1 = Some Knowledge		2 = Knowledgeable		3 = Expert Knowledge	
5				R = Required		D = Desirable					
6				TT = Test Technician		TM = Test Manager		MTE = Manual Test Engineer	ATE = Automated Test Engr		
7	Skills and Qualifications	TT Minimum Ratings	ATE Minimum Ratings	MTE Minimum Ratings	TM Jake	MTE Lin-Tsu	ATE Bob	MTE Hitesh	ATE Maria	Team Minimum	Team Average
78	**Domain Knowledge**										
79	Word Processing										
80	Windows Applications	D	1R	2R	3	3	2	1	3	1	2.4
81	Unix Applications	D	D	D	1	1	3	3	2	1	2.0
82	Macintosh Applications	D	D	D	0	1	0	3	3	0	1.4
83	Graphics and Figures	D	1R	2R	2	2	3	2	1	1	2.0
84	Tables	D	D	1R	1	2	3	2	1	1	1.8
85	Mathematical/Engineering	D	D	1R	1	3	3	0	0	0	1.4
86											
87	Document Management										
88	Windows Applications		D	D	1	2	1	0	2	0	1.2
89	Unix Applications		D	D	0	0	0	1	1	0	0.4
90	Macintosh Applications		D	D	0	0	0	1	1	0	0.4
91	Other		D	D	0	0	0	0	1	0	0.2
92	Hierarchical Storage Management		D	D	1	2	0	0	3	0	1.2
93											
94	Document Interchange										
95	Windows Applications		D	D	1	2	1	0	3	0	1.4
96	Unix Applications		D	D	1	0	0	1	3	0	1.0
97	Macintosh Applications		D	D	0	0	0	1	3	0	0.8
98											
99	Printing										
100	Color	D	D	D	0	0	1	1	2	0	0.8
101	Laser	D	D	D	1	1	1	1	2	1	1.2
102	Inkjet	D	D	D	1	1	1	1	2	1	1.2
103	Publishing/Binding		D	D	0	0	0	1	2	0	0.6
104											
105	Web Publishing										
106	HTML	D	D	D	1	3	3	2	3	1	2.4
107	XML		D	D	1	3	3	0	2	0	1.8
108	Other		D	D	1	1	3	0	2	0	1.4
109											
110	**Average Domain Knowledge**				0.8	1.3	1.3	1.0	2.0	0.3	1.3

Figure 8-4 The third page of a skills assessment worksheet

	A	B	C	D	E	F	G	H	I	J	K
1					Software Cafeteria Test Team						
2					Skills Assessment and Management Worksheet						
3											
4			Legend	0 = No Knowledge		1 = Some Knowledge		2 = Knowledge		3 = Expert Knowledge	
5				R = Required		D = Desirable					
6				TT = Test Technician		TM = Test Manager		MTE = Manual Test Engineer	ATE = Automated Test Engr		
7	Skills and Qualifications	TT Minimum Ratings	ATE Minimum Ratings	MTE Minimum Ratings	TM Jake	MTE Lin-Tsu	ATE Bob	MTE Hitesh	ATE Maria	Team Minimum	Team Average
112	**Technical Expertise**										
113	Programming										
114	C/VB (3GL)	D	1R	D	2	2	3	2	3	2	2.4
115	Java/C++(OO)	D	1R	D	0	1	3	2	2	0	1.6
116	Shell (Tcl/Ksh)Scripting	D	2R	D	3	2	3	2	2	2	2.4
117	Code Complexity and Metrics		1R	D	2	0	0	2	2	0	1.2
118											
119	Operating Systems										
120	Windows	D	1R	1R	2	3	2	1	2	1	2.0
121	Linux	D	1R	1R	2	2	1	3	2	1	2.0
122	Solaris	D	1R	1R	2	1	1	1	2	1	1.4
123	Mac OS	D	D	D	0	2	0	3	3	0	1.6
124	Other	D	D	D	1	1	0	3	3	0	1.6
125											
126	Networking/Internetworking										
127	TCP/IP, FTP, RCP (Internet Architecture)		1R	1R	2	1	1	1	1	1	1.2
128	Browsers (Firefox, Chrome, IE, etc.)	1R	1R	1R	2	3	2	2	1	1	2.0
129	Network Application Architecture (Tiered)		1R	1R	2	3	2	1	1	1	1.8
130	Network Hardware		1R	1R	2	3	2	1	1	1	1.8
131											
132	Systems and Servers										
133	Java-based Web Servers		1R	1R	1	3	1	1	3	1	1.8
134	Database Servers		1R	1R	2	3	1	1	3	1	2.0
135	Mainframe		1R	1R	1	2	1	1	3	1	1.6
136											
137	**Average Technical Expertise**				1.6	2.0	1.4	1.7	2.1	0.9	1.8

Figure 8-5 The fourth page of a skills assessment worksheet

In terms of formal education — in other words, through colleges and universities — the options are few but the trends are heartening. For example, a number of professors use my books and RBCS training materials as the texts for their courses. (If you are a professor at an accredited university and want to use RBCS training materials, send me an email, as we can usually arrange for you to use the training materials on a pro bono basis.) I hope this indicates a growing awareness of the need for educational programs in this area. Nevertheless, for the foreseeable future, most people with college degrees who come to us looking for jobs as testers will not have degrees in software testing, or even have taken a single course in software testing as part of their curriculum.

Considerable debate exists around the need for a degree in the first place, too. In some places where I've taught courses — most notably, India, Japan, and Korea — people have told me that no one even gets in the door for an interview without a degree. However, in most places in the United States and Europe, non-degreed people are considered for positions in the test team, provided that skills and experience make up for the lack of a degree. In certain organizations, though, this is not appropriate. For example, some RBCS course attendees and clients make very complex systems that require a high degree of domain knowledge. For example, our oil exploration software client requires test engineers to have degrees in geology, geophysics, petrochemistry, and the like. My rule of thumb is that engineers should either have a degree or an extra two or more years of experience, while I will hire test technicians without degrees under most circumstances.

Don't get me wrong; a degree is always a nice thing to see on a résumé — but what kind of degree to look for? That depends on which of the three specific categories of skill is most important in your organization. You might want to focus on technology, in which case you'll want software engineering, computer science, and other engineering degrees. You might want to focus on application domain expertise, like my oil exploration client, in which case a degree related to the problem the system solves is more important. However, you might think that testing is about how systems and people relate to each other and how we can know anything about the quality of a computer system, in which case psychology, logic, philosophy, math, and other fields might be more appropriate. You might choose to mix up your team, striving for diversity in educational backgrounds. A degree generally indicates an ability to persevere and to dedicate oneself to a rigorous and prolonged endeavor, which is something you want in a tester, too.

There are many different types of degrees and diplomas floating around out there, too. I find that many of my test technicians tend to hold technical or trade school certificates, or two-year degrees from junior or community colleges. At the test engineer level, the four-year bachelor's degree and beyond tend to predominate. I have had a few people working for me in various capacities with advanced degrees as well, although this is uncommon.

I've also found some atypical forms of education that some of my best testers have had. Some people have learned about computers in high school or in continuing education courses. I've had great success with former military people, especially retired noncommissioned officers. Noncommissioned officers spend their careers welding young people straight from boot camp into effective teams for disparate activities, from working on electronics to maintaining a submarine to charging into a dangerous field of battle with courage, a gun, and supreme confidence in their leaders. These human skills can be invaluable in building a test team, especially one that will include lots of inexperienced test technicians.

Training courses and seminars are another popular way for people to learn about technology, the application domain, and testing. My own company, RBCS, offers a dozen courses in testing, which are available through us and through our licensees around the world. We have many international competitors, so you have lots of options for training your team. Such courses have proven quite popular.

In some cases, you can also look for certifications for your testers. A certification might or might not involve training. The key distinction of a certification is that the person holding the certificate has passed as exam. This exam should demonstrate mastery of most of the key concepts and skills defined for that certification. The document defining these key concepts and skills is typically called either the *body of knowledge* or the *syllabus*. I'll return to this topic is just a moment, but first let's look at the various certifications applicable for testers.

Some certifications involve a technology. For example, both Microsoft and Cisco offer certification programs. Such certifications can prove useful for your testers if they involve the technologies used in your product. If you use a lot of different technologies, or if technological skills are not vitally important in your test team, then these are of limited applicability.

Some certifications involve a particular business domain. For example, paralegals and financial advisors can obtain certifications. Such certifications can prove useful for your testers if they address the specific business domain in which your product is used. If your product is used by a lot of different business domains, or if business skills are not critical in your test team, then these are of limited applicability.

Some certifications involve skills in areas closely related to testing, and which are skills that testers often need to have. For example, the International Requirements Engineering Board (IREB) and the International Institute of Business Analysts (IIBA) offer certifications in requirements engineering and business analysis. My own company, RBCS, offers a course covering both the IREB and IIBA bodies of knowledge in this area. Such certifications can prove useful for your testers if your testers are involved in creating and reviewing the specification of the product — and they should be.

Some certifications focus on general applicable testing skills. For example, the International Software Testing Qualifications Board (ISTQB), which I am involved with, offers a number of certificates at the Foundation, Advanced, and, soon, Expert level, targeting testers, test managers, test analysts, test automation, and more. The Quality Assurance Institute (QAI), Sogeti, the American Society for Quality (ASQ), and others offer such certifications, though many are proprietary.

For any certification, I believe the following considerations are essential. First, since a group of people developed the body of knowledge or syllabus underlying the exam, consider the integrity, value, and source of this document. Why should you trust these people's opinion about what is important in the field? What is the source of their expertise? Does the group of people involved in developing the body of knowledge or syllabus have real-world experience dealing with the kinds of problems and projects that are important to your team?

Second, consider the costs and benefits of achieving the certification. Is training required or can people self-study? If training is required, is the training open (with lots of competitors) or closed (only one training provider can provide the training)? Must the testers take (potentially costly) re-certification exams? How will mastery of the concepts and skills in the body of knowledge or syllabus help your team do better testing?

Third, consider the internationalism of the certification. Testing, like all aspects of software engineering, is rapidly becoming a globalized endeavor. If your team is spread across the globe (see Chapter 10), can all members of your team obtain the same certification? If not, does this create a risk of disparate ideas, terminology, and approaches to testing that might undermine the effectiveness and efficiency of your team?

Fourth, consider the degree of acceptance of the certification. Are other companies in your field using it? Are your global development and testing partners using it? Do your respected colleagues in the software testing field value it?

Fifth, and finally, consider the quality and integrity of the exams. Is the exam provider following psychometric standards of examination? Are the exam provider and the training provider the same entity (or multiple entities controlled by the same people), opening the possibility of rigging the exams? What steps does the exam provider take to ensure the person sitting for the exam and the person whose name is on the certificate are the same? [6]

All of these certification and other training programs can be beneficial adjuncts to real-world experience. I have, however, seen some technical

---

[6]Since I have written extensively elsewhere about certification, especially the International Software Testing Qualifications Board's program, I do not want to recapitulate that material here. For more information on the ISTQB program in general, I recommend the American Software Testing Qualifications Board's web site, www.astqb.org. For references to help you prepare for the exam, you can see my books *Foundations of Software Testing: ISTQB Certification, Advanced Software Testing: Volume I*, and *Advanced Software Testing: Volume II*. For an overview of the program, you can see my article, "ISTQB Certification," originally published in *Testing Experience* magazine and now on the RBCS web site (www.rbcs-us.com) in the Basic Library.

recruiters misuse certification programs by representing to their clients that the mere possession of the appropriate brightly stamped sheet of paper made a candidate an expert in the field. These programs can give attendees useful knowledge and expose them to a broader set of ideas than they would encounter in day-to-day experience, but they are not a substitute for hands-on performance of testing roles.

Finally, conferences are also a good place for testers to get education and training on testing, technology, and the application domain, both from known experts in the field and from each other. The best conferences I've attended included lots of experienced practitioners telling other attendees about what's worked — and what hasn't worked — for them. From most of the conferences I've attended, I have brought back at least one idea that paid for the cost of the conference by itself.

Steve McConnell, in *After the Gold Rush*, discusses training and education in the area of software engineering as part of a trend toward professionalization of the field. The same is probably true for testing, although training, education, licensure, or certification will never solve all of our hiring problems. Additional organizational questions exist in this area, too. Is it reasonable for an employee or employer to expect or demand some level of education and training, including support for ongoing education? Is it reasonable for employers to worry about employees taking advantage of tuition reimbursement or training course opportunities, and then leaving or demanding steep raises? Picayune though such questions might seem in the bigger scheme of things, these questions nonetheless are significant barriers to training and education in many organizations, which dampens the overall supply of trained, educated, certified testers in the job market.

Positions, Experience, and Goals

If you automate most of your testing, or if most of your testing involves the use of complex tools, you might staff your team entirely with test engineers. A test engineer is the technical peer of a programmer, a mechanical engineer, or an electrical engineer. Having chosen testing as a specialty, test engineers write tests; create, customize and use advanced test tools; and have unique skills such as test design, bug reporting, and problem isolation.

If your test execution involves simple manual operations such as loading floppy disks in response to a prompt, installing and checking PC Cards, and configuring systems according to a simple checklist, you should also have some test technicians on staff. Such straightforward, rote tasks tend to distract test engineers from their more challenging duties. In addition, some engineers do a poor job with tasks they find boring or beneath them. Having test technicians, who are less skilled and experienced — and who will find test execution, even from a written test case, challenging — handle these easier chores might well improve the quality of your test operation.

Local colleges, universities, and technical schools provide good sources for test technicians. One or two postings on their job boards can often identify a few qualified computer science students. These students enjoy working in their chosen field, usually work hard, and are likely to be bright, so you'll get excellent value for the wages you pay.

Not every student is a good fit. I try to hire computer science, computer-engineering, or engineering students. The deeper level of computer knowledge these engineers-in-the-making bring to the test organization will make a difference. Watch out, however, for hacker types, who often have trouble focusing, following a process, and staying on task. (The term *hacker* might call to mind kids who use computers with criminal intent, but I'm using the word in its original meaning: amateur computer wizards who can achieve great results but tend to follow their own muse a bit too frequently.) Worse yet, in spite of their need for guidance, these folks like to work from nine to five — but that's usually 9 p.m. to 5 a.m. For all students, monitor their work behavior for a while, especially if they have never held a job. Before turning student technicians loose on the midnight shift, make sure that they can work effectively and professionally with minimal supervision.

Speaking of late-night testing, you can use moonlighters as a good source of technicians who can keep your test resources utilized all night long. Most dual-job types are motivated. In addition, they might bring experiences from their day jobs that could make them better testers. Use caution with moon-lighters, though. Since you don't provide their sole — or even main — source of income, and your project might not be their first priority, you should give them tasks that can slip a bit in the schedule without causing disaster. With individuals who are moonlighting expressly to build an outside consulting career, you can be a little freer about moving them into key positions, pro-vided they have proven track records. (Regardless of who is on the night shift — seasoned test engineers, students, or moonlighters — keep a close eye on your night crew's productivity. Some people overestimate their ability to work effectively with little sleep, while others get stuck or veer off track without guidance.)

Finally, keep in mind that your team might need to contain other positions in addition to test engineers and test technicians. In some cases, for example, you might have a release management or configuration management engineer in your organization. As Chapter 9 describes, a variety of non-test tasks often migrate into test organizations.

The position you can put people into depends to some extent on their level of experience. Test engineering jobs will generally require someone who has experience. My rule of thumb — which varies from project to project — is two years for degreed engineers and four years for non-degreed engineers. My preference is usually that test engineers have testing experience, although you might feel application domain knowledge or technical skill are more important for your team, depending on the needs of the project and the current strengths and weaknesses of the team.

You should also consider not only what people have done, but also where they want to go. In other words, what is the career goal of each person on the test team, and how do his or her past, current, and future positions fit into that goal? The alignment of a person's aspirations with his or her position makes the difference between an inspired, dedicated, brilliant tester and a lackadaisical, bored clock-puncher.

There's a special risk for the test manager in the area of goals. Some people see testing as a temporary stepping stone, a way to gain insight into the company's products and services and a place to gain exposure to the underlying technology. Some organizations explicitly define testing as the farm team for the rest of the organization. I have a number of concerns about these approaches. For one thing, is someone likely to have the requisite critical skills and pursue growth in those skills if those skills do not align with that person's career path? Second, having artificially high turnover in the test team means that the team will always be weak, the test manager will always be hiring, and the few experienced testers will always be training new hires. This leads to reduced efficiency and effectiveness in the test team.

Specialists or Project Resources? Organizational Models

In a very small company or on a dedicated project effort, everyone works on a single project, and the question of organizational models does not exactly dominate the discussion. Suppose, however, that you have two, three, or a dozen projects going at one time. Do you break your team members into groups based on the projects they are working on, or based on the special skills they have?

Let's look at an example. You are the test manager at Winged Bytes. Two systems are in the test lab at the same time, the DataRocket server and the PortaByte laptop. Organization by skills assigns John to the BIOS, Hemamalini to Windows XP, Sandra to Windows 2x Server, Gordon to PC Card and PCI add-on cards, Crystal to networks, and Shao-Lin to environmental and reliability testing. Organization by project assigns John, Hemamalini, and Sandra to the DataRocket team, while Gordon, Crystal, and Shao-Lin work on the PortaByte. Figure 8-6 shows an organizational model based on skills, while the model shown in Figure 8-7 is based on projects.

Figure 8-6 A skills-based test organization

The skills-based model has a lot to recommend it, especially in the high-technology world. Instead of everyone having to keep up with many topics, each member of your test staff can focus on the quirks and subtleties of his or her own area of specialization. In some cases, the complexity of the tools and technology the tester must master demands a skills-based organization. The skills assessment worksheet, by the way, will tend to focus on relative strengths and the number of people strong in each skill, rather than relative weakness, because the idea is that the team be rounded as a whole but that each team member be focused on a few critical skills.

While the skills-based approach provides a test manager with a great deal of flexibility, project managers might not like it. As one project manager told me, "I don't want to hear about anyone working on anything other than my project." In an organization in which project managers are rewarded for delivering a quality product on time, such an attitude is consistent with the company's incentive structure. A skills-based organization deprives project managers of control over the allocation of test resources.

Figure 8-7 A project-based test organization

If you encounter such resistance, you have to decide whether you can persist with a skills-based approach — and whether you *want* to persist. Don't choose a skills-based model without consideration for the feelings and interests of project managers. Maintaining a positive relationship with the project managers to whom your test team provides services will boost your career and make your workday go smoothly. (Chapter 9 discusses the importance of working well with project managers in more detail.)

Besides, the second approach — a project-based organization — can have advantages for a test manager. If you have some otherwise-excellent staff members who just don't focus very well, a skills-based organization might exacerbate the problem because it would force these people to jump from one project to another during the week. Assigning them to a single project, in a project-based organization, cuts down on the interruptions and shifting tasks. In addition, if your company tracks hours spent on projects, having each person billing time to only one project makes your reporting job less confusing.

One risk posed by the project-based approach deserves mention, however. Although the test personnel report to you, they also, in a sense, work for the project managers. They probably have more contact on a daily basis with the development team than with you. Assuming that they can maintain positive, open working relationships with the developers, this contact reduces the need for you to closely manage the activities for each project. However, project managers with a strong will or lots of political clout can sometimes prevail upon your test engineers to do things they shouldn't — closing bugs that aren't confirmed as fixed, for example, or compromising test processes. If your test engineers don't have much experience with a formal test organization, they can easily go native, acting more like a developer than an independent tester. You need to monitor this situation closely.

When first setting up a test team, few test managers can use either a skills-based model or a project-based model exclusively. Some situations require experts, especially when a task involves mastery of a tricky test tool. For example, if you use graphical user interface (GUI) test tools for test automation, your team should include a GUI test engineer or two. Of course, your GUI test experts must understand how their expertise fits into the overall test architecture. However, using a GUI tester to write API tests in C++ or Java is probably not the best use of that individual's skills. Plan on using a mixed approach as your team grows. Once your organization reaches a certain size and maturity level, you will be able — and will need — to pick one or the other.

Hiring Testers

In the first half of this chapter, we looked at somewhat static and dry topics, which are necessary to lay the foundation for the test team. For the remainder of this chapter, let's look at the dynamics of test team management, starting with how we hire people to fill out that test team we've spent the last few pages characterizing and defining.

Defining the Job

To start hiring, you'll first need permission from management to hire people. This is sometimes referred to as *having a req*, meaning that a hiring requisition has worked its way through the process at your company and is now approved. If you have a human-resources department, they have likely defined this process and the various forms and approvals required. As there can be legal ramifications associated with offering a job that doesn't exist, this is a hurdle that I recommend you clear before you proceed.

Before, during, or immediately after the requisition phase, you'll need to define a job description. Job descriptions generally serve two purposes. One is as a recruiting tool. You can post the job description on the Internet and job boards, give it to recruiters, and so on. The other purpose is as a formal definition of the new hire's roles and responsibilities.

A job description should address the following issues:

- What tasks and responsibilities are involved?
- What and how much experience is necessary?
- What specific skills are needed?
- What training, education, certification, security clearances, or licenses are required?
- What are the hours and the dress code, is a drug test required, when is the starting date (if not immediately), what career path is compatible with the position, and so forth?

You should cover these issues at whatever level of specificity is required for you — and the candidates — to determine fitness for the job. You don't want to scare off applicants who could make excellent testers, but you also don't want to receive résumés from people who are clearly unqualified. For this reason, it's also a good idea to distinguish between required (must-have) and desirable (nice-to-have) credentials.

Your skills assessment spreadsheet can help you prepare a job description. In the estimate prepared in Chapter 1, the SpeedyWriter test manager identified a need for a new test engineer to work on component test development and execution, something that requires a focus on technology and the internals of the system. Figures 8-8 and 8-9 show the job description for this position. Note that this document, while useful both as a recruiting and a personnel file document, would need to be condensed if you intend to post this on a job board or in the classified ads.

Another subject you have to consider as part of defining the job is what you intend to pay the new hire. Various sources publish salary survey information. Remember that the free market for labor works, and it will continue to work tomorrow. This is especially important to keep in mind during recessions and economic hard times when the temptation to low-ball is the greatest, but any time you try to hire at bargain basement prices you can count on one of three outcomes. First, you might get exactly what you paid for; in other words, the person was not as competent as you thought during the hiring process for whatever reason. Second, you might get a bargain, but sooner or later that person will realize his true market worth and fly the coop, possibly in the middle of a tight project. Third, the person might realize that the pay is a raw deal, but consider herself stuck for whatever reason, leading to disgruntlement or poor performance.

Test Automation Engineer

Roles and responsibilities

Participate in a test automation tool selection process for an automated component testing harness in a Java/EJB/Ant environment.

Participate in project-wide reviews of requirements, system architecture, and detailed design documents.

Develop and execute automated tests using the selected tool, which will likely require programming in C, C++, Java, or some scripting language.

Perform static analysis of source code using complexity metrics.

Effectively communicate testing activities and findings in oral and written formats.

Integrate the test suites into the test management system and custom test harnesses.

The ability to participate effectively in estimation, planning, cost-of-quality, and quality risk analysis is desired.

Education

Four-year-degree in computer science, computer engineering, electrical engineering, or software engineering desired; or add two additional years experience.

Certification in testing tools or testing skills desirable.

Experience and Skills

Five or more years experience in test automation, with at least one year of that experience in a Unix Web/database/application server-side browser-based application environment.

Familiarity of the underlying architecture of a multi-tier browser-based application is required, including operating systems, servers, networking, clients, and browsers.

Programming, system administration, or database administration experience is a plus.

At least some knowledge of word processing is required, and more extensive experience with word processing, content management, and document management systems is a plus.

Figure 8-8 The first page of a job description for a SpeedyWriter automated test engineer

Career Path

A demonstrated career commitment to testing and/or quality assurance is preferred. The candidate should show a familiarity with the latest testing theory and practice, a commitment to on-going learning about the field, and a history of applying useful testing concepts in previous positions.

Other

Dress is business-casual and hours are flexible. Some weekends and evenings will be required.

A demonstrated ability to work effectively and harmoniously as part of an independent test team within a project-service-organization context is required.

Figure 8-9 The second page of a job description for a SpeedyWriter automated test engineer

You might have noticed that I set the bar pretty high in my job description in Figures 8-8 and 8-9. A person with these qualifications is a technical professional peer of a programmer, a system administrator, or other skilled technical professional. I believe in building teams of testers where the engineers are at that level, and I believe in paying them at that level, too. If a senior software engineer in your company makes $100,000 per year, say, then a senior test engineer with the same number of years of experience, education, and training should make that amount, too.

Finally, don't forget to think about the career path for your candidate. What advancement opportunities exist? How do you intend to promote growth in skills during this person's tenure in the test team, and how does that match up with potential career paths? Can you accommodate someone who wants to spend some time in testing, and then move into another area of the company, such as technical sales, marketing, programming, management, or system administration? How long would that person need to stay in testing to be a net positive to the test team? These are important questions that a serious candidate will need you to answer. You want people to remember any position that they took in your team fondly, as a valuable step on their professional ladder, not as bear trap that they had to escape to make further professional progress.

Gathering and Screening Résumés

With your proverbial ducks in a row on the job definition front, it's time to start collecting and screening candidate résumés. Candidates can be found in a number of ways, including the Internet, classified ads, college job boards, agencies and recruiters, and, not least of all, your peers. (Another benefit of going to conferences and training programs is that you meet bright, involved people you might want to hire.) You can also recruit current and former contractors, but keep in mind that usually there are conversion fees payable to that contractor's agency that can range as high as 50 percent of the annual salary.

As résumés come in, check them against the job description. Separate — but don't discard — the qualified from the unqualified. (You might decide to rethink your qualifications or consider the less-qualified for test technician roles.) Circulate the qualified candidates' résumés to other people on the test team and possibly to other peer managers. Have one or more of the team do a telephone interview of the candidates. Ask for references if they weren't provided, and check them if appropriate. In some companies, the human-resources department does all reference checks and even preliminary telephone interviews, so check with them on the precise process to follow.

During telephone (and on-site) interviews, I'm looking for people to tell me about what they've done on past projects that relates to the job description.

I go down the résumé before the telephone interview and make notes about past tasks and activities that could have taught them important skills useful for my efforts. I ask people questions such as, "Tell me about what kind of test harness you built for the XYZ system," "Talk to me a little about one or two bug reports you wrote on project ABC," and "The last time you ran a test case that was somewhat ambiguous about the expected results, how did you decide whether it passed or failed?" I also ask basic knowledge questions about testing, the technology, and the application domain. For example, "What is the difference between behavioral and structural testing?"

Sad but true, not all résumés are sterling examples of truthful self-presentation. Somewhere along the way, it became common to inflate your qualifications on your résumé. Therefore, part of the screening and telephone interview process must be looking for red flags. Does a buzzword on the résumé indicate mastery of a topic, or just exposure to it? Can the candidate back up all claims in terms of actual, meaningful work done on a project? Are the degrees, licenses, certifications, publications, and other professional qualifications substantiated?

Other warning signs include excessive job changes. This might indicate a candidate's ability to talk his way into jobs for which he's not qualified, or it might indicate an inability to get along with people, leading to rancorous departures. (Note that contractors will tend to change jobs every time their contracts end, although they should stay until they've finished their engagement.) Gaps in employment history can indicate personal or health problems — which you should steer away from discussing for legal reasons — but it could also indicate a stint in jail or other voluntary but odd choices in ways to spend one's life that might make you reconsider hiring someone. (Caveat: Criminal convictions, especially those long past or which have been expunged, set aside, or pardoned generally do not disqualify candidates, and considering such convictions as part of the hiring process can expose you and your employer to legal liability.) Frequent changes in career can indicate a flightiness and flippancy that might make you worry about someone's tendency to bolt from your project right when the pressure is highest.

While the threat of legal action has clamped down on what many past employers are willing to say about people during reference checks, most managers will *want* to help you hire their best former employees and avoid hiring their worst. Listen carefully to the words these people use — and don't use — and connect the dots. One RBCS course attendee told me that she replied to every question a manager asked her about a former employee (not a superstar, for sure) with the following deadpan words: "He was very punctual." The manager hired this person all the same! Don't bring a tin ear to the reference-checking process.

By the end of the screening process, you should be able to decide whether the person fits the basic qualification as laid out in the job description. You should also have a basic feel for whether you like the candidate, whether she'll fit into the team, and whether you think you're likely to hire her. If the answer to any of these questions is "no," then set the résumé aside and move on. The last thing you need to do during a busy test project is spend time interviewing someone who is unlikely to be a positive contributor to the project team. The best thing that can happen if you do is that you just waste a few hours of everyone's time, which is hardly good, but the worst thing that can happen is that you talk yourself into making a hiring mistake, which can cost you months of time later, damage test team credibility, and lower test team productivity.

On-Site Interviews

Interview processes tend to vary. Here's one that I've seen work well:

1. The human resources manager or the equivalent person orients the candidate to the company, salary and benefits, and "how things are done around here."

2. The test manager and other members of the test team, including test engineers and test technicians, determine the candidate's fitness for the position, including personality. This includes some mixture of one-on-one and group interviews, usually, or a group lunch.

3. Other managers might interview senior, lead, or management candidates. If a candidate will be working closely with someone in marketing, sales, business analysis, technical support, programming, or another team, then that person should probably interview the candidate. (People outside the test team should not, however, have veto power over test hiring decisions unless that's a reciprocal company policy and you likewise have veto power over other team hires.)

4. Sometimes, the HR manager will debrief the candidate at the end to see how the interview went and answer any questions about what happens next.

In some high-tech companies, before the interview even starts, the candidate must sign a nondisclosure or confidentiality agreement. Sometimes, the company has a standard form for this, which you should use if it does.

Interviewing styles tend to vary considerably. There are three basic types of interviews that I have used: the qualification interview, the behavioral interview, and the audition interview. There are also three types of interviews I don't use: the puzzle interview, the non sequitur interview, and the stress interview. Let's look at each one.

Qualification interviewing involves asking questions with well-defined right answers. Either the candidate knows the right answer or they don't. You are trying to understand whether the person possesses the skills they need for the job. These interviews should include questions about testing, technical areas, the application domain, or other relevant topics. Note the word *relevant* there. Don't ask trivia questions just because they have unambiguous answers. Also, be sure you are asking questions with truly unambiguous answers, not opinions or random bloviations posted on the Internet posing as facts.[7]

Behavioral interviewing involves open-ended questioning about past actions. You are trying to explore past behaviors and the motivations behind them. So, you use open-ended questions such as the following to start a line of discussion:

- For the last test you ran, did you expect it to pass or fail? Why?

- Tell me about the manner and tone you used to discuss a recent bug report with other members of the project team.

- Tell me about a controversial bug report that you wrote and how you ensured it got proper attention.

- Talk to me a little about what, in general, you find rewarding about working.

- Tell me about your experiences on a project where you worked XX hours per week. ("XX" being the peak number of hours I expect people to have to work during this project.)

- On your last project, how did you decide the right amount of time to spend writing a test case or isolating a bug?

- Tell me about how your past managers have helped you maintain proper focus.

- Tell me about what you learned on project XYZ that you think can help us test our product.

- Tell me about a previous test project that you really enjoyed. What did you like the most?

- Describe the career you see for yourself in testing.

- What do you like about being a tester?

Of course, feel free to add more questions to this list.

Audition interviewing involves having the candidate carry out an actual task they will do in their daily work. You are looking for a demonstrated ability to do this particular task, and possibly by extension other related tasks.

---

[7] A good source of test related questions of this sort are my three other books, *Foundations of Software Testing: ISTQB Certification*, *Advanced Software Testing: Volume I*, and *Advanced Software Testing: Volume II*, and in fact any book or exam preparation guide designed to prepare a candidate for a test related certification is a good source of such questions. You might say that the candidate can cheat by reading the book first, but I say that's not really cheating at all, because if the candidate has read books on software testing and studied the field, that's part of being a qualified tester.

For example, on my teams we've asked each candidate to run a scripted test case we know will fail. Now, we don't tell the candidate the test will fail, and we also pick a test whose failures are appropriate in complexity and subtlety for the candidate's level of experience. We put the candidate in front of the system under test, provide whatever basic orientation is necessary, and then ask the candidate to run the test. We provide the candidate with a notepad to write on to report any bugs or other interesting observations. This has been a tremendously effective technique at eliminating unqualified testers, and we typically use it as the last stage of the interview process. Of course, some wags have told me that, if you schedule enough audition interviews, you might never actually have to hire anyone, but I don't recommend audition interviews as a primary testing technique!

Let me address the three types of interviews I don't use, and I'll explain why. The puzzle interview involves posing some sort of logic problem, riddle, word- or number-puzzle, or similar exercise. You then watch the candidate squirm as she desperately tries to come up with the answer. At best, this stuff is a self-parody of the classic scene in *Monty Python and the Holy Grail* with the bridge keeper and King Arthur's knights.[8] At worst, it's a form of sadism. More importantly, I believe that the relationship between the ability to solve these kinds of puzzles and the ability to test is a weak one at best, and if you are excluding candidates based on interview questions that do not relate to the job at hand, you are getting into dangerous territory in a legal sense.

The non sequitur interview involves asking some question that seems to be analogous or related to testing. The classic example is, "Tell me how you would test a salt shaker." I find this silly. I call this a non sequitur interview style because it does not follow that, just because someone can craft a clever tale about testing simple real-world objects, they can test complex software and systems. You are hiring a test professional, not a raconteur.

The stress interview involves putting someone in a stressful position to see how they will react. I heard a story once about an interviewer at a large software company taking a hidden rubber ball out from under his desk at a random moment during an interview and bouncing it — hard! — off the wall about the interviewee's head. I also had a client whose tech support manager, who was a former police detective, liked to get up from his desk midway through the interview and engage in a long moment of eyeball-to-eyeball, uncomfortable silence with the interviewee. This is beyond silly; this is weird. If being able to handle these kinds of random, bizarre incidents is actually related to working in your test team, that says more about you as a manager than it does about the candidate, and it doesn't say anything good.

---

[8]In case you haven't seen this movie, you can find this scene reproduced line-for-line on the Internet with a simple Web search. However, if you are working in a high-tech company, you can almost certainly find someone who can recite the routine line-for-line from memory, as it is a true geek classic. In fact, if you are reading this book and you aren't at least familiar with the scene, you have some remedial geek-culture immersion studies to do as homework.

Prior to the audition interviewing, I'll use the qualification interviewing and behavioral interviewing techniques. My primary focus during an interview is to decide whether a person will fit into the test team personally, professionally, and capably. I start with describing the project at a high level, and then I start asking questions that relate past project tasks and activities to what the person will be doing should he or she get the job.

As with any interview, each question starts a line of related questions that I pursue. As during the telephone interview, I will also ask questions to probe a person's knowledge of the critical skills. The line of questions continues until I've explored the topic fully and satisfied myself as to the person's experience and qualifications in that regard — or satisfied myself that they are not qualified and should not be hired.

I have my BS antennae set to their highest level of sensitivity during the entire process, and I drill down on any answers that I find unfulfilling, wishy-washy, or vague. This can often indicate an area of weakness that a candidate is trying to paper over. If this is a weakness I can live with, I'll tell the candidate up front that I'm looking for a desirable qualification but not a required one. Whatever the case, I always react better to someone who says, "I don't know the answer to that question," than I do to someone who tries to snow me. I sometimes hire people whom I think will grow into a job, but I never hire people I think are trying to con their way into a job.

Making the Hiring Decision

I prefer to have a debriefing session together with all the interviewers at the end of the interview, to compare notes. Don't just use a checklist or form circulated via email or on paper, but actually sit down together and talk about the candidate, too. One course attendee told me once that everyone came to this debriefing meeting very positive about a candidate, but found when they discussed specific questions, that the candidate had given substantially different answers to each interviewer about what he had done on specific projects!

After you have interviewed all the candidates, you should make the hiring decision as quickly as possible, while people's recollections are still fresh and the best candidate is still available. (Remember, the good ones don't stay in the job market for very long, even in tough times.) You can extend offers of employment by telephone or through an offer letter; your HR department probably has a standard process for this.

Sometimes candidates want to negotiate the salary. I'm usually willing to do this, although I try to come to the table with my best offer up front. One thing I'm very loath to engage in is a bidding war. This happens when a candidate takes your offer letter to another potential employer, asks them to beat it, and then comes back to you with *that* offer letter and asks you to beat it. This is the type of thing that is appropriate when buying a car or a house, because ultimately it's a zero-sum game. However, I don't see hiring someone as a zero-sum game, and I don't really want to hire someone who sees it that way, either. The flip side of setting a fair salary based on prevailing and historical market value for a person's skill and experience is that I know my offer is fair. If someone wants to play games with me during the hiring process, then I'll let the other bidder win the bidding war, and good luck to both parties.

Avoiding—and Undoing—Hiring Mistakes

I am advocating that you be tough in your approach to hiring. The objective of the hiring process is to separate the qualified from the unqualified, the willing from the unwilling, the interested from the uninterested; in short, to make judgments about people and their skills, experiences, and personalities. In some ways of thinking prevalent today, it's not nice, it's not okay, it's not politically correct to judge.

It's true that you shouldn't be unduly harsh, which is why I eschew the stress interview. This just scares people off, the good along with the bad. It's also true that you should consider only factors relevant to the job at hand, and, of course, you should avoid breaking the laws that govern hiring in your local, state, and federal jurisdiction. The HR department should be able to advise you about what interview questions are disallowed, or you should consult an employment-law attorney.

I'm absolutely not recommending that you be discriminatory — as anyone who's worked with me or on my test teams will attest — or that you hold against people past mistakes, personal or professional, from which they've learned valuable lessons. To paraphrase Nietzsche, any really bad mistake is also a really important learning opportunity, so you might find that some of your best test team members have made some pretty big mistakes on past projects.[9]

As much as it's nice to be nice, though, we must keep in mind that the essence of hiring is to choose teammates. We all probably remember physical education period from our school days, so the kindest souls will know that it hurts sometimes when you're not chosen. However, you have a fiduciary responsibility to your employer or client to pick only the very best people for your test team, so you must steel yourself to that duty. To hire the wrong person is to set that person, yourself, your team, and your employer up for a failure — which isn't doing anyone any favors — but to hire the right person promotes the success of all involved.

---

[9]Nietzsche's aphorism, found in *Beyond Good and Evil*, says that the only learning experiences are bad experiences. I think Nietzsche underestimates the learning possibilities in good experiences, but he is right on the money about the need to learn from bad experiences.

To go back to our dour philosopher friend Nietzsche, though, sometimes you will — just as I certainly have — create learning experiences for yourself by making hiring mistakes or inheriting someone else's hiring mistake. Dealing with a problem employee is a test of your leadership skills and your character. Don't fail the test by trying to ignore it or pretending it will go away. It won't. Yes, it's a big unpleasant waste of time to fire someone, but just one or two inappropriate test team members can make a tough situation untenable. I will admit to having kept some testers around long after they had demonstrated their negative impact on team morale and performance. I have learned my lesson and won't repeat that mistake. Keeping a problem employee on board does no one any good. Here's why.

The rest of your staff suffers most when you keep dead weight around. The team has to compensate for this person's blunders and mistakes. Furthermore, one individual's poor work can result in a perception that the entire test team is incompetent and careless, which leads to the project team looking askance at your bug reports, metrics, and other test data. Most damaging, an individual who is not contributing usually knows it and adopts various defensive postures to camouflage the failure — for example, denigrating the work of the other team members. In such cases, productive and motivated contributors suffer disparagement to salve the ego of the inept one. Others get tired of pulling the other person's load. In both cases, qualified testers might resign rather than work with someone who is offensive, incompetent, or both. All of these outcomes are unfair to you and your team.

Your human-resources department will likely have a process by which people undergo coaching, reprimands, and ultimately involuntary separation (firing). If you are a good manager — in other words, someone who cares about the people who work for you and who wants to do right by the team — you will probably feel awful throughout this process. Nevertheless, it is *because* you are a good manager that you must do it. The person you fire might find the experience quite painful in the short run. Still, a smart person will take the opportunity to assess what he or she did wrong, and decide to do better next time. Follow the process, coaching the employee and then gradually moving up the ladder from verbal to written warnings. Once you hit the second or third written warning, it's time to make a change. You obviously aren't getting through, and after the third warning you won't be taken seriously if you don't let this person go.

Bringing the New Tester on Board

When someone accepts an offer — and sometimes even when someone already in the company becomes part of the test team temporarily or permanently — you should get moving on the logistics of having a work-station, a badge, a telephone extension, and other perquisites of employment arranged for the new hire on her first day. Are there forms to fill out? Security hurdles to leap? A drug test, fingerprints, background checks, or other such details to attend to? Nothing shouts out chaos and disorder to me like showing up on my first day at a job or an engagement and finding that no one was ready for me to arrive.

You should also think about training and orientation, especially if there's no standard program offering by the human resources department. Many people use a variant of *sink or swim* for training. Some people can handle this, while others can't, and in all cases I think it sends a questionable message to new hires that could sour them on the job from the start. RBCS provides all new hires with access to our e-learning version of our Test Engineering Foundation course so that they can quickly get up to speed on any test fundamentals that might lack. If they aren't already ISTQB-certified, we put them through that program, at least to the Foundation level.

I also generally assign a mentor to new hires. The mentor will orient the new hires and review all their work for the first few weeks. Yes, this does lead to a productivity hit, but it also leads to consistent levels of quality in test team output and sends a message to new hires that they are important members of the team whose success is instrumental to the success of the team as a whole.

Looking back on this section, you might say, "Gee, Rex, this is a pretty involved process you've laid out here, and you know, I've got a lot of testing work to do." It's very easy for me to sit here and write about spending all this time on hiring, and hard for you — and for me — to actually do it when all that other stuff is going on. Trust me, though; of all the topics addressed in this book, hiring the right people might very well be the most important one.

You can do everything else right, but if you have the wrong team, your test projects will feel like swimming through freshly poured concrete. Conversely, you can make a lot of mistakes, even some big ones, and come out smelling like a rose with the right team in place. I know it's hard to do under conditions of pressure, but do make sure you allocate plenty of time for the hiring process and use it. Rushing a hiring decision because of some externally perceived sense of urgency is a mistake. Having the wrong person on your test team can lead to tremendous problems, as discussed previously. Conversely, hiring the right people leads to nonlinear gains in effectiveness, efficiency, and credibility, because the whole is greater than the sum of the parts when you build your teams from carefully selected individuals.

Giving a Damn: Motivating Your Test Team

Maintaining morale and motivation on a test team takes some doing. In my experience, the traditional team building exercises don't work too well with test folks, since we tend to be a cynical lot. There are, however, some management styles you can adopt that will do what no amount of ersatz group bonding exercises can: convince your team members that you value their time and contributions, respect their opinions, and will stand up for them when they need you. The following sections offer tips about some techniques that have worked for me, and some that I try to avoid.[10]

Be On Your Team's Side

As noted earlier, some people regard testing as low-caste work. While you should certainly try to change this perception if it exists within your company, you might find it impossible to completely eradicate, and often the perception becomes a political reality. However, you can take some steps to minimize the extent to which this situation demotivates your team.

One of these steps is to make sure your testers know that you respect their intentions and will defend their actions, even the occasional screw-up. Every now and then, someone on your staff will put a cherry bomb in a wasp's nest. The resulting swarm of angry critters, looking to sting the perpetrator, can overwhelm the poor tester. These types of incidents usually arise from high-visibility bug reports, although hallway conversations about the tenuous connection between reality and the latest delivery date run a close second. These situations are even worse when your test engineer has in fact made a mistake. I have seen bug reports given legalistic scrutiny, and I pity the tester who mischaracterizes a bug.

When faced with angry attacks on one of your team members, never upbraid or criticize the hapless tester publicly, no matter what the mistake. You should, however, acknowledge the problem, perhaps saying something along these lines: "Yeah, we probably could have done a better job. I guess I goofed when I reviewed that report. But let's talk about this bug." This approach allows you to admit the mistake, take the blame yourself, and move to the matter at hand. (Of course, if you have staff members who habitually shoot off their mouths or write over-stated bug reports without checking the facts, you must deal with this problem on a long-term basis.)

In addition, what testers do wrong should not distract focus from what they do right. If an offending bug report lacks a few isolation steps, but the bug is undeniable, don't let people lose sight of that fact. If a tester's manner is inappropriate in the course of escalating a serious problem, shift the focus

---

[10]There are a number of excellent ideas in Rick Craig and Stefan Jaskiel's book, *Systematic Software Testing*, but the chapter on test management, which addresses many of the issues in this chapter and especially being a good leader, is worth the purchase price by itself. Especially if you are new to being a manager — but even if you're a seasoned veteran — I recommend that you read their book, and particularly that chapter. Tom DeMarco's allegorical novel, *The Deadline*, is also chock full of great management ideas, including my favorite leadership aphorism, "lead with the heart, trust your gut . . . build soul into the organization, [and] develop a nose for [untruth]."

back to the problem. Do this with the tester present. Visibly stand up for your employee in public, and then do whatever coaching is needed later, in private, after you both have had a chance to blow off steam and reflect calmly. You'll build real loyalty among your staff by displaying this type of solidarity under fire and by dealing with their failures in private.

Another step is to make sure that the goodies get doled out fairly to your team. Some years ago, a test network administrator I supervised wanted to attend a networking conference, which made good sense to me. It was appropriate for his career path, he could learn something of immediate importance, and the timing was good. We did the whole trip request tango, which also included my manager, involving two levels of management approval, HR approval, the whole works.

Several development engineers had signed up for the same conference. As the date approached, a senior manager started complaining about the large number of attendees, suggesting that perhaps some attendees should cancel. Guess who made the short list of extraneous attendees? I responded reasonably, explaining the original justifications — still valid — for sending the network administrator on this trip. I became a bit less reasonable when my own manager hopped on the dog pile. I fired off an email to my manager implying that management was singling out my engineer because of his position in test. I also asked pointedly whether she cared about this employee and about the effect that canceling the trip would have on his morale. My engineer attended the conference.

Make sure that your staff members get an equal crack at all the perks. The following list should help you keep an eye on the situation and restore a level playing field if need be. A word of warning, though: before you accuse anyone of stacking the deck against your test team, have your facts in order. You'll look paranoid if you can't document inequities.

Salaries. If the pay scale for test engineers is below that of the other engineers in your company, work with the human resources department to ensure pay parity for equal levels of responsibility, experience, and education. The old wisdom that testers should make less than developers is just that: old. Use salary surveys, as discussed earlier, to bolster your case. Be aware, however, that this can be a tough nut to crack if you have inherited an existing test team.

Job titles. If the ladder of job titles in development has more rungs, with more prestige, than the one in test, do whatever you can to resolve the inequity. Again, you'll probably need to enlist the cooperation of the human resources office. Argue for a parallel set of technical titles, such as Member of the Technical Staff, Senior Member of the Technical Staff, Principal Member of the Technical Staff, and so forth. If these parallel rungs already exist, but the test staff hold only the Member of the Technical Staff titles, not the more senior titles, investigate whether test employees are being given a lower rank than their history with the company, their years in the industry, and their levels of responsibility warrant.

Hours. If testers are expected to work unusual hours or if they get stuck testing over the weekend to meet a schedule target while the rest of the development team has the weekend off, ask for compensatory time off for your staff — or just give it to them. If testers must cede test's hardware to developers for debugging during regular business hours and consequently must perform testing after hours, discuss the matter with your development manager colleagues. Point out the unfairness, and ask to work out a schedule for debugging access that spreads the misery. If they refuse, go to your manager.

Training sessions, off-sites, seminars, and conferences. If developers frequently attend plum events in exotic locations, while testers seldom do, find a particularly useful and particularly attractive event for your best staff person to attend, and sell it to your manager. Repeat this tactic as needed to help redress any imbalance. Budget freezes sometimes restrict the number of employees who can be sent to conferences and training seminars. If these freezes affect test attendees but not development attendees, ask your manager or the human resources office to establish a training budget for each department, including yours, with demonstrable equity.

In general, your goal should be the equal treatment of your test team. It should be clear to all on your test team that you will work tirelessly on their behalf to achieve that goal.

Support a Reasonable Workstyle

Hard work, unrealistic schedules, and the occasional strange hours come with the test territory — and this lifestyle burns people out. You might encounter testers whose previous employers have overworked them ferociously. Not surprisingly, this usually makes them unwilling to be taken advantage of again.

To help alleviate some of the stress involved in testing, be sure to pace your team. Senior managers might pressure you to inflict undesirable work conditions on the team as soon as test execution begins. Resist it. Test execution is often a marathon, and you should never start a marathon by sprinting. Testing often begins behind schedule, has too few people allocated to it, and seldom ends on the date originally planned. Under these circumstances, you should avoid pushing too hard too early.

In addition, try to break up the work whenever possible. On one of my jobs, test builds for the monthly maintenance releases usually showed up on Friday afternoon around 4:00. As the build and development teams headed out for their weekends, test staff installed these builds and started automated tests, sometimes working well into the evening. Next came the weekend work to keep the tests going so that we could report on test status on Monday afternoon. Everyone loved this arrangement except us. You should pay back your staff for extra efforts like this. If people work over the weekend, give them a Friday or a Monday off. Let them go early during the week after a rough session. Try to give them breathing spells between crunches.

Clearly, one reason for the feelings of stress and overload is that most test organizations are understaffed. When your best efforts to achieve a realistic staffing level fall short, you might try shifting gears by remembering that *understaffed* can be synonymous with *overtasked* — a perspective that allows you to consider other options for reducing your team's load. Try to get support from other groups in the company for chores that might not be part of your core mission but are essential to accomplishing it. For example, you might be able to use an administrative assistant to do some of the tedious data entry work, freeing up some of your testers' time.

A second problem is that test organizations often start participating in projects too late. Ideally, one or two test people should be involved in a project right from the beginning. This gives these testers the chance to prevent bugs by participating in requirements reviews, performing quality risk analyses earlier, contributing to project planning, and so forth. You'll need to assign someone to start preparations for a new project up front rather than waiting until a few days before test execution is scheduled to begin.

As a manager, you obviously must be involved in planning the test effort, but you also need an engineer to attend to the technical details. This engineer can plan the reuse and adaptation of the existing test system (tools, cases, and suites), select whatever new tools are needed, define the changes to the test architecture, and so forth. The test engineer should also participate in technical reviews and have detailed discussions with the developers. You might not be able to spare someone full-time, but it's important enough to set aside a few hours every week. If you don't take the time to do this, you and your team will be forced into a reactive mode when test execution starts and will be chronically unable to get solid test execution under way.

Early test involvement in new projects has another benefit that feeds back into the issue of understaffing. The commencement of any new project reopens discussion of appropriate staff levels. As you demonstrate your organization's ability to add value to the delivered product, management is likely to approve more realistic staffing levels for subsequent projects.

In companies that have no experience with formal testing or with early test involvement in development projects, some care is required in implementing this up-front participation. Begin by selling the project manager on the benefits of more effective, less hectic testing. If the two of you approach senior management, you're more likely to succeed, especially since the project manager — as a person who will bring a saleable product to the company's portfolio or deliver a working system to the users — will usually have a lot more pull than you do.

A more subtle source of overload in the test organization is change. Changes in the project plan do not smite developers and test staff alike. Take scope creep for example. Adding a few simple APIs to a program can generate a whole slew of new test work, because now you need to test other programs (and maybe even hardware devices) that use those APIs. In hardware, changing the design of a moving part might call for not only re-executing a lengthy 10,000-repetition mechanical life test, but also reworking your fixtures and test tools.

Scope shrink is just as bad. This type of change can make it hard to distinguish between time well spent and a perfectly good day squandered. Suppose that one of your engineers spends 12 hours implementing a particularly nifty test tool for generating wireless network load, which seems like a good investment. Two days later, management pulls wireless network support from the system under test as part of a decision to trim features in order to hit a marketing window. Sure, it will be nice to have that test tool in the next product cycle, but in the meantime, you've let two or three other tasks languish, and those jobs are now much more important.

In addition, keep in mind that test execution occurs in the most change-rich portion of the project. As people begin to perceive how unrealistic the schedule is and yet make frantic efforts to adhere to it anyway, you'll see abrupt deletions in product functionality, reorganization of some or all of the project teams, dropping of entire test suites from the plan, and other such corrections. These changes aren't always constructive or carefully considered. "Do something! Do anything!" often becomes the project slogan as schedules start to slip, and schedule slip is most noticeable during test execution, simply because test happens to be the caboose on the project train.

Without exaggerating or overreacting, never let significant changes to the project go unremarked or undocumented. If the change is big, bring it to management's attention — not as a complaint but as a matter that should be understood and acknowledged. If someone suggests adding support for a new operating system to DataRocket, your response should be along these lines: "Great! We anticipate that will cost $1,500 in new software for our lab, require one additional engineering sample, and consume 50 person-hours. Let's talk about how we get these new resources."

Whether the change is small or large, it must be managed. Chapter 6 introduced you to a simple database that can help you track changes. While best practices call for project managers to manage all changes at a project-wide level, you should plan on tracking and managing them yourself until your organization reaches that level of maturity.

When you are faced with too few people, too much work to handle at once, and an environment of constant change, the rush to keep up can tempt you and your team to devise kludges. A kludge is any ill-advised, substandard, or temporary bandage applied to an urgent problem in the (often misguided) belief that doing so will keep a project moving forward. However, the reality is that these hasty little shortcuts usually serve only to transfer pain from the present to the immediate future — and add more pain to it in the bargain.

It often seems that performing an ad hoc, undocumented test on some one-shot feature that will never come up again almost ensures that testing this feature will become enshrined in the regular routine. Once you have a workable process in place, don't deviate from it at the drop of a hat. An engineer who devises a new test case needs to write it down. A technician who alters a test case should document the change and the reason for it. A tester who changes a system configuration must record the new setup. The cliché "more haste, less speed" is a cliché because it's true.

Foster Career Development for Each Tester

An old military recruiting slogan in the United States read, "It's not just a job, it's an adventure." Testing is sometimes an adventure, and it should be a good job, but it should also be something else: an integrated part of each test team member's career path.

This means that it is up to us as test managers to ensure skills growth in a way that is consistent with each tester's career needs as well as with the needs of the team. As I mentioned before, I like to use the skills assessment worksheet for this purpose. Have people set quarterly skills growth goals that meet their career needs and help fill in weaknesses in the test team. (This is another reason why aligning candidates' career paths with testing is so important — it prevents wide mismatches between your team's skills growth needs and those of your team members.) Provide formal and informal training opportunities as well as work assignments to help people meet these skills growth targets.

Informal training opportunities can include mentoring from strong team members. It can also include book clubs where the entire team reads a book on testing and then discusses it over weekly lunches provided by management. Formal training includes off-site and on-site seminars and training courses provided by experts, as well as some computer-based and Internet-based training courses.

As managers, we need to work with our testers to get them deserved promotions and raises. Yearly performance appraisals are the usual vehicle for this. At some point, too, someone will need to leave the test team to another position within the company to pursue her career. A good manager doesn't stand in the way, even though we always hate to see good people leave. Look at it this way, though: If you don't help the person pursue her career within the company, then she'll just leave and pursue her career somewhere else.

A good manager should work with the receiving manager to help set up the erstwhile tester for success in her new job.

Don't Offer Bonuses Based on Meeting a Schedule

Promising bonuses to staff based on whether a schedule is met is a bad idea, especially for a test team. Testing, when done properly, finds bugs, often more than expected. If the project team ignores the bugs in order to meet the schedule, the money spent on testing is wasted (see Chapter 11 for a discussion of testing return on investment). However, if the project team takes the time to fix the bugs, the test team's collective bonus can disappear. Project-wide, every test case that finds a bug reduces the odds of getting a bonus for everyone. What type of motivation does this provide? Such obvious common sense notwithstanding, these bonus arrangements do occur.

Schedule-based bonus plans usually descend from above. If the project manager proposes a scheme like this, explain the perverse incentives it will create for the testers and the negative dynamic it will set up between test and the rest of the project team. If the development team gets a bonus for meeting a schedule, you should remind management of the tension this will generate as the test team succeeds in finding bugs. The test team should have a bonus plan that emphasizes the role of testers as bug finders, confidence builders, and risk mitigaters. How about a bonus based on a high defect detection percentage, adjusted for test project scope and calculated three months after product release (see Chapter 4)? Admittedly, you will need to make some serious effort to implement this arrangement, but the path of least resistance — going along with a plan that provides an incentive for your team to do the *wrong* thing — makes no sense.

Don't Buy Bugs Like Sacks of Rice

I once heard a rumor about a test contractor who got paid by the bug and by the hour, earning over $500,000 in one year from one project. This story, while apocryphal, probably contains elements of truth.

Bug reports are not commodities. The importance of bugs and the quality of reports vary. If you want to generate a huge volume of bug reports — many of them lousy and many detailing unimportant bugs — you can award bonuses based on the sheer number of reports. If you want good bug reports, don't do this.

Expecting Thanks for Saturday Night's Pizza

When your team is working late nights and weekends, plan to pay for some meals during these overtime periods. Get approval to submit an expense report. And when you buy meals, remember that people get tired of pizza. Most American-style pizza is just about the least healthy food around. Vary the menu, and offer your staff options they'll find palatable. Instead of getting irritated when employees have special meal requests, remember that you are not doing them a favor by buying them a meal — they are doing you and your company a favor by giving up their own time. Some companies foster a macho geek chic centered on late nights, early mornings, and pizza feasts during midnight bull sessions. What exactly is the prize for winning a sleep-deprivation or junk-food-consumption contest? This seems neat for the first five or so years you're in this business, but after that it becomes obvious for what it is: a cheap way to take advantage of the employees.

Promoting an Us-versus-Them Mentality

In my opinion, the worst motivational technique is whipping up confrontational attitudes between testers and developers. This type of mock duel might inspire testers to find more bugs in the short run. However, for the same reasons that being a jerk isn't among the traits of a good test engineer, fostering mistrust and ill will between the test and development organizations won't work either.

So, What Are People Actually Doing?

It's all very well and good for me to sit here and write, "Do this, don't do that," but what are people actually doing in the field? Good question. In an interesting discussion on an Internet testing mailing list , the following ideas came up most frequently.

Some people are using management by objectives, usually in the form of yearly performance appraisals, to reward testers. Management by objectives has the risk of perverse incentives — what is called *the false customer problem* — that can create motivation problems for testers. For example, one of my peers was rated on the quality of the product being shipped and hitting the schedule. He found so many bugs that, even with the delay in schedule, they couldn't fix them all, so he ended up getting no raise that year. He quit and went somewhere where expectations were more reasonable. In another situation I'm aware of, a management dictate went down, in the form of an email memo to senior managers, that no one was allowed to achieve more than 80 percent of their objectives because they needed to cap salary expense growth at two percent that year. This memo became public knowledge in no time and contributed to immense dissatisfaction within the company. One of many people who quit — in the middle of a recession, by the way — explained, "Better to be unemployed in a lousy economy than to spend one more day at [that company]."

I have used management by objectives successfully when I align the objectives with what I actually wanted and could expect from the test team. I also require people to actively participate in the skills assessment and growth program, although I do not set numerical targets for skills growth over the year.

Some people use metrics based on test cases run versus planned or the number of bugs found. As mentioned in Chapter 3, paying people for hitting the planned number of test cases is tantamount to paying them to ignore bugs, so I don't believe this is a good idea. Paying people for bug reports means you'll get lots of bug reports, but will they be good ones? Those who report success with these approaches go to great efforts to remove the weird incentives.

The most successful were people who used defect detection effectiveness as a metric of quality achieved. Some people mentioned that they used defect detection effectiveness, schedule achievement, budget containment, and feature delivery all together across the entire project team. The idea is to put everyone on the same incentive plan and reward them for what the market would reward the company for: delivering a good enough product that offered the essential features early enough and cheaply enough.

Extending Your Talent: Using Temporary Experts and Implementers

Sometimes the list of tasks that simply must be done by a given date exceeds the capability of the test team. Sometimes you need to ramp up the test team for some peaks in workload. You might need additional expertise or just help in implementing some test development or execution effort. These situations are usually transitory and you can phase out the extra help after a period of days, weeks, or months. (For circumstances where long-term outsourcing is appropriate, see Chapter 10.) The remainder of this chapter discusses such temporary help and its use and misuse.

The Roles Temporary Workers Play

Let me start by defining the type of extra help I'm talking about. During the era of the organization man, this would be an easy exercise. Temporary agencies supplied clerical workers and other low-level interim staff to meet rush-period needs, while academia, industry alumni, and consulting companies supplied consultants to transfer expertise into the organization.

These days, though, especially in high technology, applying simplistic models such as this no longer works. Temporary agencies still exist, but they don't just supply data entry clerks; they also place six-figure-a-year programmers, test engineers, and business analysts. Some of the people who bring expertise to a company are these same test engineers, while others are the more traditional experts.

Not only is the model no longer applicable, the labels by which you could once identify the various players have become meaningless. A *temp* might very well have experience with advanced office automation tools and software that makes him or her quite different from yesterday's typist. Not all those who call themselves *consultants* work for consulting companies or bring dozens of years of unique experience and research to their assignments.[11]

Instead of relying on labels, let's break down the contributions of temporary staff along two axes: implementation and expertise. The diagram in Figure 8-10 shows the different types of assistance that temporary staff can bring to your organization. Let's go counterclockwise around the triangle to understand what each of these possible roles entails.

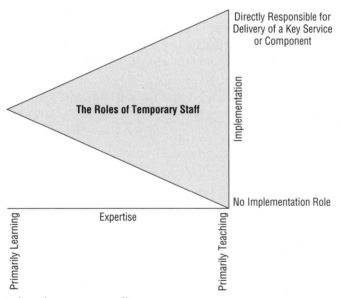

Figure 8-10 Roles of temporary staff

Toward the left apex, you find people who are best suited to being temporary test technicians. They will play an important, but not critical, role in implementation and execution. They might bring special skills to your team, but they have no role in teaching those skills to your staff. Indeed, to the extent

---

[11] In *The Computer Consultant's Guide*, Janet Ruhl, in her helpful guide to temporary staffing in the high-technology world, acknowledges the confusion that exists in the use of words like "temp," "contractor," and "consultant."

knowledge is transferred, they will spend time learning your processes and test system.

As you move toward the lower apex, you start to find the types of people who qualify as *consultants* in the traditional sense. On the mid-point of the line, perhaps, you would encounter on-site consultants who spend a few days working with your staff on a particularly tricky test automation tool, solving a few implementation problems, and then leaving. People who work near the lower apex will spend their time teaching and training exclusively. (These are people about whom Edwin Meese, a former United States Attorney General who now makes a living as an expert, quipped, "An expert is somebody who is more than 50 miles from home, has no responsibility for implementing the advice he gives, and shows slides.") For example, when RBCS consultants travel to a client's site to deliver a training course, the instructor is performing this role.

Moving toward the upper apex, you find highly knowledgeable professionals who, in addition to transferring that expertise to their clients, help their clients apply their knowledge to the implementation of technology. For example, RBCS consultants often go beyond training to work side by side with our clients. This can range from one-week engagements to jump-start risk-based testing to project-long efforts to implement a test program training the client's employee test manager to take over after we have left. Once the RBCS consultants leave, the initial release is out and we have trained our client to execute an ongoing process, implemented by RBCS associates.

Finally, moving back toward the left apex, some temporary staff, while possessed of great expertise, focus their efforts on implementing. The client might secure a black-box from them — a test tool, for example — but receive little or no training in how it works internally. The sole instruction might consist of how to use the tool.

Long-Term Temporary Workers

Notice that, to a great extent, you can place your permanent staff within this triangle as well. Your team members will probably operate more near the center than at the apexes, or perhaps along the upper edge (from left to right, think test technicians to test engineers). One important distinction will apply, though: you are not the temporary worker's employer; you are the client. This can have powerful implications in terms of how you relate to these folks.

Since we are talking about temporary workers, many of the people who fit this description will be on-site for only a few days. A trainer who teaches your engineers how to use a testing tool, for example, will probably be on-site only for a week or less. A traditional consultant who counsels you on overcoming a particular challenge might likewise spend only a few days. However, there has grown up a class of professionals who work on a contractual, rather than an employee, basis with companies for a few weeks, months, or even years. These workers are temporary in that they have no career path at your company, and will probably leave when their project or assignment is over. They look and act much like typical employees, with some important differences.

Some companies, and people within those companies, adopt dysfunctional outlooks toward these types of temporary workers, from blindness to the distinction to outright resentment at the transitory nature of their engagement. To use long-term temporary workers effectively, it's important to separate emotion and wishes from reality.

First, let's define the terms of the relationship. I'll refer to these long-term temporary workers as *contractors* in the following discussion. In this case, I mean a person who works on a contract, rather than an employee agreement, for some long period of time, usually working as an implementer as much if not more than a change agent or knowledge-transfer agent within the company. Contractors are paid by units of time, often hourly, although sometimes by the day or the week. They frequently work on-site, and side by side with employees, in a similar capacity. A contractor is generally brought on for a specific project, and his stay at the company is generally delimited by the duration of the project as well as by his contract. (By this I don't mean to imply that a contractor is not necessarily a consultant, but to emphasis the contractual rather than employee nature of his relationship.) It's usually the case that a contractor's idea of the perfect workplace differs from that of the average permanent employee. While every temporary worker is a human being with unique wants and needs, some generalizations do apply.

One is that money is a different type of motivator for temporary staff than for the average salaried employee. I realize that sounds crass, but the distinction is important. A contractor who works long hours for less than his usual rate will find it difficult to get work at his previous rate once he leaves. One implication of this is that you usually get what you pay for. If you go looking for a bargain, you might find one; perhaps a skilled contractor is new to the temporary world and doesn't know his or her own worth. More likely, though, people who have been around for a while know what they're worth. If you're paying them that much, you're not getting a bargain. If they're taking less than their usual rate because they need the money, they'll probably stick around longer than they should, but eventually they'll leave.

Unless your company works with temporary personnel directly as subcontractors, you should also be aware of agency fees and how they fit into the financial equation. Some agencies collect up-front fees as high as 50 percent of the billing rate. In other words, you might find a contractor's rate of $100 per hour to be steep, but the contractor might be getting only $50 of that rate. Again, you get what you pay for. The $50 per hour you pay to the agency is strictly to cover its profits, the risks that your company will not pay, and the costs of marketing, maintaining an office, and insurance, only the last of which does you any good. (Please note that I'm not talking about testing consultancies, test labs, and other organizations that back up their test teams with knowledgeable consultants who can help with the project — see Chapter 10 — but rather *body shops* that provide a contractor from their résumé database based on a keyword match.) In the United States, the only other benefit to your company is protection from retroactive reclassification of subcontractors as employees, either at the instigation of the Internal Revenue Service or from the contractors themselves through a lawsuit. The $50 per hour the contractor receives is for the skills that the individual brings to the job, and that's the skill level you should expect.

Suppose, however, that you are paying $100 an hour to an agency for a contractor whose skills are really worth that amount. In this case, you're actually in worse shape than in the previous example. Temporary workers talk to one another, and they either know the agency's billing rate coming in, find out about it later, or at least have a good idea of what it is. Your contractor, who is not stupid, will discern the situation and will soon leave as a result of being underpaid by the agency. You'll suffer when a key resource disappears in the midst of a project because of a conflict that has nothing to do with you.

If you feel that an agency is offering you a contractor at such a low rate that he will feel short-changed, you might want to consider other candidates, or at the least make sure that this person is not going to be the linchpin of some critical project. You should also ask yourself whether the agency in question makes a practice of such behavior. If so, their placements will probably be an endless source of grief to you. The obvious solution, rectifying the inequity to the contractor, is, unfortunately, quite difficult. First and most importantly, your management will assume you have rocks in your head, or worse, if you negotiate your contractors' rates upward. Second, the agency might increase its rate to you at your request, but pass none of that on to the contractor. (Your contract with the agency might well prohibit you from discussing the contractor's net pay with the contractor.) It might seem like simple greed for an agency to place someone at a low rate, but there are business reasons beyond money. Cheaper contractors are easier to place, and, once they've moved into a higher rate, they often resist moving back down.

Assuming that the pay rate is appropriate, good contractors will stick out almost any assignment, provided that you don't change the rules in the middle of the game or subject them to inhuman harassment. Because these workers don't care about advancement in the company, you don't have to worry about the usual motivators, and you might find that temporary personnel will work hard on assignments that might demotivate or drive out permanent employees. Two factors, however, distinguish acceptable assignments from the ones contractors will fight to keep: intellectual challenges and lots of billable hours. The first applies to all employees, of course; everyone likes to learn and grow on the job. The second, though, is unique to temporary workers. Permanent salaried workers, paid by the week, will put in a certain number of hours willingly and then begin to grumble. If they're too overworked, they'll leave. However, hourly temporary workers usually welcome as many billable hours as you can provide.

You should structure your relationship with contractors (and their agencies) to take account of this situation. On the one hand, if your main concern is meeting a deadline, and you can hire only one contractor, make sure that person is paid hourly and is very motivated by money. To the extent that hard work and long hours can keep your project on schedule, you'll get results. On the other hand, if your main concern is staying within budget, set up a daily or weekly rate. That way, even if the contractor works seven days, you will pay for only 56 hours per week.

(Unfortunately, too many managers try to have it both ways: they negotiate a daily or weekly rate and then try to have contractors work 12-hour days. This might work with some temporary staff or for a little while, but, again, you get what you pay for. Eventually, a sharp contractor will understand that seven hours is closer to a full day than 12 — so guess what you'll get for your money.)

Contractors' lack of concern with advancement in the company has a downside. Many of these folks pursue a bohemian work style because of their distaste for the office politics needed to make it in many firms. Thus, they often display a real disinclination to participate in any event or exercise that smacks of office intrigue or maneuvering. Team picnics or company dinners are usually safe, but pointless meetings, face time with management, and pain-sharing exercises aren't. Let the contractors skip these. You'll get more work out of them, and you'll keep them happy.

Speaking of keeping contractors happy, one school of thought asks, "Why bother? After all, they're leaving eventually." Temporary workers of all stripes are used to engagements from hell, but you'll get better work from happy people than from unhappy ones, regardless of their employment status. You will also earn whatever loyalty is possible under the circumstances, which you just might need some day.

Speaking of keeping people happy, treating contractors with disrespect or showing envy toward their above-employee pay rates is a mistake. I knew of one manager who openly referred to his contractors as "software whores." He was smiling when he said it, but, needless to say, some of them found it offensive. What type of work and commitment do you think he received from these people?

Should you try to convert your best contractors — that is, try to hire them as permanent employees? When I worked as an employee in management roles, I was often under pressure to convert contractors. When I've worked as a contractor, I have also felt the pressure from the other side, having turned down a number of job offers. And, of course, some temporary workers sign on with a company *hoping* to get an offer.

If you want to convert someone — or if you are under pressure from management to do so — a subtle approach is best. Contractors who want job offers won't need an engraved invitation. They might even bring up the issue themselves. However, some of them would consider an offer insulting and would resent any repeated efforts. These folks usually perceive a job offer as the company's way of saying, "We are paying you more than you are worth." Indeed, saving money is usually management's primary motivation in converting temporary staff. The oft-stated purpose, making sure that the contractors stay around because everyone loves their work so much, is less frequently the real reason.

If an interim staff member turns down a job offer, it doesn't necessarily mean that the individual is getting ready to leave. Many temporary workers are happy to have serially monogamous relationships with clients. Just letting them know that they have a home for as long as they want it will minimize the odds that they will look for other work.

Hiring Contractors

Hiring a contractor is easier than hiring a person for a permanent staff position. It's a lot easier to get permission from management to bring on temporary help because the budget impact is less and the commitment level minimal. If you make a hiring mistake, you can easily let the temporary worker go. That said, any hiring decision should be taken seriously.

The first step in hiring temporary help is realizing that you'll need it. Most project management software, for example, allows you to see your staffing needs during project planning. To revisit the SpeedyWriter project, suppose that you examine the time that will be required from Lin-Tsu to accomplish the tasks that have been assigned to her for this project. As you can see in Figure 8-11, she will be over-allocated for three weeks in the middle of the test effort. This problem needs to be resolved, and bringing on a contractor would make sense.

Although you can bring contractors on board fairly rapidly, you do need to allocate sufficient lead time. If you need someone with basic testing skills to sit in front of a keyboard and follow a manual test script, you can usually have this person on site in a week or less. However, if you need an experienced test engineer, finding the right contractor will take at least a month — or, more likely, two months if you have exacting skill requests such as the ability to use GUI automation tools, if you need someone with an advanced technical degree, or if you require specific content expertise in areas such as security or usability.

Once you find the perfect person, establishing a business relationship between your employer and the temporary worker can be quite complex, as illustrated in Figure 8-12. (The following information is primarily applicable to the United States, although similar situations apply in Canada, much of Europe, Australia, and New Zealand.) The top two circles and the upper arrow show a test manager's relationship with the company — in this case, the manager is a permanent employee of the firm. The rest of the drawing shows the various business relationships that can be set up between temporary personnel and a client. At least one of these relationship paths must exist before the temporary worker can do one billable minute's work for you.

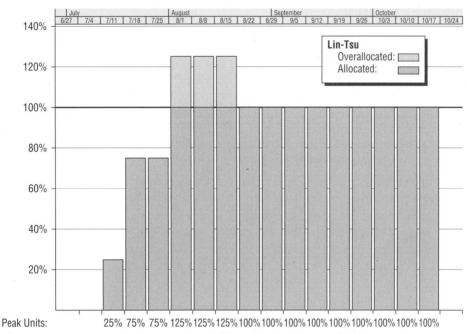

Figure 8-11 An example of resource over-allocation for the SpeedyWriter project

The simplest relationship appears in the center of the figure, directly below the client company. The temporary worker is self-employed as the sole proprietor of his or her own business. Your company, the client, has a direct relationship with this business. If you are in the United States, at the end of the year, your company sends the worker a 1099 federal tax form, not the W-2 form the test manager and other permanent employees receive. Consequently, this worker is often called a *1099 subcontractor*. This relationship is much like the one a homeowner might have with a house painter, or the one a car owner might have with an individual (independent) mechanic.

To the immediate right of this relationship is a variation in which the temporary worker's business is incorporated. In that case, he or she works for the business as an employee. At the end of the year, your company sends the worker's business a 1099.

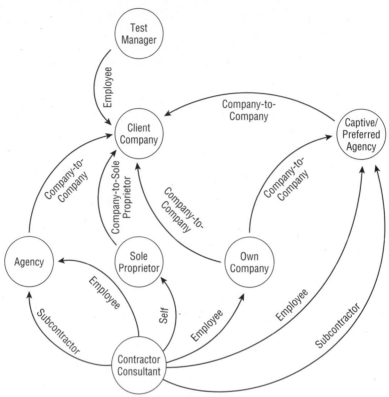

Figure 8-12 Typical business relationships between a temporary worker and a client company

The indirect relationship shown at the far left of the figure is probably the most common. Here the individual works for an agency, either as a 1099 subcontractor or a W-2 employee. It's likely that the agency received your job requirements, matched them to the contractor's résumé in its database, and sent the person to see you. If you hire that worker, your company pays the agency, and the agency — after pocketing its margin — pays the worker.

You might ask, "What's the point of the middleman?" — especially when you consider that margins can run as high as 50 percent. There are several advantages for the contractors. For example, they receive marketing services. They don't have to go out looking for clients; instead, the agency finds the clients for them. Temporary workers can also receive other benefits, such as group insurance, a 401(k) plan, and an employer-of-record, which can help with getting credit. (Especially if you have no track record, being self-employed can make buying a car or a house difficult.) Finally, contractors working for some temporary agencies are guaranteed payment on a regular schedule, regardless of when and whether the client pays.

Your company also receives benefits, in the form of three safeguards. The first is protection from the United States Internal Revenue Service. If your company works directly with temporary personnel, the IRS can, under some circumstances, retroactively classify those people as employees and then fine your company heavily for not withholding taxes from their pay.

The second is protection from the temporary personnel themselves. Some of these workers have sued past clients, claiming that they were really employees and thus were entitled to participate in benefit programs, especially stock option programs. The client companies have sometimes lost these lawsuits, to the tune of considerable sums of money. (This is an unfortunate situation whereby the litigants have, basically, taken millions of dollars out of the pockets of their fellow contractors and deposited it into the pockets of temporary agencies.) People who are the employees of an agency during their work with your company have less chance of successfully bringing such a suit.

The third protection is that the agency generally carries insurance on its contractors, which can mean that if a clumsy contractor slips and breaks a bone, your company isn't facing an expensive lawsuit. Your employees are probably covered under your worker's compensation plan and your corporate liability insurance, but contractors might not be.

To the far right in Figure 8-12 is a variation on the worker/agency/client model. In this case, your company works only with a single, internal, captive agency or a small set of preferred agencies. All temporary workers must be employed through these agencies, whether the worker operates as a sole proprietor or as an incorporated business. This arrangement provides all the advantages of the agency model just described, but with the added benefit of allowing your company to keep the accounts payable simple and, if desired, to control or at least curb the agencies' margins.

This arrangement has its drawbacks, however. It's usually true that people who don't have to compete for a client's business soon take it for granted. By limiting the pool of agencies, your company will pay a price in terms of service. The temporary workers also pay a price in that the agency, while collecting a margin from fees that arguably belong to the workers, has done little or nothing to market these people and has no incentive to keep them happy in order to place them at other companies later. Moreover, by limiting the pool of agencies, this arrangement limits the pool of available candidates. An agency's database is its most prized possession, and agencies do not all have access to the same pool of talent.

As if all this weren't complicated enough, you should be aware that the business relationship between the temporary worker and the client is often not immaterial to the contractor. Some temporary personnel work only on a 1099 basis; others work only as W-2 employees. Some will not work through agencies at all; others work only through agencies. Sometimes workers prefer or avoid specific agencies because of positive or negative past experiences. All these factors can complicate and even scuttle your attempts to hire the best temporary help.

Bringing on the Experts

On occasion, you will find yourself confronted by a situation beyond your ability. You don't need extra hands to accomplish a task; rather, you need extra knowledge. In these cases, you need someone who fits into the right sector of the triangle in Figure 8-10. This person would be a consultant in the traditional meaning of the term. How do you pick the right one? How do you find someone who can actually solve your problem?

First and foremost, it's important to be clear about the problem you want the consultant to help you solve, and how you expect her to help you solve it. In some cases, you want the consultant to assess your difficulties and advise you on possible solutions. Alternatively, you might want the consultant to train you or your team. For example, I work with an accountant in my consulting business, and I often call him with questions about how to stay out of trouble with the United States Internal Revenue Service. He tells me what I need to do, and I do it. This type of activity is *consulting* in the original sense of the word, transferring knowledge, teaching me. I use this same accountant to do my corporate and personal taxes. In this case, he is acting as a practitioner. He is still bringing special expertise to my needs — I have no aptitude for or desire of mastering the intricacies of tax law — but he is applying that knowledge directly to benefit me, rather than teaching me to help myself.

A consultant on a software or hardware development project likewise can be heavily involved in implementation or not at all. For example, the RBCS mix of consulting involves implementation as well as training and consulting for our clients. On some projects, we have put associates on-site ostensibly to teach and then found that the client actually needed help building and managing their test team.

Whatever you call an expert, the distinguishing quality is exactly that: *expertise*. This person brings knowledge to your relationship that you don't have, and that's exactly what you want. However, it is essential that you figure out whether this person or consulting group is bringing the *right* knowledge.

Making this determination is not easy. A consultant might have as much trouble figuring out how to help you as you have trouble figuring out what help you need. Most consultants want to avoid having clients that, for some weird reason, just didn't work out. However, the high fee you paid an inappropriate consultant without any tangible benefit could doom your test operation.

This requires some advance thinking. You need to define in your mind the problem you want solved. If it's an implementation problem, make sure you define it that way. I once hired a consultant to work with me on an MTBF demonstration plan without taking this important first step. He did not expect actually to have to write the plan, which was exactly what I needed him to do. It was an engagement that didn't work out at all, and I had to replace him.

Given a definition of the problem, you can assess what type of expertise you need. It also has implications on what type of person you need. A knowledge-transfer problem, such as training you to use a new test tool, requires not just a person skilled in the use of the tool, but also a person who is an effective communicator of ideas. In contrast, an implementation problem, such as building an automated test suite using a new test tool, requires the same type of skill in terms of the tool, but you can retain a person less suited to communicating if you find someone who can produce such a test suite in a short period of time.

With the problem clearly defined, you must extensively interview any prospective experts, expensive or not, before signing a contract. In addition to getting to the bottom of the softer side, such as teaching abilities and fit with the company culture, you will need to satisfy yourself that they do indeed have the right level of proficiency in terms of any tools that will be used or technology that will be involved. Because they are the expert, not you, you might not know enough about the topic at hand. In that case, you'll need to complement your discussions with them by talking to their references. If they can provide you with the name and telephone number of a past client for whom they solved a similar problem, you can satisfy yourself that they can solve your problem by talking to this person.

Interviewing an expert is different from interviewing a contractor or permanent employee. A prospective consultant might want to put on a presentation, have you visit his site, or meet with some of his associates. All these are good ideas, but it's important that you stay focused on the problem, as you've defined it in your mind, and how the expert or experts can help.

When interviewing consultants for implementation engagements, you should also be on guard against bait-and-switch tactics. Ask the person doing the pitch, "Are you the consultant who will actually do the work?" If someone else will be brought in, this might not be a problem, but you should reserve the right to talk directly to that person. Don't allow a situation in which the consulting business can put anyone who needs a few billable hours on your job. This might be just another project to the consulting company, but it's your livelihood.

Another danger is the overpaid neophyte. You might have seen the advertisements by a large consulting firm that compared their competitors' staff to elementary school children in terms of their innocence and lack of experience. This is humorous in the abstract, but you won't find it funny if you discover one day that you are paying $200 an hour for the expertise and experience of someone who just graduated from business school. Insist that the consultants on your project have a proven record of accomplishment in solving the types of problems you're facing. Again, reserve the right to interview every consultant who will work on your project.

After all, whether your staff is composed of temporary or permanent employees, technicians, or senior engineers, they are part of your test team. Far from being interchangeable bit players, each of them, and all of them together, hold the success of your test organization in their hands as much as you do. While effective management cannot be discounted, neither can the importance of any participant in a team effort. Leadership is the art of getting work done through others.

Case Study

On one project, my associates and I tested an information appliance. This system was composed of set of a back-end servers to which the clients would connect, giving the users access to the Internet, email, and other services. See Figure 8-13 for an illustration of the system under test, its basic architecture, and the test team.

Figure 8-13 System architecture and test team

Starting from the left side of the figure, one thing we wanted to test was actual user experience in the field. For this reason, one of the test engineers worked on usability testing from various outside locations.

Another thing we needed to test was scalability and performance of the servers. As commercial tools were not available to do the type of load generation and probing we needed, we had to write some of the load and performance tests, which talked directly to the servers. The two test toolsmiths were in charge of this effort.

Finally, most of the test execution was actually done by test technicians against the appliances themselves in the test lab. We used primarily scripted manual tests — albeit some were actually manual probes done while performance and load tools hit the servers hard, letting the manual testers know what the user experience would be like at full look. We also did some amount of exploratory testing. For example, the test manager (me) and the appliance and server lead test engineers would spend an hour a day each following our hunches to find bugs and simply using the system the way we thought users would. We often managed to find bugs that had eluded scripted tests this way.

Now look at Figure 8-14. Notice how the organization chart follows the architecture of the system under test and the test work being done. I believe this is fairly typical of a well-structured test team. You can achieve this type of flexibility using either the skills-oriented or project-oriented model discussed in this chapter.

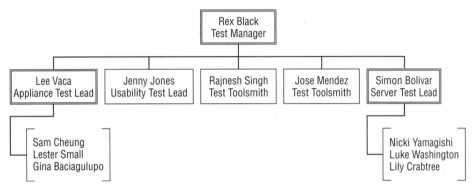

Figure 8-14 The information appliance test team organization

I thank my client, who wishes to remain anonymous, for permission to discuss this project here. I also thank my client contacts for their excellent support and steady leadership on this project. Finally, thanks to my test team for their professionalism and excellence on this project.

Exercises

1. In each of the three major skills categories (testing, technology, domain), outline the major skills that you would need on the Omninet test team.

2. Discuss how well your personal attitudes fit into the qualifications of professional pessimism, balanced curiosity, and ability to focus.

3. Sketch a critical skills worksheet for testing a video game. Sketch the worksheet for testing control software for an automated factory. Compare and contrast, commenting on the similarities and differences.

4. Calculate the defect detection percentage (DDP) for your test team on a recent project, using three months as the time window for 90 percent of the customer-discovered bugs to arrive. (See Chapter 4 for a refresher on how to calculate this metric.)

- Calculate without adjusting for scope limitations. In other words, every unique, true bug found by customers in the first three months counts against the DDP.

- Recalculate, eliminating from the customer-discovered bug count any bugs that were out of scope or could not have reasonably been found during the test effort.

- Propose and describe a reasonable bonus system based on one of these DDP calculations.

CHAPTER 9

The Triumph of Politics: Organizational Challenges for Test Managers

Office politics. We all use the phrase, usually to connote something negative about a coworker, department, or company. At one time or another, we've all undoubtedly made a comment such as this: "Oh, you know Jim — he's so *political*."

To some extent, I hesitate to use the term *politics* — the euphemisms *management considerations* or *soft skills* seem less negative — but the word is apt for three reasons. First, as a manager, you must be sensitive to political realities, some of which are unique to test management. Second, politics in the electoral sense is described as "the art of compromise," and that is certainly an art you must master in a typical hardware or software development organization. Finally, politics is also the art of managing relationships that involve power, authority, and responsibility.

Don Quixote, Champion of Quality: What's Your Job, Anyhow?

Don Quixote, the immortal character created by Miguel Cervantes, is a minor Spanish nobleman who decides that he is by birth a knight-errant. Venturing forth on a quest with his squire Sancho Panza, he stumbles into a series of misadventures, jousting with a giant who is actually a windmill, and defending the honor of a maiden named Dulcinea who turns out to be a prostitute.

I admit that I've held some quixotic positions in my career. The most notable came with the title *quality assurance manager*. I considered myself the test manager, while everyone else drew his or her own conclusions about what I was to do. With the budget I had, I was lucky to do a passable job of testing. One of my development manager peers suggested that I focus on working with the programmers to build a higher level of quality in the product, but I wasn't appropriately staffed for that role. What my managers wanted me to do, specifically, and how I would know that I was succeeding — in other words, the scope of my job — remained undefined. This was a political error on my part.

I have drawn my own boundaries too widely once or twice as well. It's tempting to decide that you, the test manager, are the lone defender of product integrity. From the point at which you make this decision, it's but a short ride to the windmill and Dulcinea. Looking back on these events, I feel vaguely embarrassed that I took myself so seriously while playing Don Quixote. Again, the error was political, in that I didn't clarify with my management what purpose my organization and I served.

The role and responsibilities of a test manager must be unambiguous. I have had the most success when I defined my role clearly and specifically with my managers and then communicated those boundaries to my peers and to my team. Whenever an issue arose that started to blur the boundaries, I reconfirmed my understanding.

Test Missions and Test Policies

Certainly, for any test team to succeed, it needs a well-defined and widely agreed mission. The phrase *mission statement* has suffered serious degradation over the years, as organizations, often at the prompting of consultants, have emitted myriad vacuous examples of the concept. So, what makes my advice here different?

What I'm talking about is a highly actionable statement, not a vague one. The mission of the test team is what the team does, day in and day out. You should not confuse this with the often even more debased phrase *vision statement*. At best, vision statements indicate long-term goals towards which a lot of, some, or no action is currently occurring. At worst, they are completely contradictory to the day-to-day activities. To me, a useful mission statement is one that actually corresponds to what we intend to do and what we indeed do.

How about an example? Here's an excerpt from an actual mission statement for an actual test team:

> *To effectively and efficiently find defects, build confidence, reduce risk, and provide timely, accurate, and useful information, within schedule and budget constraints.*

We can measure the effectiveness to which the team achieves its mission by setting key process indicators and targets in four areas:

Finding defects: Defect detection effectiveness, the percentage of bugs found by the test team relative to the number present during testing.

Building confidence: Percentage of requirements elements, design elements, supported configurations, etc. covered by the tests.

Reducing risk: Percentage of risks covered, which each risk classified as passed, failed, and not-yet-tested.

Providing information: Degree of satisfaction of test results report recipients.

We've discussed the first three of these key process indicators earlier in the book, in Chapters 3 and 5. The last of these key process indicators is one you should determine by surveying your stakeholders, especially those outside the test team. We'll discuss test efficiency in Chapter 11, but at the moment note that we can look at metrics like the cost per bug found, the cost per requirement covered, and the percentage of tests automated as efficiency measures.

By measuring the current process, its effectiveness and its efficiency, we can start to set targets for these key process indicators. Do not fall into the trap of making these targets aspirational. In other words, don't set targets that you think — or someone else thinks — you ought to achieve; set targets that you actually achieve. If your team is not performing to expectations now, that's fine: put in place and then implement process improvements that move the key process indicators — and thus the targets — to where you want them to go. Remember that exhortations like *work smarter, not harder* and other such platitudes do not change actual behavior; process improvements require constant, long-term efforts.

The last part of the mission statement, mentioning budget and schedule constraints, acknowledges that such constraints can affect our effectiveness and efficiency. This is important. If someone expects your team to achieve a defect detection effectiveness of 97.5 percent, that's perfectly achievable, provided you get the time and resources needed to achieve such a good result. Most of our clients don't hit such a target. This is not because they do not want to find bugs, but rather because various aspects of the larger software development process, especially limits on their time and resources for testing, reduce their effectiveness.

A good way to capture the test mission is in a test policy document. This is a very short, one- or two-page document. It captures the mission statement, the key process indicators, and the targets for those indicators. It should have a short statement about the strategy used to achieve the mission, such as the following:

The test team uses an analytical risk-based testing strategy. The test team works in consultation with business and other stakeholders to determine the degree of quality risk mitigation desired. The stakeholders work together to identify quality risks, and to assess risk items to determine their level of risk. The level of risk determines test effort and test sequencing. The test team reports test results in terms of mitigated and unmitigated risks. The test team uses reactive strategies like software attacks and exploratory testing to detect and fill gaps in risk coverage.

Test policies can also cover other topics, such as the sequencing of various testing and quality assurance steps in the overall software life cycle to achieve high levels of effectiveness without imposing excessive costs or delay. (I'll discuss testing in the software life cycle in Chapter 12.) Table 9-1 is an example of such integration of testing into the life cycle.

Table 9-1 Example of Test Integration into the Life Cycle

LEVEL	OWNER	OBJECTIVE(S)	KEY AREAS OF TESTING
Requirements and Design Reviews	Test team leads; entire project team participates	Detect defects in work products such as business requirements, design specifications, etc Improve testability of requirements Promote understanding, agreement, and consensus on the requirements, including their priority	Consistency, relevancy, clarity, unambiguity, traceability, testability, uniqueness, and measurability Covers both functional and non-functional aspects
Unit	Development team	Detect defective code in units Detect insecure and unmaintainable code Reduce risk of unit failure in production	Functionality, resource utilization, security, and maintainability
Unit Integration	Development team	Detect defects in unit interfaces Reduce risk of dataflow and workflow failures in production	Functionality, data quality, unit inter-operability and compatibility, performance
System	Test team	Detect defects in use cases and end-to-end scenarios Assist in mitigating risk of unmet business requirements in production Detect security vulnerabilities	Functionality, data quality, security, performance, reliability, usability, resource utilization, maintainability, installability, portability, and interoperability

(continued)

Table 9-1 (*continued*)

LEVEL	OWNER	OBJECTIVE(S)	KEY AREAS OF TESTING
Application Acceptance	Test team leads; selected developers participate	Review vendor test plans, results, defects, and other test documents Build confidence in vendor application's fitness for use Validate readiness of application for system integration	Samples of functionality, interoperability, and performance
System Integration	Test team	Detect defects in system and business interfaces Reduce risk of dataflow, control flow, workflow, and security failures in production Reduce risk of software/hardware interface failures	End-to-end functionality, usability, security, interoperability, and performance
User Acceptance	User team	Demonstrate readiness for deployment Validate user workflows	Functionality, usability
Production Verification	User team, with test team support	Validate code promotion into production	Functionality

Test Team and Manager Titles

The title you hold and the name of your group are important to drawing these boundaries. Titles and names are organizational shorthand, code words that have real implications. These abbreviations signify kinds of information discussed in the preceding section. Your title and the name of your group are short answers to the question, "What do they pay you to do?"

If your title is *test manager* or some variant of that designation, the boundaries are partially drawn right away. In such a situation, once you ensure clear ownership of the various phases of testing, you should know exactly what tasks you own. By reinforcing these perimeters in your test plans, using *is/is not* tables and entry, continuation, and exit criteria (as discussed in Chapter 2), you clarify what the test team will do. And, just as important, you clarify what your team will *not* do.

Be aware, though, that people sometimes use the word *test* to reach beyond the typical scope of writing and evaluating test cases against live, executable systems, hardware, or software. A number of books on testing include requirements reviews, design reviews, and code reviews as tests.[1] Investigate expectations in this regard. If your managers and peers include running all reviews in your job description, this expanded scope will have significant implications for the minimum skill set your test engineers must possess. The increased critical skills in the areas of application domain and technological expertise should show up in your critical skills assessment worksheet (discussed in Chapter 8).

If your title contains the word *quality*, be careful. The title *quality control manager* might be safe, because most people understand quality control to mean testing to find defects. However, the title *quality assurance manager* leaves many questions open, as I discovered. Quality assurance is not only the location of bugs through testing — it also involves the prevention of bugs. Some might say that in addition, it includes actively ensuring the continuous improvement of product quality. The way some people use the terms, *quality control* is concerned with product, *quality assurance* with process.

I won't make a blanket statement warning you never to take a job as a QA manager. If you accept such a job, however, be sure to work carefully with your managers and peers up front in an effort to understand and guide their expectations. Have a written test policy, brief perhaps but nevertheless written and approved by all key stakeholders. In the beginning, you will probably find that their expectations are not congruent with each other's or with yours. Moreover, if you are the first QA manager the company has ever had, management's expectations of your ability to affect product quality will very likely be inconsistent with its forecast of your budgetary needs.

Suppose that you are offered a job with the title *director of quality* or *chief quality officer*. However you slice it, such a job entails corporation-wide management of product and service quality. To succeed, you'll require sufficient authority and standing to work with the entire organization in defining processes, and sometimes this will involve cajoling and even dictating to your peers that process will be followed. You will also need sufficient staff and other resources to do a thorough, professional job of testing as well as the not-insignificant amount of quality management work. Don't plan on shoehorning the quality roles into the workload of your existing test engineers and technicians. Besides not having time for such tasks, they might not be qualified, either.

---

[1] The earliest example I'm aware of is Fred Brooks's *The Mythical Man-Month*, where he talks about the need for independent testers to review the requirements. Bill Hetzel's *The Complete Guide to Software Testing* includes all defect detection activities as tests. The certification programs of the ISTQB, QAI, and ASQ, mentioned in Chapter 8, also include them.

If I held the title *quality assurance manager* but believed that my authority and resources supported only test activities, I would try to change my title. I would gather some case studies about what a true quality management role entails, which would provide some ammunition to convince my manager that my role didn't match this description. If my managers insisted that I keep the title but didn't give me the requisite authority and resources, I would resign. I see no point to holding a position in which I'm bound to fail.

Finally, an aside on ethical implications: If you do accept a role that has wide-ranging quality assurance responsibilities, make sure you know enough about formal quality management. You will also need to understand the entire development process and current best practices in your industry. However, a few weeks of training will not qualify you to implement a company-wide quality program. It is, at the least, unprofessional to promote yourself as competent to perform jobs that you know are beyond your capacity. Indeed, some professional societies and organizations like the Association for Computing Machinery and the ISTQB would consider this a violation of their codes of ethics. This might strike you as trifling, but if your company becomes involved in a lawsuit, wearing a hat that's three sizes too big will at best make you look silly in court.

Where You Fit: The Test Group in the Organization

With the scope of your job defined, let's place the test group in its organizational context. A number of possible organizational models can apply. Figure 9-1 shows one basic model for a test group, in which the test manager reports to the development manager. In this case, a lead test engineer typically manages the team. (Test groups tend to be small when they service a single development team.) This lead engineer communicates test results directly to the development manager.

Some people have reported success with this model, but I've seen — and heard of — too many problems where it's used. What's wrong with including the test organization in the development team? First, it is often difficult to preserve the notion of an independent test organization giving unbiased information to the project when the test manager reports to the development manager. It's too much to expect that managers will pursue an agenda contrary to *their* manager's interests — but this model requires that test managers do just that if they are to be independent in any sense.

Why are the agendas necessarily contrary? Well, in most situations I've seen, the development manager is held primarily accountable for the delivery of a particular set of features on a predetermined schedule and within a predetermined budget. The test manager is held responsible for defect detection effectiveness and possibly some of the other targets mentioned earlier, which tend to suffer when schedule and budget constraints limit the test team's actions. This sets up a schedule-versus-quality tradeoff that tilts the field against the test organization.

Second, in this mono-team approach, testing might get short shrift in terms of access to the resources it needs. The development manager is often forced to choose between purchasing tools for development or for testing, between hiring developers or testers, and so forth. Third, testing might not keep the resources it has. In crunch mode, testers sometimes get pulled into debugging activities, tool creation, and even coding. Finally, the test team's independence and influence tends to suffer. Developers often can treat testers' bug reports as suggestions. Typically the only upward career move available to the testers is to become developers. As a practical matter, integrated test organizations often disappear over time, melting back into the development teams.

Nevertheless, this model makes sense in some situations. If you are working in a small startup with, say, a dozen or so engineers, other models can put too many layers in place. You don't want to negate the advantages of a small organization, such as shared vision and low communication overhead, by imposing unnecessary layers of management. If your company uses the approach illustrated in Figure 9-1, just keep in mind that it will require special care to preserve a separate test team.

Figure 9-1 The test organization as part of development

Figure 9-2 shows another common model, in which the test manager and the development manager both report to the project manager. This is not a perfect solution, but it is an improvement over the previous model. The test group is still not independent in a real sense, because the test manager answers to the project manager. A project manager's agenda and interests usually more closely resemble those of a development manager than those of a test manager. However, a project manager, being less involved in the creation of the system under test, can usually bring a more dispassionate outlook to the discussion of problems than a development manager can.

Under the arrangement shown in Figure 9-2, the development and test organizations usually have separate headcounts and budgets, which reduces the resource contention encountered in the first model. You must still compete for the same pool of money, but now the development manager is a peer, not your superior. Likewise, the development manager can't raid the test team's cookie jar without at least the project manager's blessing, thus minimizing situations in which you lose resources yet are expected to meet the original schedules and scope of testing. Moreover, the test organization has more stature, as bug reports and other test status reports go directly to project management.

Figure 9-2 The test organization as a development project resource

Despite these advantages, you should count on being considered a project resource and expect to participate in all the panics and crunches, even if test's involvement does not add value. For example, if the implementation falls behind schedule, your team will probably be required to commiserate with the tardy developers by suffering through the same six-day weeks, long hours, abrupt changes of priority, and all the rest. This is especially the case if your company practices the *kiddie soccer* approach to project management.[2]

Figure 9-3 shows the model I prefer. Here, the test team is truly independent. Executive management's agendas and interests promote the good of the company. (If they don't, you have bigger problems.) Therefore, management will listen to test status reports with an open mind. You might burst management's bubble in terms of the quality of the product, but in this situation it is most likely that the management team will see the quality problems as arising in the project manager's domain rather than being somehow your problem. Clout, budget, and staffing problems are minimized to the extent to which they can be, for the most part. You have a budget based on how many projects you must support — and if your project load increases, you can ask for and reasonably expect to obtain more resources.

Of course, there is no paradise on Earth. Market-driven companies make money by selling products, not by building them. IT departments must put working systems on users' desks. Deployment dates are often more closely related to marketing windows, contractual obligations, and user needs than to assessments of quality, independent or not. No matter the model, these

---

[2]In real soccer, everyone plays a specific position, and the whole team plays with grace, cohesion, and a sense of trust that each player knows his or her part. When young children first play soccer, though, the whole complement of players on both sides run around in a disoriented mob, chasing the ball around the field. There are no real positions and no sense of direction. Everyone is excited and much energy is expended, but little is accomplished.

constraints will subject you to project pressures, sometimes very strong ones. This third model, however, unlike the others, is at least structured in a way that does not actively undermine you.

Figure 9-3 The truly independent test organization

What Else Fits? Adding Other Functions to Test

In part because testing is often a misunderstood function, management might invite you to take charge of all sorts of additional duties that are more or less peripheral to testing. Test managers, in their copious free time, sometimes discharge other duties, such as the following:

- Configuration management and release management
- Customer support
- Operations such as system administration and disaster recovery
- Quality management — for example, code reviews, inspections, and enforcement of development process rules
- Management of the development lab
- Creation of training data and procedures for operations staff

The list of duties that might be attached to the test function is probably endless. However, does placing these functions in the test organization make sense?

In my opinion, the answer is usually — but not always — no.[3] The specific situations in which I recommend against such arrangements include the following:

The test team shares some responsibility for product development, or is completely integrated into the development team.
There are well-documented reasons why developers can't test their own code, in terms of subjectivity and bringing the same

---

[3] A specific case that seems to make sense is having a senior test engineer or the test manager serve as the project's risk officer. Steve McConnell makes this suggestion in his book *Software Project Survival Guide.*

blind spots to the testing as to the creating. In addition, they don't have the test expertise to test other developers' code at a system level. It is also true that many developers tend to dislike testing and give it short shrift when forced to do much of it.

Management assigns additional duties to the test team because the group is perceived to have the bandwidth. This perception is nearly always wrong: I have never managed, seen, or heard of an overstaffed test group. The extra duties will assuredly weaken the team's ability to focus on testing.

Specific tasks are assigned to a member of the test team who possesses a relevant skill set. Such assignments might make sense as temporary duties, but if the role is ongoing, your test team has been effectively downsized.

A member of the test team wants to take on additional responsibility as part of individual career growth. This might make sense for the individual, but does it make sense for your test team? This person probably belongs in another group. Perhaps now is a good time for the transition?

Even in the best-case scenario, assigning additional roles and responsibilities to the test team distracts everyone from one of the main missions: finding bugs. In the worst-case scenario, you might find yourself unable to fulfill test responsibilities competently, although you are still being held accountable both for testing and for the new duties. To avoid such a situation, be sure to draw your test group's organizational boundaries — your team's *is/is not* table — as a first step in your tenure as test manager. If you are asked to take on additional responsibilities, be sure to clarify whether these duties are permanent or temporary and to explain their impact on your ability to test.

All that said, you may have to accept certain expansions of your test group's role in order to help the company succeed. On a purely Machiavellian basis, the last thing you want is to be branded "not a team player" or "inflexible" — unless you truly don't care about advancement or permanent tenure within the company. And it's certainly true that an arrangement in which the test team works with other teams, all under the same manager, needn't be a disaster. Such an arrangement can work well when the teams are grouped together because of synergy in the kinds of tasks they perform and the kinds of expertise each group needs, as opposed to a desire to get something for nothing or to throw undesirable duties over the wall into the test ghetto. If you are faced with the suggestion that the test team take on other responsibilities, you might consider proposing an approach like the one shown in Figure 9-4. This model illustrates the structure of a development services group in which I once worked, an organization that performed very well.

Figure 9-4 A development services group

If management asks you to take on some of these extra roles, a smart political question to ask yourself is, "Why did they ask me?" There are two general possibilities. One is that management sees you as a competent manager, one who can handle non-glamorous but essential jobs well. In that case, the request is a compliment and an invitation to grow your team. Another is that management does not see testing as involving anything other than test execution, and they feel that you have extra people with nothing to do in between test execution periods. In this case, the request indicates a failure to understand the scope and complexity of the test team's job.

It's easy enough to determine which case applies. When asked to take on these extra roles, reply along the following lines, "Thanks for your trust in my ability to handle this. Let me look into way in which my team can expand to accommodate this request. I'll get back to you shortly with the budget and team-size impact required to handle it." If the response to that statement is an encouragement to do so, then you are in a good situation, politically. If the response is that you should have plenty of spare capacity in between test execution periods, then you have some educating to do.

Working with Other Managers: Directions of Test Management

Test projects must be managed in three directions:

Inward. Managing inward means defining your test team, hiring its members, organizing the team's structure, and supervising and motivating your employees.

Upward. Managing upward means summarizing the status of the test process and escalating urgent problems to the attention of the project management team, setting expectations, responding quickly but prudently to changes in direction, participating in management meetings, and selling your test effort.

Outward. Managing outward means communicating test results, clarifying problem reports, and discussing test needs and services with your management peers.

These three directions are represented in Figure 9-5. Chapter 8 focused on managing inward. Here we'll look at the other two directions.

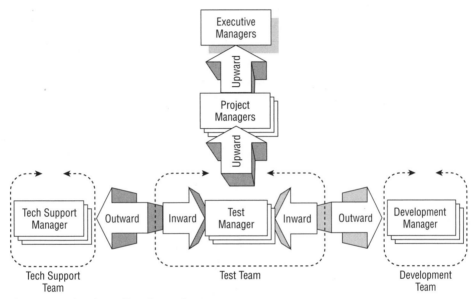

Figure 9-5 The three directions of test management

Managing Upward

Managing upward is often a difficult challenge, especially when you are communicating to people who have only a dim understanding of what testing is all about. Managing upward requires that you spend a significant amount of time preparing reports, focusing on process, and devising an effective set of test project and process metrics — the test dashboard — that your management can use to understand test status.[4]

As part of this effort, it is critical that you learn to manage your managers effectively. Perhaps this concept seems strange. Managing your managers

[4]For another, similar perspective on managing upward (and outward), see Chapter 6 of Bill Perry and Randall Rice's *Surviving the Top Ten Challenges of Software Testing,* which focuses on the need to sell management on what test can contribute and to establish clear communication and reporting.

doesn't imply that you will tell your bosses what to do. Rather, it means that your effectiveness in supervising your team's interactions with your superiors will determine your success as a manager in many ways. If you think about it, your ability to handle such interactions probably had a lot to do with why you became a manager in the first place.

Poor upward management leads to a perception among the upper echelons of the company that your team has failed. As much as the paperwork and status reporting can seem tedious and disconnected from critical tasks, remember that your managers are, in a real sense, your most important customers. (After all, we are producing information — an assessment of system quality — that should be useful to our managers, right?) From your immediate supervisor on up to the CEO, these are the people who must provide the funds you need to carry out testing. Help them understand what you're doing. Clearly explain the benefits of testing. Provide useful information in a timely and accurate fashion. If you can do these things, you'll be much more successful in obtaining critical resources and political support.

Bringing Management to Your Reality: Communicating Clearly

One of the most important demands of your job is that you communicate with upper management clearly and effectively. Every one of your managers has an individual management style, and this style should determine exactly how you approach the task of managing upward. In general, however, it's useful to keep the following considerations in mind:

Ensure that your managers do not hold you personally responsible for product quality. It should be obvious that the test organization doesn't write the code or build motherboards. However, it is hardly uncommon for unenlightened senior managers and executives to blame test managers when low-quality systems under test don't complete test phases on time. Likewise, managers of customer support or sales and marketing too frequently consider every field bug a test escape, whether testing that area was in scope or not.

Help your managers understand testing. If they lack a testing background, they might not grasp the reasons why you do (and don't do) certain things. Avoid focusing on minutiae such as boundary conditions, state machines, and load generators, which are simply a means to an end. Instead, talk about risk management and about the impact of serious test escapes on the reputation and revenues of the company.

Think ROI — return on investment. (We'll discuss this further in Chapter 11.) Your managers will regularly need to defend your budget to other managers (their bosses). If you can't explain to your superiors the business benefits gained by spending tens of thousands of dollars for GUI test automation tools or a thermal chamber, how will they explain the payoff to *their* managers?

Be ready to measure your results. The charts and reports introduced in Chapters 3, 4, and 5 provide the tools you need to summarize test coverage, the status of testing, and the quality of the system under test. Being crisp and quantitative will help your managers understand and support what you're doing. Remember, though, that we need to understand the information needs of our managers and tailor our metrics, charts, and reports to provide that information.

Keep test data, information, and reports accurate and timely. Inaccurate reporting can damage your team's credibility, making your managers' lives — as well as your own life — more difficult. Reports that show trends only when it's become too late to take remedial action will likely be more frustrating than enlightening.

Communicate in terms of moving the project forward. Most project managers aren't interested in test theory or testing as an abstract idea, but with the ways in which testing can advance the project. If you try to understand what your managers need to accomplish and then attempt to connect test's contributions to those goals, you can keep your communications with them relevant and on target. A colleague once described our mutual manager as the kind of guy who "if you told him you had a flat tire, would offer to help change your shoe." Taking actions that do nothing to promote the success of the project — or that might even actively impede it — and focusing on solving problems that are extraneous to the ones that urgently need solving will not endear you to other participants.

Be ready to participate in the dog-and-pony shows. I have spent many an hour putting together snazzy presentations for management meetings or searching for a graphic to enliven a slide — even though my spiel was sometimes cancelled at the last minute. These activities are part of your managerial selling role, so learn to enjoy them and do them well.

Address both the urgent and the important. Urgent matters require immediate action to prevent a major crisis or even the total failure of the project — for example, if you are unable to install the system under test in the lab. Important matters need focused, deliberate attention. Addressing important matters usually leads to improvements in process efficiency, quality of product, clarity of communication, and order in the workplace. Often, the two types of issues are related. On one project, we continually received builds of abysmally poor quality. We could usually install them, but they had major regressions from previous functionality. The urgent matter, repeatedly, was to get a new build to the test lab so that we could proceed with testing. The important matter, often lost in the accompanying fire drill, was that development needed to run a short regression or smoke test before delivering the product to the test group.

Remember that you are the interface between the test group and the project. For a tester, success means finding bugs, and the worse the bug, the better the tester feels. You want your team members to be diligent about finding problems and to feel a sense of accomplishment when they do. For everyone else on the project, however, news of a nasty bug is nothing to smile about. As the test manager, you must maintain a somewhat two-faced display of positive encouragement and near-celebration of bugs inside your team, while understanding the negative effect that bugs have outside your team. One talented test manager I once worked with, Reynolds MacNary, used the phrase "optimistic on the outside, pessimistic on the inside" to capture this dichotomy.

Don't let bad news wait. If there's anything a manager dreads more than bad news, it's bad news that's too old to manage effectively. The business impact of a problem almost always grows more severe as the problem festers. Nevertheless, do take the time to make sure you've gotten your story straight. Reacting and managing are different behaviors.

Escalate deliberately. Before you bring a problem to your managers' attention with a request for help, ask yourself whether they can and will make the situation better, not worse. I had a client who, when informed of a problem, would immediately begin making irate telephone calls to anyone he saw as responsible or culpable. Occasionally this solved the problem, but often it merely enraged those who were the targets of the telephone calls. In another situation, a colleague referred to the escalation process by snorting that "escalation is just another way of saying, 'Get information to Joe' [named changed to protect the guilty] so he can micromanage you." If you work for such managers, use caution.

Admittedly, managing upward can involve tedious activities, especially when it feels like you're trying to communicate with people who speak another language. How many presentations can you put together on the same topic, especially while your team is doing real work? Wouldn't you rather spend time managing your test engineers, who understand what you're talking about and admire your advanced knowledge and skills, instead of working with a bunch of managers who just don't get it? When you get caught up in one of these "leave me alone and let me work" funks, remember that upper management must either buy the end product — if it's in-house — or sell it to customers and clients. And these managers are the people who make what you and your team do possible. Although their different perspectives make communication challenging, they are paying for your test operation. In Chapter 11 we'll return to the topic of test budgets, specifically to ways you can explain the financial benefits of releasing quality systems.

"How about a Third Shift, and Weekends, and . . . ": The Effects of Lateness on Test

In addition to budgets, another major management concern is hitting scheduled project end dates. However, in the high-tech world, schedule delays are a way of life. Some argue that these delays result from the incredible pace at which technology evolves and from the fact that anything new is, by nature, somewhat unknown and unknowable. Some technical staff and development managers say that delays are simply the effects of reality biting down hard on unrealistic schedules imposed by uninformed or overly aggressive managers, salespeople, and marketers, who correspondingly often blame lazy and disorganized developers and technical people. Others hold poor planning and estimation techniques responsible. Who's right? Who cares! Although discussing culpability makes for a nice venting exercise over drinks after a long day of trying to catch up on a schedule everyone but senior management admits is unachievable, it doesn't accomplish much.

High-tech projects very often run late vis-à-vis the official schedule. As the test manager, your moment in the spotlight comes during test execution, at the end of the project — which means that, much of the time, you will be running tests just as the schedule's disconnection from reality becomes painfully obvious to all involved. Unfortunately, you are likely to suffer the consequences of management's rude awakening well out of proportion to the degree to which your team contributed to the delay.

As a schedule begins to slip, managers often impose a crunch-mode regimen in an attempt to make up time through sheer effort: this thinking assumes that if the schedule is off by 20 percent, making everyone work 50 hours a week instead of 40 will allow them to catch up. This sounds reasonable, but I have never seen it work. In addition, the test effort might well be chugging along just fine on a 40-hour-per-week schedule. It's often the case that your test team can only do 40 hours or so of work on a given deliverable, especially when quality is poor. Trying to impose extra hours on your team could actually have a negative effect in the long run, by draining energy that will be needed later.

Nevertheless, failing to participate in these exercises, or arguing openly against them, displays disloyalty to your managers and can destroy your advancement opportunities at the company. If you truly can't contribute anything by working hard, and want to conserve the test team's strength, have its weaker players put in the extra hours during the "show trial" periods of the crisis, and then bring the stronger players into the overtime mix as soon as they can be productive. If you feel absolutely compelled to dispute the intelligence of the crisis mentality, do so one-on-one with your managers. A widely distributed email or a public comment that rails against management is, politically, a suicidal maneuver.

Schedule delays tend to result in scope shrink and sometimes even in product redesign. If you begin to see significant, perhaps ill-advised changes being made to the product in an attempt to meet the schedule, it is critical that you communicate the effect of these changes to your managers. Again, though, diplomacy is important. Greeting news of an alteration by telling everyone who will listen, "That's the stupidest idea yet for rescuing this hare-brained schedule" won't win you friends in high places if the change was proposed by executive management.

If the schedule slips so far that no one — not even project management — is able to pretend that it can ever be rescued, replanning often begins. This is the rational choice, but it is not painless. You'll have to participate in planning exercises all over again, which can seriously distract your attention from managing your team.

Sometimes, management takes out its frustrations on the people involved. I've seen employees fired in these situations, especially those perceived as malcontents or flagrant contributors to the project delay. Since test execution is usually just beginning, you and your team are not likely to be pegged as responsible for the delay, but if you've spent a lot of time maligning the schedule or the management in the hallways, you are a prime candidate for malcontent status.

Along with firings, you could face a mass reorganization. A client of mine once proposed, in all seriousness, that breaking up the independent test group and having each lead test engineer report directly to the respective subsystem development manager would get us back on schedule. I had to muster a significant effort to defuse this initiative, and even then I lost about a quarter of my team to the development managers who claimed to need help with unit, component, and string testing for which they were responsible. Weird ideas become the theme as the consequences of missed schedules start to sink in.

Of course, scapegoat firings and reorganizations do not address the underlying causes of delays. Indeed, they create dysfunctional dynamics, such as fear, defensiveness, confusion, and miscommunication that actually exacerbate the fundamental problems and produce further delays. You will gain nothing by pointing this out publicly, however. If these types of actions are proposed or implemented, work behind the scenes to mitigate the damage to your team.

Even more frustration can accompany a slipping schedule if senior management succumbs to the siren song of ad hoc testing by unskilled staff, often on loan from other parts of the organization. This can happen when managers see all forms of testing as equivalent in terms of effectiveness and value. From this mistaken context, such ad hoc testing looks like a bargain: no test development is needed — just hurl a bunch of warm bodies at the product, let them bang away like monkeys, and soon enough you'll find all the bugs. In such a case, you must convince your managers that although ad hoc testing might do a decent job of finding bugs on a single release, it cannot improve product quality in the long term.

It's annoying when managers scrap best practices the moment schedules slip. Don't take it personally, however, and don't see it as a mark of irredeemable failure on the part of your managers. Remember that the end goal is to deliver a working system to users and customers — that's how we all get paid — and that management might deem it necessary to cut some corners to accomplish that goal. It's unfortunate that the corners being cut are yours in this instance, but you might still be able to make a difference at your company, so don't overreact to the crisis. We'll return to this issue of process maturity — adopting and sticking with process improvements that make long range sense — in Chapter 12.

Managing Outward

Let's assume that you work in an organization such as those modeled in Figures 9-2 and 9-3. The development managers, and perhaps the project managers, are your peers, sitting laterally across from you on a standard organizational chart. Additional peers might include the information technologies (IT), management information systems (MIS), operations, or facilities manager; the sales manager; the marketing manager; the business analyst manager; the help-desk, customer or technical support manager; the technical documentation manager; and the configuration and release engineering manager, among others. These are the people who see your test group as a team of professionals who affect their work, as opposed to seeing you simply as colleagues, coworkers, or people who happen to pick up paychecks in the same office.

Your Partners in Building Quality Systems: Development Peers

The toughest peer relationship to manage well is that between testers and developers. This relationship is often seen as inherently adversarial, but ideally it is a partnership in building a quality system. The bug reports that testers write are assertions that the system under test is not perfect. When a healthy peer relationship exists, developers will see these bug reports as helpful suggestions for quality improvement and fix the bugs. In less healthy organizations, programmers sometimes react defensively: they take umbrage at the tests themselves, considering them unfair; they claim bug reports are poorly written or unclear or that they consider the bug in question too trivial to waste precious time on.

Testers and developers must have fundamentally different outlooks to do their jobs properly. Developers must be optimistic to succeed. Why work long hours, give up weekends, and make other sacrifices to create something if you fear that the only result will be a raft of bugs? Testers, however, must pursue bugs with vigor and enthusiasm. Chapter 8 described testers as professional pessimists, who must think about ways to break the product in order to find these defects.

These differences of professional perspective can descend into rancor if you're not careful. Gloating over bugs, trying to catch developers in their mistakes, or making a point of embarrassing development colleagues will poison the well. Even though most developers and development managers do not take every bug report as a personal attack, the situation can devolve into a highly polarized one.

Despite these potential problems, there is no peer relationship in which it is more important for you to maintain open, collegial communications. Don't forget that the test team and the development team will either succeed together or fail together. A development project is like a boat headed for a port, with the entire team aboard. If the test group wastes time taking potshots at developers, they might succeed in wounding a few, but they will primarily succeed in shooting holes in the boat and sinking it.

Don't draw the definition of *developer* too narrowly, either. Anyone who provides you with products to test is a developer. A technical writer or a release or configuration engineer is also a developer. Testing finds their mistakes, too, and you must handle these relationships with care as well.

All these developers also receive a product from you: your bug reports. Most enlightened developers entertain a well-written, clear, conscientiously researched bug report with professionalism. Like your team, though, they are affected by the quality of the product they receive. A lousy bug report slows down the debugging process just as an unstable, buggy system under test slows down the test cycle. Unlike your team, however, developers' jobs do not involve helping you improve the quality of your bug reports. As I emphasized in Chapter 4, you and everyone on the test team must strive to provide high-quality bug reports to your development colleagues.

Be careful to keep your development peers honest about which test tasks *they* own and which tasks *you* own. As you begin to build an independent test organization, some development managers and staff tend to disengage from testing, assuming that your group, operating in parallel, is somehow redundant to their efforts. A colleague of mine describes this behavior as development becoming addicted to the new test organization, relying on you to perform tasks that in reality are the responsibilities of developers. Once development stops doing its own testing, an unfortunate scenario results, in which the presence of the test organization actually worsens product quality because the structural testing at which developers excel — and which complements the behavioral testing performed by most independent test organizations — disappears from the overall test program. A dysfunctional situation, indeed, but it occurs frequently. Proactive discussions with your development management peers can keep such a misfortune from befalling your company.

The Supporting Cast: Internal Service Providers

Some of your management peers are involved in providing services — usually some type of logistical or administrative support — to the test organization. If you are tempted to think of these service providers as in some sense lower on the political totem pole than the test group, don't. Because you must depend on these organizations to get, maintain, and use critical resources, managing these peers effectively is essential to your success.

The logistics database introduced in Chapters 6 and 7 can help you work with your management peers who are responsible for computer equipment, networking, and facilities. Don't be the tail trying to wag the dog, however. Before you put together a complete hardware, software, infrastructure, and staffing logistics plan using this database, be sure that the IT or MIS manager will agree to execute it. The plan you devise might conflict with the manager's other priorities, or the staff might not be available to make it happen. I have occasionally found that although I could propose a detailed plan, implementing that plan was not on the MIS manager's to-do list.

The human resources or staffing manager is another key person among your peer relationships, especially if you are building a new test organization. HR managers sometimes hold outmoded but still too common ideas about testers being low-paid button-pushers rather than skilled professionals. You will need to change this thinking before the HR manager can help you effectively. In addition, as Chapter 8 stressed, you might need the HR manager as an ally to remedy inequities that exist in your company between developers and testers.

Administrative staff and their managers are also invaluable resources. They can help with travel arrangements, procure necessary supplies for your team, and be an extra set of hands for reports, presentations, and the like. Moreover, in the more Byzantine sense of the word *politics*, don't forget that administrative assistants and secretaries often know all sorts of interesting facts. I'm referring not to gossip but to pertinent questions about staffing assignments, upcoming projects, and meeting agendas.

Help Desk, Customer Support, or Technical Support: Often Overlooked

A good relationship with the help-desk, customer support, or technical support manager serves both preventive and corrective purposes. Effective, proactive communication with the customer-support manager and team during the test design and implementation phases can add a lot of value to your tests. Most customer service managers have been on the receiving end of the fallout from a bad system, shipped way too early, with too many unknown (and even known) bugs. You can translate many of these field failures into a useful test case. To get an idea of how motivated these folks are to help you do a good job in preventing field problems, imagine the churn-and-burn atmosphere of an understaffed support organization dealing with a deluge of angry customers who just spent an hour on hold in addition to suffering some critical system failure.

The customer support manager also has a nonacademic interest in your test results. Bugs found during testing, if fixed, are bugs not reported in the field. The key phrase, of course, is *if fixed*. It's important, therefore, that you work closely with the customer support manager to communicate bugs found and bugs fixed, and that you set the manager's expectations properly. If you include customer support in your circulation list for bug reports and metrics, you give the manager an invaluable opportunity to sound off if it seems that the project is headed towards a major quality disaster.

This level of interest is a double-edged sword. If you don't include the customer service manager in discussions of bugs and test coverage, he might come to the conclusion, especially if significant field problems remain, that the test organization is incompetent. A politically well-connected customer support manager in this position might well agitate for the dissolution of the existing test team and its replacement by an organization internal to his group. I have seen such moves succeed, so beware.

This is another reason why adopting the defect detection percentage as one measure of test team effectiveness makes so much sense. This metric is based on two numbers, the bugs your team finds and the bugs that are reported to the technical support manager. The scope-adjusted defect detection percentage takes into account that management might reduce what's in scope for your test project, but either way, the customer support manager should be your partner in achieving the ideal defect detection percentage for your organization.

Business Analysts, Sales, and Marketing: Vital Allies

Like customer support managers, business analysts, sales, and marketing managers tend to have strong feelings about what you should test and what your results should be. In general, you should manage your relationship with these peers similarly. There are, however, two key differences, one negative, one positive.

On the negative side, some business analysts, sales, and marketing experts, even those with considerable experience in high-tech fields, don't really understand the complexity of testing. They might not understand your bug reports unless you are careful to describe the possible impact on customers in the summary. Even if you are, not all failures lend themselves to concise, straightforward impact assessments, especially sporadic but dangerous ones. It takes a technically sophisticated person to understand why "sometimes fails" is worse than "always fails" in such cases. In addition, sales and marketing people don't always understand why testing takes as long as it does. The "how hard can it be?" mentality can easily take root in organizations that are removed from the technical realities.

To a misguided few sales and marketing types, every field failure is a test escape. No matter how obscure a customer's problem, you and your team of knuckleheads should have found it during testing. I once took considerable heat for a bug that caused a loss of network connection on a computer running Windows. The failure occurred only in heavily loaded networks with one particular brand of network adapter connecting to one type of network server. Even when I pointed out that we couldn't very well run stress and capacity tests on every possible network, adapter, and server combination, since these combinations would surely number in the thousands, one salesperson continued to rail against my organization's lousy testing. The bug did cost the company a large sale, but this individual had unreasonable expectations about what my team could test.

I could have defused this problem politically, though, had I more carefully involved all the salespeople in discussions of test scope, which brings me to the plus side of the equation. Business analysts, sales, and marketing can provide useful support in terms of budgeting and scope. Strategically, if sales and marketing managers agree that high quality is an important brand differentiator in your market niche, and if you can then convince them that thorough testing is essential to achieve this distinction, you will have powerful backing for an effective, wide-ranging test operation, adequately staffed and funded. Business analysts who understand the mission-criticality of certain systems can help you achieve sufficient resources for complete testing of these crucial applications. Tactically, for any particular product, discussing with the business analysts, sales, and marketing people what's in and what's out of the scope of testing (and why) could spark a reconsideration of the project plan that would allow test to have a bigger impact.

Handle these opportunities with care, though. Reciting to the sales manager a tale of woe about the sorry budget you have and the screwed-up system that will be shipped or delivered because of poor testing will, at best, come off as whining. Assuming that the sales manager is not your direct superior, it could also come across as backstabbing your boss, with predictable consequences. A diplomatic opening through a telephone call or email — "Hi, I'm the new test manager, and I'd like to get your input on what we should be testing" — is much more positive. Be forthright in telling your own managers that you intend to have such a conversation to get concurrence on test priorities for the project in question. You don't have to declare your intentions to lobby business analysts, sales, and marketing managers for their strategic support of your test organization, because you're going to be subtle and indirect about that, right?

Testing in the Dark: Should You Proceed without Documentation?

In order to design, develop, and run tests, you need what's often referred to as a *test oracle*, something that tells you what the expected, correct result of a specific test should be. Specifications, requirements, business rules, marketing road maps, and other such documents frequently play this role. However, what if you receive no formal information that explains what the system under test should do?

In some organizations with mature development processes, the test department will not proceed without specifications. Because everyone expects to provide a specification to the test team as part of the development process, you are seen as reasonable and within the bounds of the company's culture when you insist on written specs.

Trouble arises, however, if you stiffen your neck this way in a company that operates in a less mature fashion. Depending on your company's readiness to embrace formal processes (and also on your personal popularity, tenure, and political clout), any one of a spectrum of outcomes could occur:

- Your management, recognizing the need to formalize processes, backs you up 100 percent and institutes formal requirements and design-specification processes throughout the organization as part of the planning phase of every new development project. Industry-standard templates for internal product documentation become the norm, and consultants are brought in to train people.

- Your management, not knowing quite how to handle this odd demand, assumes that you must know what you're talking about. The dictate goes out to all the organization's groups to support you, but since no one has any training in formal development processes, the effort produces poor-quality documents that don't help. Furthermore, because the effort is (rightly) seen as a waste of time, people are upset with you for bringing it up.

- Your management listens to your demand but then explains that the company just isn't ready for such cultural and process shifts. Perhaps things will change after the next few products go out, they speculate, but right now, process just isn't on the to-do list. Besides, this product is really critical to the success of the company, and taking big chances on unproven ways of doing things would be too risky. You are told to get back to work.

- You are fired.

The moral of this story is that you should carefully consider whether your company is ready for formal processes before you insist on requirements or design specifications and other accoutrements of mature development projects.

This situation is exacerbated by the increasing popularity of Agile methodologies.[5] Some of the people behind Agile approaches have endorsed a set of principles that include the following, "The most efficient and effective method of conveying information to and within a development team is face-to-face conversation." As you can imagine — if you are not already dealing with this situation — such a principle discounts the role of written specifications, encouraging instead an on-going dialog about the correct behavior of a system. In other words, the outcomes of discussions between stakeholders represent correct behavior. These discussions can happen in a meeting, but for some RBCS clients following Agile methods these discussions happen as one-on-ones between developers and another stakeholder.

I'm all for ongoing dialog between project stakeholders. However, unless there are written minutes from these discussions, agreed upon by all project stakeholders, including the test team, this approach has the risk that different people come to different conclusions about what the outcome of the discussion was. Of course, this is a big testing challenge if you weren't part of the discussion.

Even more challenging is the need to deal with the possibility that at any point the definition of correct behavior can change. The Agile principles including this, saying, "Welcome changing requirements, even late in development. Agile processes harness change for the customer's competitive advantage." While I can see the business value in being able to shape software like modeling clay up until the last minute, it's hard to create and maintain test cases if the definition of correctness is continually re-defined.

I will revisit the topic of development life cycle models in Chapter 12, including a detailed case study of Agile challenges on testing. When properly applied, Agile models can bring some advantages to the test team. However, they also bring challenges, not the least of which is the tendency to devalue solid, stable, documented definitions of correct behavior.

If you have to deal with a situation where the project team cannot or will not deliver written specifications well in advance, during test development, you might consider the following options for testing without specifications:

If you are testing a commercial product, remember that you have the benefit of competitors. Because your customers will expect your product to behave substantially like the products of your competitors, these competitive products are, in a sense, your test oracle. In compatibility test labs, for example, most projects have a *reference*

---

[5]For more on the Agile methodologies and their principles, you can start at `http://agilemanifesto.org`.

platform — a competitor's system, against which the system under test is being positioned, in the hope of demolishing it in the marketplace.

If your technical colleagues won't tell you what the product should do, perhaps your friends in sales and marketing will. In my experience, sales and marketing people live to create glitzy presentations showing where the product line is going. Although they can be general and imprecise, these documents might tell you which features and capabilities the product should support. If you're testing a product for which questions about supported features are harder to answer than questions regarding correct behavior, these documents might suffice for a somewhat vague but useful oracle.

Ask your customer-support colleagues. Your colleagues in customer support might not have much information about what the product *should* do, but they probably know what they *don't* want the product to do. Since your testing stands between them and the hellish scenario outlined in the previous section, they are usually happy to tell you.

Unless the product is truly unique, you can use inductive reasoning to figure out what constitutes reasonable expectations and correct behavior in many cases. The generic categories into which products fit tell you a lot about what the products are supposed to do: a word processor, a Web browser, a PC, a laptop, a server, an operating system. Some esoteric questions might arise, but a core dump, a system crash, a burning CPU, garbage on the screen, an error message in the wrong language, and abysmal performance are indisputably bugs.

If in doubt, you should consider any suspect behavior buggy. Because you don't have a crisp way of determining pass and fail conditions, you will make mistakes in result interpretation. Remember that calling correct behavior a bug and working through the bug life cycle is less detrimental to product quality than failing to report questionable behavior that does turn out to be a bug. Be sure to file bug reports when questions arise.

One thing to keep in mind about this situation is that you are definitely not alone. Many people are struggling with the right amount of documentation to gather, and errors are made on both sides. I try to maintain an open mind, even though the 20-questions approach to defining expected results is somewhat frustrating. It is a good idea, if you're working in a poorly specified situation, to make sure management understands that your test development will be less efficient due to the need to pull information from other groups. My usual rule of thumb is that the lack of clear requirements and design specifications imposes a 20- to 30-percent inefficiency on test development, and I estimate accordingly.

Pink Slips: Layoffs and Liquidation

Historically, a large number of testing and quality assurance organizations are disbanded within two years of their formation. Informal discussions on Internet testing discussion groups during the early-2000s recession suggested that testers bear a disproportionate burden in layoffs, especially in economic downturns. Anecdotally, I can attest to the credibility of these observations, having experienced multiple layoffs as a test manager. In some cases, I was asked to wield the ax; in others, I — along with most or all of my test team — got the ax.

For obvious reasons, companies don't tend to post big notices around the cube farm six months before a layoff, saying, "Get your résumés ready; here comes Chainsaw Al." In some instances, even the line managers might not know what's coming, although they usually do get a few clues. Based on my admittedly limited experience, and the shared experiences of some of my colleagues, I recount here some worrisome warning signs:

Being asked to participate in an employee ranking exercise, especially if this procedure involves every manager in the company. I have never seen these rankings used for anything other than whacking the bottom rungs off the ladder.

Noticing a decline in your company's revenues. In one firm, everyone knew that layoffs were coming when their biggest client stopped signing up new work and started to withdraw existing work. In another company, people were laid off from departments that still produced revenue, while the people who worked on a struggling, unprofitable product survived. Why? The company saw the success of that product as a "bet the farm" proposition; some bystanders lost that bet.

Noticing a sudden, unexplainable invasion of accountants or consultants, especially if they're working with the human resources department. Ask yourself whether the task at hand is figuring out severance packages.

Seeing the human resources department working long hours, even though no hiring or other obviously HR-related events are ongoing. As with the item above, there's a possibility that the long hours involve organizing a layoff.

Hearing any rumors of a layoff list. It might well include you or members of your test team. A test manager I know heard from other managers that they had seen a list of developers slated to go. He naïvely assumed that this couldn't mean testers, without asking himself how the other managers would choose to drop him a hint if it *did* mean testers.

> **Seeing signs that the independent test team will be reorganized into smaller units that will be integrated into the individual development teams.** At least one or two positions are likely to be overhead should that happen, especially the test manager's position.

Test operations can bear a disproportionate burden when it comes to layoffs. Although you can't always escape layoffs in a company that is doing poorly, the keys to keeping your test operation viable are aligning your testing with customer usage, crisply reporting the problems you find to the right people, practicing some of the political skills described elsewhere in this chapter, and demonstrating a positive return on investment (as discussed in Chapter 11).

Presenting the Results: The Right Message, Delivered Properly

As you run tests, you will find bugs. Moreover, because your test lab is the place where the product hits something like the real world for the first time, you will find all sorts of logistical snafus and poorly thought-out processes. This is especially the case when multiple development teams are involved.

Neither situation should take you by surprise. The bugs are your quarry, and when you find one, you and your team should feel satisfied. The disorderly fire drills that ensue when people fail to think through processes and logistics are less desirable, but they are hardly your fault, either. Nevertheless, you might find yourself received with dismay when the time comes to report your findings.

In ancient times, the messenger who brought bad news was sometimes executed, suggesting a human tendency that remains to this day. When you come to a meeting or approach a developer with news of bugs or unworkable test equipment, the first response might be defensiveness, anger, denial, or attack. I had a client who, in response to all the worrisome findings by a third-party test lab, seized on a few mistakes the lab had made. Every time bugs found by these folks were mentioned, the client would become infuriated at the mention of the lab's name, once sending me an email that said (paraphrased), "Get these idiots out of our life."

As dysfunctional as these behaviors are, you will have to deal with them. Even if others recognize the attacks as more appropriately directed at the problem rather than at the reporter (you), they probably won't leap to your defense. After all, they have their own problems, and getting involved in your quarrels will antagonize people. While you can't make the attacks go away, you can take certain courses of action to make the situation better — or worse.

Good Ways to Deliver Bad News

It's critical to avoid antagonizing your project teammates when discussing bugs, missed delivery schedules, support issues, and the like. Chapter 8 advocated professional pessimism, but too much pessimism approaches paranoia. The selfless, noble whistleblower who stops the evil, corrupt project team from shipping fatally flawed systems has become a mythical figure in the engineering world. When overplayed, however, such a role makes the test group the loose cannon of the development project. Loose cannons do not roll around on the corporate deck in the tempest of development for long before they fall overboard.

Likewise, you should guard against melodramatic reporting of results. It's important to maintain a sense of perspective about how a bug will actually affect a customer or user, which can differ significantly from how it affects you, your testers, and your test system. Holding up the shipment of a commercial product that is as good as or better than its competitors is a bad business decision and can cause real political damage for you. In an IT environment, delaying the deployment of an impaired but imminently useful business process automation application is likewise unwise. As a professional tester, you must keep an open mind during reasoned discussions about the business realities of delayed ship dates.

Expressing any opinion about the progress of bug-fixing efforts is also dangerous. I once made the mistake of commenting on a marathon, all-weekend bug isolation experiment undertaken by a set of developers, saying that it was "beyond my ability to understand why anyone would think that such an effort would actually locate the bug." The fact that I was right — the undertaking was indeed fruitless — did not win me any points from the developers involved, who were quite upset with me for making the comment.

Remember Don Quixote when you present your findings. Although a bug can appear quite dangerous to testers, developers often see the same bug as benign. While the truth lies somewhere between the extremes, you can easily come off as an alarmist. Worse yet, you can be accused of not being a team player if you perpetually hold the product up to unrealistically high standards of quality and rail against moving the schedule forward because the product isn't ready yet.

Sometimes you must make this argument, because it's true. However, you have to recognize that it will make you very unpopular, especially when people's bonuses are tied to hitting schedule dates. I engage in this argument only when it's likely to prevail on its own merits — the *emperor's new clothes* scenario, if you remember the children's story by Hans Christian Andersen, where it just took one person with the guts to point out the truth that everyone could see — or when failing to do so would approach professional malpractice. As the Jesuit historian Juan de Mariana wrote of his efforts to curtail the excesses of the Spanish Inquisition in the Middle Ages, "The greatest of follies is to exert oneself in vain, and to weary oneself without winning anything but hatred."[6]

Institutionalizing a Test Dashboard

One way to depersonalize the bad news is to tell the story using numbers and metrics such as the ones discussed in Chapters 3, 4, and 5. While I discussed the mechanics of gathering metrics and presenting clear, meaningful charts in those chapters, there are still strong political elements that you'll need to manage to institute a successful, useful, informative test dashboard.

First things first. The test team exists to generate useful information and effectively communicate that information to key testing stakeholders. The results reporting process is the method by which this happens, and the dashboard is the format in which the information is transmitted. Therefore, to succeed with a dashboard, we need to know who the key stakeholders are, what questions they need us to help them answer, and how best to communicate those answers to them. You already know who the key stakeholders are: the people involved in your quality risk analysis, the people who reviewed and commented on your test plan, the peer and upper managers discussed in this chapter, and the people who will attend the project status meetings. Talk to these people about the type of information you can provide to them, the charts, graphs, and reports you can present this information in, and the frequency with which they'd like to receive the information.

Based on these conversations, you can build a first draft test dashboard. Maybe it will look like the dashboard in Chapter 5, but most likely it will be different. Be sure to make the charts follow the questions you need to answer, not the other way around.

Once you have a first draft of the dashboard, take it back to your stakeholders. Explain the charts and what they mean. Make sure that you also explain the limitations of the charts. I have seen a lot of misinterpretation of test status reports — often of the wishful-thinking variety — so it's important to make sure that people know how to read the charts. It might help to also show people some examples of good and bad indicators using the charts. The sample data in the case studies, the SpeedyWriter and DataRocket charts, and the exercises at the end of this chapter can help you do that. Make sure that everyone knows what bad news looks like. Fine-tune the dashboard based on feedback from your stakeholders, but make sure people don't send you off on a wild goose chase trying to produce charts that you can't from data you don't have. This happened to me once when one of my client's managers kept asking for a

---

[6]Cited in Henry Kamen's, *The Spanish Inquisition.*

Rayleigh chart, which requires a defect removal model that didn't exist for the system we were building.

As you use the charts in status reporting, make sure that you continue to manage and fine-tune the dashboard. Ask your stakeholders about the dashboard. Is this providing useful information to you? Are you getting it often enough? Assess the credibility and accuracy of your status reports, too. Do you feel that people are taking your findings seriously? Are they acting on the reports? Do the reports paint a truthful picture of project status based on accurate data?

Don't fool yourself or others about the infallibility of the metrics, either. Since metrics can be gamed to advance a personal or political objective — anyone who's observed democracy in action is familiar with the distortion of statistics that fills each election campaign — quantitative results reporting by itself will not necessarily insulate you from your own biases or from a perception that you are biased. Therefore, even with the best dashboard, credibility is an issue.

While defining the dashboard is something you should do at the beginning of the project, the task is never completely finished. You should continue to adjust and improve your dashboards from project to project, and during each project. Think of your dashboard as a newspaper. Done right, it can be your most effective and efficient tool for delivering your assessment of quality to the project management team. As with a newspaper, credibility is key.

The Importance of Accuracy and Audience

A large part of credibility is consistent correctness. No mistake draws more attention and ridicule than telling someone else he has done something wrong when in fact *you* are the one who is wrong. You must ensure a high degree of accuracy in the test and defect data your team generates and in the information you collect and summarize from that data. The further up the corporate ladder you intend to escalate a particular bug report, defect analysis metric, or test status summary, the more critical this accuracy becomes.

Never send out a set of reports without reading every word first. Remember that typos and jargon can render your meaning unclear, causing your message to misfire. Time spent rereading these reports and fixing the errors is time well spent. Sending out accurate reports to your peers and managers is part of managing upward and outward, two key responsibilities.

Of course, accuracy is worthless if no one reads your reports or looks at your charts. This can happen if you send the wrong level of detail to your audience. For example, senior managers who need to look at trends will want to see just the dashboard. They'll also need your help understanding these reports, so you should provide high-level narrative with each chart, either as a cover sheet, as part of a presentation, or as part of the email to which the report package is attached. Individual developers, however, need to see detailed bug reports and might not care about the higher-level abstractions such as defect metrics.

Table 9-2 suggests target audiences for the reports and charts mentioned in this book. I assume that you will provide these items freely to your own test organization and expect your staff to understand at least the test status reports, bug reports, defect and test charts, and test logistics, and how these reports affect their assignments.

Table 9-2 Reports and Their Target Audience

ITEM	TARGET AUDIENCE
Formal or informal quality risks analysis	Developers, development managers, project managers, sales and marketing managers, business analysts, customer and technical support managers, executive management
Test project Gantt chart	Development managers, project managers, executive management
Budget	Project managers, executive management
Test plans	Development managers, project managers, sales and marketing managers, business analysts, customer and technical support managers, executive management
Hardware allocation plan and hardware/ software logistics database	IT/MIS managers, facilities managers, project managers, network administrators
Test coverage analyses	Development managers, project managers, sales and marketing managers, customer and technical support managers, executive management
Test results dashboard	Development managers, project managers, sales and marketing managers, customer and technical support managers, executive management
Bug detail report	Developers, development managers, project managers
Bug summary report	Development managers, project managers, sales and marketing managers, customer and technical support managers, and executive management
Test case details	Developers, business analysts

(continued)

Table 9-2 (*continued*)

ITEM	TARGET AUDIENCE
Test case summary	Development managers
Test suite summary	Development managers
Lab layout	Facilities managers, IT/MIS managers, project managers, network administrators
Staffing plan	Project managers, executive management, human-resource managers
Test organization chart	Development managers, IT/MIS managers, project managers

In addition to keeping in mind the appropriate audience, you should also consider the frequency of updates. Sending executive managers a daily update on test status, including all the items recommended in Table 9-2, is likely to exceed their ability to absorb and cope with the material. Developers, in contrast, might need access to these reports in real time; an intranet Web site, updated every few hours, might be appropriate for critical reports. Ideally, of course, you could simply give the entire company access to the tools used to generate the reports and then send out a formal update package once a week or so.

Note that *accuracy* has a different meaning to each audience listed in Table 9-2. A developer will probably tolerate jargon and less-polished grammar, provided that your data is solid and your premises and conclusions sound. However, a senior manager is much more focused on a solid summary line for a bug report, consistency between charts, and up-to-the-minute timeliness.

"You Can Tell the Pioneers . . . ": The Effect of Early Adoption on Test

As the saying goes, you can tell the pioneers in computer technology by all the arrows sticking out of their backsides. Whether they represent the first of a family of CPUs, a new way of connecting peripherals, a new generation of software, or a faster telecommunications process, complex software and hardware systems just never work as advertised early in their life cycles — a fact that creates major headaches for test managers.

As you might have noticed, sales and marketing staff love to have the latest technology bundled in their products. Nothing makes their hearts beat faster than to be able to say to a prospect or print in an advertisement, "We're first to market with this supercalifragilisticexpialidocious technology, and you can get it only from us!" Don't get me wrong. I appreciate sales and marketing people, without whom I would have far fewer job opportunities. And, in fact, they are right: being first to market with exciting new technology can make a huge difference in a product's success and, by extension, the success of the company.

Nevertheless, there's a price to pay during test execution for trying to evaluate this stuff before it is in wide use. It should come as no surprise to any test manager that some companies release products before they are fully tested and debugged. This is just as true of your vendors as it is of your employers. New products contain bugs, some subtle, some glaring. If your company incorporates those products into its products, or relies on them to produce products, it will suffer the consequences.

In addition, a new product might be fine by itself but suffer when it is integrated into another product. I once worked on a laptop-computer project that was the first to incorporate a particular generation of Intel CPUs into its systems. These chips worked well, but the increased speed and functionality meant increased power consumption, which affected battery life and increased thermal radiation, which in turn affected the heat dissipation design. These were not bugs in Intel's chip per se, but rather in our usage of it.

If you concede that lots of bugs are encountered in new technology, the logical next step would be to spend a little more time testing it. This is where yet another headache for test managers kicks in. The Gartner Group likes to talk about the *Hype Curve*.[7] When you are testing new technology during the Technology Trigger or Peak of Inflated Expectations periods, all anyone reading the trade magazines hears about is how great this new technology is. Guess what that means? When you go to your management with a request for several thousand additional dollars to test the new technology in the product, you might be met with incredulity or distrust. Even some otherwise-reasonable managers who have had painful past experience as early adopters can get caught up in the hype. As a result, you can end up woefully underbudgeted.

It's critical that you, as the test manager, remain the polite pessimist, dubious about the new technology, regardless of the enthusiasm raging around you on the project. Don't get sucked into the hype. People whose jobs involve being visionaries, product architects, and implementers must buy into it to

---

[7]You can find more on Gartner's hype curve at www.gartner.com.

some extent. After all, the desire to achieve the nearly impossible is a desirable attribute in these folks. However, test managers are professional skeptics. Even if you don't get the budget and the schedule to test new technologies properly, make the request on the record, and explain your concerns. You might manage to temper the hype a bit, and you might obtain enough resources to do a passable job of testing the new technology. At the very worst, you'll have the solace of knowing that you did your best to test the new technology thoroughly should it blow up in the customers' hands.

Note that not all companies face the risks of new technology the same way. The Gartner Group identifies three types of organizational behaviors. Type-A companies pursue new technologies aggressively, in spite of risk, to achieve predominance in a specific niche. Type-B companies wait until the earliest adopters have shaken out the most serious glitches, and then move in, mitigating some risk, but missing opportunities as well. Type-C companies linger the longest, avoiding all the risk associated. In high technology, type-C behavior is even more dangerous than type-A behavior: the business history of computing is rife with the corpses of once-strong companies that jumped at just one key technology just a little too late, and many companies have had near-death experiences this way. Again, keep in mind the greater good of the company. An organization that optimizes its processes for type-A behavior, while making your tasks more challenging, is less risky to your job security than a complaisant employer who waits until everyone else has worked out the glitches.

Ultimately, all the political advice and suggestions in this chapter come back to that theme. To feel good about your contributions as a test manager, you need to create an environment in which you and your team can do your best to find bugs. Most of the challenges are technical or managerial. Other challenges, however, are political. Any time people get together to solve problems and create products, even in the most tightly knit teams, politics are involved. Sometimes the solution is not necessarily consistent with the technical needs of the team.

Roland Huntford, author of *The Last Place on Earth*, tells the story of two teams, one English, one Norwegian, that competed to reach the South Pole in the early 1900s. The Norwegian team was the better organized and prepared, and it prevailed. However, during the expedition one of the members of the team, a man named Johansen, attacked the authority of the team leader, Amundsen. For this political offense, Johansen was excluded from the sprint to the pole and had to remain at the base camp on the Ross Ice Shelf, in spite of his skills and experience as a polar explorer, which might have been critical to the expedition's success. It was by no means a foregone conclusion that the Norwegians would beat the English.

This story illustrates the inescapable fact that, even in the best of teams, under the most perilous of circumstances, political problems will arise. You can be prepared to handle them and succeed in your overarching aims, or you can try to ignore them, which will expose you, no matter how talented you are, to the possibility of failure.

Exercises

1. What is the difference between quality control and quality assurance for software systems? Give an example of each.[8]

2. List the top three political challenges that you or your test manager face. How could you apply what you've learned in this book to meet these challenges?

3. For the following three exercises, find a partner or a small group of people who will role-play a project management team for you. In each case, you will be presenting a test status report that indicates a project in trouble. Present the status report using the dashboard charts and a verbal explanation. (The dashboard charts are available at www.rbcs-us.com for convenience, and show a variation on the quality risk coverage chart that uses absolute numbers instead of percentages.) While each of the three exercises is in a slightly different situation, some common elements apply. The project is our familiar SpeedyWriter example, the browser-based word-processing application. Second, the development team ran the component and integration test phases, component test from December 11 through December 29 and integration test from December 18 through January 12. The project is now in the system test phase. Cycle one ran from January 8 through January 14, and today is January 15. The system test phase exit meeting is planned for January 29, which leaves two more one-week test cycles.

   ▪ **Too many bugs.** In the first scenario, the dashboard for which is shown in Figures 9-6 through 9-9, the test team is working productively and finding a few more bugs than expected. A large backlog of known bugs (about 30) exists. Given the current bug find rate — which is not decreasing — and the backlog, the plan to finish testing in two weeks is in jeopardy. Furthermore, the high bug find rate forced you to skip a large number of tests in cycle one.

[8]This exercise was contributed by Dr. Deepti Suri of Milwaukee School of Engineering.

Figure 9-6 Bug reports opened and closed (too many bugs)

Figure 9-7 Test progress (too many bugs)

Figure 9-8 Planned test fulfillment (too many bugs)

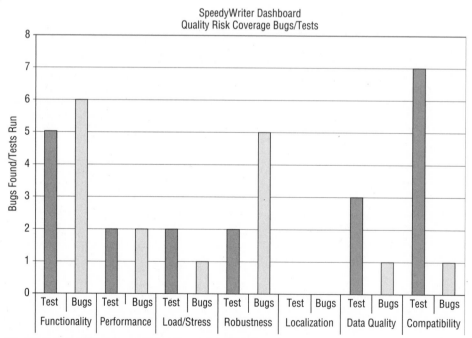

Figure 9-9 Quality risk coverage (too many bugs)

■ **Inadequate component and integration testing.** In this scenario, the dashboard for which is shown in Figures 9-10 through 9-13, the test team is finding a lot of bugs, even in basic areas that adequate component and integration testing would have found. The test manager has found out through a hallway conversation or two that component and integration testing were done very poorly if at all due to a schedule crunch in the development phase. Even with extra testers to try to get through all the tests, the number and nature of the problems block many of the sophisticated test cases.

Figure 9-10 Bug reports opened and closed (inadequate integration and component testing)

Figure 9-11 Test progress (inadequate integration and component testing)

Figure 9-12 Planned test fulfillment (inadequate integration and component testing)

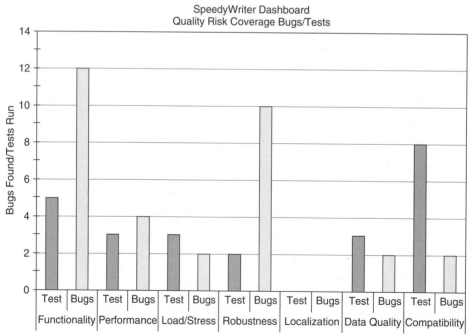

Figure 9-13 Quality risk coverage (inadequate integration and component testing)

Figure 9-14 Bug reports opened and closed (no stable test environment)

Figure 9-15 Test progress (no stable test environment)

Figure 9-16 Planned test fulfillment (no stable test environment)

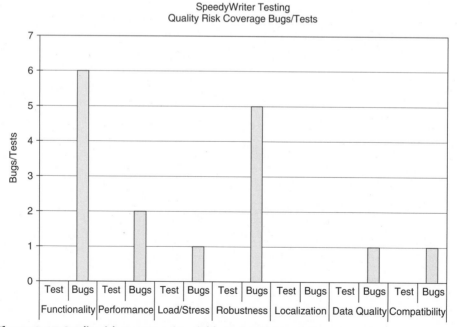

Figure 9-17 Quality risk coverage (no stable test environment)

- **No stable test environment.** In this final scenario, the dashboard for which is shown in Figures 9-14 through 9-17, the test team is totally blocked from running tests. The operations and development teams were unable to install a working test release in the test environment all week. On Monday the wrong software version was found to be on web server. On Tuesday the operations team discovered that a complete operating system reinstall was required to get the web server working. On Wednesday five different uninstallable test releases were delivered, one after another. On Thursday the server cluster appeared to be up, but the browser clients couldn't see the web server on the network. On Friday the application crashed the database server repeatedly whenever it was started. On Saturday and Sunday, when the testers came in to try to catch up from the unproductive week, the browser crashed repeatedly during testing. Pages and mobile phone calls to the operations support staff were not returned, and the manager of the operations team did not respond to escalation requests, either. Consequently, after dozens of false starts, no testing was completed during the week.

CHAPTER 10

Involving Other Players: Distributed Testing, Outsourcing, and Related Topics

Throughout this book, I've mentioned that various people and organizations in a company in addition to the test group have test-related responsibilities. Similarly, occasions arise when it makes sense to involve people and teams outside the development team or even outside the company to help with particular test challenges.

In some cases, we can distribute our testing work across various participants. I refer to this as *distributed testing*. This can involve an outsourced test team, but it doesn't necessarily. Assembling a distributed testing effort involves creating a hybrid project-matrix/skills-matrix test organization, consisting of the test team, other contributors within the company, and people who work in other companies.

Distributed testing comes in four basic flavors:

- Your vendors (those companies that provide components that will be integrated into your systems)

- Your sales or marketing offices (especially foreign offices for localization testing)

- Your business analysts, help desk or technical support, target customers or users (for alpha, beta, pilot, and acceptance testing)

- Testing service providers (especially for capital-intensive endeavors such as hardware and compatibility testing and performance testing, or for skills-intensive endeavors like test automation and security testing), either via insourced (your location) or outsourced (their location) delivery.[1]

In some cases, especially the latter, this collection of test teams doing distributed testing is called a *virtual test team*. Testing service providers sometimes speak of their offerings as *Testing as a Service*, especially when the work occurs in an outsourced fashion.

In some cases, distributed testing happens outside the scope of the test organization. Marketing teams often run the beta-test program in mass-market software and system organizations. For in-house IT projects, the accepting user organization might insist on running the acceptance tests itself. Since this book is about managing *your* testing processes, not someone else's testing process, I'll focus on situations where vendors, testing service providers, sales offices, customers, or users perform some part of the test work that is within the scope of your organization. Distributing testing in such situations means that you have extended your test operation, with all the benefits and challenges that implies.

To distribute testing successfully, you need to perform three sequential steps:

1. Choose your test partners, based on the specific testing you need to distribute and why you need to do so.

2. Plan the distributed test effort.

3. Manage the external testing as if it were your own.

The following sections examine each of these steps as well as suggest ways in which the tools introduced in this book can be extended to assist you.

Because the use of testing service providers is quite popular, throughout this chapter I will include some thoughts on how to manage outsourced and insourced testing. I've been involved in that on both sides of the relationship for about 20 years now, so I have considerable experience to share. Outsourcing of both development and testing has assumed the same role for software as it has for years in the systems business, so I'll end this chapter with a discussion about how outsourcing affects testing, including the situations where the development is outsourced. I'll also provide a couple of case studies on the appropriate use of testing service providers.

Choosing Your Partners

If you choose a Texas BBQ joint to cater your wedding, don't be surprised when brisket and beer, rather than caviar and champagne, appear on the menu. Likewise, it helps to consider your motivations and goals when choosing your

---

[1]In the interest of full disclosure, note that, among other test-related services, RBCS provides insourced and outsourced testing services. See www.rbcs-us.com for more details on our services.

test partners. Let's start with the question of why you want to use outside test resources rather than your own team exclusively.

You might want to get business analysts, help desk or technical support, target customers or users, or sales and marketing staff involved in testing to build their confidence in the quality of the system that's about to be released — or the testing that your team or some other team performed on that system. In some cases, the motivation is political, to make up for credibility deficits in the development team or your own team of testers. In other cases — especially customer involvement in acceptance testing — the motivation is contractual, since many outsource development efforts include a period of acceptance testing by the customers prior to final payment. I have worked on in-house IT projects that likewise included a user-executed acceptance test where a little bit of both applied.

More typically, though, my use of distributed testing, especially during system test, arose from one (or both) of two managerial motivations: either I was trying to leverage an external party's strength, especially one that I couldn't or didn't want to re-create in-house; or, I was off-loading work that I couldn't handle quickly enough. For example, suppose that you are the test manager on the SpeedyWriter project and that you have approached an external test lab, STC, about the possibility of performing some localization testing. Later you decide that some compatibility testing must be done with various hardware and applications, and you want to use STC for that. As for the localization efforts, Software Cafeteria's sales partner in Tokyo is willing to do the Far East localization, and your partner in Bonn can handle European localization. Your management decides that these folks will do a better job (and for free) and tells you to use them instead of STC for this aspect of testing. Finally, the marketing manager mentions to you that she has located a half-dozen customers with unusual use cases (workflows and documents) that she thinks would make good beta-test candidates.

In addition, suppose that around September 9 you receive an unpleasant surprise: Maria, a key test engineer involved in system testing, hands in her resignation. She agrees to stay through September 30 to finish developing the system test suite, but now you will need help running the suite. Because of the staffing and ramp-up turnaround time, you decide it's too late to bring a contractor on board, so you decide to have your STC test partners work with you during the system test phase, running the capacity/volume and network tests. See Figure 10-1 for a Gantt chart that shows test execution with these resources in place.

In the case of localization, compatibility, and unusual use case testing, you are leveraging the strengths of external resources. Your sales partners overseas have access to multilingual people who can help you with localization. Like many testing service providers, STC has access to more hardware than you want — or possibly can even afford — to maintain in your in-house lab. The customers' unique use cases consist of special documents they have handy and workflows they are used to performing. In this instance, it makes sense to use foreign sales offices, external labs, and users for these tasks, even if you could handle the work in-house.

Figure 10-1 A Gantt chart for test execution, showing staff resources, a contractor, foreign sales offices, and an external test lab

In the case of other system test tasks included in the three cycles of testing, you are primarily off-loading excess work to STC. However, with the load and network tests you are also exploiting a strength of the testing service providers, given the abundance of hardware these labs generally contain. However, your principal motivation is getting the work off your plate to avoid overloading your staff. You might have chosen to use a contractor, but that would have meant trying to staff a position in three weeks and then hoping that the person could hit the ground running in a critical situation three weeks before the planned release date. Using a proven testing service provider with trained, available personnel such as STC is a less risky approach. And given a small amount of work to off-load, the cost difference between using STC and using a contractor is probably minimal.

As this example shows, you can choose to distribute testing based on the factors of strength and necessity, with each decision involving different amounts of each factor. In some cases, though, necessity can tempt you to make outsourcing decisions that damage the success of your test effort. To avoid this, you should understand the strengths and weaknesses of various prospective test partners, as discussed in the following sections.

Your Vendors

When vendors are producing key components for your systems, clear-headed assessments of component quality and smart testing strategies are key to mitigating those risks. Consider this scenario. If you are the test manager for DataRocket, some of the obvious participants in your distributed test effort are your vendors. The SCSI card, purchased from a Taiwanese vendor, and the network card, purchased from a U.S. vendor, must work properly with your motherboard, with each other, with the hard drives, with any other integrated hardware devices, and with the software — but first and foremost they must work by themselves. What assurance do you have that the vendors are selling you a product that works? And, if you believe the product works, do you need to repeat the vendors' testing?

These questions apply not only to hardware, but also to software. Increasingly, software companies outsource development work to third parties, some of whom are separated from the main office by thousands of miles. Whether the outsourced effort includes hardware, software, or both, you have by definition distributed the testing. The question then becomes whether you can leverage the distributed testing to play to strengths and avoid wasted effort.

Component vendors tend to understand the testing process for their specific components. For example, I had a client who purchased custom telecommunications subsystems from a large U.S. vendor. I audited the vendor's test process to ensure that the vendor was testing sufficiently and to determine what testing my client could omit. I found that the vendor was doing a great job of testing the telecommunications subsystems themselves. The testing was focused inward, and the telecommunications subsystems, as telecommunications subsystems, worked well.

From the outward perspective of the telecommunications subsystems as part of an overall system, however, the testing was less complete. For example, the vendor did thermal testing on the telecommunications subsystems, recognizing that their customers would install them in computers. However, their test used an artificial case that didn't approximate the setting in my client's systems very well. When I pointed this out, the vendor politely but firmly declined to alter the test specifications. I received the same response concerning questions of software compatibility: the vendor wasn't interested in modifying its testing process to include the software operating environments my client intended to bundle with the computer. The vendor felt that testing the integration of the telecommunications subsystems into the system and its behavior as part of that system was clearly my client's concern.

In the case of a component such as a telecommunications subsystem, this limited focus might be acceptable. Because most telecommunications subsystems present standardized interfaces to the system, software integration occurs through this standard interface. However, for other components — even some that use standard hardware interfaces — integration could be a bigger issue. The moral is that, no matter what type of subsystem you integrate, you should consider integration issues in your quality risk analysis (discussed in Chapter 1) and plan for integration testing of those risks somewhere.

Likewise, if you buy a significant portion of your system, such as a motherboard, from a vendor, your project's success depends on the proper functioning of the component. It's fundamental to the success of your platform. Even if some parts of the system are not quite mature, you might need to begin system testing early. A fully functional prototype — even if it's missing the fit and finish aspects — is required before you assume that it will work.

Most vendors take a narrow, targeted view of their testing: they might test very deeply in certain areas, but they aren't likely to test broadly. (By this I mean testing across the entire range of features, not just those provided by the vendor's component.) Unless your product performs only limited functions — as an ATM machine does, for example — you probably need to complement vendors' testing with broad testing. Even if a vendor does a certain amount of broad testing, the tests are not likely to be as detailed as you need.

What is the risk to your system's quality related to your vendors' components? In addition to the normal considerations of risks to system quality discussed in Chapter 1, there are four additional factors, shown in Figure 10-2.

Figure 10-2 Key factors influencing component risk to system quality

Component irreplaceability. If a component such as a LAN card or a SCSI card is a problem, you can replace it easily. However, a motherboard might prove harder to replace in your system. If you need a database in your software, you should have no trouble finding various database options you can use. However, if you have a custom-developed credit-card payment-processing subsystem that doesn't work right, that will be hard to replace.

Component essentiality. Some systems include add-on components that are extraneous bells and whistles, nice to have if they work, but not key features for customers. For example, every laptop computer I've bought included a half-dozen bundled applications and other software doodads, few if any of which I've ever used. Many applications include add-on components that I know are there by the copyright notices and the packaging, but I've never used most. However, if you have outsourced the writing of the server-side software for a browser-based application, you are entirely dependent on that software working properly.

Component/system coupling. If a vendor's component is basically standalone — a LAN card, for example — and doesn't interact with the system in unique (and possibly far-flung) ways, the component is not tightly coupled. However, if it influences the overall behavior of the system, as security packages like antispyware and antivirus software do, it is tightly coupled. Software that interacts with common tables and records in a shared system database is tightly coupled. The coupling might be more than technical, too: marketing sometimes imposes constraints that couple your product to certain components.

Vendor quality problems. How much confidence do you have in the quality of the vendor's components? Smart outsourcing includes a careful assessment of the vendor's capabilities, strengths, and weaknesses — called *due diligence* — and that should include looking at quality issues such as development and maintenance practices and processes, teams, and technology, including testing. Does the test team consist of bright people, working in an orderly, planned fashion, with measurable results and repeatable processes, using appropriate tools? Are their findings taken seriously by management and used to guide the delivery of a quality product? It surprises me how few companies that purchase components or outsource custom-developed components actually include quality considerations such as these in their vendor selection and contracting processes.

You have a number of options for dealing with increased risk to the quality of your system caused by one or more of these factors. You can use the techniques described in this chapter to integrate your vendor's testing into a distributed test project starting with component testing — yours and theirs — which you track and manage. To the extent that vendor quality problems do not exist as a risk factor, you can trust their testing to deliver a working component, but make time for plenty of integration and system testing with the integrated component in your system. Most of the time, one of these two options has worked for me.

However, sometimes vendor quality problems are a significant risk factor. From a strictly problem-solving perspective, you have a couple of paths open to you. If you have the time and energy, you can fix their broken testing and quality processes by not only integrating them into a distributed test project, but also requiring the vendor to adopt process improvement measures. As a last resort, if you think the risks to system quality are huge and the vendor can't be trusted to help mitigate them, you can disregard their testing and repeat it.

From a political perspective, management will not greet either of these recommendations with great gladness. They are probably under the impression that the vendor is selling them a solid, tested component. In addition, if the vendor has a solid relationship with management, the vendor might put you in a tough political situation by accusing you of being an obstructionist or protecting your turf. Of course, you know better than to let either of these charges *be* true or *appear to be* true, right? Seriously, if you find yourself in this situation, I advise a cautious, circumspect, and politically astute approach to dealing with it.

Whichever option you end up with, you should plan on handling the bulk of the integration and system testing yourself and with other testing partners rather than your vendors. In my experience, my clients' vendors have done a poor job of integration and system testing their components with my clients' systems. Just because the component functions properly doesn't mean you have no potential problems in interfaces between the component and the rest of the system, end-to-end operations, reliability and performance effects, data quality, and most of the other integration and system test phase risks to system quality mentioned in Chapter 1.

You must also ensure that a process exists to support timely, conscientious, and unambiguous reporting, isolation, prioritization, and repair of bugs found either by the vendor or by the rest of the distributed test team. Many a bug report on a distributed project has fallen into a black hole created by an organizational boundary, never to be seen again. We'll look at some of the logistical problems associated with information flows later in the chapter. However, note that when we're talking about vendors, not only test results flow back to you, but fixes to problems must also. It can be frustrating as the test manager to get caught in the middle of an argument between your vendor and your development peers about where the bug lives. Make sure that you expand the bug life cycle discussed in Chapter 4 to accommodate the need for vendors to fix problems you find, and for your development peers to fix problems your vendors find.

Testing Service Providers

Testing service providers include any organization that offers test services to clients. Most of the time these services come at a fee, but some organizations provide some specialized services at no charge to the client.[2] The provider can offer these services on-site (insourcing), off-site (outsourcing), or both. I am excluding non-specialized staff-augmentation firms (*body shops* or placement

---

[2]For an example of the latter, the World Wide Web Consortium provides HTML standards-compliance and broken-link-detection test tools on their web site at www.w3c.org for no charge.

agencies) from my definition of a testing service provider, since they do not generally put skilled test managers on the project, offer seasoned, specialized testing experts, build turnkey test teams, provide expert test training and consulting as part of their services, or bring any other sort of thought-leadership to their clients. If a company merely gives you a contractor with the word *test* on the résumé here and there, and you direct that person as you see fit, you're dealing with a body shop, not a testing service provider. I discussed working with body shops in Chapter 8.

A testing service provider brings several key strengths to the table. The most important is expertise in test project management and test engineering. Those skills might also be specialized, tightly focused, or unique. For example, some testing service providers do nothing but computer security work, while others have usability expertise. These skills are not common and are not mastered quickly. If you need such expertise, working with a good third-party organization might be your only choice.

Another advantage is that testing service providers can often begin running tests for you more quickly than you could do it yourself. Some organizations maintain a loose confederation of subcontractors who can jump in right away; others have a staff of test experts on salary. In addition, some of these companies maintain extensive hardware inventories or software libraries that you either can't afford or don't want to replicate. For example, some test labs specialize in environmental testing, which can involve large and expensive equipment such as thermal chambers and shock tables.

A testing service provider, whether lab or consultancy or whatever, might also offer expert consulting and training services. For example, they might be able to help you through the hiring process, including putting a temporary team in place to bootstrap your growing test organization. They might have training materials for testing and test project management. They might be able to put you on the telephone with skilled and seasoned test consultants — or put those consultants on-site as needed — to help solve particularly thorny testing challenges.

A common theme runs through all these strengths: for certain assets, it's better to rent than to own. If that sounds counterintuitive, consider the following example. If you are a stable citizen of at least moderate means, you can rent a truck, a trailer, and some landscaping equipment and redo your backyard over the weekend. Alternatively, you could hire a landscaping company to come in and do it for you. Either option is somewhat expensive — the latter much more so than the former — but less expensive than buying a truck, a backhoe/trenching machine, and all the other equipment that a professional landscaping firm owns. If you only want to landscape your yard from time to time, why pay to have all that equipment sit in your garage for the rest of the year?

That said, arrangements with testing service providers can pose significant pitfalls. For the most part, these pitfalls are similar to the hazards encountered in hiring a consultant as discussed in Chapter 8. When you contract with an external test organization, you are the one bearing the risk should that organization prove incapable of discharging your distributed test needs. You might sue, but most likely a nonperforming external lab would simply walk away with one project's worth of dough and an unhappy client. You, however, could lose your job for choosing the wrong partner.

The way to avoid such a situation is for you to exercise due diligence the first time you do business with an external test team. When you hire an employee or a contractor for your own staff, you interview the individual, check references, and scrutinize the person's résumé. Retaining the right third-party test organization is not terribly different.

You begin with an interview, which is likely to be multitiered. In some cases, you'll speak to a salesperson first. This might strike you as a waste of time, but it's not. At this meeting, you can qualify (or disqualify) the company in terms of business issues such as price, turnaround time, and facilities. Remember that the salesperson is checking you out, too, gathering information about similar issues from that company's perspective.

If the results of this interview are positive for both sides, you should proceed to discussions with the project manager and the technical staff. Don't skip this step, and do insist that you talk directly to the people who will work on your project. (If the company won't commit specific individuals at this point, it might not warrant killing the deal, but you should inform the primary contact, whomever that might be, that you insist on approving any and all changes in personnel.) You already know how to hire good test project leads, test engineers, and test technicians, so you can apply similar standards to the individuals involved here. In fact, in this situation your standards should be even higher: these people will cost your company more money than the salaries of your own comparable employees, so you have a right to expect a superior level of expertise.

Be aware that the hourly rate paid for services from a third-party test organization can be more than for that for the same resource through a standard body shop. Premiums can vary from a few percent over the standard 33- to 50-percent margins of staffing agencies, to the whopping $300 to $400 per-hour rates I have seen from some particularly well-known consulting companies. You can justify such premiums when lab infrastructure, significant amounts of bundled consulting and training, or unique skills are involved. However, as a minimum the organizations should be reputable, provide seasoned people, and demonstrate a serious ability to reduce the risks to your testing project. While you will pay for quality, if you blindly pay, you might well not get quality.

Additional considerations come into play if the work is to be performed off-site. In this case, you are paying not only for people, but also for facilities and access to equipment. If you hire a test lab to perform environmental testing, for example, you are renting thermal chambers and shock and vibration tables, along with the skilled professionals who operate them.

Finally, consider the facility itself. I recommend an on-site visit if you are working with a purely off-site resource. What are your security needs? Do you require a separate lab? Do your competitors use the same facility? Is the facility geographically convenient or inconvenient? Does its location give you access to a less expensive pool of talent than you could find locally? For example, the lower labor costs you'll often find in an overseas test lab might make up for its lack of geographic proximity and the occasional trips you might have to make to coordinate the work, provided that they meet your skill requirements.

This might sound like quite an undertaking, but with luck you will need to do it only once. After you establish a solid working relationship with an external test organization, you can use it repeatedly. This trusted relationship can benefit you not only at your current place of employment, but repeatedly throughout your career. If you find a partner with whom you work well, keep the relationship going.

Sales Offices

If you sell a product internationally, you might have a local sales office or a sales partner (such as a distributor) in various regions. Alternatively, you might have a virtual sales office, with a staff member in the main sales office handling foreign sales. Either way, the sales office is singly aware of and qualified to evaluate the unique quality risks of the foreign market.

Chapter 1's list of quality risks included localization as a major category of risk for any product sold or used internationally. In some cases, testing this quality risk at the home office is well beyond challenging. With DataRocket, for example, you might need testers fluent in Japanese, Korean, Mandarin, Thai, Cantonese, German, French, Russian, Spanish, Italian, and Polish to vet your documentation and startup guides. How will you simulate foreign electrical power? If you include a modem, how about foreign dial tones? Which colloquialisms and symbols might be cultural taboos or just plain ridiculous? For example, in certain parts of Spanish-speaking South America, the verb *coger*, meaning *to get*, takes on a crude connotation that experienced speakers would avoid in polite discourse. In some countries, using an index finger as a pointer is considered rude. Few besides local people are likely to be aware of such distinctions.

As fellow employees, the staff members in a sales office have the same goals and objectives you do — they have a stake in ensuring that the test effort is successful. For example, the folks in your Tokyo sales office will want to do good job of testing the Far East localization of SpeedyWriter so that their sales numbers look good.

Unfortunately, these sales and marketing people might not have technical sophistication or a particular skill with testing. If you are responsible for the results of the testing and want specific items tested, you will need to spell out these details. Any test cases you give to nontechnical colleagues must be precise and unambiguous. As Chapter 3 explained, writing such test cases involves a great deal of hard work.

You must also remember that the salespeople, marketing staff, and sales partners do not work for you directly. They are typically peer or a peer-level manager's direct reports rather than your direct reports. Although you are responsible for ensuring the quality and completion of the testing they perform, you cannot structure their jobs, and you cannot specify standards of behavior, ways of interacting with your team, or circumstances under which you will end the relationship. As a practical matter, you might have to go to some amount of trouble to get results from them.

Users and User-Surrogates

In this category, I include business analysts, help desk, customer support, and technical support personnel along with actual target customers and users. Most commonly, these folks participate in alpha, beta, pilot, or acceptance testing efforts. (One of our clients, though, invites its customers' most-expert users of its system to participate in system test, using their own unique data and workflows.) As mentioned previously, testing by users and user-surrogates can result from considerations of credibility, contractual obligation, or from a need to broaden test coverage.

In the case of credibility problems or contractual obligation, your objective for such testing is confidence-building, not finding bugs. You do not want the test partner to locate any bugs that you haven't already seen. If you've been having trouble convincing the project team of the seriousness of some of the bugs you've found, you might want the users and user-surrogates to find those bugs, but watch out for getting on the wrong side of the project management team if you deliberately create such incidents. Ideally, involving such partners in your test effort should confirm what you and the project team already know about the quality of the system.

The most common examples of this type of testing are acceptance and pilot testing. Acceptance testing should demonstrate conformance to requirements and fitness for use. Pilot testing demonstrates readiness for production, either in terms of literally firing up an assembly line or starting to use the system to do real work. Clarity and precision about the meaning of the words *requirements*, *fitness*, and *readiness* are key to such efforts. I've seen a project terminated when the project team could not agree on the acceptance test exit criteria. To the extent that you, as the test manager for the overall development project, are involved in this, it's generally a supporting role. However, sometimes users or user-surrogates will witness acceptance testing performed by the test team, or use test cases, data, or tools developed by the test team.

In such situations, you might want to ensure that either the acceptance testers use tests you have previously created or that you have a chance to run their tests before acceptance testing starts. If the acceptance testers depart from the previously tested areas, they might well find bugs. Even if these bugs are not all that important, such discoveries could result in political issues for you and your team.

If you do need to broaden test coverage, then the focus might include finding bugs, too. Most alpha and beta programs are in this category. This type of testing can provide coverage of workflows, data sets, configurations, and deployed field conditions that might be tough to replicate in the test lab. For example, when I tested an Internet appliance, we used beta testing in part to understand how various telephone line conditions might influence connection speed and stability. These tests also give you a sense of usability issues that might not occur to testers, especially if your testers differ significantly from the users in application domain or technological expertise.

Be careful, though. Since users or user-surrogates are doing the testing, concerns might surface if too many bugs are found, especially bugs that indicate serious problems with readiness near the scheduled project end date. One of our clients told me that they developed problems over a period of time by getting beta testers involved before the products were sufficiently bug-free. This resulted in long-term reluctance to participate in beta testing.

Like acceptance and pilot testing, alpha and beta testing might not be the test manager's effort to manage. For any user or user-surrogate testing, if you don't manage the effort, be cautious about taking on the responsibility of tracking their results. Since users and user-surrogates are generally not experienced testers, the quality of the testing and test result reporting can be inconsistent. I've had people tell me that they've had great luck with such programs, and I have on occasion as well, but I've also seen indecipherable bug and test reports come out of alpha and beta programs. I also had problems with test engineers having to spend a lot of time supporting one alpha test effort that was considerably more trouble than the limited information we obtained was worth. However, with careful planning and management, you might find involving users and user-surrogates to be a valuable and economical way to leverage the substantial stores of application domain knowledge and real-world usage that they can provide.

Planning a Distributed Test Effort

You need to plan distributed testing with the same level of detail you use to plan your internal effort. It should be a straightforward process, given that you have your own operation under control. The starting point is completion of the high-level test planning discussed in Chapters 1 and 2. You should also have your own test suites fairly well defined, although a few details might remain to be settled. Your test-tracking and bug-tracking processes should be worked out, including a plan for deploying the bug-tracking system.

Assessing Capabilities

Once you've learned enough about a potential test partner to select the organization for the project, as outlined earlier, you next need to assess that partner's specific test capabilities as part of planning your overall test effort. You should approach this exercise as you approach any business meeting: with a certain expected outcome in mind. Compile a proposed list of contributions that you can check off as you go through the assessment, focusing especially on questions related to the areas of skills, staffing, and physical setup.

This is particularly important when talking to your vendors or potential testing service providers. For each proposed task, can the test partner produce an expert — or at least an experienced, competent person with the requisite skills — who will do the work? In many cases, you will be pleased with the skill levels of the people the vendor and testing service provider partner candidates will propose. However, in some cases the person you interview will not be up to your expectations. This is not necessarily a reason to eliminate the prospective partner from further consideration, especially if the person they are proposing is better qualified than any other candidates you've spoken with. Holding out for the ideal set of experts at the ideal test partner might mean having no resource available in time. As Voltaire said, "The perfect is the enemy of the good." If you must settle, make a note of this to use as a bargaining chip when price comes into the picture. In addition, as Chapter 8 warned concerning consultants, beware of bait-and-switch tactics, in which the vendor or testing service provider substitutes people with less skill than you have been promised.

With sales and marketing people, users, user-surrogates, or other coworkers or colleagues with no direct responsibility for running tests, the assessment must look not only at capability, but also at commitment. Can you be sure that, when the time comes to run tests, these folks won't be busy doing other things?

Adequate staffing is critical. It's often tempting to see vendors and testing companies as bottomless wells of skilled test experts, especially if that's what you need. However, every company has its staffing limitations. Some test labs keep client costs down by using primarily subcontractors and temporary labor, so you might find that they specialize in ramping up for test projects. Others rely on full-time staff. Assure yourself that your partner will be able to provide the entire team. It's not uncommon for a software or hardware engineering company that performs outsourced work to try to win business by overcommitting to clients in terms of the staffing resources it can bring to a project. Then, having won the business, the company is unable to execute. This is a disheartening experience for those in the company in question, but it could prove politically fatal to you if major elements of your test effort go uncompleted because you didn't fully check out your test partner.

Your assessment of your partner's physical setup should include equipment, facilities, and location. Does the company own the equipment it needs to perform the work? If not, will it be able to buy or lease it in time? Does the company have room, physically, to perform the work? Is security adequate? Is the location suitable for the tasks you are contemplating?

If the testing work will happen off-site, your assessment should be performed at the test partner's facility. For foreign sales offices and the like, you should try to travel to the remote site. Contrary to accountants' wishes, on-site assessment becomes more important the further the partner is from your home office. A partner at a less remote site is less likely to try to snow you concerning test capabilities because you can easily show up unannounced.

Understanding the Cost

Before you proceed further with detailed planning, a vendor or testing service provider might require that you begin to pay for the project. A testing service provider, of course, makes its money selling test services, not talking with prospects about test services. Your vendors might assume that further discussions are part of their deal with your company, but then again, they might not. Foreign sales partners, users, and user-surrogates might be willing to do certain testing for free, but you can't assume that their time is worth nothing.

From vendors or testing service providers, you can request a bid, which can be either a fixed-cost bid or a time-and-materials bid. If you receive a time-and-materials bid, you will need to estimate a weekly or monthly cost for your own budgeting purposes. Make sure that the bid includes some flexibility or contingency fund, not only for the inevitable changes that will occur, but also to allow for alterations you will make in the next step when you create a unified test program (as described in the following section).

In addition to the fees the test partner might charge, certain expenses are necessarily associated with distributed testing itself. Later in the chapter, we'll discuss the mapping issues that can impose some of these costs. Besides these outlays, you will have other overhead such as communication, tools, and travel. For example, if your bug-tracking or test execution tools will now have wider usage, will you need more licenses? Will you need to pay monthly subscriptions for online meeting facilities or perhaps even install new teleconferencing facilities? Gather all these associated costs and incorporate them into your budget.

This budgetary work might be tedious and can slow the process, but it's important to take care of it at an early stage to avoid getting stuck with a program you can't afford. Money always matters, and it figures significantly in distributed test efforts.

Collating, Coordinating, and Partitioning the Test Program

Your next task in distributed testing is to merge two or more test projects into a single unified test program. In general, you can think of this process as analogous to cooking and slicing up a pie. Various ingredients are involved in preparing the pie, but when the pie is served, a little of each ingredient will be on each person's plate.

Let's use another DataRocket example. Ignoring localization for the moment, assume that the players in a distributed test effort include your test team at Winged Bytes; the SCSI card vendor, Lucky Bit; and an environmental test lab, System Cookers. The goal is to produce a single set of test cases, organized into a collection of test suites, with each suite run by one of the three teams. Figure 10-3 shows the steps involved.

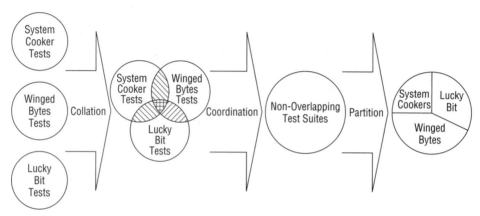

Figure 10-3 Integrating three distinct test programs into one

The first step, collation, involves creating a single list of all the test cases that will be run. You'll need to collect each team's list of test cases and add it to your test-tracking spreadsheet (discussed in Chapter 5). Use the spreadsheet's Owner column to keep track of which team is currently responsible for each test.

In the second step, coordination, you eliminate redundant test cases. For example, you notice that Lucky Bit was planning to run a thermal test on the SCSI card, but you would prefer to have System Cookers run a thermal test of the entire system with the SCSI card installed. Perhaps Lucky Bit can calculate the airflows required to keep each component operating within specifications and dispense with the test. System Cookers can attach thermal sensors to the active components and run the tests later. (Watch out, though, for partially overlapping test cases, as discussed in the section "Dealing with Mapping Issues.")

In the test-tracking spreadsheet, you can assign a *Skipped* status to each redundant test case, noting in the Comments column that the test is skipped because another team is running a preferable test. Don't forget to include the test identifiers in the comment so that people can cross-reference the other case. For example, a comment might read, *Covered by Sys. Cook. Test 3.005.*

Your third step is to partition the work, reviewing the test-tracking spreadsheet and reassigning test cases to new owners. Much of this work is done by default as you coordinate the testing, since skipped test cases are removed from a team's workload and eliminated from the list. In other cases, you simply might want a different participant to run the test case. Perhaps it is better to provide Lucky Bit with a system for thermal testing than to try to get one to System Cookers, because of engineering sample limitations.

This three-step process must take into account more than just technical matters. Budgetary concerns will surface if you change the scope of a partner's involvement drastically. Politics and turf issues can also come into play. A vendor might be happy to have you accept most of the test burden, but the vendor's test manager could feel threatened; the test manager might want to do more testing, but that could be counter to the vendor's business interests. Testing service providers always want more work, but only if you're willing to pay.

Another very important consideration if you do choose to reassign test cases to new owners is the level of detail with which those test cases are written. I discussed this topic at length in Chapter 3, but it takes on additional complexity here. Before you reassign test cases, you have to ensure that the test cases are written with sufficient detail to allow the receiving party to execute them. If the tests are not sufficiently detailed, then you must either re-write them to have the sufficient level of detail or arrange some process of knowledge transfer to ensure that the receiving party can execute them at the level of detail provided. Simply assuming you can throw test cases at another party to run without attending to this issue is a classic mistake of distributed testing.

Organizing Logistics

One of the advantages of distributed testing, when the test suites are partitioned properly, is that each partner plays to its strengths. This situation tends to minimize logistical problems. For example, if you use System Cookers to do your environmental testing for DataRocket, you have solved the logistical problems you would otherwise have in setting up your own thermal chambers, shock and vibration tables, and so forth. For SpeedyWriter, using STC to do compatibility testing frees you from having to stock and manage an extensive inventory of software and hardware.

In some cases, however, distributed testing creates unique logistical problems. The most difficult obstacles arise when a project includes one or more custom pieces of hardware, engineering samples, or other limited-availability equipment. On one project, custom-made security devices were in short supply, limiting us to two testers. In a typical laptop project, only one or two dozen prototypes are hand-built for the first test cycle. Adding partners increases the number of engineering samples needed, thus putting an extra strain on the development organizations. Expect to have to negotiate your share of the samples, and plan on making compromises.

Since these components are engineering samples, they break more easily than production hardware does. Because field support won't have any idea how to handle a damaged piece of hardware they've never seen before, the development team must repair failed components. Even when samples don't break, they might require updates to software or firmware on the devices, and to carry out those updates could require engineering skills during early development of the hardware. The support of the samples imposes an additional burden because either the item must come back to its point of origin for repair, or an engineer must travel to the remote partner's location.

Speaking of traveling hardware, someone must coordinate the delivery and return of these items. Shipping is hardly an art form, but it does require planning and consideration. A test partner of mine once returned three laptop computers — irreplaceable first-stage engineering samples out of a total population of 25 or so — that were broken beyond repair. The person who sent them neglected to use packing foam and instead placed the computers in a box, loose, and shipped them 5,000 miles. When confronted with the situation, this individual was surprised that anything had gone wrong — and expected the carrier's insurance to pay for the damage.

If computer equipment crosses an international border, you will have to deal with customs. Unlike shipping, this *is* an art form. Don't fly across the Pacific with four laptop computers in checked luggage, expecting to show up at a Taiwanese customs desk with a credit card, pay the duty, and go on your merry way, as your humble narrator once naïvely tried to do. Even with an experienced and competent customs broker, the process takes time and is not always transparent.

For these reasons, you'll want to keep the number of partners involved in your test project limited when you have custom hardware. In some cases, you might be able to give your test partners remote access to your custom hardware if their testing is primarily on the software side.

Even the software aspects are not without pitfalls, however. The problems in this area generally have to do with configuration and release management. It's critical that all testing occur against the same releases of the software at any given point in time. Otherwise, one or more of the distributed locations will be testing back-level software, and might report bugs that have been fixed and failed tests that now pass. At best, such situations cause confusion, so make sure you have solid, reliable distributed test release management.

Theoretically, this should be as simple as putting installable test releases on FTP servers or sending them via email, but it's not always so simple. Immature installation processes — which can even involve hand-placement of files into directories in some cases — often require expertise to successfully complete. For example, I participated in a project in which a remote test lab needed to have the custom software configuration of a laptop. We were forced to deliver physical disk drives because no one could come up with a workable method for delivering drive images either physically or by network download, nor could we figure out a way that the remote lab could reliably install the special software on top of a generic configuration. (Such methods exist, of course, but in this case, no one had the time to figure out the process.) If your test partners need to receive multiple software releases, you will have to spend time thinking through the delivery process.

One aspect of this release management challenge involves security. If you come up with a method of sending your software releases over the Internet, you might be concerned about someone intercepting that software. To handle that problem, you might decide to encrypt the software. However, if that encrypted software is going to be crossing an international border, all sorts of laws govern the sending of encryption technology to different countries, or using encryption within a country.

For example, at one point U.S. export laws classified some encryption tools as military weapons. France, until quite recently, actually prohibited the private use of encryption. The U.K. has considered laws requiring key escrow. In such situations, government licenses might be required. The same applies if your system includes bundled encryption functionality, which might be hiding in unsuspected places. One client whose system included a browser — which has 128-bit encryption in the secure sockets layer — had to get a license from the U.S. Department of Commerce to send the master system image to Taiwan to be put on systems there as they were produced.

You can use the logistics database discussed in Chapters 6 and 7 to help manage and keep track of the logistics of distributed testing. (You might recall that Chapter 6 included an example of distributed testing for SpeedyWriter, with testing being performed at Software Cafeteria's home office, at STC's lab location, and at John Goldstein's home office.) Of course, when you have remote partners, you might not need to use the lab logistics capabilities added in the version of this database shown in Chapter 7. Organizing their own lab is part of what you're paying your test partners for.

Dealing with Mapping Issues

If every test operation worked exactly the same way — according to the model presented in this book, for example — your planning work would be finished once the test program was unified, the work was partitioned appropriately, and the logistical problems were handled. The truth is, however, that each test team uses a different approach. You can't (and needn't) make every test partner work the same way, but you do need to recognize and manage the differences. I call these *mapping issues* because you are trying to map your partners' test efforts onto your own.

The first mapping issues usually arise during coordination, as you are comparing and sorting test cases. Figure 10-4 illustrates some of the possibilities you might encounter. Some test cases are completely unrelated to one another, and you must keep them all to maintain the desired level of coverage. In other instances, truly redundant test cases exist: either two test cases serve exactly the same purpose, or one test case completely covers another's conditions (along with additional conditions). Still other test cases overlap one another partially: test case A covers some but not all of test case B's conditions, and vice versa, but you can't drop either one without compromising coverage.

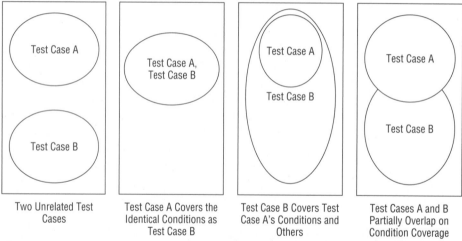

Figure 10-4 Examples of test case independence, redundancy, and partial overlap

When you discover partial overlap, you can sometimes drop one test case and then redesign another to cover the missing conditions. Often, however, you must resign yourself to some redundancy of coverage at the test case level. The amount of wasted time and effort is usually very low in comparison to the parameters of the overall project.

Test size, in terms of duration, effort, or both, can also complicate coordination and partitioning. Some test engineers write long test cases; others write shorter ones. Some test cases by nature require long duration or more effort. For example, reliability and environmental tests often run over a period of days. A three-day-long test case might happen to include some but not all of the conditions covered by a test case run elsewhere. You can't drop the test case unless you're willing to re-create all the work at the remote site.

You'll encounter other mapping issues during test execution, and you should plan solutions ahead of time. The most important is creating a process for getting all the bug reports into a single bug-tracking system. With the database presented in Chapter 4, you can use the replication feature in Microsoft Access to distribute the database to your partners, or they can connect to your servers. Many commercial and freeware bug-tracking tools include Web interfaces now, so enabling access to the bug-tracking tool in a central location is not any more complicated than enabling access to any other resource the remote team might need.

Because multiple partners are testing, you will see more than the usual number of duplicate bug reports. Even if you do a good job of coordinating and partitioning the test cases to avoid overlap, certain bugs will manifest themselves on multiple tests. (If you do independent two-party testing, in which each party is unaware of what the other is doing, you can use the number of duplicate bug reports to estimate the effectiveness of the overall program. The more duplicates, the better.)

Language can also be a major issue when it comes to bug tracking and test tracking. You can expend a lot of effort setting up a process for sharing data electronically, only to find that the teams can't communicate in the same language anyway. Unfortunately, using a nontechnical translator or administrative assistant won't suffice, since many of the questions that arise might be technical. Language can become an insurmountable barrier in some distributed test efforts. You should be sure to look into the matter before you set up such a program. Not every tester at every partner's site must speak a common language, however; usually, one or two people from each team can do the lion's share of communication work. I have successfully managed distributed test programs with vendors and test labs in Taiwan in which only one or two people on each test team spoke English.

Other mapping issues can stem from intercompany differences in work hours, conference calls, telecommuting policies, and the like. Technical challenges such as email system incompatibilities can create difficulties. Even unexpected legal and trade barriers sometimes present challenges. For example, if you plan to encrypt sensitive documents to be shared with an overseas partner, you might end up in the same bind mentioned earlier in regard to sending encrypted releases.

It's impossible to list every conceivable mapping issue. The fundamental point is that during the planning stages of a distributed test program, you must anticipate the differences — both formal and informal — between the processes you and your test partners follow, and try to put plans in place to minimize the difficulties. Once test execution starts, you will have little time to resolve these issues on the fly.

Managing a Distributed Test Effort

Once you become accustomed to it, managing your distributed test team as the work proceeds is not that different from managing your own company's team. You will find, however, that these five areas require special attention: tracking the test project and its findings; communicating test status and changes in direction; handling the political realities; being sensitive to disparate cultures; and establishing and maintaining trust.

Monitoring Test Execution

Chapter 6 stressed the importance of keeping the bug-tracking and test-tracking mechanisms accurate and current during crunch periods. You will probably find this more challenging in a distributed test effort, even if you have done a good job of attending to the mapping issues discussed earlier. Distance, time zones, and language barriers can all get in the way. If you are updating the test-tracking spreadsheet, for example, and find that you have questions about a set of test case failures found by your test partner, you could lose a few hours or even a day tracking down the person who can provide the information. If you need the data for an urgent presentation to management, this becomes a bigger problem.

Generally, you should plan for a certain lag in receiving results from external test partners, from a few extra minutes to as much as several days, depending on location. For example, when I worked with partners in Taiwan, our limited window for telephone conversations (early morning and early evening) meant that a miscommunication could go uncorrected for a full day. Email asynchronicity is convenient, but it also allows miscommunications to fester for days on end, especially when you're asking someone to carry out a task he doesn't really want to perform.

If you have a remote test partner whose work is on the critical path, there is no substitute for being on-site. A travel budget is important: a 10-day, $7,500 trip to Tokyo or Taipei starts to look pretty affordable when a loss of momentum by your test partner risks slipping the ship date by three or four weeks.

Although this might be seen as an argument against distributed testing, don't forget that there is also an upside to your test partners' isolation. Many dysfunctional events can occur at the home office during test execution, and having some of your testers insulated from the effects of those events can keep them focused on the tasks at hand. I once had a client who moved the test operation from one side of the building to another at the start of a critical 10-day test period. This was a major distraction that hurt productivity for the first two days of that period. I've also seen plenty of testers demotivated by the politics and frenzy attending crunch mode. If projects flounder, some managers have a tendency to pull people into frequent — and often ineffectual and distracting — meetings. An outside team, operating in a less crisis-driven environment, might make more headway than your own team, who is forced to react to the crisis of the moment.

Communicating Status and Changing Direction

None of your test partners can operate in a vacuum. You need a way to keep them apprised of what's going on, a way to allow them to bring problems to your attention, and a way to adjust course based on changing circumstances and test findings.

Email is not a bad communication channel for these purposes, but it can easily degenerate into flame wars and tangential discussions. If you use email to communicate status, it's useful to format messages as either a status report or a list of action items. A daily update of a short (one- or two-page) document from each test partner should suffice as a status report. (To keep it from being a running report, allow old items that have been finished to drop off.) Alternatively, you can keep a specific list of numbered action items, each with an owner and a due date.

The action item list is most effective when combined with a regular conference call at least once a week. During crunch mode, you'll probably find that such calls are necessary daily. A conference call should always have a structured agenda, with each partner reporting status and problems to the group in turn, followed by a review of the action items. At the end of every conference call, all the participants should agree on the current status of the test project and what is to happen next (i.e., the agreed upon action items).

These conference calls are also the right place to communicate changes of direction that affect multiple partners. Changes that affect only one partner can be communicated either by telephone or by email, depending on urgency. Be sure to track any alterations in plan in your change management database (discussed in Chapter 6). Changes affecting your test partners are just as important as those affecting your own team.

I've assumed throughout this discussion that none of your test partners compete with each other directly. If they do, keep the two sides separated. In one project with some logistical pressures, I needed to use two competing independent labs for testing, one in Taiwan and one in Los Angeles. I explained the arrangement to each lab manager, and both understood, although neither was happy about it. I had to avoid including both groups in conference calls, email threads, and project findings to ensure that no industrial espionage or unproductive sniping could take place.

If you end up in this situation, avoid the temptation to play one side against the other. Agitating situations in which conflicting interests exist is liable to have unforeseen and negative outcomes. In addition, both of the organizations being manipulated will come to resent and dislike you. Building up reservoirs of ill will between you and people with whom you hope to do business in the future is hardly a wise move.

Handling Political Considerations

While your off-site test partners might be insulated from the turmoil and intrigue of your development project, you will inherit their political issues. Everyone in a development project must be seen as an active, positive participant. Because third-party test companies and vendors are off-site, however, an image of them as noncontributive can gain currency. In addition, questions of competency and diligence can arise when the inevitable mistakes are made. Certainly, such concerns arose among my client's project managers after the laptop shipping incident mentioned earlier in this chapter.

Since you selected the test participants and planned the test effort, you have a stake in their success — not only their technical success (finding bugs and covering important test points), but also their political success (being perceived by the rest of the development team as effective, committed, and hard working). It is up to you to champion the external test partners among your internal colleagues on the development team.

It sometimes happens, however, that negative perceptions of the external test partners are correct. In some cases, they are a net drag on the project. Testing service providers can win contracts for which they are unqualified or understaffed. Vendors can prove unwilling to be frank about serious bugs they discover in their own products. Users, user-surrogates, and salespeople can turn out to be less interested in making a positive contribution to product quality than in carping about the lack of it — or even taking potshots at your testing effort. In spite of your best efforts, the logistics or mapping issues mentioned earlier might prove irresolvable in practice, resulting in blocked testing or useless test results at the remote location. In these unfortunate circumstances — in which, I should point out, you might never find yourself — you need to act resolutely to mitigate the risk.

Such actions might include pulling the distributed testing back in-house — a painful solution, because you will likely discover the problem in the midst of the most pressure-filled part of the test schedule. This is not a conspiracy to make your life hell. People and organizations fail under pressure, not when the going is easy.

You might also want to shift some distributed testing to other external partners. Working with two test labs, as I described in the preceding section, did make my task of managing the project somewhat tricky. However, in addition to the logistical benefits, it also gave me a safety net. If one lab had proven unable to carry out its commitments, I could have moved its work to the other partner.

Either way, severing a relationship with a test partner is likely to prove unpleasant. Lots of money is at stake, and people get emotional under these circumstances. Since you had a hand in selecting the participants and planning the effort, you stand to lose face as well. You might also fear damaging an established relationship with the test staff of the vendor or testing service provider. It's important, however, to keep your interests clear and consistent. Your ethical and fiduciary obligations are to your employer or client. If you handle it professionally, you can end the participation of a test partner without excessive rancor or unfairness.

Fairness in ending a relationship requires not only meeting financial considerations, but also maintaining an open mind in making the decision. Move slowly on such decisions, and consider the source of derogatory information you hear about external test partners. Distributed testing, while undoubtedly a good idea under many circumstances, encounters internal resistance in most organizations. Some people will resent the work being sent outside the company. These people sometimes act, both overtly and covertly, to damage the image of the distributed test program. Bashing the participants is one easy way to accomplish this. Do not disregard the concerns of such Cassandras, for they can be right, but do check out the story before making a final decision.

Being Sensitive to Culture Clashes

Any time your test organization relies on an external partner, cultural issues will become relevant, whether based in local culture or in the culture of a company. This is guaranteed by the fact that testers must, as discussed in Chapters 8 and 9, hold different perspectives than other technical contributors.

My own background provides some examples. I changed from being a programmer and a system administrator to being a tester and test project leader when I took a job with a testing service provider. All my colleagues at the lab were testers. We worked on projects for clients who were developing hardware and software, but usually we interacted with only one or two client contacts. This all served to shield me from the political and cultural cross-currents that roil test groups in broader organizational settings.

I was forced to adapt rapidly a few years later when I became a test manager in a small custom software development shop. Chapter 9 dealt with the political realities of testing within the context of a development organization, lessons I learned to a great extent in that first test manager position. I have since relearned those same lessons, with a few variations, with subsequent employers and clients.

When you implement a distributed test program, you will experience these cultural issues writ large. Perspectives, priorities, and values differ from one team to the next even within a company, depending on the personalities of the team members, the leadership skills of the manager, the integrity of the perceived technical and moral leaders of the team (not just the manager), and, not least, the mission that team serves. When you deal with external organizations, these cultural issues are intensified by the fact that the leaders of the partner companies can instill different values. Although I always emphasize the importance of individual contributors to the success of a team, I am often reminded, sometimes shockingly, of how much the vision, ethics, and leadership skills of a handful of top managers in a company can profoundly influence the way in which even the most mundane tasks are performed.

In terms of distributed testing, such differences can mean that some individuals who would fail as test technicians, test engineers, or test managers in your company are seen as consummate test professionals perfectly aligned with the company culture in your test partners' organizations. For example, I place great value on cooperative relationships between testers and developers. In contrast, however, some successful organizations use an adversarial approach, with test managers encouraging testers to catch developers in errors. I would find it too emotionally draining to work in an organization where employees sought to undermine each other's successes, but if I worked with a test partner that used such an approach, it would hardly be within my purview to try to change that culture. Nevertheless, I might find the internecine quarrels distracting, to the extent that they spilled over into my life.

More subtle but equally challenging cultural clashes can occur. For example, I had a client who (at my recommendation) used an external lab in Taipei to handle some compatibility testing. The client's vendor was also located in Taipei. The test lab's corporate culture encouraged flexible but long hours, as my client did. The vendor involved had an 8-to-5 culture. Ironically, when we needed to institute regular conference calls, the vendor's culture and my client's culture meshed, but the time difference worked against the test lab. We had to schedule the calls for 8:30 a.m. Taipei time, which was fine for the vendor but troublesome for the project leader in the test lab, who worked from noon to midnight by choice. Ultimately, I decided to excuse him from the call, making sure I understood their results and could represent their findings. This allowed the test manager to continue working his comfortable schedule. Had I insisted that he start working cumbersome hours, that could have damaged our relationship, and it probably would have made him less productive.

Building and Maintaining Trust

More fundamental than congruent cultures is the question of whether you can trust your test partners. Trust is an even more slippery concept than culture, but we all recognize people we trust or distrust. Even those who spend time building trust with us can lose it at a moment's notice. Suppose that you are the manager at Winged Bytes, working on DataRocket. A colleague of yours, the test manager for the SCSI-card vendor, has been scrupulous about reporting any problems the vendor's test team finds, not just on this project but also on two previous projects. Suppose now that the test manager delays or conceals news of a fatal bug in the card's BIOS. That trust, built up over years, will suffer a serious, perhaps fatal, setback.

All the tools and tips discussed in this chapter cannot resolve this problem. If you partition your test program to have test partners execute critical tests, you must establish a relationship of trust. You have to trust that the testing service provider won't skip a few tests because it's running behind schedule and fears that it will lose money on your project. You have to trust your vendor to be frank about even the most embarrassing bugs. You have to trust your colleagues in the foreign sales office to follow up with test results so that you aren't scrambling at the last minute to deal with critical bugs. You have to trust users and user-surrogates not to use testing results to slam your team — or the project.

Trust also involves more than ensuring that your partners won't take advantage of you. You must look out for them, too. For example, I have helped test partners on my projects work through problems with invoices and contracts. There is, of course, a narrow path to tread in such matters, as you have fiduciary responsibilities to your employer. However, assisting your chosen test partners in dealing with a nebulous or sluggish accounts payable problem shows good faith and a concern for your partner's success. When people know you are looking out for them, they'll usually look out for you.

In closing this section, it's worthwhile to point out that trust isn't an issue only for your external test partners. It is critical for the entire project team, whether those people work at one company or at several. You have to assume that people are all pulling for the success of the project, by playing their individual roles to the best of their abilities. You must also assume that people are pulling for the success of their collaborators.

The cliché about a few bad apples spoiling the barrel applies especially to trust in an organization, but it's also true that key leaders in a firm, by setting an example of trustworthiness, can set a company-wide standard. People who consistently apply their best efforts create passion and dedication. People who support all their colleagues and cooperate for the good of the team foster an environment filled with confidence and good will. No one, though, can contribute as much to a trusting and open company culture as a manager can. Managers who keep their commitments, who never let underlings take the fall for their own failings, who support and celebrate the successes of their star players, their team, and the company as a whole, who balance the company's needs with the personal needs of their subordinates and colleagues, and who consistently give and expect the truth from their staff, their peers, or their own managers, cultivate a corporate culture of trust and integrity. As a test manager, you must participate in creating and upholding an environment of trust, both within your team and across the company. The standard you set in your team is as important as anything else you do.

How Outsourcing Affects Testing

Up to this point, I've discussed distributed testing primarily in the sense that you, as the test manager, are making a decision to distribute your testing. Further, I have focused on situations where the testing itself is the key element being distributed. You could consider this a *from the inside looking out* perspective; i.e., how you manage testing when an option is distribution of testing.

Over the last 20 years, outsource development of one or more key components in the system has come to dominate software and hardware systems engineering. The trend started in hardware in the 1990s. RBCS clients like Dell, Hitachi, Hewlett-Packard, and other computer systems vendors took advantage of cheap yet educated labor overseas to compete effectively in an increasingly commoditized market.

Outsourcing spread slowly into software in the 1990s. However, in 2000, a series of events unfolded that accelerated the inevitable. The near-simultaneous bursting of the telecom and dot-com bubbles in 2000 combined with the Y2K and Euro-conversion wind-downs, making the software industry and its customers more conservative and price-conscious. This already-unsettled situation then collided with the ferocious 2001/2002 global recession. By the end of 2002, when after three years into a spectacular IT downturn computer science enrollments in the United States fell to less than half of their 1999 levels, price had become the primary determinant in most IT project decisions. Mass outsourcing of software projects took hold, and it continues unabated to this day.

As with hardware, commoditization plays a role with software outsourcing. Software as a Service (SaaS) represents one facet of commoditized software, and it is clearly a form of pay-as-you-go outsourcing. The use of open source packages represents another facet of commoditized software, being a form of pay-nothing-as-you-go outsourcing (albeit requiring potentially expensive self-support).

Another interesting factor to observe is that the Cold War ended in 1989, right as outsourcing as we know it today was born. The Cold War was a clash of ideologies between socialism and capitalism, and capitalism won. Capitalism is a system for maximizing return on capital, and one mechanism for doing that is reducing the cost of inputs required to produce an output. With the ongoing trends toward bundling applications with other applications and with computers, focusing on core competencies, commoditization of hardware and software, using cheaper offshore labor inputs to maximize return on capital, and insourcing of implementation of in-house IT systems, don't expect an end to this outsourcing trend any time soon.

I believe in the use of outsourced teams to provide key components and services as part of a project. If I didn't, RBCS would not provide outsource testing services. However, some RBCS clients have made the mistake of assuming that they could outsource without any risk, without any management or oversight, and without any implications to their practices and processes. I have seen more than one manager, beguiled by clever marketing and sales presentations, impressive client lists, or low hourly rates, who then lost control of key risks to the project. Risks to system quality are among them.

Therefore, we also need to consider a *from the outside looking in* perspective; i.e., how you manage testing when a constraint is distribution of some of the testing, all of the testing, and perhaps even the entire development effort.

So, let me draw the scope of this discussion broadly at this point, and examine the effects. By outsourcing, I mean sending work outside of the organization, with variations that include the following:

- Outsource the development, but retain the testing in-house.
- Outsource the development and the testing to one company only.
- Outsource the development and the testing to two different companies.
- Outsource the development and/or the testing, each to multiple companies.

As you can see, this includes the distributed testing scenarios discussed earlier, but also includes other possible scenarios.

In addition, let's consider situations where the management of the project might be hands-on (directly, day-to-day direction of the outsourced work) or hands-off. Further, we have to understand that the location of the outsourcing might be across the hall in the same building, across street, across the town, across the country, or across the globe.

To manage testing in an outsourced situation, we also have to understand the reasons for it. These can include both spoken, readily acknowledged reasons, and unspoken, possibly present but often unacknowledged or even denied reasons.

The spoken, readily acknowledged reasons can include the following:

- The desire to realize labor and other cost savings.
- The expertise, capital equipment, or geographical advantages of the outsource organization.
- The need for system or product certification by a qualified service provider.
- The inability to handle the work in-house, either due to a temporary spike in workload or a one-off project.

The unspoken, possibly present but often unacknowledged or even denied reasons can include the following:

- Organizational or peer pressure on decision-makers to outsource, which is the "everybody's doing it" argument.

- Dissatisfaction with the in-house team's capability, whether for service, cost, attitude, quality, or some other reason, which is the "it couldn't be worse, at least it's cheaper" argument.

Gartner Group calls outsourcing an "irreversible megatrend."[3] So, love it or hate it, outsourcing is here to stay, for reasons spoken or unspoken, fair or foul. It's pretty much an oncoming train for us in this industry. As a test manager, your choices are stark and simple. You can get on the train and make it work. You can stand in front of the train and hope for the best. Or you can change careers into a field you believe is not subject to outsourcing.

I have come to the conclusion that the first choice is the only viable one for me and my company if we are to remain in the testing business. If you agree, let's look at how outsourcing affects testing.

Increased Need for Organization

To set the stage for properly utilizing outsourcing, the project will need to achieve a great degree of organization. Chaos will not scale across multiple organizations. This can pose a special challenge to organizations using Agile methodologies like Scrum (see Chapter 12 for a discussion of various life cycle methodologies, including Agile), since many of the enablers of these will not be present on outsource projects. You can't count on chance emails or hallway discussions to give the team information or clues about what is going well or poorly.

A number of our clients have not recognized that outsourcing greatly increases project complexity. Coordinating disparate groups of people, often separated by thousands of miles and many time zones, is a complicated endeavor. Like any complex human endeavor, careful planning, precise organization, and closely tracked and managed execution are key to success. This includes the need for careful mapping, integrating, and standardizing of the activities, as discussed earlier in this chapter.

I mentioned Agile methodologies a moment ago. I don't mean to suggest that you can't tailor these methodologies to work in an outsourced situation. Whatever methodology your organization chooses, the chosen and possibly tailored development or maintenance life cycle processes must have the following attributes:

---

[3]For their full position on this, check www.gartner.com/press_releases/ pr23june2003b.html.

- They must allow for distribution of work.

- They must provide for checkpoints and course correction at regular, predictable, reasonable intervals. By reasonable I mean not too frequent or too infrequent.

- They must include ways to reduce complexity in hand-offs, touchpoints, communications, change management, and so forth.

Unsuitable or cumbersome life cycle processes can complicate, delay, or entirely block work on outsource projects.

For example, let's assume your project follows a sequential, V-model life cycle (see Chapter 12 for more explanation on this model). As shown in Figure 10-5, the project must have careful project management and change management activities in place at the end of each stage of the life cycle. Otherwise, you run the risk of serious changes and deviations from plan accumulating in the project, which might become visible only during late-phase testing.

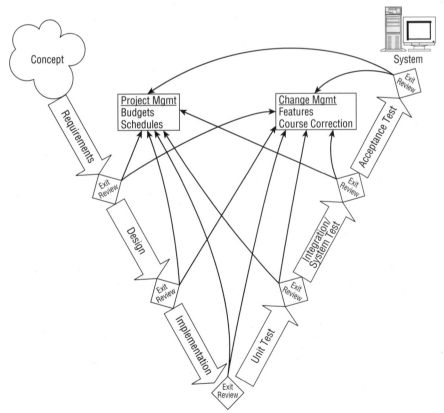

Figure 10-5 Project management and change management in outsourced projects

Selecting the Right Test Team

Testing plays a key gate-keeping role in a project. When pervasive testing is practiced, as I have advocated throughout this book, it also provides an early-warning-system role. So, in an outsourced project, you have to select the right test teams to perform the various testing tasks, keeping both roles in mind.

If you intend to outsource some or all of the testing on a project, success depends on the following factors:

- ▪ You have to select the right testers for the testing tasks, with the right skills. This includes test management skills for large chunks of testing work that will be outsourced.

- ▪ The outsourced testers must have access to the right equipment, the right tools, the right infrastructure, and so forth. If the assumption is that the outsourced testing will use equipment, tools, and infrastructure that you have in-house, this will not happen by magic, but will require careful planning and management of the logistics of that.

- ▪ The outsourced testers must have the ability to adapt their work to your project and your organization.

- ▪ The outsourced testers must have sufficient independence to tell the straight truth about their results.

This all sounds obvious, I suppose, but, in my consulting work, I have seen two really risky outsource testing assumptions arise again and again. The first is that an organization can contract with a single service provider to outsource both development and testing work, and that service provider can (and will) test competently. The second is that, failing competent testing by the service provider, acceptance testing by the contracting organization will suffice to prevent disastrous releases. As with any risks, you have to ask what the likelihood and impact will be if these assumptions are invalid.

Serious conflicts of interest occur when the service provider develops a product and then tests its own work. Similar conflicts of interest occur if you insist on outside testing but allow the service provider that developed the product to hire the test partner. To list just a few of these problems, notice that independence of testing is compromised in both cases. Fresh perspectives might not always be available, even if the test partner is external (but hired by and working for the development organization). In both cases, financial incentives can work against you.

To address the second assumption that acceptance testing by the contracting organization will suffice to prevent disastrous releases, although acceptance testing of the deliverable is necessary, by itself it is not sufficient. If you find serious problems during acceptance testing, what practical options might exist? Sure, your company could sue the development organization for failure to perform, but where does that leave your company in the interim during the lawsuit?

I suggest that, when outsourced development occurs, companies consider hiring an external testing service provider with no conflicts of interest, or handle all the testing work in-house. There are plenty of cheap, geographically convenient, and independent testing service providers available, no matter where you outsource the development. The modest increase in project cost and complexity is worth the peace of mind and reduced risk.

Another team-related challenge with outsourcing relates to the level of skills and, in many cases, the number of people at those skills levels, available in the outsource region compared to the outsourcing region. This is an issue because, in many cases, for reasons of labor pricing, outsourcing organizations choose to outsource to developing regions.

In a developing region, both the number of people with the appropriate level of skills at entry-level positions and the number of people with sufficient skills at senior technical and leadership positions might be limited compared to those in a developed region. You can see this by comparing Figure 10-6 with Figure 10-7. This is a hard matter to explore, for two reasons. First, the outsourced staff can only compare their skills relatively. Therefore, they will tend to measure their level of skills in relative terms, rather than against the level of skills available in the outsourcing region, which is often more developed. Second, the outsource organization has a strong financial incentive to inflate their skills relative to the skills available to the outsourcing organization.

Figure 10-6 Skills pyramids in developing regions

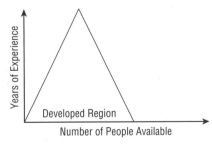

Figure 10-7 Skills pyramids in developed regions

This creates a real issue for testing, in two ways. First, the outsource organization will tend to lack deep skills and experience in fields that may be required of them, such as performance testing, reliability testing, and test management. The problem is especially acute in terms of a lack of seasoned test managers, the kind of people who have been through dozens of projects and have a good ability to intuit and manage sources of test project risks. Second, because of the lack of deep skills and experience, outsource test teams in developing regions tend to lack the access to mentoring by highly skilled and experienced staff that people take for granted in developed regions.

Finally, since this topic comes up a lot in terms of selecting outsource development organizations, let's talk about what accreditation under Compatibility Maturity Model Integration (CMMI) or some similar development process model does — and does not — tell you about testing and quality. To start with, let me say that I am not opposed to process formalization programs such as CMMI. I believe that they can result in quality improvement when used properly. However, even Bill Curtis of the Software Engineering Institute admitted (at the ASM/SM 2002 conference) that, when used purely as a marketing device, CMMI does not result in significant quality or efficiency improvements.[4]

Even if you find a vendor who is using CMMI properly and achieving quality and efficiency improvements from it, it's important to understand that CMM does not say much about testing. In other words, the various key process areas and key process indicators used in the CMM model are not the same as those one would use to assess testing capability. So, even an organization that achieves CMMI level-5 maturity for its software engineering processes can score low in test maturity.

To determine what we could and could not say about testing based on a maturity-level rating, I did an analysis by reviewing the Capability Maturity Model against my own Critical Testing Processes framework.[5] The results are

---

[4]You can find an abstract of Curtis's talk at `www.sqe.com/Events/archive /asm2002/keynotes.html`. While the talk focused on some specific issues, listening to it, I found the *meta-issue* (if I can coin a term) the most fascinating element. Here was one of the fathers of the Capability Maturity Model, developed by the Software Engineering Institute on behalf of the U.S. Department of Defense to create an ungameable system by which the Department of Defense could evaluate potential software vendors, and he was admitting that this model could be gamed. In other words, if vendors could obtain a high maturity rating by displaying to assessors the accoutrements of maturity, even while not achieving the proper outcomes, and then could serially use that rating to convince potential customers that they were obtaining the proper outcomes on evidence of the rating alone, it's hard to come to a conclusion other than that the Software Engineering Institute had failed in the mission set to it by the Department of Defense. So much for the attempt to simplify the outsource organization selection to a matter of a 1-to-5 scale. *Caveat emptor.*

[5]This test assessment and improvement framework appears in my book *Critical Testing Processes*. RBCS consultants have used this test assessment model to assess and improve test process capability for a number of clients around the world.

in Table 10-1. The 12 critical testing processes are shown in the first column. The second column shows the corresponding level of CMM maturity that addresses that critical testing process. The numbers in italics indicate the CMM level that requires the software engineering process to include activities that support testing maturity for that critical testing process. The numbers in bold indicate the CMM level at which I think you could assume, with a reasonable degree of confidence, that the organization handled that critical testing process properly.

Table 10-1 Measuring the Testing Maturity of CMM

CRITICAL TESTING PROCESS	CMM
Testing overall	*2 3 4 5*
Test team alignment	*3*
Risk-based testing	*3* **4**
Test estimation	*2 3* **4**
Test planning	*2 3*
Test team staff and skills	*3 5*
Test system development	*3*
Test releases	*2 3*
Test execution	*3*
Bug reporting	*3 4* **5**
Test results reporting	*3* **4**
Change management	*2 3 4* **5**

The bottom line is that, while CMMI and other similar models can help companies establish a foundation for quality, they do not guarantee thorough testing. When selecting the right test team, don't rely on remonstrations by the outsource development organization that, because they are CMMI level 4 or 5 or whatever, you don't need an outside testing process. For all the reasons covered in this section, while you might get away with that approach, it's at best a very risky one.

Planning and Preparing for Testing in Outsourced Projects

Okay, so you've selected an outsource development organization, and hopefully also a testing service provider located fairly near the development organization who can provide truly independent testing during the development. You've also retained some portion of the final testing as an in-house effort. That's a good high-level view of how to organize the testing work on an outsourced project. However, it will not suffice for a plan. As with any distributed testing effort, testing in an outsourced project requires a good deal of planning.

Let's start with carving up the main testing activities. To do so, you'll need to refer to the life cycle model that you are following (again, see Chapter 12 for a detailed discussion on this). For the moment, let's assume you're following the V-model approach mentioned earlier. If so, then the division of work shown in Figure 10-8 makes sense. Combined with the project management and change management elements shown in Figure 10-5, you now have a model for knowing who is supposed to do what work when, and a way for measuring progress against major milestones and managing the inevitable changes that will occur.

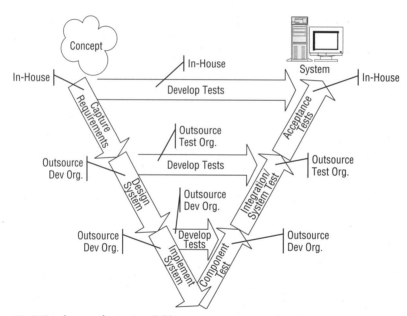

Figure 10-8 Carving up the test activities on an outsourced project

If the activities shown in Figure 10-8 were largely independent of each other, this might suffice. However, each activity generally produces a number of work products that must flow to other subsequent or concurrent activities. Further, these flows might actually be cycles, where a work product goes back and forth between various project participants, possibly spanning the organizational boundaries that exist. Therefore, you need to plan and ultimately execute crisp, efficient logistics for the testing activities.

While the specific logistical issues will vary from one project to another, there are three general categories that exist on just about any outsourced project:

- **The system being built:** This includes not only the transfer of test releases, release notes, code, and other supporting files, under proper configuration management control and as part of a solid release engineering process, but also the change management and project management elements.

- **The test system:** Due to reasons of expense or security, it is often necessary to share test environments with the outsource development and, if you have them, outsource testing partners. This includes the obvious elements of the test environment, but also access to cohabiting software, affected or linked systems or databases, and other connected elements that will be present in the customer or production environment. You'll need also to be able to exchange various testware items, such as test data, cases, and test tools, both to audit the test work of the outsource organizations and to avoid problems with gaps and overlap in the creation of the testware. Finally, you also need to coordinate the test processes, at least the major touchpoints that cross-organizational boundaries.

- **Information flows:** A tremendous amount of information should flow across organization boundaries as part of testing in an outsourced project. This includes project documents, quality risk analysis documents, estimates and plans, work assignments, bug reports, and, of course, test results reports. It also includes less-formalized but equally critical information flows like emails, project discussion enablers like wikis and newsgroups, and the like.

It's really easy to forget just one or two important logistical items. Doing so will cause immense headaches, often at a point in the project where it has become too late to resolve the logistical problem. Organizations running their first outsource project often have such logistical problems, but even experienced hands can get bitten.

On the Internet appliance project I've mentioned a few times in this book, we had a vendor who provided us with a modem integrated into the appliance. The modem consisted of both hardware and embedded firmware. During test execution, we started to experience severe unit-specific connection reliability problems. This vexed everyone, until one of the more hardware-savvy engineers compared the firmware from units without connection problems to the firmware from units with connection problems. Lo and behold, the vendor had changed the firmware without telling us. When we investigated the situation with the vendor, it turned out they had no configuration management, no source code repository worthy of the name, and no release engineering process. That one incident probably cost two person-months of project effort and could, had it happened closer to the project end date, have delayed release by up to a month.

Logistical risks are just one kind of project risk you need to manage on outsourced projects. Project risks on outsourced projects include all the usual ones (e.g., those discussed in Chapter 2), plus a number of others, such as the following:

- Political instability, especially when using outsource organizations in developing regions.[6]

- Time zones, language barriers, and other communication issues.

- Overtime and other off-hours constraints due to lack of access to the facility, lack of power or other infrastructure during off-hours at the facility, or physical safety issues associated with being at the facility during off-hours.

- Infrastructure problems and inadequacies, such as unreliable Internet connectivity, poor roads and airports, difficulties obtaining potable water and safe food during site visits, and so forth.

- Skills availability, as mentioned in the earlier section.

- Unforeseen and sometimes abruptly exposed organizational weakness, including loss of key players due to extreme rates of turnover, organizational collapse due to governance problems, and the like.

Failure of the outsourcing organization to identify and manage these risks at a project level increases the potential consequences.

One thing that can help you identify and manage risks, along with smoothing the way in which the work occurs, is to know the key participants in all parties. Ask yourself two questions. First, do you fully trust people you've never met? While you can establish trust by proxy — e.g., if someone you trust very much recommends someone else — establishing trust solely via emails and proposals is much harder. Second, is trust important for complex projects? If you've ever worked on a project with major trust issues, you know the answer to this question from having seen the results when trust is lacking. If you have to spend a lot of time and energy double-checking what people say and what they say they have done, that will reduce your efficiency, at best.

---

[6]For example, at the time of writing this book, Indian outsource companies were reeling from a double whammy. First there was a devastating terrorist attack in Mumbai. Then, just a few months later, one of the largest outsourcing vendors, Satyam, was revealed as an enormous (and almost bankrupt) piggy bank for the owner and his family, complete with fake books and gulled auditors to hide the fraud. These two incidents illustrate the risk of political instability and that of abruptly exposed organizational weakness.

At worst, trust issues lead to open or hidden enmity, possibly resulting in deliberate sabotage or undermining of other people's work and contributions in an attempt to prove a point or get even.

Trust is a major issue particularly with outsourced projects, because, frankly, the project team often starts out in a trust deficit. In many developed countries, there are reservoirs of fear and hostility among certain individual contributors and line managers who feel that their long-term financial prospects, job security, and even ability to continue to work in their chosen career are threatened by outsourcing and insourced labor from offshore organizations (e.g., H1-B visa holders working for purely offshore staff augmentation firms). I believe most people will recognize that the individuals involved, both in the outsourcing organization and the outsource service providers' organizations, are simply relatively powerless players in the enormous geopolitical and economic re-ordering of the world that I mentioned earlier. However, recognizing that intellectually and dealing with the subconscious feelings associated with the creative destruction of capitalism in action are two different things.

Establishing trust in outsourced situation is also complicated by the fact that many times, the outsource service provider is a long, long way away. Most communication occurs through email and conference calls. That can work for routine communication, but for tense, potentially fraught communications, these are problematic communication channels. You simply don't hear the whole message when you don't see the speaker's face, hands, and body.

I have frequently told clients that successful distribution of testing, including outsourcing, requires a certain amount of jet fuel and a certain number of visas in a passport. Sometimes only a physical visit to the vendor's site will do. I believe this is especially true in three situations: first, when you want to evaluate the outsource company and their staff; second, when you need to solve thorny project problems quickly; and, third, when you need to build and maintain trust and relationships.

Maintaining Focus During Test Execution

If you've gotten yourself properly organized, as discussed so far, you'll have cleared most of the obstacles from your way prior to starting test execution. I certainly won't suggest that test execution will be trivial — it never is, as discussed Chapter 6. However, beyond the usual challenges of test execution, you have a few more concerns to consider when dealing with testing on an outsourced project.

Most of these relate to the challenge of maintaining focus, including the following areas:

■ Building the various project deliverables, testing them, gathering results, and reporting useful information to project stakeholders.

- Keeping communication channels open and clear, especially those channels that flow information into testing.

- Course correcting in response to triggered project risks and unforeseen problems.

- Managing change as the needs of the project and its stakeholders evolve.

It's important not to get distracted from your key testing objectives. Opportunities for distraction often abound on outsourced projects, including petty conflicts and turf battles, one-time crises that don't really offer any long-tem lessons to learn, and minor differences in definitions, approaches, and other trivialities that don't affect anyone's ability to get work done. Remember that you can properly carry out all the stuff I mentioned earlier in this section, but if you don't manage the test execution properly, you can end up not achieving anything of value.

Conclusions about Outsourcing and Testing

As I wrote this third edition, the world economy, including software and systems engineering, had entered another tight economic period. *Reducing cost* is even more a by-word than it was previously. Furthermore, while organizations still have a lot to learn about effective outsourcing of software development and maintenance compared to their hardware and systems engineering colleagues, many organizations have learned ways to make outsourcing succeed. So, outsourcing is here to stay.

As discussed in this section, outsourcing does pose a number of challenges to testing and quality. However, none of those challenges are fundamentally that much different or harder to manage than the risks and activities on non-outsourced, collocated projects. The differences are those of degree more than of kind. So, the diligent test manager can succeed with outsourced projects if she manages the overall testing process with the same level of attention to detail that she would use to manage any other testing effort.

Indeed, I believe that, as software outsourcing matures, testers and test managers are well positioned to become essential project participants. Outsourcing might be cheaper than doing projects in-house, but it's harder, much more complex, and thus riskier. Since testing, ultimately, is composed of risk management activities, I suggest you bring your risk management skills to bear. You might well find that you are the key to outsourcing success in your organization.

Case Study 1

On the information appliance project cited in Chapter 8, I put together an in-house test team that focused on four areas: server-farm testing, information appliance testing, usability testing, and test tool development. To make sure the custom hardware worked correctly, I asked the vendor who built the system to thoroughly test the hardware. I also had a third-party test lab run some of the most critical hardware tests to make sure the quality was sufficient in these areas. Finally, the marketing manager administered various forms of user and user-surrogate testing, which, while not under our direct control, resulted in some interesting bug data that both confirmed some of our findings and added new information, especially in the area of environmental issues such as telephone line conditions.

Figure 10-9 shows the organizational chart for the distributed test team on this project. (The names have been changed to mask the project's identity.)

Figure 10-9 A distributed test project

I thank my client, who wishes to remain anonymous, for permission to discuss this project here. I also thank my client contacts for their excellent support and steady leadership on this project. Finally, thanks to my test team, the vendor, and the independent test lab for their professionalism and excellence on this project.

Case Study 2

Should we outsource our testing? What testing tasks should we outsource, and what tasks should we keep in-house? What are the chief advantages and disadvantages of outsourcing testing? As a consultant, I've been asked questions like these and other outsourcing-related questions a number of times. For a few clients, I've provided the following analysis, which should prove useful to you if you are evaluating outsourcing of testing.

In this case study, I analyze the use of outsourcing in testing, based on some 20 years of experience with outsourcing of testing in one form or another. First, I enumerate the key differences between in-house and outsourced test teams. Next, driven by these key differences, I'll analyze which tasks fit better with outsourced testing service providers, followed by a similar analysis for in-house test teams. Then I'll list some of the technical, managerial, and political challenges that confront a company trying to make effective use of outsourced testing. Finally I'll address some of the processes needed to use testing service providers effectively and with the least amount of trouble.

Key Differences between Testing Service Providers and In-House Test Teams

A number of important key differences exist between testing by an in-house test team and testing by a testing service provider. I want to start by listing these here, because I'll refer to them later in this analysis (by the labels *KD1*, *KD2*, etc.). The key differences include, most especially, the following:

KD1. Testing service providers already exist. An organization can use them almost immediately for any project. Building an in-house test team can take longer than the duration of a project.

KD2. The cost structure of a testing service provider is variable, while an in-house test team has start-up costs (infrastructure purchase), fixed costs (both labor and infrastructure maintenance), and variable costs (generally project-related contract labor).

KD3. Testing service providers spread the purchase and maintenance costs of particularly expensive infrastructures, such as network test facilities and extensive hardware/software libraries, across a large number of (customer) organizations. An in-house test team must incorporate these costs into the development budget.

KD4. Testing service providers often have existing documented test cases, suites, procedures, and processes that have proven efficient (based on the test labs' continued existence). An in-house test team may not have the competitive pressures and sufficient repetition required to hone such tools.

KD5. When the testing service provider is focused entirely on testing, typically it will be staffed by professional testers, people who choose to work in the test field. (Note that you should carefully scrutinize the test staffs of larger outsourcing firms that include a so-called testing center of excellence or testing practice before concluding that they consist of test professionals.) In-house test teams sometimes attract people who want to move into other areas in the organization.

KD6. In some cases, two or more competitors use the same testing service providers. An in-house test team can provide unique, focused services with no risk of intellectual property leakage.

KD7. Testing service providers tend to run lean. An in-house test team may fully staff a project to avoid temporary stalls in project progress.

KD8. Testing service providers are typically off-site (though some provide the services in part or in whole through on-site staff augmentation). In-house test teams are more likely to be col-located with the engineering and development facilities.

KD9. Testing service providers are most economical when used in a single-pass mode (i.e., once through the planned test suite). They are often uneconomical when used in cyclical activities, in comparison to an in-house test team.

With these differences in mind, let's now analyze how they affect outsourced testing.

Test Tasks Appropriate for Testing Service Providers

Now, let's look at how these key differences make certain tasks particularly appropriate for outsourcing to testing service providers. First, consider the *ready, willing and able* nature of external labs (KD1). Test projects that arise suddenly, contain spikes in personnel needs, or exceed the capacity of the current internal test organization are appropriate for outsourcing to a testing service provider. Also, the variable cost structure (KD2) implies that, even in cases where one could staff to meet a spike in test needs, the fixed costs associated with staffing up plus the variable costs incurred during the testing might exceed the variable cost incurred by using an external lab instead. So, RBCS recommends the use of testing service providers in most cases of atypical peaks in needed test capacity, rather than staffing to handle the peak and then eliminating staff after the peak.

Diffusing infrastructure costs across multiple customers (KD3) means that when one needs to test with particularly expensive hardware or simply a wide range of hardware or software, using a testing service provider makes sense. Network tests are a good example, because, across four or more network topologies (some with three or four protocols), six or seven server types, ten or more client stacks, and almost innumerable client network adapter options, the level of complexity and the fixed and variable costs associated with such a lab are high. Such labs require full-time network, database, and system administrators who command large salaries. Also, testing service providers maintain extensive libraries of software and hardware, having full-time acquisitions managers who keep the test tools current. Such expenses are impractical for small to mid-sized companies, yet compatibility and configuration testing are essential in many mass-market and Internet products and services. RBCS recommends the use of testing service providers to provide broad test coverage in these areas as a particularly smart reason to hire a testing service provider.

Efficient test processes and expert test professionals (KD4 and KD5) are especially useful in areas of testing that are considered unglamorous. Testing service providers generally hire and retain a greater proportion of professional testers than do hardware, software, and systems companies staffing in-house test teams, and certainly more than the average non-computer-related company hiring testers for their IT operation. In-house test team candidates sometimes have long-term goals in other fields within the company, and view testing as a stepping stone to advancement. In-house test team staff members usually enjoy testing cutting-edge technologies and developing test plans for products that use these technologies. When it comes to more mundane but equally important tasks, testing service providers will usually have an edge.

The remote location of the testing service provider (KD8), while sometimes perceived as a disadvantage, can provide benefits. First, it offers an environment where the test effort can stay focused on the overall test plan rather than getting bogged down in the crisis of the moment. Second, in conjunction with a dedicated liaison, a single contact window provides a way of channeling information from the test staff to the project team without non-test-team members interrupting testers with what they think will be (but often are not) quick questions, a significant time drain for in-house test teams. This means that one can hand off the bulk of the test tasks to a testing service provider, knowing they will proceed towards the agreed-upon goals for completion in a deliberate fashion, regardless of the tempests raging around the project on-site.

Test Tasks Appropriate for In-House Test Teams

Now, let's look at how the key differences make certain tasks particularly appropriate to retain for an in-house test team. First, a two-edged sword: the variable cost structure of external labs (KD2) implies that you need to use testing service providers carefully, and with forethought. Though the cost for a single test may be relatively low, the cost per test cycle (one complete run through all planned tests) might not be. Therefore, you need to keep the number of cycles executed at an external lab to a minimum in many cases. Handling crisis situations, especially those sparked by last-minute changes in requirements, is better suited to an in-house test team, at least at first, testing service provider responsiveness (KD1) and leveraged infrastructure (KD3) notwithstanding. In some cases, of course, the infrastructure available at the testing service provider is necessary (e.g., a complex network or a range of supported browsers). If testing service provider participation in a crisis is needed, the test manager must take time to plan carefully their role. Otherwise, you might incur excessive cycles at the testing service provider, and you'll typically pay for these services on a time-and-materials basis.

While documented, standard test processes (KD4) would suggest that testing service providers will outperform in-house test teams, this often is most true for tasks which must be done efficiently (i.e., with the minimum cost and effort). Sometimes the most important consideration is completeness of coverage and meticulousness of testing, especially for those features and functions judged by business stakeholders as critical. Although the broad client base and cross-platform service offering of testing service providers (KD6) means solid testing and technology expertise, service providers tend to be weak in highly specialized application domains, since they often cannot afford to specialize in the features, advanced functions, and peculiarities applicable to a single client's system. These two facts have a number of implications. First, some level of in-house test expertise is needed to make the decision on whether bugs reported by testing service providers have the appropriate severity and priority assigned, and, indeed, whether they are bugs at all, given the unique elements of the system. Second, in-house test staff will need to cover the unusual features in the system, or be prepared to provide direct support to the testing service provider in terms of what testing should occur. Third, in-house test staff will need to test the most critical features, even though you might also have the external labs provide double coverage for added security.

In a mass-market, e-commerce, or SaaS situation, where many of your competitors offer substantially similar products and services, the openness of the external labs (KD6) means that you can't obtain a significant competitive edge in terms of testing and quality by using testing service providers exclusively. While using a dedicated testing service provider liaison allows for a great degree of specialization and more-complete coverage, to achieve truly distinctive levels of quality, an organization must add testing in an in-house test team. Furthermore, this in-house test team should use insights from business stakeholders and others with direct interaction with customers and users, and construct realistic, end-user-like test environments, test scenarios, and usage profiles. In other words, while in-house test teams have the potential to provide a competitive edge in testing, that edge does not come free, but rather requires considerable forethought, cooperation, and hard work.

The lean staffing of testing service providers (KD7) affects handling of the critical test tasks, those in which speed of completion, accuracy of results, and thoroughness are all of crucial importance. A good example is performance testing. You should select testing service providers for specialized test types (e.g., performance, reliability, and usability) based in large part on the availability of experts in that type of testing. In most testing service providers, specialized personnel are not always available to work on your particular crisis task at the exact moment you require the service, and you or others in your organization might find it unacceptable to have the testing service provider place such crisis tasks in a queue for service based on specialist availability. Of course, the distinction here may well be one of appearance — the perception of a uniform sense of urgency — as opposed to any actual difference in the time required to complete the task. A testing service provider might, through efficiency and expertise, hold an edge in handling such tasks, but the politics of the crisis might require someone present on-site, visibly sweating the details and working long hours. Note that location (KD8) comes into play here as well, particularly when the priorities tend to change a few times a day, with the latency of communication to an off-site testing service provider making it difficult for them to keep up with rapidly evolving conditions.

The rapidly mounting costs of external labs in a cyclic mode (KD9) affects test tasks such as regression testing. While using a testing service provider to provide a final check on the product makes sense, delivering highly buggy products for testing can result in multiple passes through the test suite at considerable expense. An in-house test team should ensure sufficient quality prior to engagement of a testing service provider, using written entry criteria.

Organizational Challenges

Using a testing service provider can involve resolving a number of technical, managerial, and political challenges in many organizations. Many of these challenges apply to distributed testing in general; e.g., leveraging a vendor's test organization. Let's take a look at these challenges so that you can resolve them before they become obstacles.

First, since there is no widely accepted definition of a test case, each test organization involved will have cases consisting of a different number of conditions (granularity) and requiring a different amount of time. Also, some tests naturally break down into different-sized tasks. The test manager must ensure that they have a way to integrate tests and test information across disparate testing teams in a way that makes sense.

In addition to test case definitions, a continuum also exists in terms of where debugging tasks end and where testing tasks begin. This is multidimensional, applying to the responsibilities of developers versus testers, when testers have performed sufficient isolation to characterize a bug in a report sufficient for delivery to the development team, and when developers have performed sufficient testing to return a fix to the test team. Each organization will have a different answer. This is an issue for testing service providers in that you need an agreement in advance on the level of isolation performed for each bug report. Failure to get sufficient isolation information in the bug reports from the testing service providers will result in a lot of questions and complaints by developers about bugs reported by the testing service provider.

In development projects that have international teams, language will be an issue. You cannot assume that all testers will know the project language, nor can you assume that a project team member from another country who is conversant in the project language will read and write it as effortlessly as a native speaker. The organization must make allowances for varying levels of language proficiency, and plans must exist for translating critical documents into the project language.

Influenced by the three issues mentioned already but distinct from them is the matter of test result reporting. While there is a certain minimal set of data one expects to find in a bug report, standards and formats vary widely. In addition, the ways in which organizations track the status (pass, fail, blocked, etc.) of test cases vary both in method and in quality. The overall test results dashboard is likely to vary from one organization to another. While converting everyone to a single format is unlikely, crucial milestones prior to starting test execution include agreeing on a minimal set of data, a frequency of reporting, standards for failure reproduction procedures, and standards for updating changing status. In addition, the test manager will need to create a single, unified test results dashboard for reporting to project and outside managers, with quick, meaningful data feeds across all the test teams, both internal and external.

Testing should be pervasive, in the sense that there is a series of levels of testing and quality assurance activities embedded in the project. Each level should have established entry and exit criteria. This allows each activity to act as a bug filter, leading to the highest cumulative level of bug removal in the most efficient fashion. In contrast, a single-level approach with no formal entry or exit criteria tends to rush products into testing before they are ready, to squander a lot of time in trying to test unready, unstable products, and to release systems with low and inconsistent levels of quality. However, while this multi-filter approach is well-established in mature organizations, and general guidelines for test levels are available, organizations apply them differently. This means that a vendor might use A-Test, B-Test, and C-Test, your company might use component test, integration test, and system test, and the testing service provider might use a whole different standard. Alternatively, they might all use the same names for the levels but have different objectives, entry criteria, and exit criteria for them. The manager responsible for the master test plan on a given project must understand how all these levels fit together; otherwise, the benefits of the test levels will be defeated.

On systems projects that involve hardware prototypes, prototype allocation will usually create a headache or two. You should pay attention to this issue both during test planning and during test control. Because more organizations are involved, you'll need more prototypes. Before test execution starts, you should make sure that an agreed-upon allocation plan exists. This plan should, to the extent possible, meet the needs of all test participants. The compromises made — and you will make compromises — due to system scarcity should be understood and clearly communicated. During test execution, you must set and monitor milestones to ensure that allocated quantities are delivered on time. You should proactively anticipate and handle any delays and shortages that might occur.

With downsizing always a possibility and leading a large department sometimes seen as part of climbing the management ladder, the use of testing service providers for reasons other than pure staffing necessity tends to meet with some resistance from the in-house test team. This is less of a challenge for an organization planning to use testing service providers from the beginning than for organizations with large, existing in-house test teams that are starting to use test outsourcing. However, the political pressures exist to some degree regardless, and the organization must deal with these pressures effectively to prevent dysfunctional behavior.

Managing all of these organizational challenges can be handled by *mapping*, which involves taking the test processes of different teams and mapping them functionally into a single virtual test team. This is, of course, less efficient than having a single set of standards to which all test teams adhere from the start, but, in the case of outside testing service providers and vendors, there is no real alternative.

Processes for Effective Use of Testing Service Providers

Related to the issue of mapping is alignment of processes. While you cannot — and need not — resolve all such process alignment issues to the point where everyone involved in testing works the same as your in-house test team does, you need to ensure good process alignment in the following areas to support effective use of testing service providers.

- Someone must own the role of test coordinator or liaison to ensure integration of the test results into the test management and reporting processes.

- Processes must exist to deal with the mapping issues that arise.

- During the planning phases for the overall test project, a global plan should identify all the test work that will occur, regardless of location. The test manager should consider the testing service providers as available testing resources, and plan accordingly.

- Since no testing service provider works for free, a way of getting them paid must exist.

- Though email and phone calls can handle much of the coordinating of external testing, nothing maximizes communication effectiveness like physical presence, especially in international situations where project language issues exist. Therefore, the coordinator or liaison role must involve travel to the testing service provider's location as required. In addition, this liaison should make sure that developers address the bugs found and reported by the testing service providers.

- Whenever hardware prototypes will remain on-site at a testing service provider for any length of time, a process must exist for refreshing the prototypes as needed. Allowing the prototypes to get out of date in terms of firmware and hardware versions in comparison to the final hardware will cause test escapes and will frustrate the testers trying to use them.

All these processes must include active follow-up elements for the coordinator, liaison, and/or test manager. In any distributed project, especially one that spans time zones, multiple opportunities exist for confusion, miscommunication, lost communication, and ostrich-like reactions to bad news or undesirable requests. While distributed testing creates a matrix-like test organization, the ultimate responsibility for test task completion must remain with one person.

Bonus Case Study: People Are Not Widgets!

–Judy Mckay

I have always had mixed feelings about outsourcing. I can see the benefits of lower labor costs and I believe in building technical capabilities worldwide. On the other hand, I have also seen numerous outsource projects fail dismally, falling into many of the pitfalls discussed in this chapter. Recently though, I have had the luck to be involved in an outsourcing project that has been remarkably successful. A little background:

I work for a company that is a strong believer in outsourcing work, particularly to India, to reduce expenses. Outsourcing in my group is done to two teams in India, a set of employees at one facility and a set of contractors who are employed by a big software testing house at another facility. When I joined the group, there was little focus on the work these teams contributed and the individuals were definitely considered to be interchangeable, high-turnover widgets. While this model may have worked on less technically complex projects, it was completely unworkable for our projects that required strong domain knowledge, dedication, and a willingness to put in extra time as needed.

For my first step, I reviewed the resources we had and assessed the skill levels. The contractor group was technically strong but less committed than would be ideal. The multiple layers of management between the individuals and me made them dismissive of my efforts to create a unified team. In fairness to them, there had been a high turnover in the outsourcing team (I was only the latest in a long series of QA management) so their tendency to treat me as "temporary" was certainly warranted. For the employee outsourced team, I was able to build the group. It's usually an advantage to be able to pick your own people, but I quickly learned that while I am good at the in-person interview process, I lose a lot when the process is conducted over the phone and is complicated by telecommunication issues and heavy, sometimes indecipherable, accents. Recognizing my difficulties with this process, I formed a relationship with the person who was to be the on-site management resource for the testing team. He was somewhat inexperienced, but willing to learn and, as I quickly discovered, was stunned that someone from the U.S. would take the time to train him and help develop his managerial skills.

I worked closely with the manager and helped him hone his interviewing skills. We also worked together to develop the description of our "perfect" candidates. That done, I turned over the screening process to him. When he found a candidate that he felt was suitable, I would interview the person over the phone. The manager and I would review our observations and discuss the pros and cons of the individual. This served as both an education in interviewing techniques for him, and an opportunity for him to educate me regarding success factors necessary for that environment. If we decided we still liked the candidate, I then turned him/her over to one of my local U.S. leads to conduct an in-depth technical interview. Because this individual was also from India, he could work through any communication issues I had with the candidate. This interview technique was very strong and produced an excellent set of candidates who were hired.

The next challenge was to select the test leads for the group. It quickly became apparent that there was a natural lead in the group, and she then took over more of the management role from her manager and also became the primary screener for new candidates with some coaching from both me and her manager. Once given the responsibility to find people who would be productive and could work well together, she quickly took the task to heart and provided very thorough screening. I accepted every candidate she approved.

But what about the team of contractors? They were in the practice of doing work that was easily quantified. For example, if they were told to write a test case, it contained hundreds of highly detailed steps. Obviously, they had been trained that this was a way to provide strong metrics that would please the U.S. employers. Unfortunately, this didn't meet the needs of our project where the software was rapidly changing and time spent on detailed test cases was often wasted. I had numerous phone meetings with the team and email communications, explaining the project goals and emphasizing the need for a long-term relationship. They were distrustful at first, the veterans of many job changes, but they did do as I requested (perhaps grudgingly at first) and slowly came to realize that I meant what I said — that I valued them for their knowledge and their contribution and I didn't want their work proven by a very high pile of paper, but by the production of a quality product.

It has been interesting to watch these teams grow into their responsibilities. As I give them more opportunities, they take them willingly. This can be a problem, though. It took me at least a year to convince them that it was okay, in fact desirable, for them to say "no" when they felt something was not the right thing to do or wasn't even possible. I also discovered that they *expected* to be treated as widgets. The fact that I gave them responsibility, trusted them, invested in their training and growth, and valued them was a new concept. Soon after I had hired one employee in India, I was having a discussion on instant message with her and she said that her co-workers (all employees, but working on different projects) were jealous of her. I asked why. She responded that they were jealous that she worked for someone who said "thank you." Not only had she never experienced it before, but neither had her coworkers. And this wasn't an isolated incident. I asked one of the people in the contracting group to conduct a screening interview for a potential addition to the team and to provide his honest opinion of the candidate. His first email about the candidate was strictly a review of the candidate's technical qualifications. I thanked him for that and asked him what he thought of the candidate as a potential coworker. After a little prodding, he came forth with his opinion that the candidate didn't appear to have the drive or interest in the job, although he was technically capable. That's what I was seeking! I thanked him for his honest input, told him that I valued his opinion and appreciated his time. His response email that clearly expressed that he was surprised said that he was very pleased to have been asked for his opinion and he appreciated my asking for it and was very happy to have been able to assist in the process.

How do we treat our outsource resources? As widgets without valid opinions or deserving of our thanks? Is that how we would treat our coworkers who are on-site? People, regardless of where they are, are not widgets. They want responsibility. They want respect. They want to be valued. They want us to be interested in developing their skills and their careers, even if they work for a third-party contractor. They want feedback. I use periodic meetings, instant message, and a lot of email to keep them informed. And remember, *informed* doesn't just mean giving them assignments; it also means making them a part of the group. They should receive the promotion, birth, and marriage announcements that are circulated within a working group. They should receive general information that is available about their projects. If you want your outsource team to contribute like your on-site team, you need to treat them as if they are on-site and are actually part of the overall team. Nothing creates a feeling of isolation faster than being denied information, even information that might be considered trivial.

This also means that you may need to step into email discussions with developers where it appears the outsource testers aren't receiving the respect and attention they deserve. Follow up. Don't let your people be ignored or their contribution trivialized. I've been fortunate to have developers who do value the team's input and will periodically arrange to meet with a tester at 11:00 p.m. our time just to provide clarification and accessibility. This builds team coherence and establishes the value of the outsource teams.

You might ask how long these teams have been together. Four years. Four years with virtually no turnover. That is rare in this industry. I value these individuals. They are critical to our projects and they know it. Outsource teams can work well. You have to master communication. You have to be accessible. And, most importantly, you have to remember that they are not widgets. They are people.

Conclusion

Properly used, testing service providers can make a valuable and economical contribution to system and software projects. Categories of tests that make sense to outsource include the following:

- Tests that would cause a short-term spike in test manpower requirements, followed by downtime or layoffs
- Tests that cover a broad range of hardware and software, or otherwise use expensive or difficult-to-maintain infrastructures
- Tests that are routine and unglamorous, but important to shipping a quality product
- Large blocks of tests that might not get done in-house due to changing priorities

Some tests require in-house attention. Categories of tests that make sense to run using in-house test teams include the following:

- Tests that result from last-minute changes in requirements
- Tests and test result evaluations that require sophisticated domain knowledge
- Tests that provide a competitive advantage in terms of evaluating and improving product quality
- Tests that are time-critical and vital to project success, or that are subject to rapidly evolving requirements
- Tests that establish system stability prior to release to a testing service provider for final testing

In addition to dividing the test workload intelligently, the effective test manager must handle the technical, managerial, and political issues associated with using external and distributed test resources. Many of these problems have to do with mapping and integrating the disparate test organizations into a single virtual test team. In addition, the test manager must allocate test units effectively and make intelligent allocation compromises as needed. Finally, once the test manager has the work divided and the virtual organization mapped, the test manager must ensure that appropriate processes exist to support the execution of the project. These processes must support a single point of contact for gathering test results into a consistent test dashboard and to ensure completion of critical tasks.

Exercises

1. Suppose that an external test lab located in Taiwan and a vendor located in India are participating in your test effort. (Your offices are located in the central time zone of the United States.) They send you bug reports by email and you have a test technician enter them into the bug-tracking system.

   - Due to the time difference, bug reports get into the bug-tracking system after almost a full day's lag. How will this affect your test dashboard? Is the effect significant?

   - Assume a test release comes out once a week on Monday morning. It takes two days for the release to be transmitted securely to the vendor and the test lab. Assuming they both work from 9:00 a.m. to 5:00 p.m. local time, when is the earliest you would expect confirmation, regression, and planned testing to commence (in terms of central U.S. time) at each location?

   - Assuming that confirmation testing concludes in a day and bugs identified in the test release notes are reported by email as fixed or not fixed by the end of the day, how does this lag affect your test dashboard? Is the effect significant?

2. One of the frequently cited concerns about outsourcing testing to a third-party test company is that the consultancy's or lab's testers might not have sufficient knowledge of the application domain of the system. Based on the critical skills discussion in Chapter 8, do you feel that would necessarily be an issue for your company? Are there certain tests that your company could outsource even if application domain knowledge was in some cases an issue? Is your company sufficiently organized in terms of the areas discussed in this chapter to gain benefit from outsourcing testing?

Economics of Testing: Fiscal Context

In the last 10 chapters, I explained the key tools, techniques, and approaches that I use to manage testing projects. Some 35,000 people have read this book in its previous editions and translations, another 10,000 or so have taken courses that derive from this book in some way or another, and RBCS has over 100 clients and licensees that use materials based on this book. As you can see, these ideas have worked for lots of test managers in some form or another, and I trust that you, too, will be able to put them to good use.

To adapt these ideas to your particular situation, you need to understand the context in which you're working. Testing does not happen for its own sake, in a vacuum, because we're merely intellectually curious about the quality of some system — at least I've never been paid to do that. Rather, organizations pay for testing — they *invest* in testing — to realize benefits.

If the project management team has realistic expectations, they'll invest in testing as part of a larger investment in quality. In other words, the project management team should understand that the mere act of testing does not make bugs go away or reduce the number of bugs developers put in the system.

This investment in quality can yield benefits such as the following:

- An improved reputation for quality
- Lower post-release maintenance costs
- Smoother release cycles
- Increased confidence that the system will work well for users and satisfy customers

- Protection from lawsuits initiated by unhappy customers, users, or those otherwise affected by system failure

- Reduced risk of loss of entire missions and even lives

Your management team might want you to help them realize some of these benefits, all of these benefits, or even some benefits not on this list.

As I started to become aware of the motivating factors behind my test team's existence, I realized the difference between the tactical perspective on testing and the strategic one. Tactically, testing is the search for bugs in the system and for knowledge about what works and what doesn't work. Strategically, testing is a risk management activity that reduces the likelihood of the organization having to bear unanticipated future costs related to poor quality. Testing is something like insurance, but without actuarial certainty or the ability to pay the company for the costs of production failures. A good test team provides value in this regard by delivering a timely, accurate assessment of system quality to the organization. This assessment is usually delivered in the context of a development or maintenance project.

Various risks threaten the success of a project:

Features. Can we deliver the right set of functions to the users and customers?

Schedule. Can we deliver those features soon enough?

Budget. Can we deliver those features in a profitable or at least financially acceptable way?

Quality. Can we deliver those features with the predominant presence of satisfying behaviors and attributes and a relative absence of dissatisfying behaviors and attributes?

Successful projects mitigate and balance these risks, and the four elements converge for a successful delivery.

Because of the need to mitigate the risks and balance these competing elements, the test subproject must integrate smoothly into the sponsoring project. I discussed one aspect of this integration, aligning testing with the critical risks to the quality of each of the features in the system and the system as a whole, in Chapter 1 and Chapter 2. I also discussed the need to fit the test subproject within the economic, schedule, and process parameters of the project from a micro or local sense; in other words, the way these project parameters affect the test subproject. In this chapter and the next chapter, I'll look at the macro or global view of testing. I'll start in this chapter with the economic parameters. The next chapter will deal with the schedule and process parameters.

Is Quality Free? The Economic Justification for the Testing Investment

Let's start with economics. There's a really fascinating apparent dichotomy lurking in this topic. On the one hand, improved quality is usually — or always, depending on whom you ask — a good investment. In this chapter, I'll demonstrate that concept through a simple model called *cost of quality*. On the other hand, it is often very difficult to get adequate funding for testing, for reasons both economic and non-economic.

What Does Testing Really Cost?

Nothing. Zilch. Nada. Zero. Quality is free — at least that's what Phillip Crosby wrote in his book of the same name. Frank Gryna did his first cost/benefit analyses on quality at General Electric in 1949. Later, Gryna, together with J. M. Juran, wrote the *Quality Control Handbook*, which describes a model referred to as *cost of quality* or *quality costs*. (Gryna did not participate in the latest edition of this book.) Crosby, Gryna, and Juran refer primarily to service industries and manufacturing, but Campanella and his co-authors, in *Principles of Quality Costs*, include a case study of cost of quality at Raytheon's Electronic Systems group. Raytheon's Electronic Systems group reduced their costs associated with poor quality from a high of over 40 percent of the average project cost to 6 percent over the course of 8 years. (This was done in conjunction with a process maturity initiative called the Capability Maturity Model, which I'll discuss in Chapter 12.) When we do assessments of our clients' test processes, we typically find that testing saves the organization anywhere from 50 percent to 3500 percent more than it costs.

Creative accounting strikes again, you say? Not really. To reach this rather startling conclusion, let's look at the cost of quality model. This model says that we can divide quality costs into two categories: the *cost of conformance* and the *cost of nonconformance*.

$$Cost_{quality} = Cost_{conformance} + Cost_{nonconformance}$$

The cost of conformance includes any expenditure taken to ensure quality. This includes *prevention costs* — in other words, quality assurance — such as training, process improvement, and so forth. The cost of conformance also includes much of the testing budget, such as planning the test effort, designing and developing a test system, installing and configuring a test environment, and running each test (the first time). These test expenses are called *detection costs*.

$$Cost_{conformance} = Cost_{prevention} + Cost_{detection}$$

The costs of nonconformance arise from system problems (i.e., bugs) and process failures (such as the delays, bad test releases, and others discussed in Chapter 12). These bugs and process breakdowns result in rework, repairs, slowdowns, and other inefficiencies. In the testing effort, a common example arises any time a test case fails. You must repeat the test that found the bug or bugs to verify and isolate them, repeat tests to confirm fixes to the bug or bugs, and repeat some number of previously passed tests to check for regression due to the fixes. All this effort spent repeating tests is basically wasted time due to the presence of defects in the initial system. The time and money expended represent one cost of nonconformance arising from *internal failures*. Costs of nonconformance also include *external failures* (what happens when a bug affects a customer, end user, or society). These costs include much of the technical support group's budget, the expenses associated with creating, testing, and deploying field fixes, product recalls and refunds, liability costs, and lost sales.

$$Cost_{nonconformance} = Cost_{internal\ failure} + Cost_{external\ failure}$$

Crosby, Gryna and Juran, Campanella and his co-authors, and my own work with RBCS clients all demonstrate that, if you invest testing and quality assurance budgets wisely, you can reduce the total cost of quality by increasing the costs of prevention and detection.

A SpeedyWriter Case Study

Cost of quality is a concept that's much easier to grasp when you see an example. Let's suppose that we're working with SpeedyWriter. To keep things simple, we'll look at testing as the only cost of conformance; in other words, there are no quality assurance or prevention costs of quality, only detection. For nonconformance costs, we'll consider only the cost of fixing bugs either before or after release, without trying to quantify intangibles. The plan is for a quarterly release, which, based on defect data from past projects and the estimated size of the SpeedyWriter releases, the project management team estimates will contain 1,000 must-fix (i.e., customer-impacting) bugs. Finally, let's assume that we know that costs of failure, on average, are as follows:

$10 for bugs found and fixed by programmers during informal testing (unit and component) of their own or each other's code.

$100 for bugs found by testers during formal testing (integration and system), fixed by programmers, and confirmed fixed by the test team.

$1,000 for bugs found by customers after release, reported to technical support, fixed by supporting programmers, and run through confirmation and regression testing by the test team prior to release to customers.

Our initial situation, before an independent test team is formed, is shown in the No Formal Testing column in Figure 11-1. The programmers do a fine job of unit and component testing, finding 25 percent of the bugs, but customers still find 750 bugs per release. Our cost of nonconformance — mostly external failure — is $750,000, with a total cost of quality of $752,500. I said I'd ignore intangibles, but let me point out as an aside that it's not as if we're buying happy customers with this sizeable tab; on the contrary, customers are quite upset with us.

	A	B	C	D
1	**Testing Investment Options: ROI Analysis**			
2				
3		**No Formal**	**Manual**	**Automated**
4	**Testing**	**Testing**	**Testing**	**Testing**
5	Staff	$0	$60,000	$60,000
6	Infrastructure	0	10,000	10,000
7	Tools (amortized)	0	0	12,500
8	Total Investment	0	70,000	82,500
9				
10	**Development**	250	250	250
11	Must-Fix Bugs Found	2,500	2,500	2,500
12	Fix Cost			
13				
14	**Testing**			
15	Must-Fix Bugs Found	0	350	500
16	Fix Cost	0	35,000	50,000
17				
18	**Customer Support**			
19	Must-Fix Bugs Found	750	400	250
20	Fix Cost	750,000	400,000	250,000
21				
22	**Cost of Quality**			
23	Conformance	$0	$70,000	$82,500
24	Nonconformance	$752,500	$437,500	$302,500
25	**Total CoQ**	$752,500	$507,500	$385,000
26				
27	**Return on Investment**	#N/A	350%	445%

Figure 11-1 SpeedyWriter testing-investment ROI

Suppose that in response to this situation the project management team decides to institute a test team to do manual testing, in addition to maintaining the same standard of unit and component testing by the programmers. The analysis of this situation is shown in the Manual Testing column in Figure 11-1. Between the testing environment and the staff, this represents an investment of $70,000 per quarterly release. (The test environment can be amortized over multiple releases, let's say one year, so this represents a $40,000 initial test environment setup cost.) Assume this test team does a good job of testing and finds about half of the bugs that remain in the system during integration and system testing. Now customers find only 400 bugs — still a sizeable number, but quite an improvement — and our total cost of quality has fallen to a little over $500,000.

So, what is our return on our $70,000 investment?

$$ROI = \frac{Net\ Benefit}{Cost\ of\ Investment} = \frac{752,500 - 507,500}{70,000} = 350\%$$

Well, that's certainly a solid and respectable return on a fairly modest initial investment, right?

If you recall the defect detection percentage (DDP) metric from Chapter 4, we can put a metric on the effectiveness of our test team, too.

$$DDP = \frac{350}{400 + 350} = 47\%$$

As I mentioned in Chapter 4, this is not a very good DDP. That said, it's certainly a better situation than before, and it establishes a baseline for future improvement. This also demonstrates that even test teams that aren't very effective at finding bugs might still run very efficient operations in terms of saving companies money.

Perhaps we can improve both the ROI and the DDP? One common technique for improving the effectiveness and efficiency of testing is to introduce automated testing tools for functional regression, load, performance, and reliability testing, among other areas. The Automated Testing column in Figure 11-1 shows the analysis of that situation.

Assume we've invested $150,000 in test tool licenses, training, and expert consulting and contractor services to get our automated test effort off the ground. The licenses include 3 years of maintenance and upgrades, and the tests are expected to be usable on the average over 12 releases, so this represents a $12,500 investment per release. Thus, the overall test investment goes up to $82,500 per quarterly release. Assume this test team now finds about two-thirds of the bugs that remain in the system during integration and system testing. Now customers find only 250 bugs, which is perhaps a number we can live with at this point. Our total cost of quality has fallen to under $400,000.

Our new return on investment, including the test automation investment, is

$$ROI = \frac{Net\ Benefit}{Cost\ of\ Investment} = \frac{752,500 - 385,500}{82,500} = 445\%$$

Our new DDP has also improved significantly, becoming

$$DDP = \frac{500}{500 + 250} = 67\%$$

It's important to recognize that returns like this on the testing investment might be above or below what you will get. In addition, your returns will be negative if you test the wrong things. Finding bugs that do not relate to customer usage or critical quality risks distracts the project team from fixing real problems and can give a false sense of confidence that things work when in fact the system is teeming with bugs. However, if you follow the risk-based approach outlined in this book; apply good test system design, development, and implementation practices; and are responsible for test phases where finding bugs is the norm and the goal (i.e., not acceptance or pilot testing), then you are likely to consistently see a demonstrable, positive return on investment.

Management Obstacles to Test Funding

Given the business case we demonstrated in the preceding section, we should have no trouble getting adequate funding for our test efforts, right? Well, even armed with a convincing business case that includes a solid return on investment, you might find that you still have problems. There are a number of obstacles to getting adequate funding for testing. Some of these we create ourselves as test managers. Some are inherent in the testing reality. And some are the result of management blind spots to testing realities, usually compounded by our own mistakes. To do a decent job of testing, you must receive sufficient money, hiring requisitions, and lab equipment. However, the figure you consider adequate and the figure your managers will accept seldom coincide. In a typical situation, you will have to put together an organization that is both lean and effective.

Test Manager Budgeting Faux Pas: Obstacles the Test Manager Creates

Communication is a two-way street, as the saying goes, but as a test manager requesting funding for your test effort, the burden lies mostly on you to make the communication that occurs between you and your superiors effective. You have to explain to your manager, in terms she can understand, why you should receive a substantial sum of money to find bugs in the product. There are a number of ways to make this case, as I'll explain in a minute, but one way to *not* make this case is to argue from a moral perspective. Okay, if you're writing software where personal or public safety is involved, you have the right to play the "moral imperative" card. However, most of the time, banging the quality gong and pretending to be Don Quixote, Lone Defender of Quality, will just come off as self-righteous and disconnected from project realities. Usually, the test manager's job is not to be the lone defender of quality, but rather to put together an operation that can assess quality — as the customer will experience it — so that management can act on that information.[1]

Try to see testing through management's eyes. What motivates them to want testing? Can you make the information you can provide as a tester even more desirable to them? Do they see your testing budget as excessive? If so, why? The better you can understand the obstacles in your management's minds to giving you what you consider sufficient funds — and the forces that make them want to give you what they consider sufficient funds — the better you can communicate with them about this hotly debated topic. After all, selling is the art of making a product or service desirable to a customer, and then overcoming the customer's objections to the sale.

Regrettable Necessity: Obstacles the Testing Reality Creates

As you start to see testing from a management perspective, you'll also start to see that testing is, to paraphrase Winston Churchill's comment about democracy, the worst possible form of ensuring quality in computer products, except for all the others. Ideally, business analysts, marketing managers, software designers, engineers, and developers could, by applying preventive techniques, produce perfect systems that would require no testing.

Imagine a world where there was no crime. We wouldn't have to pay for police officers, would we? Imagine a world where houses couldn't catch fire. We wouldn't have to pay for firefighters then, right? Imagine a world where people settled their differences without fighting — okay, I'm getting into John Lennon territory here, so I promise to stop in just a second — but seriously, if people didn't fight wars to solve political problems, then we wouldn't need militaries.

The reason I bring this up is not to espouse some utopian society — I don't believe in the perfectibility of humanity, so I don't believe in utopias — but to introduce the economic concept of the *regrettable necessity*. A regrettable

---

[1] For more thoughts on the counter-productive nature of a moral argument for testing, see James Bullock's article, "Calculating the Value of Testing," originally published in *Software Testing and Quality Engineering*, Volume 2, Issue 3, now available on www.stickyminds.com.

necessity is a cost that, from an economic point of view, would be nice to do without, because that money could be spent more productively elsewhere. It's very unfortunate that people commit crimes that victimize their fellow citizens, that houses catch fire, that some people start wars and some people get dragged into wars, but these things do happen. It's too bad that we need to spend money on governments at all, because government is another form of friction and economic loss. If we all could agree on the right thing to do and simply do so, without someone forcing us to be nonviolent and honest with laws, that would be cheaper, wouldn't it?

Okay, blue sky aside, the human condition is that we play the hand we're dealt. In software and hardware engineering, programmers and other engineers can't help but create bugs. They can do a reasonable job of finding some of those bugs during unit and component testing, but they tend to do a poor job of finding those bugs during integration and system testing. This means that test teams, which can consume as much as 50 percent of the human resources budget for a project, must exist to catch these bugs. Even if you are fortunate enough to work in an organization whose executive managers understand the necessity of testing, don't expect them to be thrilled about paying for it. Testing is expensive. If the ratio of testers to developers is 1-to-3, somewhere between 15 and 35 percent of the development organization's human resources budget is going to people who, from the senior managers' bottom-line perspective, do nothing but find problems created by the people who receive the other 65 to 85 percent of the paycheck budget.

Some bugs are shy, as discussed in Chapter 6. This means that we have to construct production-like or customer-like test environments to find these bugs. The test environments can be extensive, costly, and hard to maintain. In terms of resources such as hardware and software, the ratio of costs for development environments versus test environments is tilted toward the test team. Developers can usually work on a subset or scaled-down version of the operating environment, but to be truly effective, testing must replicate end-user settings as much as possible. It's not unheard of for test labs to require resources valued at 10 times those needed by the development team. One attendee at an RBCS test management seminar told me that in his test lab he had single pieces of equipment valued at over $1,000,000, and that he had figured he would have to spend well over $1,000,000,000 to thoroughly represent the different field configuration options.

Time is money, too. Each additional test cycle is another day, week, month, or however long that cycle takes that the system will not be out in the real world. Delaying deployment or release means that some beneficial features or functions aren't being delivered. This could mean inefficiencies in some internal process for IT shops, which means lost money. This could mean lost sales — perhaps forever — in mass-market situations where someone chooses the product currently on the market and then is no longer looking to buy that product. This could mean contractual penalties in a custom development shop where your managers agreed to deliver to the customer on a particular day.

So, when a manager is looking at a testing budget, he sees all these costs that he wishes weren't there. He also probably knows — if he's been around once or twice — that testing might well end up taking twice as long as planned. Hopefully, he recognizes that this isn't the test manager's fault, usually, at least when an abysmally bad product is snuck into the testing environment. However, slips in the schedule mean more staffing costs, more test environment costs, and more opportunity costs.

"Hang on, Rex," you might say, "didn't you just tell me at the beginning of this chapter that quality is free? If so, what are all these economic objections to the huge return on investment that I can offer?"

Well, yes, I did say that quality is free, but only in the long run. Since we're talking economics, the dismal science, I'll quote John Maynard Keynes, who said that, "in the long run, we're all dead." A limited pile of cash is available for any given project. Once that money's gone, it's gone. (Ask any former employee of a failed dot-com firm or some other underfunded start-up about this fact of life.) Managers have to make prudent decisions — often trade-offs — about where to spend money. This puts limits on how much money can be spent on quality-related activities for any given project, positive return on investment notwithstanding.

Communication Breakdowns: Management Blind Spots and the Difficulty of Education

Sometimes test budgets are not approved — or are retroactively unapproved — because the management team doesn't understand the benefits of testing. Even seasoned high-tech managers occasionally fall into the rut of complacently thinking, "Oh, what could possibly go wrong?"

Some managers never get out of this rut. When you hear of organizations in which developers do all the testing, small test groups are assigned unachievable test loads and held responsible for quality, or management doesn't pay attention to the test dashboard, then you know that such organizations are run by a team of senior managers who fail to understand the complexity of software and hardware development. Frankly, there are many buggy products on the market today, and not understanding the need for an independent test organization, how it should function, or how to appropriately respond to test results has a lot to do with that.

However, I think that we test professionals need to accept our share of the responsibility for this situation. If we can't effectively articulate the test plan, doesn't that reinforce the idea that testing isn't really that hard? If we can't produce a clear set of system quality metrics, how will we convey our concerns about system quality to managers? If we can't measure defect removal trends, then how do we demonstrate how long it really takes to fix bugs — and thus to exit a test phase? If we fall into adversarial relationships, won't we come across as disruptive and negative rather than as people providing a valuable service to the project team?

Surmounting the Obstacles . . . Then Doing What We Can

I don't claim to know exactly how to communicate to your managers about the testing budget. Everyone is different. I run a testing consulting and services provider, and we don't win every engagement we propose, so I guess I haven't figured out all these angles, either. However, there are some techniques I try to get people on board. Then there are some follow-through steps I think are important.

Testing is about risk management, and you must explain the risks as part of selling management on your budget. Because a risk is the possibility of a bad outcome, your pitch for each budget item might sound something like this: "If you don't test A, you might have failures X, Y, and Z in the field; and I can't test A without buying C." Some salespeople refer to this technique as "fear, uncertainty, and doubt," which makes it sound pretty low. However, it serves the greater good of shipping a better product, and some managers just won't listen to you unless you use this technique to get their attention. Don't be an alarmist, though. Describe some realistic scenarios of bugs that could cost the company a lot of money but that could be caught by testing. The time you've spent understanding the important risks, using the techniques discussed in Chapter 1, should pay off here. Express those risks in terms of possible user experiences: "unable to complete a sale," "prevented from printing the file," "taking 10 seconds to respond to a keystroke." Avoid those dry and slightly mystical technical phrases such as "core dump," "blue screen of death," "surface overtemp condition," and other jargon.

If you consider it crass to raise alarms, at least understand that it is not dishonest. Testing can only add value when it helps the company mitigate risk. You are tying one hand behind your back if you decide to "take the high road" — whatever that might mean in this context — and eschew discussions of what could go wrong. If at some later point, you end up with so many people on your staff that everyone is playing video games or surfing the Internet half the time, then perhaps you should feel guilty.

Anecdotes are convincing, and you should use them. You should also use figures and data, too, in spite of the cliché that figures don't lie but liars do figure. Build credibility for your data, and then use defect removal models, past test results, and cost of quality to justify your budget. Just as with explaining your test results, using data to explain your resource needs can help make your presentation dispassionate.

It's important, too, to recognize that project funds are limited, so you're playing something of a *zero-sum game* — in other words, a game whose outcome involves moving around existing money, like poker or blackjack, rather than creating new wealth, like free-market capitalism — with the other managers on the project. Money allocated to testing is money your fellow managers don't have in their budgets. But don't panic. Money I spend on food, airline tickets, trash pickup services, auto maintenance, and every other thing I write checks for every month is money I don't have in my savings account either, but I don't resent the people who sell me these goods and services. On the contrary, I feel that they are providing me with useful economic options and I'm glad to pay for those options.

This is something we need to master as test professionals. How can we convince our peer managers that we are providing them with a useful service? First, let's focus on being service-oriented, on building strong alliances with our peer managers, as I discussed in Chapter 9. Developers need help finding bugs. Sales, marketing people, and business analysts want to sell or deliver quality to users and customers. Help desk, technical support, and customer support people don't want angry customers. All of these teams — and their managers — are obvious allies to help you help them.

Finally, I'm particularly careful these days to advocate but never pontificate. Even when senior managers understand the need for testing, they might not realize why it costs so much. It's not always simple to explain. Because I've been testing for many years, all these facts of testing life have become obvious to me. These facts are seldom obvious to my managers. Senior managers who understand and value the need for independent testing always give me an opportunity to justify each line item in my budget, but I am not excused from that exercise. It's up to me to respond to these legitimate questions by providing clear, to-the-point answers.

It's also up to me to do what I can with whatever I ultimately get. If I react to attempts to trim my budget by saying, "Fine, cut my budget and I'm outta here," then I'll probably spend a lot of my time adjusting to new cubicle space. Just as I said in Chapter 1, there's usually a difference between what I *should* test and what I *can* test. The difference: features, schedule, quality, and budget realities. When my wife and I had a house custom-built, we left out many features in the house that we wanted. We'll probably add these features over the coming years, and the features will cost us more than they would have if included during construction. However, we couldn't wait 6 or 12 more months to move in and we didn't want to spend another $100,000 or $200,000 on the house.

As a test manager, I make trade-offs. I always do. I'll be asked to focus on what's most critical, what no one else is testing. That's part of my job. Often, I'll make a pitch to management for some amount of testing and I'll be told to do a bit less testing with a bit less money and time. Doing a bit less testing than I'd really like to is always part of testing in the contexts in which I've worked. If I want to work as a test manager in such a context, I can't let what I can't do stop me from doing what I can. To paraphrase a much-maligned quote from Donald Rumsfeld, you have to do your testing with the test budget you have, not the test budget you wish you had.

Case Study

Table 11-1 shows the return on investment for the Internet-appliance project. In the first section of the table, I calculate the cost of detection. This involves removing costs of internal failure (regression test costs) and amortizable costs of equipment, tools, test environments, and so forth. In the second section, I calculate costs of internal failure, based on the costs of fixing bugs (a development costs) and regression testing after the bug fixes are integrated. In the third section, I calculate the costs of external failure, based on the costs of technical support, maintenance bug fixing, and maintenance release testing. In the fourth section, I calculate the return on the testing investment. Since each bug costs $1,100 to find and fix prior to release, while a post-release bug costs $3,000, each of the 1,500 must-fix bugs found by the test team offered the company the opportunity to save $1,900.

I thank my client on the Internet appliance project for the opportunity to work with them and for letting me to share this case study with readers of this book. My client contacts have asked that their organization remain anonymous.

Table 11-1 Cost of Quality Return on Investment Analysis for the Internet Appliance Project

DETECTION COSTS	
Test budget	$1,000,000
Future value of assets created	100,000
Regression test costs	500,000
Net detection costs	$400,000
Must-fix bugs found during testing	1,500
Approximate cost per bug	267
INTERNAL FAILURE COSTS	
Pre-release bug fix costs	750,000
Regression test costs	500,000
Net internal failure costs	$1,250,000

(continued)

Table 11-1 (*continued*)

INTERNAL FAILURE COSTS	
Must-fix bugs found during testing	1,500
Approximate cost per bug	833

EXTERNAL FAILURE COSTS	
Sustaining costs	3,000,000
Percentage bug-related	50%
Net external failure costs	$1,500,000
Must-fix bugs found after testing	500
Approximate cost per bug	3,000

RETURN ON INVESTMENT	
Cost of quality (w/testing)	3,150,000
Cost of quality (w/o testing)	6,000,000
Net benefit of testing	2,850,000
Approximate testing ROI	713%

Exercises

Figures 11-2 shows the reactive test budget, and Figure 11-3 shows the return on investment analysis for reactive testing, using cost of quality. Similarly, Figures 11-4 and 11-5 show the respective budget and analyses for manual scripted testing. Figures 11-6 and 11-7 show the respective budget and analyses for a test using both manual and automated testing. The source spreadsheet for these worksheets, "Exercise SpeedyWriter Budget.xls" is also available at www.rbcs-us.com.

1. Some common threads among the three projects are that each release will include 200 must-fix bugs that are either found and fixed during testing or delivered to the customers. In other words, we're not assuming any changes to the development process that would prevent defects. There will be quarterly maintenance releases and one major release every year. This allows you to amortize the test environment, test development, and any tools across 3 years, or 12 releases. For test engineer time, assume that half the time is spent developing tests or capturing testing done for later re-use, while the other half is spent in execution. Finally, assume that the test team is engaged from the start of the project in November. (Realistically, many major release projects would be longer than 3 months, but let's keep the exercise as simple as possible to focus on the key concepts.)

	A	B	C	D	E
1	SpeedyWriter Test Budget				
2	Reactive Testing				
3					
4		Nov	Dec	Jan	Total
5	**Staff**				
6	Lin-Tus Wong--Test Engineer	8,333	8,333	8,333	$25,000
7	**Total Staff**	**$8,333**	**$8,333**	**$8,333**	**$25,000**
8					
9	**Tools**				
10	Web loading/stress tool	$0	$0	$0	$0
11	**Total Tools**	**$0**	**$0**	**$0**	**$0**
12					
13	**Test Systems**				
14	Linux Client	$1,500	$0	$0	$1,500
15	Windows Laptop Client	1,000	0	0	1,000
16	Windows Desktop Client	1,500	0	0	1,500
17	Mac Client	1,500	0	0	1,500
18	Solaris Server	2,500	0	0	2,500
19	Windows Server	2,500	0	0	2,500
20	Linux Server	2,500	0	0	2,500
21	**Total Test System**	**$13,000**	**$0**	**$0**	**$13,000**
22					
23	**Grand Total**	**$21,333**	**$8,333**	**$8,333**	**$38,000**

Figure 11-2 SpeedyWriter test budget (reactive testing only)

	A	B	C
1	SpeedyWriter Test Budget		
2	Reactive Testing ROI		
3			
4	**Testing**	**Baseline**	**Testing**
5	Staff (test development amortized)	0	$13,542
6	Systems (amortized)	0	1,083
7	Tools (amortized)	0	0
8	**Total Investment**	**$0**	**$14,625**
9			
10	**Development**		
11	Must-Fix Bugs Found	100	100
12	**Fix Cost**	**$1,000**	**$1,000**
13			
14	**Testing**		
15	Must-Fix Bugs Found	0	30
16	**Fix Cost**	**$0**	**$3,000**
17			
18	**Customer Support**		
19	Must-Fix Bugs Found	100	70
20	**Fix Cost**	**$100,000**	**$70,000**
21			
22	**Cost of Quality**		
23	Conformance	$0	$14,625
24	Nonconformance	$101,000	$74,000
25	**Total CoQ**	**$101,000**	**$88,625**
26			
27	**Return on Investment**	**#N/A**	**85%**
28			
29	**Defect Detection Percentage**	**0%**	**30%**

Figure 11-3 SpeedyWriter test ROI (reactive testing only)

	A	B	C	D	E
1	SpeedyWriter Test Budget				
2	Scripted Manual Testing				
3					
4		Nov	Dec	Jan	Total
5	**Staff**				
6	Jamal Brown--Test Manager	$10,000	$10,000	$10,000	$30,000
7	Lin-Tsu Wong--Test Engineer	8,333	8,333	8,333	$25,000
8	**Total Staff**	**$18,333**	**$18,333**	**$18,333**	**$55,000**
9					
10	**Tools**				
11	Web loading/stress tool	$0	$0	$0	$0
12	**Total Tools**	**$0**	**$0**	**$0**	**$0**
13					
14	**Test Systems**				
15	Linux Client	$1,500	$0	$0	$1,500
16	Windows Laptop Client	1,000	0	0	1,000
17	Windows Desktop Client	1,500	0	0	1,500
18	Mac Client	1,500	0	0	1,500
19	Solaris Server	2,500	0	0	2,500
20	Windows Server	2,500	0	0	2,500
21	Linux Server	2,500	0	0	2,500
22	**Total Test Systems**	**$13,000**	**$0**	**$0**	**$13,000**
23					
24	**Grand Total**	**$31,333**	**$18,333**	**$18,333**	**$68,000**

Figure 11-4 SpeedyWriter test budget (manual scripted testing primarily)

	A	B	C
1	SpeedyWriter Test Budget		
2	Scripted Manual Testing ROI		
3			
4	**Testing**	**Baseline**	**Testing**
5	Staff (test development amortized)	0	$29,792
6	Systems (amortized)	0	1,083
7	Tools (amortized)	0	0
8	**Total Investment**	**$0**	**$30,875**
9			
10	**Development**		
11	Must-Fix Bugs Found	100	100
12	**Fix Cost**	**$1,000**	**$1,000**
13			
14	**Testing**		
15	Must-Fix Bugs Found	0	60
16	**Fix Cost**	**$0**	**$6,000**
17			
18	**Customer Support**		
19	Must-Fix Bugs Found	100	40
20	**Fix Cost**	**$100,000**	**$40,000**
21			
22	**Cost of Quality**		
23	Conformance	$0	$30,875
24	Nonconformance	$101,000	$47,000
25	**Total CoQ**	**$101,000**	**$77,875**
26			
27	**Return on Investment**	**#N/A**	**75%**
28			
29	**Defect Detection Percentage**	**0%**	**60%**

Figure 11-5 SpeedyWriter test ROI (manual scripted testing primarily)

	A	B	C	D	E
1	SpeedyWriter Test Budget				
2	Manual and Automated Testing				
3					
4		Nov	Dec	Jan	Total
5	**Staff**				
6	Jamal Brown--Test Manager	$10,000	$10,000	$10,000	$30,000
7	Lin-Tsu Wong--Test Engineer	8,333	8,333	8,333	$25,000
8	Emma Moorhouse--Test Engineer	9,167	9,167	9,167	$27,500
9	**Total Staff**	**$27,500**	**$27,500**	**$27,500**	**$82,500**
10					
11	**Tools**				
12	Web loading/stress tool	$20,000	$0	$0	$20,000
13	**Total Tools**	**$20,000**	**$0**	**$0**	**$20,000**
14					
15	**Test Systems**				
16	Linux Client	$1,500	$0	$0	$1,500
17	Windows Laptop Client	1,000	0	0	1,000
18	Windows Desktop Client	1,500	0	0	1,500
19	Mac Client	1,500	0	0	1,500
20	Solaris Server	2,500	0	0	2,500
21	Windows Server	2,500	0	0	2,500
22	Linux Server	2,500	0	0	2,500
23	**Total Test Systems**	**$13,000**	**$0**	**$0**	**$13,000**
24					
25	**Grand Total**	**$60,500**	**$27,500**	**$27,500**	**$115,500**

Figure 11-6 SpeedyWriter test budget (automated and manual testing)

	A	B	C
1	SpeedyWriter Test Budget		
2	Manual and Automated Testing ROI		
3			
4	**Testing**	**Baseline**	**Testing**
5	Staff (test development amortized)	0	$44,688
6	Systems (amortized)	0	1,083
7	Tools (amortized)	0	1,667
8	**Total Investment**	**$0**	**$47,438**
9			
10	**Development**		
11	Must-Fix Bugs Found	100	100
12	**Fix Cost**	**$1,000**	**$1,000**
13			
14	**Testing**		
15	Must-Fix Bugs Found	0	90
16	**Fix Cost**	**$0**	**$9,000**
17			
18	**Customer Support**		
19	Must-Fix Bugs Found	100	10
20	**Fix Cost**	**$100,000**	**$10,000**
21			
22	**Cost of Quality**		
23	Conformance	$0	$47,438
24	Nonconformance	$101,000	$20,000
25	**Total CoQ**	**$101,000**	**$67,438**
26			
27	**Return on Investment**	**#N/A**	**71%**
28			
29	**Defect Detection Percentage**	**0%**	**90%**

Figure 11-7 SpeedyWriter test ROI (automated and manual testing)

   a. If you have two colleagues or fellow students available, take turns role-playing the test manager while the other two act as the skeptical project and executive managers. Present and defend the budget using the return on investment analysis.

   b. If you don't have anyone to do exercise 1.a with, write down the justification you would use for each budget.

2. Suppose that we want to calculate the expected average cost of external failure for DataRocket. We know from past projects that the average server has 50 must-fix bugs lurking undiscovered when it ships. Customers report and receive fixes for 90 percent of these bugs within six months of first customer delivery. One full-time supporting engineer is assigned for each server during those 6 months, assuming the supporting engineer can fix on average 7.5 bugs per month. Each bug generates on average 10 calls to technical support, and each call requires one person-hour of technical support time, including any follow-up research, discussions with the supporting engineer, and providing information to the test team to create a confirmation test for the bug. Bug fixes are bundled in weekly support packs that require 20 person-hours of testing and 5 person-hours of release engineering time. Assume that the cost of a person-month, including the burden rate, is $10,000. Based on 22 workdays a month and six productive work hours in a day, assume that a person-hour costs $76.

   a. What is the expected average cost of external failure during the first six months for DataRocket?

   b. Suppose you also knew that, on average for each technical support call, the customer spent one hour before calling trying to fix the problem and one hour during and after the call implementing a workaround, installing the fix, or otherwise mitigating the effect of the bug on the system. Further suppose that for every customer who did call, one other customer chose to fix the problem herself without calling, spending on average three hours. One other customer chose to return the server for a full refund of the $2,000 purchase price. Recalculate the expected average cost of external failure during the first six months based on this additional information.

   c. In exercise 2.b, did you include the customers' lost time? Why or why not?

   d. Are any categories of external failure costs missing in this exercise?

COMMENTS ON EXERCISE 1

You might have noticed in working through exercise 1 that the return on investment is significantly lower than the 350 percent and 445 percent shown in Figure 11-1, and that it went down as we added more resources, rather than up. Why?

The reason the return on investment is lower is because the cost of conformance *per bug found* is different. In the example illustrated in Figure 11-1, the investment in testing (cost of conformance), normalized by the number of bugs found, came to about $175 per bug. In exercise 1, the cost of conformance per bug found is about $500 per bug, which is approximately three times higher. If we reduce staff costs — for example, through wise use of test technicians — we could increase the return on investment. However, it's also the case that the worse the system under test is in terms of quality, the better the return on investment will look (at least, as long as we can run enough tests to find most of the bugs). This is another example of metrics being potentially misleading and dysfunctional. If, as the test manager or as the test team, you are given a bonus based on the return on investment calculated by cost of quality, then your incentive is to file an excessive number of bugs reports, ask the development team not do any unit or component testing, or both.

The reason for the declining return on investment is the shape of the cost of quality curve. Traditional cost of quality curves look something like Figure 11-8. If such is the shape of your cost of quality curve, at some point the cost-of-conformance and the cost-of-nonconformance curves intercept. Spending exactly that amount on cost of conformance minimizes the cost of quality. (Newer thinking on cost of quality suggests that, if you invest your money in quality assurance and testing wisely, the cost of conformance never exceeds the cost of nonconformance.[2]) As you approach the cost of quality minimum, the return on investment might fall off because each additional dollar investment in testing results in less of a reduction in the cost of nonconformance.

You already have seen an example of this phenomenon at work. If you think back on the opened/closed charts shown in Chapter 4, imagine using that data along with the daily tester effort figures gathered in Chapter 5 to graph, on a daily basis, the number of person-hours required to find the next bug. You would get a curve that, instead of leveling off as you approached the end of system test, would instead go from a flat curve when bugs were easy to find to an upward-sloped and parabolic curve as bugs became more difficult to find.

(continued)

---

[2]See Campanella, et al.'s *Principles of Quality Costs.*

COMMENTS ON EXERCISE 1 *(continued)*

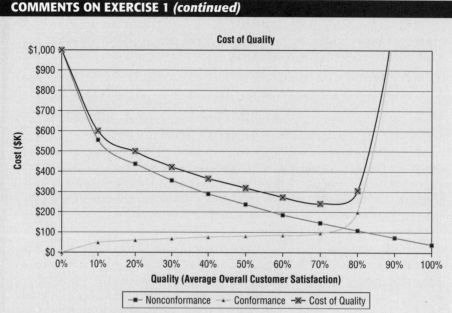

Figure 11-8 A hypothetical cost of quality graph

As you think about these topics, you might start to ask yourself, as I did at one point, a nagging question. "Gee," I thought, "isn't something missing in this approach to calculating the return on investment of testing?" The answer to this question occurred to me in the form of another question: "Is the only value of testing in finding bugs?"

I believe the answer to that question is, "No." Testing is a form of quality risk management, something like insurance. Most people who own cars carry car insurance. At the end of a policy year, if a driver hasn't made any claims, would that driver go out and run a car into a lightpost to achieve a positive return on investment on the insurance policy? Of course not.

Using the insurance model, we might attempt to quantify the value of a passed test. In insurance, the expected payout is the probability of a loss times the cost of the loss. Therefore, if we know the average cost of particular types of field failures, we can justify spending some fraction of the total costs of those types of failures that could occur, based on the chance that those bugs *could* be present in the system. The return on investment would come not from finding the bugs, but from knowing whether the bugs were there. In other words, the return on investment would come from the reduced chance of unanticipated future costs.

(continued)

COMMENTS ON EXERCISE 1 *(continued)*

I certainly haven't read every paper and book on software engineering economics, so I might have missed something. However, to my knowledge, no one has done a lot of digging into this topic yet. If you are a software engineering student looking for a senior-year project or graduate thesis, this could well be fertile ground for research.

CHAPTER 12

Testing Implications of Project and Process: Situational Context

In the previous chapter, we turned our attention from the way the test management world looks from the test manager's perspective to the way the test management world looks from the outside world's perspective. In particular, we looked at the motivation for testing as a way to reap financial and other benefits. The main benefit to you as a test manager of understanding this outside view of your value is that you can better defend your budget and your resource allocations.

There are still two important and somewhat related contextual issues to address. One is the matter of the project context, especially the life cycle. A formal or informal software life cycle model provides organizations with guidance on the way to organize a project. It is typically chosen to achieve a particular purpose or organization goal such as faster releases, regulatory compliance, and so forth. If testing is done inconsistently with the chosen life cycle, that will create major impediments for us as testers. For one thing, the large amount of friction associated with this mismatch will cause a lot of frustration and inefficiency. For another thing, we are likely to be ineffective at producing the benefits the organization wants from us, which ultimately is dangerous to the ongoing survival of the test team. Perhaps most importantly, we become an obstacle to achieving the very goals the organization set out to achieve by choosing a particular life cycle model in the first place.

The other issue — which is related — is the overall process followed, both for software or systems projects in general and for testing on those projects specifically. This is particularly significant for us as testers because processes tend to differ greatly in their level of maturity. Mature processes, through their predictability, efficiency, and effectiveness, enhance the predictability, efficiency, and effectiveness by which we achieve our objectives as testers. This is as much true for external processes for software or systems development as it is true for test processes. In fact, as I'll point out later, you can't have very mature test processes without a supportive overall development process, just as you won't find healthy fish in a polluted river.

So, in this chapter, I'll turn to these issues of project and process context.

Where Testing Fits into the Project Life Cycle

As I mentioned, a big part of understanding project context is thinking about where the testing to be done fits into the overall system life cycle, the various phases, constituent activities, and dependencies among those activities. This is important because strategies, plans, and activities for test system development and test execution that would be ideal for one life cycle can be less helpful or even counterproductive for others. There are many different life cycle models defined, and it's beyond the scope of this book to discuss each in detail. In the following subsections, I'll discuss the major types of life cycles and how they affect testing.

Common Life Cycle Themes

Regardless of the specific life cycle chosen, the most successful projects I've worked on have some common themes in this area. One is that the testing is divided into phases or levels, as discussed in Chapter 1. Ideally, each phase should find most of the bugs it can, leaving only those bugs specific to the subsequent phase to be found. For example, programmers (acting as unit testers) should find logic errors in specific functions or objects during component testing, leaving programmers and testers working together during integration testing to find data flow errors between functions or objects, which in turn leaves testers to find system performance problems during system testing.

In Chapter 1, I used the metaphor of the different coarsenesses of fishnets used to catch different kinds of fish. In Chapters 3, 4, and 10, I referred to the idea of testing as a bug filter. In both cases, the analogy is that different testing phases should catch different kinds of bugs. Letting bugs escape from the earliest phase in which you can find them to a later phase not only increases the cost of finding those bugs, but also reduces the effectiveness of the downstream testing processes, because the fishnets (or filters, if you prefer) either miss the bugs or get too clogged up with residual bugs to find the ones we should focus on in that phase. I have seen examples of this *clogged filter, low test effectiveness and efficiency* phenomenon in many, many different organizations following many, many different life cycle models, so I am convinced that the problem is universal. The degree of formality and the number of phases tend to vary, but at a minimum should include a unit or component test phase and a system test phase.

If neither the fishnet nor the bug filter metaphor works for you, think of test phases as steps in a cleaning process, each of which uses a type of cleanser and a cleaning approach that removes a particular type of dirt, grime, or soil. For example, you can remove bacon grease from a plate with a clean dry towel, but that will leave a film behind that will spoil and taint the flavor of the next meal served on the plate. You'd be better off washing the plate in hot water with dishwashing detergent and a sponge first, then rinsing the plate with warm water, and finally using the towel to dry the plate.

In most organizations in which I've worked, the developer of a unit or component was the owner of the unit or component testing for his or her unit or component. The component testing approach was primarily structural (white-box). The independent test team handled system testing. The system testing approach was primarily behavioral (black-box), with some live testing (especially live data, but also beta testing) and some structural testing (especially test tools) thrown in.

For all but the simplest of systems or the most minor of maintenance releases, I highly recommend having a separate integration test phase as well. If you don't have the time and resources to do the type of formal, risk-driven integration testing I mentioned in Chapter 1, with integration or build plans along with integration test plans, at least do informal testing of as much of the system as exists as the components are completed, looking for bugs that could arise in interfaces and dataflows for various reasons.

Remember that, as my associate Judy McKay puts it, you never actually skip a test phase; you just push the work into the next phase. Without integration testing of some sort, the initial period of system test becomes a de facto, unstaged integration test phase. I have seen this approach cause entire weeks of testing downtime when key components that seemed to work fine on their own failed to communicate — or sometimes even to compile and link — correctly when put together.

Integration testing is often an orphaned test phase. It requires some amount of structural testing and some amount of behavioral testing, so integration testing requires broader skills from a test team engaged in integration testing than one engaged in either unit testing or system testing alone. It checks behaviors and looks for bugs between pairs of components, but often programmers do not want to spend the time testing their component with other programmers' components.

Two assumptions about integration testing that I've encountered with programmers are ''I already unit tested my component, so if someone else's component doesn't work with my component then they must be using my component improperly" and "I don't mind testing my own component, but testing that stuff works together is the test team's job." The first assumption is invalid because bugs can exist *between* components, neither in one component nor the other. The second assumption is problematic, because testers don't always have the technical skills and insight required to do good integration testing.

However, it can help to ask, "Who are the immediate beneficiaries of good integration testing?" The people charged with system testing are, because, as mentioned earlier, they are the people who will be blocked if poor or omitted integration testing results in a non-working system being delivered for system test. (Even if you require the system to pass entry criteria and/or a smoke test before entering system test, as discussed in Chapter 2, you'll still end up scrambling to find productive work to do if the day before system test was to start, the system fails to meet the entry criteria or to pass the smoke test.) The development team also benefits from good integration testing, because it's easier to debug a bug found in integration test. The developers will find it less painful to isolate failures, remove bugs, and regression test when working with a limited, smaller set of components.

Therefore, if integration testing is an orphan in your organization, I encourage you to work with management to get the resources you need to adopt it. Once you get it started, try to get development involved by explaining to them that their debugging work will go more smoothly if they help you achieve good integration testing. If integration testing is already owned by the development team, I recommend that you try to get a senior test person involved, working with the development team, to help improve integration test coverage and to ensure alignment between integration test and system test.

In systems for in-house or contractual (as opposed to mass-market) customers, there is often an acceptance test phase of some sort. Pilot testing is another post-system test phase that occurs in some organizations. Often, the test manager is not responsible for the acceptance test phase directly. However, the organization will reasonably expect that good component, integration, and system testing will result in a system ready for acceptance and pilot testing when the time comes.

In some cases, though, risks to system quality covered in acceptance and pilot testing go beyond the scope of the previous testing phases. For example, pilot testing of laptop computers also tests the production line capability and the computers coming off the line, while usually the previous test phases used hand-built engineering prototypes. However, it's a good idea to understand what the acceptance and/or pilot testing will cover and make sure you cover that as well during system test.

During the planning process, look at what the acceptance or pilot testing phases involve, and escalate to management if you see any gaps in the component, integration, and system test phases that could lead to last-minute discovery of critical bugs in acceptance or pilot testing. These types of findings can create a serious conundrum for the project — sometimes even outright project cancellation — along with real political problems for the test manager if people see these bugs as test escapes. Even if these problems are avoided, as discussed in Chapter 11, finding and fixing problems gets more expensive as the project goes on, so avoiding costly bugs in the final phases of testing makes good financial sense.

Entry into and exit from test phases should represent major transitions in the readiness of the system, especially in terms of quality. If the system leaves one test phase and enters the next with all the appropriate bugs detected and repaired that could be detected and repaired in that phase, the subsequent phase will go smoothly. If a phase is done poorly or not at all and the system enters a subsequent phase buggy and untested, that subsequent phase will tend to proceed inefficiently. The subsequent phase might also be ineffective at finding the bugs it should find, due to the distraction posed by the leftover bugs that previous test phases should have found earlier. This can lead to a cascading or snowballing effect on to the next phase and ultimately on the quality of the delivered system. This is part of the reason for the importance of adopting good definitions for exit and entry criteria, as discussed in Chapter 2.

Another reason is that entry into a test phase owned by a different group than the previous test phase represents a significant handoff point in the organization. If you use the right set of test phases with the proper entry and exit criteria, these handoffs go smoothly, fostering a feeling of teamwork. If the organization omits key test phases, if criteria are poorly defined, if the criteria are defined but not measurable in an objective way, or if criteria are defined and measurable but not abided by during testing, then phase transitions will be more a matter of some poor-quality system hurled over an organizational wall, resulting in a *gotcha* experience for the receiving party. In the long run, repeated botched handoffs will lead to personal ill will and distrust between members of the project team, especially between developers and testers or between users and user-surrogates and testers.

Selecting the right set of phases, defining proper criteria for them, and abiding by those criteria (or at least only waiving any of them through well-informed, carefully considered, mutual consent of the stakeholders) is a key part of fitting the testing effort into the project life cycle context. But how do we know what the right phases and criteria are? To some extent, that is a function of the life cycle model being used, which can also have other effects on the test project.

The V Model and Sequential Projects

One common life cycle model of software development is called the *V model*, shown in Figure 12-1, which applies to sequential projects. The development work proceeds in sequential phases down the left side of the V, while test execution phases occurs up the right side of the V. Tests are planned and developed, and the appropriate test environments acquired and configured, starting as soon as the corresponding development phase begins. The three arrows crossing the V show these activities. For example, requirements being the basis for behavioral and live acceptance tests, preparatory work for that phase of test execution can commence immediately. (Of course, requirements also figure in system testing, and to a lesser extent integration and component testing, too.) Some versions of the V model allow for overlap of phases. Others call for pure sequentialism, where the entry criteria for one phase always include exiting from the previous phase.

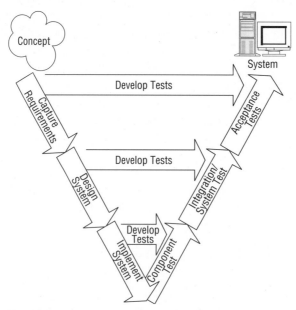

Figure 12-1 The V model

This is an intuitive model, and one that has in many ways become institutionalized in a lot of software engineers' minds and in many software development organizations. To many testers, it just looks right when they first see it. Most software engineers who received their college degrees prior to 2000 — which would therefore include many of the people involved in test, development, and project management now — probably learned this model or its less test-explicit variant, the waterfall model, when they were in college.[1]

One chief danger with this model is that it's hard to plan accurately that far in advance. To announce that the project team will deliver a given set of

---

[1]I have two copies of Roger Pressman's *Software Engineering: A Practitioner's Approach*, which is a commonly used textbook in many college software engineering courses. The second edition, published in 1987, includes eight pages of discussion on life cycles, primarily focused on variations of the sequential model. The fourth edition, published in 1997, includes an entire chapter on the topic, and has started to discuss other models. The Agile models discussed in this chapter became more common in the post-2000 period.

features — which are often cast in stone in the minds of project managers, users, or user-surrogates by the end of the requirements phase — on a specific date that might be two or three years in the future and for a specific amount of money is to presume a level of prescience most human beings don't have. Capers Jones, in *Estimating Software Costs*, cites the incidence of significant delay or even cancellation in moderate-sized development efforts as around 20 percent, and for large efforts that figure can balloon to as large as 70 to 90 percent. As Jones puts it, "[T]here is almost an infinite number of ways to fail in building software applications, and only a few ways to succeed."[2]

This life cycle model is basically driven by schedule and budget risks, with quality often taking a back seat. If the requirements, design, or implementation take longer than expected — and they often do — the pivot point at the bottom of the V starts to slide to the right, but the end date anchoring the top of the right arm of the V often remains stuck in place. This leads to what I often refer to as the *ski slope and cliff* variant of the V model. The project glides down the implementation ski slope right into the quality cliff of the test execution phases at the end of the project, which were compressed in a haze of wishful thinking about how all those test cycles planned won't be needed after all.

Nevertheless, you can mitigate the risks inherent in the V model and use it successfully. Testing tasks should start as early as possible, be cooperative between all the participating groups, and include feedback mechanisms. For example, on one project my team started working on test cases with early drafts of the requirements document. In this process, we discovered a whole raft of requirements problems that the project team then had a chance to resolve before they resulted in design and code defects.

The project team must also plan test execution cycles realistically, especially in terms of the cycles necessary to find all the bugs for each phase and give the developers ample time to repair those bugs before moving to the next phase. Defect removal models such as those discussed in Chapter 4 help, but if you don't have data, at least trust your gut instincts and the collective wisdom of the test team.

Resist the urge to put in place patently silly plans such as two cycles of component, integration, or system testing on the assumption that the first will find all the bugs, which the developers will fix in short order, and then the second cycle will simply confirm the fixes and the lack of regression. This might be a reasonable plan for acceptance testing, since you shouldn't really find any bugs during acceptance testing at all, but not for any other test phase. Such almost entirely bug-free test execution periods might happen on some projects, but it's never happened on a project I've worked on.

---

[2]See Chapter 7 of Caper Jones's *Estimating Software Costs* for his figures on project success and failure. The specific quote is found on page 114.

While good entry and exit criteria are important regardless of the life cycle model, in the V model they're even more critical, because test phase entry and exit points can provide the project team with its best indicators that the project is off track in terms of schedule and budget. Be clear about the risks to the quality of the system and perhaps to the project itself if people start talking about violating those criteria in order to stay on schedule, as this is a classic problem with all life cycle models. (See the section "Process Brake Pedals" later in this chapter.) If you are allowing overlap between phases, fine, but then you should have smoke tests defined that demonstrate readiness to enter each phase. These smoke tests, if automated, also make a handy tool for keeping broken releases out of the test environment, because you can run them before starting a given test cycle.

Finally, rather than violating or waiving entry criteria, see if you can't set up a process where the project team revisits the feature set at test phase entry points. Change control boards (CCBs) are particularly useful for this process. If a feature is not completed or is completely bug-ridden, and that will delay the start of some test phase or activity, then perhaps the team can delay that feature to a later release. Realistic feature triage like this can mitigate some of the most nasty failures of the V model.

The Spiral Model

In some cases, it's hard to determine in advance what features exactly are needed — or can be feasibly built. The spiral model relies on quick prototyping to discover and manage key project risks early in the effort. In this model, shown graphically in Figure 12-2, the initial concept is quickly translated into a prototype of some or all of the system, focusing usually on those features and design elements considered most at risk in terms of technical feasibility or satisfying the users. The prototype is put through some limited testing, again focusing on the high-risk areas. What is learned from that prototype informs a subsequent round of design, prototyping, and testing. This continues until a final set of features, known to be feasible, is selected, at which point the model becomes much like the V, with design and implementation followed by the appropriate test phases, which might include unit, integration, and acceptance testing, as shown in Figure 12-2.

This model solves the V-model problem of predicting the future on limited knowledge, because we don't commit to any particular feature set until we know what's feasible. If the prototypes include user interface prototypes and we can get the users involved in the early testing, then this model also mitigates the user interface and usability risks.

However, sometimes people get confused about which model they're following. I worked on one project that was clearly operating on a nice spiral life cycle, but none of the senior project managers seemed to understand that.

With each of the early testing phases, they became excited that we were about ready to deploy. They thought we were on a V model. This created lots of political problems when we went back to the redesign stages at the end of each test period.

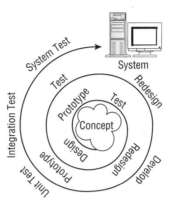

Figure 12-2 The spiral model

Another risk of this model is that schedule and budget can be hard to control. This can result in the same type of problem described for the V model, namely the immovable end date. If someone decides by fiat that the system simply *shall* ship on a particular date, then testing can once again get squeezed at the end. This brings us back to the same old schedule conundrum: ship a lousy product on time and budget, or slip the project to allow further testing, bug repair, and higher quality.

With expectations set clearly for all the stakeholders, though, this model can work really well. My associates and I built an automated test harness for a client using this model. Every two or three weeks we polished up what we were working on into a stable prototype that included some new set of features, and then did a demo for the test team that showcased those features. As the prototypes matured, the testers started using the test tool a bit, too, to get some hands-on experience. Based on the feedback from the users, we would repair, redesign, and then add some new features. There is no way that a V model would have worked in that environment, because we could never have gotten the time and focus from the testers to write good requirements. However, they were happy to attend the demos and give us input as the test tool grew organically.

Of course, you might argue that what we were following was an Agile methodology, at least one with loosely defined iterations. You could say that model applied as well as any other. After all, models are just approximations of what really happens on projects. Any model that makes sense and provides useful guidance to the project team is useful.

Evolutionary, Incremental, or Agile Models

A broad and increasingly popular family of life cycle models can be considered evolutionary or incremental in the sense that a given release grows up around a core of features that are delivered, often on a predetermined date. While that might sound like the V model, the difference is that features are added in chunks to a stable core. As the features drop in, this new system is stabilized through testing and debugging, and only then are more features added. At any point once the core features are stable, you can ship a system. The only question is what features it will include. The project team can use various methods to select the order of feature inclusion, including user or market importance, technical risk, system architecture or consistency, or some mix of all of these and other considerations.

This model covers a broad spectrum of formality, from Rapid Application Development to the Agile methods like Scrum and Extreme Programming. Some purists might object to my including Scrum, Extreme Programming, and other Agile methods in this category, but the core characteristics of evolutionary or incremental models apply to these methods. The only question is the amount of ceremony involved. The more formal variations will include what look like *mini V models* for each delivered increment (see Figure 12-3), while the less formal models will look more like a sequence of spirals.

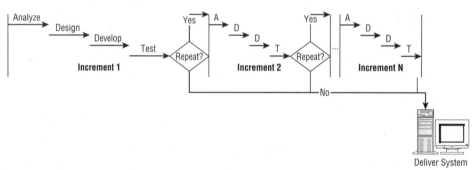

Figure 12-3 An evolutionary model, with formal increments

The fixed release dates do resemble the V model in one way, in that there's always a temptation to ship a product where the last incremental set of features really isn't quite ready. We have a number of clients that use incremental life cycles. While the features in the last increment aren't always completely done, the core features of their products are stable. Therefore, provided you pick the right set of core features and add additional increments in the right order, lingering quality issues in the final increment might be an acceptable business decision.

One aspect of incremental methods is that you'll need more testers, especially test technicians and other test execution resources, than you would for a V model, at least one of decent size. Testing, including the expansive and expensive system test phase, tends to start earlier, because we need to thoroughly test the core before adding new increments. Therefore, where the entry criteria for system test for a V model project might specify that all features are complete and unit tested and the requirements frozen, in an incremental model you can only ask that the *core features* are complete and unit tested. The requirements won't be frozen until the decision is made about which is the last (i.e., shipping) increment, and in some projects there aren't any requirements specified at all. An automated regression testing tool can reduce the need for extra staff, but it takes talented automated test engineers to develop automated tests for a system or parts of a system that are in the initial development (as opposed to on-going maintenance) stage of their life cycle.[3]

For smaller incremental life cycle projects, especially those working with Agile methods, the software engineering community seems to be feeling its way toward an understanding of where and how testing in general — and independent testers and test teams in particular — fit in.[4]

On the one hand, I find in the Agile methods positive and encouraging ideas such as writing tests first and then writing code only until those tests pass. A couple of associates and I built an automated testing harness and defined a lightweight but comprehensive process for component and integration testing for a client using freeware tools; I'm not sure they would have taken such care in this regard had they not been following an Agile method.[5]

On the other hand, I've heard this quote from some Agile practitioners with no experience or training in the field of testing: "We test everything that could break." Upon closer scrutiny, this statement turned out to mean that they tested in a purely reactive way, focused on whatever came to mind as risky in a technical sense. That approach to testing is about as far away from what I'm advocating in this book as almost anything could be. (See the case study at the end of this chapter for more on the topic of testing in an Agile project.)

---

[3]You may want to see Mark Fewster and Dorothy Graham's book, *Software Test Automation*, for ideas on how to handle this and other challenges of test automation.

[4]To learn more about Extreme Programming from the tester's perspective, see Lisa Crispin's articles, "eXtreme Rules of the Road," published in *Software Testing and Quality Engineering* magazine, Volume 3, Issue 4 (July/August 2001), and "Is Quality Negotiable?" published in *The Proceedings of the STARWest 2001 Conference*. Both are now available on www.stickyminds.com.

[5]See our article, "Mission Made Possible," originally published in *Software Testing and Quality Engineering* magazine, Volume 4, Issue 4 (July/August 2002), and now available on www.rbcs-us.com.

Code and Fix

Even though I said that a testing approach epitomized by statements like, "We test everything that could break" was almost as far from what I'm advocating as anything could be, there is one approach that is even farther away. It occurs within the context of a particular approach to software development known sometimes as *code and fix*.

While there is typically no defined goal or method, here's the process in a nutshell:

1. On the first day of the project, developers immediately sit down to write and debug code. No requirements gathering or design of any kind occurs. Often, none of the developers do any unit testing, or each developer picks their own approach, with little hope of sharing or reuse and no way to automate.

2. Within a few days, developers start to release code to an informal test team, often junior developers or other people with no training or experience in testing.

3. Even without the benefit of professional testing, the testers find many bugs. Often, the developers debug in the test environment, with the corresponding changes not always making it into the code repository. Test releases — such as they are — come hourly or more frequently, often from the developers' own systems rather than out of the build and release engineering environment.

4. The project team repeats all of the preceding steps at the same time.

This process continues until time, money, or patience runs out. The team ships or deploys whatever the team has produced at the end of this maelstrom of chaos, unless it's clearly impossible to do so, in which case the organization cancels the project. Sometimes the end result of this frenzy is that the company goes out of business without deploying anything of value. The 2000 and 2001 dot-com-failure phenomenon featured plenty of ill-conceived and poorly executed Internet applications that fit in this category, and the practice continues to this day.

What's interesting is that, in small projects, with a few minor tweaks, this process can work. Practice good source code control and release engineering, and a major source of chaos goes away. Use professional testers instead of people with no talent or motivation to do the testing, and the team can identify the critical risks to system quality and test for them. Establish a shared vision — on as little as a cocktail napkin — of the system's requirements and design, and keep people on the same page through frequent dialog. This degree of structure might be enough to avoid the "push me–pull you" that can break out between developers writing interfacing or interacting components.

The trouble is that this model does not scale — at least, I've not seen it scale — in situations where there are large or distributed development teams working on complex projects. Once you get more than a half-dozen people working together on a project, it seems that you have to start writing things down and adopting orderly processes, or chaos and confusion will begin to eat dangerously into project team efficiency and effectiveness. I have seen people try to follow the code-and-fix approach as their companies grew, and often bad things happened. I had a colleague years ago who worked at Ashton-Tate, once the predominant player in PC database software. They apparently followed the code-and-fix approach. Basically, this became a game of quality roulette. They got away with it for a while, but finally in one release enough catastrophically bad bugs were missed that the marketplace abandoned their product in droves. I have had more than one of my clients tell me similar stories.

If you work in a code-and-fix environment, I recommend that you at least adopt some of the ideas in this book to try to instill some order in the testing part of your projects. You might serve as a shining beacon of order and efficiency to the rest of the project, or you might just eliminate some of the madness and frustration from your own domain, but at least you'll know that you're no longer part of the problem.

Testing Maintenance Releases

So far, I've been talking mostly about system development projects, but that's just the beginning of the software life cycle. Once software is released, it must be maintained. These maintenance releases must also be tested. From a task list and schedule perspective, a typical maintenance release might appear as shown in Figure 12-4.

Task Name	October	November	December
Select Fixes and Features for Release			
Develop Fixes and Features			
Develop New and Update Existing Tests			
Debug Fixes and Features			
Debug Test Cases			
Smoke Test Execution			
System Test Execution			
Acceptance Test Execution			

Figure 12-4 A maintenance release task list and schedule

A major risk for a maintenance release is regression. In Chapter 3, I provided an extensive discussion about regression and options for dealing with it, but here my focus is on the process, not the test system. Yes, the new features or bug fixes in the maintenance release must work, but you sure don't want to break an important system feature or capability that has become integrated into critical workflows by users or customers.

Some organizations, through a variety of analytical methods such as module-to-feature tracing matrices, try to anticipate where the regression risk is highest for any given change. They then rerun only those tests that cover those modules (which implies that they also have to have a tracing matrix from tests to features, and that they write test cases against each release that are reusable against subsequent maintenance releases). The trouble with these matrices and other analytical regression predicting methods is that the paperwork and record keeping is time-consuming and complex. Programmers and testers alike often perceive it as low-priority drudgery. These facts can combine to result in near-instantaneous obsolescence. Furthermore, software can interact in unexpected ways, especially in the risky areas of reliability and performance or when shared databases exist. So, just because no one touched a given feature doesn't mean that a bug can't magically appear in it.

The more brute force but less hazardous way to address regression risk is to repeat a lot of tests against each release. I'm assuming you have reusable tests from the original release where the feature first appeared. One of the dangers of a purely reactive approach with no documented test coverage is that you have very limited alternatives in terms of regression testing. There are two common approaches to doing this.

The first, more whiz-bang approach is to use automation for your regression testing. You either buy a commercial test tool or build one yourself, and then automate as many of your tests as you can. You can start small and then gradually build up to having every test that you can practically automate in your automated suite. Some tests, such as usability tests, error handling and recovery tests, compatibility tests, and the like are not often automatable, so the same considerations of what you should and can test discussed in Chapter 1 should drive your testing, not what the tool can and can't do.

Some people have had real trouble with automated testing, and others might not have the budget for it. In this case, you might prefer adopting a slower release schedule. If you try to have a maintenance release every two weeks, then you might have limited time available for manual retesting outside the new and changed areas. What if the maintenance releases happened every two months, though? Yes, there'll be five times or so as much content in terms of new features and bug fixes to test, but there's an interesting thing that happens: tests often cover more than you expect.

You might remember my geological-modeling software client from Chapter 3. They have a complete set of tests that takes about 2 person-decades of effort to run. With a test team of 20, they can get through all the tests in a year. They were concerned about regression risk, so they started measuring rolling 4-week code coverage during testing. They were surprised — pleasantly so — to discover that in a given four-week period they were consistently exercising over 50 percent of the code while running less than 10 percent of the test set. Over the course of their entire course of testing, they achieved 100-percent cumulative coverage for the entire project, but the more coverage they had already achieved, the less likely each subsequent test case was to add anything to the cumulative number.

This is nothing but the old 80/20 rule of management — 80 percent of your payoff comes from the first 20 percent of your effort, and the remaining 20 percent of your payoff requires the remaining 80 percent of your effort. Perhaps you can settle for something closer to 80 percent than 100 percent? The moral of this story is that, by combining less-frequent releases with some intelligent assessment of what you might miss and the selection of appropriate test cases to fill those gaps, you can probably mitigate regression risk reasonably well even without test automation.

Whether you adopt a slow or rapid release schedule, one constant problem I've encountered in maintenance testing is the pressure to squeeze too much content into one given release. To each user, customer, salesperson, business analyst, help desk technician, or marketer, the bug fixes or new features important to them or their constituents are the most critical. Collectively, this results in a tremendous amount of pressure on the development team to increase the size of a maintenance release, but that just puts us right back in the painful trade-off of quality versus schedule and budget. This is particularly bad in maintenance testing, because stakeholders often will only accept delays based on an increase in the features in the maintenance release — which, of course, means more testing is needed not only for the additional features but also for the regression risk they bring with them — while shipping bad maintenance releases only further damages company credibility with customers and users and digs a deeper hole for the sustaining team to climb out of. Both of these are forms of vicious cycles that the organization's management team must break by establishing realistic estimation processes for maintenance releases.

Part of that process must include sufficient time for development of new tests or upgrading existing tests based on the maintenance release content. In the case of one company with an automated functional regression test harness, we received data and procedures to replicate a bug from technical support at the beginning of each maintenance release effort. We added new automated tests based on this material. We then waited to see which tests failed in the first test run, and then checked those failed tests to see which failures were actually correct results due to the changes made. That allowed us to re-establish the expected results and run the tests again. This took about a week once we got it all down.

Sometimes, though, a small change can result in a big impact on the tests, especially automated tests. In the same company, a change to some file-reading and database record-sorting logic resulted in my test team having to re-validate literally hundreds of test results, along with an entire new test suite that we had to write. The test development effort was probably almost equivalent to the programmer effort.

System, Subsystem, Commercial Off-the-Shelf Software, and Component Integration

Not every major system project involves a whole lot of system development or maintenance. Especially with the rise of outsourcing (see Chapter 10), many projects primarily center on acquiring, integrating, and perhaps customizing existing software or hardware within a new or existing system. These projects — regardless of what any vendor's salesperson said during the sales process — require testing commensurate with the business and technical risks associated with the integrated system's potential failures.

These risks tend to increase in the presence of one or more of the following factors (some of which I covered in Chapter 10):

- The criticality of the integrated component to the intended business purpose, operation, or mission of the overall system.

- The coupling between the integrated component and any critical component, especially if the integrated component is upstream in terms of workflow or data processing.

- A large degree of component customization or adaptation to a unique use.

- Any unusual or unique workflows, use cases, or data sets that the component will encounter in your environment.

- A large number of supported configurations in your environment.

- A large number of configurations supported by the component (e.g., if the vendor tells you the component supports every version of Windows, ask yourself how much testing they could have practically done on your particular desktop configuration).

- A relatively small installed customer base for the component, especially if that customer base does not include anyone using the system in ways or configurations remotely like yours.

- A brand new major release (e.g., release 1.0 as opposed to release 1.4).

- A large number of service patches, maintenance releases, and minor upgrades for the component.

- Poor vendor testing practices.

- Poor vendor support.

As discussed in Chapter 10, you can try to leverage your vendors' testing and tools to some extent, but you should remain in control of the testing and be vigilant about what's being done. The more your project involves integration of existing subsystems and components, the more you are — as a practical matter — limited to an acceptance-testing role for those components. However, I'd encourage you to try to get as much visibility as possible into the vendor testing as early as possible, and adopt a *test to fail* outlook in this case, rather than the usual *test to pass* perspective of acceptance testing.

Hardware/Software Systems

Some projects include hardware and software components, some custom, some integrated from other vendors, and some commercial off-the-shelf items. This can create some complications that affect the test effort. For one thing, the critical skills you identify for your test team will expand to include some amount of hardware knowledge, even if you're not directly responsible for hardware testing. As discussed in Chapter 2, you'll also need to ensure sufficient hardware — especially scarce engineering prototypes, if applicable — to provide for all your testing. Finally, it's often the case that custom hardware has testability issues compared to off-the-shelf hardware. You might have trouble understanding the internal states, especially error states, without tools or special skills.

Especially with custom-developed hardware, you'll see some extra time and money required during estimation. Usually, projects that involve custom hardware reveal bugs not just in software, but in the hardware, too. There's some amount of extra time required to handle each bug, of course, but it also means that proportionately more test cases fail, which adds to the overall test time as well. When tests fail, you need to isolate bugs across multiple platforms to make sure that you don't have a defective unit, rather than software, causing the bug. In some cases, hardware shortages occur when engineering prototype units die, which can block tests or require that you institute second or third shifts to utilize the remaining hardware continuously.

After you file bug reports, you might see longer turnaround times (i.e., the closure periods discussed in Chapter 4) on bugs if confusion (or outright obfuscation) arises over whether the bug resides in the hardware, the firmware, some software component, and so forth. A properly authorized CCB, bug review committee, bug triage team, or whatever name these folks go by in your organization should have the ability to assign a bug to a particular team for repair, to keep the test team out of the middle of any debate on what's broken. For test teams with a primarily behavioral testing charter, once the testers have identified a quality problem in the system, prioritizing the bug, determining the root cause, ascertaining the most appropriate subsystem in which to fix the bug, and implementing that fix are all tasks that live most properly outside of the test team.

If you're a new test manager with a primarily software background approaching a test project that involves hardware, don't worry. You don't need to become a hardware engineer overnight — if at all. The techniques and tools outlined in this book are ones that I've used for plenty of hardware/software system projects ranging from standalone laptops to complex, distributed custom-interactive-voice-response/call center systems. A little time spent brushing up on statistical quality control and possibly hardware-reliability engineering if you can spare it will make you all the more effective, but most important are thoughtful advance planning, hiring an appropriate test team, managing execution carefully, and possibly arranging for good hardware testing by a vendor or test lab as discussed in Chapter 10.[6] For a very basic introduction to typical hardware testing, see Appendix A.

Process Improvement

With all these different variations of life cycles, schedule and budgetary considerations, and other context issues affecting testing, surely every project is a unique beast, huh? Well, every project is a new thing in the sense that it's an endeavor to fill a heretofore-unfilled need with a product or service. But, as King Solomon wrote, "What has been is what will be, and what has been done is what will be done; there is nothing new under the sun." While some see Ecclesiastes as a disheartening poem, perhaps this constancy of human nature is good news to us? Since the days of the great Egyptian pyramids and even before, people have been working together to accomplish spectacular things, to implement useful tools, to make life better for each other. Perhaps there are lessons we can learn from the past, and from each other?

"But We're Different . . .": The Commonality of Solutions

In the opening sentence of his novel *Anna Karenina*, Leo Tolstoy says that "all happy families are alike, but each unhappy family is unhappy in its own way." In commenting on this passage, the historian Paul Johnson disagrees, retorting that the sources of unhappiness in families — alcoholism, infidelity, violence, poverty — are tiresome and common and lead to tiresome, common, and sad

---

[6]You may want to consider Kaoru Ishikawa's *Guide to Quality Control* and Patrick O'Connor's *Practical Reliability Engineering*.

results.[7] The commonality of problems is great news, though, because the commonality of the afflictions allows common approaches to alleviating them.

The same is true of software and hardware development companies, development projects, and test organizations. When you talk about test concepts that might help to get your organization under control, management might respond, "Oh, but we're different. That will never work here. We have to be more creative than that." Balderdash! In fact, many corporate dynamics are common not only among companies in similar sectors, but even among organizations whose only similarities are that they are groups of people working together. As Peter Drucker, management sage extraordinaire, writes, "The differences between managing a chain of retail stores and managing a Roman Catholic diocese are amazingly fewer than either retail executives or bishops realize . . . whether you are managing a software company, a hospital, a bank, or a Boy Scout organization, the differences apply to only about 10% of your work. This 10% is determined by the organization's specific mission, its specific culture, its specific history and its specific vocabulary. The rest is pretty much interchangeable."[8]

I have worked with companies and clients in various areas of the computer business, including big insurance companies, banks, and hardware companies, small systems integrators, mass-market and specialized software houses, custom programming shops working for huge and small clients, and everything in between. Although the level of maturity of the processes and the skill levels of the staff influenced the types of problems I saw, the company's particular product or service mattered much less.

I don't want to over-generalize. It's certain that you have some unique test management predicaments. But you have many more that are common. You are not alone, and you can apply solutions such as those you find in this book and others to solve your problems. Anyone who says, "Oh, but we're different . . . " is either uninformed or resisting change.

Nevertheless, you can't rush the process of change. The idealized test project models presented in this book represent organizations operating at a significant level of management maturity. The word *maturity* in this context doesn't mean that a company's senior managers are of a particular age. Rather, it refers to companies that are in a continuous process of applying, adopting, and adapting the best — or at least the better — practices of software and

---

[7]That said, don't let me deter you from reading this great book by Tolstoy, or his other classic, *War and Peace*. In fact, *War and Peace* is a great read for managers, especially those who aspire to executive levels, because its theme, ultimately, is that history's so-called great men matter much less to the outcomes than the thousands of individuals who make decisions moment by moment in all momentous events. Tolstoy is a brilliant author, but Johnson's critique of the opening sentence of *Anna Karenina* in *Intellectuals* is right on target. Ultimately, we are all human, and thus much less different than we are alike.

[8]See "Management's New Paradigms" by Peter Drucker.

hardware development professionals. In other words, they have learned from the cumulative mistakes of past software and hardware organization managers, and they continue to learn from their own mistakes.

I discussed the Software Engineering Institute's Capability Maturity Model back in Chapter 10. This model is not perfect, as I mentioned, especially for evaluation of vendors, but it does provide a useful mental framework for evaluation of your own organization.

These models measure five levels of process maturity. Level one is characterized by a completely ad hoc approach, devoid of any real processes whatsoever. People work according to their own and management's whim of the moment. At the first sign of a crisis, managers drop any pretense of process and simply make up something on the fly. According to the Software Engineering Institute, "In an immature organization, there is no objective basis for judging product quality or for solving product or process problems. There is little understanding of how the steps of the software process affect quality, and product quality is difficult to predict. Moreover, activities intended to enhance quality, such as reviews and testing, are often curtailed or eliminated when projects fall behind schedule."[9]

The really pernicious aspect of an immature organization is that many managers who operate at that level have made a conscious choice to do so. They tend to react viscerally to suggestions that adopting a set of processes, rather than relying on intrepid improvisation, might make life better. If you work in an immature organization, you need first to recognize it and then to understand whether the situation results from an unawareness of the opportunity to do better or a denial of software engineering realities. The former situation is reparable through hard work and determination from the senior executive level on down, while the latter is a matter of attitudes and belief systems that sometimes resist empirical data and logical reasoning.

The tools and techniques in this book work best in an organization striving to become a mature one, applying industry best practices. To apply the approaches described here, you must have control of your test processes. This includes controlling the deployment of resources and the methods of work in your test group. If your organization remains stuck in deliberately chosen immaturity, proclaiming individual heroics the only way, and managers — both those above you and your peers — insist on micromanaging your resources, you will find it difficult to improve your situation. Depending on your place in the organization and your personal credibility with senior management, you might not be well-positioned to be an agent of significant change to your company's processes. However, the survival of the test organization depends on your ability to educate people about — and

[9]See *The Capability Maturity Model.*

achieve — tangible benefits from testing. This can be a daunting task without some degree of formal process, both internal to the test group and at the test team's interfaces with other groups and managers.

Test organizations bear a heavy burden under unmanaged, abrupt changes in plan. A sudden about-face by management can blow away significant investments of time and money in test suite development, undermining your return on investment. The change management database introduced in Chapter 6 can help you track the impact of such changes, but you might find that no one wants to hear explanations (a typical situation in immature organizations). If, after giving it the old college try, the organization will not change, and your colleagues, peers, and managers treat the test team like the poor relation of the company, you might want to find a job that will give you an opportunity to succeed.

However, let's focus on the positive, not the negative. Yes, you might fail to effect change, but you might succeed. If you can connect with your colleagues, peers, and managers in terms of how you can really deliver valuable services to them and the organization, you will gain their ear. Sell them on testing as a valuable activity. Sell them on changes that can improve the value and the quality of the product. When you sell change, don't talk about your pain. Talk about their pain — and how better testing and higher quality can make it go away. People move away from pain much faster than they move towards idealized situations, especially when those situations don't provide immediate benefits. With that in mind, let's talk about how external factors affect your team's ability to provide services.

The Test Team Is Not an Island: External Effects on Your Productivity

Various organizational behaviors and attributes, which I call *gas pedals* and *brake pedals*, can speed up or slow down test progress. In general, all of them exercise incremental influence on your test operation: a single tap on the brake won't bring the test project to a dead stop, just as a jab to the gas won't send the system under test rocketing through the test exit criteria in a single pass. Overall, however, to make testing proceed smoothly, your company needs to press on the gas pedal and lay off the brake pedal. Although each single incident or behavior is incremental, lots of braking signals a troubling trend.

Your test project can easily suffer the death of 10,000 cuts from many little braking events. In a reactive sense, when the project takes a significant hit, document it in the change management database introduced in Chapter 6. However, the broader theme of this chapter, project and process context, has to do with understanding — and influencing — these contextual influences on your testing effort. See if you can recognize any inhibiting trends, and try to reduce their occurrence in the future. Likewise, actively promote the behaviors that make your job easier. Help your peers and colleagues understand the importance to your productivity of following certain courses of action and eschewing others.

Process Gas Pedals

The following organizational behaviors and attributes tend to accelerate the test process. Encourage these activities and values among your peers, and jump at the opportunities to perform them yourself where appropriate.

Testing throughout the project. I use the phrase *testing throughout the project* in a three-dimensional sense. The first dimension involves time: in order to be properly prepared, and to help contain bugs as early as possible, the test team must become involved when the project starts, not at the end. The second dimension is organizational: the more a company promotes open communication between the test organization and the other teams throughout the company, the better the test group can align its efforts with the company's needs. The third dimension is cultural: in a mature company, testing as an entity, a way of mitigating risk, and a business management philosophy permeates the development projects. I also call this type of testing *pervasive testing*, as I mentioned in Chapter 1.

Smart use of cheaper resources. One way to do this is to use test technicians. As Chapter 8 explained, you can get qualified test technicians from the computer-science and engineering schools of local universities and colleges as well as from technical institutes. Try to use these employees to perform any tasks that do not specifically require a test engineer's level of expertise. Another way to do this is to use distributed and outsourced testing, as explained in Chapter 10.

Appropriate test automation. The more automated the test system, the less time it takes to run the tests. Automation also allows unattended test execution overnight and over weekends, which maximizes utilization of the system under test and other resources, leaving more time for engineers and technicians to analyze and report test failures. The basic tools provided with this book will allow you to automate some key test management activities, and you can expand these tools to be even more automated. You should apply a careful balance, however. Generating a good automated test suite can take many more hours than writing a good manual test suite. Developing a completely automated test management system is a large endeavor. If you don't have the running room to thoroughly automate everything you'd like before test execution begins, you should focus on automating a few simple tools that will make manual testing go more quickly. In the long run, automation of test execution is typically an important part of dealing with regression risk during maintenance.

Good test system architecture. Spending time in advance understanding how the test system should work, selecting the right tools, ensuring the compatibility and logical structure of all the components, and designing for subsequent maintainability really pay off once test execution starts. The more intuitive the test system, the more easily testers can use it.

Clearly defined test-to-development handoff processes. As discussed in Chapter 4, two closely related activities, bug isolation and debugging, occur on opposite sides of the fence between test and development. On the one hand, test managers must ensure that test engineers and technicians thoroughly isolate every bug they find and write up those isolation steps in the bug report. Development managers, on the other hand, must ensure that their staff does not try to involve test engineers and technicians, who have other responsibilities, in debugging activities.

Clearly defined development-to-test handoff processes. The project team must manage the release of new hardware and software revisions to the test group. As part of this process, the following conditions should be met:

- All software is under revision control.
- All test builds come from revision-controlled code.
- Consistent, clear release naming nomenclatures exist for each major system.
- A regular, planned release schedule exists and is followed.
- A well-understood, correct integration strategy is developed and followed during the test planning stages.

Automated smoke tests run against test releases, whether in the development, build (or release engineering), or testing environments (or all three), are also a good idea to ensure that broken test releases don't block test activities for hours or even days at the beginning of a test cycle.

Another handoff occurs when exit and entry criteria for phases result in the test team commencing or ending their testing work on a given project. The more clearly defined and mutually accepted these criteria are, the more smoothly and efficiently the testing will proceed.

A clearly defined system under test. If the test team receives clear requirements and design specifications when developing tests and clear documentation while running tests, it can perform both tasks more effectively and efficiently. When the project management team commits to and documents how the product is expected to behave, you and your intrepid team of testers don't have to waste time trying to guess — or dealing with the consequences of guessing incorrectly. (See Chapter 9 for tips on operating without clear requirements, design specifications, and documentation when the project context calls for it.)

Continuous test execution. Related to, and enabled by, test automation, this type of execution involves setting up test execution so that the system under test runs as nearly continuously as possible. This arrangement can entail some odd hours for the test staff, especially test technicians, so everyone on the test team should have access to all appropriate areas of the test lab.

Continuous test execution also implies not getting blocked. If you're working on a one-week test cycle, being blocked for one just day means that 20 percent of the planned tests for this release will not happen, or will have to happen through extra staff, overtime, weekend work, and other undesirable methods.[10] Good release engineering and management practices, including smoke-testing builds before installing them in the test environment, can be a big part of this. Another part is having an adequate test environment so that testers don't have to queue to run tests that require some particular configuration or to report test results.

Adding test engineers. Fred Brooks once observed that "adding more people to a late software project makes it later," a statement that has become known as Brooks's Law.[11] Depending on the ramp-up time required for test engineers in your projects, this law might not hold true as strongly in testing as it does in most areas of software and hardware engineering. Brooks reasoned that as you add people to a project, you increase the communication overhead, burden the current development engineers with training the new engineers, and don't usually get the new engineers up to speed soon enough to do much good. In contrast, a well-designed behavioral test system reflects the (ideally) simpler external interfaces of the system under test, not its internal complexities. In some cases, this can allow a new engineer to contribute within a couple of weeks of joining the team. (Structural test systems, however, do require an understanding of system internals and tend to have longer ramp-up times.)

My usual rule of thumb is that, if a schedule crisis looms six weeks or more in my future, I can bring in a new test engineer in time to help. However, I have also added test engineers on the day system test execution started, and I once joined a laptop development project

---

[10]As Tom DeMarco put it in *The Deadline*, "There are infinitely many ways to lose a day ... but not even one way to get one back."

[11]See Frederick Brooks's software engineering classic *The Mythical Man-Month* for this and other useful observations. Published initially in 1975, this book still has a lot to say about software engineering and software project management.

as the test manager about two weeks before the start of system test execution. In both cases, the results were good. (Note, though, that I am not contradicting myself. Testing does proceed most smoothly when the appropriate levels of test staffing become involved early, but don't let having missed the opportunity to do that preclude adding more staff.) Talk to your test engineers to ascertain the amount of time that'll be required, if any, to ramp up new people, and then plan accordingly.

Process Brake Pedals

The following project behaviors and attributes tend to decelerate the test process. You should avoid these behaviors yourself, and help your organization avoid them as well.

Getting too clever. Because many previously independent pieces of the product come together in testing, test schedules have myriad dependencies, an elaborate critical chain (critical-path and near-critical-path task networks), and single points of failure. Even with the collective knowledge of the entire project team, test and project managers cannot easily identify all of these before they come whistling out of nowhere and whack you on the forehead. Avoid the temptation to "accelerate" the test schedule by piling one seemingly reasonable assumption on top of another, thereby building an insupportable house of cards. When the assumptions fail, the project is left de facto without a schedule, and chaos and improvisation ensue.

Unrealistic project schedules. The same types of problems associated with getting too clever also arise when project schedules are totally disconnected from reality. This situation occurs when management confuses business priorities with technical possibilities, and it is especially prevalent when marketing windows and bonuses are involved. When your managers start telling you that they intend to make up earlier schedule slips during test execution, something bad is about to happen, and you will be intimately involved.[12] (This is what I meant by the *ski slope and cliff* earlier when discussing the V model.)

Failure to provide test deliverables. Such failures include shortages of hardware or software, the release to test of incomplete software

---

[12]Robert Glass, in his *Practical Programmer* column in *Communications of the ACM*, writes of consulting with a client who had put such a schedule in place: "I said things like, 'The approach you are taking to accelerate the schedule is actually costing you long term, in that enhancements and system testing are taking such unpredictably long periods of time that it is not possible to achieve any anticipated schedule.' (Things had literally crawled to a halt in system testing, with each new bug fix generating enough new bugs that almost no forward progress was achieved)."

systems, software releases that are impossible to install or that are improperly packaged, incompatibilities, releases outside strict revision control, and so forth. The frequent follow-up to such delays can take the form of project management dictating that the test team must meet its original schedule, hobbled though it is. Therefore, proactive efforts to anticipate and prevent such problems in the first place is key.

Lack of system administration, infrastructure, and developer support. The test lab infrastructure will often require expert system administration support. An experienced system administrator can resolve in five minutes a problem that a test engineer might take five hours to figure out. For the same reason, support from facilities management is important — for example, having people on call to unlock doors that no one expected to be locked. Developer support is necessary, too. For example, during the early stages of testing, the product might have blocking bugs that need quick resolution and emergency test releases. A test team must have prompt support available from these various sources whenever tests are being run, which sometimes means 24 hours a day, 7 days a week, once test execution begins in earnest. Testers should have contact lists, with home and mobile phone numbers, including, as a last resort, the names and numbers of managers. Defining an escalation process, as discussed in Chapter 2, is important, and following that process when support breaks down is essential.

Scrimping on tools. Test tools, especially test automation tools, will pay for themselves when used wisely. (When used foolishly they cost much more in wasted time than money, but that's a different story.) Trying to economize by building your own tools, quashing the idea of purchasing a new tool because of budget constraints, using inappropriate open-source tools because they are "free," and sending test engineers on snipe hunts for bargain tools waste the test team's time, thus delaying the project *and* costing more money.

It's true that sometimes you need to build your own test tools, because no commercial tool can accomplish what you need done. In this case, you should hire a separate toolsmith (or toolsmiths) to provide the tool-building support. It's a prime example of unrealistic scheduling to assume that someone will cobble up a test tool in her spare time while writing test cases, developing test data, getting the test environment configured, hiring test technicians, and all the other tasks that test engineers do while getting ready for test execution.

Unrealistic test execution schedules. Test schedules must allocate sufficient time for each test case, understanding that the discovery of bugs will increase the time needed to run the test cases. The schedules must also include sufficient cycles, in advance, for the resolution of problems found in the first cycle. I have participated in too many projects whose schedules were blown when management assumed that test would find no must-fix bugs. As soon as the first must-fix bug surfaced, these projects had no schedule. The estimation techniques discussed in Chapter 1 are part of putting realistic test execution schedules in place.

Slow or shoddy development response. As mentioned in Chapter 4, a key metric for development response to test-reported bugs is the average turnaround time from the opening of a bug report to its resolution and closure, the closure period. Only development, by promptly debugging and fixing problems, can influence the closure period. (There are, though, process overheads such as test release schedules that introduce natural delays.) Another key metric for development response to bugs is the confirmation test failure rate, which is the percentage of bug fixes that fail to resolve the underlying bug. The longer development takes to resolve a bug, or the more times it must try to fix a bug before it succeeds, especially for the high-severity issues that can block test progress, the slower the test effort moves. The more bugs in the bug backlog, the harder it is for testers to make sense of the test results. Consequences of long closure periods and big bug backlogs include not getting through all the planned tests in a cycle and, ultimately, delaying finding bugs until late in the test phase, possibly with insufficient time to resolve the bugs.

Debugging in the test environment. Sometimes development is forced to use the test environment to reproduce bugs because the development environment is insufficiently complex. However, every minute that development uses a piece of test equipment for debugging is a minute that the test team can't run tests. There is also time required to bring the test environment back to a known configuration after debugging, which can include reinstalling software, changing network configurations, and other labor-intensive activities. Make sure project managers understand that testing is blocked while developers use the test environment for debugging and afterwards while your team restores the configuration. Escalate these situations when they occur, and make notes in your change management database (see Chapter 6).

Buggy deliverables. The more bugs in the system under test, the slower testing goes. The time that test technicians and engineers spend in bug identification and isolation is several orders of magnitude greater than the time it takes to kick off automated tests and collect passing results.

Violations of test plan entry criteria. Project management often justifies entering a test execution phase before the system under test is ready by arguing that this will accelerate testing. It usually does not. Most commonly, the test team must abort the first cycle as a result of rampant stability bugs that prevent any forward progress. During hardware testing, equipment can actually be damaged because it can't survive in the test lab environment.

Violations of test plan exit criteria. Leaving a test phase before the bug find rate has leveled off and all other exit criteria are met just passes along an immature system to the next phase of testing. This next phase will do a less efficient and less effective job of identifying the test escapes from the previous phase, because the test system operates at a coarser level of granularity as it progresses from one phase to the next.

Scope creep, crawl, and redefinition. Changes in system scope (e.g., features, capabilities, etc.) result in changes in test project scope. Test scope itself is sometimes subject to abrupt change, usually when the schedule begins to falter. Both increases and reductions in scope can create problems. Test engineers who design the test system must make certain assumptions about the functionality of the product. If some of the functionality later drops out, a domino effect can result that compromises the test system, partially or completely breaking it.

For example, suppose that you design tools and cases to test stress, volume, and capacity loads of a system based on a particular driver or interface in the system, and then that driver or interface changes. What if you invest person-months of effort in building a test tool that can scale up to hundreds of simultaneous load-generating connections, only to find that the design capacity has been dropped, in response to bugs found by your team, to an order of magnitude less? Was the time spent building a tool that could scale to that capacity wasted? Maybe not, in the long run, but it will surely feel that way in the midst of a furious schedule crunch, when those two person-months could have been devoted to many other priorities.

Test suite or phase cancellation. Like system scope shrink, test scope shrink can waste time, although in this case it's usually retroactive: the time spent developing or preparing to run a test suite or phase proves to have been wasted. Those tests won't find any bugs, mitigate any risks, build any confidence, or produce any information. So, the return on investment is shot, but the investment was already made. Fortunately, it's not impossible to see this coming. If a test phase or cycle drags on well beyond its originally scheduled exit date, start to plan proactively to shut it down and catch up the testing later, if possible.

Tester mistakes. Simply put, test managers, test engineers, and test technicians make mistakes. Clearly, as the test manager, you are responsible for minimizing these types of goofs. They include, among others, the following notable examples from my own experience:

- Failing to understand the dependencies while planning
- Developing tightly coupled, unstable, unmaintainable, incompatible, or erroneous test systems
- Picking the wrong test tools
- Doing poor or inefficient bug isolation
- Wasting time on trivial matters while the critical areas fall apart
- Reporting bugs that aren't bugs
- Failing to report bugs that are bugs
- Running automated tests with the wrong parameters or in the wrong configurations
- Skipping critical test cases

Did I put this item last on the list of brake pedals on purpose? You bet. I've worked on a few troubled projects, and tester mistakes were always the least important of the problems. However, they can attract a lot of attention, especially when someone's looking to distract the project management team from his or her own problems, or when someone has a vested interest in undermining the credibility of the information coming out of the test team. (Sorry to sound so cynical, but I've known it to happen on my own projects, during consulting engagements, and from many test management training attendees.) As I said in Chapter 9, if we are to point out the errors of others, it really does help to be right. Therefore, part of running a mature, credible test operation is working to minimize these tester errors, even if you have irrefutable evidence in your change management database that test errors are the least of the project's problems.

Project Retrospectives

So, how can project teams learn to step on the gas pedals and keep their feet off the brake pedals? It's easy to say, "Let's just do more of the gas pedals and fewer of the brake pedals." However, in the heat of a project, especially as projects get closer to the end, project teams often find they have engaged in behaviors that now have consequences. Some of those consequences accelerate testing; others retard it. And, in the heat of a project, you often must set aside the question of why situations arose so that you can deal with the situations.

Yes, when you're in a situation, you should deal with the situation. Too much reflection on the situation distracts you from the solutions. However, if you never reflect on the situations in which you find yourself over and over, then you are doomed to a Sisyphean existence, pushing a rock up a hill on each and every project only to have it roll back down on you.

A colleague once told me that his company motto was *make interesting, new mistakes*. If you're not making mistakes, you're not innovating, and that's a road to disaster. However, you should make only new mistakes, because repeating past mistakes is foolish. And you should hope that your mistakes are interesting, because interesting mistakes offer important learning opportunities.

One good way to learn from what we did well and what we did poorly on our projects is to hold *project retrospectives*. Project retrospectives are also called post-mortems and postpartums, though each of these terms has negative connotations that many people like to avoid. Ideally, these retrospectives are cross-functional meetings held after the project is over, after the terrific sense of urgency has ended, so we can reflect on what happened and why.

While you could hold such a meeting with just that for the agenda, it often helps to put a bit more structure around it. I suggest making sure that retrospectives address at least the following three questions:

- What went well (and how can we do more of it next time)?

- What went badly (and how can we prevent it next time)?

- What unexpected risks and opportunities did we encounter?

Feel free to add more questions to this list, but try not to add so many that you distract people from these key issues.

What contributes to a good retrospective meeting? I suggest the following ground rules or expectations for the meeting:

- Encourage open exchanges of ideas. This is not the same as encouraging people to criticize others. The point is to understand why something happened, not who did or didn't do something.

- Have participants come ready to present data to illustrate their points. As a consultant, I have heard many people offer explanations for why things happen. Often, those explanations are not based on data, just on feelings. People try to have reasonable explanations for why things happen, but sometimes these explanations are wrong. The most dangerous kind of wrong is the kind of wrong that sounds reasonable, as I've said elsewhere in this book. You can and should use data that can test people's hypotheses.

- Have people bring ideas on how they can do better on future projects. It's easy for retrospectives to devolve into a group wail when projects went badly. Instead, focus on how to make things better. A good refocusing statement to keep in mind is: So what? Now what?

- Build a library of data, presentations, reports, and minutes from retrospectives. Remember the motto I cited above about making new mistakes. It's not a new mistake if some other project team made the same mistake on an earlier project. You want to make this information readily available so it serves as a future project resource.

- Make sure that management will commit to implementing good ideas from retrospectives. I went to one retrospective where one attendee reacted at the end by saying, "I've been in the exact same meeting three or four times now. Same set of things we will do, same set of things we won't do. The next project will be exactly the same as this last project because management won't change the process." That's just depressing. You don't want these meetings to degrade into the management equivalent of the movie *Groundhog Day*, where Bill Murray's character relives the same day over and over again.

Now, if you convince the project team, especially the managers, to have retrospective meetings, there's still value in having a test retrospective with the test team alone. As a test manager, you can make this happen. However, if the testing went badly, this could have more to do with external factors than with factors under your control. If so, you should focus the test team on those things you can control or improve, so that the meeting doesn't become a venting session for people's frustrations. There's a time and a place for such venting: The time is after work, and the place is typically a bar. Blowing off steam at the workplace is at least a waste of time, and more often is counterproductive, because it damages project team cohesion when your colleagues hear about a meeting where the test team spent time disparaging the idiotic actions of their coworkers on the last project.

Improving Your Test Process

If you wanted to measure and improve your development or maintenance process — at least as it affects the testing process — and your testing process, too, you could use the gas pedals and brake pedals to informally assess your last few projects. How many of the gas-pedal types of events occurred? How many of the brake-pedal types of events occurred? What does the data in the change management database (from Chapter 6) tell us about the efficiency of course correction? On a project following mature processes, there'd be few brake-pedal events, many gas-pedal events, and limited or even positive testing impact of changes.

Such an assessment would be useful, but it's rather unstructured. Further, the basis for improvement is primarily reactive, since you derive your assessment of what needs to change from what happened in the past. It can deal with the *known unknowns* — e.g., we know that we don't know how to write good bug reports — but not with the *unknown unknowns* — e.g., what percentage of our customers will not do business with us in the future because of bugs we didn't find. So, what can we do to lay a better framework for assessing and improving our test process?

First, let me firm up the terminology a bit. When I say *process* you can interpret that as "the way things are done." Your processes might be written, passed on through oral tradition, embedded in institutional knowledge, or made up by each participant from scratch as needs demand and fancy suits.

A number of factors influence the maturity of a process. One is the degree to which all the participants and stakeholders understand and support what is going on. It also involves the degree of transparency and simplicity associated with process knowledge transfer to a new project team member. Successful process maturity improvement doesn't involve management dictates about how things will be done, but rather arises from ground-level consensus about how the team can effectively and efficiently execute projects. (Of course, management can and should provide guidance, support, and direction in achieving process maturity.)

A mature process should also be reproducible and measurable. Reproducibility means that we do the same thing the same way on subsequent projects. Measurability means that we gather important project management and engineering metrics on the process. Measurability supports reproducibility because we can use those metrics to estimate and guide the upcoming projects.

We also should use these metrics not only to reproduce the processes from one project to the next, but also to improve them. W. Edwards Deming and Walter A. Shewhart, two of the fathers of modern quality control, described a four-step process for continual improvement:

1. **Plan.** Develop a plan for improving the process, either to improve quality, save money, accelerate schedules, or some combination of all three. Set quantifiable goals to measure whether the plan succeeded.

2. **Do.** Execute the plan, gathering metrics that will allow you to judge process improvement success.

3. **Check.** Evaluate the metrics at key points to check the success of the change.

4. **Act.** Course-correct the plan to make it more effective in implementing improvements.

This cycle should repeat throughout the project and especially from one project to the next. In the most mature organizations I've seen, this Plan/Do/Check/Act process has become permanently ingrained in the way they work.

For example, one of my clients analyzes the bugs reported by customers within the first six months of the release of their computers. (Such bugs are called *initial field incident reports*, or IFIRs.) They do a Pareto analysis of the bugs, the affected subsystems, and their root causes to see where to focus their attention. Then, for the most significant problems, the most likely-to-fail subsystems, the most frequent root causes, they introduce what they call *closed loop corrective actions* to ensure that these problems do not occur on future systems.

Notice, though, that the Deming/Shewhart cycle remains primarily reactive. In other words, we are reacting to observations and metrics from our current process to improve that process. It will tend to lead to incremental changes. This is important, but will only sometimes result in major advances in your process. If you want to effect major changes in your process, you need some form of assessment of your process against a framework of best practices.

If you want a more extensive assessment of test process maturity, you have a number of options to choose from. These fall into two general categories. Some test process assessment models are *non-prescriptive*. They give you a framework for assessing your test process, key metrics to look at for each constituent process, and key assessment questions to ask for each constituent process. This will allow you to identify sources of pain, ineffectiveness, and inefficiency in your test process. However, non-prescriptive models do not tell you the order in which to attack these problems. You need to understand the particular business value that will accrue to your organization from attacking each problem. The value will vary from one organization to another. You should attack the problems in order of decreasing value; i.e., start with the problems that offer the biggest value boost by their resolution.

Some test process assessment models are *prescriptive*. They offer not only the framework, the assessment questions, and the metrics, but also they give the order in which you should improve constituent processes. This is typically done by assigning a maturity level to an organization based on which processes that organization does well. You have to have achieved adequacy in one set of processes before you get any credit for the next set.

Which approach you pick depends on what you are trying to accomplish. If what you need most is a measure of where you currently stand, especially for marketing purposes — either internal marketing of your test process within the company or external marketing of your test process to external clients — then a prescriptive assessment will arm you with such a measure. This is typically either as a one-dimensional measure, such as a 1-to-5 scale, or a two-dimensional measure, giving specific maturity ratings for each of 10 to 20 processes. If you score low on maturity and need to raise that maturity number, then the prescriptive model will provide a detailed roadmap.

However, if what you need most is to understand how the test process can provide more value to the organization or can better help alleviate organizational pain, then prescriptive models don't necessarily connect with that. It's true that the prescriptive models have a philosophy behind why the improvements they propose occur in the order in which they propose them. If that philosophy is consistent with what's causing your organization the most pain right now and with what changes could cause the greatest increases in effectiveness and efficiency, then following that prescriptive model's roadmap happens to make business sense. However, absent some compelling business reason or a marketing need for a particular maturity rating, the organization will not fund changes to achieve progress on these maturity scales.

The non-prescriptive models focus on what is most important to provide more value or to alleviate organizational pain. What changes could you make in the future to reduce organizational pain and to increase effectiveness and efficiency? Those are the questions a non-prescriptive assessment model answers. Changes that can reduce organizational pain, increase testing effectiveness, and improve testing efficiency are connected to value. You can make a business case to management for such changes.

So, with that in mind, what are your options for test process assessment models? There are a few in both categories. The following are ones I've used or encountered clients using:

- **Prescriptive:** TMM and TPI

- **Non-prescriptive:** CTP, STEP, and TMap

Let's take a quick look at each one, in no particular order other than the order that seems to make them all easiest to explain.[13]

TMM stands for *Test Maturity Model*. Professor Ilene Burnstein and her colleagues designed TMM as a way to complement the Capability Maturity Model (CMM). Burnstein and her colleagues had noticed the absence of detailed coverage of testing in CMM and sought to address that with TMM. It uses the same five-point maturity scale as CMM, with a score of 1 indicating little or no testing that is chaotic at best, and a score of 5 indicating well-organized, continuously improving, highly valuable testing. As with CMM, there are groups of processes for which an organization must achieve at least adequate capability to advance from one maturity level to another.

TMap stands for *Test Management Approach* and grew out of the testing practice of the European-based consulting company Sogeti. In its latest incarnation, it includes four main elements: 1) business-driven test management, where business priorities determine test focus; 2) a structured test process embracing all test work on the project, including unit testing; 3) a set of checklists, templates, and other items to support testing; and, 4) existing adaptations for various situations and life cycle models. A test team would need to have these various elements properly in place to assess high on a TMap assessment.

---

[13]Each of these models is described in detail in the following books: CTP in my own *Critical Testing Processes*, STEP in Rick Craig and Stefan Jaskiel's *Systematic Software Testing*, TMM in Ilene Burnstein's *Practical Software Testing*, TMap in Tim Koomen, et al.'s *T-Map: Next*, and TPI in Tim Koomen and Martin Pol's *Test Process Improvement*.

TPI stands for *Test Process Improvement*. Tim Koomen and Martin Pol build TPI on top of the TMap testing methodology. For each of the 20 process areas, Koomen and Pol designed typically not just one maturity rating — adequate or inadequate — but a scale of maturity ratings, measuring how well you carried out the process. Through a complex table, you can aggregate these individual process ratings into an overall maturity score ranging from 0 to 13, with the lowest number again being the worst score and the highest number being the best. I'll show you an example of TPI applied to an actual project in a case study later in this chapter.

STEP stands for *Systematic Test and Evaluation Process*. Just as TMap grew out of Sogeti's consulting practice, STEP grew out of Software Quality Engineering's (SQE's) consulting and training practice. It also grew out of the work of its original author, David Gelperin, on the IEEE 829 standards committee. It decomposes each level of testing into what it calls *phases* (planning, acquisition, and measurement), with those phases decomposed into activities, so you can think of STEP as a generic work-breakdown structure for each level of testing. You can assess based on which of the activities you carry out, and how well. Alternatively, you can combine STEP with TPI to obtain a maturity rating as well as recommendations, as some SQE consultants have told me that they often do. This has the effect of transforming STEP into a prescriptive model.

CTP stands for *Critical Testing Process*. I wrote the underlying book and developed the framework based on my own work as a test manager, consultant, and trainer, which as you can see hardly sets it apart among these other models! However, I focused on those processes that my consulting experience convinced me had the greatest effect on a test team's success. I selected 12 critical testing processes based on meeting one or more of four criteria: 1) frequently repeated; 2) highly collaborative; 3) visible outside of the test team; or, 4) directly connected to project success. An assessment involves examining the capability of a test team in each of the 12 critical testing processes, using both qualitative and quantitative factors, and including taking into account external factors that influence the team's capabilities. Recommendations for improvement derive from the relative benefits associated with improving a particular factor.

If you decide to assess your testing using one or more of these models, here's something important to keep in mind. When I first read about the Testing Maturity Model, I thought, "Hey, I'm a pretty organized, methodical test manager, I'll self-assess a few of my projects and see how great I am." I was disappointed to find that I scored mostly threes and fours, rather than fives, the maximum. As I thought about why I had scored low in certain areas, I realized that many testing processes are very collaborative and very sensitive to chaos in the project. For example, I can only finish all the planned tests if I'm in control of the test release process, especially timing. If I get test releases at the whim of the development manager — say every hour or so like we did on one project — then I'll have no time to do anything but confirmation testing. If someone asks later, "Why didn't you run all the tests you planned?" my answer will be, "Because I spent all my time reacting to bug fixes." A mature process should be proactive, not reactive, but sometimes the test manager is not in control of the upstream and downstream processes that influence the testing process.

Therefore, while you can use test process maturity models as a way to institute incremental improvements in your critical processes, the only way to have a world-class test process is in concert with a world-class company-wide process. Some formal models for company-wide process improvement include the International Standards Organization's ISO 9000 and 14000 family of standards, the Software Engineering Institute's Capability Maturity Model (CMM) and Capability Maturity Model Integration (CMMI), and the United States Department of Commerce's Malcolm Baldridge National Quality Award, along with others such as SPICE, TickIT, and Six Sigma.[14]

Like test process assessment models, an organization can use these models for self-assessment and lay the groundwork for implementing process improvements. One of my clients had a small team who focused on working with the entire organization to define and improve processes. This was not one of the test managers, but she reported to the same vice president as the test managers. The existence of a separate organization focused entirely on process improvement, reporting to an executive level in a company, is one sign of organizational commitment to improving quality by improving processes. Another sign of organizational commitment is when everyone recognizes — and managers and executives articulate — that process improvement is a serious, prolonged undertaking.

In some cases, organizations will choose to have that process maturity certified by an outside assessor. These consultants will come in and verify compliance with whatever maturity model you have followed. If you meet the criteria, they will certify you to as ISO-compliant, CMM level 4, or whatever approach you've chosen. Bear in mind that these assessors don't work cheaply. Moreover, in this case, the customer is *not* always right. Assessors can't afford to be pushovers, as their reputations are at stake as much as yours is when they do an assessment. A successful certification effort allows the organization to use that certification and the certifying organization's name in sales and marketing material.[15]

---

[14]If you're interested in these topics, you may want to check out Pankaj Jalote's *CMM in Practice*, Mark Paulk, et al.'s *The Capability Maturity Model*, and Charles Schmauch's *ISO 9000 for Software Developers*, as a few starting points.

[15]The American Society for Quality's monthly journal, *Software Quality Professional*, generally includes a number of advertisements for assessor consultancies. As with any consultant, interview carefully and check references if you are involved in the assessor selection process. If you are pursuing certification in order to do business with a particular client — e.g., the United States Department of Defense — then you should probably check with your client to see if they have "preferred assessor" or "recognized assessor" lists.

Over the years, a certain amount of cynicism has grown in regard to these company-wide process improvement programs. I recall hearing a company president in the early 1990s say to his management team that he was committed to winning the Malcolm Baldridge National Quality Award the next year. This comment revealed a significant level of unawareness, as the company would have scored at best a two out of five on the Capability Maturity Model. IBM, whose Rochester, Minnesota development team that created the AS/400 has actually won the Malcolm Baldridge National Quality Award, also had a division that was rated as CMM level five, which gives you an idea of the type of serious and mature organizations that win this award. Mercifully, this executive's plan for world-class quality in world-record time was silently dropped a few months later, but this further fed the skepticism many of us felt.

You might also remember my discussion about CMM and CMMI in Chapter 9. To briefly recap, even the prime movers in the invention of that maturity model acknowledge that, if used only as a marketing device, it doesn't tell you much about the quality or efficiency of that organization's work. In other words, while the assessors are not supposed to be pushovers, somehow some organizations win (and heavily tout) CMM maturity ratings that don't reflect their actual capabilities.

Eileen Shapiro, in her book *Fad Surfing in the Boardroom*, described in ruthless — and humorous — detail how total quality management, right-sizing, reengineering, and other management trends have blown into organizations — often along with lots of high-priced consultants — and then blown out again after a few months. Then the next big thing comes along, escorted by its coterie of consultants and sycophants. Scott Adams, creator of the *Dilbert* characters, ran a sequence of cartoons lampooning the efforts of Dilbert's employer, a fictional high-tech company, to achieve ISO 9000 certification. People in organizations with will-o'-the-wisp executive management develop a defensive posture of agreeing (often unenthusiastically) to whatever the new trend is, but then doing as little as possible in regard to the effort and waiting for it to go away. This type of behavior is what Deming describes as *lack of constancy of purpose*, which he includes in his list of Seven Deadly Sins in *The Deming Management Method*.

Such fickle management behavior and the justifiable cynicism it breeds are unfortunate and sad, I think. These process improvement models *can* work. I mentioned **Raytheon's** Electronic Systems group in Chapter 11 in the discussion on cost of **quality**. Raytheon, as part of the CMM process improvement and cost of **quality** programs, reduced their overall cost of quality from about 70 percent of project cost to down around 20 percent. Those types of improvements add up to saving around $500,000 on a medium-sized, million-dollar project. I consider myself a professional pessimist and a somewhat cynical guy, but I can get pretty optimistic and not a bit cynical about half a million dollars.

Managing the Testing Process: A Retrospective Conclusion

Whew! That's it. Just the case studies and exercises at the end of this chapter to go, and you have finished the book. I hope you enjoyed reading this third edition of *Managing the Testing Process* as much as I enjoyed writing it. Before you put it down, though, let me spend a few final paragraphs looking back at the book and putting it all in context.

Over the last 10 years, since the publication of the first edition, my associates and I have taught a course based on this book, with the clever and unexpected title of "Managing the Testing Process." Sometime course attendees remark, at the end of the seminar, "Nice course, but where was the test process?" The first few times I heard this, I slowly realized that, while this entire book is about the test process, I've told the story from the inside of the process without ever looking at it from the outside. Of course, the same process looks different from the inside than from the outside, just as the process of doing laundry looks different depending on whether you're the sock in the washing machine or the frazzled business traveler at the hotel self-service laundry.

So, to tie this all together, let me outline the test process as it might appear from the outside, and refer each piece of that process back to the chapter that addressed it.

1. Plan: Understand the testing effort.

   A. Discover the broader context of the testing effort (Chapters 11 and 12).

   B. Assess and prioritize the risks to system quality (Chapter 1).

   C. Estimate testing tasks, cost, and time (Chapters 1 and 11).

   D. Develop a test plan (Chapter 2).

2. Prepare: Assemble the people and the tests.

   A. Assemble the testers (Chapters 8 and 10).

   B. Build the test system (Chapter 3) and the test environment (Chapters 6 and 7).

3. Perform: Assess the quality of the system under test.

   A. Acquire a test release (Chapter 2).

   B. Execute tests (Chapters 3, 5, and 6).

4. Perfect: Guide the adaptation and improvement of the system under test and the testing itself.

   A. Report bugs to the appropriate stakeholders (Chapter 4).

   B. Report test results via an appropriate test dashboard (Chapters 4, 5, and 9).

   C. Manage changes to the project and product (Chapter 6).

This is shown graphically in Figure 12-5, and is the same process framework I discuss in my book *Critical Testing Processes*.[16]

Figure 12-5 The testing process

The point of this book is to give you some basic tools, tips, and techniques that you can use to manage this process and each constituent activity. These approaches have worked well for me over my career as a test manager, consultant, and trainer. I hope you find them useful as well. As you continue to build your own career as a test manager, I'm sure you'll come up with your own methods and practices. To the extent that you build off my ideas, I'm glad I could help you. Perhaps someday, you'll share some of your own ideas on testing and test management with me, too, whether by email, in a conference presentation, an article, or a book. I'd like that.

This book is by no means the last word on the topic. There's a lot of work to do still, figuring out all the ins and outs of managing testing of hardware and software systems. It's our unique privilege to work in the early days of an emerging discipline, computer systems engineering. The ancient Egyptians that built the pyramids were pioneers in the field of civil engineering. The construction of a pyramid was an enormous project, involving a small city of workers and incredible logistics, made all the more complicated by the fact that the only real power available was human power. However, some of the management techniques — assembling specialized teams to handle particular tasks and adopting a hierarchical management structure to organize and control the work — would be familiar to civil engineers today. Likewise, some of our current test management techniques will be abandoned, just as today civil engineers use large trucks to move stones rather than having people roll the stones over logs. Nevertheless, like specialized teams and hierarchical management, some of what we do now will survive this first full millennium of systems engineering, becoming part of the best practices of the future.

I'm not sure how many of the ideas in this book will end up in that future body of knowledge, if any. Even if none do, I feel fortunate to work in this

---

[16]If you are interested in a process-centric view of the testing process, please look for my book *Critical Testing Processes*.

unique field at this moment of its development. I also feel fortunate to work among colleagues like the many test managers and practitioners I've met as RBCS clients, other authors on this topic, the thousands of people around the world who've taken RBCS training courses live or via e-learning, and the people like you who've read this book.

Case Study 1: Agile Testing Challenges

A number of our clients have adopted Scrum and other Agile methodologies. Every software development life cycle model, from sequential to spiral to incremental to Agile, has testing implications. Some of these implications ease the testing process. We don't need to worry about these implications here.

Some of these testing implications challenge testing. In this case study, I discuss the challenges of Agile methodologies. This will help readers understand the issues created by Agile methodologies, distinguish those from other types of testing issues, and start to identify ways to deal with those issues.

Throughout this book, I recommended a blended testing strategy consisting of three types of test strategies:

- Analytical risk-based testing
- Automated regression testing
- Reactive testing (also referred to as *dynamic testing*)

The blended testing strategy I recommend aligns well with Scrum and other Agile methodologies. In some cases, this strategy will mitigate the testing risks and reduce the testing challenges associated with these methodologies. However, it does not resolve all of the risks and challenges. In this case study, let's examine some of the challenges that RBCS consultants have observed with other clients using Scrum and Agile methodologies.

Before we start, though, I should note that these challenges fall broadly into two categories. The first category is the set of challenges that arise from Agile itself; i.e., they are inherent in it. For example, within the difficult, dynamic balance between too much documentation and not enough documentation lives the test oracle problem I mention later in this section. Even though not all of these problems are exclusively found on teams following Agile methodologies, I'm including them here because this case study examines challenges facing teams using Agile methodologies.

The second category is the set of challenges that arise from improper or incomplete implementations of Agile. For example, I mention a problem related to tester overtime. According to some Agile advocates, this problem should not happen in a "true" Agile project. I'm including these challenges here because this case study also examines the challenges facing teams using a methodology they think of as Agile and call Agile. Through usage, I expect the term *Agile methodology* will come to encompass these practices, just as the term *risk-based testing* has come to include a lot of ideas that I might not consider proper risk-based testing.

Dealing with the Volume and Speed of Change

One of the principles of Agile development is that project teams should "welcome changing requirements, even late in development."[17] Many testing strategies, especially analytical requirements-based testing, become quite inefficient in such situations.

However, risk-based testing accommodates change, since we can always add risks, remove risks, change risks, and adjust the level of risk. If test execution is underway, we can adjust our plan for the remaining period based on this new view of quality risk. Since risk-based testing provides an intelligent way to decide what to test, how much, and in what order, we can always revise those decisions based on new information or direction from the project team.

The automated testing of the sort I discuss in Chapter 3 is quite able to accommodate ongoing change. With care, automation at the graphical user interface can be maintainable. Automation at stable command line interfaces does not tend to suffer severe maintainability problems. The reactive testing that I recommended, not requiring much documentation, is also quite resilient in the face of change.

However, change can impose challenges for testing that are independent of the use of these test strategies. Many of these challenges arise from changes in the definition of the product and its correct behavior (discussed later).

The project team must keep the test team informed of these changes as they happen. In addition, certain changes can affect testing more significantly than development, and the project team must take that into account. Otherwise, changes can impose inefficiencies on the development, execution, and maintenance of tests.

Remaining Effective during Very Short Iterations

In sequential life cycles, test teams can have a long period of time in which to develop and maintain their tests, in parallel with the development of the system, prior to the start of system test execution. Some more formal iterative life cycle models, such as Rapid Application Development and the Rational Unified Process, often allow substantial periods of time between test execution periods for each iteration. These intervals allow test teams to develop and maintain their test systems.

---

[17]See www.agilemanifesto.org.

Agile methodologies like Scrum are less formal and faster-moving. Consistent with the evocative name, *sprints*, these methodologies use short, fast-paced iterations. For a number of clients, RBCS consultants have seen this pace and brevity further squeeze the test team's ability to develop and maintain test systems, compounding the effects of change noted earlier. Testing strategies that include an automation element have proven particularly sensitive to this challenge.

The risk-based element of the recommended strategy can help. Risk-based testing focuses on the important areas of test coverage, and de-emphasizes or even cuts less important areas, relieving some of the pressure created by the short iterations. This ability to focus proves especially helpful for test teams also under tight resource constraints. Test teams in an Agile world should develop, maintain, and execute tests in risk-priority order. Using risk priority to sequence development and maintenance efforts allows the test team to have the most important tests ready at the beginning of each sprint's test execution period.

Receiving Code after Inconsistent (and Often Inadequate) Unit Testing

Many of the authors, practitioners, and academics involved with Agile methodologies stress good, automated unit testing. Open-source test harnesses such as JUnit and CppUnit minimize the tool costs of doing so, overcoming one key obstacle to automation. Such automated unit tests allow what Agile proponents call *refactoring*. Refactoring is the redesign of major chunks of code or even entire objects. The automated unit tests provide for quick regression testing of refactored code. Some Agilists recommend substituting automated unit tests for design, as in Test Driven Development.[18]

While this sounds good in theory, there are two problems that we tend to observe with this approach in practice.

First, unit testing has limited bug-finding utility. Capers Jones has found 25 to 30 percent average defect removal effectiveness for unit testing. RBCS assessments have shown that good system testing by an independent test team averages around 85 percent defect detection effectiveness. So, while unit testing helps, the main filter to prevent excessive field failures remains system testing.[19]

Second, we find that, under the guise of excuses both valid and not-so-valid, many programmers do not create automated unit tests and in some cases don't

---

[18]Test Driven Development has its own set of challenges, some of them related to testing. See Bjornvig, Gertrud, et al.'s, "A Story about User Stories and Test Driven Development," at `www.rbcs-us.com/UserFiles/File/Articles/Test Driven Development.pdf`.
[19]For a discussion of defect detection effectiveness, see my book *Advanced Software Testing: Volume II*. Note that the defect removal effectiveness of system testing is less than the detection effectiveness, because the project team will typically defer some bugs rather than remove them.

do any unit testing at all. This creates a great deal of trouble for the system test team, which, as mentioned earlier, remains a critical bug-removing filter. The short test execution periods on Agile sprints, compared to sequential projects, means that the degree of damage caused by one or two days' of test progress blockage due to highly buggy code is greater than in a sequential project.[20]

Delivery of unstable, buggy code will undermine one of the key benefits of the risk-based testing portion of the recommended strategy, which is the discovery of the most important defects early in the test execution period. It also inevitably leads to a large degree of code churn during testing, since so much must change to fix the bugs. The amount of change can ultimately outstrip even the ability of the best automated regression test system to keep up, which would then lead to lower defect detection effectiveness for the test team.

Managing the Increased Regression Risk

Capers Jones has found that regression accounts for about seven percent of bugs. In iterative life cycles like Scrum, though, code that worked in previous sprints gets churned by new features in each subsequent sprint. This increases the risk of regression. Agile methodology advocates emphasize good automated unit testing in part to manage the regression risk inherent in such churn.[21]

However, good unit testing has limited defect removal effectiveness, as cited earlier. So, automated regression testing via unit tests will likely miss most of the regression bugs. Therefore, we need effective regression testing at the system test level (which has a higher level of defect detection effectiveness). By combining risk-based testing with the automated regression testing, test teams can effectively manage the increased regression risk.

Making Do with Poor, Changing, and Missing Test Oracles

Agile methodologies de-value written documentation. Special scorn is reserved for specifications. For example, the Agile manifesto suggests people should value "working software over comprehensive documentation." This creates real challenges for a test team. Testers use requirements specifications and other documents as *test oracles*; i.e., as the means to determine correct behavior under a given test condition. We have seen testers in Agile situations given documents with insufficient detail, or, in some cases, given no such documents at all.

---

[20]See Jones's article, "Measuring Defect Potentials and Defect Removal Efficiency," found in the Basic Library at www.rbcs-us.com.

[21]See, for example, Jones's figures in *Estimating Software Costs, Second Edition*.

Even if the project team provides the test team with adequate documents, two other Agile development principles keep the test oracle challenge alive. First, Agile methodologies require teams to embrace change, as I discussed earlier. Second, Agile principles state that "the most efficient and effective method of conveying information to and within a development team is face-to-face conversation." For many of our clients following Agile methodologies like Scrum, these two principles allow the project team to change the definition of correct behavior at any time, including after testers have tested to confirm a particular behavior and after testers have reported bugs against a particular behavior. Further, the definition of correct behavior can change in a meeting or a discussion which might not involve the test team and which might produce no documented record of the change.

No known test strategy can resolve this challenge. Resolving the challenge requires change management. The percentage of rejected bug reports provides a measurable symptom of this challenge. Rejected bug reports are ones that the team ultimately discarded because the reports described correct behavior. Projects with well-defined, stable test oracles enjoy bug reject rates below five percent. Projects with poor, changing, or missing test oracles often endure bug reject rates of 30 percent or more.

We have estimated imposed test team inefficiencies from such test oracle problems at around 20 to 30 percent. Further, the inability to determine precisely whether a test failed affects both the efficiency of the testing and the defect detection effectiveness. When testers spend time isolating situations that the project team ultimately chooses to define as correct behavior, that takes away from time they could have spent finding and reporting real bugs. These unfound and very real bugs create subsequent problems for customers, users, and technical support staff, and distractions for developers and test teams.

Further, the situation creates frustration for the testers that reduces their morale and, consequently, their effectiveness. Testers want to produce valid information. When much of the information they produce — in the form of rejected bugs reports — ends up in the figurative wastebasket of the project, that tends to make people wonder why they bother.

It's important to realize that this reduction in test effectiveness, efficiency, and morale is a potential side effect of Agile methodologies. Organizations using Agile methodologies must assign responsibility for these outcomes in the proper place. Bad problems can get much worse when the test team is held accountable for outcomes beyond their control.

Dealing with a Shifting Test Basis

Requirements-based testing strategies cannot handle vague or missing requirements specifications. Missing requirements specifications would mean a test team following a requirements-based testing strategy not only can't say what it means for a particular test to pass or fail, but also won't have a *test basis*. The test basis is that which the tests are based upon. Requirements-based testing strategies require test teams to develop test cases by first analyzing test conditions in the requirements, and then use those test conditions to design and implement test cases. A missing or poor requirements specification won't work for such analysis.

The test basis also provides a means to measure the results. In a requirements-based test strategy, testers can't report test results accurately if the requirements are missing or poor. Testers can't report the percentage of the test basis covered by passed tests, because the requirements won't provide enough detail for meaningful coverage analysis.

With the risk-based testing strategy recommended in this book, test teams can evade both problems. Testers design and implement test cases based on the quality risk items. The level of risk associated with each risk item determines the number of test cases and the priority of the test cases derived from that risk item. The test team can report test results in terms of quality risks mitigated versus not mitigated.

From Detailed Documentation to Many Meetings

As the Agile manifesto quotation cited earlier puts it, people should focus on creating working software rather than comprehensive documentation. However, the information that was, under the *ancien régime*, captured and exchanged in these documents must flow somehow, so Agile advocates promote "face-to-face conversations." This, of course, is another name for a meeting. From a marketing perspective, it was smart of the Agile advocates not to use the word *meeting* in the Agile manifesto, but the reality remains.

I mentioned in an earlier section on test oracle issues with Agile methodologies the problem of a meeting or a discussion that changes the definition of correct behavior, which did not involve the test team, and which did not produce a documented record of the change. The flip side of this problem, in some organizations, is that everyone gets invited to every meeting, the meetings balloon in number and duration, managers and leads are not available to manage and lead their team because they are in meetings much of the day, and effectiveness and efficiency drop.

One manager jokingly described this situation as follows: "Scrum is a heavyweight process. I'm surprised at the name *Agile* — it should be called *couch potato*. There are too many meetings. There's too much jawboning. I find it really ironic that there are all these books explaining how simple it is."

To be fair, having too many meetings is a problem that any project following any life cycle model can suffer from. I've worked on classic waterfall projects as a test manager where I spent four hours or more per day in meetings. I had one client relate a hilarious anecdote where a senior manager, in response to a complaint from a line manager about how attending meetings was negatively impacting his ability to lead his team, shouted, "We're going to continue to have these meetings until I find out why nothing is getting done around here!"

That said, every organization, every project, and every life cycle has to strike the right balance. In some cases, organizations and projects following Agile methodologies react too strongly to the Agile manifesto's comments on documentation and face-to-face "discussions." Further, embracing change should not mean throwing out or re-considering previous decisions to the extent that it paralyzes the team. Teams using Agile methodologies must achieve the right balance between documentation and meetings — they must have crisp, efficient meetings that move the project forward and course-correct, not meetings that grind the team down and go around in circles.

Holding to Arbitrary Sprint Durations

Some of our clients following Agile methodologies like Scrum tend to ritualize some of the rules of the process. The time deadlines for sprints seem particularly subject to this ritualization. At first, I was puzzled that these same clients discarded some other rules, such as the requirement for unit testing, often with less reason than the reasons for which they held tightly to the deadlines. However, deadlines are tangible, while the benefits of unit tests are not as well-understood and clear, so I can now see the reasons behind the selective emphasis on certain Agile process rules over others.

For example, suppose that a project team follows four-week sprints. A systemic problem in our industry is related to software estimation, particularly the tendency to over-commit in terms of the number of features (*user stories*) for that sprint. So, on the last Friday of the sprint, with development ending late for the sprint, the arbitrary deadline remains intact at the expense of the test team's weekend. This is actually a situation where one rule of Agile is being used to justify the violation of another rule of Agile, since the Agile manifesto calls for reasonable, sustainable levels of work for the entire team.

Fully resolving this challenge requires team and management maturity. When people habitually and systematically over-commit, management should require use of historical progress metrics for estimation. Many Agile practitioners use metrics like *burndown charts* and *story-point velocity*. The Scrum process includes gathering and using such metrics.

If the software estimation problems cannot be fixed, risk-based testing helps the test team deal with systematic and constant over-commitment. To start with, when the test team is time-crunched over and over again at sprint's end, the test team should accept that the project team's priorities are schedule-driven, not quality-driven. The test team should revise the risk analysis approach to institute an across-the-board reduction in the extent of testing assigned to each quality risk item during risk analysis for subsequent projects. That way, at least the test team won't over-commit.

In some cases, in spite of reducing the scope of testing, the test team still can't execute all the tests in the available time at the end of a sprint. If so, rather than ruining their weekend to run every test, the test team can select the most important tests using the risk priority number. Less-important tests can slip into the next sprint. (You'll notice that Scrum and other Agile methodologies allow user stories to slip from one sprint to the next in the same way.) Of course, if the test team must consistently triage its tests in this fashion, they should again adjust the test extent mapping downward for future sprints.

Dealing with Blind Spots in the Sprint Silos

Not all experts on Agile methodologies agree on the need for independent test teams. Some seem to think of testing as a subset of the tasks carried out by programmers on an Agile team, specifically creating various forms of auto-mated unit tests and/or acceptance tests. This might exclude an independent test team, or it might transform the role of that team.[22]

Most of our clients adopting Agile methodologies have retained the inde-pendent test team, or at least the independent tester, to some extent. For those retaining the independent team, most have chosen to partition the team across the sprints in some way, often making each tester answerable on a day-to-day task basis to the Scrum master or other sprint leader, rather than to the test manager. In the case of having independent testers but not an independent test team, there is no test manager.

This provides some advantages, especially to the person leading the sprint:

- Each tester focuses entirely on sprint-related tasks, with minimal outside distractions.

- Each tester allocates time entirely to the benefit of the sprint and its exigent goals.

- The sprint leader can re-direct any tester to focus on what is most important to the sprint team, often without having to consult the test manager.

- The sprint leader can — and, at the end of a sprint, often will — call on the tester to put in extra effort to hit sprint targets.

---

[22]See, for example, the abstract of Kent Beck's talk, given at the Quality Week 2001 conference, www.soft.com/QualWeek/QW2001/papers/2Q.html. Beck claimed that unit testing by programmers might eventually make the defect detection role of independent test teams (referred to as "QA" in the abstract) superfluous, transforming testing into a role similar to a business analyst's. My earlier comments about unit testing, and the figures I cited from Caper Jones's work on the limits of the effectiveness of unit testing, make me skeptical that we will see substantially bug-free code delivered to test teams, no matter what the life cycle model, but I'd enjoy working on projects where someone managed to prove me wrong.

- The amount of test effort allocated to the sprint does not vary once the number of testers for the sprint is determined, and the test manager cannot surprise the sprint leader with a sudden reduction in test effort to serve other test team priorities.

As you can see, some of the advantages have zero-sum-game elements that carry within them the seeds — if not the actual fruit — of various potential problems.

The challenges of this approach — some of which are obvious corollaries of the advantages — include the following:

- The tester thinks of himself as — and conducts himself as — less of a tester and more of a specialized developer. This can include a loss of interest in growing test-specific skills in favor of growing technical skills.

- The tester has less contact with people outside the sprint team, reducing the wider, system-level perspective provided by an independent test team.

- In the absence of coordinative guidance from the test manager, the tester starts to make mistakes related to gaps and overlaps. The tester fails to perform some test tasks that make sense, especially longer-term investments that don't necessarily benefit the current sprint. The tester redundantly performs test tasks done by other testers on other sprints, because she wasn't aware of the other testers' work.

- The test manager, having lost the ability to manage the workload of their resources, finds the morale suffers and turnover increases as unsustainable workloads at the end of each sprint take their toll.

- The ability of the test team to grow a consistent, powerful, maintainable test system — the test scripts, the test tools, the test data, and other stuff needed for effective and efficient testing in the long term — goes down because of the exigent focus on the sprint's immediate needs.

- Testers display a tendency to "go native" and lose some of the objectivity that an independent test team normally provides, suffering a loss of defect detection effectiveness.

None of these challenges (or advantages, for that matter) arises from Agile methodologies per se; it just happens that Agile methodologies as typically practiced tend to accentuate them. I have observed similar problems for years on projects following sequential models or no model at all, when the test team adopted what I refer to as the *project resource* approach to test team organization.

The challenges are not insurmountable if an independent test team exists. The test team, lead by a good test manager, can introduce centripetal forces that will bind the team together and make its actions consistent and congruent. These forces then balance the sprint-specific centrifugal forces that tend to push the test team members into sub-optimizing for their sprint as well as isolating the test team members from broader testing considerations.

One approach to managing these challenges is to have a separate test period that follows the development sprint. (To keep the terminology clean, some like to call this approach an alternation of *development sprints* following by *test sprints*.) Some of our clients have pursued this approach. It does seem to work for them when the test team remains engaged in the development sprint. In other words, if the test team disengages from the development team during the development sprint, you are just exchanging one form of siloing for another.

Managing Expectations

To close this discussion, let's look at a psychological challenge to test teams on Agile projects. Gartner, the industry analysts, say that IT-industry adoption of new technologies and ideas goes through a *Hype Cycle* that consists of five distinct phases, as they describe on their Web site:[23]

1. **Technology Trigger.** The first phase of a Hype Cycle is the "technology trigger" or breakthrough, product launch, or other event that generates significant press and interest.

2. **Peak of Inflated Expectations.** In the next phase, a frenzy of publicity typically generates over-enthusiasm and unrealistic expectations. There may be some successful applications of a technology, but there are typically more failures.

3. **Trough of Disillusionment.** Technologies enter the "trough of disillusionment" because they fail to meet expectations and quickly become unfashionable. Consequently, the press usually abandons the topic and the technology.

4. **Slope of Enlightenment.** Although the press may have stopped covering the technology, some businesses continue through the "slope of enlightenment" and experiment to understand the benefits and practical application of the technology.

5. **Plateau of Productivity.** A technology reaches the "plateau of productivity" as the benefits of it become widely demonstrated and accepted. The technology becomes increasingly stable and evolves in second and third generations. The final height of the plateau varies according to whether the technology is broadly applicable or benefits only a niche market.

As we head into the 2010s decade, we are seeing Agile methodologies in the Peak of Inflated Expectations phase. RBCS clients have inflated expectations for Agile methods that relate to quality, productivity, and flexibility.

---

[23]See www.gartner.com/pages/story.php.id.8795.s.8.jsp.

Some test teams on Agile projects report to management that the product quality is no higher than normal, and sometimes even lower than normal. Some test teams on Agile projects report to management that the challenges discussed in this case study have reduced their efficiency. Some test teams on Agile projects report to management that, while development might not experience negative consequences or pain from change — which is a key promise of Agile methodologies and one of the key management selling points — testing will still endure problems when coping with unlimited, unmanaged change.

When these test teams on Scrum projects report these negative outcomes to management, management experiences a psychological phenomenon called *cognitive dissonance*. Cognitive dissonance involves feelings of mental tension between the incompatibility of their expectations of Agile methodologies and the observed results. Ultimately, these cognitive dissonance experiences, across the various adopters of Agile methodologies, will push these approaches along the Hype Cycle, out of the Peak of Inflated Expectations phase. In the short run, though, management might engage in another psychological phenomenon called *projection*. This involves projecting onto others how you feel about something they are associated with, but perhaps not responsible for. The experienced test professional knows this phenomenon better under the phrase *killing the messenger*.

The test strategies I've recommended in this book will support the stated goals of Agile methodologies. Risk-based testing supports increased quality, since it focuses testing on high-risk areas where testing can significantly reduce the risk. Risk-based testing supports increased productivity, since it reduces or eliminates testing where the quality risk is lower. Risk-based testing supports flexibility, since it allows regular revision of the quality risk items, which re-aligns the remaining testing with the new risks and their new levels of risk. Automated regression testing helps to contain the regression risks associated with Agile methodologies, allowing a higher rate of change. Reactive testing allows testers to explore various aspects of the system that risk-based testing and automated regression testing together might miss.

However, the test strategies recommended in this book cannot fully resolve the challenges covered in this case study. In the long run, people will come to recognize that, and rational trade-offs will prevail. In the short run, though, while Agile methodologies remain on the peak of inflated expectations, the test team must carefully communicate any testing issues that arise due to Agile methodologies and their effect on testing rather than from testing itself.

I wrote in the second edition of this book, "I think the onus is on us as professional testers to help develop a proper role for systematic but lightweight test processes and adapt the best practices of testing within the context of Agile methods. Hopefully, this will happen before the end of this decade." Unfortunately, I think we still have a fair amount of work to do to figure this out. Realistically, it could well take another 10 years, because it took about 20 years total to properly integrate testing into the waterfall to produce the V model.

Case Study 2: Maturity and ROI

Let's revisit the ROI case study from the previous chapter. To refresh your memory, Table 12-1 shows the return on investment for the Internet appliance project.

Retrospectively, I self-assessed the maturity of the test process on this project using Tim Koomen and Martin Pol's Test Process Improvement. The testing maturity matrix is shown in Figure 12-6. The source spreadsheet, "Case Study TPI Test Maturity Assessment.xls," which includes the worksheets that assess compliance with each level in each key area, is available at www.rbcs-us.com.[24] In this figure, I've marked the upper levels of capability — which we did not achieve — for the three processes where we fell short, using an asterisk. Because our rating on low-level testing — basically, the unit testing by the developers — stops us from attaining level 8, we rank at level 7, in the Efficient band.

As you can see, while we did not achieve a perfect score in some of the areas — we missed out in the areas of some long-term metrics and quality assurance for the test effort — the maturity of the test process we built and handed over to the client at the end of the project was quite good and certainly fit for their purposes. At the risk of pounding our own drum too strenuously, please allow me to point out that the level-of-maturity measure was achieved by an outstanding team of test professionals who applied the tools, tips, and techniques described in the previous 11 chapters.

---

[24]I thank Will Franklin and Allen Sell for sharing their Microsoft Word template for TPI assessment with me. It and Koomen and Pol's book formed the basis of the worksheet provided on the RBCS' Web site.

Table 12-1 Cost of Quality Return on Investment Analysis for the Internet Appliance Project

DETECTION COSTS	
Test budget	$1,000,000
Future value of assets created	100,000
Regression test costs	500,000
Net detection costs	**$400,000**
Must-fix bugs found during testing	1,500
Approximate cost per bug	**267**
INTERNAL FAILURE COSTS	
Pre-release bug fix costs	750,000
Regression test costs	500,000
Net internal failure costs	**$1,250,000**
Must-fix bugs found during testing	1,500
Approximate cost per bug	**833**
EXTERNAL FAILURE COSTS	
Sustaining costs	3,000,000
Percentage bug-related	50%
Net external failure costs	**$1,500,000**
Must-fix bugs found after testing	500
Approximate cost per bug	**3,000**
RETURN ON INVESTMENT	
Cost of quality (w/testing)	3,150,000
Cost of quality (w/o testing)	6,000,000
Net benefit of testing	2,850,000
Approximate testing ROI	**713%**

ID	Key Area	0	1	2	3	4	5	6	7	8	9	10	11	12	13
		Ad Hoc	Controlled					Efficient					Optimizing		
1	Test Strategy	A						B				C		D	
2	Lifecycle Model	A			B										
3	Pervasiveness			A				B				C		D	
4	Estimation and Planning				A							B			
5	Test Specification Techniques	A		B											
6	Static Test Techniques					A		B							
7	Metrics						A			B			C		D*
8	Test Tools					A			B		C				
9	Test Environment			A					B						C
10	Office Environment			A											
11	Commitment and Motivation	A				B						C			
12	Test Function and Training				A			B		C*					
13	Scope of Methodology				A						B				C
14	Communication		A	B								C			
15	Reporting	A		B		C						D			
16	Defect Management	A				B		C							
17	Testware Management		A			B					C				D
18	Test Process Management	A	B									C			
19	Evaluation							A			B				
20	Low-level Testing					A		B		C*					

Figure 12-6 An assessment of test maturity based on the TPI model

Exercises

1. For as many current and past positions, engagements, or projects as practical, calculate your bug-finding effectiveness with the defect detection percentage (as in Chapter 4), your bug-finding efficiency using cost of quality (as in Chapter 11), and your test maturity using TMM or TPI. Do you see a positive correlation between test maturity and effectiveness, between test maturity and efficiency, or between effectiveness and efficiency?

2. Refer to the case study change management database from Chapter 6, and to the lists of *brake pedals* and *gas pedals* in this chapter. In a spreadsheet, classify the delaying problems against one of the brake pedals and the accelerating events against one of the gas pedals. (Add *another* category for anything that doesn't fit.) Create a Pareto diagram of the influences of process maturity issues on that project.

Appendices

In This Appendices

Appendix 1: Hardware Testing Fundamentals: An Introduction for Software Testing Professionals

Appendix 2: Omninet: The Internet Everywhere Marketing Requirements Document

Appendix 3: Omninet: The Internet Everywhere System Requirements Document

Appendix 4: Bibliography, Related Readings, and Other Resources

NOTE Both the Omninet Marketing Requirements Document and the Omninet System Requirements Document contain some defects. I introduced most of these accidentally when writing them, but I deliberately left them in. That may seem strange, but I want to ensure that you work from realistic source documents, not unrealistically polished ones. Also, in some of the static and black-box exercises, you will find these mistakes, which emphasizes that testing as a preventive activity. I have been told by course attendees around the world that the quality of these two requirements documents is about the same as the quality of requirements documents they typically receive when they are lucky enough to receive requirements documents!

Hardware Testing Fundamentals: An Introduction for Software Testing Professionals

Many people involved in computer hardware testing, myself included, fell into that role as part of testing systems that consist of both hardware and software, while having primarily a software background. While I did take some electrical, electronics, circuit, and engineering courses in college, I certainly don't consider myself a computer hardware or electronics engineer. However, I've found that, armed with a few basic concepts, those of us with extensive software test management experience can usually manage hardware testing as well, provided the right people are put in charge of the actual testing. The following brief introduction will give you some ideas of what to look for in a competently executed hardware testing effort. If you need to become a competent hardware tester yourself, I recommend that you read O'Connor's *Practical Reliability Engineering* and Ishikawa's *Guide to Quality Control* as a starting point.

Test Management

From a purely test management point of view, the same tools I introduced in the last 12 chapters will work for a test project that involves both hardware and software. You still have to track tests and bugs, assemble a test environment and team, get releases into the test environment, and possibly work with a distributed test team. That doesn't go away.

However, if you are a big test automation buff, know that many of these tools won't help you in the hardware and systems testing world. You can use load generators of various sorts as part of a reliability testing (more to come), but the failures you see will differ from the type of functional regression bugs most people use the automated tools to catch.

That's not to say you won't need tools. On the contrary, whomever ends up doing the actual hardware testing — the hardware vendor, a third-party test lab, someone else, all of the above — will need lots of tools: thermal chambers, oscilloscopes, voltage/amperage meters, shock and vibration tables, mechanical life harnesses, and more.

When testers find bugs using these tools, you'll soon learn that sometimes hardware systems behave differently, one to the next. Bad unit failures happen. They can be perplexing until you stop and think about the nature of a bug in hardware instead of software. In two hardware systems, bugs can arise because one system has a bad solder connection, a broken wire, a faulty chip, or for any number of other unique reasons. In software, the copy of the software distribution you use to install the software under test doesn't matter. That's hard for some software professionals to get used to, so internalize that fact as soon as possible.

It's also important to understand that test conditions can take longer to create in hardware testing. Some thermal tests can last days. A classic hardware reliability demonstration can take weeks. It's important to plan accordingly. Just because you'd like all the tests to last the same length of time — and indeed I encouraged such a standard in Chapter 3 — doesn't mean that's practical for all hardware test cases.

Basic Functionality and Self Tests

The most fundamental hardware tests are those tests, often embedded in a system's firmware, that run whenever the system reboots or powers up. The tests, often called system diagnostics, generally are nothing more than a basic subsystem sanity test. A good test will cover not just one subsystem, but all of them. (I have seen embedded communication subsystems be especially problematic in this area.) It's also a good idea for the test team — possibly through a special keystroke combination if you want to hide this capability from users — to be able to launch these tests. A basic subsystem sanity check should be the first line of defense in isolating bad unit failures.

Electrical Testing

This is one type of testing that, unlike almost all software tests, poses an actual risk of physical danger to the test and the system under test. Even a system that is not powered up can have potentially deadly electrical charges stored in capacitors or batteries. Only qualified professionals should perform any type of test, but in running electrical tests, this fact is especially critical.

Electrical tests come in many flavors. One type of electrical test is making sure the signal waveforms are correct on running systems. This type of testing, called *signal quality* testing, also includes checking for inappropriate voltages or potential current flows in various places, especially externally accessible ports. With systems supplying power to external devices such as USB ports and peripherals, the possibility exists for dangerous (to the hardware) situations.

Another type of electrical testing involves checking to see how the system responds to various types of power conditions. In the United States, Canada, and Taiwan, 120 volts and 60 hertz are the nominal voltage and frequency coming out of the wall, but in Europe and much of Asia, 240 volts and 50 hertz are the norm. Temporary losses in voltage (*sags* or *brownouts*) happen in various locations around the world, including even the high-tech state of California in 2001. How will voltage spikes affect your system? The best software in the world doesn't do any good if the host system crashes every 15 minutes because it can't eat the AC power coming out of the wall.

Some systems, such as laptops, mobile phones, and other portable devices, spend a lot of time away from the AC power coming out of the wall — or the DC power coming out of the car dashboard or the airplane armrest. For these devices, how they work — and how long they work — under battery power is a major concern. It also matters how long they take to charge. Do the batteries maintain consistent performance over multiple charge/discharge cycles? Does power run out without warning?

Environmental Tests

Environmental tests are those tests designed to see how the system responds to various types of insults and strenuous conditions the system will encounter in the real world. One type of such tests involves shocks and vibrations. Systems tend to get bumped, transported across rough roads, shaken, swung around in briefcases, and so forth. Rather than try to mimic these conditions exactly, the usual procedure is to mount the system under test to a shock table or vibration table, and then subject the system to certain accelerations and vibrations. The intensity of these shocks and vibrations are calibrated often in *G*'s for gravitational acceleration, like jet pilots measure tightness of turns at high speed.

Vibrations happen across various frequencies, with a gradual change usually (sweeping) across the frequencies in the course of the test. Shocks, occurring as incidents rather than over a period of time, have pulse shapes and durations. It is often somewhat difficult to imagine exactly how a particular shock or vibration test relates to an actual (potential) field incident, but most of the hardware test labs and reputable vendors have standard tests that they run. You'll need to consult an expert to understand how two different tests relate to each other, especially if they're measured in different units.

A related type of test is a drop test. Unlike the somewhat mystifying shock and vibration tests, this test involves simply dropping a system from a given height onto various types of surfaces in various configurations to see what happens. For example, a laptop computer might be dropped with the lid shut and the lid open onto a carpeted and a cement floor from a foot or two in the air onto its flat surfaces, edges, and corners.

Environmental tests can also include other nasty surprises the system is likely to encounter. For example, on several laptop and information appliance projects, the systems were subjected to juice, coffee, water, and cola poured into the device. The test involves not only correct operation during or after the spill, but also a reasonable cleanup process that does not damage the unit; strip legends off of keys on the keyboard; warp or crack mice, trackballs, pointers, and the like; or cause any other physical damage to the unit. Battlefield computers are often subjected to smoke, sand, bullets, fire, and other severe insults.

Altitude is another potential factor, especially in systems that rely on convection cooling rather than cooling fans. For example, an information appliance we tested did not include a fan on its CPU, but rather had special vents and heat sinks designed to wick heat away from active components. Thin air at altitude can reduce the effectiveness of such schemes. PDAs, mobile phones, and other such devices might need such testing. Systems that operate at high altitudes or in space — for example, aeronautical systems on jets (especially supersonics jets that can operate in extremely thin air) and satellites must be tested in such environments.

The effect of pollutants might be another factor to consider. A home telephone system or information appliance designed to work in a kitchen will be subjected to smoke from hot or burned food, including smoking oil, which leaves heavy deposits behind.

One last environmental test to mention is electrical conductivity and resistance. Can a simple static discharge onto a user interface or user-accessible component route through to a sensitive component such as a chip, causing damage? One way to find out is to test static discharges onto the exterior of the system. Can the device create dangerous shorts? If the system somehow comes in contact with a hot wire or electrified surface, that voltage should not travel through the case to a point where the user might receive a shock.

All of these environmental tests can — and perhaps in your case should — involve both operating (powered up) and non-operating units. The non-operating tests are generally of at least equal intensity as the operating tests, since it is assumed that non-operating units will be moved, while operating units tend to be more sedentary. This assumption does not hold for laptop computers, battlefield computers, integrated weapons electronics, mobile phones, PDAs, and other portable devices. In addition, for such portable devices, the shock, vibration, and drop tests should be considerably more severe than those used for a non-mobile system such as a server, a telephone switch, a rack-mounted router, or the like.

These tests often destroy one or more units. Therefore, if you must run such tests against scarce engineering prototypes (see Chapter 2), you might want to run those tests toward the end of a hardware test cycle, when new systems are soon to come. However, if environmental risks are considered a particularly high risk, then you should run these tests right away. Plan for extra units. Do not plan to use a system that has been through an environmental test for any other testing, especially not any of the testing discussed in this appendix. Even if the unit is not destroyed, it might be damaged in subtle ways that influence the outcome of other tests, including software tests.

Mechanical Life

Any part of the system that can move, flex, rotate, bend, latch and unlatch, plug and unplug, toggle, switch, open and close, click, press and depress, or is in any way subject to opposing forces will be subject to strains and wear. Prime examples of this are hinges and latches, keyboards, touchpads, touchscreens, mice, trackballs, power switches, removable drives, CD/DVD players, and so forth. These items can have multiple moving parts. For example, a CD/DVD drive has the spindle, the laser and read head, the soft eject button (that works when the system is on), the hard eject button (that works when the system is off), and the platter. Any connector (e.g., the RJ-45 connector for a LAN) or a regularly touched surface such as a keyboard or trackpad or touchscreen is subject to the wear associated with regular use.

For any of these moving parts, the hardware test experts must make some reasonable assumption about how many motion events the part will experience over the course of its life. For keyboards, for example, test cases are often based on an assumption that each key will be pressed between 1 million and 10 million times. Range of motion is another consideration, especially for latches, hinges, and the like. The test cases should also take force of motion into account. Often, frustrated computer users will bang on or sharply actuate computer keys or buttons during failure of the system. Finally, consider shearing or torque forces. For examples, suppose a user of a laptop always tends to open the lid by one corner or the other rather than the middle.

Thermal Tests

Thermals tests check to see whether the system can stand up to the temperature and humidity conditions it will experience in both operating and non-operating modes. The testers place the system in a thermal chamber and run it through a series of temperature and humidity cycles as shown in Figure A-1. (Temperature is shown on the y-axis in centigrade scale, humidity is shown in percentages above the temperature graph, and durations of the dwells [flat lines] and transitions [sloped lines] in hours are show on the x-axis.) Often, active and heat-producing components such as CPUs and power supplies are instrumented with thermal sensors to check, over the course of the test, whether these components exceed their maximum operating temperatures. These tests are sometimes referred to as *four corners* tests, because graphs of maximum and minimum temperatures and humidity under operating and non-operating conditions produce a rectangle or parallelogram with four corners.

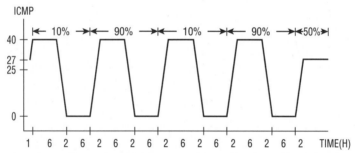

Figure A-1 A graph of temperature and humidity over time in a thermal test

Another type of thermal test involves thermal shocks, where temperatures are changed rapidly. For example, consider the circuitry in a satellite, where ambient temperatures and humidity will go from the balmy launch pad to frigid and desiccated upper atmosphere and then outer space in a period of minutes.

Reliability

Hardware systems, unlike software, wear out and fail over time. When software works under a particular condition it tends to work under that same condition indefinitely, but hardware can work under a particular condition one day and then fail the next. These failures can often be repaired and the unit put back into service, although the very act of repair tends to result in a lessening of future reliability. The rate of failure in a population of systems is often measured in terms of the *mean time between failures* (MTBF). If the more important consideration is availability, then this can be measured in terms of uptime, which is a function of the mean time between failure and the mean time to repair (MTTR). A test for reliability is often referred to as a *reliability demonstration* or *MTBF demonstration*.

One common technique for such a test is to gather a fairly large number of units, power them up, and then leave them in a running state, with some load test cycling indefinitely, under periods of maximum operating temperature and humidity. Given a desired level of statistical MTBF in the production units, some small number of units can fail during the demonstration period, which generally lasts weeks. The higher the level of reliability you want to demonstrate, the larger the sample, the longer the demonstration, and the fewer the units that can fail. These tests are based on an assumption that failure rates are constant over time, which is generally valid during the expected life of the system.

Understanding reliability is very important if you intend to offer a warranty on your systems, because you can predict, with great statistical accuracy, the exact cost associated with returns over the life of the warranty. Extended warranties sold with the system can be a significant profit center for your company, provided that you know the MTBF and can charge customers well above the expected payout per unit in repair costs. This is why consumer electronics stores tend to push these warranties so heavily, and why, statistically, you are rooking yourself out of good money if you let them talk you into buying one.

Some people use what are called *highly accelerated life tests (HALTs)* to predict the reliability and the lifetime of a system. These tests subject a small sample of systems to extreme operating temperatures, humidity, shock, and vibrations until they fail. Not only is the time to fail interesting in predicting the longevity of the system, but the failure mode is often interpreted as indicating which component or components are most likely to fail. Because of the elevated temperature, the lifetime of the system is accelerated (hence the name) according to the Arrhenius equation, which calculates the speeding up of chemical reactions under conditions of higher temperature. Unlike a traditional MTBF demonstration, which involves a basic grasp of statistics, a highly accelerated life test involves a very sophisticated understanding of the system under test and the specifics of running a valid HALT.[1]

---

[1]Patrick O'Connor's *Practical Reliability Engineering* explains the standard MTBF demonstration process, while Harry McLean's *HALT, HASS & HASA Explained,* uh, like the title says, explains HALTs. There is some controversy about HALT and other related tests now, so do your research if someone suggests using them.

Packaging Tests

An important variant of thermal, shock, drop, and vibration testing involves a non-operating test of the system in its packaging, especially for computer electronics and computer systems such as mobile phones, laptop and desktop computers, PDAs, and the like. In these tests, you put the systems in their packaging as they will be shipped to the customer and run through a sequence of tests designed to check for problems that could occur during shipping and delivery to the customers. The circumstances of shipping and delivery affect this testing.

A system shipped on an airplane will experience different modes of vibration than one shipped on a boat or a train. Propeller-driven planes have different vibrations in their frames than jet planes do. This might seem picayune, but the wrong vibration over a period of hours can shake a board, a chip, or a screw loose, resulting in reliability problems — and potentially warranty costs — after the system is delivered and installed.

A system shipped in a heated truck and then transported on a forklift in a warehouse in Alaska or Siberia in the winter will undergo dramatic thermal shocks, and might undergo significant mechanical shocks if the forklift operator is less than gentle when removing the palette of systems from the tines of the forklift. I once saw two movers drop a $250,000 IVR server in its packaging off the lip of a loading ramp. It fell two inches and hit with a loud boom. I made sure to get the number of the moving truck just in case; fortunately, the system powered up and worked fine in the test lab later.

The packaging tests are run much like the corresponding non-operating thermal, shock, drop, and vibration tests, except that the system is inside its packaging. Thermal, humidity, and motion sensors are generally attached to the inside of the package, and then the test is run. These sensors record maximums and minimums and you can examine them after the test is over. The testers typically power up the system and give it a basic functionality test, along with conducting a visual inspection.

Acoustics

Systems with built-in speakers and microphones are supposed to reproduce and capture sound with some level of quality. That is subject to testing, often in anechoic chambers with precise instruments for measuring sound across the audible spectrum of frequencies.

Systems also tend to produce sounds, especially the noise of spinning hard disks, CD/DVDs, and other drives. Cooling fans are generally not silent, either. Keyboards, mice, and other mechanical parts can make noise as they move. Sometimes warning noises are irritating or disruptive. For example, I once had a laptop computer that emitted a very loud, repetitive tone when the battery got low, which frequently disturbed fellow passengers on airplanes. There was no way to customize the volume or type of warning tone emitted.

The best systems will have limits on how much noise they can produce, and these systems should be tested against these limits. Testing should take into account any factor that affects the noise a system makes. For example, to save power, some laptop computers, rather than switching on a fan to cool a CPU, will downshift the processor speed when operating on battery power. An acoustics test run on a laptop not connected to AC power will fail to detect a noisy fan.

Safety

Systems are often used by people or in an environment in which people are present. This means that systems can hurt people, especially when they fail or are used in an unusual way. Understanding customer usage, the environment, and potential failure modes is key to running a safety test. For consumer products, a classic example is small parts such as keys on a keyboard that can fall off or be plucked off and subsequently swallowed by a small child, resulting in choking.

Many portable computers contain batteries, which frequently include dangerous substances. Adequate care must be taken to ensure that these devices do not leak dangerous chemicals under foreseeable failure modes, and that warnings are included for safe disposal of the units after their life cycle is complete. And, of course, sometimes rechargeable batteries can catch on fire. Testing should address this risk, too.

The NEBS test for telephony servers, telephone switches, and other devices to be located in central telephone offices specifies a fire test that actually involves taking a gas torch to various components on the system in a sealed chamber. (The tester should have a safety suit and an outside air supply for this test.) The resulting fumes are tested for toxicity, and the system is watched carefully for any signs of combustibility.

Radiation

In the course of operation, most system will emit — and be subject to — various forms of radiation, especially electromagnetic radiation in the radio spectrum due to the frequencies in clocks that control bus speeds, CPU speeds, screen refresh rates, and so forth. Emitted radiation must be limited to avoid interference with other devices, and incoming radiation that is within normal limits should not interfere with the operation of this device.

Some radiation can be more magnetic than electromagnetic. Computer-controlled magnetic resonance imaging (MRI) medical systems have been involved in fatalities when their powerful magnetic fields caused ferrous (iron-based) metal objects to abruptly fly through the air and strike occupants and bystanders with tremendous force. One patient was killed by a flying oxygen tank, and a police officer's gun was involved in another incident.

Some systems are designed to emit radiation. One such system, the nuclear-medicine device Therac-25, caused treatment accidents. Two software bugs interacted to result in fatal dosages being delivered to some patients. The United States Department of Defense is now considering the construction of extremely high-powered lasers mounted on aircraft for the purposes of shooting down ballistic missiles, and the United States Department of Energy replaced the nuclear testing of bombs with simulated nuclear explosions through the action of computer-controlled lasers at the Lawrence Livermore National Laboratory in California. Understanding usage conditions, the environment, and potential errors and failure modes is important to thorough testing of any system, especially complex computer-controlled systems that have the potential to affect human safety and health.

Standards and Regulations

Especially in the case of safety and radiation, testers have standards that specify the testing to be performed or at least what constitutes success or failure. In telecommunications, the NEBS standard applies to servers or other systems to be installed in telephone system central offices. Most governments have standards for safety and radiation, such as the United States Underwriters Laboratories and Federal Communications Commission, respectively. The bottom of a portable system to be sold in many countries often looks like a high-tech alphabet soup of the seals and logos of various regulatory agencies scattered around the globe.

One thing to remember about standards enforced by regulatory bodies is that government bureaucracies are not stakeholders in the success of your product. They will not care much if, say, your system's failure to pass a particular test is blocking its delivery to paying customers and costing your company thousands of dollars per day while the window of opportunity to capture the market closes. As a test manager, this means you must pay careful attention to these standards, allow for plenty of time to complete testing (including cycle time should the tests fail), and escalate blockages to management quickly. No matter how well-functioning your bug triage committee is, it cannot decide to waive or defer a bug related to the failure to meet government regulatory standards.

Not all regulations and standards are enforced by governments. For packaging, the various shipping and transportation associations have voluntary standards that you can apply for testing. While no one will force your company to adhere to these standards, they represent good ideas that you won't need to reinvent for your testing. Why not give them a try?

Components and Subsystems

Complicating this whole matter of hardware testing is that systems are often composed of various components and subsystems. These need to be tested separately before they're integrated into your system, but they also need to be tested in the system. Special tests might be required, depending on the subsystem.

Video cards, networking cards, USB controllers, and other I/O components are a prime example of this. Signal quality testing of the incoming and outgoing signals is important, even on pins that are supposedly not used. I once worked on a project where the vendor had assumed that that words *not used* associated with a particular pin in the requirements specification for the connection to a monitor meant they could use that pin to adjust the monitor's image size on the assembly line. The vendor learned during testing that the words should have been *not to be used*, because an internal video chip controller signal was present on that pin, causing sporadic resizing of the image when the pin was used!

Thermal testing can also be a concern. On the IVR project I've referred to in this book, the telephony cards included high-speed processors. These cards were packed together in a VME bus in the system rack with four fans to move air over the cards. During thermal testing, I had the testers instrument these chips so that I could check for overtemp conditions during high-heat portions of the test cycle.

Systems often include screens — ranging from simple LCDs to advanced TFT color displays — and these are subject to testing for defective pixels, contrast, color, power consumption, and readability under various lighting conditions. Screens also have implications for other tests, especially shock, vibration, drop, environmental, and battery life tests. Finally, a touchscreen, being both an input and an output device, needs special testing of the input facilities, including mechanical life testing.

External mice, keyboards, printers, monitors, and other bundled devices should also be considered for testing. In many cases, you can rely on the vendor's testing if this is a widely used commercial product, but you still must consider any unique usage conditions or environments. For example, if you're testing a battlefield system, just assuming that you can plug a standard monitor, keyboard, and mouse into that system and have those components work correctly with sand, smoke, bullets, and bombs flying around is probably a mistake.

Shocks and vibration can damage or loosen components and subsystems. Drops might cause bending or warping, even if the subsystem isn't at the point of impact, due to transmitted vibrations. Radiation might affect the component, and, if the component is inside your system, it might not be protected by radiation screening installed in the chassis or case of the system. Components might have moving parts that are subject to mechanical life tests. The failure of a component can affect the overall reliability of your system.

Integrated Software

While not directly related to hardware testing, it bears mentioning that many components of your system will have integrated software, especially firmware or BIOS code that starts the system or guides its operation during use. This includes networking cards, video cards, hard drives, CD/DVDs, and other items. I mention this because insufficient testing or unmanaged change in these software elements can seriously affect the reliability and functionality of the subsystem, which can ripple through to affect your system. It can also affect the interfaces that a subsystem presents to your system or other subsystems within your system. On one project, poor testing and a total lack of configuration management and change control practices resulted in the firmware on an embedded subsystem causing all sorts of connection reliability issues for the system under test. When talking to hardware vendors about their testing, don't forget to ask about how they control the quality of their firmware. Even the most diligent and careful hardware engineers might not understand good software engineering practices, especially if the company is too small to have a dedicated software engineering team.

Supplier Quality Engineering

The best way to deal with vendor quality issues — including testing of hardware and software — is to build long-term relationships with vendors, apply the distributed testing ideas I discussed in Chapter 10, and also assign someone to work with the vendor to ensure the quality of their products during design, development, and production. This practice is often referred to as *supplier quality engineering.* A supplier quality engineer works with the vendor to ensure thorough testing and prompt resolution of any quality problems that arise throughout the life cycle of the subsystem. My most successful clients who buy subsystems to integrate in their systems have mature, well-run supplier quality engineering programs as part of their design, development, and production processes.

Pilot Testing

Once software is written and run through final system and perhaps acceptance testing, production is often as simple as copying bits onto a CD or DVD, or posting the software to a web site. However, there is a distinct difference in hardware between skilled engineers hand assembling an engineering proto-type system and multiple people on a semi-automated assembly line doing the same thing for dozens or hundreds of systems per hour. Production of hardware systems is a complex endeavor. The quality of the outgoing products is influenced by the quality of the components and subsystems, the assembly process, the production environment, the training given to the assembly line team, and potentially myriad other factors.

To figure out what these factors are and whether the vendor is able to manufacture systems of an acceptable quality level and in an acceptable volume, a pilot test is often run during the initial production period. During the pilot test, heavy sampling and testing of the systems — sometimes as high as 100 percent — is performed. The appropriate period for burn-in testing (i.e., tests run to screen out those systems that will suffer infant mortality) is determined. I have sometimes been involved in this testing, even though my official role was as the development system test manager.

Case Study

On the information appliance project discussed in earlier case studies, we had to test not only the client and server software, but also the information appliance hardware. That testing involved primarily the vendor's test team and an external test lab. However, as shown in Figure A-2, testing also involved the vendor's engineering team, the vendor's production test team, and the two subsystem vendors making the keyboard and the power adapter (a.k.a. "brick"). The case study hardware test tracking spreadsheet, "Case Study Info Appliance Device Test Tracking.xls," is available at www.rbcs-us.com.

	A	B	C	D	E	F	G	H	I	J	K	L	M	N	O
1			Device Test Case	Tracking Worksheet											
2		Test			System	Bug	Bug	Bug		Plan	Act	Plan	Act	Test	
3	Owner	ID	Test Suite/Care	Status	Config	ID	RPN	Status	By	Date	Date	Hrs	Hrs	Hrs	Comment
4															
5	Owner														
6	Vendor Test	1.000	Electrical												
23															
24	Vendor Test	2.000	Reliability												
54															
55	Vendor Engr.	3.000	Regulatory/Standards												
64															
65	Vendor Engr.	4.000	Engineering Test												
67															
68	NTS	5.000	Reliability/Correlation												
84															
85	Vendor Test	6.000	Functionality												
110															
111	Vendor Prod.	7.000	Manufacturability												
118															
119	Kbd Vendor	8.000	Keyboard												
133															
134	Brick Vendor	9.000	Power Adapter												

Figure A-2 Information appliance hardware test suites and assigned organizations

I thank my client, who wishes to remain anonymous, for permission to discuss this project here. I also thank my client contacts for their excellent support and steady leadership on this project. Finally, thanks to my test team, the vendors, and the independent test lab for their professionalism and excellence on this project.

Omninet:
The Internet Everywhere
Marketing Requirements
Document

VER.	DATE	AUTHOR	DESCRIPTION	APPROVED BY	APPROVAL DATE
0.1	June 13, 2009	Rex Black	First Draft		
0.2	June 13, 2009	Rex Black	Second Draft		
0.3	July 1, 2009	Rex Black	Third Draft		

Table of Contents

1 Scope

This document specifies the requirements for a family of Internet kiosks called Omninet. These kiosks shall provide cash, credit card, and debit card customers with simple, fast, reliable Internet access in public places for reasonable prices per minute of usage.

1.1 Terms Acronyms and Abbreviations

For the purposes of this project, the following abbreviations apply:

AS	Application Server
Cable	Cable high-speed Internet connection at least 128 KBPS
CC	Credit card (for payment): American Express, Visa, or MasterCard
CS	Communication Server
DBMS	Database Management System (server)
DC	Debit card (for payment): PLUS or Cirrus networks.
DSL	Digital Subscriber Line high-speed Internet connection (either asymmetric or symmetric) at least 128 KBPS
IE	The Internet Explorer Internet browser
KBPS	Kilobits per second
Kiosk	The free-standing Omninet Internet access point
Linux	Red Hat Linux operating system
Opera	The Opera freeware Internet browser
PIN	Personal Identification Number (for debit card)
PSTN	Public Switched Telephone Network Internet connection (ordinary dial-up connectivity) at least 50 KBPS
URL	Universal resource locator
WS	Web Server
WXP	Windows XP Professional operating system

1.2 Applicable Documents

[1] See the Omninet System Requirements Document for system design requirements

[2] See the Omninet Screen Prototype Document for the kiosk and call center screens (currently unavailable).

2 Required release date

The first set of 1,000 Omninet kiosks shall be live, accepting payment and accessing the Internet, as of the financial third quarter.

3 Description of requirements

3.1 General technical requirements

Omninet shall give customers in airports, malls, theaters, and other public places access to the Internet.

Omninet shall provide call center agents with access to information about current and past kiosk sessions, as well as the ability to control current sessions.

3.1.1 Welcome

Between sessions, each Omninet kiosk shall display an inviting welcome message (see screen prototype K.1).

3.1.2 Payment

Once a user navigates past the Welcome screen, the kiosk shall give the user the option to purchase a block of browser time in the Payment screen (see screen prototype K.2). The kiosk shall sell blocks of time in five (5) minute increments, up to one (1) hour.

The system accepts the following forms of payment:

- Cash (bills only) (see screen prototype K.3)

- Credit card (American Express, Visa, or Mastercard only) (see screen prototype K.4 and K.7)

- Debit card (PLUS or Cirrus networks only) (see screen prototype K.5 and K.7)

Once the current block of time is within sixty (60) seconds of expiration, the kiosk shall pop up a message asking if the user wants to purchase more time (see screen prototype K.9).

3.1.3 Internet Browser

At the Welcome screen, each Omninet kiosk shall provide the user with a choice of the latest version of Firefox, Opera, or Internet Explorer (available on Windows kiosks only).

3.1.4 Performance

On kiosks operating with a PSTN connection, users shall have greater than 50 KBPS connection speed.

On kiosks operating with DSL or cable connections, users shall have greater than 128 KBPS connection speed.

3.1.5 Localization

Each Omninet kiosk shall be configured to operate in the primary local language for its installed locale.

In locales where multiple languages are commonly used, the Welcome screen shall present the user with the option to select the language for the session.

Each Omninet kiosk browser shall be configured to support all languages supported by the operating system and browser.

3.1.6 Content Control

Because Omninet users will access the Internet in public places, Omninet shall implement site blocking that prevents the display of pornographic, objectionable, lewd, obscene, or violent material.

Omninet shall protect each kiosk against sending or receiving a virus, worm, or other malicious code.

3.1.7 Session Termination

Users may terminate sessions in one of two ways:

Logging out (no refund is given for unused time)

Allowing time to expire.

3.1.8 Confidentiality

To protect user confidentiality — e.g., URLs visited — once a session terminates, each kiosk shall clear all cookies and other downloaded files, clear the URL history, exit the browser, and restart the browser at the Welcome screen.

3.2 Administration

3.2.1 Software Updates

Under ordinary circumstances, software updates will take place automatically. At 2:00 AM local time, each kiosk shall connect to the server farm and ask for updates. Those updates include:

- Operating system or browser patches
- New network, modem, or graphics drivers
- New logos
- Updated per-minute payment rate tables
- Virus, worm, malicious code, or other firewall definitions
- Blocked Web sites.
- If there are no updates available, the kiosk shall disconnect.

If the update application on the application server tells the kiosk that it is overloaded, the kiosk shall disconnect, then retry at a later time. The delay for retry is a random period between ten (10) and sixty (60) minutes.

Call center agents may also push software updates to kiosks.

3.2.2 View Kiosks

Call center agents shall be able to browse a list of kiosks. For each kiosk, call center agents shall be able to see:

- Current operating system version
- Current browser version
- Total uptime since installation
- Total uptime since last software update
- Number of crashes, reboots, or other hard failures since last software update.

Kiosks shall connect to the server farm once per hour to report status.

If a kiosk is not connected to the server farm, the call center agent may force a connection to check status.

If a kiosk is down, that kiosk shall show up at the top of the list of kiosks, highlighted in red.

3.2.3 *View Users*

For those kiosks that have active users, call center agents shall have access to the following information:

- Current and past URLs.
- Credit or debit card number (if applicable)
- Name (if available from credit card validation)
- Amount paid for this session
- Blocks of time purchased
- Previous session (if available from credit card number and name)
- Paid time remaining

3.2.4 *Modify User*

Call center agents shall be able to modify a user's session by adding blocks of time.

Supervisory override is required for an agent to add more than sixty (60) minutes of time per day.

3.2.5 *Terminate User*

If a call center agent believes that a user is engaged in illegal, inappropriate, or fraudulent use of a session, the agent may terminate that session.

The user shall receive a refund for any unused time at the point of termination.

The user shall receive a message that the session was terminated for inappropriate activity. The message shall specify the amount of the refund.

Omninet: The Internet Everywhere System Requirements Document

VER.	DATE	AUTHOR	DESCRIPTION	APPROVED BY	DATE
0.1	June 14, 2009	Rex Black	First Draft		
0.2	July 1, 2009	Rex Black	Second Draft		

This document contains proprietary and confidential material of RBCS, Inc. Any unauthorized reproduction, use, or disclosure of this material, or any part thereof, is strictly prohibited. This document is solely for the use of RBCS employees authorized RBCS course attendees, and purchasers of Managing the Testing Process.

Functionality System Requirements

The capability of the system to provide functions which meet stated and implied needs when the software is used under specified conditions.

ID.	VER	MRD	DESCRIPTION	PRIORITY*
010-010			Suitability	
010-010-010	1.0	3.1	Kiosk design shall be suitable for installation in public places.	1
010-010-020	1.0	3.1	Kiosks shall allow access to Internet sites through all supported URLs.	1
010-010-030	1.0	3.1	Kiosks shall provide a standard keyboard-video-mouse graphic user interface.	1
010-010-040	1.0	3.1	Call center desktops shall provide agents with a standard keyboard-video-mouse graphic user interface.	2
010-010-110	1.0	3.1.6	Kiosks shall accept payment in local currencies.	2
010-010-210	1.0	3.1.5	Kiosks shall be configured to interact with customers entirely in the primary local language from the Welcome screen until session termination.	1
010-010-220	1.0	3.15	At the Welcome screen, kiosks shall allow users to select a secondary local language where appropriate. Once this language is selected, the kiosk shall interact with customers entirely in this language until session termination.	2
010-010-230	1.0	3.15	All kiosk Web browsers shall be able to display Web pages in (US) English, (Mexican) Spanish, and (Canadian) French in addition to all primary and secondary local languages for which the kiosk is configured.	2

*Priorities are: 1 Very high 2 High 3 Medium 4 Low 5 Very low

ID.	VER	MRD	DESCRIPTION	PRIORITY*
010-010-240	1.0	3.15	All kiosk Web browsers shall be able to display Web pages in Hebrew, Arabic, German, (Mandarin) Chinese, (Hong Kong) Chinese, Japanese, and Russian.	3
010-010-250	1.0	3.15	All kiosk Web browsers shall be able to display Web pages in languages other than those specified in 010-010-230 and 010-010-240.	4
010-010-910	1.0	3.1.7	Kiosks shall allow users to terminate sessions at any time by clicking the "Log Out" icon on the taskbar.	1
010-010-920	1.0	3.1.2	At any time while the user is browsing the Web, kiosks shall allow users to purchase more time by clicking on the "Buy Time" icon on the taskbar.	3
010-010-930	1.0	3.1.2	Exactly 60 seconds before a session expires, kiosks shall present users with a message that gives them the option to return to the payment screen and purchase additional time. The user may accept the option or decline.	1
010-010-940	1.0	3.1.7	Kiosks shall automatically terminate a user's sessions within 1 second of the expiration of the user's currently purchased blow of time.	1
			[More TBD]	
010-020			*Accuracy*	
010-020-010		3.1.3	All supported e-mail attachments and Web pages (see section 010-030) shall be visible on kiosks without any noticeable distortion from their sources on their originating systems. Scrolling shall not be considered distortion.	2
			[More TBD]	
010-030			*Interoperability*	

Continued

*Priorities are: 1 Very high   2 High   3 Medium   4 Low   5 Very low

(continued)

ID.	VER	MRD	DESCRIPTION	PRIORITY*
010-030-010		3.1.3	The kiosks shall allow users to send and receive e-mail to and from other Omninet kiosks.	1
010-030-020		3.1.3	The kiosks shall allow users to send and receive e-mail to and from other Windows and Linux PCs running e-mail and operating system software not more than two years old.	2
010-030-030		3.1.3	The kiosks shall allow users to send and receive e-mail to and from Macintosh PCs.	3
010-030-040		3.1.3	The kiosks shall allow users to send and receive e-mail to and from other systems such as mainframes, Unix servers, VMS servers, PCs (those running e-mail or operating system software more than two years olds or those not running Windows, Linux, or Mac) and other systems.	5
			[More TBD]	
010-040			*Security*	
010-040-010	1.0	3.16	A firewall running on the kiosk shall protect each kiosk against inbound or outbound virii, worms, other malicious code, and hacking via a firewall. Upon detection of any such item, the firewall shall report such security events to the application server.	1
010-040-020	1.0	3.16	Filtering software running at the server farm shall protect each kiosks against inbound or outbound pornographic, objectionable, lewd, obscene, violent, or other inappropriate material. Upon detection of any such item, the filtering software shall report such security events to the application server.	1
010-040-030	1.0	3.16	Upon report of a security event, the application server shall send a log entry to the database server to place the event in a database table.	1

*Priorities are: 1 Very high   2 High   3 Medium   4 Low   5 Very low

ID.	VER	MRD	DESCRIPTION	PRIORITY*
010-040-040	1.0	3.16	Logged security events in the database table shall be maintained for at least one year.	3
010-040-040	1.0	3.16	Upon report of a security event, the application server shall escalate the event to an active call center agent desktop. (Active is defined as currently logged in and not locked.) The agent so alerted shall take action in accordance with the current security policies for handling security events.	1
010-040-050	1.0	3.16 3.2.5	Subject to the current security policies for handling security events, a call center agent shall be able to terminate the session for a user who sends malicious code or inappropriate material, or who uses the kiosk to hack other systems. The user whose session is so terminated shall receive a message that includes a toll-free number to call to appeal the decision.	2
010-040-060	1.0	N/A	Subject to the current security policies for handling security events, a call center agent shall be able to log in to their desktop system at the beginning of each shift and log out at the end of each shift.	1
010-040-070	1.0	N/A	Subject to the current security policies for handling security events, a call center agent shall be able to lock their current login session on their desktop system prior to leaving their desk.	2
			[More TBD]	
010-050			*Compliance (functionality standards/laws/regs)*	
			[TBD]	

*Priorities are: 1 Very high   2 High   3 Medium   4 Low   5 Very low

Reliability System Requirements

The capability of the system to maintain a specified level of performance when used under specified conditions.

ID.	VER	MRD	DESCRIPTION	PRIORITY
020-010			Maturity	
020-010-010	1.0	3.1.3	Except as noted in 020-010-030, the server farm shall make available to the kiosks the latest drivers, patches, and other updates for Linux or Windows (as appropriate) only after each update has been available for at least 30 days, Technical Support has documented all known issues, and the Change Control Board has approved the update.	3
020-010-020	1.0	3.1.3	Except as noted in 020-010-030, the server farm shall make available to the kiosks the latest drivers, patches, and other updates for Internet Explorer, Firefox, or Opera (as appropriate) only after each update has been available for at least 30 days, Technical Support has documented all known issues, and the Change Control Board has approved the update.	3
020-010-030	1.0	3.1.6	The server farm shall make available to the kiosks the latest virus, worm, malicious code, and blocked Web site definitions.	1
			[More TBD]	
020-020			Fault-tolerance	
020-020-010	1.0	3.1.2	Should the network connection fail during payment approval, the kiosk shall complete the transaction if the customer has been charged. The kiosk shall not complete the transaction if the customer has not been charged.	1

ID.	VER	MRD	DESCRIPTION	PRIORITY
020-020-020	1.0	3.1.2	Should the network connection fail during payment approval, the kiosk shall not complete the transaction if the customer has not been charged.	2
			[More TBD]	
020-030			Recoverability	
			[TBD]	
020-040			Compliance (reliability standards/laws/regs)	
			[TBD]	

Usability System Requirements

The capability of the system to be understood learned, used, and attractive to the user and the call center agents when used under specified conditions.

ID.	VER	MRD	DESCRIPTION	PRIORITY
030-010			Understandability	
030-010-010	1.0	3.1	The kiosk user interface shall preserve the commonly-understood Microsoft Windows look-and-feel.	2
030-010-010	1.0	3.1	Call center agent desktop user interface shall preserve the commonly-understood Microsoft Windows look-and-feel.	2
			[More TBD]	
030-020			Learnability	
			[TBD]	
030-030			Operability	
030-030-010	1.0	3.1	The kiosk user interface shall not require the user to navigate through more than five unique pages before accessing the Web browser.	2

Continued

(continued)

ID.	VER	MRD	DESCRIPTION	PRIORITY
030-030-020	1.0	3.1	The call center desktop agent user interface shall not require the user to navigate through more than five unique pages before accessing the any of the major call-center functions.	2
			[More TBD]	
030-040			Attractiveness	
			[TBD]	
030-050			Compliance (usability standards)	
	1.1		System shall comply with local handicap-access laws.	5

Efficiency System Requirements

The capability of the system to provide appropriate performance, relative to the amount of resources used under stated conditions.

ID.	VER	MRD	DESCRIPTION	PRIORITY
040-010			Time behavior	
040-010-010	1.0	3.1.1	The kiosk shall present the Welcome screen within 120 seconds of initial kiosk power up 95% of the time. In no case shall the time exceed 240 seconds.	1
040-010-020	1.0	3.1.1	The kiosk shall present the Welcome screen within 15 seconds of completion of the previous session 95% of the time. In no case shall the time exceed 30 seconds.	1
040-010-030	1.0	3.1.2	The kiosk shall present the first payment screen within 0.5 seconds of a potential customer touching the screen, mouse, or keyboard, 95% of the time. In no case shall the time exceed 1.5 seconds.	2

ID.	VER	MRD	DESCRIPTION	PRIORITY
040-010-040	1.0	3.1.2	Excluding any user and credit/ debit card approval delays, the kiosk shall complete payment processing no more than 15 after presenting the first payment screen 95% of the time. In no case shall the time exceed 30 seconds. Should any credit/debit card approval delay exceed 30 seconds, the kiosk shall present the user with the option of canceling the transaction.	2
040-010-050	1.0	3.1.2	In the case that any user or credit/debit card approval delay reaches 60 seconds, the kiosk shall cancel (time-out) the transaction. The user may re-attempt the transaction.	2
			[More TBD]	
040-020			Resource utilization	
040-020-010	1.0	2	The server farm shall support 1,000 kiosks, all of which may be simultaneously active.	2
040-020-020	1.0		The server farm shall support 25 call center agent desktops, all of which may be simultaneously active.	2
			[More TBD]	
040-030			Compliance (performance standards)	
			[TBD]	

Maintainability System Requirements

The capability of the system to be modified. Modifications may include corrections, improvement, or adaptations of the software changes in environments, and in requirement s and functional specifications.

ID.	VER	MRD	DESCRIPTION	PRIORITY
050-010			Analyzability	
	1.0		The development and maintenance organizations shall maintain traceability between marketing requirements, system requirements, quality risks, test suites, and test cases.	1
			[More TBD]	
050-020			Changeability	
050-020-010	1.1		The server farm shall support up to 100 call center agents.	2
050-020-020	1.1		The server farm shall support up to 5,000 kiosks.	2
			[TBD]	
040-030			Compliance (performance standards)	
			[TBD]	

Portability System Requirements

The capability of the system to be transferred from one environment to another.

ID.	VER	MRD	DESCRIPTION	PRIORITY
060-010			Adaptability	
060-010-010	1.0		The kiosk hardware shall support Linux.	1
060-010-010	1.1		The kiosk hardware shall support Windows XP.	2
			[More TBD]	
060-020			Installability	

ID.	VER	MRD	DESCRIPTION	PRIORITY
060-020-010	1.0		The server farm shall push appropriate updates (for OS, browser, and kiosk software) to the kiosks upon identifying a back-level version of software in a kiosk.	1
			[More TBD]	
060-030			Co-existence	
060-030-010	1.0		The kiosks shall support viewing Adobe Acrobat documents on Web pages.	3
			[More TBD]	
060-040			Replaceability	
060-040-010	1.0		The server software shall be written to be portable across Web server, application server, and database server vendors.	2
			[More TBD]	
060-050			Compliance	
060-050-010	1.0		The kiosk software shall be implemented to work on any standards-compliant browser.	3
060-050-020	1.0		The server software shall be written using industry-standard database and programming languages.	1
			[More TBD]	

Design Models

Omninet System Architecture

Figure C-1 shows the Omninet system architecture.

Figure C-1 Omninet System Architecture

Payment Processing Decision Table

Table C-1 shows the business rules that govern processing of payments. The processing of payments logic that authorizes credit and/or debit cards runs on the application server. The processing of payments logic that verifies legitimate currency or correct card runs on the kiosk.

Kiosk Module Flow

Figure C-2 shows the kiosk module flow.

Table C-1 Payment Processing Decision Table

CONDITION	BUSINESS RULE					
	1	2	3	4	5	6
Valid money	No	Yes	-	-	-	-
Valid card	-	-	No	Yes	Yes	Yes
Valid PIN (for debit) or no PIN required (for credit)	-	-	-	No	Yes	Yes
Amount approved	-	-	-	-	No	Yes
Action						
Reject cash	Yes	No	No	No	No	No
Reject card	No	No	Yes	Yes	No	No
Prompt for lower amount	No	No	No	No	Yes	No
Sell time block	No	Yes	No	No	No	Yes

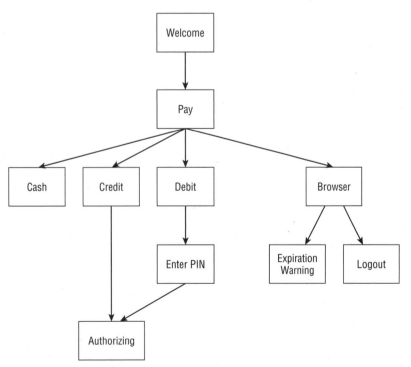

Figure C-2 Kiosk module flow

Kiosk State-Transition Diagram

The following diagram shows the states that the kiosk can be in, the transitions that can occur between states, and the events, conditions, and actions associated with those transitions.

TBD

Kiosk State-Transition Table

The following table shows the state transitions that can occur based on the events and conditions that can influence the kiosks behavior.

NB: The following events can occur:

Logout:	The user terminates the active kiosk session.
Terminate:	A call center agent terminates the active kiosk session.
URL:	The user enters a URL (which may be browseable or blocked)
Pay:	The user submits some form of payment (currency, credit card, or debit card) to the kiosk (which may be valid or invalid) to begin or continue a kiosk session

TBD

Starting State	Event [Condition]	Action	New State

Kiosk OS/Browser/Connection Speed Configuration Orthogonal Array

The following orthogonal array shows the configuration options (singletons and pairs) that will need to be tested.

TBD: One of these arrays will work.

	Factors		
Config	**1**	**2**	**3**
1	0	0	0
2	0	1	1
3	1	0	1
4	1	1	0

	Factors			
Config	1	2	3	4
1	0	0	0	0
2	0	1	1	2
3	0	2	2	1
4	1	0	1	1
5	1	1	2	0
6	1	2	0	2
7	2	0	2	2
8	2	1	0	1
9	2	2	1	0

	Factors				
Config	1	2	3	4	5
1	0	0	0	0	0
2	0	1	1	1	1
3	0	2	2	2	2
4	0	3	3	3	3
5	1	0	1	2	3
6	1	1	0	3	2
7	1	2	3	0	1
8	1	3	2	1	0
9	2	0	2	3	1
10	2	1	3	2	0
11	2	2	0	1	3
12	2	3	1	0	2
13	3	0	3	1	2
14	3	1	2	0	3
15	3	2	1	3	0
16	3	3	0	2	1

Bibliography, Related Readings, and Other Resources

While this book should provide you with enough information to manage a test project, it is not exhaustive. I encourage you to continue to augment your knowledge. The following subsections provide you with some places to go for more information, including the bibliography of references and recommended readings. Like the book, this appendix is not complete, nor does the presence or absence of a particular company, book, organization, or individual reflect my endorsement or opinion.

Bibliography and Related Readings

The following is my suggested reading list for test managers. Many of these books and articles are referenced somewhere in *Managing the Testing Process*. However, some I have included simply because I feel that you might benefit from a familiarity with the material presented, or with the author's point of view. Over the last decade, we have gained a wealth of materials we can use as test professionals. I encourage you to stay current and involved with the latest thinking and research in the field. Today's wacky idea is tomorrow's best practice, and the day after's expected minimum skill set.

Andrews, Mike, and James Whittaker. *How to Break Web Software.* Boston, MA: Addison-Wesley Professional, 2006.

Batini, Carlo, Stefano Ceri, and Shamkant Navathe. *Conceptual Database Design.* Redwood City, CA: Benjamin/Cummings, 1992.

Beizer, Boris. *Software System Testing and Quality Assurance.* New York, NY: International Thomson Computer Press, 1996.

Beizer, Boris. *Software Testing Techniques, Second Edition.* New York, NY: Van Nostrand Reinhold, 1990.

Bjornvig, Gertrud, et al. "A Story about User Stories and Test Driven Development," originally published in *Better Software* magazine, November 2007, now available in the Basic Library at www.rbcs-us.com.

Black, Rex. *Advanced Software Testing: Volume I.* Santa Barbara, CA: Rocky Nook, 2008.

Black, Rex. *Advanced Software Testing: Volume II.* Santa Barbara, CA: Rocky Nook, 2008.

Black, Rex. *Critical Testing Processes.* Boston, MA: Addison-Wesley, 2002.

Black, Rex. "ISTQB Certification," originally published in *Testing Experience*, Nov. 2008, now available in the Basic Library at www.rbcs-us.com.

Black, Rex and Greg Kubaczkowski. "Mission Made Possible," *Software Testing and Quality Engineering*, Volume 4, Issue 4, now available in the Basic Library of www.rbcs-us.com.

Rex, Black. "No More Bad MBOs," originally an online article on www.stickyminds.com, now available in the Basic Library at www.rbcs-us.com.

Black, Rex. *Pragmatic Software Testing.* New York, NY: Wiley, 2007.

Black, Rex. "Software Test Estimation," originally in *Software Testing and Quality Engineering* magazine, Nov./Dec. 2002 (vol. 4, no. 6), now available in the Basic Library at www.rbcs-us.com.

Brooks, Frederick P., Jr. *The Mythical Man-Month.* Reading, MA: Addison-Wesley, 1995.

Burnstein, Ilene. *Practical Software Testing.* Berlin: Springer, 2003.

Campanella, Jack, ed., with the American Society for Quality's Quality Costs Committee. *Principles of Quality Costs, Third Edition.* Milwaukee, WI: ASQ Quality Press, 1999.

Carroll, Sue, and Taz Daughtrey, ed. *Fundamental Concepts for the Software Quality Engineer: Volume 2.* Milwaukee, WI: ASQ Quality Press, 2007.

Craig, Rick, and Stefan Jaskiel. *Systematic Software Testing*. New York, NY: Artech House Publishers, 2002.

Crosby, Phillip. *Quality Is Free: The Art of Making Quality Certain*. New York, NY: McGraw-Hill, 1979.

DeMarco, Tom. *The Deadline*. New York, NY: Dorset House, 1997.

Drucker, Peter. "Management's New Paradigms." *Forbes*, October 5, 1998, pp. 52–76.

Drucker, Peter. *The Practice of Management*. New York, NY: Collins Business, 2006.

Ensworth, Patricia. *The Accidental Project Manager*. New York, NY: Wiley, 2001.

Fewster, Mark and Dorothy Graham. *Software Test Automation*. Harlow, England: Addison-Wesley, 1999.

Graham, Dorothy, et al. *Foundations of Software Testing: ISTQB Certification*. London: Cengage, 2008.

Hadden, Rita. "Credible Estimation for Small Projects," *Software Quality Professional* 3, no. 2, March 2001.

Hetzel, Bill. *The Complete Guide to Software Testing*. New York, NY: Wiley-QED, 1988.

IEEE Standards Committee. *IEEE Standard for Software and System Test Documentation*, 2008.

Ishikawa, Kaoru. *Guide to Quality Control*. Tokyo, Japan: Asian Productivity Organization, 1982.

Johnson, Paul. *Intellectuals*. New York, NY: Harper and Row, 1988.

Jones, Capers.*Estimating Software Costs, Second Edition*. New York, NY: McGraw-Hill, 2007.

Jones, Capers. "Measuring Defect Potentials and Defect Removal Efficiency," found in the Basic Library at www.rbcs-us.com.

Jorgensen, Paul. *Software Testing: A Craftsman's Approach, Third Edition*. New York, NY: Auerbach Publications, 2008.

Juran, J. M. *Juran on Planning for Quality*. New York, NY: Free Press, 1988.

Juran, J. M., and A. Blanton Godfrey. *Quality Control Handbook, Fifth Edition*. New York, NY: McGraw-Hill, 2000.

Kamen, Henry. *The Spanish Inquisition*. New Haven, CT: Yale University Press, 1999.

Koomen, Tim, and Martin Pol. *Test Process Improvement*. Boston, MA: Addison-Wesley Professional, 1999.

Koomen, Tim, et al. *TMap: Next*. Utrecht: UTN Publishers, 2006.

Kan, Stephen. *Metrics and Models in Software Quality Engineering, Second Edition*. Reading, MA: Addison-Wesley, 2002.

Kaner, Cem, James Bach, and Bret Pettichord. *Lessons Learned in Software Testing*. New York, NY: Wiley, 2001.

Lyu, Michael, ed. *Handbook of Software Reliability Engineering*. New York, NY: McGraw-Hill, 1996.

McConnell, Steve. *After the Gold Rush*. Redmond, WA: Microsoft Press, 1999.

McConnell, Steve. *Software Project Survival Guide*. Redmond, WA: Microsoft Press, 1997.

McKay, Judy. *Managing the Test People*. Santa Barbara, CA: Rocky Nook, 2007

McLean, Harry. *HALT, HASS & HASA Explained: Accelerated Reliability Techniques*. Milwaukee, WI: ASQ Press, 2000.

Myers, Glenford. *The Art of Software Testing*. New York, NY: Wiley, 1979.

Neumann, Peter. *Computer-Related Risks*. New York, NY: Addison-Wesley, 1995.

Nietzsche, Friedrich. *Beyond Good and Evil*. Cambridge: Oxford University Press, 2009.

O'Connor, Patrick. *Practical Reliability Engineering, Fourth Edition*. New York, NY: Wiley, 2002.

Paulk, Mark C., Charles V. Weber, Bill Curtis, and Mary Beth Chrissis. *The Capability Maturity Model: Guidelines for Improving the Software Process*. Reading, MA: Addison-Wesley, 1995.

Perry, William, and Randall Rice. *Surviving the Top Ten Challenges of Software Testing*. New York, NY: Dorset House, 1997.

Pressman, Roger. *Software Engineering: A Practitioner's Approach. Seventh Edition*. New York, NY: McGraw-Hill, 2009.

Ruhl, Janet. *The Computer Consultant's Guide: Real-Life Strategies for Building a Successful Consulting Career*. New York, NY: Wiley, 1997.

Sabourin, Robert. *I am a Bug!* Roxboro, Quebec: Self-published, 1999.

Shapiro, Eileen. *Fad Surfing in the Boardroom: Reclaiming the Courage to Manage in the Age of Instant Answers*. New York, NY: Perseus Press, 1995.

Stamatis, D. H. *Failure Mode and Effect Analysis, Second Edition*. Milwaukee, WI: ASQ Quality Press, 2003.

Walton, Mary. *The Deming Management Method*. New York, NY: Putnam Publishing Group, 1986.

Whittaker, James. *How to Break Software*. Boston, MA: Addison-Wesley, 2002.

Whittaker, James, and Herbert Thompson. *How to Break Software Security*. Boston, MA: Addison-Wesley, 2003.

Wysocki, Robert, Robert Beck, Jr., and David Crane. *Effective Project Management, Fourth Edition*. New York, NY: Wiley, 2006.

Online and Hard-Copy Publications

Publications come and go. A review of this list from this book's second edition will show that few of the entries from the second edition remain active now. At the risk of becoming dated overnight, though, here's a list of periodicals, magazines, and online resources that you might find interesting as someone working in the areas of software and hardware testing and quality assurance.

- Software Quality Engineering, *Better Software*, www.bettersoftware.com.
- Association for Computing Machinery, *Communications of the ACM*, www.acm.org.
- Quality House, *Quality Matters*, www.quality-matters.org.
- The newsgroup comp.risks, also available as a mailing list risk-request @csl.sri.com.
- American Society for Quality, *Software Quality Professional*, www.asq.org.
- Redwood Collaborative Media, *Software Test & Performance*, www.stpmag.com.
- Díaz & Hilterscheid, *Testing Experience*, www.testingexperience.com.
- Various IEEE-published periodicals that pertain to testing and quality assurance. See ieee.org.

Many, many, many others exist. New ones seem to come about every day, so you can search the Internet to find these and others. However, check out their backgrounds. Who is sponsoring the site? How do they make money? Can they offer unbiased advice?

Contacting RBCS

Rex Black Consulting Services (RBCS) is a premier international testing consultancy specializing in consulting, outsourcing, and training services. Led by one of the most recognized and published industry leaders, Rex Black, RBCS is an established company you can trust to deliver results, and with the track record to prove it.

Since 1994, RBCS has been both a pioneer and a leader in quality hardware and software testing. Through its training, consulting, and outsourcing services, RBCS has helped hundreds of companies improve their test practices and achieve quality results. RBCS has offices in the United States, New Zealand, Australia, and Sri Lanka, with partners around the world.

Our Value

RBCS utilizes deep industry experience to solve testing problems and improve testing processes. We help clients reduce risk and save money through higher-quality products and services. Our goal is to help clients avoid the costs associated with poor product quality — such as product recalls, tech support calls, lawsuits, and reputation damage — by helping them understand and solve testing and performance issues and build better testing teams. Whether it's customizing a program to fit your company's needs or providing the hands-on experience and resources that will allow your testing team to grow professionally, RBCS helps companies produce better products and increase ROI. RBCS pours its resources into ensuring our clients become successful.

Our People

Employing the industry's most experienced and recognized consultants, RBCS conducts product testing, builds and improves testing groups, and hires testing staff for hundreds of clients worldwide. Our principals include published, international experts in the area of hardware and software testing. Our skilled test managers and engineers all hold International Software Testing Qualifications Board (ISTQB) certifications and are highly trained.

RBCS believes in the value of real-life experience and leadership, which is why the RBCS team is always striving to improve and perfect the testing process. Every employee is ISTQB-certified and encouraged to write articles and books, share leading ideas through presentations, and continually advance the state of the testing profession. In addition, as former president of ASTQB and ISTQB, Rex Black has more than a quarter-century of software and systems engineering experience and strongly leads the company with the most recent, proven testing methodologies and strategies. For complete bios on RBCS principals and project managers visit www.rbcs-us.com.

Our Clients

Our client-centered approach helps companies deliver better-quality products and reduce costs by improving the effectiveness and efficiency of their test practices. The difference? Our recognized industry experts started their careers in our customers' shoes — they have the real-world knowledge required to deliver the best services with proven practices. From Fortune 100 to small and mid-size organizations, RBCS works with a variety of companies, in industries such as technology, finance, communications, retail, government, and education.

Consulting

RBCS offers customized consulting services that will not only help you solve your testing challenges, but provide you with the tools and framework for managing a successful testing organization. Our consulting methodology is based on successful, peer-reviewed publications with a customized approach that focuses on the individual needs of each client. Plus we have a long list of happy, reference-able customers around the globe that have benefited from RBCS expertise.

Assessments

RBCS provides assessments, which will identify opportunities to improve the effectiveness and efficiency of your testing team and processes, along with detailed recommendations on how to do so. All assessments look at the tools, processes, and deliverables under review from both a tactical, individual contributor perspective and a strategic, managerial/executive perspective.

Test process: Following Rex Black's professionally acclaimed book, *Critical Testing Processes*, we examine the 12 critical testing processes for effectiveness and efficiency, including defect detection and return on investment metrics.

Test tools: RBCS will evaluate and make recommendations for existing or proposed test automation efforts, including consideration of commercial, open-source, and custom-made tool options. We'll also evaluate test tool design concepts, maintainability, and return on investment goals.

Quality methodology: RBCS will evaluate and make recommendations for the best overall approach. This will ensure high-quality deliverables, from requirements, design, and code reviews to unit, integration, system, and acceptance testing. We also compare financial and project time-lines of your current practices against the industry's best practices.

A typical assessment engagement involves about one week per site, plus one week of off-site analysis and report preparation.

Jump-Starts

RBCS provides jump-starts, which are short engagements that bring best practices into your test processes. All jump-starts enable you to introduce a new technique, tool, or process in your organization quickly, bypassing common mistakes and pitfalls.

Risk-based testing: Deal with schedule and budget constraints in a way that intelligently and transparently manages risk. Focus your test effort via detailed risk analysis and proven techniques developed by the pioneers in the field.

Unit testing: Increase quality, accelerate delivery, and save money by removing bugs earlier in development.

Test engineering: Take your test team to the highest levels of test proficiency.

Test automation: Incrementally introduce automated tools using proven approaches for low-risk, high-return on investment, successful testing of regression, performance, and other areas.

Test management: For better management of a testing effort, learn how to introduce comprehensive, lightweight, proven techniques and how to best apply them to your test project.

Acceptance test: Mitigate the risk of outsource development through careful, proactive means.

A typical jump-start engagement involves anywhere from one week to two months of on-site services, generally include a blend of training, consulting, and hands-on mentoring on a pilot project.

Project Test Services

RBCS provides complete testing services for projects, either at your place or ours. Projects involve planning, design, implementation, execution, and results reporting for any or all levels of tests (e.g., unit test, system test, acceptance) and may involve setting up a team and transitioning that team into your organization.

Functional test: Testing for accuracy, suitability, completeness, and correctness in the area of a system's functional requirements.

Non-functional test: Testing of areas beyond functionality, such as performance, security, usability, compatibility, accessibility, and more.

Test automation: Testing via commercial, open-source, and custom-built tools, where one deliverable is the automated solution as well as the result.

Technical test: Testing focused on the technology you're using to implement the system under test, such as white-box testing, Linux testing, Web testing, embedded/real-time system testing, and so forth.

Our lead consultants on these engagements are proven industry experts, with years of experience and typically a record of publications in industry journals.

Test Recruiting, Staff Augmentation, and Outsourcing

RBCS provides recruiting, staff augmentation, and outsourcing services to companies, too. Building a top-notch testing team takes more than sifting through a stack of resumes. RBCS outsourcing services work to screen applicants, prepare them for the job, and stay engaged to make sure things run smoothly. Whether on-site, off-site, or off-shore, RBCS has a worldwide team of trained test engineers to complement your testing group, reduce operating costs, and help you scale to meet changing needs.

RBCS outsourcing services include test technician, test engineer, test expert, and test manager resources for on-site staff augmentation as well as outsourcing to our U.S., New Zealand, Australia, Sri Lanka, Korea, or Japan facilities.

Training and Certification

Whether you are seeking testing certification or better test management skills, RBCS has a broad range of hands-on, practical test training courses. These courses have proven successful with thousands of attendees in dozens of countries. Each course is taught by one of RBCS's top industry consultants, who are seasoned test professionals *and* skilled, experienced trainers.

RBCS has the worldwide capabilities and experience to ensure you get the best training possible. Our most popular courses are also available in e-learning modes. In addition, all clients receive access to RBCS high-quality testing tools and resources developed by industry leaders. Our goal is to not only prepare you to pass ISTQB exams, but to give you real-life insight to help you build a successful testing career.

The Bottom Line

Many business applications are not tested properly before being released into the market, costing organizations huge sums of money and wasting time and resources. Smart companies are figuring out how to save this money by making software testing an independent, professional discipline in their shops. Professional testers bring objectivity and transparency to quality assessment and improve the core business strategy. After working with RBCS, you will understand the opportunities to improve your testing organization, have a plan for making those improvements, and have the assistance of a world-class consultancy to help you along the way. Let us know how we can help you transform your company into a smart producer of quality products.

Contact RBCS, Inc.:

www.rbcs-us.com

info@rbcs-us.com

US: +1 (866) 438-4830

Worldwide: +1 (830) 438-4830

Glossary

Following is a list of terms that can be helpful to know when you are dealing with hardware and software testing.

acceptance testing A software or hardware development test phase designed to demonstrate that the system under test meets requirements. This phase is unique in all test activities in that its sole purpose is to build confidence in the quality of the software. Acceptance testing should not find bugs. Acceptance testing is usually the last test phase before a product is released.

ad hoc testing Testing without written test cases, documented expected results, a checklist, a script, or instructions. Ad hoc tests often are not captured, which leads to questions about coverage and makes it impossible to do proper regression testing. Ad hoc testing can, however, be useful as a way to develop tests if records are kept. Also called ad-lib testing. Contrast with exploratory testing or software attacks.

behavioral tests Tests based on what a computer system, hardware or software, is supposed to do. Such tests are usage-based and frequently functional, at the levels of features, operational profiles, and customer scenarios. Also called black-box tests or functional tests.

black-box tests See behavioral tests.

bug A problem present in the system under test that causes it to fail to meet reasonable expectations; also called a defect. The symptom of a bug is a failure. The reasonableness of an expectation can be determined by iterative consensus or management fiat if it is not obvious or defined (in the design specification or requirements documents). Notice that the test team usually sees only the failure, the improper behavior, but the bug itself is the flaw that causes the failure.

bug crawl A meeting or discussion focused on an item-by-item review of every active bug reported against the system under test. During this review, the participants can assign bug priority, fix dates, defer insignificant bugs, and assess the progress of the development process. Also referred to as a bug scrub, change control board (CCB) meeting, bug triage meeting, bug review meeting, and many other different names.

closure period For an individual bug that has been fixed and closed, the time between the initial bug report and the confirmation of the fix. The daily closure period is the average number of days between the opening of a bug report and its resolution for all bug reports closed on the same day, and the rolling closure period is the average for all closed bug reports. Closure period is a measure of development's responsiveness to test's bug reports.

component testing A software development test phase (often referred to as subsystem testing in hardware development) that finds bugs in the individual pieces of the system under test before the pieces are fully integrated into the system. Component testing can require support structures such as stubs or scaffolds. Sometimes also called unit testing.

confirmation tests A selected set of tests designed to determine whether a bug fix has failed to address the reported issue fully. A typical confirmation test involves re-running the test procedure and isolation steps, per the bug report.

congruent A description of test system architecture in which all elements of a test system align with one another and with the objectives of the test system. In a congruent test system, each component contributes to the functioning of the test system, without contradictory or destructive interfaces, outputs, or side effects.

continuation criteria A set of decision-making guidelines that indicate whether a particular phase of testing is proceeding effectively and efficiently. Conversely, when called stopping criteria, these guidelines are expressed in terms of determining whether testing should stop due to poor quality of the system under test or logistical problems related to performing tests. Continuation or stopping criteria tend to become more rigorous in later test phases such as integration testing and system testing. See also entry criteria and exit criteria.

debugging   The process in which developers determine the root cause of a bug and identify possible fixes. Developers perform debugging activities to resolve a known bug either after development of a subsystem or unit or because of a bug report. Contrast isolation.

deployment   The point at which the first system under test, now a completely tested, finished product, ships to the first user or is installed onto the production systems. Also called release, cut-over, or migration, among other names.

distributed testing   Testing that occurs at multiple locations, involves multiple teams, or both.

due diligence   Informally, the requirement that responsible employees and business associates, especially managers, not be negligent of the consequences of their decisions and the attendant risks to their employers or clients. This term has legal connotations; you should consult legal counsel for a precise definition.

entry criteria   A set of decision-making guidelines that indicate whether the project is ready to enter a particular phase of testing. Entry criteria tend to become more rigorous in the later phases, such as integration testing and system testing. See also continuation criteria and exit criteria.

error seeding   A theoretical technique for measuring the bugs remaining in the system under test and thereby measuring the effectiveness of the test system itself, by deliberately inserting known defects (hidden from the testers) into the system under test, and then checking the proportion of these defects that are detected. Not commonly used and subject to widespread doubts about its accuracy.

escalate   To communicate a problem to a higher level of management for resolution.

exit criteria   A set of decision-making guidelines that indicate whether the project is ready to exit a particular phase of testing, either to move on to the next phase or to complete the project. Exit criteria tend to become more rigorous in later phases, such as integration testing and system testing. See also continuation criteria and entry criteria.

experience of quality   The customers' and users' opinions about whether a system is fulfilling their expectations and needs.

exploratory testing   Simultaneous design, development, and execution of tests, usually coupled with learning about the system under test, with generally lightweight documentation. Exploratory testing can be entirely self-guided, but can also proceed according to a high-level direction about the area to test (called a test charter). Contrast with scripted testing and ad hoc testing.

fault injection   A theoretical technique for measuring the effectiveness of a test system, in which errors are created in the system under test by deliberately damaging, or perturbing, the source code, the executable code, or the data storage locations and then analyzing the test results. This technique is limited to finding bugs present in code that exists; in other words, bugs arising from missing, ambiguous, or incorrect items in requirements or design specification can generally not be detected. Fault injection in code is not commonly used, but fault injection in data is a well-recognized technique.

fidelity   With respect to a test system, the degree to which it accurately models end-user hardware, software, and network environments and simulates end-user activities.

field-reported bug   A failure in a released, deployed, or shipping product, usually reported by a user, customer or a salesperson, that either affects the ability of the user or customer to use the product or involves side effects that impair the user's or customer's ability to use other products on the same system.

first customer ship   For mass-market systems, the point at which the first system under test, now a completely tested, finished product, ships to the first paying customer. Also called release or general availability.

flexibility   The extent to which a test component can handle minor changes in the system under test's behavior without reporting bugs that don't exist or failing to report bugs that do exist.

FMEA   Acronym for *failure mode and effect analysis*, a technique for identifying and defining potential quality risks, ranking them by risk priority, and assigning action to prevent and/or detect related problems.

functional tests   Sometimes this phrase has the same meaning as behavioral tests, but it can also connote testing that focuses strictly on correctness of functionality. In these cases, it must be augmented with other test approaches to deal with potentially important quality risks such as performance, load, capacity, volume, and so forth.

GA   Acronym for *general availability*. See first customer ship.

goat rodeo   Any confused, disorganized, and chaotic group event, generally held under pressure or duress, that results in little forward progress, thus frustrating many participants. Derived from the children's rodeo events where youngsters attempt to rope and tie goats, calves, and other small farm animals.

granularity   Fineness or coarseness of focus. A fine-grained test allows the tester to check low-level details; a structural test is fine-grained. Behavioral tests, which are coarse-grained, provide the tester with information on general system behavior, not details.

integration testing   A software development test phase (often referred to as product testing in hardware development) that finds bugs in the relationships and interfaces between pairs and groups of components in the system under test, often in a staged fashion. This test phase ideally occurs as all the constituent components of the system under test are being integrated, and is closely coordinated with and also helps coordinate the integration plan.

isolation   Repeating the steps needed to reproduce a bug, possibly many times, with precise changes in system configuration, permission levels, background load, environment, and so forth, in an effort to understand the levers that control the bug and its behavior — in other words, to confirm that the bug is a real problem and to identify those factors that affect the bug's manifestations. Good isolation draws a bounding box around a bug. Isolation requires the tester to make intelligent guesses about the root cause of the problem. Contrast debugging.

kludge   Any ill-advised, substandard, or temporary fix applied to an urgent problem in the (often misguided) belief that doing so will keep a project moving forward.

maintainable   In terms of the test system, the extent to which a test engineer versed in the operation of the system can make changes in a test component without undue risk of damaging that component or other components.

MEGO   Acronym for *my eyes glazed over*; referring to a loss of focus and attention, often caused by an attempt to read a particularly impenetrable or dense technical document, or attending a meeting where off-agenda discussions and minutiae dominate the proceedings.

MTBF   Acronym for *mean time between failures*. Demonstrating a particular MTBF or discovering a statistically meaningful MTBF is often an important part of a hardware development project, as this figure predicts the financial impact of various warranty policies and has important implications for field defect rates and a company's reputation for quality.

MTTR   Acronym for *mean time to repair*. Like MTBF, this figure has implications for a company's warranties and reputation. A problem that takes longer to repair will generally be a higher priority than one that takes less time to repair, all other factors being equal.

oracle   Any way of determining the expected (correct) result for a test case, a test suite, or a test operation. This term is usually synonymous with output oracle or test oracle, which, for a given input under a given set of test conditions, tells the tester what the expected output should be. However, oracles are also needed to describe non-output behaviors, especially when testing performance, load, capacity and volume, and error handling.

orthogonal   A description of the relationship between two or more variables or set members in which the value of one does not influence the values of others.

peer review   A quality improvement technique common in software development, in which one or more participants reads and comments on a development or test deliverable such as the requirements specification, the code, a bug report, a test suite, or a test plan. The reading is followed by a review meeting in which the deliverable is discussed. Based on this discussion, the deliverable is updated, corrected, and re-released.

pilot testing   In hardware development, a test phase generally following or accompanying acceptance testing, which demonstrates the ability of the assembly line to mass-produce the completely tested, finished system under test. In software development, pilot testing is a test phase that demonstrates the ability of the system to handle typical operations from live customers on live hardware. First customer ship or deployment often immediately follows the successful completion of the pilot testing phase.

priority   The business importance of a bug, especially its effect on the viability and acceptability of the system from a user and customer perspective. Contrast severity.

product testing   See integration testing.

quality risk   The possibility of undesirable types of behaviors, or failure modes, in which the system under test does not meet stated product requirements or end users' reasonable expectations of behavior; in plain terms, the possibility of a bug.

quality risk management   The process of identifying, prioritizing, and managing risks to the quality of the system under test, with the aim of preventing them or detecting and removing them.

railroading   A technique that continues test execution in test suite order when a new test cycle starts. Rather than restarting the testing or moving on to a new set of suites, the testing simply continues from where it was when the test cycle began. The goal of this and similar techniques is to achieve an acceptable level of test coverage and minimize regression test gaps when the test team cannot run all tests against every test release.

ramp-up   A hardware production phase that immediately follows a product release, in which the assembly line learns the process and product foibles associated with mass-producing the completely tested, finished system under test. This phase usually is accompanied by a spike in field-reported bugs, unless this phase precedes general availability.

regression   A problem that occurs when, as a result of a change in the system under test, a new revision of the system, S_{n+1}, contains a defect not present in revisions S_1 through S_n. In other words, regression occurs when some previously correct operation misbehaves. (If a new revision contains a new piece of functionality that fails without affecting the rest of the system, this is not considered regression.) Usually, you'll detect regression when test cases that previously passed now show failures.

regression tests   A set of tests selected to find regression introduced by changes in component, interface, or product functionality, usually associated with bug fixes or new functionality. Regression is a particularly insidious risk in a software maintenance effort, because there is seldom time for a full re-test of the product, even though seemingly innocuous changes can have knock-on effects in remote areas of functionality or behavior.

regression test gap   For any given change or revision in the system under test, the difference between the areas of test coverage provided by the entire test system and the test coverage provided by the portion of the test system that is actually re-run. For a system release, a regression test gap is the extent to which the final release version of every component and change in the system did not experience the full brunt of the test system.

reporting logs   Raw test output produced by low-level test tools, which is human-readable in varying degrees. Examples include text files containing test condition pass/fail results, screen shots, and diagnostics.

reporting tools   Special test tools that can process reporting logs into reports and charts, given some information about the context in which the log was produced.

root cause   The underlying reason why a bug occurs, as opposed to the observed symptoms of the bug. Root cause data is most useful in the aggregate; analyzing a breakdown of the root causes of all bugs found in a system under test can help to focus the attention of both test and development on those areas that are causing the most serious and frequent problems.

scalable   The extent to which a test component's parameters of operation can expand without necessitating major changes or fundamental redesign in the test system.

scripted testing   Manual testing that follows a written test procedure, test case, or test script. These tests are written to some level of precision; the less precise the test script, the greater the number of details that are left to the discretion of the tester. I would be hard-pressed to distinguish chartered exploratory testing from imprecise scripted testing. Confusingly enough, since automated tests are often implemented in interpreted programming languages (called scripting languages in programming parlance), the programming instructions to an automated test tool are often called test scripts.

severity   The impact of a bug on the system under test, regardless of the likelihood of its occurrence under end-user conditions or the extent to which the failure impedes use of the system. Contrast priority.

shotgunning   A technique that distributes test suites randomly across test cycles, or distributes test configurations randomly across test suites throughout a test phase. Shotgunning test suites across test cycles means that the test suites are preassigned to each cycle and are run as the new cycles begin. Shotgunning test configurations across test suites means that test system configurations (combinations of hardware, software, operating system, and infrastructure) are arbitrarily selected to run specific test suites. In both cases, the goal is to achieve an acceptable level of test coverage and minimize regression test gaps when the test team cannot run all test suites or test configurations against all test releases.

software attacks   A technique for lightweight, reactive testing, notably described by James Whittaker in his books. Testers use generalized, logical test cases that are designed to reveal the presence of certain kinds of bugs.

spinning disk release   A software revision that is sent by development to test so hastily that supposedly the CD or DVD is still spinning.

straw man plan   Any lightweight or incomplete plan, such as the first draft of a test plan or a hardware allocation plan, that serves as a starting point for discussion and a framework for coalescing a more concrete plan.

string testing   A software development test phase that finds bugs in typical usage scripts and operational or control-flow strings. This test phase is fairly unusual.

structural tests   Tests based on how a computer system, hardware or software, operates. Such tests are code-based or component-based, and they find bugs in operations such as those that occur at the levels of lines of code, chips, subassemblies, and interfaces. Also called white-box tests, glass-box tests, code-based tests, or design-based tests.

subsystem testing   See component testing.

SUT   See system under test.

SWAG   Acronym for *scientific wild-ass guess*; an educated guess or estimate. SWAGs abound in test estimation activities early in the development process.

system testing   A software or hardware development test phase that finds bugs in the overall and particular behaviors, functions, and responses of the system under test as a whole operating under realistic usage scenarios. These various system operations are performed once the system is fully integrated.

system under test   The entirety of the product, or system, being tested, which often consists of more than the immediately obvious pieces; system under test is often abbreviated *SUT*. Test escapes can arise through misunderstanding the scope of the system under test.

TBD   Acronym for *to be determined*; a useful placeholder in test documents to indicate a work-in-progress.

test case   A sequence of steps, substeps, and other actions, performed serially, in parallel, or some combination of consecution, that creates the desired test conditions that the test case is designed to evaluate. In some styles of documentation, particularly IEEE 829, these elements are referred to as test specifications and test procedures.

test case library   A collection of independent, reusable test cases.

test case (suite) setup   The steps required to configure the test environment for execution of a test case or test suite.

test case (suite) teardown   The steps required to restore the test environment to a clean condition after execution of a test case or test suite.

test condition   A system state or circumstance created by proceeding through some combination of steps, substeps, or actions in a test case. The term is sometimes also used to refer to the steps, substeps, or actions themselves.

test coverage   There are two types of test coverage:

- In a structural sense, the extent to which the test system covers, or exercises, the structure — the code or components — in the system under test. The metric is usually expressed as a percent of the total count of whatever structural element is being covered, such as lines of code or function points.

- In a behavioral sense, the extent to which the test system covers, or exercises, the behavior — quality risks, operations, activities, functions, and other uses — of the system under test. Coverage can be measured qualitatively against the uses to which the users and customers will subject the system, or quantitatively against requirements, quality risks, design specification elements, configurations, and so forth. Achieving thorough test coverage both behaviorally and structurally is necessary for good testing.

test cycle   A partial or total execution of all the test suites planned for a given test phase as part of that phase. A test phase involves at least one cycle (usually more) through all the designated test suites. Test cycles are usually associated with a single release of the system under test, such as a build of software or a motherboard. Generally, new test releases occur during a test phase, triggering another test cycle.

test environment   The setting in which testing happens, including the test platforms, the test infrastructure, the test lab, and other facilities.

test escape   Any field-reported bug that could reasonably have been caught during testing but was not. The term can also refer to a bug that makes its way into a subsequent phase of testing, although it should have been caught in a previous phase. A field-reported bug that was found during testing but that was not fixed because of a project management decision is not a test escape. A bug that could be found only through unusual and complicated hardware configurations or obscure operations is often not considered a test escape, either.

test pass   A period of testing consisting of the complete set of all the test suites planned for a given test phase. A test pass includes one or more test cycles, depending on the frequency of test releases and how long it takes to run all the tests.

test phase   A period of testing that addresses a particular set of quality risks and consists of one or more test passes.

test platform   Any piece of hardware on which a test can be run. The test platform is not necessarily the system under test, especially when testing software.

test release   Some subset of the overall system to be developed that is delivered for installation in some test environment and subsequent testing during a single test cycle. In later phases, such as system and acceptance testing, a test release should be as close as possible to being identical to the final customer release in terms of process, format, and completeness.

test suite   A framework for the execution of a group of test cases; a way of organizing test cases. In a test suite, test cases can be combined to create unique test conditions.

test system failure   Any failure of the test system. A test system failure can result in reporting bugs that don't exist, or failure to report bugs that do exist, or it can simply cause unpleasant side effects that nevertheless do not compromise the validity of the test results.

test yield   The degree to which a test case or test suite finds bugs. A high-yield test suite, for example, results in many bug reports of a serious nature, while a low-yield test suite results in few or trivial bug reports.

test to fail   The mind-set involved in designing, developing, and executing tests with the aim of finding as many problems as possible. This attitude represents the right way to think while designing, developing, and executing tests.

test to pass   The mind-set involved in designing, developing, and executing tests with the aim of proving compliance with requirements and correctness of operation. Such an attitude not only misses opportunities to increase product quality, but also is demonstrably futile. It represents the wrong way to think while designing, developing, and executing tests (except in the case of acceptance testing).

test system   An integrated and maintainable collection of items used to find, reproduce, isolate, describe, and manage bugs in the software or hardware under test. The items consist of the test environment, the test processes, and the testware.

test tool   Any general-purpose hardware, software, or hardware/software system used during test case execution to set up or tear down the test environment, to create test conditions, or to measure test results. A test tool is separate from the test case itself.

tester failure   Any failure caused by a tester using the test system, often the misinterpretation of a test result. Tester failures can result in reporting bugs that don't exist, or failing to report bugs that do exist, or they can simply be irritating yet immaterial.

unit testing   A software development concept that refers to the basic testing of a piece of code, the size of which is often undefined in practice, although it is usually a class, function, or subroutine. Unit testing is generally performed by developers. See also component testing.

white-box tests   See structural tests.

Index

A

abbreviations. *See* acronyms/abbreviations
accept or ignore option, 69
acceptance (user-acceptance) testing, 2, 7–8,
 500–501
  defined, 601
  jump-start for, 598
  project life cycle and, 500–501
  quality risk categories and, 21–24
Access (Microsoft), 154, 271, 271n4, 272
accountability
  bug-tracking database and, 160–161
  test lab and, 305
  tragedy of the commons and, 305
accuracy
  audience and, 407–409
  bug reports and, 151
  bug-tracking database and, 194
acoustics tests, 560–561
acronyms/abbreviations
  defining, 53
  Omninet Marketing Requirements
   Document, 569
action components, 82–84
action verbs, test plans and, 76
Actual Date column, 207
Adams, Scott, 320n2, 533
"AddValidUser.case", 135
ad-hoc testing, 4, 394, 395, 601
Advanced Software Testing (Black)
  Volume I, 105n4, 335n6, 348n7
  Volume II, 179n7, 335n6, 348n7, 538n19

Aesop's fables, 68n4
After the Gold Rush (McConnell), 336
Agile methodologies, 5, 16, 401, 401n5,
  450, 502n1, 506–507, 536–547. *See also*
  sprints
  case study, 536–547
  challenges, 401, 536–547
  Extreme Programming, 5, 506, 507
  online information, 401n5
  Scrum, 450, 506, 536, 538, 539, 540, 541, 542,
   543, 546
alarm card, 18
all things held equal (*ceteris paribus*), 189
allocation of effort, 15
all-pairs tables, 115, 115n7. *See also* orthogonal
  arrays
alpha tests, 8
altitude, 556
American Society for Quality (ASQ), 335,
  382n1
American Software Testing Qualifications
  Board, 335n6. *See also* ISTQB
analytical risk-based testing. *See* risk-based
  testing
Anderson, Hans Christian, 405
Anna Karenina (Tolstoy), 514, 515n7
anomaly, 147
anomaly reports (bug reports), 75, 177, 177n6,
  223. *See also* bug reports
anomaly-report (bug-report) template,
  176–178
anonymization process, 136–138